# Jewish Life in Small-Town America

*The Moses Montefiore Temple in Bloomington, Illinois, ca. 1889. Courtesy of the Jacob Rader Marcus Center of the American Jewish Archives.*

# Jewish Life in Small-Town America: A History

Lee Shai Weissbach

Yale University Press
New Haven & London

Published with assistance from the Committee on Academic Publications of the University of Louisville.

Designed by Mary Valencia.
Set in Veljovic type by Keystone Typesetting, Inc.
Printed in the United States of America by Sheridan Books.

Library of Congress Cataloging-in-Publication Data

Weissbach, Lee Shai, 1947–
Jewish life in small-town America : a history / Lee Shai Weissbach.
p. cm.
Includes bibliographical references and index.
ISBN 0-300-10671-8 (alk. paper)
1. Jews—United States—Social conditions—19th century. 2. Jews—United States—Social conditions—20th century. 3. Cities and towns—Religious aspects—Judaism. 4. City and town life—United States—History. 5. United States—History, Local. I. Title.
E184.36.S65W45 2005
307.76′2′089924073—dc22

2004051195

A catalogue record for this book is available from the British Library.

The paper in this book meets the guidelines for permanence and durability of the Committee on Production Guidelines for Book Longevity of the Council on Library Resources.

10   9   8   7   6   5   4   3   2   1

**For Sharon**

# Contents

# Acknowledgments

**M**y research and writing on the history of America's smaller Jewish communities have occupied me in one way or another for more than a decade and a half. Over this long period I have incurred a great many debts of gratitude. Most of the thanks I owe are to those I encountered during my travels in connection with this project, at numerous small-town libraries, historical societies, archives, and synagogues, as well as at the facilities of several major research institutions. In all these places, I invariably came upon people who were amiable, forthcoming, and eager to aid me in my work: librarians and archivists who went out of their way to help me find relevant material, rabbis and other congregational officials who took an interest in my project and did what they could to facilitate it, individual residents of small towns who met with me, pointed me to documentary evidence, and sometimes even offered a cup of tea or a meal, and colleagues who encouraged my research and shared their insights with me. Given the scores of individuals who have rendered help over the years, I hesitate to try to name them all lest I inadvertently forget some. I expressed my gratitude in person to all the people who helped me along the way, and I hope that if and when they see these words in print, they will know that I have not forgotten their kind assistance.

Although I cannot thank by name each of the individuals who provided help, I do want to acknowledge explicitly the various agencies that have provided financial support for my project. Major funding for my research came from the National Endowment for the Humanities, which awarded me a Senior Scholar Fellowship for 1995–96. Also providing research funding at one time or another were the Lucius N. Littauer Foundation, the Kentucky Humanities Council, and the University of Louisville and its College of Arts and Sciences.

Although I could not have completed my work without traveling widely and visiting dozens of repositories of research materials, there is no question that the single most valuable institution for my research has been the Jacob Rader Marcus Center of the American Jewish Archives in Cincinnati. I do not think a year has gone by over the last decade and a half when I did not make at least one visit to that remarkable institution, and I am most grateful to its staff, including its current executive director, Gary Zola, and its chief archivist, Kevin Proffitt, for their liberal and gracious assistance. In 1990 the Archives awarded me a Rapoport Fellowship, and in 2002 a Loewenstein-Wiener Fellowship.

Over the years, my articles concerning various aspects of small-town Jewish life have appeared in several journals: *American Jewish History,* the *American Jewish Archives Journal, Shofar, Jewish History,* and *Western Pennsylvania History.* My essays on the history of small communities have appeared also in the *Proceedings of the Eleventh World Congress of Jewish Studies* (Jerusalem, 1994); in the volume *Patterns of Migration, 1850–1914,* edited by Aubrey Newman and Stephen W. Massil (London, 1996); and in the exhibition catalogue *We Call This Place Home: Jewish Life in Maryland's Small Towns,* edited by Karen Falk and Avi Y. Dechter and produced at the Jewish Museum of Maryland (Baltimore, 2002). I have also contributed a chapter on rabbinic leadership in small-town America to the second volume of *Jewish Religious Leadership: Image and Reality,* edited by Jack Wertheimer (New York, 2004). The editors of each of these publications have always been generous in their encouragement of my project and supportive of my efforts to publish portions of my research findings even as I worked on the present book. For all this I thank them sincerely.

I thank also my children, Maya and Cobi, and my new daughter-in-law, Shira, for the interest they have shown in my work, for their affection, and for helping me to keep my efforts as a historian in perspective. Finally, I thank all the people at the Yale University Press who have been involved in preparing this book for publication. It has been a pleasure to work with them.

I dedicate this volume to my wife, Sharon, with profound appreciation and eternal love. For over three and a half decades, Sharon has been not only an ideal spouse, but also a willing advisor and a discerning critic. I owe her more gratitude than I can possibly express in words. She has helped me to develop and grow not only as a historian but as a person.

Louisville, January 2004

# Introduction:
# Searching for Patterns

A t the end of the 1920s, the Jewish population of the United States stood at about 4.25 million people, the vast majority of whom were immigrants who had come to America in a huge wave of migration from Eastern Europe during the previous half-century, or the children of those immigrants. The immense influx of Jews that had begun in 1881 was stimulated both by severe economic hardships in Eastern Europe and by an increase in discrimination and persecution there, following the assassination of the Russian czar Alexander II. East European Jewish migration to America had slowed to a trickle during the most difficult years of World War I, and, after a brief recovery in the early 1920s, it was again curtailed, this time permanently, when the U.S. Congress, motivated by nativism and xenophobia, introduced severe restrictions on immigration, culminating in the Johnson-Reed Act of 1924.[1]

The wave of immigration that ended soon after World War I not only increased the Jewish population of the United States dramatically, but also altered its geography by greatly expanding the number of individual Jewish communities in the country. Of course, the principal centers of Jewish life in America in the 1920s were large ones, most of which had been established in major cities long before the era of mass migration began. These were communities at coastal locations such as Boston, Philadelphia, Baltimore, and, of course, New York, and in substantial inland cities such as Cleveland, Cincinnati, Chicago, and St. Louis. According to the available statistics, by 1927 there were eleven great cities in the country with Jewish populations of 50,000 or more, thirty-four other cities with Jewish populations of at least 10,000 but fewer than 50,000, and yet another 152 cities with Jewish populations of at least 1,000 but fewer than 10,000.[2] In addition, by the late 1920s there were also a substantial number of Jewish communities in the United States com-

---

posed of no more than a few hundred individuals. These less visible centers of Jewish life were almost invariably in smaller cities and towns, and it is with their largely untold story that this book is concerned.

The history of smaller Jewish communities has remained for the most part unexplored because ever since the study of local Jewish history emerged as a serious academic pursuit around the middle of the twentieth century, scholars have focused their attention almost exclusively on the more populous Jewish communities of America's large and midsize cities. Thus, we now have many significant and often erudite accounts of communities that were already notable in the nineteenth century or that mushroomed during the era of mass migration. New York has received the lion's share of attention,[3] but admirable studies of other sizable communities also have been produced.[4] By contrast, penetrating studies of the history of smaller communities remain extremely rare. A very few scholars, such as Lance Sussman and Ewa Morawska, have produced excellent works that represent a start in the study of less populous Jewish centers.[5] However, even the communities about which Sussman and Morawska have written, those of Binghamton, New York, and Johnstown, Pennsylvania, had Jewish populations of over 1,000 by the 1920s and were located in rather substantial smaller cities. Both Binghamton and Johnstown had populations of about 67,000 in 1920.

To the extent that the stories of truly small communities have been chronicled, most have taken the form of brief congregational histories and local studies prepared by amateur researchers. Such accounts have usually focused on familiar topics such as the development of hometown Jewish institutions and the biographies of locally prominent personalities. Moreover, the authors of these accounts generally have been unfamiliar with specialized techniques such as demographic analysis, and unconcerned with the need to verify and document their findings. As the historian Louis Swichkow once observed, studies of the history of small Jewish communities have tended to be "hastily conceived, haphazardly compiled, and hurriedly published."[6]

Another problem with most existing accounts of smaller Jewish communities is that they lack attention to context. Occasionally, those chronicling the history of a small community have recognized that it is part of a larger story. Helene Gerard, for example, who wrote about the small-town Jewish enclaves of eastern Long Island in New York, suggested that these communities "might be considered prototypes of similar villages throughout the country"; and Dennis Devlin, who wrote about the Jews of Muskegon, Michigan, maintained that their community was "in essence a microcosm of American Jewry." Similarly, the authors of the catalogue for an exhibit on Jewish life in Charlottesville, Virginia, declared that the history of their community "shares much in common with the broad sweep of the Jewish experience in the South and throughout America"; and Rabbi Solomon Jacobson, in his introduction to a study prepared by a local merchant, observed that the Jewish community of Petersburg, Virginia, was "a fragment of the entirety of the Jewish population in the smaller towns of the land" and he argued that "this fragment, like the archeologist's potsherd, enables one to readily reconstruct and visualize the complete vessel."[7] Nonetheless, even those authors who have acknowledged that their stories are part of some larger narrative have retained a rather narrow focus, and few of their works have become known beyond the communities whose stories they recount. Until now, there has been no comprehensive analysis of the experience of America's small Jewish communities as a class.

One manifestation of the fact that little scholarly research has been done on smaller Jewish settlements is that general surveys of American Jewish history have largely ignored small-town Jewish life, except perhaps in their coverage of early American Jewry up until the middle of the nineteenth century. Even historians who have recognized the importance of looking at Jewish life outside the confines of New York and the other great cities of the East usually have reported on midsize Jewish communities rather than smaller ones. Gerald Sorin's approach in his fine book *A Time for Building,* the third volume of the series The Jewish People in America, provides a case in point. When Sorin moves "beyond New York" to write about Jewish communities in what he calls "smaller cities and towns," he nonetheless focuses on places such as "Providence, Hartford, Sioux City, Kansas City, Cincinnati, Richmond, and New Orleans," all of which were actually very big cities by the standards of their regions and all of which were home to several thousand Jews by the beginning of the twentieth century.[8]

Of course, the scholarly focus on major communities in large and midsize cities is to a great extent justified, for American Jewry has always been a highly urbanized minority heavily concentrated in Jewish settlements of considerable magnitude. Around 1878, for example, fully 71 percent of all the Jews in the United States lived in those twenty-six American cities that had Jewish populations of 1,000 or more. Fifty years later, 92 percent of American Jews lived in places with Jewish populations of 1,000 or more. Still, in all the scholarly attention paid to Jews in larger communities, something essential has been missed, for small communities have always been fundamental features in the American Jewish landscape. These communities played a crucial role in American Jewish settlement and mobility patterns not only in the era of mass migration, but before and after as well. Indeed, even while a huge proportion of America's Jews lived in major Jewish centers, throughout the late nineteenth century and into the twentieth, the vast majority of the country's individual Jewish communities were, in fact, smaller ones in less prominent cities and towns. It would be a mistake to think that the full story of the

American Jewish experience can be told without considering the history of small-town Jewish life.

Furthermore, the history of small Jewish communities demands attention because in the late nineteenth century and in the early decades of the twentieth, many of those concerned about the nature of American society perceived the smaller cities and towns in which these communities were located as the nation's heart and soul. After all, until about the time of World War I, the United States was essentially a rural country in which most people were far more familiar with small towns than they were with big cities. The census of 1920 was the first to reveal more people living in places with populations of at least 2,500 than in manifestly rural areas. Moreover, even in the period between World War I and World War II, there was still a sense that small-town life was fundamental to the American experience. For some social critics, often worried about the encroachment of urban and industrial influences, the small town represented a sort of ideal, with its unhurried pace and its strong sense of rootedness and intimacy. This view was closely connected with an American mythology that glorified rural life and values, its pedigree going back all the way to Thomas Jefferson's distrust of urban life. For other commentators, small towns represented problematic characteristics such as puritanism, provincialism, and naiveté. Either way, throughout the first half of the twentieth century, few thoughtful observers of American society were unconcerned about small-town life.[9]

It was in the years between the outbreak of World War I and the start of World War II, for instance, that several of America's best-known writers produced masterworks exploring the character of small-town America. Some of these literary classics reaffirmed the myth of its idyllic nature while others, in what has been called "the revolt from the village," challenged that myth. This was the era of Willa Cather's *My Antonia* (1918), Sherwood Anderson's *Winesburg, Ohio* (1919), Sinclair Lewis' *Main Street* (1920), and Thornton Wilder's *Our Town* (1938).[10] Furthermore, just as some of the country's foremost novelists and playwrights looked for the real America in smaller cities and towns, so too did many of those whose examination of society took a more systematic approach. It was not by chance that when social reformers developed the concept of scientific urban surveys that would diagnose the problems of a modernizing society, they probed the situation not only in metropolitan areas, but also in relatively small cities such as Springfield, Illinois. The reformers who were behind the study of Springfield considered the focus of their investigation to be a more or less "typical" American town and expressed the wish that their work would "spread beyond their own borders and thereby mean a contribution . . . to the welfare of other cities than their own."[11]

Similarly, as academic sociology developed in the early decades of the twentieth century and its practitioners searched for settings in which to conduct their inquiries, many of them gravitated to smaller cities. Indeed, in the 1920s sociologists began to create a sort of cottage industry in community studies focusing on small towns. Among the most famous of these were the ones conducted by Helen and Robert Lynd in Muncie, Indiana, which they called "Middletown," and those carried out by Lloyd Warner and his team in Newburyport, Massachusetts, identified with the pseudonym "Yankee City."[12] Although each community survey of the early twentieth century examined the experience of a particular place, all were predicated, as the essayist Richard Lingeman has written "on the idea that the small town was a laboratory where American life could be dissected and studied." When the Lynds chose Muncie for their project, for example, they explained that they were looking for a community that was not only "compact and homogeneous enough to be manageable" but also "as representative as possible of American life." As late as 1949, Lloyd Warner could write that the 10,000 citizens of one of the small towns he had studied "express the values of 180 million Americans."[13]

Even the budding enterprise of market research that emerged in the first years of the twentieth century tended to look for the authentic America in her smaller cities as it developed the technique of sampling in a representative community. In a pathbreaking marketing study in 1925, for example, the *Literary Digest* launched an intensive effort to identify the most typical place in the United States, reasoning that "if it is possible to find out what the inhabitants of the average American town eat, what they wear, how they spend their money, where they seek pleasure, [and] how they study to advance themselves, then we are much nearer to a solution of the answers to these questions when they are applied to our whole nation." The *Digest*'s search led to Zanesville, Ohio, which promptly began to promote itself as "America's Typical City."[14]

Despite the intense interest in small towns during the first half of the twentieth century and despite the ubiquity of small Jewish communities in that era, most of the social reformers, sociologists, and other observers of small-town life at the time had little to say about Jews. Indeed, these researchers, scholars, and writers apparently assumed that in order for a place to be characteristically American, it had to be relatively free of ethnic and religious minorities and of foreign-born residents. Thus, they tended to select the towns they studied for the uniformity of their populations. The organizers of the Springfield, Illinois, social survey, for example, commented that their community was "unusually American," with an extremely high percentage of inhabitants who were both white and native born. The Lynds quite consciously selected for their study a city without any distinctive ethnic minorities because they wanted to focus upon the effects of industrialization without encountering other potentially disruptive aspects of urbanization. Even the Warner team in Newburyport, which had much more to say about Jews than most other social scientists working in small towns, and which eventually published an entire volume on "the social systems of American ethnic groups," nonetheless set out to study minorities in what they believed was "a town whose population was predominantly old American."[15]

In a sense, then, the modest Jewish communities whose stories unfolded in America's small towns have been doubly invisible. During the first half of the twentieth century, they were largely ignored by those concerned about the changing nature of American society, even while so many of them focused their gaze on small-town life. During the second half of the century they were overlooked by scholars exploring the American Jewish experience, even as many of them crafted sophisticated studies in local history. Thus, by telling the story of smaller Jewish communities and revealing how closely it was bound up with the history of small-town America, this book is intended both to expand our knowledge of the American Jewish experience and to enhance our awareness of the complex character of America's smaller cities and towns in times past.

This book is concerned, above all, with what I have called the "classic era" of small-town Jewish life. This period, covering the late nineteenth and early twentieth centuries and corresponding to the time of greatest salience for America's small towns, was an era when Jewish immigrant pioneers, first from Central Europe and later from Eastern Europe, created scores of small Jewish communities in the secondary cities that sprang up all across the continent as the population of the United States grew and expanded. This classic era ended soon after World War II, when the immigrant experience ceased to have a pervasive influence on American Jewry and when the nature of small-town life (and with it small-town Jewish life) changed dramatically, thanks largely to advances in technology and transportation and to changing demographic realities, all of which left small towns far less isolated from larger urban areas than they had been previously.

As the titles of the chapters of this book suggest, our exploration of small-town Jewish history will center on the patterns of development, organization, and behavior that emerged in small communities. As we shall see, these patterns were not identical from one small community to another, but the range of basic characteristics that these communities shared was remarkably narrow. This was true in terms of the migration and settlement patterns that led to the creation and the perpetuation of these less-noticed Jewish centers; it was true in terms of their occupational profiles, their family and kin networks, and their cultural contours. We will discover, for example, that small-town Jewish communities were composed overwhelmingly of families involved in mercantile pursuits of various sorts, and we will see that all over America the relationship between Jews and gentiles in small towns involved a certain tension between ready acceptance and lingering suspicion.

The tendency of Jewish life to develop along similar lines from one small town to another also will become evident in terms of the congregational structures of small communities, their synagogue histories, and their systems of rabbinic leadership, all subjects that will occupy us extensively, given the centrality of religious concerns within America's smaller Jewish settlements. We will find, for instance, that in small communities only two basic patterns of synagogue structure obtained, one in which the entire community cooperated to support a single congregation, and the other in which communal rifts persisted, but always in the face of forces that militated against internal division. Ultimately we will come to recognize that small Jewish communities were not simply miniature versions of larger Jewish centers but, rather, alternative types of settlements in many respects. How particular patterns of Jewish life in small communities differed from those in larger ones is part of the story that this book will tell.

Scholars have long recognized that geography is a vital factor in determining the way history unfolds, and in this connection many have considered the impact of sectionalism on the history of the United States. Indeed, students of the Jewish experience in the Deep South and in the frontier West have shown that sectional identity had an influence on the Jews of America, just as it had on other groups. Melvin Urofsky has written, to take but one example, that "the Southern-Jewish experience differed both qualitatively and quantitatively from that of Northern Jewry" and that Jews "did not affect the South so much as they imbibed its values and became part of it." By the same token, Hal Rothman has argued that for the Jews of Wichita, Kansas, "the meaning of [their] faith and its bearing on day to day Jewish life were changed by the circumstances of living in the American West." Still, as the historian Mark Bauman has argued persuasively, regional variations in the American Jewish experience can easily be exaggerated, and focusing too much attention on sectionalism can obscure the impact of other environmental factors that may have conditioned Jewish life across regional boundaries.[16]

The following chapters will demonstrate that living in a small community, which invariably involved an encounter with small-town America, was one of the most powerful environmental factors that could influence American Jewish life, overshadowing (though not necessarily obliterating) many other possible influences, such as the specific origins of a community's settlers, a community's proximity to other Jewish centers, and even its regional location. Although one of the goals of this book is to explore the story of small-town Jewry because of its inherent interest, another goal, equally important, is to interrogate in a new way the role of "place" in the drama of American

Jewish history. At a very fundamental level, this book addresses the question of how the limited size of some Jewish communities and their location in small-town settings helped to shape Jewish life in those communities.

This book is grounded in research at several different levels. It is based in large part on a thoroughgoing and comprehensive investigation of the history of a dozen representative small-town Jewish settlements, chosen for a certain degree of diversity and geographic spread. But this study also relies heavily on an intensive if less exhaustive examination of the history of scores of other communities, including a few, such as those of Muskegon, Michigan; La Crosse, Wisconsin; Topeka, Kansas; and Durham, North Carolina, that have been the subjects of in-depth studies by previous writers.[17] Finally, this project rests as well on an examination of composite data covering hundreds more small-town Jewish centers. Although this book reports details about many of the less visible Jewish communities that dotted the American landscape in the decades before and after the turn of the twentieth century, it cannot, of course, tell the whole story of any one community. Rather, this study synthesizes information about a great multitude of small communities in order to discover the characteristics they shared and to describe them as a class. Those interested in the broad sweep of American Jewish history or in the saga of small-town life in the United States will learn how the experience of smaller Jewish settlements fits into these narratives. Those with an interest in the history of a specific small community will be able to understand the extent to which that history conformed, or failed to conform, to basic patterns of small-town Jewish life; that is, they will be able to discover just how typical or atypical that community was.

To be sure, in searching for commonalties and patterns, there is always a danger of losing sight of particularities and uniqueness, and perhaps even of conveying the impression that the history of each of America's small Jewish communities was to some extent predestined. This was certainly not the case. A determinist view of the history of America's small-town Jewish settlements would not be an accurate one, for each of these communities was at least in part a product of its specific time and place. Indeed, not only were there several basic patterns of development and organization to which small communities might conform, but here and there individual communities actually defied standard trends and expectations, at least in some respects. From time to time, this book will call attention to deviations from established norms, but its primary goal remains to highlight the general patterns of Jewish life that were most apparent in small-town America and to construct a multidimensional model against which a detailed history of any individual small community can be examined.

In a social scientific study that describes general historical trends, there is also a danger of conveying the impression that there is only one set of objective "truths" about the subject at hand, in this case the experience of small Jewish communities. As modern scholarship has come to recognize, however, this simplistic view of history can no longer be supported. Events that took place in the past were undoubtedly perceived differently by individual participants in those events, and both contemporary narratives and subsequent reports of what happened are bound to be conditioned by preexisting assumptions. Still, just as it would be illogical to contend that modern scholars can construct historical accounts that are totally objective, it would be unreasonable to surrender to the notion that nothing coherent can be said about times gone by. Although both those who conduct historical research and those who consider its results must remain aware that the work of the historian is always colored by subjective elements, there is certainly much of interest that can be discovered about the past, and much of value. By preserving and analyzing the history of small Jewish communities, this book is intended to contribute new insights into the development of American Jewry while also broadening our understanding of the character of small-town America.

# 1  Patterns of Evidence: Identifying Small Communities

Eng'd by W.T. Barber, N.Y.

William B. Hackenburg

Any account of the history of the hundreds of small Jewish communities that existed in the smaller cities and towns of the United States in the past must depend to a large extent on the availability of comprehensive data describing how America's Jewish population has been distributed and organized over the years. Without such data, it would be impossible even to identify the country's smaller Jewish settlements, let alone examine their characteristics and analyze their development over time. Unfortunately, detailed sources of information about the dispersal of America's Jews from the middle of the nineteenth century onward are not abundant, and there are many questions to be raised about the reliability of the population figures and the data on communal structure that are available.

A rather complete picture of the size and distribution of America's limited Jewish population in the very early nineteenth century does exist. On the basis of a painstaking reading of manuscript census materials, the historian Ira Rosenwaike has concluded that America's total Jewish population was about 4,000 in the year 1830 and that the vast majority of Jews at that time were concentrated in just a few urban centers. Only seven cities in America had Jewish populations of over 100, and some 80 percent of the country's Jewish inhabitants were living in these places. The main centers of American Jewish life in 1830 were New York, Philadelphia, Baltimore, New Orleans, Charleston, Cincinnati, and Richmond.[1]

Soon after 1830, however, immigrants coming to the United States, mainly from Central Europe, began to expand the country's Jewish population into the tens of thousands. This development makes it essentially impossible to use Rosenwaike's method to reconstruct a similarly detailed picture of the distribution of America's Jews during the middle decades of the nineteenth century, and contemporary sources of information are not of much help, either. Be-

---

*Photo previous page: William B. Hackenburg, chairman of the Committee on Statistics of the Union of American Hebrew Congregations. In 1880 Hackenburg oversaw publication of the first detailed census of American Jewry. Courtesy of the Jacob Rader Marcus Center of the American Jewish Archives.*

cause the government always considered it inappropriate to inquire into the faith of individual Americans, the U.S. Census never asked about religious affiliation, and even though the Census Bureau did begin to collect data about American Jewish congregations in 1850, the reports that it published concerning religious bodies do not reveal much about the exact size of the country's various Jewish settlements, chiefly because the bureau's definition of congregational membership was inconsistent and because it paid no attention to places without organized assemblies.[2] Moreover, throughout most of the nineteenth century, American Jews themselves were not much concerned about gathering detailed population data, and only occasionally did individuals attempt to estimate even the total number of Jews in the United States.[3]

The most complete guide to America's various Jewish communities at the midpoint of the nineteenth century was compiled by Jacques Lyons and Abraham de Sola on the basis of various firsthand reports and gleanings from the Jewish press. Lyons and de Sola published their guide in Montreal in 1854 as an appendix to their *Jewish Calendar for Fifty Years*. Along with eleven Canadian and Caribbean locales, the Lyons and de Sola inventory lists sixty-five places in the United States with organized Jewish communities, including such small towns as Cumberland, Maryland; Wilmington, North Carolina; Danville, Pennsylvania; Lafayette, Indiana; and Marysville, California. Nonetheless, although it records fairly detailed information about the number and nature of congregations and other communal organizations in the places it catalogues, the guide provides almost no information about the number of Jewish individuals in these places.[4] In fact it was not until after the Civil War that the first serious efforts were made to collect comprehensive demographic data on American Jewry.

The earliest attempt at a systematic Jewish population survey in the United States was undertaken in 1873 by the Board of Delegates of American Israelites, an organization that had been founded in 1859 to create a stronger sense of unity among American Jews. This survey was apparently initiated at the urging of the Paris-based Alliance Israélite Universelle, but its findings were incomplete and its results disappointing.[5] However, from 1876 to 1878 the Board of Delegates undertook another population study, this time working in conjunction with the newly established Union of American Hebrew Congregations (UAHC). This second survey, directed by William B. Hackenburg, president of the Board of Delegates and later chairman of the UAHC's Committee on Statistics, was far more comprehensive than the first and ultimately more successful.

The organizers of the inquiry of the late 1870s conducted their research by sending standardized questionnaires to individuals in every place in the United States where Jews were known to reside. In many cases, the forms went to the heads of Jewish institutions, and where no such institutions were known to exist, they went to "influential citizens." Those who received the questionnaires were asked to provide information both about the number of Jews in the local population and about whatever local Jewish organizations existed. In 1880, after the Board of Delegates and the UAHC had merged, the results of the study the two groups had conducted were published as *Statistics of the Jews of the United States.*[6]

Unfortunately, the 1880 report is not without its problems, many of them stemming from the way Hackenburg and his staff collected data. It seems, for example, that questionnaires never even reached some places where Jews were living by the late 1870s and that quite a few of the people who received forms did not respond, "notwithstanding urgent solicitation." As a result, the information published in *Statistics of the Jews* is somewhat spotty. The report contains almost no data on Massachusetts Jewry outside Boston, for instance; and even though its section on Delaware reports "Jewish population outside of Wilmington, about 500," it accounts for only 85 Jews living in Wilmington and 47 living in five other towns. So, too, without any explanation, *Statistics of the Jews* provides two separate population figures for Mobile, Alabama, and for Wilkes-Barre, Pennsylvania, and it lists at least a dozen cities (including Schenectady, Hartford, and Los Angeles) without providing any population data. Even where the *Statistics* is less confusing, it appears that many of the population figures it provides are no more than rough approximations. The Jewish population of New York City is simply "estimated at 60,000" and that of Philadelphia at "about 12,000." So, too, the original manuscript ledger on which the published *Statistics of the Jews* is based reveals that population numbers for over a dozen towns in Florida were estimated by a single individual living in Jacksonville.[7]

The work of researchers who have explored the history of some of America's individual Jewish communities provides further evidence that the Board of Delegates–UAHC survey produced results that were far less than perfect. Judith Endelman's study of Indianapolis Jewry suggests that there were already 500 Jews in that city by 1870, for example, while *Statistics of the Jews* reports only 400 Jews there several years later. Benjamin Band's research into the history of the Jewish community of Portland, Maine, reveals that the first congregations there were not founded until 1884, but the *Statistics* reports the existence of a congregation in Portland in the late 1870s. Perhaps this explains why, when Hackenburg's office sent a questionnaire to the purported Portland congregation, it received in response "no returns."[8]

Despite its various shortcomings, however, *Statistics of the Jews* remains an extremely valuable document. It contains the first systematic compilation of population data on the Jews of the United States, and it also provides some basic information about American Jewry's various communal institutions.

Thus, it is an essential guide to the general pattern of Jewish settlement in the United States just as the mass migration of East European Jews to America was about to begin. The importance of the census published in 1880 is further enhanced by the fact that there would be no further attempts to enumerate the Jewish population of America's various cities and towns throughout the rest of the nineteenth century.

The first twentieth-century attempts to survey the Jewish population of the United States were undertaken within two years of each other, in 1905 and 1907. Both were conducted largely by Henrietta Szold while she was editor of the *American Jewish Year Book*, an annual that was then still in its infancy but would become a staple in American Jewish publishing. The results of the 1905 survey overseen by Szold appeared as part of the entry entitled "United States" in *The Jewish Encyclopedia*, the first major reference work on Jewish subjects published in English. The results of the 1907 survey appeared in the *American Jewish Year Book* itself, in conjunction with a directory of all national and local Jewish organizations in the United States.[9] The *Year Book* had provided a similar directory of organizations in its second annual volume, published in 1900, but the earlier compilation had not included any information on the size of America's various Jewish settlements.[10]

Both of the population surveys conducted during the first decade of the twentieth century aimed for broad coverage and accuracy, but neither had a foolproof method for achieving these goals. These studies, like that undertaken by the Board of Delegates and the UAHC three decades earlier, suffer from some serious deficiencies. For one thing, neither the tabulation of 1905 nor that of 1907 tried to discover population figures for all points of Jewish settlement in the United States. *The Jewish Encyclopedia* reported figures only for what it called the "chief towns in each state," while the *Year Book* included population data only for those places that supported some sort of Jewish institutional life. Indeed, the *Encyclopedia* conceded not only that its figures were "estimates . . . likely to be somewhat above the reality" but also that the figures were "incomplete." Likewise, Henrietta Szold explained that in conducting research for the survey of 1907, her office dispatched circular letters, employed canvassing agents, solicited the intervention of local dignitaries, and sent out "a mass of personal correspondence," but that "in spite of these various efforts to obtain guaranteed reports . . . it proved impossible to secure official data in all instances." Szold also reported that in some cases her office received conflicting population estimates from different individuals in the same locale. When this happened, Szold made decisions about which data to use based on "the position of the correspondents in their communities."[11]

The shortcomings of the reports published in *The Jewish Encyclopedia* and in the 1907 *American Jewish Year Book* are reflected in the fact that for several cities and towns, population figures are provided in one source but not in the other. For example, although the *Encyclopedia* indicates the existence of Jewish communities in Mobile, Alabama, and in Bridgeport, Connecticut, it gives no population data for either of these places. The *Year Book,* on the other hand, reports that Mobile had 1,000 Jews in 1907 and that Bridgeport had 3,500. Moreover, several places that probably should have been included among the "chief towns" surveyed for the census published in *The Jewish Encyclopedia* are not mentioned in that study at all. These include Stamford, Connecticut, which had 500 Jews according to the *Year Book* of 1907; Greenville, Mississippi, also with 500 Jews; Harrison, New Jersey, with 659 Jews; and Portsmouth, Virginia, with 700 Jews.

Nor is it clear that the *Year Book* is always the more comprehensive source. Even though the 1907 census was supposed to represent Szold's expansion of the survey she had conducted in 1905,[12] sometimes it is the earlier study that furnishes more information. For example, while the *Encyclopedia* provides population figures for Canton, Ohio (600 Jews); Alexandria, Louisiana (600 Jews); and Reading, Pennsylvania (800 Jews), the *Year Book* does not. There are also certain places for which neither *The Jewish Encyclopedia* nor the *Year Book* provides population data, even though the *Year Book* makes it clear that Jewish communities were functioning there. These places include Gloucester, Massachusetts; Covington, Kentucky; Jackson, Michigan; and Council Bluffs, Iowa.

Yet another indication of problems with the data reported in *The Jewish Encyclopedia* and in the 1907 *American Jewish Year Book* is that sometimes these two sources give wildly divergent population figures for the same place. For example, the *Encyclopedia* indicates that Sheffield, Alabama, was home to 3,000 Jews, whereas the 1907 *Year Book* states that it was home to only 34. According to the two sources, Springfield, Massachusetts, had 300 Jews in 1905 but 1,500 in 1907. Des Moines, Iowa, was reported to have 500 Jews in 1905 but 3,000 in 1907; and Savannah, Georgia, was reported to have 1,500 Jews in 1905 but 3,500 in 1907. It is true that Jewish immigration to America was proceeding at a very brisk pace during the two years that elapsed between the publication of *The Jewish Encyclopedia's* figures and those that appear in the 1907 *Year Book.* In fact, the peak year for Jewish immigration in the early twentieth century was 1906, during which some 154,000 Jews entered the United States. Nonetheless, the pace of population change indicated by some of the figures published in 1905 and 1907 must raise suspicion. It is likely that at least some of the huge discrepancies between the figures reported were due to inaccuracies in one or both of the studies overseen by Szold, rather than to truly enormous changes in population.[13]

By the second decade of the twentieth century, the collection of population data on American Jewry was on a firmer footing because the American

Jewish Committee, created in 1906 primarily to defend Jewish rights, had by then established a Bureau of Jewish Statistics. In the years that followed, that office was known variously as the Bureau of Jewish Statistics and Research or the Statistical Department of the American Jewish Committee, and the office eventually came under the auspices of the Synagogue Council of America. At times the Bureau of Jewish Statistics cooperated with U.S. Census authorities in collecting data on American Jewish congregations, and throughout the period of its existence, the bureau published reports of its findings in the *American Jewish Year Book*, itself a joint venture of the American Jewish Committee and the Jewish Publication Society of America. Indeed, the *Year Book* soon became the single most important source of information on the size and distribution of America's Jewish population.[14]

Early evidence of the work of the Bureau of Jewish Statistics appeared in the *American Jewish Year Book* issued in 1914. In that volume the bureau's Joseph Jacobs provided a listing of all towns in the United States "in which Jews were known to exist in 1912," together with a compilation of the population data available for those places. Jacobs included figures for 1877 taken from *Statistics of the Jews*, figures for 1905 taken from *The Jewish Encyclopedia*, and figures for 1907 based on the survey that had appeared in the *American Jewish Year Book* at that time. To all this information, Jacobs added population estimates for 1912 furnished by the Industrial Removal Office, an agency that played a significant role in the dispersal of Jews throughout the United States and whose work we shall consider later.[15]

Although the report prepared by Jacobs indicates a growing interest in information about the size and distribution of American Jewry, it was a rather careless effort, full of omissions and errors. For example, in the tables published by Jacobs, population figures available from the 1880 *Statistics of the Jews* are missing for several places, including Syracuse, New York; Augusta, Georgia; Lexington, Kentucky; and Little Rock, Arkansas. So, too, the figures from the *Statistics* for Harrisburg, Pennsylvania; Logansport, Indiana; Mobile, Alabama; and Portland, Oregon, are republished incorrectly. Jacobs' recapitulation of data from 1905 mistakenly reports the Jewish population of Glens Falls, New York, and of Gary, Indiana, as "1" and omits entirely the population figure for Hagerstown, Maryland. In reporting the data from 1907, Jacobs missed the figures for Zanesville, Ohio; Kokomo, Indiana; and Trinidad, Colorado, among other places. He also miscopied the figure for Butte, Montana, and reported the 1907 Jewish population of Albuquerque as 800, whereas this is the figure for all of New Mexico in the original source. Beyond all these problems, the new population estimates for 1912 that Jacobs obtained from the Industrial Removal Office covered fewer than 400 of the nearly 1,600 cities and towns identified as points of Jewish settlement on the eve of World War I.

The first major population survey that the American Jewish Committee's statistical bureau undertook on its own account was conducted during 1917 and 1918 under the leadership of Samson D. Oppenheim, then the bureau's head. Backed by a Jewish establishment eager to demonstrate American Jewish patriotism just after the United States entered World War I, this survey was motivated in part by a desire "to obtain an idea of the proportionate contribution of American Jews to the war." The study focused mainly on securing an accurate assessment of the number of Jews in New York City, home to about half of all the Jews in the United States at the time. Nonetheless, the survey was concerned with the rest of the country as well, and in fact its attempt to arrive at Jewish population statistics for the American hinterland was both more sophisticated and more exhaustive than any previous effort.[16]

Like earlier surveys, the population study initiated by the Bureau of Jewish Statistics in 1917 began with questionnaires. The bureau sent a request for information about the size of the local Jewish community to every rabbi in the country and to many other Jewish leaders as well. It then compared the returns it received with one another and with information from the Industrial Removal Office and other national organizations. On this basis, the bureau fixed a population figure for a great many places. The system worked best for large urban centers, of course, for there the number of respondents was greatest, as was the amount of information available from other sources. But the bureau got replies to its inquiries from numerous small towns as well, and ultimately it was able to devise a rule of thumb that it believed would allow an accurate determination of the number of Jews in any locale, even if no first-hand data were available.

On the basis of the information that it was able to gather, the bureau concluded that in all American cities that had populations of 100,000 or more, the Jewish population averaged 4.5 percent of the total. The only exceptions it cited were New York, where Jews made up about 27 percent of the city's total population, and nine other large manufacturing centers, where the Jewish population approached 10 percent of the total. The bureau also determined that in cities of at least 50,000 inhabitants but fewer than 100,000, Jews made up about 3 percent of the total population and that in cities of at least 20,000 but fewer than 50,000, Jews made up about 2 percent. Finally, it determined that in cities that had fewer than 20,000 inhabitants but over 1,000, Jews made up between 1 and 2 percent of the population and that in places with populations of fewer than 1,000, Jews usually made up between one quarter and one half of 1 percent of all inhabitants. The bureau claimed that the accuracy of the "rule" it had formulated to arrive at the Jewish population of any settlement had been validated on many occasions. It explained that "frequently, after an estimate had been made [using the 'rule'], a return would come in from some little town, and in hardly any instance did the detailed report vary materially . . . from the estimate that had been made."[17]

Results of the population census conducted in 1917 and 1918 appeared in the *American Jewish Year Book* both in 1918 and in 1919. In the year the survey was concluded, the *Year Book* carried a lengthy review of the census, accompanied by eleven tables containing a wealth of population data. This account was incomplete in at least one respect, however, for even with all its tables, it did not report the population of every Jewish settlement in the country. In 1919 the *Year Book* used the results of the population survey conducted during World War I in conjunction with a new directory of local Jewish institutions that was intended to update the one that had appeared in 1907. Again, however, the population information reported was incomplete, as figures were provided for many of the cities listed in the directory, but not for all. Apparently the compilers of the 1919 directory were reluctant to employ the estimation "rule" so highly touted by the Bureau of Jewish Statistics in 1918. Moreover, the 1919 directory ignored any point of settlement where no Jewish institutions had been established.[18]

The directory published in the *American Jewish Year Book* in 1919 contains what is without question the most comprehensive listing of local Jewish organizations to appear in the first half of the twentieth century. As such, it is of incomparable value for the study both of major Jewish communities and of smaller ones in small towns. Still, even this resource has its limitations. For one thing, as they themselves admitted, the compilers of the 1919 directory did not always get responses to the survey questionnaires they circulated, despite "repeated requests for information."[19] Furthermore, many of the particulars published in the directory are contradicted by information available from other sources. For example, whereas the 1919 directory indicates that Congregation Bnai Israel in Keokuk, Iowa, was founded in 1853, the 1880 *Statistics of the Jews* gives the date of the congregation's establishment as 1864, the *American Jewish Year Book* directory of 1900 indicates 1856, and the *Year Book* directory of 1907 suggests 1865. Similarly, the 1919 directory gives 1888 as the year in which Congregation Beth Tefilloh was founded in Brunswick, Georgia, but the *Universal Jewish Encyclopedia*, published in the 1940s, indicates 1885 as the date of Beth Tefiloh's establishment, and the temple's own seventy-fifth anniversary history gives 1886. To cite but one more example, the 1919 directory indicates that the United Hebrew Congregation of Keyport, New Jersey, was organized in 1902, while a recent study covering the Jewish history of that town reports that the congregation was founded in 1880 and cites 1902 as the year in which it converted a private house for use as a synagogue.[20] In cases such as these, it is always difficult to know which source to believe, and we are left simply to make educated guesses.

---

### RALEIGH (Jewish pop. 120)

Cg.  **House of Jacob.** Org. 1912. Pres., J. Kline, S. Wilmington; Sec., H. Kaplan. Members, 25; income, $1500. *Services:* Weekly, Hebrew. *School:* Classes, 2; teachers, 1; pupils, 35; sessions weekly, 3.
**House of Or,** 210 Wilmington. Rabbi, William Loewenberg; Pres., M. Rosenthal; Sec., I. Emanuel. Members, 30. *Services:* Sabbath, English and Hebrew. *School:* Classes, 5; teachers, 5; pupils, 35; sessions weekly, 1. *Auxiliary Society:* Sisterhood.

Educ. **Young Men's Hebrew Association.** Pres., Solon Jacobs, 309 Fayetteville.

Cem.  **Hebrew Cemetery,** County of Wake. Inc. March 25, 1870.

### STATESVILLE (Jewish pop. 55)

Cg.  **Emanuel.** Pres., J. Stephany; Sec., Sig. Wallace.
Cem.  **Oakwood Cemetery.**

### TARBORO (Jewish pop. 55)

Cg.  **B'nai Israel,** Main. Sec., G. L. Heilbronner.

### WILMINGTON (Jewish pop. 400)

Cg.  ***B'nai Yisroel,** 116 Dock. Org. April 20, 1906.
**Temple Israel,** 511 Orange. Rabbi, Samuel Mendelson.

Educ. **Young Men's Hebrew Association,** 212 N. Front. Org. 1910. Pres., B. May; Sec., H. Joffe. Members, 30.

Char. **Hebrew Relief Association,** 511 Orange. Pres., B. Solomon; Sec.-Treas., S. Mendelsohn. Members, 30.

Cem. **B'nai Yisroel Burial Ground.** Inc. April 20, 1906.
**True Brothers Society.** Inc. 1852. Cemetery, Oakdale.

### WINSTON-SALEM (Jewish pop. 116)

Cg.  **Winston-Salem Hebrew Congregation,** N. Cherry. Org. 1912. Rabbi, P. Berlin; Pres., Frank Urband; Sec., T. Sosnik. Members, 30; income, $1200. *Services:* Weekly, Hebrew. *School:* Classes, 3; teachers, 1; pupils, 9; sessions weekly, 5.

## NORTH DAKOTA

### ASHLEY

Cg.  **Congregation.** Rabbi, ——— Ostrowsky.

### DEVILS LAKE

Cg.  **B'nai Israel.** Rabbi, Simon Rapoport.

### EDMORE

Cg.  **Hebrew Aid Society** (in Jewish colony, 12 miles from Edmore, N. D.). Sam Yaffee, Starkweather, N. D.

Cem. **Cemetery,** Sullivan township. Used also by Jews of Devil's Lake, N. D.

### FALLON

Cem. **Cemetery.**

### FARGO (Jewish pop. 600)

Cg.  **Fargo Hebrew Congregation.** Org. 1896. Cantor, J. Klitzner. *Services:* Hebrew. *School:* Talmud Torah, teachers, 2; pupils, 122.

Char. **Associated Jewish Charities.** Sec., Dave Naftalin, 318 Front.
**Hebrew Ladies' Aid Society.** Mrs. M. Seigel, 1019 4th Av., S.

Zion. **Fargo Zionist Society.** Pres., Dave Naftalin.

Cem. **Cemetery.** Owned by Fargo Hebrew Congregation.

---

*A page from the "Directory of Jewish Local Organizations in the United States" that appeared in the* American Jewish Year Book *in 1919. The 1919 directory is one of the few comprehensive inventories of local Jewish institutions ever published. Reprinted by permission of the American Jewish Committee.*

For some years after 1919, the *American Jewish Year Book* continued to supplement and update its directory of local organizations,[21] but it never again published a complete listing of all of American Jewry's local institutions. On the other hand, the *Year Book* did report on two exhaustive population surveys undertaken by the Bureau of Jewish Statistics during the period between the two world wars, when that office was under the direction of Harry S. Linfield. The first of these enumerations was conducted in 1927, and its results were published in the *Jewish Year Book* twice. They appear in a city-by-city listing in the volume that came out in 1928 and again in the volume published in 1929, where they accompany a report focusing on Jewish congregations throughout the United States. The bureau's second Jewish census of the interwar period was conducted in 1937, with the results included in the *American Jewish Year Book* that appeared in 1940.[22]

As in previous studies, many of the Jewish population figures generated by the 1927 and 1937 surveys are open to question. To take one example, it is almost certain that the figure of 450 Jews reported for San Mateo, California, in 1927 is incorrect. A review of local city directories from that era reveals that Jews operated very few San Mateo businesses of the type commonly owned by small-town Jewish merchants, and this result makes it difficult to believe that San Mateo was home to several hundred Jews in the interwar period. In 1930, for instance, San Mateo had seven ladies' wear shops, nine men's clothing stores, and about a dozen furniture stores, but no more than two of these establishments were owned by local Jews. Moreover, San Mateo's first synagogue, Peninsula Temple Beth El, was not established until after World War II, and the history of that congregation suggests that significant Jewish settlement in the area began only in the late 1940s, as young families came there to buy homes with the aid of the G.I. Bill. Perhaps the report of hundreds of Jews in San Mateo is somehow related to the fact that San Francisco's Jewish elite had established the Beresford Country Club there in 1912. Only a handful of its members became residents of San Mateo, but the presence of the club may have prompted whoever reported on the town to exaggerate the size of its Jewish population. Similarly, the figures of 800 Jews reported for Paducah, Kentucky, in 1927 and of 600 in 1937, are also open to challenge. The records of Paducah's only synagogue, Temple Israel, reveal a total congregational population of only 232 individuals in 1927, when synagogue membership seems to have been the norm. So, too, a 1937 report dealing with Jewish Federations and Welfare Funds gives Paducah's Jewish population as only 350.[23]

Aside from questions about the accuracy of the data collected, there are problems with the way the results of the 1927 and 1937 surveys were reported. The account of the 1927 census published in 1928 lists over 3,000 places in the United States where Jews were living, but even this exhaustive account inadvertently omits at least some towns that were centers of Jewish life in the late 1920s. Tupper Lake, New York; Kittaning, Pennsylvania; and Waukegan, Illinois, are all absent from the 1928 report, for instance, even though Jews supported a synagogue in each of these places and even though the survey of congregations published in 1929 provides a Jewish population figure for each of these towns. So, too, Ottumwa, Iowa, which was reported to have 400 Jewish residents in 1918 and 195 in 1937, is missing from the published accounts of the 1927 census.

Another indication of the imperfect nature of the 1928 and 1929 *Jewish Year Book* reports is that in some cases they provide different population figures for the same place. The Jewish population of Warren, Ohio, for example, is given as 710 in the 1928 city-by-city report, but as 400 in the 1929 report on congregations. Similarly, the figure for the Jewish population of Norristown, Pennsylvania, is 750 in the 1928 report, but 600 in the 1929 report. Marion, Indiana, is said to have 500 Jews in the 1928 report, but 5,000 in the report on congregations. In one table published in 1929, Bristol, Tennessee, is shown as a place with seventy Jews and a congregation. However, in another table in the same *Year Book* volume, Bristol is listed as having 108 Jews and no congregation. Even if some of the differences that show up in the census figures published in 1928 and 1929 are simply typographical errors (this is certainly true in the case of Marion, Indiana), their appearance suggests a certain laxity on the part of those involved with the population study.[24] Nonetheless, the Jewish population surveys of 1927 and 1937 seem to have been handled more carefully than previous tabulations, and they remain the most detailed studies ever undertaken of the number of Jews in the United States and their geographic distribution. Among the most impressive features of these surveys is that they attempted to solicit data from every Jewish settlement in the United States and to provide an exact population figure for every place in the country that was home to more than ten Jewish inhabitants.

When the *American Jewish Year Book* resumed publishing information on the Jewish population of the United States after World War II, it was no longer able to base its reports on the kinds of exhaustive studies that had been undertaken in the interwar period. The Bureau of Jewish Statistics established early in the century had disappeared as a separate agency by the late 1940s, and population estimates available after that time were based only on data from large communities in which there were affiliates of the Council of Jewish Federations and Welfare Funds, and from a few centralized Jewish agencies that had offices in New York. Thus, whereas the last Jewish population survey conducted before World War II had benefited from reports received from "4,694 cities, villages, and rural areas," the census taken in 1948 could claim only that it relied primarily on "a poll of over two hundred Jewish community organizations." The population update conducted in 1950 was based on reports from only 159 communities, in most of which, the compiler of the statistics lamented, "interest in basic population data did not seem to be very marked."[25]

Generally speaking, in the decades after World War II, demographic studies of large and midsize Jewish communities became more sophisticated and more reliable, while the population statistics for smaller communities became less precise, if they were available at all. In the second half of the twentieth century, the *American Jewish Year Book* adopted the practice of publishing data only on places with Jewish populations of at least 100, and it increasingly consolidated the figures for many metropolitan areas. Sometimes it lumped together population data for even larger geographic regions. In the listings that the *Year Book* published in 1984, for example, the section on Illinois grouped together all the towns of the "Chicago Metropolitan Area" and gave only a single population figure for "Southern Illinois." The 1984 listings for New Jersey supplied figures for entire counties such as Bergen, Essex, Gloucester, Monmouth, and Ocean, rather than for the individual cities and towns in each of these counties. It also gave a consolidated figure for twelve towns in two different counties under the heading "North Jersey" and for sixteen towns in three different counties under the designation "Raritan Valley."[26] As the *Year Book* itself conceded, the method of gathering and reporting Jewish population data after World War II permitted "a substantial range of error," especially where small towns were concerned.[27] All this made the task of following population trends in towns adjacent to each other or near larger cities difficult, if not impossible. It also ended any chance of systematically tracking the demographic situation in small towns where the number of Jews dropped below 100.

Despite the less than perfect nature of the various Jewish population studies conducted over the years, the aggregate data they assembled are tremendously useful. Each of these studies at least tried to be complete and accurate, and, in the absence of statistics gathered with the full resources of the American government, they provide the most reliable information available about America's Jewish population in times past. Ultimately these studies afford a highly detailed view of the patterns of Jewish settlement in America at several points in time, especially for the period between the 1870s and World War II.[28]

Of course, discovering and assessing the demographic data available on America's various Jewish centers is only a part of what is required for a comprehensive study of the small Jewish communities of small-town America. To conduct such a study, we must also find a precise way of distinguishing small communities from other centers of Jewish life, and we must identify a set of communities whose history can be taken as representative. Although some vague notion of what constitutes a "small community" or a "small-town community" may be sufficient for very general discussions of the American Jewish experience, a more rigorous definition is needed if these communities are to be examined as a class, and especially if their history is to be subjected to some sort of systematic analysis.

Although scholars studying human society have never reached complete agreement on a definition of the word "community," many widely accepted applications of the term assume not only that such an entity is composed of individuals who routinely interact with each other and have a certain sense of social connectedness, but also that these individuals inhabit a defined geographic area.[29] Thus, we should first take note of the fact that the identity of each of America's smaller Jewish communities was very much bound up with its location in a particular urban locale. This was especially true in the decades just before and after the turn of the twentieth century, when cities were strongly promoting municipal pride and when geographic features that now impose few impediments to long-distance contacts acted as significant physical and psychological barriers, even between places that were not very far apart. Only after the middle of the twentieth century did advances in transportation and communication, and the advent of urban sprawl, begin to blur the boundaries between individual cities and towns, and between big cities and the small towns around them.

In identifying small communities with the specific towns in which they existed, it is important to recognize that, in most instances, even Jewish settlements in municipalities directly adjacent to each other created their own institutional frameworks and forged their own distinct self-images. A case in point is the situation that developed in the towns of Lewiston and Auburn, Maine. These two municipalities are just across the Androscoggin River from each other, and the first Jews who moved to Auburn in 1899 actually came from Lewiston. Nonetheless, as early as 1902 the Jews of Auburn began to establish their own identity. In that year they incorporated their own synagogue, Beth Abraham, created their own burial society, and secured for their use a section of the cemetery that Lewiston's Beth Jacob congregation had established earlier. Thus, throughout much of the twentieth century, the Jews of Lewiston and those of Auburn remained members of two separate communities, both in life and in death.[30]

Still more to the point is the fact that, in the past, even the Jewish communities of small towns that were in the shadow of major cities maintained their own identities. Of course, it is true that major urban centers have always had a palpable influence on the small towns in their immediate vicinity. As early as 1910 the U.S. Census Bureau asserted that "in the case of many cities there are suburban districts . . . which, from many standpoints, are as truly a part of the city as the districts which are under the municipal government." In keeping with this conviction, the Census Bureau designated twenty-five "metropolitan districts" that were centered on cities with populations of 200,000 or more and included all other densely populated municipalities within ten miles of those cities. This meant, for example, that from early in the century, small Massachusetts towns such as Framingham, Lexington, Norwood, and Waltham (all of which were home to small Jewish communities) were considered by the Census Bureau to be within the Boston Metropolitan District, and that small

Illinois towns such as Chicago Heights, Cicero, Evanston, and Glencoe (again, all with Jewish communities) were considered to be within the Chicago Metropolitan District. By 1930 the Census Bureau had increased the number of metropolitan districts to ninety-six.[31]

Nonetheless, despite the special economic and social ties that always existed between major metropolitan centers and the towns around them, much evidence suggests that smaller cities on the perimeter of great ones maintained a strong sense of their own individuality. The historian Michael Ebner has shown, for example, that throughout the late nineteenth century and into the early twentieth, even as the concept of Greater Chicago's "North Shore" was evolving, towns such as Glencoe and Evanston strove mightily to maintain their detachment both from the huge city just to their south and from each other. More generally, the research of James Borchert has revealed that in the last decades of the nineteenth century and in the first half of the twentieth, many smaller cities adjacent to large ones were what he calls "city suburbs." These were not simply bedroom communities, but rather complex urban places with self-images that set them apart from their core municipalities. The sociologist Daniel Elazar has gone so far as to argue that even after World War II, the larger a metropolitan area was, the more likely the small cities within it were "to value their autonomy and their separate identities."[32]

In much the same way, at least until the middle of the twentieth century, most Jews in towns adjacent to big cities maintained a sense that their communities were quite self-contained and that they had their own individual characters. Before midcentury it would not have occurred to the Jews of the various mountain valleys of southwestern Pennsylvania to think of themselves as Jews from "Greater Pittsburgh," for example. Even late in the twentieth century, many of those who grew up in places such as Ambridge, Canonsburg, or Donora, Pennsylvania, retained their identification with these specific towns, though they may have moved to Pittsburgh or to other large cities long before. Nor did the Jews of northern Kentucky think of themselves as part of the Jewish community of "Greater Cincinnati," even though they could literally see that city just across the Ohio River. The Kentucky Jewish communities of both Newport and Covington had more or less disintegrated by the 1960s, but the consciousness of veterans of these communities remained connected with their places of origin. Not only did they hold a reunion as recently as 1994, but at that gathering a distinction was still being made between families that had been based in Newport and those with roots in Covington.[33]

Around New York City in the period before World War II, even Jews in Westchester Country towns such as Mount Vernon and Yonkers, which are directly adjacent to the Bronx, very seldom commuted into the metropolis, and this fact suggests that the Jews of small Westchester towns even farther away tended to maintain their isolation from the city as well. Similarly, one Jewish resident of Englewood, New Jersey, just across the Hudson River from Manhattan, described his town in the 1920s and early 1930s as being "cut off from New York" because there was no bridge to the city, while the Jewish residents of pre–World War II Kearny, New Jersey, were so detached from the adjacent city of Newark, to say nothing of New York, that they supported two kosher butcher shops of their own. As late as 1947, when Jerome Fien moved to Caldwell, New Jersey, his father-in-law worried that it would take him forty minutes to get to Newark, which was actually only about nine miles away, and he proclaimed Caldwell to be at "the end of the world."[34] It seems that no matter how imposing a major Jewish center was, the communities of the smaller towns around it resisted its pull.

Recent historians writing about America's primary Jewish centers seem to have recognized that small communities adjacent to larger ones were quite distinct entities. Seldom have they argued that the Jews of a core community and those of the small towns in its orbit represented a single, tightly integrated system. In his study of Cleveland's Jewish history, Lloyd Gartner reports that in the mid-1920s some 7,000 of Greater Cleveland's 78,000 Jews lived outside the city proper, and he gives the impression that the Jewish settlements of towns such as East Cleveland and Lakewood were essentially appendages of the Cleveland Jewish community.[35] But Gartner's approach in his study of Cleveland is anomalous. Much more commonly, scholars who have chronicled the pre–World War II history of America's more substantial Jewish communities (including Gartner himself in some of his works) have tended to ignore the smaller Jewish settlements that existed in their shadows.

For example, in their book on the Cincinnati Jewish community, Jonathan Sarna and Nancy Klein make no mention of Norwood, Ohio, or of Covington and Newport, Kentucky, even though these towns were centers of Jewish activity in the decades before World War II and all were within the Cincinnati Metropolitan District defined by the U.S. Census as early as 1910. Similarly, the exhaustive study of Milwaukee Jewry prepared by Louis Swichkow together with Lloyd Gartner chronicles how, beginning just before World War II, the city's Jewish population expanded into new areas of settlement such as White-fish Bay and Shorewood along Lake Michigan, but it never considers the Jews of the adjacent city of West Allis, even though that municipality was within the Milwaukee Metropolitan District from the time the Census Bureau first defined it. In recounting the history of the Jews of Los Angeles, Gartner and Max Vorspan describe the dispersal of Jews to areas such as Beverly Hills, Westwood, and Brentwood in the second half of the twentieth century, but they say nothing about the prewar Jewish settlements of places such as Alhambra, Glendale, and Santa Ana, all of which were within the Los Angeles Metropolitan District by 1920.[36]

Some local historians have remarked explicitly on the separate identities of small communities adjacent to the larger cities about which they have written. Sidney Bolkosky, the historian of twentieth-century Detroit Jewry, has identified the Jewish communities in places on the outskirts of the city, such as Pontiac and Mount Clemens, as "peripheral" and "autonomous" in the 1920s and 1930s. Likewise, in the preface to his book on the Jews of St. Louis, Walter Ehrlich declares that he did not feel compelled to treat the Jewish history of Hannibal, Missouri; Belleville, Illinois, and other nearby towns, because "although located near St. Louis physically, Jews residing in these places have never been viewed as part of the 'St. Louis' Jewish community." Each small-town community near St. Louis, he adds, "has had its own independent albeit isolated identity."[37] Insights such as these only reinforce the notion that small communities were invariably identified very closely with the towns in which they developed, even if those town were near much larger Jewish centers.

There still remains the matter of identifying a representative sample of small communities on which to base a study of small-town Jewish life. Virtually every small Jewish community in America was a small-town settlement, but exactly how shall the term "small community" be defined? Unfortunately, previous discussions of American Jewish demography do not provide much guidance in this regard, for those who have written about the subject have tended to avoid categorizing various Jewish settlements by size. The sundry Jewish population surveys conducted in the first half of the twentieth century, for example, essentially ignored community size as an organizing principal. When Samson Oppenheim reported on the population survey undertaken by the Bureau of Jewish Statistics in 1917, he presented nearly all its findings either in state-by-state listings or according to categories based on the total populations of the cities in which America's various Jewish communities were located.[38]

Similarly, Harry Linfield's work on the distribution of Jews across the United States in 1927 divided America's cities and towns into categories by size and reported on the number of municipalities that had Jewish residents. (Of the 2,790 urban places in the United States with populations of 2,500 or more, some 89 percent had at least some Jewish inhabitants.) Linfield's work did not, however, distinguish between places that had only a handful of Jews and those that had recognizable communities.[39] Elsewhere in his writings, Linfield designated any point of Jewish settlement where a congregation has been established as a "principal" or "independent" community and any place without a congregation as a "subordinate" community. Although this scheme recognized that the existence of religious institutions is important in defining communal life, it not only lumped small communities together with large ones, but also resulted in the labeling of some points of settlement with only tiny Jewish populations as "principal communities." For example, Linfield counted Dickinson, North Dakota; Forrest City, Arkansas; Troy, Alabama; Archbald, Pennsylvania; and Old Orchard, Maine, among America's "principal" Jewish centers, even though none of these towns had a Jewish population of over 30 individuals in 1927. By the same token, Linfield's criteria for classifying communities relegated some Jewish centers that had quite substantial Jewish populations to the status of "subordinate" communities simply because they happened to be without functioning congregations in 1927. Among these were Evanston, Illinois, with 315 Jews; Chicopee, Massachusetts, with 430 Jews; and Clifton, New Jersey, with 625 Jews.[40]

More recent scholars also have avoided using size as a criterion for defining Jewish communities. When, in the 1970s, the historian Rudolph Glanz wrote about the spread of Jews across America before the Civil War, for instance, he defined Jewish communities simply as places where "local settlers were possessed of a will to continue their communal Jewish existence through the creation of some kind of Jewish institution." Again, this broad definition not only failed to differentiate between major Jewish centers and secondary ones, but it also labeled many clusters of a few individuals and families as "communities" when they probably did not warrant that designation. Glanz's study suggested that Jewish communities existed before the Civil War in places such as New Bedford, Massachusetts; Port Carbon, Pennsylvania; Marietta, Ohio; Bolivar, Tennessee; and Grand Gulf, Mississippi. However, none of these towns was reported to have any Jewish residents at all when the first comprehensive survey of American Jewry was conducted in the 1870s, so it is unlikely that they were home to more than a handful of Jews before 1861.[41]

In the absence of any previously developed and widely accepted definition of what constitutes a small Jewish community, I have identified a specific sample of Jewish settlements that might be considered exemplars of small communities (and thus of small-town communities) in general. Specifically, this study focuses on the communities of those 490 urban places in the United States with reported Jewish populations of at least 100 but fewer than 1,000 individuals in 1927. Because our concern here is with urban settings and because the experience of Jews in agrarian environments has received a fair amount of attention in recent years,[42] agricultural colonies and rural localities with triple-digit Jewish populations, places such as Norma and Rosenhayn, New Jersey, and Colchester, Connecticut, have been excluded from consideration. An inventory of the 490 communities that constitute the sample upon which this study rests, together with their reported Jewish populations at several points in time, appears as table 1 in the appendix.

Several considerations influenced the way I selected the model Jewish settlements for this study. The decision to define "small communities" as those with triple-digit populations was in part a matter of convenience, but it relied also on the premise that in the late nineteenth and early twentieth centuries, the classic era of small-town Jewish life in America, settlements of fewer than 100 Jews were unlikely to have attained the critical mass necessary to constitute full-fledged communities. The criteria I used also assumed that once a place achieved a population of 1,000 Jews, it was already on the verge of becoming a midsize Jewish center. The presumption that at least 100 Jews were needed for the maintenance of an active communal life is borne out, at least in part, by the fact that a triple-digit population seemed to be a good predictor for the presence of fundamental communal institutions in the decades before World War II. For example, even though there were reported to be some 251 towns in the United States with at least fifty Jewish residents but fewer than 100 in 1927, the comprehensive data collected about these places indicate that only about half had established congregations. Moreover, some of the congregations counted in these towns were barely functioning in 1927 or had in fact disappeared. Temple Bnai Shalom in New Bern, North Carolina, had erected a synagogue building in 1906, but it soon began holding services only a few times a year, and it was hardly a significant presence by 1927, when New Bern was reported to have a Jewish population of sixty. In Helena, Montana, with seventy-nine Jews reported in 1927, the last rabbi of Temple Emanu-El had departed in 1917, and the congregation was so weak in the interwar period that in the 1930s its few remaining members deeded their synagogue building to the state. The town of La Porte, Indiana, with a reported Jewish population of fifty, was still listed as having an active congregation in 1927, but in fact the local Jews had ceased supporting their temple B'ne Zion in 1886 and had sold off its synagogue building in 1898.[43] By contrast, of the 490 cities and towns with triple-digit Jewish populations in 1927, 89 percent were reported to be home to at least one Jewish congregation.

At the other extreme of the standard used to categorize our small communities, growth beyond triple digits seemed to be a good predictor for the development of an increasingly complex communal infrastructure. Of the 490 triple-digit Jewish settlements in our sample, only eight were reported to have three congregations functioning in 1927, and none had any more. By contrast, of the 197 Jewish communities of 1,000 or more people reported in 1927, 124 had three or more congregations functioning, and only twenty had fewer than two congregations.

Despite the fact that scholars in the past have not attempted to define small Jewish communities in terms of numbers, over the years there have been indications that many observers of American Jewish life intuitively adopted the triple-digit standard applied in this study. In 1919, for example, the *American Jewish Year Book* implied that a population of 1,000 individuals was the dividing line between small communities and primary ones when, among the summary materials it published on Jewish population, it uncharacteristically included a table of all U.S. cities "having one thousand or more Jewish inhabitants."[44] Similarly, when, after World War II, the *Year Book* ceased reporting population data on municipalities with fewer than 100 Jews, it implied that such places were not worthy of notice as independent Jewish centers. So too, when Rabbi Lee J. Levinger published his very perceptive article on "The Disappearing Small-Town Jew" in *Commentary* magazine in 1952, he expressed particular concern about those living in communities of "a hundred Jews or less," thus distinguishing those tiny Jewish enclaves from more developed small-town communities. A decade later, the commentator Erich Rosenthal argued that any Jewish community of fewer than 1,000 individuals "necessarily lacked the esprit de corps essential for maintaining the communal institutions needed for group survival," thus implying once again that 1,000 Jews was the minimum required to constitute a community of the first order.[45]

In choosing the sample communities for this study, I took the decade of the 1920s as a point of departure because that was such a crucial time in the development of American Jewry. The era of mass migration was coming to an end, and the development of individual Jewish settlements was reaching a sort of crescendo. Furthermore, there is no period in American Jewish history for which better composite information is available about the geography of Jewish life. Using data from the 1920s also has the advantage of identifying only communities that remained small from the time of their founding until at least the middle of the twentieth century. Of the 490 Jewish centers in our sample, no more than twenty-one were reported to have Jewish populations over 1,000 as late as 1950, and these twenty-one include only seven with Jewish populations over 2,000. By contrast, selecting small communities on the basis of population data from some time before the 1920s would have swept into our sample many Jewish settlements that were simply in the process of growing into far more populous Jewish centers. After all, every large and midsize Jewish community went through a period as a small settlement sometime in its history. Even New York had a Jewish population only slightly greater than 1,000 in 1830, while Philadelphia had a Jewish population of only 750 in that year. Of the 197 cities that were home to 1,000 or more Jews in 1927, some 37 percent had supported only triple-digit Jewish settlements during the first decade of the twentieth century. Of course, major communities in the early phases of their growth had certain things in common with persistently small communities, and the experience of the one group can shed light on the experience of the other. Still, the early history of prominent communities is often well known, and it seemed appropriate in this study to focus only on smaller Jewish settlements that endured as such throughout the first half of the twentieth century, if not longer.

There is no denying, of course, that the parameters used to select representative Jewish centers for this study are to some extent arbitrary and that they exclude some settlements that might well have been counted among America's typical small Jewish communities. For example, the communities of the thirty-five American towns that were home to somewhere between ninety and ninety-nine Jews in 1927 no doubt functioned much like those of towns with triple-digit Jewish populations. Jewish life in a place such as Gastonia, North Carolina, with a reported Jewish population of ninety-nine in 1927, surely was very similar to Jewish life in a town such as High Point, in the same state, which had a reported Jewish population of 101. Likewise, Jewish life in the south Texas town of Victoria, where ninety-six Jews were said to be living in 1927, was undoubtedly much like Jewish life in Laredo, also in south Texas, where 120 Jews were reported. By the same token, some Jewish centers whose populations hovered just above 1,000 undoubtedly operated much like triple-digit communities, especially if they were in relatively small cities. Among the Jewish communities of the United States in 1927, sixty-nine were composed of between 1,000 and 2,000 Jews and located in cities with total populations under 50,000. There was probably not much difference between the Jewish experience in Homestead, Pennsylvania, whose reported Jewish population in 1927 was 1,100, and the Jewish experience in nearby Duquesne, whose reported Jewish population was 920. Jewish life in Superior, Wisconsin, with 1,050 Jews, was probably much like that in Kenosha, with 900 Jews.

Also excluded from the set of communities selected for this study are some settlements whose populations may have been misreported in 1927 or those that may have reckoned their populations in triple digits just before or soon after that year. In Massachusetts alone, for example, according to the available data, there were as many as nine triple-digit communities in 1937 that had not been in that category ten years earlier.[46] Still, it remains reasonable to base an analysis of the patterns of history in the smaller Jewish communities of small-town America on a study of the 490 places that constitute our sample. The standard used to identify our exemplary small communities is consistent, it relies upon one of the most complete surveys of America's Jewish population ever conducted, it produces a very large number of cases, and it rests on a number of carefully considered truths about the American Jewish experience. Despite all the questions that can be raised about how best to define small communities and despite all the problems that the available data on population and communal structure present, there can be little doubt that studying the experience of communities whose population was in triple digits as the era of mass migration came to a close will also reveal a great deal about similar nineteenth- and early twentieth-century Jewish centers that are absent from our sample. Ultimately, an investigation of the Jewish experience in our 490 sample communities will lead to a rather complete understanding of small-town Jewish life in America.

# 2  Patterns of Settlement: The Early Years

The population information collected by the American Jewish Committee's Bureau of Jewish Statistics in 1927 reveals that by the time the mass migration of East European Jews to America had come to an end, small communities were playing an extremely important role in defining the geography of American Jewish life. Cities and towns with Jewish populations of at least 100 but under 1,000 (the places on which our attention is focused) were widely distributed across the United States, and there were hundreds of other points of settlement with less significant concentrations of Jews as well. Except for Delaware and Oregon, each of the forty-eight states in the Union had at least one town with a triple-digit Jewish community, and several of the country's more rural states were home to a number of triple-digit communities even if they did not have a single major Jewish center. North Carolina, for example, had no Jewish communities of 1,000 or more individuals in 1927, but the state had thirteen triple-digit Jewish settlements. Mississippi, which also had no city with as many as 1,000 Jews, nonetheless had nine triple-digit communities. In the Upper Midwest, North Dakota had no major communities, but the state was home to five triple-digit settlements; and in New England, neither New Hampshire nor Vermont had any highly visible Jewish communities, but between them the two states counted eleven triple-digit Jewish centers.

A pattern of multiple small communities was also evident in several states with only one or two larger Jewish centers. In Kentucky, where the only substantial Jewish community in 1927 was in Louisville, there were five triple-digit Jewish settlements; and in Arkansas, where only the city of Little Rock was home to over 1,000 Jews, there were seven triple-digit communities. In Maine, where Jewish settlements of over 1,000 could be found only in Portland and Bangor, there were nine other towns with triple-digit Jewish populations; and in West Virginia, where Charleston and Huntington had achieved Jewish populations of slightly over 1,000 by 1927, nine other towns had Jewish populations of at least 100 but fewer than 1,000.

On the other hand, small Jewish communities were abundant in states with several large or at least midsize Jewish settlements as well. Indeed, as table 2 in the appendix indicates, the states with the greatest concentration of substantial communities were also the ones with the largest number of triple-digit settlements. Thus, in 1927, Massachusetts, New York, New Jersey, and Pennsylvania were not only the four states that had the greatest number of Jewish communities with populations of 1,000 or more, but also the four with the greatest number of triple-digit Jewish communities. In fact, when the distribution of America's Jewish communities in the 1920s is examined on a regional basis, a certain similarity between the dispersal of larger and smaller communities becomes evident. In 1927, one of every three cities in the United States with a Jewish population of 1,000 or more was located in the country's Middle Atlantic region, and so was one of every three towns with a triple-digit Jewish population. Similarly, the Midwest (the U.S. Census Bureau's East North Central and West North Central regions) had 21 percent of the more populous Jewish communities in the country and 24 percent of the country's triple-digit communities. Nineteen percent of America's Jewish communities of 1,000 or more were located in the South (the Census Bureau's South Atlantic, East South Central, and West South Central regions), as were 21 percent of the country's triple-digit communities. The Far West (the Mountain and Pacific census regions) claimed 8 percent of the nation's larger communities and 7 percent of its triple-digit Jewish centers.

Of course, the dispersal of both larger and smaller communities across the country reflected the regional distribution of America's Jewish population more generally. However, the pattern of distribution of small communities depended also on the character of the cities and towns in which they were located and on the nature of the various factors that drew Jewish settlers into the American hinterland. As we consider how Jewish pioneers created the earliest of America's classic small-town Jewish communities, we shall discover the important part played by local transportation networks and by connections of kith and kin in the formation of those settlements, and we shall learn about the key role a town's economic vitality played in determining the fate of the Jewish enclave within it.

A careful analysis of the distribution of America's various Jewish settlements confirms the very close relationship that existed between the magnitude of a city's total population and the size of its Jewish population.[1] In other words, it substantiates the observation that large and midsize Jewish centers were in more substantial urban environments, while small communities were typically in small-town settings. In New York, for example, there were ten cities with total populations of 75,000 or more according to the 1930 census, and each of these had a Jewish population of at least 1,000 in 1927. These cities were Albany, Binghamton, Buffalo, Niagara Falls, Rochester, Schenectady, Syracuse, Utica, Yonkers, and, of course, New York City itself. Of the state's thirteen other cities with total populations over 25,000, eight had Jewish communities of at least 1,000 individuals, while five had triple-digit communities. Furthermore, of the forty-seven municipalities in New York with total populations of between 10,000 and 25,000, three had Jewish communities of 1,000 or more, and twenty-two had triple-digit Jewish communities.

The situation in other states also reflected the strong relationship between the size of a city and the size of its Jewish community. In Indiana, the seven largest cities (Indianapolis, Fort Wayne, South Bend, Evansville, Gary, Hammond, and Terre Haute) were home to the seven Jewish communities of at least 1,000 in the state. Among Indiana's eleven cities next in size, nine had triple-digit communities. In Georgia, the only Jewish communities of over 1,000 were in the state's two largest cities, Atlanta and Savannah. However, seven of the nine Georgia towns next in size were home to triple-digit communities. Out in the West, in Colorado, Jewish communities of over 1,000 individuals existed in Denver and in Pueblo, the state's largest urban centers, and there were triple-digit communities in Colorado Springs, Greeley, and Trinidad, the state's three cities next in size. In Montana there were no large or midsize Jewish communities at all in 1927, but the most populous urban centers in the state, Butte and Great Falls, each had small communities in triple digits. Taking into account all urban places with 100 or more Jews, the coefficient of correlation between the Jewish population of a city in the late 1920s and its total population was a very high .92, where a coefficient of 1.00 indicates a perfect linkage between the population of a city and the size of its Jewish community.

The generalization that America's smaller Jewish centers were essentially small-town communities is borne out by actual population figures as well. On average, the total number of inhabitants in an urban place with a triple-digit Jewish community in 1927 was 18,044 in the census year 1920 and 22,986 in 1930. By contrast, the average total population of a city with a Jewish community of 1,000 or more in 1927 was 171,348 in 1920 and 210,711 in 1930. Even with New York City removed from consideration, the average population of cities with large and midsize Jewish communities was 143,549 in 1920 and 176,427 in 1930. Judging by 1920 census figures, only 18 of the 490 urban Jewish settlements in the United States that had at least 100 but fewer than 1,000 individuals were in cities of over 50,000 inhabitants. Moreover, even the largest of the cities in which triple-digit communities were found (Manchester, New Hampshire; Rockford, Illinois; and Wichita, Kansas) were not generally regarded as great urban centers.

The very oldest of the small Jewish communities that were scattered across America by the 1920s could trace their origins back to the arrival of a few Jewish settlers in the middle decades of the nineteenth century, and in a few cases even earlier. These pioneers were most often aspiring merchants who were looking for economic opportunities in what were almost invariably frontier outposts of one sort or another. Thus, Manus Israel opened a dry-goods and millinery shop in Kalamazoo, Michigan, around 1840, when the place was still little more than a village, while Michael Hyman, the first Jew to settle in Wabash, Indiana, opened a small grocery there in 1846. In Paducah, Kentucky, there were four Jewish entrepreneurs conducting business on Front Street in 1851, and in Pine Bluff, Arkansas, there were about a dozen Jewish businesses by 1860. In 1867 Joseph Perlinsky became one of the first Jewish businessmen in Canton, Mississippi, opening what was then the only tailor shop in town.[2]

It was not unusual for the first Jewish settlers who arrived in America's various small towns to have started out as peddlers, for in the middle decades of the nineteenth century peddling in the countryside was a common occupation for Jews newly arrived in America and searching for a way to establish themselves economically. Peddling was an attractive option for these immigrants because it required neither much training nor much command of the English language, and because they could usually find an established merchant, often a fellow Jew or even a relative, who would provide the capital or the goods needed to make a start. Moreover, there was a great need for peddlers among the scattered farmsteads and villages of the American countryside, for until the early twentieth century much of the population lacked ready access to major commercial centers, where the peddlers themselves obtained their wares, or even to country stores, where the peddlers sometimes kept their stock. As a result the itinerant merchant, whether with a pack on his back or driving a horse-drawn wagon, was the most immediate source many people had for commodities such as dry goods, hardware items, and novelties.[3]

Indeed, even though their names are often lost to history, it is very likely that roving peddlers were the first Jews to encounter the various towns that would eventually become the sites of small Jewish communities. So ubiquitous were Jewish peddlers in frontier areas that Jacob Rader Marcus, often regarded as the dean of American Jewish historians, was fond of saying that no matter who was identified as the first Jew in a given place, it was certain that another Jew had been there before him. Those peddlers whose names are recorded in the annals of America's small communities are ones who did more than simply wander through town. Some are identifiable because their lives took an unexpected turn. Evidence that a Jewish pack peddler named Solomon Huffman was plying his wares around the central Pennsylvania town of

Williamsport, for example, comes from the fact that he was robbed and murdered there in 1838.[4] Other itinerant peddlers became associated with specific towns because they chose those places as the centers of their peddling operations. Before the Civil War, three Weil brothers alternated peddling with running a local store in Alexandria, Louisiana, for instance; and around 1870 the peddlers Aaron Bornstein and Alexander Weinberg were based in Titusville, Pennsylvania.[5] Still other roving merchants are connected with specific small towns precisely because they gave up their peddling in order to establish themselves permanently in those places. In the 1840s Nathan Grossmayer opened a business in Macon, Georgia, after peddling in the area to accumulate the necessary capital, and around 1857 Michael Raphael established himself in Davenport, Iowa, after four years of peddling in the region. Similarly, Aaron Basch first encountered the town of Danville, Illinois, during his days as a pack peddler, and in 1877 he opened a clothing store there.[6] A time-honored, though unlikely, explanation for the establishment of a Jewish presence in one small town or another was that it was simply the place where some peddler's horse had died.[7]

Despite the sentimental image of poor peddlers settling down to become solid citizens and the founders of Jewish communities, the first Jews in America's small towns were not always individuals at the very beginning of their careers as entrepreneurs. Some Jews came to small towns not to get a start in business, but rather to expand their wealth. Already in the late eighteenth century, for example, Samuel Myers, a man well established in business in Norfolk, became the first Jewish resident of Petersburg, Virginia. At about the same time, David Isaacs, originally from Frankfurt in Germany, arrived in Charlottesville, Virginia, after having spent time as a trader for his brother Isaiah's very successful firm in Richmond. In Charlottesville, David soon became a prominent Main Street merchant and an associate of Thomas Jefferson. Isaiah Isaacs himself, who had helped finance Daniel Boone's surveys of Kentucky and who had served on the Richmond city council, eventually made the move to Charlottesville as well. Similarly, the first known Jews in Natchez, Mississippi, were Benjamin Monsanto and his wife, Clara, a prosperous couple who dealt in real estate, slaves, and farm animals, and who acquired a plantation in the 1790s.[8]

The nineteenth century yields stories of prosperous Jews migrating to small towns as well. In 1819, for example, Benjamin Gratz, scion of one of Philadelphia's most successful merchant families, became the first Jewish resident of Lexington, Kentucky. A graduate of the University of Pennsylvania, an army officer during the War of 1812, and a lawyer, Gratz was probably attracted to Lexington because his family had land holdings there, and he soon established himself as a prominent hemp manufacturer and civic activist. So, too, in 1845 the London-born John Levy arrived as the first Jewish settler in

La Crosse, Wisconsin, then a hamlet of only five log cabins. He brought with him a wagonload of goods and the intention of opening a store, but he too was already an established businessman. By the time he arrived in La Crosse, Levy was married, the father of a son, and an experienced entrepreneur who had been a retailer in St. Louis.[9]

Typically, the small towns that attracted Jewish settlers in the middle decades of the nineteenth century, or even earlier, were locally important market centers whose development created concentrations of consumers who needed the kinds of goods and services that budding Jewish entrepreneurs or business people attempting to increase their fortunes could provide. In every region of the country, these towns often lay along important routes of commerce, and the growth of their Jewish communities was frequently linked to the development of effective transportation networks. Petersburg, Virginia, for example, was attractive to Samuel Myers and to the other Jewish settlers who followed him because it was a tobacco shipping port and manufacturing center whose contacts reached all the way to Europe. Williamsport, Pennsylvania, lured Jewish settlers because it was an important lumbering center on the Susquehanna River. Farther west in the state, Titusville attracted Jews when it began to prosper after oil was discovered there in 1859.[10]

A number of the triple-digit Jewish centers of the nineteenth century were in small-town river ports of some regional stature. Along the Ohio River, these included Wheeling, West Virginia; and Paducah, Kentucky. Along the Mississippi, they included Davenport, Iowa; Quincy, Illinois; Helena, Arkansas; and Greenville, Vicksburg, and Natchez in the state of Mississippi itself. Lafayette, Indiana, was an important commercial center because it was at the head of navigation on the Wabash River and, after 1843, connected to Lake Erie by the Wabash and Erie Canal. Wilmington, North Carolina, attracted Jews because it was the state's main port on the Atlantic Ocean, while Mobile was Alabama's main port on the Gulf of Mexico. Bay City, Michigan, was a major lumbering center and port on Lake Huron's Saginaw Bay. In early California, the inland town of San Bernardino drew Jewish settlers after Mormon pioneers developed a thriving agricultural economy there. As early as 1861 there were already twenty Jewish-owned businesses in that town.[11]

America's railroad network, expanding rapidly in the period just before the Civil War, also helped spur the growth of many small towns and guide Jewish settlers to places in which small communities were being established. Cumberland, Maryland, became a major transportation hub early in the nineteenth century because it was both the western terminus of the Chesapeake and Ohio Canal and the eastern terminus of the National Road that led through the Appalachian Mountains into the Ohio Valley. It maintained its significance after midcentury as an important rail center. Meridian, Mississippi, a backwater village of only fifteen families in 1860, became a boom town when the railroad arrived a short time later and was home to at least ten Jewish families by 1869. The important role played by railroads in the development of America's oldest small-town Jewish settlements is suggested by the fact that, in our sample of 490 communities, 76 percent of those that were already home to at least 100 Jews by the late 1870s could be reached directly by rail as early as 1868.[12]

The first Jews who planted themselves in towns that would one day host small Jewish communities found themselves initially isolated from Jewish contacts, and many divorced themselves from Jewish life as a result. If they had arrived as bachelors, they often married non-Jewish women and saw their children raised as Christians. In Charlottesville, Virginia, David Isaacs maintained a long-term common-law relationship with a mulatto woman named Nancy West. They had seven children together, all of whom became identified with the local free black community. In Maryland at the turn of the nineteenth century, the town of Frederick was the home of David Levy, an English Jew who had married a gentile, and of the brothers Israel and Joseph Israel, the sons of a Jewish father who had been raised by their mother as Quakers. Benjamin Gratz married a gentile woman named Maria Cecil Gist soon after he arrived in Lexington, Kentucky, and when she died in 1841 he married her widowed niece, Anna Maria Shelby. Altogether, Gratz had eight children, none of them raised as Jews. Henry Hyams, a cousin of Judah P. Benjamin and lieutenant governor of Louisiana during the Civil War, married into a prominent Christian family in Donaldsonville, Louisiana, around 1828 and then spent a quarter-century as a lawyer and plantation owner in Alexandria.[13]

Still, some early Jewish settlers in the secondary urban centers developing in nineteenth-century America did attempt to maintain their religious traditions and to establish Jewish homes. As soon as their towns had attracted more than a handful of individuals and families who wanted to perpetuate their Jewish identities, they established the beginnings of Jewish communal activity. Indeed, in the oldest of America's persistently small Jewish communities, the origins of organized Jewish life often went back to the period before the Civil War. Several general accounts of the American Jewish experience have observed that community formation in the cities and towns of the American hinterland usually began with the creation of some sort of mutual benefit institution, most often a benevolent society concerned with care of the sick and burial of the dead, and that Jewish congregational activity came only later.[14] Some contemporaries, as well, assumed that this was the normal course of events. In 1858, for example, a correspondent in Jackson, Michigan, wrote to *The Israelite*, the newspaper published in Cincinnati by Rabbi Isaac Mayer Wise, explaining that a "Hebrew Benevolent Association" had recently been formed in his town and that it had purchased a piece of land for a cemetery. "As a Burial Ground is the usual forerunner of a Congregation," the correspondent continued, "it would not be surprising if we should soon have Israelites enough amongst us to enable us to form a permanent congregation." Jackson's Beth Israel was in fact established in 1862, and the next year the congregation absorbed the original benevolent society.[15]

There are other examples of the progression from burial society to congregation as well. Jews began to arrive in Macon, Georgia, in the 1840s, while that town was growing as a port on the Ocmulgee River and as an important rail center in the heart of the state's cotton country. As early as 1844 Macon's Jews arranged for the interment of their dead in a section of the city's Rose Hill Cemetery, and for well over a decade their cemetery compound was maintained by a voluntary association called the Hebrew Burial Ground Society. It was only in 1859 that the Jews of Macon created a full-fledged congregation, and it was not until 1863 that the Burial Ground Society and the congregation were consolidated. So, too, in Paducah, Kentucky, the first communal organization was the Chevra Yeshurum Burial Society, established in 1859. Worship services were not held in Paducah until 1868 and formal congregational activity was not inaugurated until 1871.[16]

Nonetheless, a comprehensive examination of the histories of the earliest of America's paradigmatic small Jewish communities suggests that the initiation of congregational activities in small towns did not always lag so clearly behind the establishment of benevolent associations. Not surprisingly, the same people who felt a sense of kinship with fellow Jews and who were concerned with burial according to Jewish rites were also likely to feel the need to participate in Jewish worship, at least occasionally. Thus, in many places prayer services and other communal activities were organized more or less simultaneously with the establishment of confraternities concerned with illness and burial. The origins of small-town congregational life are sometimes obscured by the fact that prayer services were commonly conducted under the aegis of benevolent associations and by the fact that congregations often obtained their formal charters only some time after they began their activities. So, too, because communities frequently found it necessary to acquire land for a cemetery well before they gave any thought to buying or erecting a synagogue building, burial societies were more likely than congregational bodies to leave an early paper trail. Still, there is abundant evidence that in many small communities, early Jewish settlers initiated holiday observances and prayer services at just about the same time that they made provisions for the care of the sick and the burial of the dead.

In Vicksburg, Mississippi, for example, the first Jews appeared during the early 1820s while the town was beginning to develop as a military outpost and trading port, and there were about twenty Jewish families there when the town was incorporated in 1825. These early settlers apparently began holding worship services as early as the 1830s, even though it was not until 1841 that they formally organized as the "Hebrew Benevolent Congregation of the Men of Mercy," choosing a name that suggested the dual purpose of their society as both a mutual benefit association concerned with burial and a congregation of worshipers. The formal charter for this organization was not granted by the state until 1862. Similarly, in Lafayette, Indiana, where the first Jews were present by the mid-1840s, the first Jewish cemetery and the first congregational body were established at essentially the same time, in 1849, and the two bodies were officially consolidated in 1852.[17]

The statement of purpose of the first Jewish institution created in San Jose, California, also reflects the fact that benevolent societies often saw themselves as serving more general religious needs as well. When the San Jose organization was created in 1861, it adopted the name Bickur Cholim (a reference to the Jewish obligation to visit those who are ill) and stated that among its purposes were "to assist the needy and sick" and to look to "the burial of the dead." However, it also proclaimed as goals the "furtherance of our Holy Religion and to encourage the education of the Hebrew Youth in the Hebrew Religion and Language." Moreover, just a year after it was founded, the Bickur Cholim Society inaugurated a fund for the erection of San Jose's first synagogue. In Lexington, Kentucky, the Spinoza Burial Society, which was organized by twenty-eight men in 1872, also saw itself as fulfilling all the religious needs of the community it served. In a resolution unanimously adopted in 1877, the members of the society specifically rejected the idea of having any body in Lexington besides their association function as a congregation. It is "contrary to all custom, usage, rule and harmony," they declared, "that a Congregation and a burial association, both wholly composed of members of the same faith and organization, should exist apart from each other in the same place."[18]

So closely were the operations of benevolent societies linked to early congregational activities that local synagogues routinely drew attention to this early relationship and traced their beginnings to the acquisition of a cemetery. The Jewish settlers who purchased a burial ground in Wheeling, West Virginia, in 1849 held their first High Holiday services on the third floor of a downtown house in the same year, and these individuals have been described as "the nucleus" of the city's Congregation L'Shem Shomayim. Congregation Anche Chesed in La Crosse, Wisconsin, which did not hire its first rabbi until 1864 or erect its first synagogue until 1867, nonetheless always traced its origins to the local "Hebrew Indigent, Sick, and Burial Society" that had bought land for a cemetery around 1857. As early as 1880 the published history of Kalamazoo County, Michigan, reported that those who founded Kalamazoo's original Jewish congregation, B'nai Israel, in 1866 "began their organization by laying out a piece of ground for a burial-place." Sometimes the close connection between mutual aid and early congregational activity in a small community was revealed when a benevolent or burial society altered its name after a few years to reflect its broader functions. Thus, in Virginia, the Charlottesville Hebrew Benevolent Society that purchased land adjacent to the city-owned Oakwood Cemetery in 1870 simply changed its name to Congregation Beth Israel in 1882.[19]

In some of America's small communities of the mid-nineteenth century, the beginnings of Jewish congregational life actually preceded the acquisition of a cemetery by some time. So, for example, in Williamsport, Pennsylvania, where the first Jewish settlers began to arrive in the late 1830s, religious services were already being conducted on Sabbaths and holidays in the homes of several families in the early 1840s. As the number of Jews in Williamsport increased, they rented rooms for services on the third floor of the Ulman Opera House, a building owned by one of the founding members of the community. For Rosh Hashanah and Yom Kippur in the period before the Civil War, the community rented other spaces, including a church building, and it occasionally welcomed itinerant rabbis to lecture and conduct services. Thus, even though Williamsport's Jews did not seek a state charter for their congregation, Beth Ha-Sholom, until after the Civil War, the congregational life of the community was well under way by the time it purchased a burial ground in 1863.[20]

As in Williamsport, the first Jews probably began to arrive in Plattsburg, New York, in the 1830s, and the first Jewish child was born there in 1842. Here also religious services were already being conducted by the 1840s. Although a Plattsburg congregation was not formally incorporated until 1861, and it did not engage its first salaried rabbi until 1862, it clearly had been functioning for quite some time before one of its members, William Cane, presented the group with land for a cemetery in 1859. In Natchez, Mississippi, the first Jewish services were probably held as early as the 1830s, even though the community did not purchase a cemetery lot until 1840 and did not formally establish its congregation, B'nai Israel, until 1845.[21]

In some cases, it was not only the inauguration of prayer services that preceded the acquisition of a burial ground, but even the formal organization of a synagogue. In Cumberland, Maryland, Congregation B'er Chayim was chartered in 1853, a year before it acquired a cemetery. In Petersburg, Virginia, the town's first Jewish congregation, known originally by the misconstrued name "Rod of Sholem," was founded in 1858, six years before the local community purchased a burial ground. In Springfield, Illinois, it appears that a group of about twenty families was already functioning as the Springfield Hebrew Congregation by 1858, several years before the first formally authorized Springfield congregation was chartered as Brith Sholom in 1865 and well before the Jews of Springfield acquired a section of the Oak Ridge Cemetery as a burial ground in 1866.[22]

As in the larger Jewish communities of the United States in the middle decades of the nineteenth century, in smaller Jewish settlements most of the early residents were immigrants from Central Europe. They had come from the various German states, from Alsace in France, from parts of the Austrian Empire, or from Posen, the region of Poland controlled by Prussia during much of the nineteenth century. The backgrounds of these people were by no means identical. The Jews of Alsace had enjoyed the status of full citizenship in their homeland, for example, while the Jews of Posen had emerged from a cultural milieu that was in many ways more Polish than German.[23] In small-town America, however, these Central European immigrants were generally thought of collectively as "German Jews," and in the oldest small communities of the country they and their descendants constituted the bulk of the Jewish population throughout much of the nineteenth century. For example, among the thirty-eight male Jewish heads of household who can be identified in Alexandria, Louisiana, in 1880, twenty-seven had been born in Prussia, Bavaria, or France, and another six were the American-born sons of Central Europeans. By contrast, Jews born in Hungary or Russia headed only four of Alexandria's identifiable Jewish households, while a Sephardic Jew from the island of St. Thomas headed another. The wives of these householders generally had backgrounds similar to those of their husbands, although they were somewhat more likely to have been born in the United States. Fifteen of the thirty-one wives of Jewish householders in Alexandria had been born in Central Europe, while six were American-born daughters of Central Europeans and five were third-generation Americans. There were also six widows who headed households in Alexandria's Jewish community, of whom five were born in Central Europe and one was born in Louisiana to parents from Bavaria.[24]

Similarly, in Hamilton, Ohio, fifteen of the sixteen heads of Jewish households in 1880 were immigrants from Germany, and the wives of all these men were from Germany as well, except for one Ohio-born daughter of German immigrants. The only Jewish householders of Eastern European background in Hamilton were the notions dealer Myer Nathan and his wife, Fannie. Among the sixteen heads of Jewish households in Appleton, Wisconsin, in 1880 (fifteen married men and one widow), there were ten whose place of birth was listed in census records as either Germany or Prussia, four whose birthplace was listed as Austria, and one whose birthplace was Hungary (this was the community's rabbi, Samuel Weisz, the father of the future escape artist Harry Houdini). Only one Jewish head of household in Appleton had been born in Poland. Of the three unmarried Jewish men who can be identified as boarding in various homes in Appleton in 1880, one had been born in Prussia, one in Austria, and one in New York to Prussian-born parents.[25]

All this is not to say that it was impossible to find small towns in America where concentrations of East European Jews had arisen even before the era of mass migration from Eastern Europe had begun. Some Jews from Russia and Poland were already arriving in America before 1881, and even though most of them gravitated to the country's larger cities, some established an East European presence in a few small towns as well. In Bradford, Pennsylvania, for instance, of the thirty-nine men known to have headed Jewish households in 1880, seventeen had been born in one of the German states and two had been born in New York to parents from Germany, but fully nineteen had been born in either Russia or Poland. One other householder was from Hungary.[26]

Although it is impossible to trace the routes taken by all those who settled in towns where small Jewish communities were in formation during the middle decades of the nineteenth century, it appears that most had sojourned elsewhere in America and that many had come to their small-town destinations by rather circuitous routes. Henry Loevenhart, for instance, was born in the German state of Nassau and came to Cincinnati with his widowed mother in 1851. He then went to work as an apprentice, a peddler, and a shopkeeper in Knoxville and Nashville, Tennessee; in Covington and Nicholasville, Kentucky; in Danville, Illinois; in Indianapolis, Indiana; and in Ottumwa, Iowa, before finally settling down and becoming a community leader in Lexington, Kentucky. Similarly, the German-born S. M. Siesel came to America at the age of fifteen around 1857 and took a job in a dry-goods store in LaGrange, Georgia. A few years later he journeyed to the Far West to seek his fortune, but by 1864 he was back in the South, this time in Nashville with his brother. From Nashville he moved to Dawson, Georgia, and from Dawson to Americus. Finally, in 1867 he came to Macon, where he settled down.[27]

To judge from census information about where their children were born, it seems that Jacob Hammel and his wife, Julia, both originally from Prussia, had lived in New York and in Canada before arriving in Wisconsin around 1867 and settling in Appleton. Phillip Weinfeld and his wife, Fannie, both Austrian born, had lived in New York and in Alabama before arriving in Appleton in the late 1870s. The Bavarian David Heuman married his wife, Celine, born in Louisiana to immigrants from France, in 1844, and they had children both in Celine's home state and in Mississippi before moving to Michigan about 1873 and establishing themselves in Jackson, David as a saloonkeeper and his wife as a language teacher. The Prussian-born Bernhard Wolff and his wife, Henrietta, had lived in Iowa and Illinois before they too ended up in Jackson, Michigan.[28]

Although the wanderings of many early members of America's small Jewish communities may at times have seemed serendipitous, there were a number of factors at work to influence their destinations. The fact that developing market towns were by definition hubs of transportation certainly helped guide some settlers to these places as they ventured into the American hinterland looking for economic opportunity. Apparently a number of the earliest Jewish settlers in La Crosse, Wisconsin, ended up there because they took a liking to the town while they were on their way up the Mississippi River to St. Paul, Minnesota.[29] Perhaps the most important single factor in drawing Jewish migrants to a specific community, however, was the previous settlement there of a relative or acquaintance. The presence of even one Jewish pioneer in a town could create a powerful attraction for those who knew that person, because early arrivals served as very good sources of information about local employment opportunities. Often the pioneers themselves would send for relatives and friends to join them.

Stories of how this sort of "chain migration" brought Jewish settlers to America's far-flung small towns in the mid-nineteenth century are almost limitless. When they were orphaned in 1857, for instance, Isidore and Morris Reinach came from Sinsheim in Baden to join an uncle in Petersburg, Virginia. Isidore, fourteen years old when he arrived, later served in the Confederate Army, but even before the Civil War had ended, he and his brother had opened a store in Petersburg and were selling clothing to the occupying Union troops. Both Isidore and Morris remained in their adopted hometown and continued to prosper in business after the war. Isaac, Bernard, and Lewis Stern also came to Petersburg because of the presence there of an uncle, in this case a man named Anthony Rosenstock. Rosenstock had come to Petersburg from Germany in 1859, starting out in business with a shop called the Temple of Fancy and later opening one of the first true department stores in the region. He had sent for his nephews because he needed additional employees to work in his business.[30]

In Cumberland, Maryland, two Sonneborn brothers were present by the beginning of the 1840s, and eventually they arranged for nine of their eleven siblings to join them. One of the Sonneborn brothers also brought over a nephew. Leopold Dreyfus ended up in Lafayette, Indiana, because his uncle Jacob Mayer had established himself as a butcher there and had paid young Leopold's passage from Bavaria in 1867. Eventually Leopold's brother Ferdinand also settled in Lafayette, and together the two developed an extremely successful meatpacking and provision business.[31]

In Bloomington, Illinois, the migration of the Livingston clan began when the brothers Aaron and Samuel opened a clothing store there in 1856. After the Civil War their cousin, another Aaron Livingston, joined them, and in 1880, when the first Aaron became ill, his father came and then two more brothers. Other members of the extended family arrived in Bloomington as well, and within half a century Livingstons were said to fill "a whole page of the phone book." The brothers Alphonse and Joseph were the first two members of the Meis family to arrive in Danville, Illinois, from Ingwiller in France, toward the end of the nineteenth century. They were followed by cousins Jack, Lee, and Oscar, all of whom either worked in the family enterprises, which included a department store and a furniture business, or struck out on their own.[32]

Out west, the Jewish community of Marshall, Texas, had its origins with the arrival there, around 1850, of members of several families that had come to the United States from Germany and settled initially in Syracuse, New York. The earliest Jewish inhabitants of Marshall were probably Meyer and Daniel Doppelmayer and their brother-in-law Isaac Wolf. Soon after settling in town, the Doppelmayers brought their nephew Joe Weisman to Marshall, and five of his six siblings eventually moved there as well. What brought the brothers Sam and Sol Jaffa to Trinidad, Colorado, around 1872 was an invitation to manage a store owned by their friend Henry Biernbaum. Levi Gildmacher established a shop in Santa Ana, California, in 1878 and not long afterward sent to Germany for his brothers-in-law. These four men, Max, Julius, Morris, and Gustav Reinhaus, also brought their sisters Theresa, Emilie, and Pauline with them; they soon constituted the largest Jewish family in town.[33]

Sometimes the presence of immigrants from a particular place in Europe set in motion chain migration to a small town, even if some or all of those who followed them were not relatives or close acquaintances. Members of the Ulman family had come to Williamsport in the 1830s and 1840s, for example, and of those they induced to join them, some were family members but others were unrelated Jews from Mannheim, the Ulman hometown in Germany. Similarly, nearly all of the thirty or so German-Jewish families in Appleton in the late 1890s traced their origins to the German village of Gemünden, even though not all of these families were interrelated. Of the fifty German-born individuals buried in the old Jewish cemetery of Brownsville, Tennessee, forty-eight had been born in Bavaria, and of these, seventeen had come from the village of Menschweiler. Zanesville, Ohio, seems to have attracted all its earliest Jewish residents from Hungary, and Ann Arbor, Michigan, drew Bohemians from the town of Ckyn.[34]

The pattern of large and small Jewish communities that resulted from the dispersal of Jews across the United States by the 1870s foreshadowed, to some extent, what the Jewish geography of the country would be like half a century later. According to the data compiled by the Board of Delegates of American Israelites and the Union of American Hebrew Congregations, the United States already had twenty-six cities with Jewish populations of 1,000 or more by 1878. These substantial communities were located in seventeen states and the District of Columbia. In addition, there were 136 places in the country with Jewish settlements of at least 100 but fewer than 1,000.[35] Of the forty-six states and territories that made up the United States in the late 1870s (North and South Dakota had not yet been divided, and Oklahoma was still an unorganized territory), all but eleven could claim at least one triple-digit Jewish center, and there was also a triple-digit community in Georgetown in the

District of Columbia. As table 3 in the appendix indicates, Jews had not yet penetrated the New England hinterland to any great extent, nor had they established many small communities of note in the area west of the Mississippi River Valley. However, in the South, in the Midwest, and in the Middle Atlantic regions of the United States, small communities with triple-digit populations were ubiquitous.

Only a handful of the individual Jewish communities that existed in America toward the end of the nineteenth century had been established before the middle of that century. Nearly all had been planted as pioneer settlements in the decades just before or after the Civil War and, as the historian Hasia Diner has suggested, for these settlements it is possible to articulate "a paradigm for Jewish community development" involving "multiple migrations, youthful founders, . . . small business, and the connectedness between family and community formation."[36] Indeed, the origins of nearly all of America's early Jewish communities were so similar that a decade or so after the Civil War it would have been difficult to distinguish between those settlements that were on the verge of growing into substantial centers of Jewish life and those that were destined to remain relatively small well into the future. Nonetheless, the details of America's Jewish geography in the 1920s make it clear that not all the small communities that could be identified in the 1870s followed the same trajectory.

Of the 136 triple-digit Jewish enclaves that existed in the late 1870s, sixty would be transformed into Jewish centers of at least 1,000 individuals by the late 1920s, and the growth of some of these was quite dramatic. Atlanta's Jewish population grew from 525 to 11,000 between 1878 and 1927, for example, and that of Minneapolis expanded from 172 to about 22,000. In the same half-century the Jewish population of Denver increased from 260 to 17,000, and that of Los Angeles soared from about 330 individuals to some 65,000. The Jewish populations of Providence, Buffalo, and Kansas City were all counted only in triple digits in the 1870s, but each of these cities, too, was home to well over 10,000 Jews by the 1920s.

The main factors that determined which early Jewish settlements would develop into more substantial ones and which would remain quite small were the economic vitality and the concomitant demographic transformation of the cities in which those settlements were located. In other words, among the urban centers in which Jews had begun to congregate, those that grew into large or at least midsize cities generally saw their Jewish communities expand accordingly. This is why there was such a high correlation between the population of a municipality and the size of its Jewish community once the era of mass migration had come to an end in the 1920s. What drew Jews to the various cities and towns of the United States at the end of nineteenth century and in the first decades of the twentieth was, above all, economic opportunity, and this opportunity only increased with urban expansion. Moreover, not only were large cities more apt to be economic magnets, but they also were liable to be more easily accessible to new arrivals and more likely to be home to relatives or acquaintances who could welcome them.

The dramatic growth of Atlanta's Jewish community, for example, was related to that city's development as an important rail center in the final decades of the nineteenth century and its transformation into one of the premier cities of the South. Atlanta's total population jumped from around 37,000 in 1880 to about 270,000 by 1930. In the same half-century the population exploded in other cities whose Jewish communities mushroomed as well. Minneapolis went from being a city of about 47,000 people to one of over 464,000, and Denver grew from a city of about 36,000 to one of about 288,000. The total population of Los Angeles increased from only 11,000 in 1880 to over 1.2 million fifty years later. On average, the sixty cities where the Jewish population went from triple digits to over 1,000 in the half-century after 1878 experienced a total population growth of nearly 700 percent between 1880 and 1930, achieving an average population of 173,108 thirty years into the twentieth century. By contrast, in those fifty-four American cities where a triple-digit Jewish community of the late 1870s was still only in triple digits half a century later, the average population growth was slightly under 300 percent, and the average population size in 1930 was only 34,663.

The relationship between the importance of a city and the size of its Jewish community was, in fact, already quite apparent even before the era of mass migration began, for in the late 1870s, America's larger Jewish settlements were consistently in cities that were among the county's main urban centers. At that time, twenty-one of America's twenty-six communities of 1,000 or more Jews were in cities that were among the twenty-six largest in the country. The average total population of a city with at least 1,000 Jewish residents was 243,454 in the census year 1880, and even with New York and Brooklyn excluded, the average total population of a city with 1,000 or more Jews was 189,868. Smaller Jewish communities, on the other hand, resided in second-level cities and towns, just as they would later. Of the 136 triple-digit communities identifiable around 1878, 101 were found in towns with populations under 25,000 in 1880, and forty-six of these were in towns of fewer than 10,000 inhabitants. Only 10 triple-digit communities were in cities with total populations over 50,000. The average population of a city with a Jewish community in triple digits was 20,528 in 1880.[37]

The tremendous power of general population trends to influence the fate of small communities is reflected also in the story of those few triple-digit Jewish centers that went into decline even as the overall Jewish population of the United States soared in the era of mass migration. As table 3 reveals, there were twenty communities of 100 or more Jews in existence around 1878 whose Jewish populations diminished in subsequent decades to such an extent that they stood at under 100 by 1927.[38] Two of these communities, that of Santa Fe, New Mexico, and that of Santa Cruz, California, would undergo a revival in the second half of the twentieth century, but most of these declining communities never recovered from their turn-of-the-century deterioration. What stunted the growth of the seemingly robust Jewish communities that began to flag during the era of mass migration was some sort of economic downturn in the towns where they were located. The declining economic health of these towns simply dried up the local consumer market on which so many small-town Jews depended for their livelihoods. The Jewish community of Keokuk, Iowa, for example, went into decline when that town's role as a key Mississippi River port diminished. The construction of a canal in 1877 to circumvent twelve miles of rapids on the Mississippi eliminated the need to unload and reload cargo at Keokuk. In addition, railroad expansion shifted Iowa's commercial center farther west. Keokuk's difficulties are reflected in the fact that its total population increased only 25 percent between 1880 and 1930. Similarly, the decline of Jewish life in Madison, Indiana, mirrored the diminishing role of Ohio River traffic in the commerce of the region and the emergence of Indianapolis, farther north, as Indiana's primary urban center. Madison's total population actually declined by 27 percent between 1880 and 1930.[39]

The clearest illustrations of how closely the vitality of small Jewish communities was linked to the economic health of the places in which they were located come from towns that were built on extractive industries such as mining or oil drilling, for here the general economic pattern tended to be one of boom and bust. The vigorous Jewish communities of these towns were established in the boom periods, as Jews arrived to take advantage of the business opportunities that were presented by a burgeoning population. These communities tended to disappear, however, when the bust came, dissipating local markets for goods and services. A case in point is the community of Franklin, Pennsylvania. Like several other oil towns in the northwestern part of the state, Franklin prospered for only a decade or so before the area's deposits of oil were depleted and more productive wells were sunk elsewhere. Moreover, Franklin's economy suffered from a drop in oil prices that came in 1880.[40] Consequently, Franklin's Jewish population, which stood at 131 around 1878, was not even recorded in the early years of the twentieth century, and was reported to be only thirty-four in 1927.

The pattern observable in Franklin can also be seen in some of the gold and silver mining towns of the West, where the death of a Jewish community could at times reflect the complete ruin of the city in which it had been located. Even before the 1870s, the Jewish communities of several Gold Rush towns in California had withered away, leaving behind little besides cemeteries as evidence of their brief flowering.[41] Similarly, the communities of Eureka and Virginia City, Nevada, with Jewish populations around 1878 of 172 and 305, respectively, were gone entirely by the turn of the century, just as Eureka and Virginia City themselves became virtual ghost towns.[42] The mining economy on which the survival of these cities was based had simply collapsed.

Of course the circumstances in places such as Keokuk, Franklin, and Virginia City were unusual around the turn of the twentieth century. In general, the trend in the United States was toward greater urbanization, and smaller cities and towns retained their roles as crucial elements in America's urban network. By the end of World War I the country had over 450 towns in the population range of 10,000 to 25,000, for example, three times as many as there had been in 1880. Of the hundreds of thousands of Jews who arrived in America in the final years of the nineteenth century and in the early decades of the twentieth, a great many gravitated to these kinds of places. Thus it was that as the number of locally important small towns in America multiplied, so too did the country's secondary Jewish settlements. By the decade of the 1920s, as we know, there were nearly 500 small-town Jewish communities in the United States with triple-digit populations, over three and a half times as many as there had been half a century earlier.

# 3 Patterns of Settlement:
## The Era of Mass Migration

As we consider the experience of America's smaller Jewish communities, it is perhaps natural to pay special attention to those with the longest history. Certainly in the past, the saga of those communities whose origins lay in the middle decades of the nineteenth century has been the story most often told. This was especially true in the period immediately after World War II, when American Jewry was intent upon promoting its status as an integral part of society with deep roots in the soil of the United States. With so much of the focus on the venerable communities of small towns such as Williamsport, Pennsylvania; Bloomington, Illinois; and Vicksburg, Mississippi, it is tempting to generalize from the experiences of these older settlements and to assume that the way they developed was the normal pattern for most of the small communities that were part of the American Jewish landscape in the classic era of small-town Jewry. The fact that the Jewish communities of most of America's great cities were founded by German Jews in the middle decades of the nineteenth century only reinforces the tendency to think that the same was true of smaller Jewish communities as well.

Nonetheless, as the population data presented in table 1 reveal, among the triple-digit communities that can be identified in the United States in 1927, those that already had appreciable Jewish populations on the eve of mass migration were actually only a small minority. In fact only fifty-four of the classic small-town communities in our sample of 490, or 11 percent, were already substantial centers of Jewish life with 100 or more residents in the late 1870s. Moreover, the findings published in the 1880 *Statistics of the Jews* suggest that of those communities in our sample that were home to fewer than 100 Jewish souls in the late 1870s, only 111 had any Jewish residents at all, or at least any that were noticed by the Board of Delegates of American Israelites

---

*Photo previous page: The synagogue of the United Hebrew Congregation, Newport, Kentucky, ca. 1930. Orthodox congregations like the one that occupied this former church building beginning in 1905 were established by East European Jews in scores of small towns around the turn of the twentieth century. Photo by Myron Benson, courtesy of the Jewish Federation of Cincinnati.*

and the Union of American Hebrew Congregations. These very small assemblages ranged from the two or three Jews reported in places such as Montpelier, Vermont; Salem, New Jersey; Fairmont, West Virginia; and Greeley, Colorado, to the ninety-four reported in Baton Rouge, Louisiana.[1] What this means is that the vast majority of the smaller Jewish communities that existed in the United States in the first half of the twentieth century were not well-established settlements that had been around for many decades, but rather the products of an East European Jewish migration to small towns, prompted by many of the same factors that had drawn German Jews to similar places earlier.

To be sure, the picture of Jewish dispersal painted by *Statistics of the Jews* on the eve of mass migration is a bit hazy, and it is possible that Jews had appeared at one time or another in some places where the Board of Delegates–UAHC survey failed to locate them. Perhaps they had come through a particular small town and then moved on. Or, given the problematic nature of America's first comprehensive Jewish census, they may simply have been missed by those collecting data. There are in fact several examples of towns in our sample where Jews are known to have arrived at some time before 1878, even though these places are not even mentioned in *Statistics of the Jews*. Thus a onetime pack peddler named Jacob Baer settled down in Marion, Indiana, in the early 1840s, and when he died in 1863 his brother-in-law Morris Blumenthal came from Illinois to take over his store. A local newspaper advertisement for the dry-goods firm of Lipman and Henry Marks indicates the presence of at least one Jewish family in Muncie, Indiana, as early as 1850. In 1852 Simon Goldman opened a business in Middletown, Ohio, which he had come to know while peddling in the area from a base in Cincinnati. In Albuquerque, New Mexico, the first Jewish storeowner appeared in 1863, when Aaron Zeckendorf opened a branch of Jacob Spiegelberg's Santa Fe merchandising firm there.[2]

There are even a few cases of towns not mentioned in *Statistics of the Jews* in which some sort of Jewish communal activity had taken place before 1878. An article in Rabbi Isaac Mayer Wise's newspaper, *The Israelite*, tells about the observance of Yom Kippur by eleven Jews in Manchester, New Hampshire, in 1862, for example; and in Topeka, Kansas, Simon Barnum and Moses Snattinger, two storeowners who had arrived by way of Indiana in 1868, established a Jewish cemetery association in 1872.[3] Still, despite these scattered examples of places apparently overlooked by those compiling *Statistics of the Jews*, the best comprehensive data available from the nineteenth century indicate that of all the towns that would be home to triple-digit Jewish communities in the late 1920s, only one in three could be recognized as a point of Jewish settlement in any sense fifty years earlier, and only one in five had a Jewish population that exceeded even fifty individuals in the late 1870s.

Moreover, a few of the towns that had been settled by Central European Jews before the turn of the twentieth century had largely been abandoned by these early pioneers before a new wave of East European immigrants began to arrive. Such was the case in Ann Arbor, Michigan, for example, where most of the original Jewish settlers, members of the Weil family, departed during the 1860s, and where the last nineteenth-century Jewish family, the Fantles, left in the mid-1880s. In Frederick, Maryland, which was home to about seventy-five Jews in 1878, the population shrank to such an extent that the local congregation was forced to suspend its operations from 1890 until 1910. In Iowa City, Iowa, the original German-Jewish community became so small that around 1900 it moved those buried in its cemetery and sold the ground.[4]

The significance of East European immigration for the development of America's major Jewish centers has, of course, long been recognized, and the important role of East Europeans in building midsize communities has been acknowledged as well.[5] Certainly, vital Jewish centers of 10,000 people and more would never have flourished in places such as Providence, Buffalo, Jersey City, Pittsburgh, and Kansas City had the early communities in these places not been augmented by huge numbers of East European immigrants. Moreover, it is clear that in the first part of the twentieth century, East Europeans created some highly visible Jewish communities more or less from scratch in several cities, either by settling in these places as soon as they arrived in America or by migrating there from nearby metropolitan centers. Of the 197 U.S. cities with communities of 1,000 or more Jews in 1927, 37 percent appear to have had no identifiable Jewish residents in the late 1870s, and 12 percent seem to have been devoid of Jews even as late as the first decade of the twentieth century.[6] Generally missed in all the attention given to the role of East European immigrants in the development of large and midsize Jewish centers, however, is the crucial part they played in the creation of smaller Jewish communities throughout the American hinterland.

This is not to say that German Jews played no role in peopling the new settlements that were established in America in the half-century after 1881. On the contrary, in their search for economic opportunity, some Jews of Central European background continued to be drawn to small-town communities, both old and new. When the German-speaking Rudolph Anker arrived in the United States from Prussian Poland in 1882, for example, he chose to settle near a cousin in San Bernardino, California, because, at a time when Los Angeles was no larger than San Bernardino, he believed his newly adopted city would develop into the largest urban center in southern California. So, too, when members of the Rosen family came to the United States from the town of Thorne in Prussia in the 1870s, they settled first in Syracuse, New York, and then went on to Detroit. By 1881, however, most members of the family were living in the small town of Battle Creek, Michigan, and Samuel

Rosen had been hired as a clerk in a clothing store in Muskegon. Samuel's brother Isaac followed him in 1883, opening a small tailor shop, and the next year the two brothers arranged to bring their parents and the rest of their siblings to Muskegon.[7]

Indeed, because the incremental migration that characterized the odyssey of the Rosen family was so common, and because East Europeans, too, tended to arrive in small towns only after a sojourn in a larger Jewish center, Germans continued to predominate among Jewish newcomers in at least some small communities even in the final decades of the nineteenth century. While the mass migration that began in 1881 affected the makeup of America's major Jewish centers almost immediately, it took perhaps a decade, and sometimes longer, for East Europeans to begin arriving in smaller cities and towns in significant numbers, especially in regions away from the eastern seaboard. Thus, in some of America's smaller Jewish communities, what has been called the "German period" of American Jewish history lasted a bit longer than it did in New York and in other major cities.

In Alabama, for example, Anniston, originally a closed company town built around an ironworks, began to attract newcomers only after 1883, when the railroad came through. The first Jews to arrive there were all of German background, most of them coming from other cities in the region. Among these were Leon Ullman, who arrived in 1884 and was probably the first Jewish resident of Anniston, and his four brothers, August, Abe, Leopold, and Solomon, who followed him. In Albuquerque, New Mexico, as well, most early members of the Jewish community, arriving in the 1880s and 1890s, were of Central European background. This is one reason that when the Jews of Albuquerque established a congregation in 1897 it adopted the Reform practice so widely accepted by German Jews with seemingly little controversy. It was only after the turn of the century that East Europeans began to appear in Albuquerque. In Trinidad, Colorado, also, as late as 1900, most of the adult Jews in town had been born in Alsace or one of the German states, or were the daughters of German immigrants married to German-born men. Having arrived in the United States in the middle decades of the nineteenth century, the vast majority of the Jewish men of Trinidad had resided in the country for several decades. Although there were some Russian-born Jews in Trinidad by 1900, it was not until around 1910 that they became as numerous as the Central Europeans, and by then both groups were outnumbered by native-born Jews.[8]

The continuing visibility of German Jews in some small towns notwithstanding, by the time of World War I East Europeans made up the bulk of the Jewish population in those small communities that were created in the 1880s or later. For example, of the seventy-two identifiable Jewish heads of household in Newburyport, Massachusetts, in 1920 (sixty-nine men and three widows), sixty-five had been born in Russia, and another three had been born to Yiddish-speaking parents in the Austrian Empire. Only four were native-born, and of these, only two were of German-Jewish background. Of the sixty-four identifiable heads of Jewish households in Fitchburg, Massachusetts, in 1920 (sixty men and four widows), fifty-eight had been born within the borders of the former Russian Empire. The other six included Edward Dunn, born in England to a father from Kovno; Max Sarkin, born in Germany to a father from Vilna; and Sarah Feingold, born in Germany to Yiddish-speaking parents who were themselves from Germany. Only three Jewish heads of household in Fitchburg were native-born, and of these, only one was a third-generation American.[9]

Similarly, at the other side of the continent, in Modesto, California, in 1920, twenty-four of the thirty-five identifiable Jewish heads of household had been born in Russia, while two others had been born in Austrian Galicia, one had been born in Rumania, and one had been born in England to Yiddish-speaking parents. Only one Jewish head of household in Modesto had been born in Germany, and another was reported simply to have been born in Europe. Of the thirteen Jews who were living in Modesto as boarders in the homes of others, six were Russian-born, two had been born in Germany, and one had been born in Rumania. Modesto's boarders also included four native Jews, two of them the children of immigrants from Germany, one the son of an immigrant from Russia, and one the son of an immigrant from Hungary.[10]

Although it is clear that the most significant role that East Europeans played in the history of America's small Jewish communities was in the creation of literally hundreds of new Jewish centers in the decades after 1881, they also had an important impact on small-town communities that were already firmly in place before the era of mass migration began. For one thing, even in established communities where the Jewish population did not rise beyond triple digits, the arrival of East Europeans sometimes meant notable growth. In the Midwest, for example, the Jewish population of Bloomington, Illinois, grew from 115 around 1878 to 350 in 1927, and that of Springfield, Illinois, jumped from 150 to 600 in the same period. The Jewish population of Bay City, Michigan, climbed from 153 in 1878 to 695 fifty years later, while the number of Jews in Springfield, Ohio, rose from 148 to 580, and that in Davenport, Iowa, went from 204 to 690. In the South, the Jewish populations of Charlotte, North Carolina, and of Monroe, Louisiana, each stood at about 100 before the start of East European migration, but by 1927 Charlotte's Jewish population had risen to 400 and Monroe's to 500. In the same period the Jewish community of Augusta, Georgia, grew from 240 to 970, and that of Wheeling, West Virginia, climbed from 300 to 750. Only an infusion of East Europeans could have led to expansion of this magnitude.

The information on nativity contained in the 1920 census records for several of the triple-digit communities that had been established in the era of German-Jewish settlement reveals unmistakably the demographic impact of East European migration on these communities. In Hamilton, Ohio, for example, where the Jewish population grew from 110 around 1878 to 450 half a century later, thirty-nine of the sixty-seven Jewish heads of household identifiable in 1920 (sixty-three men, two single women, and two widows) had been born in the Russian Empire. Another three were from Rumania, one was from Austrian Galicia, and one was from Hungary. By contrast, in 1920 there were only five Jewish heads of household in Hamilton who had been born in Germany, and at least one of these was a Yiddish-speaker from Posen. There was also a Belgian-born householder whose native tongue was Yiddish. The remaining Jewish heads of household in Hamilton were all American-born, and their background reflects the changing nature of the Hamilton Jewish community. Of the seventeen American-born Jewish householders in town, eleven were the children of immigrants from Central Europe and four were third-generation Americans, while only two were the children of East Europeans.[11] We can observe a similar demographic pattern in Lexington, Kentucky, where the Jewish population rose from 140 around 1878 to about 750 in 1927. There, too, East European immigrants or their children headed the vast majority of Jewish households in 1920. Of the eighty-nine Lexington Jewish householders for whom information is available, fully fifty-eight were immigrants from Eastern Europe, and another two were the children of East Europeans.[12]

In Alexandria, Louisiana, where the Jewish population increased from about 200 in 1878 to about 560 in 1927, East Europeans were not yet the dominant element in the local Jewish population in the first quarter of the twentieth century, but they were nonetheless extremely important to its growth. Census returns reveal that as the twentieth century entered its third decade, about one in three of the Jewish households in town was headed by an individual of East European background. Of the ninety-seven Jewish heads of household identifiable in the records (ninety-one men and six women), twenty had been born in Austria, Germany, or France (presumably Alsace), and another three had been born in Hungary. Also among Alexandria's Jewish householders were thirty-seven American-born children of Central European Jews. At the same time, thirty of Alexandria's householders were East European Jews born abroad, and another two were the American-born children of East Europeans. Four of Alexandria's Jewish householders were third-generation Americans, and one was the New York–born son of parents born in England.[13]

Even in older communities that did not experience dramatic growth, the arrival of East Europeans was vital, for many small-town communities that did not expand appreciably in the decades after 1880 nonetheless depended on East European immigrants simply to sustain themselves. For example, the total Jewish population of Vicksburg, Mississippi, was around 500 in the late

1870s and about the same in the 1920s. However, in 1920, individuals born in Russia or Poland headed at least a dozen Jewish households in the city, and immigrants from Austrian Galicia headed at least two others. In Appleton, Wisconsin, where the Jewish community grew from 143 to only 215 in the half century between 1878 and 1927, eight of the forty-five identifiable Jewish heads of household in 1920 had been born in Central Europe, and four or perhaps five were the American-born children of German Jews. However, fully thirty-two of the identifiable Jewish householders in Appleton had been born in Eastern Europe. So too, of the four Jews who can be identified as boarders in Appleton, three were of East European heritage, while only one was of German background.[14]

Some of the East European immigrants who settled in small communities, like some of the German Jews who preceded them, had traveled extremely convoluted routes to their ultimate destinations. Morris Nasatir, born near Dvinsk in Lithuania, spent fourteen months in South Africa before coming to America in 1888. Upon his arrival, he went first to Chicago (he had asked for passage "to the next place after New York") and then peddled for a while in downstate Illinois. When he had earned enough money, he opened a store in Omaha, Nebraska, but in 1898 he decided to move once again, looking for a small town not too far from a major Jewish center. That search brought him to Santa Ana, California, where he opened a men's clothing store. Isaac Gartner began life in Cairo, Egypt, where his parents had gone from their native Austria. When he was in his teens, Gartner came to America and made his way to Chicago to work as a tailor's apprentice. In 1893 he met and married his Russian-born wife, who had come to Chicago with her parents by way of England. The Gartners started their family in Chicago and then moved to New York, where the last seven of their nine children were born. Only then did the Gartners move to Topeka, Kansas, at the suggestion of a distant cousin who told Isaac of a job available there as a custom tailor.[15]

Similar odysseys undertaken by East European immigrants form a part of the history of just about all of America's small Jewish communities. Eli Woolfan, for example, had left Vilna for England when he was fifteen, around 1879, and two years later he continued on to Canada, where he lived for about a year. In 1882 Woolfan moved to Pittsburgh, and from there he migrated to the Upper Midwest. He lived in St. Paul for five years and in Superior for twelve years before finally settling down in the small Iron Range town of Hibbing, Minnesota. Around the turn of the century, Leon Kislin and his brother left Poland by way of Russia, traveling on foot, by rail, and by boat across Siberia, China, Japan, and the Pacific Ocean before landing in Seattle, Washington. From there they continued across the entire United States, ending up in the small town of Red Bank, New Jersey. Abe Gellman left Russia in 1897 to join his uncle and aunt in Baltimore. From there he moved to Richmond, and from

Richmond he went on to Chicago, where he stayed for five years. Only in 1903 did he come back to the region where he had got his start in America, establishing himself in Petersburg, Virginia, and remaining there until his death in 1948. William Kritt came to America from Ukraine around 1907 and sent for his wife, Bessie, and their daughter shortly thereafter. He and his family lived first in Iowa, working in scrap metal, and then in Wisconsin, where Kritt added fur trading and tobacco farming to his business ventures. It was only when the Kritts made one more move, this time to Benton Harbor, Michigan, that the family finally settled down permanently.[16]

However they made their way to America's smaller cities and towns, the East European Jews who ended up in these places came for the same kinds of reasons that earlier immigrants had come. Like a good number of their German-Jewish predecessors, for instance, some first arrived in small towns as peddlers and decided to stay. When Edel Spodick arrived in New York City from Lithuania around 1880, for example, he found that there was little demand for his Old World skill of brushmaking, and so he took the advice of a *landsman* (a fellow countryman) and become a peddler. Plying his wares on Long Island, he eventually settled down in Sag Harbor, a town that had just under 100 Jewish residents in 1927. Jacob Gartner, who arrived in America in 1884, spent perhaps two years as a pack peddler in Michigan before opening a department store in Hancock, then an important copper mining center on the state's upper peninsula. Harry Endlich, not actually a peddler but rather a traveling representative for his uncle's New York clothing factory, encountered Topeka, Kansas, on his periodic sales trips, and decided to settle there and open a ladies' ready-to-wear shop in 1909. He later served three terms as president of Topeka's synagogue, one in the 1920s, one in the 1930s, and one in the 1940s.[17]

Other East Europeans were simply passing through one small town or another when they found a reason to stay. Simon Schiffman settled in Greensboro, North Carolina, in 1892 because he noticed a jewelry store for sale there while he was changing trains. Sometime around 1910 a Jewish drifter named Cohen arrived in Champaign, Illinois, looking for a handout. The local Jewish leadership insisted that he go to work instead and got him a job in the kitchen of the town's Young Men's Christian Association. Cohen ended up settling in Champaign, becoming manager of the YMCA at a "large salary" and prompting the administration there to conclude, somewhat ironically, that "Jews are the only people to depend upon to make a success of an institution of this kind." David Maidenberg, who had worked in a bakery in Odessa and had fled Russia for America as a teenager in 1905, was intending to join relatives in Marion, Ohio, after having spent several years in Maryland and Pennsylvania. On his travels west in 1916, however, he took a train to Marion, Indiana, by mistake, and when he got off there he simply decided to stay. A peddler by trade, he sold off the items he had with him and went on to build a successful retail business. Maidenberg and his wife, Rosa, eventually raised four sons in Marion, and one of his grandsons became mayor of the city in the 1970s.[18]

In at least a few cases, it seems that Jews who came to settle in small towns were drawn to their rustic settings. The first Jews who arrived in Norwood, Massachusetts, around 1899 were coming to escape the crowded city of Boston and to buy reasonably priced homes in a rural area. Similarly, when Vivian Barnert's Russian-born father wanted to get out of the city and to become his own boss, he boarded a commuter train in Hoboken and rode to the last stop, Dover, New Jersey, where he settled down. Harry Goodwin, who later founded the Mother's Gefilte Fish Company, moved from Brooklyn to Caldwell, New Jersey, in 1919 because his son suffered from asthma and he wanted to find an environment offering more fresh air. In like fashion, Morris Brody, a native of Lvov who spent time as a garment worker in Cleveland, moved to Geneva, Ohio, in 1924 because he had developed ulcers. As his son later explained, "in those days if a city dweller had something incurable, the fashion was to send him 'to the country' to a healthier environment."[19]

The quest for a healthier place to live also brought Sam Eisberg from San Francisco to Modesto in the San Joaquin Valley of California. A tailor and a heavy smoker who had developed breathing problems, Eisberg moved around 1915 in search of fresh air. A decade later Alec Carlin, who had stomach problems, moved to Modesto for the clean water. Like Modesto, Colorado Springs, Colorado, attracted Jews because it had a reputation as a healthy place to live. For this reason, unlike many other mining towns, Colorado Springs continued to attract Jewish settlers even after the local mining industry went into decline.[20]

Ultimately, of course, like most Central European Jews who came to small towns, what most East European immigrants were seeking in these places was economic success. Even those who arrived by chance or were attracted to a rural environment remained only if they found a way to make a living. The necessity of finding work helps explain why small Jewish communities continued to develop mainly in those secondary cities and towns that prospered as local or regional centers of economic activity. One survey conducted in the 1970s among Jews in towns with total populations of under 150,000 in five southern states discovered that 92 percent of those who responded reported that business was what originally brought their families to settle where they did.[21]

The link between economic opportunity and Jewish migration was perhaps most readily apparent in cases in which Jews flocked to a town that was newly established or one that was undergoing some sort of dramatic economic upswing. In other words, the creation of new small-town Jewish communities often went hand in hand with the development of the towns themselves. In western Pennsylvania, for example, Jews were drawn to the town of Jeannette when it was founded as a glass manufacturing center in 1888, and they came to Ellwood City when it became a resort town in 1889. Similarly, when Farrell was established as a steel-mill town at the turn of the century, a fair number of Hungarian Jews came there to make a living; and when the U.S. Steel Corporation laid out Ambridge as the site of a bridge building plant in 1903, Jewish merchants rapidly moved in to take advantage of the newly created consumer market there. In Minnesota, it was an upsurge of activity on the Iron Range that attracted Jews to towns such as Chisholm, Eveleth, Hibbing and Virginia. In Texas, it was the oil boom of the 1920s that brought Jews to small towns such as Port Arthur, whose 1927 Jewish population was 173, and Beaumont, which in the same year had a Jewish population of just over 1,000.[22]

Indeed, substantial growth characterized just about all the towns in which small Jewish communities were established after 1881. A fair number of these municipalities actually were founded or first incorporated only in the last two decades of the nineteenth century or in the early years of the twentieth. As we have seen, of the 490 towns with triple-digit Jewish communities in 1927, only 54 were reported to have 100 or more Jewish residents in the late 1870s. Of the remaining 436 towns, fully 60 percent were either nonexistent or had total populations under 4,000 in 1880. By 1930, however, only 12 of these 436 towns (3 percent) were still villages of fewer than 4,000 inhabitants. Exact population figures for both 1880 and 1930 are available for 173 towns that had Jewish populations below 100 around 1878 but in triple digits in 1927 (places with total populations under 4,000 in 1880 are excluded here). The average population of these 173 towns was 8,818 in 1880 but 27,998 fifty years later, thus indicating again the crucial role of urban expansion in those places where small Jewish communities developed.

In some of the towns where small communities arose during the era of East European migration, the overall population increase was really quite spectacular. To cite just a few examples: Everett, Massachusetts, grew from a town of only 4,159 inhabitants in 1880 to one of 48,424 by 1930 (a growth rate of 1,064 percent); Warren, Ohio, grew from a town of 4,428 in 1880 to one of 41,062 in 1930 (a growth rate of 827 percent); Pontiac, Michigan, grew from a town of 4,509 people to one of 64,928 (a growth rate of 1,340 percent); and Waterloo, Iowa, grew from a town of 5,630 to one of 46,191 (720 percent). Roanoke, Virginia; Asheville, North Carolina; Lorain, Ohio; Phoenix, Arizona; and Fresno, California, were all towns with triple-digit Jewish communities in 1927 that had recorded total populations under 4,000 in 1880 but over 40,000 in 1930. No wonder Jews on the lookout for a chance to get a start in a burgeoning urban center were attracted to these kinds of places.

Because no city or town could develop into a market and service center of even local significance unless it was served by good transportation, railroad networks, far more developed around the turn of the century than they had been earlier, continued to play a tremendously important role in determining where small Jewish communities would be established. Triple-digit Jewish settlements arose in the towns of Freehold and Red Bank in Monmouth County, New Jersey, for example, because both were important rail centers. In addition, Red Bank, the county's largest commercial hub around the turn of the century, was also accessible by water. So, too, in West Virginia, coal-mining towns were reached one after another by Jews as the railroad arrived: Williamson in the mid-1890s, for example, and Logan soon after 1910. A Jewish community flourished in Trinidad, Colorado, because by the 1880s that town was served by both the Atchison, Topeka and Santa Fe Railroad and the Denver, Texas, and Fort Worth line. The railroad town of Ogden was said to be "the clearinghouse for all arrivals in Utah," and its role as a gateway promoted the development of a Jewish community there. Indeed, in some cases, such as those of Kankakee and Champaign in Illinois, it was railroad companies themselves that helped create the towns in which triple-digit Jewish communities arose.[23]

Robert Davis, an architect who has used computer graphics to accomplish "virtual restorations" of several small-town synagogues in Texas and who has studied the history of the Jewish communities in which these synagogues were located, has observed that in the heyday of Jewish settlement in the small towns of the Lone Star State, the period between 1880 and 1920, railroads created two distinct groupings of small Jewish communities (some of triple digits and some even smaller). One of these groupings ran westward from Texarkana, along the routes of the Union Pacific Railroad, and the other ran farther south, along the routes of the Santa Fe.[24]

Small towns that served as terminal points for important rail lines were especially likely to become the sites of small Jewish communities, if not large ones. Wichita, which had a Jewish population of about 700 in 1927, had become a terminus for the Rock Island Railroad serving the Kansas cattle trade in the 1870s, for example. The first rail line to connect Memphis with Little Rock terminated across the Arkansas River from the city, leading to the development of a commercial center and, consequently, a Jewish community in the town of North Little Rock. The development of a triple-digit Jewish settlement in Santa Ana, California, was tied to the fact that it had become the end of the line for the Southern Pacific Railroad in 1878, just as the era of mass migration from Eastern Europe was about to begin. Of the 490 towns with triple-digit Jewish communities identifiable in 1927, at least 451 could be reached directly by rail as early as 1893, and by 1910 at least 480 of these 490 towns had direct rail service.[25]

The huge significance of railroads as factors in the creation of small Jewish communities is strikingly illustrated by what happened in several towns that were important railheads for only a short time. In New Mexico, for example, the Atchison, Topeka and Santa Fe Railroad reached the village of Las Vegas in the 1870s, several years before it was extended to Santa Fe and Albuquerque. As a result, a small but significant Jewish community developed in Las Vegas. New Mexico's first synagogue, Congregation Montefiore, was established there no later than 1886, and in the opening decade of the twentieth century the town had a Jewish population of perhaps 250. By the 1920s, however, with the status of Las Vegas as a rail terminus in the distant past, the Jewish population of the town had dropped considerably (there were only seventy Jews in Las Vegas proper and another eighty-six in the nearby town of East Las Vegas). Albuquerque, by then the undisputed commercial hub of New Mexico, was the only city in the state with a Jewish population above 100 in 1927.[26]

The coming of the railroad also was significant in the history of the Jewish community of Tupper Lake, New York. That upstate lumbering town became the terminus of the New York Central Railroad around 1890, and by 1907 the town's Jewish population was reported to be about 125. When the New York Central line was later extended to Montreal, however, Tupper Lake became a less significant town, and its Jewish community began to decline. In 1927 the community was no more than half the size it had been twenty years earlier. The situation in the coal-mining region that straddles the border between Virginia and West Virginia also provides an example of the impact that extending rail lines could have on a Jewish settlement. In Pocahontas, Virginia, a triple-digit Jewish community developed when the Norfolk and Western Railroad reached there in 1883, making that town the first in the area to be served by trains. Pocahontas had a reported Jewish population of 120 around 1907. As rail lines spread throughout the Appalachian coalfields, however, and as other coal towns became more important than Pocahontas, the community there lost its prominence and shrank to only about two dozen people by the 1920s.[27]

Jews on the lookout for places in which they would be able to earn a decent living could find out about the opportunities available in small towns in several ways. However, the main sources of information about employment or business possibilities remained relatives and acquaintances who had arrived previously. Indeed, these people often provided the jobs that brought new Jewish settlers to small towns in the first place. Thus, for East European newcomers, as for the Central Europeans who had arrived earlier, chain migration remained the single most important factor in explaining the movement of Jews into the smaller cities and towns of the American hinterland. As early as 1881, for example, Israel Goldstein arrived in Kearny, New Jersey, because his brother Jack had opened a dry-goods store there two years before.

In 1893 Jack Levenson came to Petersburg, Virginia, from Grodno in the Russian Empire, because his *landsman* Morris Levy had gone there earlier, and in 1896 Levenson's two brothers came to Petersburg as well. Oscar Winski's parents came from Poland to Lafayette, Indiana, in 1886 to join their son, who had settled there in 1882.[28]

Yet another example of the impact of chain migration comes from Bogalusa, Louisiana. In 1906 Max Marx opened a store there, apparently specializing in hardware, when the Great Southern Lumber Company established a sawmill in Bogalusa and ushered in a period of economic expansion. Marx ran his business together with his seven children, and over the years he convinced a number of other relatives and friends to settle in his adopted hometown. At about the same time, Jack Steinberg, his sister and brother-in-law, Manya and David Gerson, and David Gerson's sister Esther all followed Jack and Manya's sister Rose Levitt to Wichita, Kansas. Eventually the Sheffreys, cousins of the Gersons, arrived as well, and when Osip Yabrof fled Russia to avoid conscription into the czar's army, he and his wife, Rose, ended up in Wichita, too, because Rose was Mrs. Sheffrey's sister. One resident of Chisholm, Minnesota, went so far as to suggest that every one of the Jewish families of his parents' generation had come to town "because they had relatives" in Chisholm; and when the rabbi of Temple Beth Israel in Clarksdale, Mississippi, summed up the history of his community, established by immigrants who had arrived mostly from Lithuania in the 1890s, he could have been describing the situation that obtained in scores of other small towns, as well. "Relatives helped relatives immigrate," he said, "and a large number of our congregation are related to one another."[29]

Even as late as the 1930s, after the era of mass migration, there were instances of Jews in small communities bringing their relatives to join them. Norbert Kahn, for example, had arrived in Hancock, Michigan, in the 1920s and married into the most prominent Jewish family there. In the 1930s he helped bring to America over three dozen of his relatives from Nazi Germany, including Ted Reiss, who settled in Hancock in 1937 and eventually married a sister of Norbert Kahn's wife. Similarly, the Nuremberg-born Jack Stiefel, who had arrived in Green Bay, Wisconsin, in 1914, brought a brother and two sisters to his adopted hometown some twenty-five years later, and, as the threat of Nazism grew in Eastern Europe in the late 1930s, Abe Pozez was able to bring several relatives to Topeka, Kansas, the town in which he had settled after arriving from Brest-Litovsk, Poland, in 1915.[30]

Not only long-standing personal connections but even chance encounters could become the basis for relocation to a small town. Jacob Berman, who had been born in Lithuania in 1887 and had come to the United States by way of Copenhagen and Montreal, settled in Clarksburg, West Virginia, in 1908 because the brother of someone he had met in Baltimore offered him a position managing a store there. Mayer Brauser emigrated from Poland in 1910 and ended up in Bradford, Pennsylvania, because a visitor from near that town wandered into the New York synagogue where Brauser was working as a caretaker and in the course of a conversation offered him a job. Maurice Cohen came to Pine Bluff, Arkansas, in 1924 because he was given a position there by a man his mother had nursed back to health in a boardinghouse in Minneapolis several years earlier.[31]

As with Central European Jewish immigrants before, connections with places of origin in Europe, even without close ties of family and friendship, continued to channel migrants to specific towns in America. The village of Latskivah in the Kovno district of Lithuania seems to have had a direct pipeline to Muscatine, Iowa, for example, and one resident of the town in the 1950s had the impression that everyone who arrived there "came because of letters from the 'landsleite' [fellow countrymen]." Similarly, Lexington, Kentucky, had a large contingent of Jews from the Lithuanian town of Pushclot. In Newburyport, Massachusetts, in 1920, no fewer than fifteen of the sixty-five Russian-born Jewish heads of household came from the city of Odessa; and in North Adams, Massachusetts, it seems that a great many of the original Jewish settlers came from the district of Minsk, and "even from the same town, Kletzk."[32]

As the forgoing examples suggest, most cases of chain migration from a previous home to a specific small town in America involved places of origin in Europe. However, as the example of early Jewish settlers who came to Marshall, Texas, by way of Syracuse, New York, illustrates, there were also instances of individuals from the same city in the United States establishing a conduit to a small town. There are even examples of chain migration involving resettlement from one small town in America to another. In 1925, for instance, the livestock entrepreneur William Smith moved from Mount Pleasant, Pennsylvania, to Danville, Illinois. One year later, he was joined by his brother Joseph, whose wife Diana was the sister of William's own wife, Ada. They too came from Mount Pleasant. Seven years after that, Abe Margolin, a friend of William Smith, moved to Danville from Mount Pleasant, as well, and he, in turn, brought to the city Rabbi David Blaustein, who was employed in the Margolin meat packing plant. Blaustein served as ritual slaughterer for the community and also from time to time as the spiritual leader of Danville's traditionalist congregation.[33]

Alongside the various informal networks of relatives and friends that guided so many Jews to small towns, there was one particular Jewish agency operating in the early years of the twentieth century whose specific mission it was to disperse Jews widely to cities and towns throughout the country. This agency was the Industrial Removal Office (IRO), created in 1901 by the Baron de Hirsch Fund, a major philanthropic organization founded by the German-

Jewish banker and railroad tycoon Maurice de Hirsh, with input from several other philanthropies concerned with immigrant absorption. The well-established German Jews who spearheaded the IRO were motivated both by their sense of responsibility to their East European coreligionists and by self-interest. They wanted to forestall the increase in antisemitism that they feared might result from the public's growing unease over the concentration of large numbers of immigrants in the county's urban centers. The goal of the IRO was thus to relieve the density of the Jewish population in New York and the other great cities of the East by resettling Jewish immigrants, and especially the unemployed, in locations beyond the major cities of the Atlantic seaboard.

The IRO also cooperated in what came to be called the Galveston Movement, an effort organized by the German-born banker and philanthropist Jacob Schiff to bring East European Jewish immigrants to the United States not by way of New York or other northeastern ports, but rather by way of the Gulf of Mexico. Schiff was convinced that settling immigrants west of the Mississippi River was the best way to facilitate the absorption of the hundreds of thousands of distressed Russian Jews who were seeking refuge in America, and he realized that dispersing them across the country would be much easier if they were brought from Europe without being exposed to the attractions of Jewish life in the major metropolitan areas of the East. While Schiff worked with various European Jewish agencies to route immigrants to Galveston, Texas, the IRO took on the task of moving them from that port city into the interior of the country, and it sent Morris Waldman, an assistant to the IRO's general manager, David Bressler, to oversee the project.[34]

In order to fulfill its mission, the IRO sought out volunteer representatives who could help coordinate aid for new immigrants at the local level. These agents were recruited in many of America's more substantial Jewish communities, those whose Jewish populations were counted in the thousands, and sometimes even in the tens of thousands, but they were enlisted also in scores of smaller cities and towns throughout the country. Local IRO representatives included officers of the B'nai B'rith fraternal order, rabbis, and prominent communal leaders, and they often organized local committees to help in their efforts. Sometimes, assisting immigrants dispatched by the IRO became the project of an entire B'nai B'rith lodge or some similar group. In Topeka from 1904 to 1906, for instance, the Ladies' Benevolent Society undertook the placement of eight immigrant families from Russia and Rumania in cooperation with the IRO.[35]

In addition to relying on local volunteers, the IRO sent its own field workers (called traveling agents) to tour the country from time to time and to report firsthand both on the fate of individuals who had been relocated by the agency and on the potential for future placements. The IRO was especially interested in learning what kinds of job opportunities existed in the towns to

*Stanley Bero, field agent for the Industrial Removal Office, 1926. The IRO dispatched Jewish immigrants to small towns all across America in the early years of the twentieth century. Courtesy of the Jacob Rader Marcus Center of the American Jewish Archives.*

which it was planning to transfer immigrants so that they could match the people they sent accordingly. For example, a 1907 letter from the IRO field worker Stanley Bero, traveling in Michigan, reported that "a baker who can make kimmel bread and german rolls—(bagels too, I suppose) can do well in Kalamazoo" and also that "tackless cobblers are always in demand." Likewise, in 1910 Bero reported that he had met a junk dealer in Ashland, Kentucky, who would "gladly send away a negro [who] works about his yard" in order to "give a chance to a Jew."[36]

The IRO also tried to become aware of the general environment in the Jewish communities to which it contemplated sending its charges. On his inspection tour of 1907, for instance, Stanley Bero wrote from Jackson, Michigan, that "no family would feel at home here and I do not believe it would be advisable to send any." He recommended instead that only unmarried men be dispatched to Jackson and that they be told in advance that they would not be able to "live kosher" there. In 1908 the field worker Elias Margolis reported that there was little hope of placing immigrants in Champaign, Illinois, because the Jewish families there were "of the particularly selfish sort and not one of them could be interested in cooperating with us." On the other hand, in Bloomington, Illinois, prospects were better, and Margolis had recruited two men there to serve as IRO representatives. In October 1912 Abraham Solomon, another IRO field worker dispatched by the agency's New York office, reported that in Danville, Illinois, the prominent Jews were "indifferent and of limited horizon," but that he nonetheless found "potential for real co-operation, if the start is right."[37]

Besides a great deal of general correspondence that passed between local IRO representatives and the agency's New York office, there were communications concerning arrangements for the "removal " of specific individuals. For example, a report from an IRO representative in Cedar Rapids, Iowa, in 1904 advised that there was no problem in sending one Sam Miller there, because "he will not be a burden to our community as he has friends here who will take care of him but are too poor to advance him money for R.R. fare." Similarly, in 1905 Rabbi Julian Morganstern of Lafayette, Indiana, advised David Bressler in New York that sending Rosie and Francis Fishlesohn to his town was reasonable, since they had a relative in Lafayette who would help them adjust and since "work is assured them by Levy and Rice, shirtmakers of this city." In 1906 a letter from the IRO finalized arrangements to send Isidor Schlossberg to Demopolis, Alabama, because a family there had specifically "made requisition" for a boy whom they could employ and assist. Schlossberg was a newly immigrated fifteen-year-old whose father was dead and whose mother had not been heard from since a recent pogrom in Zhitomir.[38]

Altogether the IRO relocated some 75,000 Jewish immigrants from New York between its founding in 1901 and the suspension of its operations in 1922. Many of these transplants landed in one or another of America's major cities beyond New York, and others ended up in midsize urban centers. However, the IRO's work had a significant impact in small-town America as well. One indication of the scope of the IRO's influence on the smaller Jewish communities of the United States is that in the first ten years of its work alone, the organization placed people in at least half of the 490 triple-digit Jewish centers that make up our sample, and it sent individuals to dozens of even smaller Jewish settlements as well.[39]

In the end, of course, the IRO played only a small role in creating the vast network of Jewish communities that had been woven across America by the time the era of mass migration came to an end. Nonetheless, the activities of the IRO serve as a potent reminder of the complex nature of America's Jewish geography in the early part of the twentieth century. In considering the pattern of Jewish settlement across America, there may be a tendency to identify the various regions of the United States with specific types of Jewish communities. The Northeast has often been thought of as a region of big-city Jews living in huge concentrations in places such as New York, Boston, and Philadelphia. On the other hand, the South and the developing West have often been perceived as regions in which small-town Jewish life was the norm, and in which substantial Jewish communities were few and far between. There is, of course, a certain amount of truth behind these general impressions. Massachusetts, for example, had twenty-three cities with Jewish populations of 1,000 or more in 1927, mostly in the greater Boston area, and some 94 percent of the state's Jews were living in those places. At the same time, Pennsylvania had twenty cities with Jewish populations of 1,000 or more in which 91 percent of the state's Jews were living. In New York, fully 93 percent of the state's Jewish residents lived in New York City alone. By contrast, in states such as South Carolina, Kentucky, Arkansas, Utah, and Oregon, there was only a single city with a Jewish population beyond triple digits in the 1920s, and, as we have seen, some southern and western states did not have even a single urban center with a Jewish community of over 1,000.

Nonetheless, general impressions about the differences between regions should not obscure the fact that Jewish settlement patterns were characterized by a mixture of larger and smaller communities in every part of the United States. It is true that few Jewish centers anywhere in the country could compare with the huge concentrations of Jews to be found in America's dozen or so largest cities, but Jewish communities of a few thousand individuals located in substantial urban centers could be found in every region, and they were invariably the most important elements in defining the configuration of Jewish settlement in every section of the country. In the southern states of Georgia and Louisiana, for example, two-thirds of the Jewish population in the late 1920s lived in cities with Jewish communities of 1,000 or more, and even the smallest of these midsize settlements, in cities such as Savannah and Shreveport, were often robust Jewish enclaves that had a lot in common with their somewhat larger counterparts. By the same token, smaller communities in typical small-town settings were important components of the Jewish landscape even in areas generally considered the realm of big-city Jews. Pennsylvania counted eighty-four small towns with triple-digit Jewish populations in 1927, for example, and Massachusetts counted thirty-three. Ultimately, small Jewish communities far outnumbered larger ones everywhere in the United States. In the decades before World War II, there were thousands of men, women, and children experiencing small-town Jewish life in every section of the country.

Although most of the individuals who helped to create America's various small Jewish communities had not been born in the United States, a great many of those who came from overseas and gravitated to America's secondary urban centers sank firm roots in these places and identified closely with their adopted hometowns. In every small city where a fair number of Jews gathered, it was possible to encounter Jewish residents who spent many decades of their lives as active members of their communities. Finding the small-town environment welcoming, they set up successful businesses, engaged in civic activity, and often established families that remained a part of local society from one generation to another. Still, the peopling of America's small Jewish communities in the late nineteenth and early twentieth centuries was not simply a story of initial settlement followed by stability and continuity, but rather one of fluidity and change. Individuals were constantly coming into these communities, and because small towns were too insular to provide unlimited economic and cultural opportunities, individuals were constantly departing as well. There were always families settling down and families being uprooted. Thus, even though there were Jews who spent their entire lives in small communities and Jewish kin networks that remained integral to those communities over long periods, the Jewish enclaves in America's small towns were in a perpetual state of flux.

The stories of Jewish settlers who developed strong bonds to their communities and remained pillars of local society are told in a multitude of biographies, and a few examples from the era of Central European immigration can provide a sense of the nature of these stories. Moses Ulman, for instance, was born in the German city of Mannheim in 1830 and migrated to the United States at the age of eighteen. He first worked as a peddler based in Liberty, Pennsylvania, but in 1856 he started a clothing business in Williamsport,

---

*Photo opposite page: The future rabbi Joshua Liebman, born in Hamilton, Ohio, in 1907. A remarkable number of American Jews, including many Reform rabbis, had small-town backgrounds or experience. Courtesy of the Jacob Rader Marcus Center of the American Jewish Archives.*

where other members of the Ulman clan had already settled. Over the years, Moses acquired a great deal of real estate, became director of a local bank, contributed to many charitable endeavors, and served as president of Williamsport's Temple Beth Ha-Sholom. He retired in 1882 and turned his business affairs over to his two sons, although he stayed on in Williamsport until his death in 1905, just after he and his wife had celebrated their fiftieth wedding anniversary.[1]

Albert Hirshheimer was born in Wurtemberg in 1840 and arrived in La Crosse, Wisconsin, with his parents and several other relatives in 1856. He worked first in his father's lumber business and then got a job steamboating on the Mississippi. To help support his family during the Civil War, Hirshheimer found work with a blacksmith, learning his trade on the job. In 1865 he bought the shop in which he had been trained and thus laid the foundation for a plow factory and foundry that would become one of La Crosse's major manufacturing concerns. Hirshheimer remained in La Crosse and involved in his business enterprises until his death in 1924, after which two of his sons and one of his grandsons continued to run the family firm. The Hirshheimer business was finally dissolved in 1947, when its last elements were sold to the Allis-Chalmers Company.[2]

Sigmund Eisner was born in Bohemia in 1859 and came to America in 1881. Settling in Red Bank, New Jersey, he started making clothing with a lone sewing machine. His business prospered, and he slowly expanded his operations. His big break came at the time of the Spanish-American War, when he won a contract to provide military uniforms to the U.S. government. During World War I Eisner secured orders from Great Britain, Belgium, and Italy, as well as from the United States, and by the time he died in 1925 he was head of a veritable uniform manufacturing empire. Eisner was considered one of Red Bank's leading citizens, and his home was eventually bequeathed to the city for use as a public library.[3]

The Alsacian Lazar Kahn arrived in America in 1866 and spent nearly two decades doing business in several cities in the Midwest and in the South, including Marshall, Illinois; Nashville, Tennessee; Selma, Alabama; and Ironton, Ohio. In 1884 he relocated the foundry that he owned in partnership with his brother to Hamilton, Ohio, where it became the nation's largest manufacturer of stoves, and Kahn became an internationally prominent figure. He had additional business interests outside Hamilton, acted as an official juror at the Paris Expositions of 1889 and 1901, and served as president of the National Association of Stove Manufacturers from 1895 to 1897. Nonetheless, Kahn played an active role in local affairs as well. He was a member of several Hamilton fraternal lodges and clubs and helped found the Hamilton Chamber of Commerce.[4]

*The Bohemian-born uniform manufacturer Sigmund Eisner of Red Bank, New Jersey, ca. 1900. Every small Jewish community had at least some individuals, like Eisner, who became closely associated with their towns. Courtesy of the Jacob Rader Marcus Center of the American Jewish Archives.*

Among the East European immigrants who arrived in small-town America in the years shortly before and after 1900, just as among their Central European counterparts, there were also individuals who became fixtures in their communities and whose families remained locally prominent over many decades. One example is Isaac Cohen, an early Jewish settler in Green Bay, Wisconsin, who was among the organizers of the Cnesses Israel congregation there in 1898 and later its president. Soon after coming to Green Bay, Cohen established a department store with a capital of $800 that he had amassed by peddling, and he remained in town until his death in 1929. Cohen's widow and four of his children continued to be active in the Green Bay Jewish community at least into the 1950s, while his department store business was carried on under the management of his son Samuel.[5]

Jules Levinsohn established himself as a coat and suit manufacturer in Englewood, New Jersey, early in the twentieth century and became perhaps the wealthiest Jewish resident of the city in the period before World War II. Known in the local community by the affectionate Yiddish nickname "Yudel" and widely recognized for his magnanimity, Levinsohn served as president of Englewood's Orthodox congregation, Ahavath Torah, continuously from 1923 until 1944. Another East European immigrant who left his mark on a small town was Sam Stein. Arriving in Greenville, Mississippi, by way of Ellis Island around 1905, Stein began his career as an itinerant peddler of notions and piece goods, "calling on wealthy cotton planters and tenant farmers alike," and he eventually opened a store that expanded over the years to occupy an entire city block. This business was taken over by Sam's son Jake, and in 1949, as Jake was liquidating merchandise in order to move to a new location in Greenville, he realized the advantages of selling at reduced prices. Thus was born the Stein Mart chain of discount stores, which began handling more upscale merchandise in the 1970s. Although Stein Mart grew to have branches in twenty-eight states from coast to coast by the end of the twentieth century, the firm's headquarters remained in Greenville until 1984.[6] Of course, for every highly successful Jewish family that established itself as a presence in one small town or another, there emerged also a host of less prominent families that were not as visible, but that were no less grounded in their small-town communities.

One factor that smoothed the transition of so many immigrants into small-town life was that the vast majority of these individuals chose their new homes of their own free will. For those who had less of a say in selecting their small-town destinations, however, and especially for those "removed" by the IRO, it was perhaps harder to adjust. Indeed, many of those who were dispatched to smaller cities by the Industrial Removal Office never even tried to acclimate themselves to their small-town environments. Those who cast aside the opportunity to make a life for themselves in small communities may have been disappointed with the jobs they were offered, or they may have found themselves uncomfortable far from their families and from the social advantages offered by great urban centers or even midsize cities. Often those who left small communities moved to larger Jewish centers not far from the secondary ones to which they had initially been sent. There they could find a wider array of employment opportunities, seek out a more diversified Jewish milieu, or simply lose themselves in greater anonymity. The records of the IRO are full of reports about removals who disappeared from the small towns to which they had been dispatched almost as soon as they arrived.

In 1904, for example, a college professor who served as the IRO agent in Greeley, Colorado, reported that an immigrant named Lipschitz had left town only a few days after he arrived and had later written from Denver, "maintaining . . . that he could do better there." A few months after that, the rabbi in Leavenworth, Kansas, reported that of the carpenter, the shoemaker, and the baker recently sent out by the IRO, two had left for Chicago and only the shoemaker was still in town. At about the same time, the IRO agent in Marshalltown, Iowa, reported that of the five immigrants recently relocated to his community, two had left for Des Moines, one for Chicago, and another for parts unknown. "It seems there is not much of a show for these people in small country towns," the Marshalltown correspondent reflected.[7]

In some cases, it appears that IRO removals were leaving the towns to which they were assigned at a faster pace than they could be replaced. A report from the IRO field agent Stanley Bero indicated that of all the removals sent to Hamilton, Ohio, by 1910, only one, a cobbler named Max Horrenstein, was still there. Various communications from Beloit, Wisconsin, reported that of the unusually large contingent of thirty-five men sent to that town between July and October 1912, only thirteen were known to be working there by November of that year, most of them for the same large firm. Of those no longer in Beloit, many had left for the nearby cities of Milwaukee, Chicago, or Rockford, Illinois. In another report from 1912, the IRO representative in Bay City, Michigan, indicated that two immigrants recently sent there were already gone. One had moved with this family to the nearby small community of Saginaw, but the other had "left for Detroit—and might be back in New York." Even in cases in which placements eventually succeeded, extra efforts by IRO agents were often needed. In June 1904, for instance, the IRO's local contact in Vicksburg, Mississippi, wrote concerning a tinsmith and a locksmith who had been sent there. "I have [only] by perseverance kept these two men in our city," he reported, complaining that one of them "can not and seems unwilling to speak English."[8]

The character of individual immigrants was often a factor in determining how they would deal with the prospect of resettlement in a small community. It seems that some clients of the IRO were less willing than others to try to adjust to new circumstances, and that at least a few simply abused the good intentions of their benefactors. The story of Hersch Ellowitch provides a case in point. Ellowitch was sent by the IRO to Pine Bluff, Arkansas, in 1905 and set up as a fruit peddler there. According to Ephraim Frisch, the rabbi in Pine Bluff at the time, Ellowitch worked for only a week or so before he stole some money and "left secretly" for Memphis. On the way, he tricked a rabbi in Little Rock into buying him a return ticket to Pine Bluff, which he promptly sold to someone else. When Ellowitch arrived in Memphis, however, he found that city not to his liking either, and he made his way back to Pine Bluff. There,

Rabbi Frisch refused to provide further assistance. In the interim Frisch had learned not only that Ellowitch had made off with some of the community's funds and deceived the rabbi in Little Rock, but also that he had walked away from a previous IRO placement in Chicago. Nonetheless, perhaps out of compassion, an individual member of the Pine Bluff Jewish community found Ellowitch a job, which he kept for only two weeks before disappearing once again, this time headed for St. Louis.[9]

Unfortunately, complaints about individuals like Ellowitch were not unusual. The IRO agent in Cedar Rapids, Iowa, declared in 1904 that of the four immigrants recently sent there, three were working out fine, but that the fourth was "inclined to be a shnorer [moocher]." The IRO representative in Macon, Georgia, referred to one recent arrival as "a *dead beat* not worthy the waste of a minute's consideration"; and the agent in Lake Charles, Louisiana, protested about "a rascal" sent by the IRO who committed theft, contracted debts, and then skipped town. "The people here are thoroughly disgusted with the whole proposition," the Lake Charles agent grumbled, "and they blame me for having induced them to import Russian immigrants." An IRO contact in Lafayette, Indiana, once complained to the head office of the organization that "all the scandals that took place on account of the people you sent here would be enough to fill a book."[10] Clearly, the results of many of the IRO's efforts to place immigrants in small communities were disappointing.

Nonetheless, among the East Europeans relocated by the IRO there were also plenty who adapted willingly to their new surroundings and remained permanently in the small communities to which they had been sent. In 1905 Rabbi Emanuel Kahn of Joplin, Missouri, reported that both of the removals about whom the New York office had inquired "have proven excellent men" and that one of them "has given me valuable assistance with those that came after him." In the same year the IRO agent in Paducah, Kentucky, reported that three recent removals "are doing very nice." He went on to explain that established members of the local Jewish community had advanced these three men the money to bring their wives and families from Europe, and he urged the IRO to provide these women and children with transportation to Paducah when they arrived in New York, asserting that "such people must be assisted because they are deserving." The IRO seems to have had notable success in sending immigrants to Bellaire, Ohio, as well. In 1907 Stanley Bero met in the local Orthodox synagogue with some fifteen heads of families whom the agency had sent to that Ohio River town. These men not only professed their satisfaction with their new situation but also promised to help resettle other immigrants; they even drew up a resolution of thanks to the Industrial Removal Office.[11]

Another expression of gratitude came from Dubuque, Iowa, where a transplanted immigrant named Sachs penned a letter, with the aid of an acquaintance who had better command of English, explaining why he felt so comfortable in his new home and urging the IRO to continue sending people. "There are about 40,000 people in this city," Sachs explained, "and there is no feeling against us [the Jews]." He noted also that "there is a synagogue here, which we have built," and that he had a good job in a factory where many other immigrant Jews could also be employed. "The Jews and people of other religions live together quietly and comfortably," he concluded; "I and those of my race, are on the same footing as anyone else in the shop or anywhere else in the city."[12]

Also expressing satisfaction was an immigrant who wrote to the IRO from Meridian, Mississippi, to say that he was gratified to be in a place where the seventy-five local Jewish families were "all well to do," with most "doing business in millions." He noted that the majority of those in the Jewish community were of German background, but that the Russian Jews in town were attempting to emulate their success. As he put it, "every one of them is trying [to] get the title of German Jew." Enthusiastic about his own experience, the writer from Meridian urged those he called "the enslaved Jews in New York" to leave the city "as quick as they can and come to get the benefit of a good climate and to conduct a good living."[13]

Not surprisingly, the IRO itself was eager to tout is triumphs, and it used the pages of its *Monthly Bulletin* to publicize the stories of immigrants who had successfully established themselves in the outlying communities to which the organization had dispatched them. Among those featured in the journal were some immigrants who had ended up in smaller towns. In August 1914, for example, the periodical reported on one of its removals who had lived in New York City for nine years before seeking the aid of the IRO. Starting out as a tinsmith's helper and then working at various odd jobs, this immigrant had "inhaled the Ghetto poetry and the Ghetto slop and after epical struggles sent for his family." Still, times were hard. He was often unemployed, and he lived five flights up in a rear tenement. The IRO inspector who investigated his condition had reported "small rooms, littered [,] derelict, the children (sick), half dressed, the hot sun baking germs." Eventually the IRO had relocated this unfortunate man to Macon, Georgia, where he had established himself as the proud proprietor of a tinware shop on Main Street. "He makes a decent living," the *Monthly Bulletin* reported, and his once sickly child was "straight as a stalk, and if the heart ever pounds, it is from joy."[14]

The accounts that have come down to us of immigrant Jews adjusting successfully to small-town life, like the stories we have of community founders becoming attached to their adopted hometowns, serve to remind us that in the classic era of small-town Jewry, every small community could boast of well-established families and accomplished native sons. These were kin groups and individuals that were likely not only to have done well economically but also to have been crucial to the continuity of local Jewish life. Indeed, lay leaders were especially important as guiding lights in smaller Jewish centers because, as we shall see, these communities often had to do without stable rabbinic leadership. The biographies of some of the individuals already mentioned make clear their involvement in the activities of their synagogues, and other examples of men and women who volunteered their time and effort to keep this or that small-town institution afloat are abundant, as well. In Alexandria, Louisiana, Julius Levin served as president of Congregation Gemiluth Chassodim from 1861 to 1871, again from 1886 to 1888, and again from 1904 to 1906, while Will Hochbaum served for the entire period from 1927 until 1952. In Annapolis, Maryland, Louis Stern was president of Congregation Kneseth Israel for almost the entire decade from 1910 to 1919, and then he was back again in 1923. Joseph Lipman was president of Kneseth Israel in the early 1920s, and his wife, Bessie, headed the congregation's sisterhood in every year from 1916 until 1931.[15] Naturally, it is the story of community stalwarts such as these that is most often recounted in the annals of smaller Jewish settlements, and it is not uncommon for local lore to link a town's Jewish history to the biographies of its most prominent Jewish residents.[16]

Nonetheless, it would be a serious mistake to lose sight of the fact that the mix of individuals and families in the small Jewish communities of the American hinterland was constantly being altered. Obviously, one thing that kept the composition of any given community from remaining stable was the continual arrival of new settlers even after these communities were well established. The membership rosters of small-town synagogues provide one hint about the impact of the continual arrival of new residents. Of the seventy individuals who held seats in the only synagogue in Paducah, Kentucky, in 1893, for example, only twenty-seven had been members of the assembly as recently as 1886, and of the thirty-six family names represented in the congregation in 1893, only twenty-two had been represented just seven years earlier. Similarly, of the fifty-two individuals assessed for dues by the only congregation in Danville, Pennsylvania, in 1924, only thirty-two were either members or the widows of members who had been assessed eleven years earlier, in 1913. Of the thirty-two family names represented in the Danville congregation in 1924, only twenty had been represented a decade or so earlier.[17]

Information about the origins of Jews whose lives came to an end in America's small towns also reflects an ongoing migration into these places and provides a sense of the patterns that this migration followed. For example, of the 169 individuals buried in the Jewish cemetery of Brownsville, Tennessee, between 1860 and 1975, 40 percent had been born abroad. That a large proportion of Brownsville's Jews were foreign-born might have been anticipated. However, even among the American-born Jews buried in Brownsville, one-third were individuals who had came there from elsewhere in the United States. Eighteen of those buried in the Brownsville cemetery had been born in other cities or towns in Tennessee, six had been born in the adjacent state of Kentucky, and ten had been born farther afield, in cities as distant as Newark, Philadelphia, Chicago, New Orleans, and Montgomery.[18]

It was not only the continual arrival of people from elsewhere, however, that kept the blend of individuals and families in America's small Jewish communities almost constantly in flux. Just as important for the dynamic demographic history of these settlements was the constant departure of Jewish residents. In many cases, even individuals who were counted among the founders of their communities or among their most prominent members did not remain in their towns permanently. Julius Hammerslough, for example, was the first Jewish resident of Springfield, Illinois, a friend of Abraham Lincoln, and a founder of the city's earliest congregation, but after living in Springfield for several years, he departed for New York City in 1865. Isaac W. Bernheim established a very successful distillery, together with his younger brother, in Paducah, Kentucky, in 1872 and was one of the town's leading citizens. After a decade in Paducah, however, he moved to Louisville, where his firm continued to prosper and where he became a noted philanthropist.[19]

Moses Cohen, who arrived in Muncie, Indiana, around 1880 to become the town's pioneer Jewish scrap dealer moved to Chicago after twenty-six years in order to take advantage of expanded business opportunities there. Similarly, the brothers Heine and Louie Kern departed from Lafayette, Indiana, even though they had done quite well there. The Kerns had arrived in Lafayette in the early 1890s and established a highly lucrative meat market and packing company. Nonetheless, around 1912 both brothers decided to leave. Heine relocated to Chicago, where he became a real estate investor, while Louie moved to Toledo. Seymour Heymann, associated for over two decades with the landmark Heymann Department Store in Oshkosh, Wisconsin, nonetheless moved to New York City around 1929.[20]

A fascinating indicator of how common it was for Jews to move away from the small communities in which they had spent a part of their lives is the fact that some of America's most famous and influential Jewish retailers started out in small towns. It seems that for many of these ambitious entrepreneurs, small-town surroundings were simply too stifling. Julius Rosenwald, who became president of Sears, Roebuck and Company in 1909 and helped build that firm's huge mail-order empire, was born in Springfield, Illinois, in 1862 and lived there until 1879, when he moved first to New York and then to Chicago. Both Augusta Nusbaum, who became Rosenwald's wife, and Augusta's brother Aaron Nusbaum (later Norman), who became Rosenwald's partner, grew up in the small town of Plattsburg, New York, before moving to Chicago with their parents in 1882.[21]

The Gimbel brothers, who eventually opened department stores in Milwaukee, Philadelphia, New York, and Pittsburgh, and who came to control the

Saks Fifth Avenue department store chain as well, also had small-town life in their backgrounds. In 1842 their father, Adam Gimbel, had opened a dry-goods store in Vincennes, Indiana (a town that was reported to have just under 100 Jews both in the late 1870s and in the 1920s), and he operated that business for forty years as his children matured. The two eldest Gimbel sons, Jacob and Isaac, got their own start in retailing by establishing a department store in Danville, Illinois, in the 1880s. David May, whose firm had acquired stores in St. Louis and in Cleveland by the turn of the twentieth century and whose May Department Store Company would eventually control Hecht's, Kaufmann's, Filene's, and Lord and Taylor, opened his first store in 1877 in the silver-mining town of Leadville, Colorado, not long before the Jewish population there rose to about 200. Indeed, in the nineteenth century especially, it was quite usual for Jewish merchants who succeeded in larger cities to have spent some time in the hinterland on their way up. The historian of Cincinnati Jewry, Stephen Mostov, has discovered, for example, that "it was rare for a Jew to successfully establish a business in Cincinnati without having had previous experience in a smaller town somewhere else."[22]

Nor were retail store magnates the only notable Jews who emerged from America's small towns. Abraham Kuhn, the cofounder with his brother-in-law of the phenomenally successful New York banking house of Kuhn, Loeb and Company, had been one of the first settlers of Lafayette, Indiana, arriving there around 1849 by way of New Orleans. Edna Ferber, the Pulitzer Prize–winning playwright and author of novels such as *So Big* (1924), *Show Boat* (1926) and *Giant* (1952), was born in Kalamazoo, Michigan, in 1887 and got her first job in journalism in Appleton, Wisconsin. As we have seen, another celebrated Jew who grew up in Appleton was Eric Weisz, a son of the town's first rabbi, more famous under his stage name Harry Houdini. The Warner brothers first ventured into the film industry with a movie theater in New Castle, Pennsylvania, in 1903. As one account explains, "Sam Warner handled the projection machine, eleven-year-old Jack sang before and after the movie, and Albert, Milton, and Harry rewound the film."[23]

A random sampling of other prominent Jews who began their lives in small towns during the late nineteenth or early twentieth century might include the musician, business executive, and philanthropist Max Adler, born in Elgin, Illinois, in 1866, who provided funds for America's first planetarium; the financier, statesman, and presidential advisor Bernard Baruch, born in Camden, South Carolina, in 1870; the film producer Jesse Lasky, whose credits include *Sergeant York* (1941) and the *Adventures of Mark Twain* (1942), born in San Jose, California, in 1880; the novelist Fannie Hurst, author of *Imitation of Life* (1933) and over two dozen other books, born in Hamilton, Ohio, in 1889; the mathematician Norbert Wiener, who invented the science of cybernetics, born in Columbia, Missouri, in 1894; the conservative economist

*Playwright and novelist Edna Ferber, who was born in Kalamazoo, Michigan, and began her career as a writer in Appleton, Wisconsin. Ferber, pictured here ca. 1950, represents the many notable American Jews with small-town beginnings. Courtesy of the Jacob Rader Marcus Center of the American Jewish Archives.*

Milton Friedman, born in Rahway, New Jersey, in 1912; and the bandleader Harry James, born in Albany, Georgia, in 1916.[24] Also emerging from American small towns was an array of prominent Reform rabbis who made their mark in the early decades of the twentieth century. These include David Philipson, professor at Hebrew Union College and president of the Central Conference of American Rabbis from 1907 to 1909, born in Wabash, Indiana, in 1862; Sidney Goldstein, a founder of the Jewish Institute of Religion in New York, born in Marshall, Texas, in 1879; Julian Feibelman, longtime rabbi of Temple Sinai in New Orleans, born in Jackson, Mississippi, in 1897; Abraham L. Feinberg, spiritual leader of Holy Blossom Temple in Toronto, born in Bellaire, Ohio, in 1899; and Joshua Liebman, rabbi of Temple Israel in Boston and, in 1946, author of the widely read book *Peace of Mind*, born in Hamilton, Ohio, in 1907.[25]

Calculating the precise rates at which Jews moved into and out of small towns in the classic era of small-town Jewry is impossible, and even studies of mobility in specific communities are difficult to conduct, primarily because there were several reasons besides relocation that might have caused individuals to disappear from the records of these communities. Some of those whose names vanished from sources such as census lists, city directories, and congregational membership rosters may have died, for example, while others may simply have been overlooked by those preparing these documents. So, too, some small-town Jews may have changed the spelling of their names, or changed their names entirely. Typical of this phenomenon was the modification of the name "Schilkerat" in the 1920 census of Appleton, Wisconsin, to "Shilcrat" later on. This kind of alteration is relatively easy to spot, but other, more radical changes are not. Rabbi Nathan Krass, who served in several small communities in Louisiana, Indiana, and Kentucky before moving on to larger cities, began his career as Nathan Krasnowitz, for example; and the Krakofsky family of Newburyport, Massachusetts, became the Kray family in the 1920s. Similarly, Max Shubovitz of Burlington, Vermont, changed his name to Shubert, while his nephew Sam Shubovitz, who moved to Fitchburg, Massachusetts, changed his name to Stevens. Of course, women almost always adopted the surnames of their husbands when they married and thus became difficult to follow in any kinds of records.[26]

Nonetheless, there are many suggestive research findings, as well as much anecdotal evidence, to substantiate the assertion that a large proportion of those Jews who peopled America's small-town Jewish communities at one time or another did not remain in those settings throughout their lives. In his study of the Jewish community of Trinidad, Colorado, for example, the historian William Toll found that about half the Jewish families present in town in 1890 and in 1900 left during each succeeding decade, with most going to larger cities such as Denver or Chicago.[27] An examination of the available records of other small communities suggests a similar pattern of continual emigration.

The records of Beth Israel, the only Jewish congregation in Jackson, Michigan, for instance, reveal that the congregation had thirty-one members when it adopted its first constitution in 1863. Of these thirty-one, however, only fifteen or perhaps sixteen were listed in the Jackson city directory published only ten years later. It is possible that some members of Beth Israel were unlisted because they lived near Jackson but not in the town. Others, of course, may have died. Nonetheless, it is remarkable that Jackson's congregation could have witnessed the departure of as many as half of its members within just ten years of its founding. Similarly, the same records of the congregation in Paducah that reflect the continual migration of Jews into the city also attest to the departure of others. In 1880 the assembly had forty individual seatholders bearing thirty-one different surnames. Just six years later, however, fully one-third of these seatholders were gone from the congregation, and nine of the family names of 1880 were no longer represented. Paducah's congregation changed its name from Bene Yeshurum to Temple Israel in 1893, and in that year only twenty-two of the forty seatholders present in 1880 were still among its members, and only twenty of the thirty-one surnames of 1880 were still represented.[28]

Tracking Jewish residents who appear in the 1880 census records for some of the small communities in our sample also reveals a pattern of ongoing departures. Of the thirty-seven individuals identifiable in the 1880 manuscript census as Jewish heads of household in Lafayette, Indiana, for instance, only twenty-five (68 percent) can be located in the city directory published for Lafayette just nine years later, in 1889. Moreover, it is unlikely that many of those absent from the directory would have died, since the average age of the twelve missing householders was only forty-nine in 1889. Of the sixteen Jewish heads of household identifiable in Appleton, Wisconsin, in 1880, only seven men and the widow Babetta Silverfreund (50 percent of the householders) were listed in the city directory of Appleton published in 1891.[29]

Tracking Jewish householders identifiable in 1880 over longer periods reveals an even higher rate of attrition. Of the twenty Jewish men who can be identified as heads of household in the 1880 manuscript census for Lexington, Kentucky, only six were still present in the Lexington city directory published in 1902, although two others were represented by their widows. Even more revealing of high mobility, however, is the fact that none of the householders of 1880 who disappeared from Lexington by 1902 seems to have been survived by a son or sons still living in town. Although daughters who married and had new surnames may have been missed in this analysis, and although Howard Gratz, the gentile son of Lexington's first Jewish resident, was still around, it is safe to say that perhaps half of the households that made up the Lexington Jewish community in 1880 were no longer represented in the city two decades later.[30]

An examination of congregational membership patterns in Lexington also points to continual migration out of the city. Lexington's Reform temple, Adath Israel, allocated seats in its sanctuary for the first time in 1907, and of the congregation's fifty-one original seatholders, thirty-nine can be located in the Lexington city directory of 1908 (one reason some seatholders were missing is that they were from small towns surrounding Lexington). By 1919, however, only twenty-eight of Adath Israel's original seatholders could be found in the Lexington city directory, and by 1927 no more than fourteen were listed, together with four widows of original seatholders.[31] These findings only reinforce the notion that even those people who made a positive commitment to local Jewish life did not necessarily stay in their communities permanently.

Information on membership from congregation B'nai Zion in Danville, Pennsylvania, also reflects an ongoing population turnover. Of the thirty-six individuals who were assessed for annual dues by B'nai Zion in March of 1896 (most from Danville, but some from other small towns in the vicinity), thirteen were no longer recorded as dues payers by December 1900, although three of those missing were represented by their widows. Furthermore, of the forty individuals who were members of the Danville congregation in 1900, only half were still listed as members in 1913, with three of the missing represented by their widows and one man who had been on the B'nai Zion membership list in 1896 but not in 1900 reappearing. Of the forty-five individuals who were members of B'nai Zion in 1913, in turn, only thirty-two were either still present or represented by their widows ten years later, at the end of 1923. Moreover, a few of the congregants of 1923 were maintaining their membership while living in larger cities in the East. Emanuel Wolf was by then in Philadelphia, for example, and Simon Dreifuss was in Yonkers. Of the twenty-four surnames represented among B'nai Zion members in 1900, seven were completely absent in 1923.[32]

Analyses that take the manuscript census returns of 1920 as their point of departure reveal the same trends as those based on returns from 1880 and testify that migration out of small towns remained a significant element in the history of small Jewish communities throughout the first half of the twentieth century. For example, of the seventy-two Jewish heads of household in Newburyport, Massachusetts, in 1920, only fifty-two (72 percent) can still be located in the town's city directory just five years later, and only thirty-nine (54 percent) can be located eleven years later. Tracking a set of 105 Jewish male heads of household identifiable in Bradford, Pennsylvania, in 1920 reveals that there, too, Jewish residents were far from certain to remain in town. As early as 1925, twenty-six of the householders of 1920 (25 percent) were already absent from the town's city directory, although six of these men were survived by widows still living in Bradford. By 1929, thirty or thirty-one of the 105 householders of 1920 (29 percent) were neither listed in the directory nor represented by their widows. By 1940 nearly half of those tracked were neither listed in Bradford nor survived there by widows. In Jackson, Michigan, the rate at which Jews abandoned the town after 1920 was quite astonishing. Of the twenty-eight Jewish heads of household identifiable in Jackson on the basis of the 1920 census, only twelve (43 percent) were listed in the Jackson city directory published just five years after the census. Here, too, death is unlikely to explain the disappearance of so many householders, for the average age of the twenty-eight individuals followed was only forty-three in 1920, and only four of them were over fifty-five.[33]

As the disappearance of certain surnames from the records of various small towns attests, it was not uncommon for children who had grown up in these places to seek greener pastures elsewhere. Indeed, much of the migration of Jews out of small towns took the form of the departure of children as they matured. Within Lafayette's Jewish households of 1880, for instance, there were nineteen identifiable sons who would have been twenty-one or older in 1889. Of these, only ten (53 percent) appear in the Lafayette city directory of that year. Ten years after that, in 1899, only six of these nineteen sons (32 percent) appear in the city directory. The sixteen Jewish heads of household in Appleton in 1880 had thirty-two sons among them, all of whom would have been at least twenty-one years old in 1901. According to the city directory published in that year, however, only four of these sons (12 percent) were still in Appleton in the first year of the twentieth century, although Joseph Hammel, a son of Jacob and Julia Hammel who would have been forty-one years old in 1901, was represented by his widow, Ellen. Of twenty-eight sons who lived in the Jewish households of Hamilton, Ohio, in 1880, only half (either thirteen or fourteen) were still in Hamilton in 1902, when the youngest of these children would have been twenty-three and the oldest, forty-four.[34]

In the twentieth century, the departure of children from small communities continued apace. Of the forty-two Jewish boys under twenty-one years of age identifiable in Appleton in 1920, only seventeen were still listed in the local city directory published two decades later (40 percent, assuming that Leo Solinger and Lee Solinger are the same person). At the time, the youngest of these individuals would have been twenty years old and the oldest, thirty-nine. Nine of the seventeen sons remaining in Appleton were still listed as living with one or both of their parents, but three of those nine were away at college, two at the University of Wisconsin in Madison and one at Marquette University in Milwaukee. As late as 1950, only ten of the forty-two individuals followed in this study (24 percent) appear to have married and set up their own households in Appleton. A study following 101 male children of Jewish householders in Bradford, Pennsylvania, in 1920, reveals that at least fifty-one of them were missing from the Bradford city directory published for 1940, when the youngest of these sons would have been twenty and the oldest, forty. Of the 101 sons followed, it seems that a mere fifteen were married heads of household in their original hometown two decades after they had been recorded in the 1920 census.[35]

The evidence available from quantitative studies showing that young people frequently left the small communities of their childhood is reinforced by information from the obituaries of Jews who died in small towns, for these death notices often indicate the whereabouts of children. When Lena Malachowsky Pincus died in Alexandria, Louisiana, in 1915, for example, she had two unmarried daughters living in town, but her son S. E. Pincus was living in Memphis and her son Herman was living in Fort Worth. When Lena Allen died in Bradford, Pennsylvania, in 1921, she had one daughter and one son living near her, but she also had a daughter in Rochester and three sons in Calgary, Alberta. When Bettie Netter Benjamin died in Natchez, Mississippi, in 1925, she had a daughter living in that city, but three other daughters living elsewhere: one in St. Louis, one in Albuquerque, and one in Columbus, Ohio.[36]

A set of obituaries pasted into the minute book of Temple Israel in Lafayette, Indiana, covering the period from August 1932 through June 1937 illustrates more systematically some of the patterns of migration typical of Jewish children leaving small towns. Some children of small-town families moved to other secondary cities, usually nearby; others moved to the major metropolitan centers of their regions; and still others relocated to one of the great urban centers of America where the country's largest Jewish communities were found. When Gustav Truman died, for instance, he left only one son in Lafayette, but three sons living out of town: one in Evansville, Indiana; one in Greenup, Illinois; and one in Allwood, New Jersey. When Bernhardt Born died, his son was living in Detroit. Henry Rosenthal's survivors included one son who had been in business with his father in Lafayette, one son living in Indianapolis, and two daughters in Chicago. The Lafayette cigar manufacturer Nathan Sobel died in New York City in 1935, rather than in his hometown, because he had left Indiana after he retired to be near his son, the theater historian and publicist Bernard Sobel. Nathan's other children were gone from Lafayette as well. A second son was in Dayton, Ohio, and a daughter was in Fort Wayne, Indiana. When Solomon Loeb died at age eighty-four in 1937, he left two sons in Lafayette running the department store he had helped to found, but a third son was a manufacturer living in New York. When Maurice Levy died in the same year, he left two daughters, one in Lafayette and one in Columbus, Ohio. The survivors of Hannah Pottlitzer were the daughter with whom she had been living in Lafayette, and a son in Louisville. The survivors of Marian Pottlitzer were a son in Lafayette and a daughter in Reading, Pennsylvania.[37]

A review of the obituaries of twenty-eight men and women who were among the founders of the Reform and Orthodox congregations established in Lexington, Kentucky, early in the twentieth century reveals that only 46 percent of the children of these early settlers were living in Lexington at the time their parents died there. This figure is slightly skewed by the fact that several Lexington synagogue founders died while their children were serving in the armed forces during World War II (one was a prisoner of war held by the Japanese), but the information from Lexington, like much of the other data available, clearly supports the contention that the departure of Jewish children from their small hometowns was a routine occurrence. At the time of their deaths, only two of the twenty-eight Lexington Jews studied had all of their children living in Lexington.[38] Again, neither quantitative studies based on data whose reliability is open to question, nor surveys of representative obituaries can furnish precise measures of the rate at which people departed from America's small Jewish communities, but they provide a clear indication that the composition of these communities was far from stable.

The motivations that drew individuals and families away from their small communities were as varied as those that initially attracted Jews to small towns. Probably the most frequent cause of departures was a sense that the economic climate was better elsewhere. Whether it was well-established business people who believed that even greater prosperity awaited them in larger cities, downtrodden immigrants disappointed with their lack of success in their current circumstances, or the children of small-town Jews who were drawn to job opportunities in other places, the hope that relocation would mean an improved economic situation was a very powerful force. Indeed, as we have seen, where adverse developments such as mine closings or the depletion of oil wells caused the local economy to become stagnant or even to collapse, entire small-town Jewish communities could go into decline. Even in places where communities survived, moreover, short-term economic reverses could lead Jews to leave their towns in noticeable numbers. In Muskegon, Michigan, for instance, the influx of Jewish settlers in the 1880s was tied to the town's development as a lumbering center. However, when the area's great lumber boom came to an end and the economic downturn experienced by the country as a whole in the mid-1890s affected the town's economy, some of the Jews who had come to Muskegon left, and the community ceased to expand. Only at the turn of the century, when Muskegon began to attract industrial development, did the local Jewish community begin to grow anew. Similarly, the impact of short-term economic change was felt in Columbus, Mississippi, from which many Jews were forced to depart in the 1920s because Prohibition destroyed the liquor trade in which they had been involved.[39]

Not unexpectedly, analyses of the composition of several small communities suggest quite consistently that economic prosperity was a key factor in keeping some Jews in town while others left. For example, in Lexington, Kentucky, three of the six men whose names are recorded both in the census of 1880 and in the city directory of 1902 were the heads of successful clothing firms throughout the final two decades of the nineteenth century. Among the seven male householders who seem to have been present in Appleton, Wisconsin, continuously from 1880 until at least 1901 were David Hammel, Jacob Hammel, and Fred Loeb, all of them well-to-do horse and cattle dealers, sometimes in partnership with one another. As a prosperous businessman, David Hammel gained such prominence in Appleton that he was elected mayor of the city in the 1890s and served into the early twentieth century. Also among the most entrenched Jews of late nineteenth-century Appleton were Gabe and Joseph Ullman. In 1880 Gabe had been a clothing merchant and Joseph a sewing machine agent, but by the turn of the century they, too, had built a thriving business as "dealers in horses, mules and cattle."[40]

The records available for congregation B'nai Zion in Danville, Pennsylvania, provide further evidence that there was a positive correlation between individual prosperity and a propensity to remain in a small town. The membership fees paid by those affiliated with B'nai Zion reflected their level of wealth, and so it is significant that all nine of the B'nai Zion congregants who were assessed annual dues of thirty-six dollars or more in 1896 were still present in the congregation in 1900 or represented by their widows. Of the fourteen congregants who were assessed eighteen dollars in 1896, eleven (79 percent) were still present in 1900. However, of the thirteen less affluent Danville congregants who were assessed somewhere between six and fifteen dollars in 1896, only six (46 percent) appear on the list of dues payers prepared at the end of 1900. B'nai Zion dues seem to have been set at levels to make them affordable to all, so the disappearance of congregants is unlikely to have resulted from their resignation. It was far more likely a consequence of their relocation. To judge from the B'nai Zion records, prosperity continued to correlate with an inclination to stay in Danville or one of the surrounding small towns as the twentieth century progressed. Of the twenty-six B'nai Zion members who were assessed annual dues of eighteen dollars or more in 1913, twenty-one (81 percent) were still members of the congregation themselves or had widows who were members in 1923. By contrast, of the nineteen B'nai Zion members who were assessed dues of less than eighteen dollars in 1913, only eleven (59 percent) were still members of the congregation ten years later.[41]

Support for the contention that persistence in a small town was related to economic success comes also from information about home ownership in several of our sample communities. On the assumption that owning one's home was at least a partial indicator of economic stability and well-being, it is not surprising that, at least in some communities in the years after 1920, those Jews who had been able to purchase their homes were more prone to stay in their small towns than were those who rented their homes or boarded with others. In some places, it is true, homeowners and renters seem to have persisted at about the same rates. In Lafayette, Indiana, for example, about 53 percent of those who owned their homes in 1920 were either still in town or represented by their widows in 1929, while 52 percent of those who rented in 1920 were still in town. Similarly, in Newburyport, 57 percent of Jewish homeowners in 1920 were either still in town in 1931 or are known to have died there in the previous decade, while 60 percent of renters were still in town in 1931. In Vicksburg, Mississippi, which had an unusually high persistence rate in the first half of the twentieth century (perhaps because of the presence of so many well-established German-Jewish families even in the interwar period), 80 percent of the Jewish homeowners of 1920 were either still in town in 1929 or are known to have died in Vicksburg by that year. At the same time, 81 percent of those Jewish heads of household who rented their homes in Vicksburg in 1920 were either still in town about a decade later or are known to have died.[42]

Still, the available evidence indicates that nowhere did homeowners leave their small towns with any greater frequency than renters did, and data from some places suggest a positive correlation between home ownership and relatively high levels of persistence. In Jackson, Michigan, where the overall rate of departure of Jewish householders was very high after 1920, renters nonetheless left at a faster pace than homeowners did. While ten of the twenty-one Jackson Jewish homeowners of 1920 (48 percent) are known to have still been in town in 1925, only two of the seven heads of household who rented (29 percent) were still present. In Alexandria, Louisiana, at least 69 percent of those Jews who owned their own homes in 1920 were either still in town or represented by their widows in 1931, while the comparable figure for renters was a somewhat lower 57 percent. In Bradford, Pennsylvania, it appears that 78 percent of those who owned their homes in 1920 were either still living or survived by widows in Bradford about a decade later, in 1929. By contrast, the comparable figure for those who rented their homes in 1920 was 60 percent. By 1940, it appears that 60 percent of those who owned their homes in 1920 were either still living or survived by widows in Bradford while the comparable figure for those who rented their homes in 1920 was only 40 percent.[43]

Boarding in the home of a nonrelative suggested even greater economic uncertainty than did renting a home, and attempts to follow Jewish boarders in small towns, usually single men, indeed indicate that they had a high rate of geographic mobility. Of the three Jewish male boarders identifiable in Appleton in 1880, for instance, only one was listed in the city directory of 1891. He was Rudolph Schwarz, a thirty-three-year-old clerk in a clothing store in 1880 who was the owner of his own clothing business a decade later. Of the seven boarders in Lafayette in 1920 who can be tracked, all but the physician Samuel Pearlman were gone from the city directory as early as 1924. Of the six boarders who could be tracked in Jackson, Michigan, in the same period, all but two were absent from the city directory of 1925. As might have been expected, the two boarders who were still around had relatively good jobs in Jackson. One was the manager of the Liberal Credit Clothing Company, and the other was the manager of the American Lady Corset Company.[44]

Tracking a set of fourteen Jewish male boarders in Bradford in 1920 suggests that four were absent by 1925, seven were absent by 1929, and nine were absent by 1940. The average age of these boarders was only thirty-nine in 1920, and only three of them were over fifty, so even though two-thirds of these boarders were gone from Bradford within twenty years, it is unlikely that a great many of them had died. In Newburyport, of the seventeen boarders identifiable in the 1920 census, Hyman Walters is known to have died in 1923, but nine others are missing from the city directory prepared for 1925 as well (assuming that Nathan Abraham and Nathan Abrams are the same person). When a new city directory was prepared for Newburyport at the end of 1930, nine of the seventeen boarders of 1920 were missing, although those present included two who had not appeared in the 1925 directory. These two may have left town and then returned, or they may simply have been missed by those collecting information in the middle of the decade.[45]

In general terms, using city directories to track boarders requires even more caution than using them to track heads of household, for it is likely that boarders were more readily ignored than householders when city directories were prepared and that this likelihood colors the impression that those who lived with nonrelatives were highly mobile. In Newburyport, for instance, the names of six of the seventeen boarders identified in the 1920 census appear in neither the city directory of 1919–20 (actually prepared in 1918) nor that of 1922–23 (prepared in 1921). This absence may mean that these six people were in Newburyport only for an extremely short time, but it could also indicate that they were missed by the compilers of the directories just before and after 1920. Still, there is a lot of evidence to suggest that directory information is a fairly good guide to the fate of the residents of the towns they cover, including the fate of boarders. Faith in the accuracy of the Newburyport directories is bolstered, for instance, by the fact that even though George Rosenfield, one of the men boarding with Max Traister according to the 1920 census, does not show up in the directories of the period, Traister's other boarder, Louis Shamesman, does appear as a harnessmaker in the directory for 1922–23 before disappearing from later volumes. It is also encouraging to be able to discover details about the fortunes of other boarders in Newburyport. Louis Ossen, a junk dealer boarding with Isaac Lubeowitz in 1920, was listed in the directory of 1922–23 as a boarder in a different home, before disappearing from later directories. Louis Bornstein, a peddler known to have been boarding with Jacob Woodman in 1918, 1920, and 1921, was living in his own place with his wife, Rose, by 1924 and operating a grocery store, which apparently specialized in meats by 1930.[46]

Although the search for better economic circumstances was the consideration most likely to prompt individuals to move out of small towns, this was not the only possible motive. For some of those who abandoned secondary cities, a fundamental change in the course of their lives was the catalyst. Marriage could be the occasion for a relocation, for instance, as young women who wed outside their own communities were especially likely to move to the hometowns of their husbands. Again, evidence of this pattern can be found in the obituaries of small-town Jews. When L. M. Krienson died in Bradford, Pennsylvania, on the first day of 1921, for example, he had a son living in Bradford, but his two married daughters were in larger cities, one in Montreal and the other in Chicago. Abraham Geisenberger of Natchez, Mississippi, was survived by several sons and brothers in his hometown when he died in 1923, but he also left a daughter who had married and moved to Meridian, Mississippi, and a sister who had married and moved to Dallas, Texas.[47]

Retirement was another event that could occasion a move to a larger city with more to offer, especially for those who were kept in their small communities primarily by their business interests. For example, around the turn of the century, several merchants who had made their mark in the commercial life of Frederick, Maryland, moved to Baltimore when they stopped working. One was James Landauer, who had spent thirty-seven years in Frederick before relocating. Another was Joseph Stern, who had spent forty years in Frederick. The community's longtime rabbi, Sussman Goebricher, also moved to Baltimore when he retired at the age of sixty-four in 1891, and he lived there until his death in 1908.[48]

It is certain, also, that some of the East European immigrants who settled in small towns left, either sooner or later, because they found their new environments unconducive to the intensively Jewish lifestyles with which they had been familiar in Russia or Poland, or perhaps even in New York or some other large American city. Among those who could not abide small-town life in the American hinterland were individuals for whom Orthodox religious practice was extremely important. The story of Nathan Blecker's family provides a case in point. Blecker arrived in Jonesboro, Arkansas, around 1890 and established a dry-goods business there that soon had branches in several other towns. Although he did not want to give up his thriving commercial enterprise, he craved a more intensively Jewish environment for his family. His solution was to move his wife and children from Jonesboro to Memphis and to arrange to be at home with them on each Sabbath. Blecker preferred to have his children reared in a community with an extensive Jewish infrastructure, even if it meant he had to be apart from his family all week long. The biography of Julius Friedland is illustrative here as well. Friedland came from Minsk, in the Russian Empire, to serve as a rabbi, *mohel* (ritual circumciser), and *shochet* (ritual slaughterer) in Meridian, Mississippi, around 1904. Later he and his family moved to Tyler, Texas. Before long, however, they transplanted themselves once again, this time to New York, where they could find a huge like-minded community of which to be a part. The relocation of Morris Nasatir and his family was also motivated by a search for surroundings in which their Orthodoxy could be accommodated more easily. A highly observant Jew,

Nasatir spent some seventeen years as a merchant in Santa Ana, California, before moving his family to Los Angeles in 1915, around the time his children reached dating age.[49]

Other kinds of commitments also could motivate small-town Jews to seek out like-minded peers in larger communities. Among those who were unlikely to find much of a support network in small towns were people ideologically committed to secularism or to radical socialism. In Gloversville, New York, which was a place with only slightly over 1,000 Jews in the late 1920s, for example, uncompromising secularists were said to be quite uncomfortable, and so they often "fled to the anonymity of New York City." Similarly, storekeepers with leftist leanings in the triple-digit Jewish communities of the Minnesota Iron Range understood that in order to survive in business, they had to remain silent on political issues. Although left-wing political opinions were common in some truly rural Jewish agricultural settlements, perhaps the only one of the towns in our sample in which radical views were the norm was the community of Petaluma, California, to which dozens of Jewish families flocked in the early decades of the twentieth century to take up chicken ranching and to form an ethnic enclave devoted to socialist and Jewish internationalism. In short, those with a strong desire for an extensive network of individuals deeply committed to a specific worldview, be it Orthodoxy, secularism, or some other philosophy, were unlikely to find what they wanted in a small town. As the historian Deborah Dash Moore has observed, those who adapted most successfully to American Jewish life outside New York and the other major port cities of the East were the ones for whom "the desire for economic independence and individual achievement" outweighed the need for "psychological security and cultural fulfillment."[50]

In their propensity to move both into and out of small towns rather freely, Jews in the late nineteenth and early twentieth centuries were not all that different from other groups of people living in America at the time. Studies of general population trends in several small towns around the turn of the twentieth century have demonstrated that the people living in these places, like people living in big cities, were frequently on the move. The persistence rate for gainfully employed males who were either first- or second-generation Americans in South Bend, Indiana, was only 26 percent between 1870 and 1880, for example; and the persistence rate for adult males in Holland, Michigan, in the same period was 55 percent. In one Pennsylvania steel town studied by the historian John Bodnar, the persistence rate for all property owners was no more than 50 percent between 1905 and 1915 and 53 percent between 1915 and 1925.[51]

The constantly changing composition of America's smaller Jewish centers had important implications for the character of these communities. New arrivals always brought with them the influences of the places from which they had come, be they in Europe or elsewhere in America; as a result, the cultural mix in small communities was constantly being altered. At no time was this clearer than when East European Jews arrived in communities that had been founded and previously dominated by German Jews. The ongoing population change witnessed by small communities also helped to keep the people living in these communities from feeling completely isolated. After all, they were frequently coming into contact with Jews arriving from other places, and they themselves knew that there was always the prospect that they, too, would move on. Although this was by no means the only factor that kept smaller Jewish settlements in touch with the larger world, it was an important element in maintaining that connection.

The ongoing migration of Jews into and out of small communities had significance for American Jewry more generally, as well, because, just as Jews arriving in small towns brought with them the influences of the places from which they had come, those departing took some of their small-town outlook to other places. Although only a tiny minority of American Jews lived in small communities at any given time, especially after the turn of the century, the transiency that helped shape these communities meant that a much larger percentage of America's Jews encountered a small-town environment at some point in their lives. Thus, in late nineteenth- and early twentieth-century America, there were many thousands of Jews besides those who spent all their years in small towns who had experienced one of the country's smaller Jewish centers, places with rather limited Jewish infrastructures and with their own singular social dynamics, as we shall see. Whether these Jews were immigrants who spent a part of their lives in small towns, American-born individuals who passed through small communities, or natives who were brought up in these places and then left, they remained at least in part products of the small-town Jewish experience. All those who had sojourned in small communities remained aware that, for better or for worse, an alternative existed to life in a large or midsize city.

# 5  Patterns of Livelihood and Class

The quest for economic well-being that motivated most Jewish men who took up residence in small towns meant, more than anything else, a search for a place where they could go into business for themselves. This reality is what lay behind the creation of small-town Jewish centers that were very different from larger Jewish communities in their occupational and socioeconomic profiles. In large communities such as those of New York, Baltimore, Pittsburgh, and Chicago, the range of economic activities in which Jews were engaged was more diverse than it was in small towns, and the same was true in midsize Jewish centers such as those of Passaic, Indianapolis, Louisville, and Memphis. Most significantly, large and midsize Jewish communities all included a substantial and highly visible Jewish working class.[1] Indeed, in the very early years of the twentieth century, some 60 percent of the Jews living in cities with populations of 250,000 or more were workers in manufacturing, with over half of these people engaged in the production of clothing, hats, and other items of apparel. Moreover, even in a city such as Providence, Rhode Island, which the historian Joel Perlmann has inaccurately characterized as a place with a "small Jewish community" (the city's Jewish population was 15,000 in the era of World War I), some 23 percent of Russian Jewish immigrant fathers were blue-collar workers in 1915.[2] By contrast, triple-digit communities, and certainly smaller ones, were essentially middle-class enclaves devoid of a Jewish working class. Both in the nineteenth century and in the early decades of the twentieth, small communities were ones in which just about every head of household was involved in business, usually as a retailer, a wholesaler, or a skilled artisan meeting the basic consumer needs of small-town society.

To begin with, even the work of peddling that introduced so many nineteenth-century German Jews to the towns where they would eventually

*Photo oppsosite page: David Spector and his son in front of Spector's Clothing Store, Bristol, Pennsylvania, 1907. Jews commonly sold clothing and dry goods in small towns, both in mainstream establishments and in more modest stores. Courtesy of the Margaret R. Grundy Memorial Library, Bristol, Pennsylvania.*

settle was itself a sort of entrepreneurial undertaking, for peddlers generally worked for themselves, rather than for those who supplied their merchandise. Moreover, few peddlers wanted to continue earning their living as itinerants. Most viewed peddling only as a way to begin their working lives in America, and as soon as they gained the necessary capital and experience to open their own stores or launch other kinds of business ventures, they did so. The same might be said about Jews who arrived in small towns to be store clerks. Whether these young men came to work for a relative or for someone with whom they had no previous connection, their goal was almost invariably to strike out on their own as soon as they could.[3]

Tales of Jews at the turn of the twentieth century who were peddlers when they first encountered the small towns in which they eventually settled suggest that for East Europeans, too, peddling was not an uncommon way of earning a living in the American hinterland. Rudolph Glanz, one of the great historians of nineteenth-century American Jewry, has written that railroads changed the way goods were distributed to such an extent that by the time East European immigrants began to arrive in the United States in large numbers they "could no longer start out as peddlers."[4] Contrary to this assertion, however, well into the twentieth century a great many East European Jews used peddling in and around America's small towns as a way to broaden their opportunities. Like their German-Jewish predecessors, they adopted the itinerant life as an expedient, hoping to give it up as soon as possible.

In Fitchburg, Massachusetts, for example, many of the earliest Jewish residents were East Europeans who initially came to town as peddlers. Among the first, arriving around 1882, were Barney Goldstein and Lewis Rome, who journeyed to Fitchburg by train from Boston and then roamed the countryside. These men were followed by individuals such as Jack Shack, who dealt mainly in pots and pans; Joseph Cohen, who sold notions; Moritz Dubinsky, who traded in dry goods; Morris Bauman, who peddled bread; Hyman Penan, who sold stationary; and Hyman or Herman Segal, who began by going door to door repairing umbrellas. Lewis Rome later established the Rome Clothing Company in Fitchburg, and the umbrella mender Segal later opened a Fitchburg store as well. The bread peddler Bauman opened a bakery in Fitchburg, and the stationary hawker Penan opened a shoe store there in 1898. A little later Fitchburg saw the arrival of Simon Winthrop (a Jew despite his aristocratic New England surname), who began by peddling household items from a wagon. When he had saved enough money, he opened a variety store, and later he branched out into groceries and meat. In 1912 he added paper goods to the products he handled, and soon after that he established a new firm, the Fitchburg Paper and Bag Company. Barnet Fine and his son Simon were still peddling around Fitchburg with a horse and cart into the 1920s.[5]

Perhaps the stories of East European peddlers such as the first Jews of Fitchburg have been eclipsed by the tales of nineteenth-century German-Jewish peddlers because peddling was more common among German Jews than among East Europeans starting out. Nonetheless, accounts of small-town East Europeans who began their working lives going door to door are abundant. Lewis and Henry Harris began peddling in Virginia and North Carolina from a base in Richmond in the mid-1880s, and in the early 1890s they settled in High Point, North Carolina, where they bought land and opened a store. Joseph Kamenensky came to the United States in 1892 and four years later arrived in Wichita, Kansas, as a peddler. Beginning with a pack, he moved on to selling from a wagon and then to junk collecting. By 1902 he had set up his own junk yard, and this enterprise laid the foundation for a family that was soon calling itself Kamens and that remained prominent in Wichita for the rest of the twentieth century, producing, as a local history reports, "civic leaders, mayors, and other local notables."[6]

Isidore Katz came from Lithuania to Englewood, New Jersey, at the age of eighteen in 1909 and began his working life as a vegetable peddler working for his brother. After three years, Katz went into business for himself. In 1914 he finally was able to buy a truck and eventually to move from retail sales to wholesale. Still later, Katz and three partners began operating a bus service. Even as late as 1920, in Lexington, Kentucky, the thirty-eight-year-old Russian-born Sam Bederman, who had immigrated in 1903, was working as a dry-goods peddler, and the forty-eight-year-old Polish-born Louis Horne, who had come to America in 1886, was working as a "mercantile peddler." In Nashua, New Hampshire, the thirty-one-year-old Maurice Weisman, who had emigrated from Russia in 1913, was working as a fruit peddler; and in Bradford, Pennsylvania, forty-year-old Sam Elasky, who had arrived from Russia in 1900, was working as a peddler as well.[7]

Whether they were German Jews or East Europeans, whether they found their initial employment as peddlers, as store clerks, or in some other pursuit, the Jews who set up businesses in small-town America had a fairly good chance of achieving success, at least on a modest scale. Although it is always dangerous to accept any stereotype too readily, there is certainly some truth to the generalization that those Jews who came to small towns brought with them a certain predisposition to accomplishment in trade. After all, they were highly literate, the European milieu from which they had come had often provided them a familiarity with both business practices and risk-taking, and they embarked upon some of the same kinds of economic activities in which Jews had engaged in the old country. Moreover, certain Jewish cultural traditions tended to promote upward economic mobility as well. As the historian Daniel Soyer has demonstrated, even among East Europeans who took their

*Jewish peddlers, location unknown, ca. 1900. Peddling was one way for both German and East European Jews to encounter the towns in which they would eventually settle. Courtesy of The Jewish Museum of Maryland, 1996.79.8.*

place within the urban working class, including many of those who were labor activists, there always lingered the dream of becoming "a boss."[8] Thus, the story of an East European immigrant such as the vestmaker Dave Gordon is not all that unusual. Gordon had come from Russia to Baltimore around the turn of the twentieth century and had married there, but in 1913, "looking for a future away from the sweat shops," he moved to Frederick, Maryland, and opened a store.[9]

Also significant in explaining Jewish success in smaller communities is the fact that at the same time that Jews were fanning out across the American hinterland, small towns were rife with opportunities for business expansion. The country's population was growing by leaps and bounds in the late nineteenth and early twentieth centuries, the national economy was becoming more complex and segmented, and small towns were increasing their importance as centers of trade and commerce. By their very nature, these places served as points of distribution for consumer products not only to their own inhabitants but also to the residents of their rural surroundings. The possibility of doing well was abetted further by the availability of a number of credit mechanisms for financing the very kinds of businesses that Jews often established. Clothing suppliers commonly sent goods to small stores on credit, for example, and large-scale furniture manufacturers often financed dealers' stocks in order to maintain high levels of production. Cooperation between suppliers and local merchants was only enhanced when the parties were linked by their Jewish identities or even by ties of kinship. The Baltimore Bargain House in Maryland, a Jewish-owned supply firm, maintained an ongoing relationship with merchants in the small towns of several nearby states, for example, even providing free transportation, business services, and management advice to store owners on buying trips.[10]

Most of the stores that Jewish merchants in small towns operated dealt in basic necessities such as clothing and other dry goods, shoes, furniture, and hardware. Jews also frequently owned tobacco shops, grocery stores, and fruit markets. In some places, it seems that food retailers actually rivaled apparel and dry-goods merchants for primacy amongst Jewish shopkeepers. Looking back over the first half of the twentieth century, one commentator on the Jewish history of Iowa City, Iowa, concluded that the synagogue membership there was "a congregation of grocers," although in truth the East European families that established the community also included proprietors of clothing stores and shoe stores, and several junk dealers and peddlers.[11]

As new consumer products appeared, Jewish entrepreneurs became involved in their marketing as well. The sale of electrical appliances was not far removed from the sale of furniture, for example, and in the early decades of the twentieth century, auto supply houses, tire stores, and automobile dealerships owned by Jews appeared in small towns as well. One study conducted by the B'nai B'rith fraternal organization in 168 American communities with Jewish populations under 1,000 at the midpoint of the twentieth century revealed that 66 percent of employed Jews in these communities were owners or managers of businesses, and that the vast majority of these individuals (80 percent) were working in the wholesale and retail fields. Of all the owners and managers in the study, 31 percent sold clothing and shoes; 10 percent dealt in food, confectionery, and beverages; 7 percent sold furniture and home furnishings, and 5 percent sold jewelry. Among those who were over age fifty when the B'nai B'rith study was conducted, the proportion of owners and managers rose to 71 percent, attesting to the fact that in the decades before World War II, mercantile activity was even more prevalent among small-town Jews than it was in the years just after the war.[12]

While many small-town Jewish entrepreneurs were happy to sell to the general buying public, others catered to a more specific clientele. Often they directed their efforts toward poorer socioeconomic groups, both because consumers in these groups tended to be underserved by the mainstream business community, and because opening a store featuring lower-priced goods and fewer amenities required less capital than establishing a more traditional type of store. Jewish businesses catering to those in more precarious circumstances were likely to take into account the seasonal nature of many rural economies, which depended on agricultural cycles, allowing customers to buy on credit and to pay their debts only after crops were harvested and sold. So, too, if they had working-class patrons from other immigrant ethnic groups, Jewish shop-keepers would hire salespeople who knew their languages, or would learn those languages themselves (sometimes they knew them already).[13]

Jewish businessmen serving a poorer clientele often gave their stores names that stressed reduced prices and honest trading practices, although these attributes could have appealed to better-off shoppers as well. Joseph Cohen's turn-of-the-century business in Middletown, New York, for example, was called the Bargain Clothing Store ("Everything in Reliable, Up-to-Date Clothing and Gents' Furnishings. Our Prices are the Very Lowest"). The shop that Nathan Einstein opened in Topeka in 1910 was called Economy Men's Clothing, and the business established by James Cohen in Frederick, Mary-land, around the time of World War I was called the Frederick Savings Store. Leonard and Sidney Wolf's clothing store in turn-of-the-century Phoenix ad-vertised that it was "right in town but away from the high-rent district," and in Vicksburg, Mississippi, the Feld Furniture Company announced "Easy Terms for All."[14] Sometimes a local general store dealing in commodities such as clothing, notions, and other dry goods, often at a discount, was referred to colloquially as a "Jew store," reflecting the fact that Jewish merchants were closely identified with general merchandizing and with discount retailing in many smaller cities and towns.[15]

In the South, the prospect of opening a store with very little capital was enhanced by the presence of a large African-American population that seemed to offer a ready customer base for Jewish entrepreneurs. As Abraham Isaac-son, an immigrant storeowner from Clarksdale, Mississippi, once explained, "the average negroe [sic] has a grudge against the native white man and he thinks that he has been mistreated in some way or another ever since slavery days." It was for this reason, according to Isaacson, that "the negroe will rather patronize a store operated by the foreigner than the one owened [sic] by a native Amercan [sic]."[16] Moreover, as the commentator on southern Jewish life Harry Golden has suggested, Jews did well catering to African Americans in the South because, more than other shopkeepers, they were prepared to let blacks try on clothing and because they were willing to haggle with them, a practice that other white storeowners considered beneath their dignity. Jew-ish shopkeepers often showed African Americans other courtesies as well. Local lore in Paducah, Kentucky, for example, preserves the memory of a time when the only downtown drinking fountain blacks were permitted to use was the one in the hardware store of the Michael brothers on Broadway.[17]

Despite the ubiquity of low-overhead stores operated by Jews, the most highly visible Jewish businesses in small-town America were mainstream department stores. By the early twentieth century, it was possible to find at least one substantial Jewish-owned establishment carrying a wide range of clothing and related merchandise in just about every American town with a triple-digit Jewish community, and in scores of towns with even smaller Jewish populations as well. These stores generally started as small enterprises controlled by members of the same family or by a few partners, and developed over time into major local institutions. In Charlottesville, Virginia, for example, the brothers Isaac and Simon Leterman established a retail store on Main Street in 1852, and by 1898 five of Simon's sons had pooled their own business interests to create the largest department store the city had ever seen. "To enumerate every-thing carried in this vast establishment would require a volume," observed a local magazine in 1906, and an illustrated advertisement for the Leterman's store depicted a train bringing goods from Baltimore, Philadelphia, New York, and Boston.[18]

In Lafayette, Indiana, a similar story of business success unfolded. Julius Loeb began as a peddler when he came to Lafayette sometime around 1870, following friends who had arrived earlier. By 1872 he had saved enough money to open a small shop on Lafayette's main square, and by the late 1880s Julius had been joined in business by two partners: his brother Sol, who had arrived in America at the age of fourteen and had spent time as a bootblack and shoe polish salesman in Erie, Pennsylvania; and his brother-in-law Sam Hene. The three men opened a larger store selling piece goods, furnishings, and millinery, also on Lafayette's main square, and over the years the Loeb and Hene Company became the largest department store in northwestern Indiana. When Sam Hene died in 1912, Sol Loeb acquired his interest in the business, and he took sole control in 1927 when his brother Julius died. By the middle of the twentieth century, the enterprise, reincorporated as Loeb's and run by two of Sol's sons, was a household name in Lafayette.[19]

As the examples of Leterman's and the Loeb and Hene Company suggest, the stores of Jewish merchants often bore the names of their owners, thus reinforcing the visibility of Jewish merchant families in their small-town environments. Examples of prominent Jewish establishments bearing their founders' names abound. In Danbury, Connecticut, there was the Harris Heyman Department Store ("Clothiers, Dry Goods, Shoes, Hardware, Floor Coverings, Stoves, Paints, Oils and Glass"); in Macon, Georgia, there was S. Waxelbaum and Son; in Alexandria, Louisiana, Weil Brothers and Bauer; in Meridian, Mississippi, Winner and Klein. In Marion, Indiana, there was Blumenthal's, so successful that it made its proprietor, Morris Blumenthal, "something of a legend, even in his own time." In Jonesboro, Arkansas, there was Heinemann's Department Store, and in Marshall, Texas, there was Joe Weisman and Company. In Hibbing, Minnesota, there was Lippman's, and in Leavenworth, Kansas, there was Ettenson, Woolfe and Company, and its offshoots such as Henry Ettenson and Sons, and Woolfe and Winnig.[20]

Another common approach of Jewish merchants in naming their stores was to allude to the great cities from which they imported their goods. This practice gave their businesses a cosmopolitan feel and suggested to their small-town customers that they could keep up with the fashion trends and the standards of the country's leading urban centers. The first true department store in La Crosse, Wisconsin, was Herman Berger's Boston Store, for example; and when Levi and Julius Oppenheimer founded their store in Lafayette, Indiana, in 1870, they called it the Baltimore Clothing House. In Wichita at about the same time, there was Morris Kohn's New York Store, as well as its competitor, Aaron Katz's Philadelphia Store. Wichita had a Boston Store as well. Owned by Charles Cohn and Henry Wallenstein, it eventually became the most fashionable clothing outlet in the city. In Phoenix, too, there was a New York Store, opened by the Polish immigrant Sam Korrick in 1895, and yet another Boston Store, this one founded by Nathan Diamond in 1898.[21]

In Devil's Lake, North Dakota, Morris Glickson opened a Chicago Store in 1906, and when his cousin Julius arrived two years later, the two men opened a shop that gave small-town America yet one more Boston Store. In Mobile, Alabama, in the early years of the twentieth century, Samuel Goldstein was selling clothing, dry goods, boots, and shoes at yet another New York Store. When the Austrian immigrant Marcus Hoff opened his business in Santa Ana, California, he named it not for a specific city but, more broadly, the Great Eastern Dry Goods and Clothing House. Saul Hutner looked even beyond Boston and New York when he established his women's apparel shop in Marion, Indiana, in 1902. He called it The Paris.[22] Yet another approach taken by Jewish entrepreneurs when they opened their stores was to give them names suggesting their importance and their popularity. Thus, there was Hugo Baer's Smart Shoppe in Bristol, Connecticut; Morris Rakov's Royal in Oswego, New York; Leon Kaufman's Leader in Frederick, Maryland; A.A. Cohn's Palace in Oshkosh, Wisconsin; and Henry Deutsch's Bee Hive in Davenport, Iowa.[23]

Closely related to the retail stores established by so many small-town Jews were the businesses set up by skilled tradesmen whose emphasis was on services rather than on merchandise. In one small town after another, especially in the era of East European migration, Jewish tailors, cobblers, and other artisans catered to the needs of the public. Among the Jewish heads of household in Lafayette, Indiana, in 1880, for example, were a tailor, a shoemaker, and a painter; and in 1920 there were at least six Jewish tailors and three Jewish cobblers in Newburyport, Massachusetts, as well as a Jewish blacksmith, all with their own shops. Among the independent Jewish artisans in Modesto, California, in 1920 were two shoemakers, a tailor, and a signmaker.[24]

Services of a different sort were offered occasionally by Jewish businessmen in small towns as well. The 1880 census for Jackson, Michigan, listed a Jewish steamship agent and a Jewish insurance agent. In Lexington, Kentucky, in 1880 there was a Jewish hotelkeeper, and in Vicksburg, Mississippi, there were three Jewish stable keepers. In 1920 Fitchburg, Massachusetts,

MANDEL & SCHWARZMAN
GENERAL MERCHANDISE
WHOLESALE AND RETAIL

MY STORE

BLOOMINGTON, ILLINOIS.   *Feby 5/14*

*Rev Dr K. K. Kohler*
*Rev Sir*
*I am instructed by our Trustees*
*to ask you to provide us with a*
*student Senior, to Officiate here*

*Letterhead of the Mandel and Schwarzman department store in Bloomington, Illinois, 1914. Department stores bearing the names of their proprietors and proclaiming a welcoming message ("My Store") were the most visible Jewish businesses in small towns. Courtesy of the Jacob Rader Marcus Center of the American Jewish Archives.*

Herman Coffman was a pawnbroker, and in Bradford, Pennsylvania, Lazer Halprin and M. L. Mendelsohn provided cleaning and dyeing services. The census of Alexandria, Louisiana, in 1920 listed at least two Jewish insurance agents, as well as a building contractor, a road contractor, and an electrical contractor who were Jews. Jewish entrepreneurs sometimes ran taverns and restaurants as well. Vicksburg had at least five Jewish saloonkeepers in 1880, for example; and in the mining community of Keystone, West Virginia, in 1898, when the local Jewish population numbered about 110, Jews owned five of the town's seventeen taverns. In the period after World War I, Sam Schiller was the proprietor of a restaurant in Hamilton, Ohio, and Rose and Joseph Bales were Jewish restaurateurs in Washington, Pennsylvania.[25]

Just as local lore is replete with stories of individual Jews who succeeded in the retail sector, there are many stories of accomplishment in the service sector as well. Representative is the saga of Isidore Lehman. Born in Jackson, Mississippi, in 1879, Lehman began his working life around the turn of the century as an agent for a laundry in Memphis, Tennessee. He would go door to door collecting dirty clothing, send it to be cleaned in Memphis, and then return it to his customers. After a few years working for the Memphis firm, Lehman was hired to manage a local laundry and dry cleaning establishment. He accepted his new position, however, only on condition that if he proved effective, he would become half owner of the business. By taking advantage of the goodwill he had developed among his former clients, investing in state-of-the-art equipment, and engaging in some spirited advertising ("When Clothes Are Dirty Ring Seven Thirty" or "Let Izzy Do It"), Lehman soon had the Jackson Steam Laundry and French Dry Cleaning plant functioning at full capacity and was made president of the company. By the 1920s Lehman was also on the board of directors of an insurance company, a bank, a bakery, and the Jackson chamber of commerce. He was a member of the local draft board during World War I and later served on the Jackson board of education. A member of at least seven fraternal orders, Lehman was at one point president of Jackson's Beth Israel synagogue, as well, reminding us again of how frequently those who succeeded in small-town business ventures were called upon to serve as the lay leaders of local Jewish institutions.[26]

Perhaps the most glamorous service-oriented pursuit undertaken by Jews in small towns was entrepreneurship in the entertainment industry. In the nineteenth century this often meant building and running an opera house, and in the twentieth century it frequently meant owning or managing a movie theater. The Jaffa brothers, prominent in both Jewish and civic affairs in New Mexico and Colorado, opened the ornate Jaffa Opera House on Main Street in Trinidad, Colorado, in 1882, for example, and this building, which included some office space as well, remained "both the cultural and commercial center of the city" for a quarter of a century. Similarly, the first theater in Modesto, California, was Plato's Opera House, occupying the second floor of a commercial building constructed in 1882 to house a store owned by the Plato family, which was the first Jewish kin group in town.[27]

In Charlottesville, Virginia, Jefferson Monroe Levy, a onetime New York congressman, the owner of Thomas Jefferson's estate, Monticello, and a nephew of the famous naval officer Commodore Uriah P. Levy, transformed the old town hall into the Levy Opera House in 1887, and engaged Jacob Leterman and Ernest Oberdorfer, two of Charlottesville's leading merchants, both Jews, to manage the facility. In 1896 Letterman opened his own theater, the Jefferson Auditorium, and in 1907 he established the Wonderland amusement park, whose many attractions included early motion pictures. In Topeka, Kansas, at about the same time, the Russian-born George Gordon and his brother Hyman, who started out as pawnbrokers, established the town's first movie theater, the Best, and in 1913 the Gordon brothers built the Orpheum Theater and Office Building as well. In the same city, Simon Galitzki began with a department store but later opened the Kaw Theater downtown and soon afterward built the first neighborhood theater in Topeka. On the Iron Range of Minnesota, Joseph Roman in Virginia, Frank Rabinowitz in Eveleth, J. Edelstein in Hibbing, and Henry Sosnosky in Chisholm all ran movie theaters in the second and third decades of the twentieth century, some of which booked live shows as well. At the same time Max Gutstadt managed the Lyceum Theater in Ithaca, New York, which brought both serious drama and vaudeville to town. Leo F. Keiler, whose family in Paducah, Kentucky, operated one of the largest distilleries in the country, moved into the theater business when Prohibition began to take its toll on the liquor industry.[28]

Jews never even approached constituting the bulk of business owners in small-town America, and there were certainly many secondary cities and towns in which the Jewish presence in retail trade and related activities was not particularly striking. Nonetheless, whether they were operating on a large scale or more modestly, whether they were selling to the general public on one of the main streets of downtown or marketing to a more specific clientele in a poorer neighborhood, those who made up America's small Jewish communities were often highly visible in the mercantile hustle and bustle of their towns. They frequently played a disproportionate role in supplying local residents with basic consumer goods and with basic services such as tailoring and shoe repair. Even though, on average in the 1920s, Jews in towns with triple-digit communities constituted only about 2 percent of the general population, it would have been difficult for a citizen of any of these towns to conduct the normal activities of daily life without encountering at least some Jewish merchants or business people. Thus, the positions Jews occupied as middlemen in small towns kept them centrally involved in maintaining the ties that the ordinary citizens of these places had with the larger consumer culture of the country. Quite illuminating in this context is the story Edna Ferber told about how her mother Julia, who ran the family dry-goods store in Appleton, Wisconsin, came back from a buying trip to Chicago at one point in the 1890s to introduce local women to skirts that did not drag along the ground. Also instructive in this connection is the way Lippman's Department Store in Hibbing, Minnesota, informed its customers in 1916 that it was keeping them abreast of the latest fashions. Its new spring lines, Lippman's announced, were "carefully selected from the foremost designers and creators of authentic styles of two continents." Moreover, by establishing places of public accommodation, theaters, and newsstands, the Jews of small communities also played a key role in providing the inhabitants of America's small towns with news, in general, of what was going on in the world beyond the city limits.[29]

Indeed, in many small towns throughout the late nineteenth and early twentieth centuries, some people had the mistaken notion that Jewish merchants nearly monopolized the local market for goods and services. One resident of Charlottesville, Virginia, recalled that in the early part of the twentieth century "on Rosh Hashanah and Yom Kippur, you couldn't go outside because none of the stores were open. Everybody would close," she remembered; "there ain't nothing but Jewish stores back then." Likewise, a review of the Jewish history of one small town in western Pennsylvania reported that "the commercial area of Donora was effectively closed down by the Jewish holidays. The Jewish merchants closed their stores, and there were very few non-

Jewish storekeepers in the town." Thinking back at the end of the century to the situation around World War II in Englewood, New Jersey, one woman who grew up there had the impression that "ninety percent of the businesses at that time were owned by Jewish people."[30]

Reinforcing impressions such as these were certain realities about the way Jews did dominate some occupations in some places. In Trinidad, Colorado, in the mid-1870s, for instance, five of the six dry-goods stores in town were owned by Jews, and in 1881 seven of the eight shops listed in the city directory of Paducah, Kentucky, as dealing in hats and caps were Jewish-owned establishments. In 1898, ten of the eleven retail clothing stores in Leavenworth, Kansas, were Jewish businesses, and the only three pawnbrokers in town were Jews as well: Simon Bernstein, Myer Goldsmith, and Nathan Kantrowitz. In 1909, five of the nine retail furniture outlets in Leavenworth were operated by Jews. Similarly, in 1900 the only three pawnbrokers in Mobile, Alabama, were Jews, and in 1931 at least twelve of the eighteen retail dry-goods businesses in Alexandria, Louisiana, were Jewish-owned firms.[31]

In Vicksburg, Mississippi, in 1929, at least seventeen of the thirty-six purveyors of dry goods were Jewish concerns, and walking along downtown's Washington Street a shopper would have encountered a large number of typical small-town Jewish businesses. In the 1000 block there were Paul Kestenbaum's grocery and David Feder's shoe store; in the 1100 block there were the Meyer Dry Goods Company, Feith and Salter's Variety Store, and the Rose Drug Company; in the 1200 block there were the Baer and Brother Department Store, Schlesinger's leather shop, the Marcus Furniture Company, and Stern's Ladies' Shop. Albert Fischel's Central Smoke House, J.M. Fried's electrical appliance store, and Louis Herman's shoe store were in the 1300 block, and in the 1400 block were Sartorius and Fried's Style Shop (ladies' ready-to-wear, millinery, and hosiery), Metzger and Company shoes, Ben Warren Clothing, the huge Valley Dry Goods department store, and Mozart Kaufman's Electrik Maid Bake Shop.[32]

Similarly, in Marion, Indiana, among the Jewish businesses on the courthouse square in the mid-1920s, aside from Blumenthal's Department Store and The Paris women's wear shop, mentioned earlier, were the jewelry store operated by the partners Meyer and Alexander, Albert Rosenbaum's shoe store, Morris Witcoff's tailor shop, the tire company that Mark and Myer Savesky owned together with Joseph Kuppin, Nathan Shiff's men's store, and other Jewish-operated clothing businesses such as the Phil Lyons Clothing Company, the Richard Clothing Company, the Union Store, and the Leon and Strauss store. Indeed, one review of the Jewish history of Marion observed that "Jewish-owned retail businesses were the backbone of the business activity around the square, which was the very hub of activity for the entire city." The review concluded that in the years after World War I "a trip around the courthouse square would have convinced any newcomer that the Jewish community was closer to a majority of the population than [to] the small but successful minority it really was." Likewise, a retrospective look at Jewish life in Ashland, Kentucky, observed that "it is impossible to separate the story of Ashland's Jewish community from the story of the city's business community" and recalled a time when, downtown, "voices with Eastern European accents drifted out of clothing shops and furniture and jewelry stores" and when "names like Isaac, Jacob and Saul called out in greeting on the street."[33]

Of course, entrepreneurship did not have to involve running a shop or a store, and, indeed, some small-town Jews undertook commercial ventures that did not entail dealing directly with the public. Among these were businessmen who became wholesalers. The biography of Isaac R. Brunn is representative here. An immigrant from Prussian Poland, Brunn began by selling general merchandise in San Bernardino, California, in 1856, but he soon started specializing in liquor and tobacco products and eventually became one of the most prominent wholesalers of these goods in his region. Similarly, around the turn of the century, A. M. Landauer ran a wholesale notions and grocery distributorship based in Frederick, Maryland, that supplied much of the western part of the state, and at about the same time there were over thirty Jewish wholesale houses in Wilmington, North Carolina. In Oshkosh, Wisconsin, the Segal family operated a wholesale distributorship that carried an eclectic mix of food products and related items, including "canned goods, nuts, paper, produce, cheese, oleomargarine, dried fruits, salt fish, shortening, confectionery [and] oysters."[34]

Livestock trading was yet another type of enterprise in which Jews were involved conspicuously. In Appleton, Wisconsin, for instance, around 1880 there were more Jewish heads of household involved in horse and cattle dealing than there were those involved in retail trade. Edna Ferber later recalled that many of the Jewish men in town "smelled too pungently of the horse barns" even when they came to the synagogue "dressed in their Sabbath blacks." In Lexington, Kentucky, the Weil family, which was transplanted from Alsace and which produced two presidents of the city's Reform congregation during the first decade of the twentieth century, was said to operate one of the largest and most innovative cattle businesses in the country by the time World War I had begun. Similarly, one of the largest distributors of livestock in New England in the interwar period was Morris Levin of Fitchburg, Massachusetts. In Modesto, California, around 1920, as in Appleton several decades earlier, cattle dealing was the leading occupation among Jewish heads of household.[35]

Also among small-town Jews not involved in retail trade were some who set up manufacturing plants, very often producing textiles or specific items of apparel. In the middle decades of the nineteenth century, enterprising Jews

established clothing factories in the secondary cities of the American hinterland so that they could conveniently provide peddlers and small shopkeepers
with their wares and mitigate the dependence of these people on textile firms
in the great cities of the East or in the major river cities of the interior such as
Cincinnati, Louisville, St. Louis, and New Orleans. Thus, the Hungarian Jew
Henry Deutsch, who later opened the Bee Hive clothing store, established a
factory in Davenport, Iowa, around 1870 to manufacture coats and suits. So
too, by the beginning of the twentieth century, Lafayette, Indiana, had its
Levy and Isaac shirtmaking firm, and at about the same time Nathan Meyer's
hat factory in Wabash, Indiana, was employing 270 workers and turning out
well over 3,000 hats a day. Similarly, Danville, Illinois, had its Rissman Brothers jacket factory, where Harry Friedman, a Jewish employee who had moved
to Danville from Chicago in 1917, designed the first Windbreaker, the light
jacket whose brand name soon became a generic term.[36]

In creating a manufacturing enterprise based in a small town, perhaps no
other Jewish family was as successful as the Cones of Greensboro, North
Carolina, whose patriarch, Herman, had arrived in the United States from
Bavaria in 1854, and whose members had initially prospered in wholesale
trade in Baltimore. As suppliers to many small stores in the South, the Cones
already had important connections in North Carolina, and when, in the 1890s,
the brothers Moses and Caesar Cone set out to establish a textile mill, they
chose the town of Greensboro in which to locate. They developed a variety of
cotton products in Greensboro, and by the 1950s the Cone Mills were operating some 600,000 spindles. At one point they were the world's leading producers of denim and corduroy cloth.[37]

Although the idea of manufacturing clothing in smaller cities first developed among Jews of Central European background, some East European
immigrants adopted the practice as well. Among these entrepreneurs were
former laborers from the New York clothing industry who wanted to go into
business for themselves in places where they might escape the strike activities and the difficult conditions they had encountered in the metropolis. "It
took only a small investment to set up a business," recalled Jack Habacht, describing circumstances in South River, New Jersey, in the 1920s; "rent space
and (buy) some second-hand sewing machines and you were in business." In
the decade of the Great Depression, Manchester, New Hampshire, witnessed
the establishment by Jews of several manufacturing ventures. These entrepreneurs were taking advantage of the factory space and the skilled labor
made available inexpensively when the Amoskeag Manufacturing Company,
already hurt by the migration of cotton textile production to the South, went
bankrupt and shut down its great cotton mills in 1935.[38]

Those Jewish manufacturers in America's smaller cities and towns who
were not producing textiles or wearing apparel were involved with a variety of

other products. Some, like Henry Hess in Mobile, Alabama, and Jacob and Samuel Goldenberg in Chisholm, Minnesota, set up cigar factories, while others manufactured more unusual items. In Leominster, Massachusetts, Morris Falk ran a company making barrettes and plastic hairpins using a machine process he had invented around 1905. When women began to bob their hair and the demand for hairpins dried up, Falk retooled to produce automobile keys and related items. In 1926 he moved his small firm, which he had named the Independent Lock Company (ILCO), to nearby Fitchburg, Massachusetts, where it continued to grow and prosper, acquiring several other firms and even surviving the worst years of the Depression. By the end of World War II, during which the ILCO plant manufactured fuses for the military, Falk's company was a multimillion-dollar concern. In Muskegon, Michigan, Harold Rosen, who had moved from working in his family's clothing store into real estate and then into automobile servicing, developed a new type of lubricating oil, and in 1931 he and his brother Leo founded the American Grease Stick Company to manufacture the multipurpose dripless and stainless lubricant he had invented.[39]

Of course, starting a manufacturing enterprise, launching a livestock business, or even opening a small retail outlet required more capital than many Jews could muster when they migrated to small towns. Thus, numerous immigrants who undertook independent business ventures entered upon more lowly pursuits. A remarkable number of Jewish men in small-town America, especially among the East Europeans, got their start as junk collectors, buying up cast-off scrap metal, household goods, paper, rags, animal fur, and other waste, and then preparing it either for sale as used merchandise or as cleaned and sorted raw material to be marketed to large reprocessors in commercially viable lots. Junk dealing was a business that took almost no start-up capital and yet allowed for a certain level of independence. Another advantage of the occupation was that it allowed a great deal of flexibility when it came to scheduling work. This was a benefit especially important to those who wanted to observe the traditional restrictions concerning work on the Sabbath. Indeed, many of those who chose to remain junk dealers all their lives, rather than moving on to other occupations, did so in order to continue observing a day of rest on Saturday.[40]

Jews were so much involved in the junk trade that they essentially cornered the market on scrap in a great many small towns. In Leavenworth, Kansas, it appears that all five of the firms collecting junk early in the twentieth century were owned by Jews. In Colorado Springs, all six of the junkyards operating in the mid-1920s were Jewish concerns, with four of these yards located on the same creekfront street as the city's Orthodox synagogue. Of the six junk dealers operating in Oswego, New York, at the beginning of the 1930s, five were Jews. In Oshkosh, Wisconsin, at the same time, firms with impressive names such as the Badger Iron and Metal Company, the Winnebago Iron and Metal Company, the Wisconsin Iron and Metal Company, and Wisconsin Hide and Fur were all scrap yards owned by Jewish businessmen. Just as livestock trading was the primary occupation of Appleton Jews around 1880, junk collecting was the dominant Jewish trade in that town forty years later. Of the thirty-five East European–born heads of Jewish households listed in the census of Appleton in 1920, a remarkable 40 percent were in the junk business.[41]

In Modesto, California, in 1935 at least four of the five junk companies listed in the city directory were owned by Jews, and the entry for the scrap business run by Philip and Benjamin Plotkin provides a good sense of the range of items that junk dealers commonly collected and the kinds of complementary activities in which they engaged. The entry reads: "Junk, Hides, Wool, Auto wrecking, Blacksmithing, Welding, Auto Repairing, Pumps, Motors, Pipe, Plumbing supplies, Second Hand Furniture." Indeed, the combination of scrap collecting with related activities was a common feature of small-town junk businesses. In 1906, for example, Moses Atlass' Sons, a scrap business in Lafayette, Indiana, advertised that the firm would not only buy iron and hides (those who hauled their scarp themselves could "save the middlemen's profit") but also handle poultry sales and repair farm machinery. By 1914 the firm had become the Atlass Produce Company, but it still advertised that it was "always in the market for Scrap Rubber, Scrap Iron, Metals, etc."[42]

Jews attempting to start out in small towns gravitated so readily to junk collecting that at times it seemed that there could not possibly be enough work to keep all of them employed. No wonder that in 1913, when the Industrial Removal Office was making plans to sponsor an immigrant who wanted to become a junk man in Jackson, Michigan, the organization heard from Adolph Traub, himself a scrap dealer in Jackson, with a warning: "The only thing I can say is that the business is overdone here and the market is very poor."[43] Still, junk collecting provided a starting point for many of the careers of small-town Jews, and like small-time store owners and other entrepreneurs, some who began as scrap dealers became very successful and extremely wealthy. The annals of numerous small towns yield stories of junk dealers who prospered even without leaving the scrap business.

In La Crosse, Wisconsin, for example, Abraham M. Goldish, probably the pioneer East European Jew in town and for a long time a mainstay of the Orthodox congregation there, established a junk yard that not only directly controlled a great deal of the scrap business in the area, but also bought the junk collected by several other peddlers. The Hungarian-born Louis Glick, who arrived in Jackson, Michigan, by way of Saginaw with little more than "a sledgehammer and a chisel," began a scrap iron business in 1916 that had sales of $131,000 as early as 1923. In Kalamazoo, Morris Friedman became the first provider of an automobile towing service in the city. He had started out as a junk peddler with only a horse and wagon. "A good horse in those days was like a member of the family," Friedman's son remembered; "when he took sick and died, my Father cried." Isadore Mervis bought an existing scrap yard in order to help support his parents and siblings when his family moved to Danville, Illinois, in the 1930s, and Isadore's son eventually turned the business into Mervis Industries, a conglomerate of thirteen corporate divisions and four affiliated companies that had interests all across central Illinois and western Indiana.[44]

Because one could be a clothing merchant or a grocer or a junk dealer almost anywhere, the economic pursuits of Jews in small communities were seldom tied directly to distinctive features of the local or even the regional economy. Nonetheless, some small-town Jewish business operations were linked at least loosely to particular aspects of the local economic environment. In the Deep South, for example, both before and after the Civil War, Jews were among the region's cotton brokers. Around the turn of the twentieth century, the cotton factors of Mobile, Alabama, included the Jewish firms of S. Haas and Company and of Bernard Kahn and Company.[45] So, too, beyond the Mississippi River there were Jews who adapted to the unique environment of the American frontier and became involved in some of the economic activities associated with the late nineteenth-century "Wild West." In Wichita, Kansas, in the 1860s the brothers Leopold and David Hays were traders in buffalo skins. Later they began finishing hides themselves and at one point had a stock of over 12,000 cured buffalo robes and wolf skins. Pioneer Jewish merchants in Phoenix, men such as Benjamin Block, Hyman Mannasse, and Michel Goldwater, were often paid in grain for the goods they sold, so some of them secured government contracts to sell it to the army and to Indian reservations. A few Jews in Phoenix also moved into farming and cattle raising. Michael Wormser, an Alsacian immigrant who had started out as a storekeeper, amassed over 7,000 acres of land on the south bank of the Salt River by the time of his death in 1898, and Wolf Sachs was one of the founders of the Phoenix cattlemen's association. In 1901 he was referred to as one of the "ten cattle kings of Arizona."[46]

In parts of the country where liquor production was big business, Jewish distillers could often be found. Thus, among the most prosperous makers of alcoholic beverages in late nineteenth- and early twentieth-century Paducah, Kentucky, were firms such as Loeb and Bloom; Friedman, Keiler and Company; Bernheim Brothers and Uri; and Dreyfuss, Weil and Company, whose products included Devils Island Endurance Gin and Hacudap Spearmint Whiskey.[47] In the various oil-producing regions of the country, Jews could be found associated with drilling. In Marietta, Ohio, for example, Dave Rabinovitz owned an oil well supply business during the first decade of the twentieth century, when the local oil economy was booming. In Bradford, Pennsylvania, at least nine Jews were listed as oil producers in the census of 1920, while twenty-two-year-old Harry Mendelson was listed as a chemist for an oil company, thirty-one-year-old Helen Nesselson was listed as a book-keeper for an oil concern, and thirty-six-year-old Julius Shear was listed as a traveling salesman handling oil well supplies. In Hancock, Michigan, a major center of copper mining around the turn of the century, Harry Benedict was an engineer in charge of a copper smelter, and Frederick Hirschman was a mining company physician.[48]

In resort towns at the seashore, on a lakefront, or in the mountains, Jews could be found catering to the tourist trade, especially when the vacationers who came were Jewish as well. For example, during the first three decades of the twentieth century, Belmar, New Jersey, served as a summer gathering place for "the New York Jewish intelligentsia," and the social center of this group was the Atlantic Hotel on Ocean Avenue, owned by the Strunsky family. Among the vacationers in Belmar were the Yiddish writers Sholem Aleichem and Sholem Asch, the dramatist Peretz Hirshbein, and the Russian revolutionary and later Zionist leader in Palestine Pinhas Rutenberg. Benton Harbor and South Haven, Michigan, directly across Lake Michigan from Chicago, served as tourist havens for Jews from that midwestern metropolis, and in these small towns, too, members of the Jewish community could be found making their living serving the needs of visitors. The vacationers' demand for kosher food provided work for three kosher butchers in Benton Harbor alone at one point early in the twentieth century. The curative baths of Hot Springs, Arkansas, and of Mount Clemens, Michigan, attracted Jewish visitors who helped support the businesses of the local Jews there, and towns with even fewer than 100 year-round Jewish residents in the Catskill Mountains of New York brimmed with Jewish vacationers during the summer.[49]

Although Jews in small towns tended to concentrate in a limited number of business activities, with retail trade predominating, certain factors broadened and complicated the occupational and economic profiles of America's small Jewish communities. One of these was the propensity of small-town Jews to be involved in several economic ventures in succession or even at the same time. Among both German Jews and East Europeans, these multiple activities were sometimes motivated by necessity. Perhaps the income from only one job was not enough to meet expenses, or perhaps one way of making a living did not work out, so another was attempted. Although many small-town Jews whose businesses failed moved elsewhere, others decided to stay on even if doing so meant experiencing downward economic mobility. One Jewish immigrant in Hibbing, Minnesota, was a clothing store owner in 1910 but a wage-earning salesman in 1920, for example, while another was a junk dealer in 1918 but a common laborer for the municipality two years later.[50] On the other hand, in many instances the movement from one economic activity to another or the multiplication of concurrent activities reflected a desire to improve continually upon an already comfortable economic standing. Success in one endeavor could provide the capital necessary to embark on another. Many small-town Jews realized that one route to prosperity was investment in real estate, for instance, so even though few individuals made real estate investing their primary source of income, some who rose into the upper levels of the middle class did so by acquiring buildings, city lots, or farmland against a background of activity in other enterprises.

Examples of successful small-town Jews with multiple business activities, often involving investment in real estate, are not difficult to discover. John Levy, who was the first Jew in La Crosse, Wisconsin, and who lived in his adopted hometown for sixty-five years, was once described as "an Indian trader, storekeeper, hotelkeeper, warehouse owner, storage and forwarding commission merchant, grain dealer, Indian agent, banker, grocer, real estate operator, mail carrier, weed commissioner, circuit court doorkeeper, eight times alderman, city supervisor, three times mayor of La Crosse, and synagogue cantor." Apparently Levy "earned and lost several fortunes" as a result of his various business activities.[51]

Similarly, David Bach of Wabash, Indiana, went through a variety of occupations during his lifetime. He arrived as a peddler in 1854, but after a period of ill health forced him to give up that strenuous occupation, he began an overland delivery service, carrying mail, light freight, and passengers. By 1856, however, he had sold his wagon and taken a job as a grocery clerk, only to open his own grocery store with a partner shortly thereafter. Over the next decade he bought out his partner, expanded his grocery business, and then, in 1866, sold it in order to go into the clothing and men's furnishings trade. By 1869 Bach had built up his clothing business to such an extent that he decided to sell it at a profit, and in 1872 he again entered the grocery business, building his food store into the most extensive in the city. He finally retired in 1885 and died in 1899. In Marion, Indiana, not far from Wabash, the German-born Leo Nussbaum arrived in the 1880s and established a dry-goods store called the Trade Palace. He sold this store in 1896, however, in order to found the National Metallic Bedstead Company, which he sold two years later in order to found the Indiana Brass and Iron Bed Company. Two years after that he organized the Pacific Oil Company in Marion, and in 1902 Nussbaum also acquired the town's Canton Glass Company.[52]

Out west, in the years before and after the Civil War, Marcus Katz was not only proprietor of a book and stationary store in San Bernardino, California, but also a Wells Fargo agent, a notary public, the county treasurer, and a highly successful real estate speculator. In Phoenix, Arizona, Emil Ganz began as a hotelkeeper and restaurateur in 1879, but in later years he became a wholesale and retail liquor distributor, an investor in the local streetcar system, an insurance agent, and a banker. In Fresno, California, Louis Slater arrived around the time of World War I and began his working life as a peddler. He then opened a furniture store, and from the furniture business he moved on to found a bank that eventually had five branches and was ultimately purchased by the Wells Fargo Corporation.[53]

Back east, Moses Kaufman of Charlottesville, Virginia, owned a clothing store on Main Street toward the end of the nineteenth century, but he also maintained a whiskey warehouse and operated factories manufacturing pencils and cigars. In Frederick, Maryland, at about the same time David Lowenstein was president of the Union Manufacturing Company, a firm that turned out 2,400 pair of hose a week, but also the founder of the Frederick City Shoe Manufacturing Company and the Homestead Building Association, which established its own subdivision of houses. Lowenstein was also on the board of a local bank and of a regional milk company. In Ithaca, New York, Nathan Kramer began as a peddler around 1909, then moved on to become a junk dealer, then a furniture retailer, and finally a grocer and food wholesaler whose specialty products attracted many Cornell University faculty as customers.[54]

The multiplication of business interests on the part of small-town Jews was only made easier when partnerships were forged. Sam Roosth had come from Poland in 1907 by way of Galveston, for example, and after a few years as a baker's helper in Marshall, Texas, he and his wife opened their own bakery in Tyler. In 1931, however, Roosth went into partnership with his friend Aleck Genecov, and their firm soon had interests in real estate, cattle, and oil. In Muskegon, Michigan, in the 1920s Harry Fisher owned his own valve manufacturing firm, but he was also treasurer of Isadore Rubinsky's Muskegon Scrap Material Company, and the two men had several other joint ventures as well, including a pool hall that was reputed to be an outlet for bootleg liquor.[55]

It would be difficult to overemphasize the importance of store ownership and other commercial pursuits in defining the occupational patterns that obtained in America's small Jewish communities. Nonetheless, in these settlements there were also likely to be a few Jews involved in the liberal professions, and this was yet another factor that added nuance to the profiles of America's small-town Jewish centers in their classic era. Throughout the final decades of the nineteenth century and during the early decades of the twentieth, it was possible to find Jewish physicians, lawyers, journalists, and the like in a great many small towns. For example, in 1866 the physician Rudolph Alberti, a graduate of the University of Berlin, opened an office in Davenport, Iowa, and in 1872 Mordecai Davis was practicing medicine in Aurora, Illinois. In the 1890s August Kohn, a graduate of South Carolina College, was the Columbia bureau chief for the *Charleston News and Courier*, then the state's preeminent newspaper. Aaron Kern, who had studied medicine at Northwestern University, opened a medical practice in Wabash, Indiana, in 1900. He had grown up in that town, the son of a Bavarian immigrant who had made his fortune in the livestock business. In Lafayette, Indiana, Samuel Pearlman was practicing medicine in 1920, while Louis Pearlman was practicing dentistry. In the same year there were two Jewish lawyers listed in the census of Vicksburg, Mississippi, and one physician as well.[56]

David Cohn, son of a merchant who had immigrated from Cracow, Poland, was born in Greenville, Mississippi, in 1894 and went on to study law at the University of Virginia and at Yale. He then returned to Greenville to become first a businessman but later a prolific and highly respected writer. In Fitchburg, Massachusetts, Samuel Golden, the son of Russian immigrants, went to Tufts Medical School and then opened an ophthalmology practice in his hometown, while Seymour Nathanson, the son of a shoeshop owner, opened a medical practice there in 1936. Both Samuel and Philip Salny, sons of the Fitchburg junk dealer Harris Salny, became lawyers, and each served for a time as Fitchburg city solicitor. In Wichita, Kansas, Henry Lampl, the son of East European immigrant grocers, became an attorney and mayor of the city. Jacob Pinsker, also the son of immigrant grocers, became a Wichita physician.[57]

In small towns where colleges or universities were located, Jews could at times be found as faculty members, although Jewish professors were almost invariably few in number and often resisted becoming involved with the local Jewish community. Exceptions such as the economist Simon Litman, who came to Champaign to teach at the University of Illinois in 1908 and later served not only as a founder of the first chapter of the Hillel student organization in America, but also as a fundraiser for the local synagogue and as president of the local B'nai B'rith lodge, were scarce.[58] Many Jewish professors even tried to conceal their ethnic backgrounds; such was the culture of academic life in the decades before World War II. At the University of Virginia in Charlottesville, for example, it seems that there were only two Jewish faculty members hired during the first half of the twentieth century: Linwood Lehman, who taught Latin from 1920 until 1953, and Ben-Zion Linfield, hired in 1927 to teach mathematics. At Purdue University in Lafayette, Indiana, there were no Jewish faculty whatsoever before 1920, and over the following two decades only five Jewish professors were hired, two of whom did not openly identify as Jews. Purdue's first Jewish professor, the Vilna-born engineer Andrey Abraham Potter (né Polanski), apparently attended church regularly, at least for part of his life, and raised his children as Protestants. At the University of Iowa in Iowa City, by contrast, there were already a few rather visible Jewish faculty members by the late 1920s, and by 1927 the university had even cooperated in the creation of an affiliated School of Religion, which housed, among other positions, a chair in Jewish studies. Even at

Iowa, however, the first incumbent of the Jewish studies chair, Maurice Far-bridge, was a man described by one alumnus as "aloof and detached" who avoided any meaningful involvement with Jewish students and left after only two years.[59]

Although the number of university-trained professionals among the Jewish residents of small towns in the era before World War II was never large, it did tend to increase over the years. In general, those who entered professions such as medicine, law, and higher education were the children and grand-children of immigrants, rather than immigrants themselves, so there were few professionals of German-Jewish background in small-town America be-fore the end of the nineteenth century, and few of East European background until the middle of the twentieth. The B'nai B'rith study conducted in 168 small communities around 1950 revealed that among all the employed Jews in these places, about 20 percent were professionals, but among those over age fifty, the proportion of professionals was only 11 percent.[60]

One final element that complicates the story of Jewish occupational pat-terns in small communities is the fact that, even though entrepreneurship was without doubt the goal of the vast majority of the Jewish householders living in these settlements, there were always some Jewish men and women in small towns who were wage-earners, far removed from positions of author-ity or ownership. Those working under the tutelage of others might have been clerks or bookkeepers in clothing establishments or groceries, tailors or stitch-ers in shops they did not own, or simple laborers in junk yards or livestock barns. For some, of course, their humble status was only temporary. They might have been the children of local Jewish families preparing to take over a business or to move out of town. Or they might have been recent arrivals. In Wichita, Morris Chuzy, Ben Witrogen, Nathan King, and Jake Glickman all worked as meatpackers when they first arrived as Yiddish-speaking im-migrants in 1908, until the first three of these men opened their own gro-cery stores and Glickman launched a scrap metal business that became the basis for an "economic empire."[61] However, other small-town Jews continued throughout their working lives without ever achieving the status of indepen-dent businesspeople or even of store managers or company officials.

More to the point, even semiskilled or unskilled industrial workers, though highly anomalous, were not entirely absent from small Jewish com-munities in late-nineteenth and early twentieth-century America. Some East European Jews from New York City were attracted to the mills of the Ameri-can Lace Manufacturing Company that had been established by the Jewish entrepreneurs Einstein and Wolf in 1890 in the small town of Patchogue on Long Island, for example. Daniel Davidow, a former peddler, had a grocery store near the mills and a good relationship with the mill owners. Whenever "greenhorns" showed up in Patchogue looking for work, he would help them find jobs in the factory. Likewise, some East Europeans who had landed in New York went to Red Bank, New Jersey, to work in the uniform factories established there by the German-Jewish entrepreneur Sigmund Eisner. In Norwood, Massachusetts, some of the Jewish residents worked in the local tanneries; and in Newburyport, a town with no fewer than seventeen shoe factories just after World War I, at least sixteen Jewish men and women were identified in the 1920 census as factory hands in the shoe industry. In other places also, there were scattered Jews in essentially working-class roles. Norman Neuberger, the son of an immigrant furrier, was working as a boiler-maker in the railroad shops of Lafayette, Indiana, around 1920, for instance; and a woman who grew up in Plymouth, Pennsylvania, recalled that in the 1930s "mostly, the Jewish men were merchants," but that there was also "one person in the Jewish community who had worked in the coal mines."[62]

Occasionally there would be a large enough collection of Jewish workers in a small town to constitute an identifiable Jewish working-class subcommunity. A hundred or more Jewish cigarette rollers, originally from Russia and Poland, constituted one such subcommunity in Durham, North Carolina. Recruited in New York in the 1880s by the budding tobacco magnate James Duke and by his competitor W. T. Blackwell, these workers congregated in one section of town, conducted their lives in Yiddish, and may even have established their own communal institutions. In Setauket on New York's Long Island, a Jewish working-class circle developed around the local rubber industry at the very end of the nineteenth century. The Jewish laborers of Setauket not only established their own congregation, but a socialist society as well. Around the turn of the twentieth century, many of the Jews of Middletown, Connecticut, were employed at the New England Enameling Company and Nathan Meyer's Pioneer Hat Works in Wabash, Indiana, attracted a fair number of Jewish workers as it became a major employer there. In Northumberland, Pennsylvania, where the Jewish population was reported to be 125 around 1907, most of the local Jews were laborers who had relocated from New York to work at the Seff and Lauterstein cap factory.[63]

Still, large concentrations of Jewish laborers in small towns usually depended on a single industry, and sometimes on a single factory, so these enclaves of working-class Jews could easily be disrupted, and most were quite short-lived. As cigarette-making machinery became more reliable and as cigarette manufacturers began to prefer more docile local laborers, the Jewish cigarette rollers of Durham were driven out of work, and nearly all left town, taking up peddling or other pursuits in the South or returning to New York. The labor community of Setauket more or less disappeared when the rubber industry that had attracted Jewish workers went into decline. Likewise, when the Pioneer Hat Works went out of business in Wabash, many of its Jewish employees left for other communities; and when the Seff and Lauterstein cap factory in Northumberland went up in flames in 1909, most of its Jewish workers returned to New York. Northumberland's Jewish population was reported to total only fourteen in 1927.

In the end, then, we can confirm the generalization that America's smaller Jewish communities in their classic era were overwhelmingly composed of entrepreneurs working in retail trade or in commercial ventures such as livestock sales or junk collecting, together with their families and their white-collar employees. Thus, nearly all small-town Jewish families were part of a broadly defined middle class, or very near its edges, with good prospects of upward mobility. Looking back from the perspective of the mid-twentieth century, it was clear that only a few small-town Jews had gained the economic and social status of the upper class and that only a very small number could be identified with the working class. Those Jews who had risen into the upper echelons of local society were primarily from Central European families whose members had been present long enough to become extremely well established in the local economy. Edna Ferber described the German Jews of Appleton, Wisconsin, in the 1890s, for example, as people who "owned big comfortable houses, richly furnished," who "lived well," and who had carriages with coachmen and horses, although she also noted that although there were several millionaires in Appleton, none of these was a Jew. Similarly, the historian of the Jewish community in La Crosse has reported that in the early part of the twentieth century, only one East European Jewish family had a maid, but that "nearly all of the German Reformed Jews were well-to-do and had beautiful homes and servants."[64]

As the observations offered about Appleton and La Crosse suggest, the employment of household help was an important mark of middle-class status around the turn of the twentieth century, and a systematic inquiry into the presence of servants in the Jewish households of several small towns tends to confirm the impression that many Jewish families in these places were very solidly middle class. As table 4 in the appendix indicates, in the eight communities for which information is available for 1880, the percentage of Jewish families that had servants actually living in their homes ranged from a low of 20 percent in Alexandria, Louisiana (where African-American domestic helpers were plentiful but generally did not live with their employers), to a high of 81 percent in Appleton, Wisconsin. On average in the eight towns surveyed, 39 percent of Jewish families had live-in servants in 1880. Unfortunately, it is impossible to know how many small-town Jewish families had maids or housekeepers who did not live with them, but if we assume that even more families could afford to hire nonresident household help than could afford to employ live-in domestics, the substantial percentage of Jewish households with resident maids or servants around 1880 becomes even more impressive.

In 1920 having live-in help was far less common than it had been during the late nineteenth century, and the figures available for twelve triple-digit Jewish communities from our sample reflect this fact. In the New England towns of Newburyport, Fitchburg, and Nashua, live-in domestic help was almost unknown in Jewish homes, while in another seven of the twelve towns surveyed, somewhere between 5 and 7 percent of Jewish households had resident servants. Only in Appleton, Wisconsin, and in Lafayette, Indiana, among the towns surveyed, did the percentage of Jewish families with resident help rise into the upper teens. What all this tends to confirm is that in the period after World War I, very few small-town Jewish families were at the very highest levels of the local economic elite, but that in some small communities there were at least a few families affluent enough to have live-in domestic servants even as this practice was dying out. Those communities with more frequent occurrences of live-in helpers tended to be somewhat older, with a substantial numbers of household heads who were born in Central Europe or in America and were thus from better-established families. In the twelve towns surveyed, of the fifty-nine households identified as having live-in help in 1920, fourteen were headed by individuals born in Central Europe, thirty-three were headed by native-born Jews (twenty-four of these of Central European background), and only twelve were headed by immigrants from Eastern Europe. Nonetheless, in places with an abundant supply of domestic workers from poorer immigrant ethnic groups, even immigrant Jews could employ live-in helpers at a relatively high rate. On the Minnesota Iron Range, for instance, there were plenty of young Scandinavian and Slavic immigrant maids available, and so some 16 percent of Jewish households in the towns of Hibbing, Eveleth, Chisholm, and Virginia had live-in domestics in 1920, even though nearly all the Jewish families in these places were of East European background.[65]

Obviously, information about domestic servants, though suggestive, is of only limited value in helping describe the socioeconomic status of small-town Jewish families in the early decades of the twentieth century. Fortunately, however, other sources of information exist to indicate that most small-town Jewish families of that era were either in the middle class or at its fringes. For instance, in what is by far the most sophisticated study of a small Jewish community in the interwar period, the sociologists W. Lloyd Warner and Paul Lunt concluded that in Newburyport, Massachusetts, 48 percent of the Jews were in the upper levels of the lower class, 42 percent were in the lower levels of the middle class, and another 3 percent were in the upper levels of the middle class. No other group in Newburyport was more heavily represented in the middle class except the native Yankees. Only 8 percent of Newburyport's Jews were in the very lowest ranks of the local socioeconomic structure. By contrast, 44 percent of Newburyport's Italians were in the lowest social ranking, as were 46 percent of the city's French Canadians, 56 percent of its Greeks, 70 percent of its Russians, 89 percent of its Poles, and 100 percent of its blacks.[66]

Less precise commentaries on other small communities make much the same point. The rabbi of Temple Israel in Springfield, Missouri, reported in 1943 that over the previous half-century "the Jews in town enjoyed economic prosperity but there were no large fortunes among them." Herschel Rubin observed that in the early decades of the twentieth century in East Liverpool, Ohio, the "middle-class town" where he was born, "Jewish families were not at the top or bottom of the income levels." Likewise, the historian of Ithaca Jewry, writing in 1955, maintained that the local Jewish heads of household in his New York town were "neither men of great wealth nor dependent folk."[67]

The general impression conveyed by contemporary observers about the occupational contours and economic status of Jews in America's small-town communities is consistently confirmed by nineteenth- and early twentieth-century accounts of the composition of various Jewish institutions in these communities. Especially in cases in which most or all household heads were involved in these institutions, information about their composition can be very revealing. In Macon, Georgia, in the early 1860s, for example, the local Jewish congregation adopted a fee structure that provided for married men with their own businesses to pay fifty dollars per year in dues, single men with their own businesses and married men working as employees to pay twenty-five, and unmarried "daily laborers or clerks" to pay twelve. Thus, a good sense of the occupational profile and economic structure of the Macon community is reflected in the fact that of the twenty-eight original members of the congregation there, fourteen committed themselves to fifty dollars per year, seven to twenty-five dollars per year, and only six to twelve dollars per year. One man, perhaps unsure of his status, committed himself to contribute thirty-six dollars per year.[68]

A similar picture of the Jewish occupational structure in small towns emerges from evidence about those who became the first seatholders at Temple Adath Israel in Lexington, Kentucky, in 1907, when that congregation was the only one in the city. These early seatholders numbered fifty-one, of whom a handful were from surrounding towns such as Paris and Versailles, whose Jews looked to Lexington as the local hub of Jewish life. Two of the first seatholders at Adath Israel were women: Minnie Blumenthal, a widow; and Rosalie Shane, an unmarried cousin of a prominent Lexington businessman who boarded with his family and worked as a dry-goods clerk. Of the forty-nine male seatholders at Adath Israel, it is possible to discover the occupations of thirty-eight, and of these fully fifteen were proprietors of stores selling clothing, dry goods, or notions. Another ten individuals held managerial or sales positions, and most of these were also in clothing establishments. Other seatholders included members of the Weil family, the cattle traders mentioned earlier, and members of the Speyer family, who were junk dealers. Two other Adath Israel seatholders were partners in a bottling plant, and one was a professor at the Kentucky Agricultural and Mechanical College, the forerunner of the University of Kentucky. There were also a furrier, a jeweler, a tailor, and a grocer among Adath Israel's first seatholders.[69]

The composition of the local IRO committee in Danville, Illinois, in 1912 is also instructive. Although the nature and the size of this committee make it less reflective of the occupational profile of the community as a whole, it nonetheless provides a good sense of the kinds of professions represented among the people who dominated just about all small-town Jewish communities in the early decades of the twentieth century. The account available of the men who made up the Danville IRO committee was prepared by the field worker Abraham Solomon, who provided not only a description of their positions within the community, but also his assessment of their character. On the committee were Sam Goldberg, owner of a wholesale liquor business ("Bluff-hearted, good-natured, *Reliable*"); Sam Sincere, a restaurateur ("a very fat man, hence very good natured"); Sam Zeppin, the owner of a big shoe repair firm; Louis Goldman and Joseph Blumberg, dry-goods merchants ("amiable—but harmless"); Alphonse Mies, a "leading merchant" and "pillar of [the] community"; I. H. Louis, a merchant "Prince"; Jules Strauss, Louis's partner and "a splendid man"; James Greenebaum, the young and "enthusiastic" owner of the Royal Cloak Company; N. J. Basch, owner of the Bell Department Store ("A hustler"); Sam Levin, a lawyer; and Otto Newman, owner of a large clothing store and a "self-made man" who had come to Danville on a freight train fourteen years earlier.[70]

Even more helpful in painting a picture of small-town occupational patterns than membership lists such as those of Adath Israel in Lexington and the IRO committee in Danville is the membership roster of the Barzillai Lodge of B'nai B'rith in Lafayette, Indiana, which covers several decades rather than only one point in time. Of the 158 men who were initiated into the Barzillai Lodge between its founding in 1868 and the year 1920, seventy-nine, or exactly half, were described as merchants at the time of their initiation. In addition, twenty-nine inductees were described as clerks or salesmen, two as managers, five as traveling salesmen, and four as peddlers. Among those who joined the lodge were also seven manufacturers (two of these were cigar-makers), and several skilled artisans (two shoemakers, two tailors, one machinist, and five butchers, one of whom was listed specifically as a *shochet*). Not unexpectedly, the number of professionals joining the Barzillai Lodge in the half-century before 1920 was quite limited: there were three engineers, one doctor, one dentist, one teacher, one publisher and another newspaper man, one cantor, and six rabbis who served in Lafayette at various times.

Among those initiated were also a bookkeeper, a timekeeper, a "credit man," and two students. The number of simple laborers inducted into B'nai B'rith in Lafayette was limited to two men who were listed as painters.[71]

Just as accounts of the membership of individual small-town institutions can provide a sense of the occupational structure of these communities, so, too, can evidence from various census records. Although, like some of the institutional data available, census records provide only "snapshots" of the occupational patterns in individual communities, their potential to be comprehensive makes them very rich sources indeed. William Toll, for example, found that, according to the census of 1900, thirty-nine of the adult males in Trinidad, Colorado, in that year were entrepreneurs, ten were salesmen or clerks, while only two were skilled or semiskilled laborers and only one, the town's rabbi, was a professional. It was largely from these data that Toll concluded that the Jews of Trinidad around the turn of the twentieth century constituted "a small mercantile enclave of brothers, cousins and friends who owned general stores or dry-goods and clothing stores serving the general public." Toll found that the number of professionals in Trinidad had risen to eleven by 1910, but that the vast majority of the town's men were still in the world of business. Of the sixty-seven men in town in 1910, thirty-one were entrepreneurs and thirteen were salesmen or clerks. Only five were laborers. Similarly, research into census records by the local historian Jane Manaster has revealed that in Corsicana, Texas, in 1900, twenty-two of the sixty local Jewish heads of household were in the dry-goods business and eleven dealt in liquor, either as retailers or tavernkeepers. The community also included two hardware merchants, two pawnbrokers, two tailors, and two furniture salesmen.[72]

Investigations of the populations of other triple-digit communities reveal similar patterns. According to census material from Alexandria, Louisiana, in 1880 there were thirty-eight Jewish men living in their own homes whose occupations can be determined. Of these, twenty-two were retail merchants of one sort or another and eleven were clerks. By contrast, there were no professionals among the male Jewish householders in Alexandria in 1880, and only one peddler and one skilled worker, a tinsmith. The three Jewish men who can be identified as boarders in Alexandria in 1880 were two store clerks and a cooper. In Hamilton, Ohio, in the same year, the sixteen Jewish male heads of household included seven merchants, three cattle dealers, a notions peddler, three rag dealers, and one metal dealer, presumably collecting scrap. The only professional in town was the community's rabbi. In Bradford, Pennsylvania, in 1880 the thirty-nine Jewish men who were living in their own homes and whose occupations can be determined included twenty-one retail merchants, four restaurant or saloon keepers, two tailors and two peddlers. Also in Bradford were three oil producers, two liquor wholesalers, and a cigar manufacturer, along with the town's Jewish physician and a rabbi.

The twenty-three Jewish heads of household in Jackson, Michigan, in 1880 included twelve store owners, two saloonkeepers, four dealers in hides and fur, and one retired liquor merchant.[73]

One of the most striking things revealed by systematic studies of small-town census materials is that the basic Jewish occupational structure in small communities did not change appreciably during the early part of the twentieth century, despite the influx of East Europeans and the consequent growth of many of these communities. In 1920 in Alexandria, for example, forty-nine of the eighty-three Jewish men who headed their own households and whose occupations are known were retail merchants, with fully thirty-one of these selling clothing, dry goods, or general merchandise. In addition, thirteen male Jewish householders held white-collar jobs such as clerk or bookkeeper, and nine provided services of one sort or another. Only two Alexandria Jewish householders were in the liberal professions, while Mayer Hirsch was a horse dealer, Dave Mayer had a dairy, and Nathan Gamburg owned a milling concern, the Central Louisiana Rice and Corn Meal Company. Of the fifty-nine Jewish male heads of household in Hamilton, Ohio, in 1920, twenty-five were retailers, nine were junk dealers, and eight were skilled artisans, six of them self-employed. Also in Hamilton were a manufacturer and a livestock dealer. Only two Jewish heads of household in Hamilton were professionals in 1920, the town's rabbi and a teacher, and only five were wage-earning laborers.[74]

In Bradford, Pennsylvania, the 106 identifiable Jewish male heads of household included, aside from the nine oil producers mentioned earlier, four professionals (two rabbis, a physician, and a music teacher), a cigar manufacturer, a textile manufacturer, a wholesale merchant, forty-one retail merchants (among these were six shoe store owners, six clothiers, six dry-goods dealers, four grocers, two furniture store owners, and two stationers), ten clerks or salesmen, six tailors (four with their own shops), and five junk dealers. There were no industrial laborers among Bradford's Jewish householders, although there were a machinist in a machine shop, a fireman on the Erie Railroad, a junk yard worker, and a worker on the city streets, all being paid by the hour.[75]

The rather slight impact of the arrival of East Europeans on occupational patterns in America's small Jewish communities is revealed even more clearly when the vocations of East Europeans are analyzed apart from those of longer-established German Jews. Of the thirty-one Russian-born heads of household in 1920 Alexandria, for example, at least twenty-two were merchants of one sort or another, half of them in the dry-goods business. Other Russian Jews included a junk dealer, a buyer of hides and furs, a watchmaker, a traveling salesman, two shoemakers, the horse dealer Mayer Hirsch and the miller Nathan Gamburg. In Lexington, Kentucky, the fifty-three Russian-, Polish- or Rumanian-born Jewish heads of household identifiable in the 1920 census included twelve clothing merchants, twelve dry-goods merchants, seven tailors, four grocers and two junk dealers. Among these East Europeans were also a produce wholesaler, a cobbler, and a pawnbroker. Only a handful of the East European Jewish householders of Lexington were employed in what might be considered atypical jobs for small-town Jews: one was a farmer, one a barber, one a radiator repairman, and one a simple laborer.[76]

Fitchburg, Massachusetts, had a Jewish community composed almost entirely of East Europeans. Of the sixty Jewish male heads of household there in 1920, fifty-five had been born in the Russian Empire, and four of the five household heads born elsewhere had Russian-born parents. Nonetheless, even in Fitchburg, Jewish occupational patterns were notably similar to those of small-town Jewish communities in the nineteenth century. The sixty householders of Fitchburg in 1920 included some sixteen retail merchants (six of them clothiers), three cattle dealers, several skilled workers with their own shops, two peddlers (one selling clothing and the other with a lunch cart), and twenty-one men in the junk business. There was only one professional among Fitchburg's male Jewish householders, the community's Hebrew teacher, and only three or four wage-earning laborers, including a helper in a blacksmith's shop and a railroad worker. Similarly, of the sixty-five male heads of household in the Jewish community of Nashua, New Hampshire, in 1920, sixty had been born in Russia or Poland, and the other five were the children of East Europeans. Of the sixty-five householders in Nashua, at least fifty-three were owners of their own businesses. They included eight clothing store owners, four dry-goods merchants, three shoe store owners, and two owners of stores selling secondhand goods. They also included eleven grocers, four proprietors of meat markets, nine junk dealers, and a cattle dealer. The handful of wage earners among Nashua's East European householders included the manager of a dry-goods store, the manager of a newsstand, a shoe salesman, and the town's rabbi, but only a very few true laborers: two men were cotton mill workers and one was a cement worker.[77]

The remarkable similarity between the occupational choices of nineteenth-century German Jews and twentieth-century East Europeans in America's smaller Jewish communities, regardless of region, helps explain why there is a certain constancy in the image of small-town Jewish life across the decades, with little distinction being made in popular perceptions between communities founded by Central European Jews and those established by East Europeans in the era of mass migration. After all, the East Europeans who arrived in small towns often began as peddlers, or clerks, or small-scale business owners, much like their German-Jewish predecessors, and those who remained, more often than not, became entrenched as part of the commercial middle class of their towns. The similarity between the occupational profiles of small communities both before the era of mass migration and near its end also underscores the rather narrow range of occupations in which most small-town Jews were engaged and serves as a reminder of the distinctiveness of their communities. That small-town Jews took their place so overwhelmingly in the mercantile niche of their local environments was a key element in making America's smaller Jewish centers alternative types of Jewish settlements, rather than ones that replicated the characteristics of larger Jewish communities.

# 6  Patterns of Family Life

The earliest Central European Jews to make their way to America's small towns were often unmarried young men looking to establish themselves in a new land, and some of the pioneer East European Jews who fanned out across the country in later decades also migrated without wives or families. In Wichita, Kansas, for example, immigrants from the Russian Empire began to arrive in large numbers in the first decade of the twentieth century, and the 1910 census shows that of the 111 addresses at which East European Jews lived, thirty-three were the homes of single men, and several families boarded unattached Jewish males as well.[1] Nonetheless, soon after the creation of each of America's small-town Jewish settlements, family ties emerged as fundamental elements in the organization of these communities. After all, it was common for early settlers to attract relatives to their towns, and at least some members of successive generations of a community's core Jewish kin groups were likely to stay on, despite the pattern of continual migration out of America's smaller Jewish centers. In essence, small-town Jewish enclaves quickly took on the character of collections of families, rather than of individuals. Nearly all small-town Jews were linked to others in their communities in some way, and everything from housing arrangements, to business decisions, to concerns about finding marriage partners involved considerations of family and kinship. To remain unattached and anonymous in a small Jewish community was difficult, if not impossible.

That America's small-town Jewish settlements quickly became populated by contingents of men and women who were related to one another was already evident in many places during the middle decades of the nineteenth century. The twelve individuals who founded the first Jewish congregation in Galesburg, Illinois, in 1867, for example, included three men named Mayer, three named Spear, and two named Jacobi. Among the Jewish merchants of

---

*Photo opposite page: Mr. and Mrs. Harry Moses and their children Alfred and Ethel, Trinidad, Colorado, ca. 1890. Small Jewish communities were collections of family units rather than of individuals. Courtesy of the Jacob Rader Marcus Center of the American Jewish Archives.*

mid-nineteenth-century La Crosse, Wisconsin, were two Steinman brothers, two Cantrovitz brothers, three Gutman brothers, and Herman Langstadt and his sister Bertha, who was the first woman in La Crosse to open her own shop. Similarly, among the thirty-six charter members of the Kesher Shel Barzel fraternal lodge founded in Zanesville, Ohio, in 1874 were two men named Cohn, two named Frosh, two named Levy, two named Witkosky, three named Freedman, three named Stern, and four named Klein.[2]

In Alexandria, Louisiana, the manuscript of the 1880 census reveals that among the forty-four identifiable Jewish heads of household in the city, eight were named Weil, three were named Rosenthal, three were named Levy, and two each were named Ehrnstein, Gehr, Heyman, Malachowsky, Meyer, and Sachman. Among the twenty-three heads of Jewish households in Jackson, Michigan, in the same year there were at least two Cohns, two Hanaws, two Langs, two Levys, two Weils, and three Weigers. In Appleton, Wisconsin, among the sixteen identifiable Jewish heads of household were three named Hammel, two named Ullman, and two named Weinfeld. No wonder that when Edna Ferber arrived in Appleton in the late 1890s, she described the local Jewish community as "a snarl of brothers, sisters, uncles, cousins, very puzzling to the outsider." In Boise, Idaho, in 1895 the twenty-five charter members of the Beth Israel congregation included two individuals named Seller, three named Grunbaum, four named Falk, and five named Spiegel.[3]

As East Europeans came to dominate small-town Jewish life, kin connections remained highly significant. The congregation organized by East European Jews in Petersburg, Virginia, in 1908, for instance, comprised thirty-seven members, but these thirty-seven represented only nineteen families, with three families supplying sixteen of the congregants. Among the Russian-born heads of Jewish households in 1920 Alexandria, Louisiana, there were two each named Caplan, Goldberg, Posner, Rubin, and Walder. Among the Russian-born heads of Jewish households in 1920 Lexington, Kentucky, were two each named Ades, Kaplan, Kravitz, Levin, Paritz, Rosen, and Wides. Also living in Lexington were three Russian-born heads of household named Grossman, four named Rosenberg, and five named Levy. In Newburyport, Massachusetts, where nearly the entire Jewish population was of East European background, seven different surnames were represented twice among the seventy-two identifiable Jewish heads of household in 1920, and among those householders were also three Barths, three Fellmans, three Trebacks, and six Checkoways. In North Adams, Massachusetts, in the 1930s, there were some fifteen Jewish families with the surname Kronick.[4]

To be sure, some individuals with the same last names in America's various small communities may not have been related to each other, especially if their names were very common ones such as Cohen or Levy. Nonetheless, the duplication of surnames within communities was so frequent that it cannot but attest to the importance of kinship there. Moreover, there were many Jewish families in small-town America that were related even though they bore different surnames. This was especially the case where connections through marriage were involved. An example from the Jewish community of Frederick, Maryland, in the decades just before 1900 illustrates just how intricate small-town Jewish kinship ties could be. There, Samuel Kingsbaker was the brother-in-law of Samuel Wineberg, having married Jennie Lowenstein, a sister of Wineberg's wife, Amelia. David Lowenstein was a brother-in-law not only of Samuel Wineberg and of Samuel Kingsbaker, but also of Philip Stern, since he had married Stern's sister. Meanwhile, Solomon Kingsbaker, the brother of Samuel and thus connected to the Lowensteins, was also the brother-in-law of Bernhard Rosenour, since he had married the sister of Sarah Rosenour, Bernhard's wife.[5]

Similar complex marriage connections existed in most other small towns as well. In Sharon, Pennsylvania, in the late 1880s the Rabinovitz family was related to the Grossmans, and the Rosenblum family was related to the Bearmans. In the same period in Natchez, Mississippi, the marriages of the fourteen children of John and Jeanette Mayer created links between the local Beekman, Frank, Katz, Levy, Marx, Mendelssohn, Moses, Roos, and Weis families. In Albuquerque, the three daughters of the Westphalian immigrant Herman Block married three brothers from the Seligman family, creating a complex network of relatives involving both Blocks and Seligmans. Hyman Berkowitz, who arrived in Lexington, Kentucky, about 1925, had relatives in town with the surnames Goller, Herman, Gordon, and Levy; and at about the same time in Benton Harbor, Michigan, the Flamm, Frank, Pink, Radom, Sax, Tobiansky, and Walper families were all interrelated.[6]

Aside from the ties of blood or marriage that connected so many of those who lived in small Jewish communities, another factor that created the feeling that these settlements were composed of families rather than of individuals was the propensity of Jews who grew up in small towns, or who migrated to them, to find spouses and raise children. As early as 1880 a published history of Kalamazoo, Michigan, reported that the Jewish congregation there had between twenty-five and thirty members and that "nearly every member has a family." Although it is possible that married individuals would have been more likely than the unmarried to affiliate with a synagogue, the composition of congregations in places such as Kalamazoo nonetheless reflected the basic character of the communities in which they functioned. William Toll found that in the Jewish community of Trinidad, Colorado, in 1900, for example, there were only two bachelors living in rooming houses and that "the great majority of men and women lived as families in their own homes." Similarly, the historian of La Crosse Jewry had the notion that among the East European Jews in that town "the majority had large families of six to eight children." The membership of Congregation B'er Chayim in Cumberland, Maryland, in 1935 consisted of fifty families, eight individual women (presumably widows), and only a single unmarried man.[7]

A systematic review of census data from several cities reinforces the impression that family life was the rule in small Jewish communities. Even if we take into account the possibility that unmarried individuals were over-looked more often than married people, both when census takers did their work and in later analyses of census records, the paucity of unattached Jewish adults in small-town census documents is remarkable. In just about every community investigated for this study, boarders living in the homes of others or in hotels or rooming houses were quite rare, and single individuals living in their own homes were almost unknown. As tables 4 and 5 in the appendix indicate, both in the eight communities of 1880 and in the twelve communities of 1920 that were surveyed, boarders and hotel residents averaged only 4 percent of the total Jewish population, and even some of these were living in family groups. In 1880 Vicksburg, for example, the thirty-two-year-old cigar dealer Henry Mayer was living in the Washington Street Hotel with his wife, Rosa, and his two daughters, Hattie, aged five, and Clara, aged three. More-over, a very large proportion of the boarders identified (actually a majority in 1880) were living in households headed by Jews who may well have treated them as members of a sort of extended family. The number of adult Jews living in their own homes with no other family members did not exceed five in any of the towns studied, either in 1880 or in 1920, and at least some of these individuals, such as the seventy-year-old Sarah Berwald, who was living alone in 1920 in a house she owned in Bradford, Pennsylvania, were widows or widowers who had obviously lived in family settings earlier in their lives.[8]

To judge from an analysis of the eight communities of 1880 and the twelve of 1920 that were studied, the domestic arrangement of the nuclear family was by far the most common in the small-town Jewish centers of late nine-teenth- and early twentieth-century America. On average in the communities investigated, 62 percent of all Jewish households in 1880 and 68 percent in 1920 were composed exclusively of a married couple, or perhaps a widow or widower if one spouse had died, and the couple's children. Furthermore, again as reflected in tables 4 and 5, nearly all the remaining Jewish house-holds in the towns studied were composed of relatives other than, or in addi-tion to, the children of the household head.

The familial configurations that went beyond the nuclear family in small-town Jewish households were many and varied. In Appleton in 1880, for example, Mark and Bertha Lyon's family circle included five children be-tween the ages of one and thirteen, but also Bertha's sister and her brother. In Lafayette, Indiana, in the same year, the household of the clothier S. N. Ullman and his wife, Agnes, included their daughter Rosa, their son-in-law

Henry Rosenthal, who was probably a clerk in Ullman's store, and the Rosenthal's infant son, Milton. In Bradford, Pennsylvania, Harry Sondheim and his wife, Alice, had two sons, a daughter, and Alice's mother in their home, as well as a boarder and a servant.[9]

In 1920, too, the household groupings of extended Jewish families took many forms. In Hamilton, Ohio, D. M. Silver and his wife, Stella, provided a home not only for Silver's brother, Harry, but also for his sister, Pauline, and for Pauline's husband and fifteen-year-old son. The Silvers also had a boarder in their home: Fred Mayer, the manager of a local theater. In Fitchburg, Massachusetts, the thirty-two-year-old widow Nellie Hurvitz provided a home not only for her four-year-old son, Leon, but also for her twenty-one-year-old brother, David Posner, and for her two unmarried sisters, Reba, aged twenty-five, and Nettie, aged twenty-two. In Nashau, New Hampshire, the thirty-nine-year-old shoemaker Frank Marcus, who had come from Russia in 1890, shared his home with his wife, Annie, and their four children but also with his brother-in-law, Simon Goldman, Goldman's wife (Annie's sister), and their one-year-old son.[10]

In Alexandria, Louisiana, in 1920 the Russian-born Joseph Goldberg and his French-born wife, Laura, had at home not only their two young daughters but also Mrs. Goldberg's parents, Elias and Fannie Moch. The household of Charles and Minnie Frenkel consisted of their two daughters; Minnie's widowed mother, Bertha Sackman; and Charles's two brothers, Dietrich and Joe, both in their forties and both clothing merchants. The Russian-immigrant couple Simon and Sarah Caplan had in their home not only two sons, both in their late twenties, and a teenage daughter, but also the wives of the two sons and a grandson. The Alexandria household of Isaie and Ricka Weil included the couple's thirty-six-year-old widowed daughter and her two children, an unmarried thirty-two-year-old son, a twenty-four-year-old daughter, also unmarried, and Ricka's sixty-five-year-old brother, Samuel Warshauer.[11]

Sometimes the extended Jewish families in small towns encompassed as many as four generations. In Vicksburg, where complex groupings of relatives rivaled nuclear families for importance in the makeup of the community, the insurance agent Rudolph Weil and his wife, Ida, headed a household that in 1920 included not only their sons, Samuel and Philip, but also Samuel's wife, Inez; the couple's son, William; and Ida's mother, Sybil Teller. In the same year in Appleton, the Russian immigrant junk dealer Sam Cohen and his wife Esther had in their home two sons, aged eleven and sixteen, their twenty-year-old married daughter and her newborn infant, and Esther's parents, Rose and Isaac Greenspon.[12]

In the vast majority of Jewish households with children present in the sample communities studied, both in 1880 and in 1920, the youngsters in the home were all under twenty-one years of age. Nonetheless, as some of the

examples of extended households already cited suggest, it was not unknown for older children to be living with their parents as well, especially if these children had not married. Thus, in 1880 Jackson, Michigan, the retired liquor dealer David Cohen had three sons still living with him, all in their twenties. Two of these were saloonkeepers and the third was a tobacconist. In Vicksburg the rather large household of Jacob and Fannie Reis included their thirty-year-old son, Benjamin, and their twenty-seven-year-old son, Samuel, both unmarried and working as butchers. In Alexandria in 1920 the twenty-eight-year-old dry-goods merchant Harry Levine and his twenty-four-year-old brother Aaron, a bookkeeper, were still living with their parents, and the thirty-one-year-old schoolteacher Leah Levin was living with her widowed father. Among the children of Barnet and Ida Rose Fine who were still living at home in 1920 in Fitchburg, Massachusetts, were twenty-nine-year-old Abraham, the proprietor of a clothing store; twenty-seven-year-old Simon, an itinerant clothing salesman; twenty-five-year-old Joseph, a physical education teacher; and twenty-three-year-old Samuel, a dentist. In a few cases, older children turned up in the homes of their parents because they had come back after the death of a spouse or the failure of a marriage. In 1920 Vicksburg, for instance, fifty-year-old Alfred Adler, who had been divorced, was living in the home of his widowed mother, Fanny; and the forty-five-year-old widow Hannah Fishel was living with her mother, Rosalee Brown, also a widow.[13] One way or another, small-town Jews almost always found themselves sharing a hearth with kith and kin, a situation that both reflected and reinforced the family-centered atmosphere of small-town society in general.

Not surprisingly, home ownership seems to have been an ideal among the family-oriented Jews of small communities. When the sociologist Lloyd Warner and his team studied this matter in Newburyport, Massachusetts, during the 1930s, they concluded that the East European immigrants in that town believed that acquisition of a house, as well as other property, was a fine way to build security. Indeed, already in 1920 several Jewish residents of Newburyport owned multifamily dwellings, earning income by renting out the units they did not occupy themselves. At least five families in town owned and lived in two-family houses, and the household of Harry Coltin occupied one section of a four-unit building that belonged to him. Still, the ideal of home ownership was not always realized immediately. In Trinidad, Colorado, in 1900, for instance, most of the German Jews in town owned their homes, but most of the more recently arrived Russian Jews were still renting their residences. Even in Newburyport as late as the mid-1930s, only about 63 percent of the Jewish families in town owned the house in which they lived.[14] In general, as our earlier consideration of stability and mobility has suggested, there was a mix of homeowners and renters in each of America's small Jewish communities, and although the available data reveal no clear correla-

tion between the preponderance of recent immigrants and the degree of pro-
prietorship in a town, there are some hints that established families were
more likely than recent arrivals to own the houses they occupied. Home
ownership in the twelve communities of 1920 selected for our study ranged
from a high of 75 percent in Jackson, Michigan, where many families of
German-Jewish background had had several generations in which to become
established, to a low of 34 percent in Modesto, California, where nearly all the
families that made up the Jewish community were headed by East European
immigrants who had arrived in town fairly recently. Overall, 54 percent of all
Jewish families in the twelve towns studied were living in homes that they
themselves owned in the census year 1920.

In middle-class circles during the late nineteenth and early twentieth centuries, earning a living was viewed primarily as the responsibility of the male
head of the family, while women were charged with taking care of the children
and maintaining the household. This broadly defined "separate spheres" philosophy seems to have been adopted by most Jewish families living in small
communities. After all, most of these families had come to small towns in
order to achieve a middle-class social and economic status, and because few
heads of Jewish families had come to small communities directly off the boat,
most had had some time to become familiar with American mores even before
settling in these places. The power of the "separate spheres" model of domestic life may help account for the fact that in various late nineteenth- and early
twentieth-century census reports, the wives of Jewish householders are almost invariably described as housekeepers or as having no occupation at all,
whether they were of Central European or Eastern European background,
whether they were well settled or more recently arrived. The persistence of
this description may be explained, in part, by the fact that even the newer
paradigm of middle-class womanhood that was emerging by the early decades
of the twentieth century, a model stressing the independence of women and
their more public involvement in club organization and philanthropic activity,
still maintained the ideal that women should be spared the burden of direct
concern with the world of work.[15]

Nonetheless, the actual relationship of husbands and wives in the economic management of small-town Jewish households was not always quite so
simple. While there were certainly many families in which wives were not
directly involved in the financial affairs of the household, there is also much
evidence to suggest that even in families in which wives did not take an active
role as breadwinners there was a genuine sense of economic partnership, at
least by the interwar period. Studies undertaken in Newburyport, for example, reveal that during the 1930s the relationship between Jewish husbands
and wives was a more egalitarian one than between spouses in other immigrant groups, especially in families in which the adults had been raised in

America. Americanizing Jewish wives of the middle classes not only developed social networks and identities independently of their husbands, but also had a great deal of control over family finances. As the team of sociologists who described the situation in Newburyport observed, the wife in most Jewish households became "the purchasing agent and business manager of the family corporation" while the husband filled "a position akin to banker."[16]

Moreover, in many Jewish families in small communities, the practical requirements of running a business, especially a fairly modest retail operation, often demanded the participation of wives as well as husbands. Indeed, despite what census documents attest, it is likely that only the most successful Jewish business owners in small communities could afford to manage their enterprises without any help at all from their wives, and there is much anecdotal evidence to indicate that many small-town Jewish businesses were quite literally "mom and pop" operations. From as early as the 1840s there are stories of husbands and wives working as teams in one small town or another. For example, the diverse set of business activities that occupied John Levy in early La Crosse, Wisconsin, depended heavily on the participation of his wife, Fredericka, who joined him just a few months after he had set up shop on the frontier and who helped turn the family home into a combination residence, store, trading post, tavern, and inn. Similarly, a careful study of Wichita's East European immigrant community in the World War I era has revealed that many women there played crucial roles in supporting the family economy. Belle Pinsker worked together with her husband in the family grocery, for instance, while Manya Gerson was active in the family pawnshop. Ida Smed actually ran her family's waste paper operation, and Sarah Kamenensky sold dishes and other housewares in a business separate from that of her husband.[17]

In Topeka at about the same time, Sarah Galitzki, one of the most active women in local Jewish affairs, was also a business partner with her husband in the family department store. The Galitzkis lived at the back of the store, and Sarah even gave birth to two of her three children there. In Virginia, Minnesota, Yetty Dorfman worked with her husband in the family candy store while in nearby Hibbing, Sarah Isenberg was a clerk in her husband's tailor shop. According to the city directory for Alexandria, Louisiana, in 1931, Fannie Gold actually controlled the clothing store in which her husband, Harry, worked as a salesman. In the same period in Rockville Center, New York, Susan Breitburg's grandfather owned two kosher butcher shops (one a chicken market and the other a meat market), and her grandmother drove the pickup truck for the business and delivered most of the meat.[18] No doubt, participation in the world of work by aspiring middle-class women was made somewhat more palatable in Jewish circles by the lingering influence of the Old World tradition of women working, although in the European setting the declared motivation for this was to allow husbands to spend more time in study.

Even though the economic roles of women are frequently obscured in records produced while their husbands were living, the involvement of wives in family enterprises is more transparent in records produced after their husbands' deaths. For example, widows who were identified as storeowners in various census documents had almost certainly taken over businesses in which they had earlier been involved with their spouses. This was probably true of seventy-one-year-old Eva Malachowsky, listed in the 1880 census of Alexandria, Louisiana, as a grocer, and of thirty-nine-year-old Jane Lehman, who was listed in the 1920 census of Alexandria as the owner of a general merchandise business. Also running concerns in which their deceased husbands had probably been involved were forty-year-old Nehama Chudacoff, listed in the 1920 census of Appleton as the proprietor of a grocery store, and forty-three-year-old Sarah Feingold, listed in the census of Fitchburg as the manager of a clothing store. In all these census records there is an echo of accounts such as that penned by Evelyn Rose Benson of Plymouth, Pennsylvania, who reported that when her father died in 1932, her mother "found the strength, courage, and determination to carry on [her] father's business in order to keep [her] family together."[19]

As the case of the Galitzkis in Topeka suggests, in many instances, reliance on the shared labor of husband and wife, and of children as well, was facilitated by the fact that family businesses often operated from the same buildings that served as family homes, or perhaps from storefront locations nearby. In 1915 Wilmington, North Carolina, for example, nearly twenty stores owned by East European Jews lined Fourth Street, with most of the families of these merchants living above the stores or not far away. Often the storeowners would peddle their wares in the countryside near Wilmington during the day, while the shops themselves were tended by other members of their families, a situation made possible by the fact that in this southern city, even struggling immigrants could afford the services of black maids to help them with domestic chores.[20]

As in Wilmington, so, too, in other towns, the homes and shops of Jewish families were often at the very same location. In Lafayette in 1924, for example, Isidore Kornstein's living quarters and his tailor shop were at the same address. So also were Louis Friedman's home and his delicatessen, Samuel Roston's home and his food store, and Sam Elkin's home and the Samuel Elkin and Son Grocery. Isador Miller had a tire store at 216 Columbia in Lafayette and lived at 216 1/2, while the owner of the Bargain Clothing Store at 1600 North Thirteenth Street lived just a few doors away, at 1526 North Thirteenth. The 1925 city directory for Bradford, Pennsylvania, reveals at least eight Jewish householders whose home address and business address were one and the same. These included the shoemaker Harris Levine, the shoe store owner Joseph Bergman, the fishmonger Jacob Rogalsky, and the grocers Harris Cohen and Solomon Engelsky. Even businesses as potentially disruptive of family life as junk collecting were not necessarily located away from the family home. In Fitchburg, Massachusetts, where three Winthrop brothers were all in the scrap business, the huge pile of waste metal that Harris Winthrop accumulated in his backyard was clearly visible through the windows of the town's synagogue.[21]

The same drive for economic success and middle-class respectability that colored the attitude toward work of most small-town Jewish families also inclined these families to promote the schooling of their children. The traditional Jewish respect for learning only reinforced the high priority placed on education. Judging from the available census data, even around 1880, when the average American child was attending school for only four years, it was quite rare to find school-age youngsters in America's small Jewish communities who were under age sixteen but not in school.[22] Indeed, many children continued on to complete high school in the small-town Jewish communities of the late nineteenth century. In the early decades of the twentieth century, the educational attainments of small-town Jewish youngsters advanced even further.

By the end of World War I, compulsory education laws, progressive schooling reforms, and the demand for a more highly educated workforce had expanded educational opportunities for all Americans. Nonetheless, the rate of school attendance for youngsters between the ages of fourteen and seventeen still stood at only 28 percent around 1920. It was not until the era of the Great Depression of the 1930s that even the majority of high-school-age youngsters were enrolled in classes. Among small-town Jews of this period, however, high school graduation was nearly universal. In the twelve representative communities surveyed for this study, nearly every teenager under the age of eighteen in 1920 was in school. The few exceptions were mainly seventeen-year-olds, and at least some of these may already have completed high school before going to work.

Not only census records but also individual narratives about small communities point to impressive levels of high school graduation by the early decades of the twentieth century. The historian of the Jewish community in La Crosse, for example, maintained that immigrant parents there "were determined that their children would get fine educations," and he reported that in the first half of the twentieth century only one Jewish high school student in La Crosse ever dropped out without graduating. Moreover, even that person returned to finish high school when he was nearly thirty years old and then went on to college. Similarly, the intensive study of Newburyport's Jewish community conducted during the 1930s found that, unlike the situation among some other ethnic groups, it was "unusual for a Jewish child not to finish high school." As one Newburyport school official observed, "The Jewish parent is anxious for the child to speak English, go to school without exception, and is always willing to cooperate." Indeed, high levels of achievement in small-town high schools become sources of great pride for the entire community. Young people such as Ida Rosen, who was born in Poland and grew up in Asheville, North Carolina, to become the valedictorian of her 1936 high school class, were widely recognized as local heroes. Perhaps it was this kind of pride in accomplishment that prompted the same Newburyport school official who observed that "Jews do not become problems" to complain that "the trouble with the young Jew is the swell-headed attitude."[23]

Not only did small-town Jews complete high school at a very high rate but, when family resources allowed, at least some went on to college. The attainment of a college education by some local youngsters, combined with the fact that Jewish professionals sometimes moved to small towns from elsewhere, meant that by the interwar period it was common to find at least a few college graduates in just about every one of America's smaller Jewish settlements. A student rabbi in Muskogee, Oklahoma, for example, reported that there were ten Jewish college graduates in that town in 1935, when the local Jewish population stood at about 125. Three of these graduates were physicians, two were dentists, and one was a lawyer. The 300-person Jewish community of Greenwood, Mississippi, was also home to ten college graduates in 1935; and in Harrisonburg, Virginia, whose Jewish population was somewhere between 100 and 150, a visiting seminarian reported that college degrees had been earned by "perhaps eight of the younger men in town." From Kalamazoo, Michigan, came a somewhat surprising, and unconfirmed, report that "practically all" of the young people in the Jewish community had gone to college, about forty individuals in all.[24]

Some small-town Jews who attained a higher education did so by attending institutions at or near their homes. Sara Landau, who later went on to teach economics at the University of Louisville, at Wheaton College in Massachusetts, and at Roosevelt University in Chicago, graduated from high school in Crowley, Louisiana, in 1906 and went on to study business at Southwest Industrial Institute in nearby Lafayette. In 1920 Fitchburg, Anita Lang, the stepdaughter of a clothing store salesman; Samuel Salny, the son of a junk dealer; and Hyman Klebanov, who lived with his widowed mother, were all university students, presumably at the local state college. David Gladstein and Benjamin Lovenstein of Durham, both of whom had been unsuccessful as dry-goods merchants, were eventually able to go to school at the University of North Carolina and became attorneys.[25]

Other high school graduates from small communities, and especially those seeking to enter the liberal professions, went off to universities farther from home, including some of the most prestigious. Gertrude Weil, for example, left Goldsboro, North Carolina, for Smith College in 1897, later to return to her hometown and become an influential social activist there. The daughter of Rebecca and Samuel Rosenblum, East European immigrants who, in 1893, had been the first Jewish couple to be married in Manchester, New Hampshire, attended Radcliffe College. Her three brothers went off to university as well, with two of them eventually becoming dentists and one becoming a physician. In the years before 1925, young people from Wilmington, North Carolina, went to such prestigious schools as Princeton, Smith, Vassar, Williams, and the University of Pennsylvania, as well as to Duke University and the University of North Carolina in their home state.[26]

Because economic circumstances were sometimes precarious and because so many small-town Jewish businesses were family affairs, there was always a certain tension between the desire of parents to provide for the education for their children and their need to take advantage of the labor of their offspring. As youngsters matured, they were frequently expected to help manage the household, to find jobs in order to supplement the family income, or to work in the family business. After all, the ability to employ the unpaid labor of family members was fundamental to many small-town enterprises, as was the security provided by knowing that all those involved in running a business shared the same collective values and goals. Thus, a great many small-town families found it necessary to compromise their desire to allow their children to continue their education through high school and beyond in complete freedom.

In some cases (probably many more than are revealed in the documentary evidence), children took on work responsibilities while they remained in school. Census records for Appleton in 1920 show Lester Chudacoff, the fifteen-year-old son of the widow Nehama Chudacoff, as both a student and a grocery delivery boy, for example. The records for Hamilton, Ohio, show seventeen-year-old Phillip Cohen as both a student and a junk peddler. One woman who grew up in Williamson, West Virginia, in the pre–World War II era recalled that she and her siblings began working in her parents' store "as soon as we could see over the counter"; and in Suffolk, Virginia, in the early 1930s, the adolescent Sam Shilsky would open the grocery store run by his parents at 7 A.M., stock the shelves, stack meat, cut ice, and saw lumber, all before going off to school for the day. His younger sisters Rachel and Dee-Dee worked in the grocery store as well.[27] Especially in the decades before World War I, a family's economic situation could even result in a youngster's dropping out of school altogether at a fairly early age. The available evidence suggests that throughout the late nineteenth century, many Jewish girls were taken out of school at around age sixteen, and 1880 census documents generally listed girls under eighteen who were no longer attending school as being "at home" with their parents, presumably helping with domestic chores. On the other hand, boys who interrupted their education before finishing high school usually took jobs outside the home, often working in their fathers' businesses.

In every town for which census data were examined for our study, there were at least a few boys who had left school at a relatively early age in order to contribute to the family coffers. In Hamilton in 1880, for example, there were four boys under eighteen who held regular jobs. These youngsters were seventeen-year-old Max Grabenheimer, a cattle dealer like his father and his older brother; seventeen-year-old Albert Levi, a clothing clerk, probably in his father's store; sixteen-year-old Abram Hirsch, a dry-goods clerk; and the unusually young Jacob Grossman, only fourteen years old, who drove a wagon, most likely for his rag dealer father. In Lafayette, Indiana, in 1880 there were two boys under eighteen not in school. One was Louis Wolf, a rag peddler like his father, and the other was Henry Faust, working as a telegraph messenger. In late nineteenth-century Vicksburg, more than in the other towns surveyed, sending youngsters to work at an early age seemed to be a fairly common practice. In that town in 1880 there were at least seventeen Jewish boys under the age of eighteen working as store clerks, including three thirteen-year-olds, one twelve-year-old, and one ten-year-old.[28]

Even in the early decades of the twentieth century, amid ever-increasing rates of school attendance, there were still a few small-town Jewish boys who had to stop their educations in order to help their parents make ends meet. In Newburyport, Abe Edelstein ended his formal schooling after sixth grade in order to help support his family. He worked first for a baker and later for a shoe store owner, eventually establishing himself in the shoe business on his own. In the largely immigrant community of Nashua, census records reveal that in 1920, sixteen-year-old Harry Kamenski was working as a laborer in a foundry (probably under the tutelage of his father), although he may have been going to school at the same time. In the Jewish community of Vicksburg in 1920, three teenagers under the age of eighteen can be identified as working at regular jobs. These youngsters were the dry-goods clerk Elbert Joel, the laundry clerk Leon Fischel, and the gas station attendant Henry Haas.[29]

It appears that most Jewish youngsters who finished high school in small communities remained in the homes of their parents until they either married or left town. Evidence from 1880 and 1920 indicates that sons who remained in their parents' homes after graduation were expected to be gainfully employed, except if they were from the very wealthiest of families. Of the nine young men aged nineteen or older found to be living with their parents in Lafayette, Indiana, in 1880, for example, one was a manufacturer, one a clothing merchant, one a confectioner, and one a traveling salesman, while two were cigar merchants and three were store clerks. In Lexington, Kentucky, in 1920 those sons aged nineteen or older living in their parents' homes comprised a pawnbroker, a dry-goods merchant, a manufacturer, two cattle buyers, two brothers in the poultry business, two brothers who were lawyers, three salesmen, three grocers, three clothing merchants, as well as two students, presumably pursuing higher education.[30]

The arrangements for young women who stayed at home past the age of eighteen were somewhat different. During the final decades of the nineteenth century, daughters who remained in their parental households continued to refrain from outside employment. In the 1880 census records for the eight representative communities surveyed for this study, girls over eighteen who were living at home were almost invariably listed as having no occupation, as "keeping house," or (like most out-of-school girls under eighteen) as being simply "at home." Similarly, in Trinidad, Colorado, in 1900 only two unmarried young women were working outside their homes. Both of these, the daughters of Sam and Amelia Jaffa, were employed as telephone operators.[31]

By the time the twentieth century had ended its second decade, however, the situation for older girls living at home had changed somewhat. In the 1920 census records available for twelve representative towns, Jewish girls who remained at home after age eighteen were still listed quite frequently as having no occupation, but by then it was far more common for daughters, like sons, to be out in the general workforce. Not only had work outside the home become more socially acceptable by the end of World War I, but the need for daughters to help in the family store or to earn actual wages was probably more pressing among the East European immigrant families that made up most small Jewish communities in America in the 1920s than it had been among the German-Jewish families that dominated around 1880. Of the eighteen never-married daughters aged nineteen or older found living in their parents' homes in Alexandria, Louisiana, in 1920, for instance, seven had no occupation and three were still students, but two worked as bookkeepers, two as stenographers, two as salesladies, one as an office clerk, and one as a teacher. In Hamilton, Ohio, in the same year, of twenty-five never-married daughters aged nineteen or older living in their parents' homes, ten had no occupation, two were in school, and two more were working as salesladies while studying. The others comprised four store clerks, three office clerks, two stenographers, a bookkeeper, and a teacher.[32]

In the same way that many small-town entrepreneurs considered the businesses they were building to be family projects, they also assumed that their children would carry on those businesses. Although this did not always happen, there were many cases in which it did, both among German Jews and among East Europeans. In Muskegon, Michigan, in the decade or so after World War I, for example, the two sons of Henry Rubinsky took over their father's scrap business; Komma Gudelsky took over his family's clothing and tailoring shop, employing most of his brothers; and Milton, Carl, and Irving

Steindler became partners in their father's paper company. Similarly, in 1941 Muskegon's leading department store passed from the hands of Isaac Grossman into those of his sons Herman and Louis and his son-in-law Sam Klayf.[33]

Because of the great concern with continuity among small-town entrepreneurs, the fate of the family business always had to be considered when the prospect of sending children to college arose. Again an example from Muskegon is illustrative. There, around the turn of the twentieth century, Samuel Rosen ran the family clothing and shoe store, while his father and two of his brothers worked there as tailors and his four sisters served at various times as bookkeepers. The youngest two siblings in the family, David and Goldie, were not needed in the business, however, so they were able to depart for studies at the University of Michigan. Similarly, in Fitchburg, Massachusetts, around 1910, Abe Rome was accepted at Dartmouth, but instead of going to college he remained in town because he was needed to keep the family clothing business afloat. On the other hand, Abe Rome's younger brother, Oscar, moved on from part-time work in the family store during high school to take an undergraduate degree at Harvard in 1927 and then enter the insurance business. A still younger brother, Harold, also went to Harvard and stayed there to complete a professional degree, eventually returning to Fitchburg to practice law.[34] Clearly, in most small-town Jewish homes, business strategy and planning for the future of the family were inexorably intertwined.

Perhaps the most fundamental issue of domestic life to face Jews in small communities was finding marriage partners for the young people growing up there. In any town with more than a handful of resident Jewish families, there were, of course, opportunities for hometown matches to be made. These must have been very gratifying for the members of small-town communities, for they demonstrated the viability of these Jewish settlements and were symbols of hope for the future. Even in the mid-nineteenth century, when most secondary Jewish centers were smaller than they would become with the arrival of East European immigrants, circumstances existed under which future spouses could meet. David Bach arrived in Wabash, Indiana, as a peddler in 1854, for example, and there he met and married Rachel Hyman, a Rhinepfalz native who was living in Wabash with her brother.[35]

There is no shortage of stories involving local courtship and marriage. In La Crosse, Wisconsin, in 1869 the industrialist Albert Hirshheimer married Dora Fox, daughter of another La Crosse Jewish pioneer. When Dora died twenty-six years later, Hirshheimer married her sister Sara. In Charlottesville, Virginia, also in 1869, Moses Kaufman married his cousin Hannah, the daughter of his aunt Matilda and her husband, Isaac Leterman, the merchant who had helped sponsor Kaufman's immigration to America. Around 1880 Aaron Lehman and Celestine Wolff met and married in Jackson, Mississippi, the city to which each had come independently from different towns in France.

Israel Gudelsky, a native of Russian Poland, arrived in Muskegon, Michigan, in 1884, got work as a traveling salesman for the dry-goods entrepreneur Israel Goldman, and eventually married Goldman's niece, Bessie. Goldman's son, who was the first Jewish child born in Muskegon, later married Rachel Rosenthal, the daughter of another pioneer Jewish couple in the city. In Danbury, Connecticut, Bertha Dick wed Abram Feinson in 1926, uniting two of the most prominent local Jewish families "in a manner reminiscent of dynastic marriages."[36]

Still, the pool of eligible singles in small communities was unlikely to be large enough to allow local matches to be taken for granted. Moreover, as a number of studies conducted around the middle of the twentieth century demonstrated, young people who grew up together in small communities knew each other so intimately that they became averse to the idea of marriage within their group. As one observer concluded, children brought up together in small towns "looked upon their Jewish playmates and chums more as brothers and sisters than as future spouses."[37] Nor was the courtship situation helped by the fact that young men were more likely to be anchored to family businesses than young women, thus making it easier for the females to leave home in search of mates in larger communities.

In addition, there seemed to be quite a bias among Jewish men in favor or younger wives, and this preference complicated the search for a spouse even further. Once a woman passed a certain age, it was likely that she would become less desirable as a marriage partner. In 1880, for example, married Jewish men in Hamilton, Ohio, had wives who were, on average, 4 years younger than they were. In Bradford, Pennsylvania, in the same year, the average married Jewish man had a wife 4.6 years his junior. In Vicksburg, where 44 percent of married Jewish men had wives at least 10 years younger than they, women were 8.6 years younger than their husbands on average. Similarly, in 1920, Jewish wives in Hamilton were on average 4.2 years younger than their husbands. In Bradford they were 4.3 years younger and in Vicksburg they were 6.4 years younger. In Nashua, New Hampshire, and in Modesto, California, Jewish wives in 1920 were on average 3.6 and 4.1 years younger than their husbands, respectively.[38]

One result of the restricted number of eligible partners in small towns was that, despite the strong inclination of Jews in these places to wed, some remained unmarried throughout their lives. This reality was reflected in the presence of unattached adults in some of the extended households of America's small-town Jewish communities, and there were even some family units in these communities made up solely of older adults who had never married. The highly successful merchant Bertrand Weil, born in Louisiana around 1860 to parents from Germany, was still living as a bachelor in Alexandria in 1920, for example, sharing his home with one sister who also had never married and a second sister who was widowed. The lawyer Lester Simons, born in Pennsylvania around 1870 to Polish parents, was living as a bachelor in Bradford fifty years later, also sharing his home with a widowed sister. In Hamilton, Ohio, in 1920 the Sauer family circle was made up of several siblings who had come to America as youngsters in 1879 and had never wed: the brothers Albert (sixty years old and a cigar store owner), Sigmund (a soft drink merchant), and Morris (the owner of a tailor shop), and the sisters Johanna and Rosa.[39]

Another result of the relative scarcity of Jewish marriage partners in small communities was the selection of non-Jewish mates. Just as some early settlers in small towns married gentiles in the days before a local Jewish community took shape, young people eager to find spouses and start families continued to select marriage partners whose religious and ethnic background was different from their own. Those Jews who chose to marry outside the faith were usually men, but whether they were of German origin or East Europeans, their intermarriage usually did not result in their conversion to Christianity. Indeed, small-town Jews married to Christians often maintained some sort of Jewish identity, and if they were members of a Reform congregation, which would have been relatively tolerant of assimilationism, they may even have continued to attend services at the local temple. Sometimes they were even accompanied by their non-Jewish wives. One set of statistics from around the middle of the twentieth century indicates that in a period when thirty-four Jewish men married gentile women in Charlotte, North Carolina, only four Jewish women married gentile men. In the marriages involving a Jewish man and a gentile woman, no more than four of the men converted to Christianity, and only seven of the women converted to Judaism. On the other hand, all four of the Jewish women who married gentile men adopted the Christian faith of their husbands.[40]

One reason intermarriage was not completely rejected in small communities was the belief that it would help preserve some Jewish settlements that would otherwise face extinction. After all, there were at least some cases in which the children of intermarried couples were raised as Jews. A student rabbi reporting from Zanesville, Ohio, in 1935 wrote that in the four or five local cases of intermarriage of which he was aware, the children had remained Jewish. There were even a few small-town Jewish leaders who were willing to temper their opposition to intermarriage because of their concern over the very survival of their communities. The problem of communal continuity was apparently so great in early twentieth-century Meridian, Mississippi, that in 1913 the Reform rabbi there, Max Raisin, declared that even though there were grave dangers inherent in mixed marriages, an even greater threat to Judaism was "the unhealthy indifference" of many men toward marriage in the first place. He was concerned that Jews were in danger of becoming "a childless people," and argued that as long as Jewish men continued to create families, there was hope for Jewish survival. Not being married at all, Rabbi Raisin concluded, was worse than intermarrying.[41]

The reality, however, was that children born to couples in which the wife was a gentile were far more likely to be raised in the Christian faith of their mothers than as Jews. The situation in Zanesville in 1935, if reported accurately, seems to have been highly anomalous. In the same year the student rabbi serving Hamilton, Ohio, reported that he knew of twelve marriages there involving Jews and gentiles, and that in none of these did the children remain Jewish. The student rabbi in Muskogee, Oklahoma, in 1935 reported that of the fifteen or so intermarried couples in his town, only four had "aligned themselves with [the] Jewish community" and that only two of the eleven children of these couples attended his congregation's religious school.[42]

Indeed, there are even cases in which, far from being linked to the survival of a Jewish community, intermarriage was a factor in its demise. For example, in Donaldsonville, Louisiana, which had a reported Jewish population of 179 in 1878 but only eighty in 1927, many Jews married local Catholic women of French or Spanish ancestry and, to quote from a local newspaper, "headed families in which the children were baptized and reared in the Catholic faith." In Ligonier, Indiana, where the Jewish population dropped from 133 around 1907 to only fifty twenty years later, there seem to have been three intermarriages before 1910, and at least four after that year, with the non-Jewish spouses often rejected by the small Jewish community that still existed in town. In Madison, Indiana, whose Jewish population was 253 in 1878 but only twenty-four fifty years later, the most prominent local Jewish figure, Marcus Sulzer, married the daughter of a Baptist minister in 1893, and when she died, he married her sister. Although Sulzer's son attended temple with his father on Friday nights as well as church with his mother on Sundays, he eventually became an Episcopalian.[43]

The actual incidence of intermarriage in smaller Jewish communities during the late nineteenth and early twentieth centuries is impossible to quantify with precision. In 1904 one observer placed the rate of mixed marriages in small-town America at no more than 5 percent in the North but somewhere between 20 and 50 percent in the South. However, this commentator was speaking about the situation in places with only a handful of Jews, as well as places where a small community existed, and even he admitted that he was unable to explain the regional disparity he perceived.[44] Still, the fact that there are so many examples of marriages between Jews and gentiles in smaller communities makes it safe to conclude that, in an era when the rate of mixed marriages nationally was well below 10 percent (actually below 2 percent in the 1920s), intermarriage was nonetheless a factor in the demography of just about every one of America's small-town Jewish settlements, and one that was likely to be more noticeable there than in larger communities, which provided greater anonymity to their residents.[45]

Despite the threat that intermarriage posed to Jewish survival, an active involvement in small-town Jewish life was no guarantee that it would be avoided. Bernard Yoste, who provided space for services in one of his buildings and acted as "rabbi" of Vicksburg Jewry in the period before the Civil War, nonetheless married a Catholic woman and watched his six children become "lost to Judaism." Similarly, Lazard Lion was an active member of the San Jose Jewish community in California during its early development, but neither his wife nor his offspring were Jewish. Of the five children of Marcus Katz, a pioneer Jewish merchant and communal leader in San Bernardino, California, two married Jews, one never married, and two others married gentiles. Joe Pottlitzer, a third-generation member of Temple Israel in Lafayette, Indiana, married his wife, Madonna, in a Catholic ceremony in 1933, and although he retained his identity as a Jew, he agreed that his children would be raised in the church. "In all our married life," Joe explained, he and his wife of fifty-five years "never once had an argument about religion, never. She respected my religion," he reported, and "I respected hers."[46]

Although intermarriage was probably more common among Reform Jews of German stock, there was no shortage of mixed marriages among nominally Orthodox small-town Jews of East European background as well. One of the first East Europeans to come to Red Bank, New Jersey, was married to a non-Jewish woman in 1889, in a ceremony that was reportedly conducted by an itinerant rabbi. Ten years later, a "hitherto unheard of event" occurred in the Orthodox community of Manchester, New Hampshire, when a local insurance agent and congregational leader divorced his Jewish wife and married a Christian woman. The 1920 census records for Fitchburg, Massachusetts, show that the Vilna-born Yiddish-speaking Peter Smith was married to an Irish immigrant named Margaret, almost certainly a Catholic. Of the nine children of Ben Zeff, a leader of the Orthodox community in interwar Modesto, California, four married Jews, but five married gentiles, only one of whom later converted to Judaism.[47]

Intermarriage was such a salient factor in many small Jewish communities that their institutions often had to address the issue in some formal context. When the two dozen or so Jewish men in Galesburg, Illinois, chartered their Hebrew Congregation in 1867, for example, they found it necessary to stipulate that "any individual whose wife is a non-Jewess shall not become a member." So, too, the late nineteenth-century constitution of Congregation Rodef Sholem in Wabash, Indiana, decreed that in order to be buried in the temple's cemetery, "the Deceased must have been an Israelite at the time of death." Even those who drafted the constitution adopted by the East European founders of Congregation Brith Achim in Petersburg, Virginia, in

1908 found it necessary to state that "no person shall be eligible to member-ship who is married outside the Jewish faith, and any member so married forfeits all rights and benefits of the congregation." The founders of the Jewish cemetery in Racine, Wisconsin, were forward-looking enough in 1918 to desig-nate portions of their burial ground that might be used by non-Orthodox con-gregations in the future, but they, too, stipulated that non-Jews must never be interred even in those sections. Of course, some Jewish institutions had more liberal policies regarding the intermarried from the outset, and others that at first had strict rules later relaxed them in the face of developing reali-ties. In Columbia, South Carolina, the Hebrew Benevolent Society considered a constitutional amendment in 1924 to allow for the burial of non-Jewish spouses in its cemetery. Although this amendment was initially rejected, it was adopted ten year later.[48]

As the tendency to exclude the intermarried from small-town congrega-tions and to deny Christians burial in Jewish cemeteries demonstrates, the ideal in small communities always remained marriage within the faith. In advocating marriage to a non-Jew over childlessness, even Rabbi Raisin of Meridian had declared that intermarriage "must always be looked upon as a potent factor of disintegration, one to be dreaded and with main and might discouraged." Because of the strong desire to maintain endogamy, and be-cause intermarriage was in any case not readily accepted in mainstream America until the second half of the twentieth century, Jewish families that knew their children could not be certain of finding mates in the local commu-nity had to devise strategies to bring their sons and daughters into contact with marriageable young Jews from elsewhere.

One tactic that small-town residents employed was arranging visits to and from relatives and friends in places outside their own communities. Most small-town Jews had out-of-town kin, and the fact that many individuals had sojourned in small towns before moving out only increased the number of contacts that Jews in small communities had elsewhere. Some families that wanted to en-courage their children to find Jewish mates simply sent them to live for a time with relatives in larger cities. This was easiest to do, of course, with daughters, who were deemed less essential to family businesses. In early twentieth-century Wilmington, North Carolina, a sort of "Philadelphia-Wilmington axis" seems to have facilitated the strategy of sending children off to the big city. There were also instances in which entire families relocated to larger commu-nities just because their youngsters were reaching the age at which they would begin serious dating. This was said to be the case in Devil's Lake, North Dakota, for example.[49]

In any case, there is no question that Jewish families in various small communities kept in close contact with relatives and acquaintances else-where. In one issue of the local paper in Hibbing, Minnesota, in 1916, for instance, the "Personals" column contained news that "Reverend B. Gusse, of the Jewish synagog," had gone on a trip to Duluth; that "Miss Goldie Edelstein, . . . clerk at the Boston Bargain store," had spent six weeks with relatives in the Minneapolis area; and that the merchant Eli Woolfan had visited family in New York for two months. In the same year an issue of the monthly *Jewish Community Journal,* published in Lafayette, Indiana, noted that Florence Greensfelter of Logansport, Indiana, had visited her sister in town, that Maurice Levy was making an extended business trip through the West, that Isaac Rice had returned from a business trip to the South, and that Mrs. Rice's sister and her husband had visited from Indianapolis. The journal also reported that Mrs. J. Cadden and her daughter had visited from Terre Haute; that the family of Mr. and Mrs. David Fishman was visiting in Los Angeles; that Mrs. J. Spector, Mrs. Fishman's mother, was visiting in Texas; and that Mrs. Louis Loeb was the guest of her daughter in Detroit. So, too, Florence Levy of Peru, Indiana, had just left after a short stay with the Solomon Loebs, Mrs. Edward Pottlitzer was hosting her niece from Cincinnati, Mrs. Joseph King was entertaining her sister from out of town, and the Stern family of Indianapolis had been Thanksgiving guests of the Oppenheimers. All this during the single month of November.[50]

Yet another indication of how frequently small-town Jews were in contact with friends and family members in other places comes from the April 1936 issue of the *American Jewish Times*, a newspaper published in Greensboro, North Carolina, and coving the Jewish South. In reporting on the activities of members of the Jewish community of Charlotte, that issue revealed that Mr. and Mrs. II. Policr were spending a few days with relatives in Atlanta; that Mrs. Jack Fred and Mrs. Ben Sheftal were entertaining a guest from Baltimore; that Mrs. Ralph Malever and her daughter, Hilda, were vacationing in Florida, while Miss Sara Nelson had just returned from there. Furthermore, Mrs. Harry Schwartz had left for two weeks in New York City, while Mrs. I. D. Blumenthal had also departed for New York and was then continuing to Canada. Mrs. Louis Schlanger was reported to be visiting relatives in Wilkes-Barre, Pennsylvania.[51]

With all this kind of travel going on, there was no shortage of opportunities to make matches based on family connections and visits involving relatives in small communities. Abe Kobre, whose Kiev-born father had opened a shoe store in Charlottesville, Virginia, in 1922, met his future wife, Faye, when she came from Baltimore to visit her uncle and aunt, owners of a discount store in Charlottesville. Florence Shubert, whose parents had moved from Lowell, Massachusetts, to Plattsburgh, New York, met her future husband, the Plattsburgh liquor dealer Aaron Scheicr, on a family visit around 1933. In Ithaca, New York, the home of Mary and Nathan Kramer was a gathering place for the couple's unmarried Jewish relatives and friends as they arrived in the area. "The women lived in one room and the men in another," a member of the Kramer family reported, and in that situation "many a romance caught fire." So complex were the marriage ties that developed in Ithaca that "newcomers were always befuddled by the intricate relationships."[52]

Just as ties of kinship and friendship often facilitated the introduction of potential marriage partners, so, too, did business connections. Networking that combined commercial and social concerns was an extremely important resource for small-town families, and young men whose work took them on buying trips to larger cities often used these trips as opportunities to meet likely spouses. By the same token, the visits of young men making business calls in small communities could also lead to introductions and eventual betrothals. The parents of Anita Behn, for instance, met when her father stayed at the home of her mother's parents while making a call in Batavia, New York, as the representative of a furniture firm. Sidney Steiner met his future wife when he came to Topeka, Kansas, as a traveling representative for a millinery concern and presented his wares at her parents' store. Similarly, one of the daughters of Ben Zeff in Modesto married a young Jewish man from Fresno who used to come to town to pick up hides from the slaughterhouse her father owned. Local lore tells of an extremely enterprising storeowner in a small town in the South sometime in the first half of the twentieth century who notified his suppliers in the North that if they wanted him to continue buying their merchandise, they would have to send only unmarried Jewish salesmen to solicit his business. In this way, it is said, he helped all six of his daughters find suitable husbands.[53]

Of course, given the nature of small-town Jewish occupational patterns, business connections and family connections sometimes worked in tandem to facilitate courtship and marriage. Such was the case with the Cohen family of Jackson, Mississippi, around the turn of the twentieth century. The Cohen Brothers clothing store was in the territory served by Ike Levy, a suit distributor based in Memphis, Tennessee. During his sales calls, Levy became acquainted with Moise Cohen and soon came to believe that Moise might make a good husband for his sister-in-law, Etta. Etta had come from Rochester, New York, to live in Memphis so she could be with Levy's wife, Ida, while he was on the road. Levy introduced Moise and Etta, and they married in 1908 after only a brief courtship. With Etta now relocated to Jackson and otherwise occupied, Ida Levy asked another of her sisters, Nell, to come to Memphis to keep her company. Not long after she arrived, Nell was introduced to Moise's brother Sam, and the two of them were married only four months after Nell's arrival in the South.[54]

Some of the marriages arranged by residents of small Jewish communities involved connections over rather long distances. Philip Drachman of Tucson, for example, married Rosa Katzenstein while he was on a visit to New

York City in 1868, and they went back to Arizona by way of the Isthmus of Panama, San Francisco, and Los Angeles. Similarly, the Romanian-born father of Rose Orenstein settled in Farrell in western Pennsylvania in 1905, but when he was ready to wed three years later, he went all the way to New York City to find a wife. The woman he married there, after a courtship that lasted only three weeks, was a Polish immigrant working in a shirt factory and sleeping on a cot in her cousin's kitchen. She agreed to move to Farrell because there, as her daughter explained, "she felt her life could only improve." Even European connections figured in some marriage strategies. Leopold Hays of Wichita, Kansas, went back to his native Trier in Germany to find a wife in 1873, for example; and Morris Nasatir sent for a wife from his native Lithuania soon after he settled in Santa Ana, California, around 1898. Also in the 1890s, Moses Walper brought his niece, Gertrude Tobiansky, from Lithuania to Benton Harbor, Michigan, in the hope of matching her up with a local resident named David Sax. Walper's plan worked; Gertrude and David married, settled down in Benton Harbor and eventually had nine children.[55]

Still, it was easier to make contacts and to maintain them if the geographic distances involved were not too great. For this reason, proximity seems to have facilitated a great many out-of-town matches. Thus, in 1886, for example, at least two Jewish weddings took place in Baltimore in which women from that city married men from Frederick, Maryland, only about fifty miles distant. Rudolph Weil, born in Jackson, Mississippi, in 1866, moved to Vicksburg, not far away, and there married Ida Teller in 1891. When their children were ready to wed, their son Felix married Ernestine Stein from his own hometown, while their son Sam married Inez Isenberg of Greenville, Mississippi, just upriver from Vicksburg. Lillian Rosenberg of Gardner, Massachusetts, found her mate in nearby Fitchburg and was married on Armistice Day in 1920. In four "representative marriages" reported in Wilmington, North Carolina, in the quarter-century after 1885, Wilmingtonians married partners from four other Jewish centers in the region: Atlanta, Charlotte, Richmond, and Raleigh.[56]

The power of relative proximity is also revealed in a survey of fourteen marriages involving Jews from Lafayette, Indiana, and reported in the local press between 1905 and 1925. In four of these marriages, both partners were from Lafayette. In the other ten, either the bride or the groom was from outside the city, but most were still from within the region. One bride of a Lafayette man was from Toledo, one was from Louisville, one was from Chicago, and two were from Cincinnati. The two Cincinnatians were sisters, one of whom married into the Loeb department store family, and the other of whom married a bookkeeper at the Loeb store. Two of the grooms who married Lafayette woman were from Fort Wayne, one was from Chicago (this was Rabbi Arthur Zinkin, who had once served in Lafayette), and one was from

Indianapolis (Rabbi Morris Feuerlicht, who also had served in Lafayette). Only one young man involved in the fourteen marriages recorded was from farther away. He came from Wilkes-Barre, Pennsylvania, but had gone to school at Purdue.[57]

Another manifestation of the influence of proximity can be found in a review of the eleven marriages involving Jews that took place during the year 1912 in the town of Meridian, Mississippi. In two of these marriages, both bride and groom seem to have been from Meridian, while in six other cases one partner was from Meridian and the other was from another town in Mississippi or in the adjacent state of Alabama. Yet one more marriage involved a man from Meridian and a woman from Florida. Only two of the eleven marriages seem to have involved partners who came from places quite far from Meridian, although both were cities in which individuals from small towns were likely to have contacts. In one of these two marriages, Dr. Leo Bohm wed Carrie Steinhart in New York City, and in the other Dr. Leo Strousse wed Essie Myer in Philadelphia.[58]

Among the factors that account for the marriages of small-town Jews to partners from within their own regions is the involvement of organizations within small communities that designed activities specifically to foster contacts between young people from their towns and Jews from elsewhere. Organizations such as Young Men's and Young Women's Hebrew Associations and synagogue youth groups sponsored social events that brought together Jewish youngsters from several communities so that they could get to know each other. Samuel Stahl, a dentist in Manchester, New Hampshire, met his future wife, Sadie Flaxman, at a YM/YWHA convention around 1925, for example. In Topeka, a chapter of Aleph Zadik Aleph, the B'nai B'rith youth auxiliary, was organized in 1929, and the group regularly traveled to Kansas City to promote interests such as "debates, basketball, and girls." The young people of Modesto, California, had a chance to meet potential mates during barge rides on the San Joaquin River organized by the AZA chapter in Stockton.[59]

So, too, invitations to social events in the synagogues of small towns often went out to members of the congregations of other towns not far away. This was not only because there were likely to be ties of family and friendship between these congregations, but also because it gave teenagers and singles from the communities involved a chance to encounter each other. As Esther Gorwitz Palmer of Oshkosh, Wisconsin, recalled, the Jews of her community often attended congregational functions in places such as Fond du Lac, Appleton, and Green Bay because these occasions "afforded our young people an opportunity to meet and socialize with other young people of their own faith." Nor did it always take formal arrangements to create situations in which young people could meet. It was common knowledge in Newburyport, Massachusetts, and other towns along the Merrimack Valley, for example, that

Salisbury Beach was a gathering place for Jewish singles in the period around World War I.[60]

When young people from small towns went off to school, most commonly in their own parts of the country, they had another opportunity to meet their future mates. Sadie Rubinsky left Muskegon, Michigan, in 1905 to attend finishing school in Chicago, and there she met Isaac Grossman, a young clothing merchant from Wisconsin. After a two-year courtship the couple married, and, contrary to what normally happened in such situations, Grossman sold his business in Wisconsin and moved to Muskegon. Herschel Rubin of East Liverpool, Ohio, met his future wife at Ohio State University, where he was a member of the Jewish fraternity Zeta Beta Tau. Seymour Flamm of Benton Harbor met his wife, Elaine Resnick, at a Hillel mixer at Michigan State University in the early 1940s. At the University of North Carolina, the Hillel chapter served as a meeting place for young people from small towns all over the state, even if they were not students at the school.[61]

Family life in the various small Jewish communities of late nineteenth- and early twentieth-century America clearly had a certain familiar rhythm involving the centrality of kinship ties, the demands of work, the pursuit of schooling, and the excitement of courtship. Nonetheless, it goes almost without saying that each family in these communities faced its own individual joys and sorrows, and that no two small-town Jewish households shared exactly the same experience. So, too, the ebb and flow of larger historical events often disrupted the more routine existence of the families that constituted America's small-town communities. Those Jewish centers that were in existence at the time of the Civil War, for example, invariably felt the impact of that conflict. They sent their men into the service—the small community of Wabash, Indiana, dispatched at least five soldiers to fight for the Union, for instance—and they endured the social and economic dislocations that the conflict brought in its wake. In Wilmington, North Carolina, the Jews felt the scorn of their neighbors because so many of them were involved in trade at a time when the Union blockade of that port city drove consumer prices ever higher. The situation of the Jews in Rome, Georgia, was so precarious that they are reported to have packed up their households and businesses, lock, stock, and barrel, and relocated to Nashville for the duration of the war.[62]

Catastrophes such as the yellow fever epidemic of 1878, which claimed some 20,000 victims, mainly in the Mississippi River Valley, also had a profound effect on a great many small-town Jewish families. In Vicksburg, for example, the 1878 outbreak led to a strict quarantine of the city and took the lives of perhaps forty-six local Jews, including the town's rabbi, Bernhard Henry Gotthelf, and one of his sons. The great influenza epidemic of 1918 also took its toll on Jewish families in small towns across America. In Jackson, Mississippi, for instance, the future Reform rabbi Julian Feibelman lost his

*Wedding portrait of Lena Joffee and Louis Kotzin, Annapolis, Maryland, 1908. Finding marriage partners for the young people growing up in small towns was a fundamental concern for the Jews living there. Courtesy of The Jewish Museum of Maryland, 2001.113.108.*

uncle Fred to the scourge; and in Owensboro, Kentucky, whose Jewish population was still in triple digits in 1918, Clemmie Wolf became something of a local legend when she herself died as a result of her volunteer work nursing victims of the flu.[63]

World War I again saw small Jewish communities sending their sons into military service, and many families suffered tragic losses. From the small community of Muskegon, two sons of Israel Gudelsky served with the army in France, and two sons of Isaac Rosen saw duty in the navy, while Homer Grossman was killed at Belleau Woods toward the end of the war. The first young man from Chisholm, Minnesota, to be killed in the fighting was a Jewish soldier, Louis Press; and Nate Nesselson of Bradford, Pennsylvania, lost his life in France while carrying messages from his company to battalion headquarters. The triple-digit Jewish community of Burlington, Vermont, sent sixty-eight men to serve in World War I; and the community of Port Chester, New York, sent fifty-four to the colors, one of whom was killed in action.[64]

The Great Depression was another event that took its toll on many families in small-town Jewish communities. It both imperiled businesses and disrupted family lives. A student rabbi in Hamilton, Ohio, perceived that the economic situation of his congregants in the mid-1930s was "at present not so good, only fair," and he observed that the storekeepers who headed the Jewish families of Hamilton faced the usual "struggles of petty merchants today." Rabbi Jerome Folkman, serving in Jackson, Michigan, found himself welcoming the homeless on a regular basis. He later recalled that "indigents were always welcome at our table and the word was soon spread around that we had no money and no 'discretionary funds' to distribute but that we were always good for a meal at the conventional hours." Some middle-class households, such as that of Vivian Barnert in Dover, New Jersey, and that of Bea Weill in Greensboro, North Carolina, had to dismiss their domestic help during the Depression, and some individuals even had to sell off personal items just to buy food.[65]

The economic crisis also could mean store closings. Rose and Sam Wolpert lost their Peoples Clothing establishment in Leominster, Massachusetts, for example, and they had to move to Fitchburg where Sam could work for the Rome Clothing Company, owned by relatives. In Muskegon the Depression brought about the demise even of a few very well-established businesses, such as the Goldberg family's downtown clothing store and that of the Gudelsky brothers. Having lost his business, Komma Gudelsky started selling insurance, and for a while his wife worked as a receptionist for a county welfare agency. Komma's brother, Benjamin, opened a store called Ben's Resale Shop, which he operated with his wife, while brother Joseph Gudelsky went to work for a beer company, and brother David took a job with a scrap yard. Hard times also meant that Komma's son Marvin had to leave the University of Michigan and look for work. Similarly, in Durham, North Carolina, E. J. Evans went to work in his father-in-law's business rather than beginning his studies at Harvard Law School, and Sam Margolis had to give up graduate study at Duke in order to support his family. In Muncie, Indiana, the response of some Jewish business owners to declining sales was to keep their stores open for longer hours, and this practice eventually forced other shopkeepers to follow suit.[66]

Still, small-town Jews probably suffered less during the 1930s than did their counterparts in larger communities. In general, unemployment was slightly lower in smaller cities and towns than it was in big cities, and it was the very kinds of businesses in which small-town Jews engaged that tended to fare better than the economy as a whole during the Depression years.[67] After all, even in hard times there was still a need for basic consumer goods, and the demand for services such as alterations and cleaning probably increased in an era when replacing old items was less of an option. The student rabbi in Harrisonburg, Virginia, in 1935 asserted that in his town "most families are either comfortable or a little better off than this even," and he indicated that the president of the local congregation had a fund to aid needy Jewish transients, but that as far as he could discover, there were "no Jewish poor" in town. At the same time the student rabbi in Zanesville reported that the economic condition of the Jews there was "fair to good," with "none destitute" in his community. Remembering the 1930s, the son of a shoe store owner in Cumberland, Maryland, reported that although his town "was hard hit by the Depression," he himself was "hardly aware of it."[68]

One consequence of the relatively easier circumstances in smaller communities during the Depression was that these places attracted some big-city Jewish families hoping to escape the worst effects of the economic crisis. As one women who grew up in Warren, Ohio, recalled, unemployed urban Jews often "headed for the 'greener pastures' of the small towns." Their strategy, she explained, was to settle "in areas close enough to be within a few hours of their families . . . in the cities, yet far enough to bring their skills and entrepreneurship to these fertile areas." It was because of the Depression that young Howard Fink and much of his extended family ended up in Marion, Indiana. Fink's maternal grandfather left the jewelry business in Chicago to buy a roofing concern in Marion around 1931, Fink's parents made the move to Marion in 1933, and his uncle and aunt came as well when their Chicago-area clothing store failed. Similarly, Nathan and Fannie Price came to Muskegon, Michigan, from Chicago so that Nathan could go to work in his brother-in-law's furniture store. It was also the Depression that brought the family of the future radio commentator Faye Moskowitz from Detroit to Jackson, Michigan, around 1938.[69]

World War II, that great watershed in the history of the United States and in the saga of the Jewish people, also had a tremendous impact on small Jewish communities. Not only did the families in these communities share the agony of world Jewry as they followed events in Nazi-dominated Europe, but they also witnessed the departure of nearly all their able-bodied young men (and of some of their young women) for military service. The Jewish community of Plymouth, Massachusetts, sent twenty-one of its children to fight, and at least seven young Jews from Fitchburg, Massachusetts, were killed during the war. The B'nai Abraham congregation of Hagerstown, Maryland, sent forty congregants to the fighting, two of whom lost their lives. One hundred Jewish men and women from Englewood, New Jersey, were in the service during World War II, and eight were killed in action. The Jewish community of Michigan City, Indiana, lost Donald Kottler, Marshall Kottler, Milton Soloff, and Gerald Kadet. The community of Racine, Wisconsin, sent nearly 150 of its young people into the service, and four were killed, including the brothers David and Norman Gordon and their cousin Leonard Hulbert.[70]

Whether in the era of World War II or in earlier times, the linkages that tied together so many Jewish households in America's small towns meant that the hardships and the tragic losses suffered by individual families were felt throughout the entire community. In riding out the great undulations of late nineteenth- and early twentieth-century history, as in nearly everything else small communities experienced, the intense interconnectedness of the individuals and kin groups in these Jewish enclaves played a role. There was no escaping the fact that within the local Jewish circle everyone was likely to be known to everyone else, so that, whether in their daily lives or in their confrontations with extraordinary events, small-town Jews never felt alone or anonymous. In this way, as in so many others, America's smaller Jewish communities were quite unlike those of the country's large or even midsize cities.

For those who constituted the smaller Jewish communities of the United States, a sense of communal cohesion depended in part on factors such as a shared history and family ties, but even more so on the establishment of congregations. In the larger communities of the country, Jews could interact with one another, as Jews, in a variety of settings. In fact in some big-city neighborhoods the street itself became a Jewish space. In smaller communities, however, it was extremely difficult to maintain any kind of consistent Jewish identity without synagogue affiliation. The mid-twentieth-century comedian and social critic Lenny Bruce certainly exaggerated when he observed that "if you live in New York or any other big city, you are Jewish . . . even if you're Catholic" but that "if you live in Butte, Montana, you're going to be goyish [gentile] even if you're Jewish."[1] Nonetheless, his observation did make the valid point that Jewish identity was not easy to preserve in a small-town setting. Thus, if they felt the need for any specifically Jewish connections, even Jews who did not have strongly held religious convictions were inclined to affiliate with local congregations. Jews in small towns tended to establish synagogues as soon as a minimal number of their coreligionists were present, and these institutions almost always became the essential foci of local Jewish life.

Indeed, the congregations of small communities often became magnets for Jews in surrounding rural areas as well. There were, after all, thousands of points of settlement in America that were home to so few Jews that they could support little or nothing in the way of communal life, and for many of the Jewish families and individuals who lived in virtual isolation from other Jews, it was a nearby small community, rather than a major Jewish center, that served as their lifeline to the Jewish world. So, for example, the congregation in Danville, Pennsylvania, served Jews in places such as Berwick,

---

*Photo opposite page: Sunday school class of the Reform congregation Keneseth Israel, Zanesville, Ohio, ca. 1912. The small size of this class reflects both the limited Jewish population of Zanesville and divisions within the community. Courtesy of the Jacob Rader Marcus Center of the American Jewish Archives.*

Bloomsburg, Milton, and Selinsgrove as well, just as the congregation in Columbus, Mississippi, served Jews in places such as Aberdeen, Starkville, and West Point.[2]

The critical importance of congregational life in America's small Jewish communities is reflected in the fact that of the 136 triple-digit Jewish settlements that can be identified in the United States in the late 1870s, at least 113, or 83 percent, had functioning congregations by 1878. Furthermore, the creation of congregations was just over the horizon for many of those triple-digit communities that were without them in that year. At least eight more of these communities had established congregations by 1884.[3] In the late 1920s, as well, some sort of organized religious life was in evidence in nearly all urban places with triple-digit Jewish populations. We should recall that, for this study, one factor that helped define Jewish settlements of 100 or more individuals as true communities is the fact that of the 490 triple-digit Jewish settlements in the United States in 1927, no more than 11 percent were reported to be without congregations.

Most of America's triple-digit Jewish communities were home to only a single congregational body in the classic era of small-town Jewry, but, for a variety of reasons, a significant minority of small communities supported more than one assembly at some point before the middle of the twentieth century. Both the account of why most small-town Jewish communities united to maintain a single congregation and the account of why others found themselves internally divided despite their limited size are intriguing stories worthy of detailed consideration.

We should begin by recognizing that a great many of the triple-digit communities lacking even one formally organized congregation in 1927 were in towns not far from larger cities. Among such small communities were those of Evanston and Cicero, Illinois, a short distance from Chicago; those of Alhambra, Pomona, and Santa Ana, California, all quite near Los Angeles; and those of Chicopee and Longmeadow, Massachusetts, adjacent to Springfield. Despite the fact that small communities in the shadow of larger cities generally had independent identities, the proximity of metropolitan centers where synagogues were available obviously mitigated the urgency of creating local congregations in some smaller Jewish settlements. Even so, it is likely that the residents of some small communities without congregations had organized informal prayer gatherings by the 1920s and that others were in the process of establishing synagogues. The Jews of Lakewood, Ohio, for instance, thought of themselves as being at a "great distance to any Temple" even though their town was adjacent to Cleveland, and they were already discussing the formation of a Lakewood congregation as early as 1918, though they were still without one in 1927.[4]

The oldest small-town congregations functioning in the period between the two world wars were typically ones that had been established by Jews of Central European origin in the middle decades of the nineteenth century. Usually these had begun as congregations adhering to traditional religious norms, but by the turn of the twentieth century nearly all had been attracted to the principles and practices of Reform Judaism, which was attempting to create a form of the Jewish faith that was better suited to an American milieu. One after another, these congregations adopted innovations such as sermons in English, choral singing with organ accompaniment, and seating in family pews. They also introduced an abbreviated liturgy and placed new emphasis on maintaining decorum during services.

More often than not, the transition to Reform in small-town congregations was accompanied by a fair amount of controversy and turmoil. In his memoir of Jewish life in Paducah, Kentucky, for example, the distiller and philanthropist Isaac Bernheim recalled that soon after the local congregation was founded and its first synagogue dedicated in 1871, "the question of family pews almost disrupted the little struggling organization, and when the question of removing hats during Divine Worship was raised it created a perfect storm of opposition." The Paducah congregation eventually reached a compromise over hats, allowing "members who conscientiously believed that it was a sin to bare one's head during worship" to keep their heads covered, but in the end it seems that only one man in the community continued to take advantage of this privilege. Similarly, at Rodef Sholem in Petersburg, Virginia, which had been founded in 1852 and reconstituted after the Civil War, an 1877 decision to pray bareheaded in the congregation's newly erected synagogue was made despite bitter opposition from some members. At Beth Israel in Macon, Georgia, the period between 1880 and 1894 has been described as one "characterized by a lack of agreement over leadership and ritual," and it was only after a decade and a half of rancor that the congregation emerged with a clear Reform identity and "firmly established" as a member of the Union of American Hebrew Congregations, which had become by then the umbrella organization of Reform temples.[5]

The transition to Reform was without question the main point of contention within a great many Jewish congregations all over the United States during the late nineteenth century. However, there is reason to believe that battles over the adoption of Reform were especially intense in small communities. In those settings, control over congregational policy was more important both for the supporters of Reform and for its opponents, because the limited size of smaller settlements inhibited the establishment of dissident congregations when conflicts arose. Nonetheless, feelings were so strong that multiple congregations sometimes did appear even in very tiny communities when nineteenth-century arguments over Reform could not be resolved. In Illinois, for instance, the Springfield Hebrew Congregation, which was established in 1858 and chartered in 1867, worshiped at first according to *minhag ashkenaz,* the traditional rite of German Jews. By 1876, however, that assembly, having erected its first synagogue and adopted the name B'rith Sholom, introduced a number of liturgical reforms. This was the signal for those Jews in Springfield who still adhered to Orthodox practice to withdraw from the congregation. They began meeting informally on their own, and then, in 1886, established the Young Men's Hebrew Congregation as an alternative to B'rith Sholom.[6]

In Quincy, Illinois, too, the community was divided by the controversy over Reform, at least for a time. There, philosophical and liturgical innovation were introduced not through the transformation of the town's original congregation, B'nai Avraham, which had been founded in 1856, but rather through the establishment of a new congregation, B'nai Sholom, created in 1864. Both B'nai Avraham and B'nai Sholom supported their own rabbis and maintained their own synagogues for several years, and the two groups merged only in 1872, after fire had destroyed the home of B'nai Avraham's spiritual leader and damaged its synagogue.[7]

Arguments over Reform created a rift in the community of Zanesville, Ohio, as well. Although there is conflicting information about the exact course of congregational formation there, the most likely scenario is that Jews of Hungarian origin organized an assembly in Zanesville around 1868 that eventually took the name Keneseth Israel. This body was initially Orthodox, but it adopted Reform practices quite early, and so in 1874 some of its original members seceded and helped to establish a Hungarian Benevolent Association that, despite its name, functioned also as a congregation maintaining traditional practice. By the mid-1890s the Benevolent Association had adopted the name Beth Abraham and erected a synagogue of its own.

Despite the contentious process of innovation and the occasional establishment of alternative assemblies, toward the end of the nineteenth century most small-town congregations were firmly within the Reform camp, which was especially strong in the South and the Midwest. Even in the first decade of the twentieth century, as East European Jews were arriving in small towns and organizing their own synagogues, Reform congregations remained highly conspicuous throughout America's Jewish hinterland. Among the 490 communities that are the focus of our study, 143 were reported to have populations of at least 100 individuals in the very first years of the twentieth century, and data from 1907 indicate that in that year there were Reform congregations operating in at least half of these 143 communities. In fifty-four of the 143 settlements there was a temple formally affiliated with the UAHC, and in at least twenty other communities there was an unaffiliated synagogue that can be identified with Reform on the basis of its name or its practices. Examples include the Reform Congregation of Danville in Illinois and the Greensboro Hebrew Reformed Congregation in North Carolina.[8]

In some small communities, Reform temples continued to dominate local religious life well into the twentieth century, and where they did so it was generally by attracting as members the East European Jews who were arriving in small towns in the decades after 1881. The centennial history published by Congregation B'er Chayim of Cumberland, Maryland, in 1953, for instance, explains that the Bavarian, Bohemian, and Austrian Jews who made up the assembly's original membership had been drawn to Reform during the nineteenth century, and that when East Europeans began to arrive in Cumberland they were readily absorbed into B'er Chayim because "to them too the newer pattern of religious services and the new decorum had a greater appeal than the older forms." Similarly, according to one student of small-town Jewish life in the Ohio Valley, East Europeans arriving in Portsmouth, Ohio, were simply "folded into" the town's Reform congregation.[9]

This kind of uneventful absorption of East Europeans may have occurred to some degree in Cumberland and in Portsmouth, but if it did, it was unusual. In most small communities, by contrast, East Europeans were initially reluctant to affiliate with congregations that were unabashedly Reform. The sensibilities of these immigrants were offended by a religious philosophy that rejected the traditional concept of a binding Jewish law and that adopted Christian forms such as family pews and organ music. Even those East Europeans who were not personally observant were put off by Reform's rejection of the concept of Jewish peoplehood and of ethnic cultural norms that were rooted in an Orthodox consciousness. Indeed, despite the way their sentiments are described in the B'er Chayim centennial history, many East Europeans in Cumberland were reluctant to join that congregation, and they established their own Beth Jacob synagogue in 1913. Furthermore, arguments over the elements of Reform to be adopted at B'er Chayim split even that congregation for about three years in the 1920s, with a dissident group going its own way and identifying itself as Congregation Beth El. As B'er Chayim's own history admits, this was an "intense, almost feverish, period" during which "a schism developed within the Congregation which resulted in considerable bitterness and was not healed until some years later."[10]

Clearly, Reform congregations could not simply assume that East European Jews would affiliate when they arrived in town. If these congregations wanted to attract traditionalists, they had to make a concerted effort to do so. Thus, in Charlottesville, Virginia, the town's lone congregation, Beth Israel, determined to tread lightly where its fundamentally Reform practice was concerned in order to accommodate the East Europeans who began arriving in town during the 1890s. The synagogue occasionally allowed the traditionalists to conduct Hebrew-language Torah readings, for instance, and to organize separate High Holiday services in the temple's basement. Moreover, Beth Israel delayed joining the UAHC until 1927 in an apparent gesture of goodwill toward its more traditional members. In the words of the chroniclers of the congregation's history, over the years Beth Israel was faced with "divisions along the line of . . . country of birth, religious practice, social standing or economics," but "those fissures were negotiated" within a "remarkably flexible and tolerant community."[11]

In Vicksburg, Mississippi, Sol Kory, who was rabbi of that town's Reform congregation, Anshe Chesed, from 1903 until 1936, seems to have made the integration of East European families a high priority. Although Reform Jews at the time were hostile to the trappings and ceremonies of more traditional Jews, Kory allowed head coverings at Anshe Chesed for many years, and he occasionally got old-timers to attend traditional *minyanim* (prayer services with a quorum). Anshe Chesed also kept traditional burial shrouds on hand for families that wanted to make use of them. Stanley Brav, Kory's successor, wrote that "Rabbi Kory must have gone out of his way . . . to enarm in welcome every new Jewish family, as it arrived in the city; at the time making that family feel 'at home' in Anshe Chesed [as much] as humanly possible, and guaranteeing that whatever traditionalist needs they may personally feel, he would assist them to fulfill."[12]

In San Jose, California, too, the essentially Reform congregation Bickur Cholim made arrangements to satisfy the needs of Jews from a variety of backgrounds and thus to maintain its position as the only synagogue in town. When Rabbi Harvey Franklin arrived there in 1920, he reported finding "a very mixed group of Reform, Orthodox and Conservative," and he implemented a rather unusual order of service to accommodate his congregants. On Friday evenings, for instance, the president of the congregation would conducted a traditional prayer service first, and then the rabbi would conduct a second service using the *Union Prayer Book* of the Reform movement. The traditionalists would stay for this second service so they could hear the sermon the rabbi had prepared. Franklin eventually published a pamphlet detailing his "San Jose Plan," suggesting that "the great antagonism" he encountered between the Reform and the Orthodox groups at his temple made it necessary. Franklin described how "the wearing of hats at divine service" was made optional; how two days of certain holidays were observed, instead of the single day adopted in Reform Judaism; how separate "orthodox" and "modern" services were held on the High Holidays at hours that did not conflict; how a number of traditional prayers were inserted into the Reform service (these included *kol nidre* on the evening of Yom Kippur), and how traditionalists in the congregation had "willingly yielded" to a non-Jewish choir.[13]

Other Reform congregations came up with yet other creative methods of accommodating a diverse membership. Throughout the 1930s, East European Jews who preferred a traditional service were permitted to meet early on Saturday mornings at Texarkana's Mount Sinai synagogue, while members of the Reform congregation's core constituency cooperated by providing any extra worshipers the traditionalists might need to complete a quorum for prayer. In Laredo, Texas, when the predominately Reform B'nai Israel congregation erected a synagogue in 1938, it commissioned a double-decker building with two assembly halls so that it could accommodate both Reform and Orthodox services. The raked floor of the upper hall was appropriate to the decorum and theatricality of a Reform service, while the flat floor of the lower hall was more suited to the participatory style of an Orthodox *minyan*. Nonetheless, the bylaws of the Laredo congregation stipulated that whichever group started its Sabbath services first could determine the form of liturgy in the upper hall, while the other group went downstairs.[14]

A variety of factors motivated small-town Reform congregations to reach out to East European immigrants. Certainly there was some goodwill involved in these efforts, and there may also have been some doctrinal fervor, with advocates of Reform intent on bringing their understanding of Judaism to the newcomers. But established congregations in small towns must also have been motivated in part by the fear that their communities could not support more than one place of worship. Only by winning over new arrivals and forestalling the creation of competing congregations could they hope to perpetuate their existence. For their part, the East Europeans joined existing Reform temples not so much because of their attractiveness but rather because the newcomers realized that they lacked the numbers and the resources necessary to create the kind of traditionalist congregations they preferred. Indeed, in a few places East Europeans attempted to establish their own congregations despite the outreach efforts of Reform temples but gave up after only a few years. For example, in Vicksburg, where Anshe Chesed made such a concerted effort to attract East Europeans, the Orthodox congregation Ahavas Achim lasted only from 1900 until 1906. In Jackson, Michigan, too, a group of newly arrived East European Jews attempted to organize their own *minyan* sometime after World War I, but there, also, they soon gave up. Several of the traditionalists departed for Detroit, and the field was left open to the city's established Reform congregation, Beth Israel.[15]

The mid-nineteenth-century origins of most Reform temples that remained the only congregations in their towns has given those venerable assemblies and the communities they dominated great visibility and a sense of special significance. Nonetheless, because so many of America's small Jewish communities were established by East Europeans arriving in the 1880s and after, in the majority of small-town settlements that had only a single synagogue in the early twentieth century, that synagogue was established along

Orthodox lines and perpetuated an East European liturgical style. Indeed, in smaller cities and towns where Jewish residents were few in number or completely absent in the period before 1880, the clearest indication that a full-fledged Jewish community had come into being around the turn of the century was the establishment of an Orthodox prayer group. Thus, East European Jews founded Beth Abraham in Nashua, New Hampshire in 1896; B'nai Israel in Hampton, Virginia, in 1899; Beth Israel in Washington, Pennsylvania, in 1902; Keneseth Israel in Annapolis, Maryland, in 1906; Sons of Israel in Belmar, New Jersey, in 1907; Beth Jacob in Plymouth, Massachusetts, in 1909; B'nai Abraham in Aurora, Illinois, in 1910; Sons of Israel in Derby, Connecticut, in 1915; and scores of similar congregations in other small towns all across America.[16]

The Orthodox congregations established in America's smaller Jewish communities generally developed in the same way that small-town congregations had before the era of mass migration. First there was a period of informal worship activities, sometimes only for the High Holidays and often contemporaneous with the development of mutual aid and burial societies. This period was followed by the formal establishment of a congregation, frequently in connection with a decision to move into permanent quarters. Shortly thereafter came the acquisition or construction of a synagogue building. The histories of many individual communities founded by East Europeans provide illustrations of this common chain of events. In Leominster, Massachusetts, for example, the first known Jewish resident arrived in 1896, and the first religious services took place ten years later. A formal congregational body, calling itself Agudas Achim, was created in 1915. This assembly hired its first rabbi in 1923 and erected a synagogue building the following year. In South River, New Jersey, the local Jews began to meet for services in 1910, using a Torah scroll borrowed from a synagogue in Perth Amboy. Shortly thereafter they established the South River Hebrew Benevolent and Sick Association and purchased land for a cemetery. Then, in 1919, they adopted the name Anshe Emeth for their congregation and began raising money for a synagogue building, which they dedicated in 1920.[17]

In most small communities composed entirely or almost entirely of East European Jewish immigrants and their children, there was little need to even consider the beliefs and practices of Reform Judaism. Still, in essentially East European communities where there was an identifiable Reform minority of German-Jewish background, newly created Orthodox congregations often did make an effort to be inclusive. In much the same way that small-town temples often adopted a tolerant attitude where adherents of Reform were in the majority, traditionalist synagogues sometimes tried to accommodate nontraditionalists in their community as well. B'nai Israel, a congregation established in 1902 by the East European Jews of Muskegon, Michigan, provides a case in point. This congregation, initially called Beth Abraham, was led exclusively by Orthodox rabbis until 1945, but the assembly always thought of itself as "mixed" and attempted to be considerate of non-Orthodox members. As a former president of the congregation commented in 1973, the compromises adopted at B'nai Israel "worked beautifully" as he and the other members of the synagogue "learned tolerance among ourselves."[18]

An understanding of how difficult it would be to support rival congregations where both the local Jewish population and its resources were limited accounts for the inclination of small-town Jews from various backgrounds to cooperate and compromise and helps explain why in most of America's small Jewish communities, only a single congregation became entrenched, whether that body was essentially Reform or nominally Orthodox. To judge from the situation reported in 1927, when no more than 11 percent of America's triple-digit Jewish centers were without any organized congregations, fully 69 percent of these communities were home to only a single congregational body as the twentieth century entered its second quarter. As the 1927 figures suggest, however, cooperation did not always prevail among small-town Jews, and small-town synagogues were not always able to satisfy the needs of the entire local constituency. There were in fact a fair number of triple-digit communities in which at least two congregations coexisted, at least for a time. The information available from 1927 reveals that about 18 percent of America's triple-digit Jewish centers were served by two rival congregations in that year, and this figure does not take into account the possibility that some communities had alternative *minyanim* meeting on an informal basis. In just under 2 percent of America's triple-digit communities, as many as three formally organized congregations were reported in 1927.[19]

Understandably, in most cases in which two congregations were present in the same small community, one was Reform in its ideology and the other Orthodox. In a very few locales, both types of congregations were already in place even before the era of mass migration began, with turn-of-the-century immigrants from Russia and Poland reinforcing rather than establishing an Orthodox presence. In Springfield, Illinois, for instance, immigrants arriving in the late 1880s encountered the Young Men's Hebrew Congregation that had been formed by those who had objected to the adoption of Reform in the town's original congregation, B'rith Sholom. With the support of these newly arrived East Europeans, the Hebrew Congregation reconstituted itself in 1896 as B'nai Abraham and purchased a synagogue building. Struggling financially at first, B'nai Abraham was finally on a sound enough footing to hire a full-time rabbi in 1927. B'rith Sholom, in the meantime, continued to flourish as a Reform congregation. It had moved into a new synagogue building in 1917 and in 1919 reported that it was holding weekly services, operating a Sunday school with six teachers and fifty students, sponsoring a temple sisterhood, and supporting its own full-time rabbi.[20]

Usually, however, the existence of an Orthodox congregation alongside a Reform temple was not the legacy of a nineteenth-century communal rift, but rather the result of the arrival of East Europeans to a town where a Reform congregation was already functioning. Notwithstanding the fact that in many places Reform temples made an earnest effort to attract newcomers, East Europeans settling in small towns far preferred to establish synagogues of their own. Indeed, while there were instances of pioneer East Europeans attending Reform services until enough like-minded individuals arrived to allow them to go their own way, frequently such early arriving immigrants simply did without any local synagogue affiliation for a time. In at least some places, Reform temples were so alien to arriving East Europeans that these institutions were virtually invisible to them.

Examples of the founding of new Orthodox congregations in towns where Reform assemblies were already in place are legion. In the South, East Europeans established Brith Achim in Petersburg, Virginia, in 1896 to function independently of Rodef Sholem, which had been organized by German Jews as early as 1858. In Macon, Georgia, East Europeans chartered Sherah Israel in 1904 to satisfy their needs in a town where there had been a German-Jewish congregation since 1859. In Wilmington, North Carolina, where the Temple of Israel had been founded in 1867, the Orthodox Bnai Yisroel was established in 1906. In Pine Bluff, Arkansas, East European Jews created B'nai Israel in 1907 because they were not comfortable at the Reform Anshe Emeth, organized in 1866.[21]

Elsewhere in the country, Beth Israel came into being in Hamilton, Ohio, in 1911 as an Orthodox alternative to the Reform B'nai Israel, which had been founded in 1866. In Danville, Illinois, where German Jews had organized the Reform Beth El congregation in 1902 and built a substantial brick synagogue in 1914, Russian and Polish Jews incorporated the Anshe Knesses Israel congregation in 1916 after meeting for worship in private homes for several years. In Plattsburg, New York, Ahavas Sholom was organized in 1917 as an Orthodox alternative to Beth Israel, which had been founded in 1865 and had joined the UAHC in 1913. Out west, in Wichita, Kansas, where the early German Jews had founded a congregation they called Holy Emanu-El (renamed Congregation Emanu-El in 1928), the East Europeans arriving in town founded Ahavat Achim in 1906. In Boise, Idaho, Ahavas Israel was organized in 1912 alongside the local Reform congregation, Beth Israel, which had been founded in 1895.[22]

Although in the classic examples of small towns with both Reform and Orthodox congregations the founding of the Reform assemblies predated the arrival of appreciable numbers of East Europeans, this was not the only scenario that could account for the coexistence of Reform temples and Orthodox synagogues. In a few small towns, German-Jewish Reformers and East European traditionalists arrived at about the same time in sufficient numbers to allow for two subcommunities to develop simultaneously. In fact, under these circumstances it appears that the creation of a congregation by one element in the community may have helped galvanize support for a rival congregation. Thus in Bradford, Pennsylvania, both Beth Zion, supported primarily by Jews of German background and following Reform practice, and Beth Israel, an Orthodox body, were founded around 1880. In Michigan City, Indiana, East European immigrants created the Adath Israel congregation perhaps as early as 1892 and dedicated their first synagogue in 1907, when it had about thirty-five members. By then the city's Reform Jews had already begun meeting for High Holiday services in rented spaces, and around 1911, on the heels of the dedication of Adath Israel's building, they organized the Sinai Congregation under the leadership of Moses Moritz, whose family had been in Michigan City since the middle of the nineteenth century.[23]

By the 1920s there were even some small towns supporting both Reform and Orthodox congregations where the usual pattern by which this situation arose was completely reversed. On occasion, in towns where all or nearly all of the earliest Jewish settlers were East Europeans, it was the original congregation that maintained traditional practice, with dissidents, often more acculturated members of the original group, establishing a Reform temple somewhat later. In New Castle, Pennsylvania, for example, Tiferet Israel, founded in 1894, was the original assembly, and it continued to adhere to traditional practice; the Reform Temple Israel was founded only after World War I with encouragement from rabbis such as Samuel Goldenson of Rodef Shalom in Pittsburgh and Abba Hillel Silver of The Temple in Cleveland. Similarly, in Steubenville, Ohio, Bnai Israel, an Orthodox congregation, was created around 1890, but the Reform Temple Beth El was not established until 1922.[24]

The difficulty of fostering cooperation between those in a small community who advocated Reform and those who were at least nominally Orthodox is perhaps best illustrated by the failure of many of the attempts that were made to work out compromises that would avoid communal rifts. In Columbia, South Carolina, for instance, the Tree of Life Congregation that was organized in 1896 had intended to serve those with both Reform and Orthodox leanings. Initially it described itself as "a Liberal Orthodox Congregation," obviously trying to please all its constituencies. By the first decade of the twentieth century, however, control over the congregation's policies had become such a volatile issue that it led to contested elections, a lawsuit, and a power struggle within the community's Hebrew Benevolent Society. The final result was the creation in 1908 of a new Orthodox congregation in Columbia, Beth

Shalom. As the historians of Columbia Jewry explain, "the factional fighting left a residue of bitterness that lasted a lifetime for many involved . . . . Families split over the issue and former friends never spoke to each other again."[25]

Similarly, in Colorado Springs, Colorado, the Reform and traditionalist factions in town apparently were able to cooperate when they formed the Sons of Israel Association in 1902 and began planning for the erection of a synagogue. Within a few years, however, the two groups found it impossible to continue their joint effort. As the Jewish newspaper in Denver, sympathetic to the Reformers, put it, the liberal faction objected to the commitment of the Sons of Israel Association "to worship according to the obsolete and incomprehensible tenets of the now effete Jewish Orthodoxy of the Middle Ages." By 1910 both Reform and Orthodox groups had broken away from the Sons of Israel, constituting themselves as Temple Beth El and Congregation B'nai Abraham, respectively. Even in Laredo, Texas, where cooperation between Orthodox and Reform factions had allowed the community to build a two-story synagogue in 1938, the two camps had a falling out soon afterward, resulting in the creation of a new congregation, the Orthodox Agudas Achim, alongside the Reform B'nai Israel.[26]

The problems inherent in bringing Reformers and traditionalists together were reflected not only in the failure of joint ventures here and there, but also in the reluctance of established small-town congregations with differing ideologies to merge, even when practical considerations compelled them to consider doing so. The situation in Marion, Indiana, provides a case in point. There the Jews had apparently sustained two congregations during the first decade of the twentieth century, when the town's Jewish population was probably somewhere between 50 and 100. In 1924, however, leaders of the community gathered to discuss the formation of a congregation that would serve the needs of all the town's Jewish inhabitants. At that gathering, those who wanted the new body to affiliate with the Reform movement carried the day, and in response the Orthodox contingent withdrew. Into the late 1930s, the traditionalists continued to hold their own religious services in a second-floor hall in Marion's downtown business district. Similarly, in Bradford, Pennsylvania, a merger between the Reform Beth Zion and the Orthodox Beth Israel was first contemplated as early as 1923, when a group of local leaders produced a document titled "In Unity There Is Strength." But in Bradford, also, the traditionalists and the followers of Reform had so much trouble negotiating the terms of consolidation that a merger of the two congregations was not consummated until thirty-five years later, at a time when there was no longer any serious demand that traditional Judaism be maintained in the city.[27]

It is indeed quite striking how often the division between Reform and Orthodox factions persisted even in places with a population that was barely large enough to support one active congregation, let alone two. In the years following World War I, the Jews of Michigan City persisted in supporting their two assemblies, for example, even though the Reform Sinai Congregation had only nineteen members as of 1919, and the Orthodox Adath Israel had only twenty-eight. In the same period the Jews of Corsicana, Texas, supported both the Reform Beth El and the Orthodox Agudas Achim, even though the first of these congregations had only twenty-six members and the second only twenty-one. In Boise, Idaho, too, both a temple and a synagogue survived. The former, Beth Israel, had only twenty members in 1919, and the latter, Ahavas Israel, had only twelve.[28]

Struggling congregations that adhered to the principles of Reform seem to have been even more reluctant about merger than their traditionalist counterparts. They could not see their way to reverse their radical departures from Orthodoxy. Thus, in Zanesville the Reform congregation carried on a precarious existence apart from the local Orthodox body well into the twentieth century, even though it was reported to have no more than twelve members as early as 1907 and to be meeting for services only on alternate Sundays. In Appleton, Wisconsin, the Reform Temple Zion, the city's original congregation, was still functioning as late as midcentury, even though its last full-time rabbi had departed in 1921, its membership was down to no more than eighteen families by 1938, and for High Holiday services it had to borrow back its synagogue from the Gospel Tabernacle Church, to which it had sold the building.[29]

All this is not to say that in small towns with rival Reform and Orthodox congregations there were never any bridges built between the subcommunities that supported them. On the contrary, from early on, the two factions in many towns realized that even if they could not agree on congregational unity, they could and should not live in total isolation from each other. Thus, for example, in the early days of the Orthodox Brith Achim congregation in Petersburg, Virginia, the Reform Rodef Sholem would send over some of its members to help constitute a *minyan* when necessary. By the same token, when Reform-minded Jews living in Benton Harbor, Michigan, established Temple Beth-El in 1934, they met for their first two years in the school building of the Orthodox Ohava Sholom congregation. In Fresno, California, the Reform Temple Beth Israel, which was incorporated in 1919, shared its building with the traditionalist Beth Jacob congregation. Beth Jacob had been founded soon after Beth Israel's establishment, but met for services only on the High Holidays or when a member of the group wanted to commemorate the anniversary of a death by reciting the *kaddish*. Moreover, during World War II, when the presence of many soldiers stationed in the area necessitated both liberal and traditional services each Saturday, these were held simultaneously in different parts of the same building. Only after the war did Beth Jacob hire its own rabbi and embark on its own building campaign.[30]

Another sign of cooperation was the willingness of well-established Reform congregations to open the doors of their Sunday schools to the children of rival Orthodox groups that lacked the resources to organize their own education programs. This was the case in Bloomington, Illinois, after the turn of the century, for example, where the Moses Montefiore congregation was a firmly rooted institution, but where East European immigrants were meeting on their own only for the High Holidays and engaging in an ultimately unsuccessful struggle to establish their own synagogue. This was also the case in Springfield, Missouri, during the 1930s and in Williamsport, Pennsylvania, where the Reform temple was ordinarily served by a rabbi while the Orthodox congregation often was not. In Columbia, South Carolina, where the Tree of Life Congregation adopted Reform practice after its Orthodox faction broke away, the children of the Orthodox families in town nonetheless continued to attend the Tree of Life Sunday School. Reform Sunday schools were so welcoming, no doubt, both because they felt they were providing a needed service for the young and because they hoped to familiarize the children of the Orthodox with Reform practice and perhaps even entice their families to affiliate.[31]

Indeed, toward midcentury there was mounting evidence that local Jewish leaders were coming to recognize that the separate congregations of persistently small communities could not afford to remain distinct from each other indefinitely. The trend toward cooperation was only encouraged by the increasing acculturation of small-town Jews from East European backgrounds. In Hamilton, Ohio, for instance, the two synagogue youth groups functioning in town had members from both local congregations. In 1939 perhaps fifteen or sixteen of the twenty members of the Hamilton chapter of the Reform movement's National Federation of Temple Youth were actually members of the town's Orthodox congregation. Even in Springfield, Illinois, where both the local Reform and Orthodox congregations were on a solid foundation, Rabbi Herman Snyder of Temple B'rith Sholom led a move to bridge the gap between his congregants and members of B'nai Abraham by establishing a Jewish Center for the entire community, located in a house adjacent to his synagogue. Opened in 1930, this center had its own governing board and sponsored a wide range of communal activities, creating a situation in which "young people in both congregations met for the first time."[32]

Although a lack of agreement between Reform Jews and those who favored Orthodox rituals was the primary reason that separate congregations sometimes existed in the same small community, this was not the only possible explanation. The presence of multiple congregations could also be based upon divisions within the ranks of local traditionalists. While Reform Jews in small towns always seemed to be able to gather under one roof, those with Orthodox leanings had several possible motives for organizing disparate assemblies. For one thing, in small towns, just as in larger cities, traditionalists who had migrated from different parts of Europe and who brought with them different liturgical traditions often wanted to perpetuate their own customs. Thus, in Zanesville, for instance, when Jewish immigrants of Polish background arrived in the early 1880s to discover that the existing Orthodox congregation was dominated by Hungarians, they established their own assembly, Rodef Shalom, which functioned until about 1905. In Farrell, Pennsylvania, too, it was Hungarian settlers who in 1902 obtained a charter for the town's first synagogue, the Orthodox Ahavas Achim, but it was Russian and Rumanian settlers who established Farrell's second Orthodox congregation, B'nai Zion, in 1916. The existence of separate Orthodox congregations in Manchester, New Hampshire, was also based in part on divergent places of origin. There, Congregation Adath Yeshurun was founded around 1889 by immigrants from Lithuania, while the breakaway congregation Anshe Sephard, established ten years later, was dominated by immigrants from Ukraine. Anshe Sephard even established its own cemetery adjacent to that of Adath Yeshurun and insisted that the two burial grounds be divided by a fence, a "visible sign of dissension" that was removed only in the late 1920s.[33]

Yet another factor that could lead to the creation of multiple Orthodox congregations in the same small community was the simple matter of local geography. Where there were Jews living in different parts of the same town, different synagogues sometimes developed as a matter of convenience, related to the continued adherence of some individuals to the prohibition against driving on the Sabbath. In the years before World War II, the primary synagogue in North Adams, Massachusetts, for example, was Beth Israel, but a splinter group established a second congregation, called Chai Odom, so that they could hold services nearer their homes in the "swamp" area of town. Similarly, in Aliquippa, Pennsylvania, the Jews living in the older part of the city along the Ohio River supported one Orthodox assembly, while those living on higher ground away from the waterfront supported another. In Newport, Kentucky, in the 1920s the meeting place of the United Hebrew Congregation was known as the "Big Shul," employing the Yiddish term for a synagogue generally favored by East Europeans, and it was considered an institution for the "more affluent." At the same time, at least one other small synagogue was located in the West End, a less well-to-do section of Newport. In Benton Harbor, Michigan, the original Children of Israel congregation, incorporated in 1895, built its first synagogue on Eighth Street in 1900 and its second on Lake Avenue in 1923, both locations near the center of the city. Meanwhile, in 1911 its sister Orthodox congregation, Ohava Sholom, erected a house of worship on the eastern edge of town, where it could better serve the needs of the Jewish farmers and resort owners in the area.[34]

Even though congregational divisions based on local geography may have arisen out of practical considerations alone, the cleavages they created some-times developed a life of their own. In North Adams, for instance, when mem-bers of Chai Odom purchased tickets to attend High Holiday services at Beth Israel, which had a larger facility, there was "much vocal objection" to those viewed as "free-riders" who did not support the town's primary synagogue year round. Similarly, in Benton Harbor, while some traditionalists main-tained an affiliation with both of the Orthodox congregations in town, there were others who would not even speak to members of the shul to which they did not belong. One longtime resident of Benton Harbor considered the ob-vious antagonism between the two local Orthodox factions an embarrassment before his non-Jewish neighbors, "a shame for the goyim."[35]

One other matter that created fault lines within many nominally Ortho-dox communities was the proposed alteration of traditional religious prac-tices. As in the nineteenth century, when a great many small-town syna-gogues founded by German Jews wrestled with the introduction of Reform, in the twentieth century, too, traditionalist congregations found themselves torn over questions of theological leniency and liberalization. Again, the stakes were high in communities where it made little practical sense to maintain more than one congregation. In some places, internal disputes within tradi-tionalist synagogues were resolved with compromises. In Port Huron, Michi-gan, for instance, differences surfaced within the town's sole congregation, Mount Sinai, as it prepared to construct a new synagogue building in the early 1920s. Those committed to strict Orthodox practice wanted to retain gender-segregated seating, while a more liberal faction wanted to initiate family seat-ing and organ music. By the time the new Mount Sinai building was dedicated in 1924, however, a settlement had been reached: women were seated to-gether with men, but no organ was installed. In Newburyport, Massachusetts, also, a controversy over seating developed in 1933 when the congregation left its run-down building in a lower-class neighborhood and moved into a new, worthier building in a better part of town. At the time, many young families that had dropped their membership in the Newburyport congregation reaffili-ated, but many of the women in these families demanded to sit with their husbands. Here, too, the conflict over this matter was resolved with a compro-mise. Three sections of seats were designated in the community's new syn-agogue, one reserved for men, one reserved for women, and one with family seating.[36]

Still, disagreements within traditionalist congregations did sometimes be-come too difficult to manage, and intractable disputes provided yet another reason for the appearance of multiple congregations in the same small town. In Sharon, Pennsylvania, the House of Israel, founded in 1888, experienced frequent arguments over the direction the congregation should take. As the congregational history relates, there were "constant clashes" between individuals "with little or no decorum in the Services or in the business meetings." The records of these meetings were "dotted with disturbances created by different members" and with indications that disorderly participants were subject to fines. In this atmosphere, desertions on both the left and the right occurred during the early decades of the twentieth century. For a while an extreme Orthodox group broke away and established a separate synagogue it called Shaarah Torah, while those members of the House of Israel who were attracted to Reform, primarily congregants of German background, held services in private homes and established their own Sunday school. [37]

Similarly, in Appleton, Wisconsin, the year 1932 saw the creation of Beth Israel, organized by former members of the Moses Montefiore congregation who "disputed" the Orthodoxy of that body and charged that "it was leaning to the reformed." In Iron Mountain, Michigan, on the other hand, it was a more liberal faction that broke away from the town's established Orthodox prayer group, attempting in the process to gain control of that assembly's Torah scroll. Initially it was the dissidents who won the struggle over the scroll (it helped that they had a sheriff's deputy among their members), although eventually the two groups in Iron Mountain were able to reconcile and reintegrate. In Ashland, Kentucky, the rift between the two factions that developed within Congregation Agudath Achim, established by East European immigrants in the 1890s, was longer lasting. There the majority introduced Reform practices during the era of World War I and took the congregation into the UAHC in the early 1920s. In the meantime the Orthodox minority of Agudath Achim formed their own congregation and went their own way, continuing to proclaim that the reformers "stole our name and our Torahs."[38]

Although in many cases it is possible to trace divisions within small-town Orthodox communities to substantive matters such as liturgical distinctions, considerations of topography, or fundamental philosophical arguments, in other cases rifts developed because of rather obscure local squabbles. In Davenport, Iowa, for example, a disagreement over the performance of the community's *shochet* led a faction of the local Orthodox Congregation, B'nai Emes, to break away and create Anshe Sholom, a body that survived for about three years. In Torrington, Connecticut, where the Sons of Jacob had been formally organized in 1916, it seems to have been a quarrel involving the location of the congregation's synagogue that led to a rupture. In 1918 Sons of Jacob moved from the private dwelling it had been using as a place of worship into a former church building, and in 1929 it purchased yet another property in preparation for yet another move. At the meeting held to ratify the purchase of the new property, however, a major dispute erupted, and the congregation split in two. One group, still calling itself Sons of Jacob, moved to the new property, while the other, calling itself Beth El, remained in the old Sons of Jacob building. Although both Torrington shuls remained Orthodox in practice, and although

Harry Radunsky, who had led the Sons of Jacob since 1916, found himself officiating at Beth El as well, both Sons of Jacob and Beth El survived until 1945, when the older of these congregations finally dissolved.[39]

Sometimes even simple personality conflicts could split a community. In Bradford, Pennsylvania, a feud between the Nichols family and other members of the local Orthodox congregation led to the creation of a dissident assembly, complete with its own cemetery, at some point after World War I. In Sheboygan, Wisconsin, whose Jewish population peaked at just over 1,000 in the 1920s, it was also an individual family that instigated the formation of a dissident congregation. There, when the Holmans became upset with both of the Orthodox shuls that already existed in Sheboygan, they founded Ohel Moshe, yet a third congregation.[40]

Beyond all this, there is no shortage of writings on local Jewish history that recount small-town congregational ruptures without any hint as to their actual cause. It is not clear, for example, why the Jews of Plymouth, Massachusetts, divided into two separate *minyanim* at the beginning of the twentieth century, overcoming their differences to form Congregation Beth Jacob only in 1910, when they realized that they would have to unite in order to afford the cost of constructing a synagogue. Nor is it clear why a group of members broke away from Agudas Achim, the original congregation in Red Bank, New Jersey, soon after that assembly was organized in 1908. Whatever the reason, their objection to Agudas Achim was serious enough to keep the rift in Red Bank from being healed until 1922, when the two groups reunited under the name Congregation B'nai Israel.[41]

Other communal divisions and subdivisions are shrouded in even greater mystery, their existence sometimes suggested by no more than tantalizing hints in the often fragmentary records that survive to tell the story of America's various small-town Jewish settlements. For example, the 1907 *American Jewish Year Book* indicates the existence in Vineland, New Jersey, of the twelve-member Ahavas Achim congregation, founded in 1905, but it also lists a second congregation claiming the name Ahavas Achim, described as having twenty-five members and "dissenting from [the] above." How this situation arose is unexplained. Similarly, the *Year Book* for 1919 reveals that in Grand Forks, North Dakota, where the Children of Israel had been established in 1891 and where a second congregation, calling itself Talmud Torah, had taken root by 1907, yet a third congregation was organized in 1912, this one with the provocative name Independent Children of Israel. The 1919 *Year Book* also lists three different synagogues operating in Auburn, Maine, at a time when the town was home to only about 300 East European Jews. These were Beth Abraham, Beth Jacob, and Tiferes Israel Anshe Sfard, itself apparently the result of a merger between two preexisting bodies. The origins of Beth Abraham are well documented; the other congregations listed as Auburn institutions are otherwise unknown. Although it is possible that shadowy references such as these in the *American Jewish Year Book* are the result of errors, it is also possible that at least some of them are true indications of communal division.[42]

In the end, then, the history of congregational organization in the small Jewish communities of the United States is one of substantial complexity. Because small communities lacked the critical mass necessary to easily sustain multiple congregations, Jews living in small towns often overcame their ideological and liturgical divisions so that they would be able to sustain some kind of local congregational life. Small-town temples and synagogues in the late nineteenth and early twentieth centuries were far more likely than their counterparts in larger cities to function on the basis of negotiation and compromise. At the same time, however, it is striking how frequently small communities were split into subcommunities along congregational lines, despite the difficulties communal division presented. Just as in big cities, there was enough animosity in small towns between Reform Jews, generally of Central European background, and traditionalist Jews, mainly East Europeans, to keep the two groups from presupposing that they could cooperate in congregational organization. Similarly, an estrangement between *landsleit* from different parts of Europe or even between feuding factions within a congregation sometimes split small-town Jewish populations, at least temporarily, in ways that would not have been expected in settlements of no more than a few hundred people. In other words, the history of small communities suggests that a small-town locale could be such a powerful environmental factor that it fostered high levels of cooperation and accommodation. However, the story of these communities also indicates that divisions within Jewish society were at times so entrenched that they persisted even in the face of conditions that should have promoted their moderation.

How likely a community was to support multiple congregations in the decades before World War II does seem to have been influenced to some extent by certain demographic factors. For example, even among settlements whose Jewish populations were only in triple digits, those that supported two or more congregations in 1927 tended to be somewhat larger than those that were home to only one. The difference was about 200 people on average. So, too, communities whose history stretched back to the middle decades of the nineteenth century seem to have had a greater chance of maintaining multiple congregations because longevity meant that early arriving German Jews had more of an opportunity to establish themselves and to found synagogues before East Europeans began to put down roots. Of the ninety triple-digit Jewish communities that were reported to have two congregations in 1927, 27 percent already had populations of at least 100 individuals as early as the

1870s. By contrast, of the 392 triple-digit communities that had only a single congregation in 1927, only 7 percent had populations of 100 or more on the eve of mass migration.

Neither of these factors, however, was decisive in determining patterns of congregational organization. Towns such as Galesburg, Illinois; Ann Arbor, Michigan; El Dorado, Arkansas; Raleigh, North Carolina; and Alexandria, Virginia, supported two congregations in 1927, even though none of these places had a reported Jewish population of over 150. At the same time, only a single congregation served towns such as Burlington, Vermont; Port Chester, New York; Warren, Ohio; Cheyenne, Wyoming; and Baton Rouge, Louisiana, even though each of these places had a Jewish population of between 700 and 1,000. So, too, of all the triple-digit communities of 1927 that were already home to at least 100 Jews in the late 1870s, the number that had two congregations a decade after World War I was about equal to the number that had only one. Ultimately, all of this points to how crucial the human element was in determining cohesiveness or division within a community.

In the same way that congregations were the fundamental institutions of America's small Jewish communities, synagogue buildings were the prime physical manifestations of a Jewish presence in small towns all over America. These structures provided both tangible evidence of a firmly established Jewish community and the physical facilities that local Jews needed in order to conduct their activities. Every small-town Jewish congregation aspired to acquire a home of its own, and, as the early development of small-town congregations suggests, these institutions generally followed similar paths in their search for the facilities they needed. Once within the walls of their synagogues, small-town congregations toiled to keep up their buildings and to consolidate the role of these structures as the centers of local Jewish life. Ultimately, as the middle of the twentieth century neared, those congregations established as Orthodox assemblies also witnessed the liberalization of their practice, a development that often coincided with the ascendancy of a younger leadership and sometimes involved a merger with local Reform temples.

Of course, in their very earliest years, small communities generally had very modest requirements for meeting facilities. When the Jews of these communities first gathered informally for prayers, they usually did so in the homes of communal leaders, or perhaps at their stores. The local history of Kalamazoo, Michigan, reports that before 1875 Jewish services were held in a synagogue space fitted out in the home of a Mr. Rosenberg, for instance; and in Nashua, New Hampshire, the first services were held in 1892 in the home of Aaron Borofsky. In Amsterdam, New York, services were held in 1873 on the third floor of a building owned by Julius Wasserman, and they were later moved to a building owned by Moses Behr. Having a Torah scroll was essential for the proper conduct of Sabbath and holiday services, and somehow, there always seemed to be at least one person in every small community who had

*Photo previous page: The 1901 Temple of Israel building in Amsterdam, New York, pictured ca. 1948. This Reform temple stood in a town that had an Orthodox congregation as well. Courtesy of the Jacob Rader Marcus Center of the American Jewish Archives.*

brought a Torah with him or was willing to purchase one. In Bloomington, Illinois, members of the Livingston clan who arrived in the 1880s were the ones who possessed a Torah scroll, and in late nineteenth-century Wichita, two entrepreneurs, Leopold Hays and Sam Goldstein, each owned a Torah. In Engelwood, New Jersey, eight men gathered in 1895 to organize services for the upcoming High Holidays, and each contributed ten dollars so that two of their number could go to New York City to buy a Torah. When they discovered in New York that the minimum cost of a scroll was $130 they made partial payment and decided that if they could not raise the additional fifty dollars they needed within ninety days, they would hide their newly acquired treasure in order to keep it from being repossessed.[1]

As they gained a sense of greater permanence, fledgling small-town congregations tended to graduate from private homes and stores to rented halls or other semipermanent meeting spaces, especially for the High Holidays. Often these were in commercial buildings downtown or in the halls of fraternal organizations. In Petersburg, Virginia, for example, Rodef Sholem met from 1867 until 1876 on the lower floor of the local Masonic Hall, which had been "consecrated" by the congregation's minister, while in Macon, Georgia, Beth Israel was meeting in a rented room over Horn's Confectionery. In Newburyport, Massachusetts, around the turn of the century, congregation Ahavas Achim met at the Old Music Hall or in second-floor rooms on Market Square, where worshipers sometimes found themselves next door to rehearsals of the Cadet Band. "As they would practice the National Anthem," a local writer recalled, "the men would try to say the Shemah [a fundamental part of the Jewish liturgy]."[2]

Without question, there were many headaches associated with renting space from others, and this fact only accelerated the desire of small-town congregations to find adequate facilities of their own. In Manchester, New Hampshire, Adath Yeshurun had bought a cottage and remodeled it as a synagogue in 1902, but for the High Holidays the congregation still had to rent the lodge hall of the Knights of Pythias or of the Odd Fellows. The members of the Manchester congregation were motivated to erect a genuine synagogue in 1910, however, when they were abruptly forced to vacate the hall they had reserved for evening services on Yom Kippur, the holiest day of the year, in order to accommodate a previously scheduled lodge meeting. A similar story is told about the Ohavay Zion congregation in Lexington, Kentucky, whose founders decided to organize formally and to secure a permanent place of worship on the very night in 1911 that they were put out on the sidewalk before finishing their service on the eve of Yom Kippur. Here, too, the Odd Fellows from whom they had rented space were not willing to wait for the Yom Kippur liturgy to conclude before they convened for their regular meeting. It seems that the same scenario was played out in other places as well. No wonder that when a member of the Jewish community of Auburn, New York, looked back to the time when his congregation acquired its first permanent home in 1912, he remembered the joy of having a place "to use as we pleased, and when we pleased." He recalled with satisfaction the realization that his congregation would no longer "be pushed about by some lodge or Labor organization waiting at the door."[3]

Besides solving the practical problem of where to hold services, acquiring a synagogue was important because it symbolized the permanence of a congregation and helped create a sense that Jews were a part of local town life, in the same way as citizens of other faiths. In the open atmosphere of America's secondary urban centers, where the affairs of local institutions were likely to be widely known, every self-respecting religious body wanted to have appropriate quarters. Especially because they were such a tiny minority in their small-town environments, congregants must have had a great feeling of satisfaction when they saw their synagogues listed with other houses of worship in local city directories, or when they saw them pictured alongside area churches in the promotional books and brochures that proliferated in late nineteenth- and early twentieth-century America in order to boost the reputations of various cities and towns. Because small-town Jews tended to cluster in areas convenient to the central shopping districts where most had their businesses, synagogues were generally situated near the commercial centers of their towns, and in this way the very location of these structures reinforced the impression that Jews were a pivotal group within the larger community. That acquiring a building, or preparing to do so, often provided the occasion for a congregation to seek a charter from the state only heightened the sense of permanence and belonging with which synagogue buildings were associated. The feelings of many small-town Jews were summed up by Marjorie Abrams and Meyer Cohen of Green Bay, Wisconsin, around 1951, as they recalled the synagogue their community had dedicated in 1904 and observed that "there is no way to accurately describe the bond between the building and its builders except [to say] that they loved it—it was an object of actual affection."[4]

As synagogues went up in small towns all over the United States in the classic era of small-town Jewish life, they tended to follow general trends in American synagogue design. Where congregations lacked the resources to put up elaborate buildings, their synagogues were simple and functional, often consisting of little more than a sanctuary on the main floor and a basement social hall, frequently referred to as a vestry in Reform circles. However, where resources allowed, small-town synagogue buildings could be quite grand. Occasionally congregations built houses of worship that were designed to reflect their identification with the local cultural milieu. One commentator has suggested that in the mining town of Hancock, Michigan, the copper dome that crowned the 1912 Congregation of Israel synagogue (commonly called Temple Jacob) was "a visible symbol of the desire of the local Jews to be part of the Copper Country." So, too, congregations sometimes erected buildings far larger than they needed, suggesting both their optimism and their desire to make a statement about their place in the local religious culture. The brick and granite synagogue erected by Petersburg's Rodef Sholem in 1876 had a seating capacity of 400, even though its actual members at the time represented no more than thirty households. Similarly, in 1891 the Jews of Helena, Montana, dedicated a 300-seat temple for Congregation Emanu-El with a sanctuary designed so that it could be expanded to seat 500; this, even though Helena's Jewish population was to peak at only about 150 individuals in the early years of the twentieth century and to fall below triple digits by the 1920s.[5]

Congregations with adequate means could also afford to take into account the latest stylistic developments in synagogue architecture. Architects and builders throughout the American hinterland seem to have been aware of the dominant conventions in synagogue design and often erected houses of worship that were in keeping with evolving synagogue styles. In the latter decades of the nineteenth century, for example, synagogues of an Oriental character came into vogue. These so-called Moorish buildings, often with horseshoe arches, minarets, and bulbous or elongated domes, were erected first in Central Europe, where they came into fashion because they recalled the Near Eastern origins of Judaism; and they soon began to appear in America as well, where the predominantly Reform congregations that commissioned them saw in these structures a certain expression of self-confidence. An apprehensive minority would not have been willing to build such conspicuous and exotic houses of worship. Important U.S. examples of Moorish synagogues were erected in prominent Jewish centers such as New York, Cincinnati, and San Francisco, but such buildings appeared in small towns as well. B'nai Sholom in Quincy, Illinois, dedicated a brick and stone Moorish temple seating 651 in 1870, and in Bloomington, Illinois, a Moorish building was erected in 1889 by the Moses Montefiore congregation, named in honor of that renowned Anglo-Jewish leader at the request of a substantial donor to the building fund. Temple Israel of Paducah, Kentucky, built a Moorish synagogue in 1893, and Congregation Beth El in Corsicana, Texas, dedicated a temple in the same style in 1900.[6]

While some American Jewish congregations were building elaborate Moorish houses of worship, others, though perhaps no less confident of their place in the local environment, were choosing to build synagogues that more nearly resembled the churches of their Christian neighbors. Indeed, although few synagogues were built in a pure revival style of any sort and no one set of conventions ever held a monopoly on synagogue design, Romanesque motifs of one kind or another were probably the most commonly employed for synagogue buildings both in the second half of the nineteenth century and in the early decades of the twentieth, both in larger cities and in small towns. Ahavath Achim in Lafayette, Indiana, dedicated a Romanesque temple in 1867, and in Warren, Ohio, Beth Israel built a Romanesque house of worship in 1918. Other Romanesque synagogues were constructed by B'nai Israel in Plymouth, Pennsylvania, in 1924 and by Children of Israel in Benton Harbor, Michigan, in 1925. The Romanesque synagogue erected by Adath Israel in Middletown, Connecticut, in 1929 exhibited touches of Art Deco, and the Romanesque building put up by Shaarey Zedek in Lansing, Michigan, in 1932 apparently borrowed its form from the same prestigious Detroit synagogue that had given the Lansing congregation the idea for its name.[7]

Gothic architecture, with its characteristic pointed arches, was too much associated with the medieval Catholic Church to become tremendously popular with Jewish congregations, but some Jewish groups that wished to have their houses of worship fit seamlessly with the local ecclesiastical building stock used elements of this style, nonetheless. The first temple constructed in Vicksburg, Mississippi, dedicated in 1870, was essentially Gothic in style, and a local newspaper at the time noted that its interior was arranged "something similarly to the Presbyterian church on Walnut Street." So, too, the main features of the Beth Israel building in Charlottesville, Virginia, designed by the local architect George Spooner in 1882, were its Gothic windows. Gothic windows also dominated the simple synagogue built in Stevens Point, Wisconsin, in 1905.[8]

By the early part of the twentieth century, various Neoclassical architectural styles were becoming fashionable among the designers of churches and public buildings, and this mode was adopted by some leading synagogue architects as well. Once again, a trend that influenced the look of Jewish houses of worship in major cities was also reflected in small towns. In Macon, Georgia, Beth Israel erected a Neoclassical temple in 1902, and in Greenville, Mississippi, the United Hebrew Congregation built one in 1906. B'Nai Israel in Monroe, Louisiana, dedicated its Neoclassical building in 1915, and B'rith Sholom in Springfield, Illinois, dedicated its own in 1917.[9]

Of course, the synagogues commissioned by various small-town congregations reflected the liturgical practices of the assemblies they were to serve. Reform congregations built temples with family pews and with a *bimah*, a pulpit, designed so that those leading the service could face the congregation. They also adopted layouts that would accommodate an organ and a choir. Although building materials and specifications varied widely from place to place, the description Edna Ferber has left of the temple she attended in Appleton, Wisconsin, around the turn of the twentieth century would probably have sounded familiar to members of many other small-town Reform congregations as well: "The temple was a neat and dignified building in a good residence section of the town. It was a frame building, double-porched, with stained-glass windows, a charmingly proportioned pulpit completed by the ark and its twin seven-branched candlesticks. The choir loft was at the back. . . . [The rabbi appeared] lost in the embrace of the stately oak and crimson-velvet chair on which he sat enthroned as the choir held forth in the hymns."[10]

On the other hand, although this could later stir controversy, East European immigrant congregations built their shuls to conform to the norms of Orthodox custom. These buildings were designed for gender-segregated seating, with women often relegated to a balcony, and with a *bimah* placed either in the center of the sanctuary or at its front, but always configured so that those who led services could face toward the ark containing the Torah scrolls, rather than toward the congregation. The description of the synagogue that Congregation Adath Yeshurun dedicated on Central Street in Manchester, New Hampshire, in 1911 echoes the way scores of other small-town synagogues might have been described as well: "In the male preserve on the main floor, pews in a central section and two side sections under the balcony all faced . . . toward the *bimah*. . . . Immediately adjacent to the *bimah* on either side the pews were faced toward it. The women and young girls sat upstairs in the balcony which surrounded the hall on three sides. The balcony had three rows of seats along the sides facing into the sanctuary and eight or nine rows in the rear."[11]

Despite their ardent desire to erect houses of worship, some congregations in triple-digit Jewish communities had to wait a long time before they could afford their own buildings. As in many other matters, the limited size of these congregations was often the deciding factor. It took Temple Israel in Springfield, Missouri, some thirty-seven years of meeting in rented spaces before it was able to construct its own synagogue in 1930. Indeed, some small-town congregations never were able to occupy purpose-built synagogues. Still, nearly every congregation serving a small community was able to acquire a structure that it could call its own temple or shul at some point in its history. Even those assemblies that could not erect new buildings were usually able to purchase previously existing structures and to convert them for use as synagogues. Most often they bought vacant churches. In 1883 in Wabash, Indiana, for instance, the Rodef Sholem congregation, after having met in private homes for over a decade, purchased a vacant church that had originally been the home of a Christian sect called the New Lights. In 1902, B'Nai Israel in Oshkosh, Wisconsin, bought the school building of the Peace Lutheran Church and moved the frame structure several blocks to a corner lot that the congregation had purchased a short time earlier. At about the same time the Sons of Israel in Colorado Springs moved into a former church of the United Brethren, and in 1912 the Temple of Israel in Portsmouth, New Hampshire, purchased and refurbished a former Methodist Church. The members of Ohavay Zion in Lexington, Kentucky, who had found themselves standing on the sidewalk in front of the Odd Fellows hall on Yom Kipper eve in 1911, finally acquired a vacant Presbyterian church and moved into that converted building in 1914. Ahavas Achim in Newburyport, whose members had braved a band next door when they met in rented space, purchased a private home for use as a synagogue in 1907, and in 1933 moved into the former Washington Street Methodist Church, built in 1865.[12]

Besides former church properties, other kinds of buildings as well were converted for use by small-town Jewish congregations. In Bakersfield, California, the members of the B'nai Jacob Congregation met in the Woodmen of the World Hall from 1910 to 1914, at a facility called Taylor's Hall from 1914 to 1916, and in the Knights of Pythias Hall from 1918 to 1920. Finally they were able to buy the building of the Bakersfield Women's Club and turn it into their own place of worship. In Santa Barbara, California, Congregation B'nai Brith made a down payment on a former grocery store in 1930, and the congregants themselves spent two years renovating the space for use as a synagogue. At the other end of the country, in Frederick, Maryland, the synagogue dedicated by the Beth Sholom Congregation in 1923 was the town's former Elks Club. In North Adams, Massachusetts, the Beth Israel congregation was housed in a former theater during the interwar period, and the shul was commonly referred to as "the Bijou."[13]

Some converted buildings continued to serve their congregations throughout the period before World War II, but from time to time converted buildings did give way to purpose-built synagogues. In Lexington, Kentucky, while the Orthodox Jews of Ohavay Zion were working to find their own place of worship, the Reform Jews of the Adath Israel congregation were meeting in a former German Lutheran Church that they had purchased in 1905. In 1926, however, Adath Israel was able to move into its own structure, designed by a professor at the University of Kentucky who was a member of the congregation. In Auburn, Maine, Beth Abraham acquired a former schoolhouse soon after the congregation incorporated in 1902, and its second building was originally the home of the Union Musical Society. After two disastrous fires in this second facility, however, Beth Abraham finally constructed a purpose-built synagogue in 1934.[14]

Throughout the late nineteenth and early twentieth centuries, the acquisition and upkeep of synagogue buildings was the greatest financial burden faced by small-town congregations of all stripes. In order to acquire their buildings in the first place, congregations turned primarily to their own members to make whatever financial commitments they could. Some congregations were fortunate enough to get help from major donors. In Frederick, Maryland, Leo Weinberg and his wife bought the local Elks Club building and donated it to the Jewish community in memory of Weinberg's parents. In

Warren, Ohio, Jacob Knofsky and his wife paid for the foundation of the town's new synagogue and provided an additional $2,500 for construction of the building itself. In Lexington, Kentucky, it was a $25,000 donation from Leo Marks in memory of his father that enabled Adath Israel to construct its temple in 1926. The catalyst for building a synagogue in Rome, Georgia, in 1938 was a $6,000 bequest from the brothers Abe and Harrison Abramson.[15]

Still, because financing a building was often a struggle, congregations frequently turned to sources beyond their own small communities for the monetary support they needed. Some solicited their Christian neighbors. This was true when Bnai Israel built is first temple in Kalamazoo around 1875, for example. Later, when the Orthodox Jews of Kalamazoo's Congregation of Moses needed help with their building fund, they turned to their non-Jewish neighbors as well. In North Carolina, Christian donations helped build synagogues in Wilmington, Raleigh, and Durham, among other places. In Plymouth, Pennsylvania, local lore has it that it was actually a Catholic priest who provided the impetus for the erection of a synagogue when he urged the Jewish merchants of the town to build a sanctuary to house their "beautiful religion" and contributed $100 to get the ball rolling.[16]

Small-town congregations with building campaigns also looked for help from beyond their own cities. When the Moses Montefiore congregation of Bloomington, Illinois, was raising funds for its first synagogue in the 1880s, it got a part of the $15,000 it needed from out-of-town manufacturers and wholesalers who did business with Bloomington's Jewish merchants. When the Jews of Anniston, Alabama, were raising funds for the construction of their temple in 1892, they wrote to Jewish congregations all over the country, soliciting a donation of a dollar from each. They got responses from Charleston, Chicago, and Spokane, among other places. When Tree of Life in Columbia, South Carolina, was seeking to erect its first building at the turn of the twentieth century, one member of the congregation was dispatched to New York to solicit funds from his grandson's synagogue there, and another was sent on a similar trip to secure backing from prominent New York Jewish families such as the Schiffs and the Warburgs. Funds for the Columbia synagogue were solicited through a national advertisement in the *American Israelite* as well. Similarly, when the Jews of Virginia, Minnesota, sought to erect a house of worship in 1909, they looked for financial help in larger cities where they had connections. Clearly, the same kind of networking that helped small communities cope with their limitations of size when it came to matters such as negotiating business deals and finding mates for their children, also provided some assistance when it came to synagogue construction.[17]

To meet their ongoing monetary needs, congregations collected dues, held fundraising events, and sometimes sold synagogue honors. No issue was discussed at synagogue board meetings more often than finances: how much members were to pay, who would be threatened with expulsion for being in arrears, where money would be found for specific projects, often ones involving repair or renovation.[18] Congregations sometimes even resorted to a system of fines to increase revenues. In the period after the Civil War at congregation B'er Chayim in Cumberland, Maryland, for instance, members could be fined for talking during services, for chewing (presumably tobacco), for gathering in front of the synagogue, for bringing children under five to services, or for leaving services without the express permission of a congregational officer.[19] Again, however, despite all the financial burdens involved, no small-town community wanted to be without a synagogue building.

Beyond the usefulness of having synagogues in which to hold worship services, and beyond the great symbolic value of synagogue buildings, these structures were vital for small-town Jewish life in another way. Unlike the situation that prevailed in larger urban centers, synagogues in smaller cities generally served as the venues for all the communal activities of the local Jewish population. Most often, a single synagogue building was the only Jewish address in a small town. The synagogue was nearly always the place where an educational program was offered, for example, whether it was a Reform temple's Sunday school or an Orthodox community's afterschool *cheyder* classes. Synagogue buildings were also the main social centers in small communities. For some East Europeans of the immigrant generation, these buildings could even be a sort of refuge. Sociologists studying the synagogue in Newburyport, Massachusetts, described it as the "club and home" for the original East European Jewish settlers in town. For many years the immigrant men in the community would come there for morning services, which lasted from about 6:30 to 7:00, but they would remain to socialize, not leaving to go to breakfast for another hour or more. In the same vein, the architect Robert Davis, a student of the small Jewish communities of Texas, has observed that in the years before World War II, the small-town synagogue was often "a haven for those whose English might still be heavily accented and others for whom acculturation was painful."[20]

In a great many small towns, synagogue buildings performed their multiple functions even though their ancillary physical facilities included little more than a basement gathering place with a small kitchen. In other small towns, however, foresighted congregations designed buildings that took into account the variety of roles that they would be expected to fulfill. When the Jews of San Bernardino, California, began to plan a home for their congregation in 1920, for example, they spoke in terms of erecting a "Jewish Community Center," and when their temple was dedicated in 1921, its layout reflected the fact that it was intended to be the hub of local Jewish life. Off the main entrance hall of the building was a lodge room that could serve as a meeting place for groups such as the local B'nai B'rith chapter, and above its main sanctuary was a large multipurpose social hall. Similarly, the leaders of Agudas Achim in Newburyport thought of the church that they converted into a synagogue in 1933 as a facility designed "to house not only a place of worship, but also all the activities of a well organized community." By midcentury the Agudas Achim building was home not only to the congregation's sisterhood and brotherhood groups, but also to the Newburyport chapter of the women's organization Hadassah, founded in 1917; the Credit Union sponsored by the community, organized in 1934; and the city's central Zionist organization, founded in 1943. When a chapter of the Jewish War Veterans was formed in Newburyport in 1948, it got space at the synagogue as well, as did the local Young Judaea Zionist youth group, organized in 1949.[21]

The synagogue dedicated in 1936 by Congregation Adath Israel in Dover, New Jersey, provides another example of a building conceived as a multipurpose facility. Construction of this synagogue had progressed slowly over two years during the Great Depression, but when it was completed, it became Dover's "center of Jewish religious and social activity," accommodating, to quote from the synagogue's own literature, "dinners, dances, parties, lectures, [and] a wide assortment of [other] happenings." The synagogue was also the scene of regular Boy Scout and Girl Scout meetings, and it even had a gymnasium with a basketball court. Because synagogues served so many purposes in small towns, those that were constructed as worship halls and little else often had to be expanded over time in order to accommodate increasing activities. In Freehold, New Jersey, Agudath Achim erected a small wooden synagogue in 1911 but added a second floor in 1916 and made other improvements in 1920. Bickur Cholim in San Jose, California, added a "community house" to its temple in 1923 "because it was impossible to hold a graded Sunday school in the single room of the synagogue." By 1928 the rabbi of Bickur Cholim was able to boast that his new facility was being used by all the Jewish organizations in town and that it was bringing together various factions within the community.[22]

To be sure, smaller Jewish settlements were occasionally able to support communal buildings apart from synagogues. However, these facilities always existed in a symbiotic relationship with local temples or shuls. The events that took place in them were very commonly viewed as extensions of synagogue activities, especially in communities dominated by a single congregation. In Belmar, New Jersey, for instance, a community center was created in 1926 as an adjunct to the town's small synagogue, built in 1908, and soon "all educational, social and athletic activities in the community were held there." Among the organizations that were based at the center were the community's Hebrew school, the congregational sisterhood, the Hebrew Ladies Community Circle, and the Young Men's and Young Women's Hebrew Association. In South River, New Jersey, a Jewish Community Center functioning as a congregational facility was established in 1941 in a building near the town's 1920 synagogue. In that same year a Jewish Community Center was founded in Annapolis, Maryland, as well. "Although a separate organization," the community's history records, "the center from the beginning cooperated with the [Kneseth Israel] synagogue." Indeed, the offices of Kneseth Israel's rabbi and cantor were housed at the center, as well as the congregation's Hebrew school. In Sharon, Pennsylvania, a Jewish Center building was donated to the House of Israel Congregation around 1943, and even the Montefiore Country Club, established by a group of Jewish men who had bought farm property in nearby Orangeville, Ohio, was under the auspices of the congregation.[23]

Many of those who were residents of small communities in the decades before the middle of the twentieth century recognized the centrality of the synagogue in small-town Jewish life. Joseph Goodkovitz, the brother of Alexander Goode, who was one of the celebrated "four chaplains" who went down with the troopship *Dorchester* during World War II, recalled that when his father was the rabbi of Brith Achim in Petersburg, Virginia, in the early 1920s, "community life was simple, centering more or less about the synagogue." Similarly, a woman who grew up in Plymouth, Pennsylvania, described the Jews of the 1930s there as "a fairly close-knit group with a communal life centered around the synagogue (or as we called it, our shul)." One resident of Englewood, New Jersey, has observed succinctly that before midcentury, "the Shul was a social center, religiously oriented." Thus in a great many small towns, synagogues became, perhaps inadvertently, the very kinds of multifaceted institutions that were being actively promoted in big cities, and especially in New York, as "synagogue centers."[24]

Through all the complexities of congregational formation in America's small Jewish communities, and through all the efforts involved in acquiring and maintaining houses of worship, one of the clearest trends visible in small-town Jewish life was a decided drift away from Orthodoxy as the middle of the twentieth century approached. This pattern had already played itself out once, during the middle decades of the nineteenth century, as so many small-town congregations followed the general movement toward Reform. In the early decades of the twentieth century the pattern emerged again, as more and more congregations founded by East European immigrants broke even their nominal ties with Orthodox Judaism. In some places, such as Vicksburg, Mississippi, and Jackson, Michigan, the difficult position of Orthodoxy was evident early on, as East Europeans failed in their attempts to inaugurate Orthodox congregations, or did not even try. The weakening of Orthodoxy in small communities was also manifested in cases in which Orthodox synagogues that were established alongside Reform temples simply folded after a few decades. Several cases from the state of Arkansas can serve as illustrations. In Jonesboro the Orthodox assembly that had been organized in 1892 was disbanded by 1927, and its remaining members became affiliated with the town's older congregation, the Reform Temple Israel. In Pine Bluff the Orthodox B'nai Israel discovered that it could support a full-time rabbi for only about ten years after its establishment in 1907, and by the 1930s the congregation was barely functioning. The Orthodox congregation in Fort Smith, also called B'nai Israel, had disbanded completely by the end of the 1930s. Years later a member of the surviving congregation in Fort Smith still recalled the poignant moment when "several Orthodox men brought B'nai Israel's two [Torah] scrolls to the temple . . . [and] joined their lot with the Reform."[25]

Sometimes the Reform congregations that absorbed Orthodox bodies made a few concessions to their new, more tradition-minded members, just as, earlier, Reform temples in some places had reached out to the more observant in an effort to keep them from establishing their own prayer groups in the first place. In Albuquerque, for example, the Reform Temple Albert took in the town's nominally Orthodox congregation in 1930 in a bid to broaden its membership as the Great Depression deepened, and it promised the traditionalists that they could hold their own services in the temple's vestry room if they wished. In Quincy, Illinois, it took a bit longer for a separate Orthodox congregation to disappear, but when its remaining members finally did join the Reform B'Nai Sholom, the temple became so dependent on traditionalist Jews that by the 1940s the services there were described as "Conservative rather than Reformed."[26]

In some small towns where Orthodox congregations found themselves in precarious circumstances, they saw the negotiation of mergers with their local Reform counterparts as preferable to simply disbanding, even though they understood that they would be the weaker partners in such alliances. While Reform congregations often held on to their independence rather than enter into agreements that would force them to make major concessions to Orthodoxy, they welcomed opportunities to join with Orthodox bodies when it was clear that it would be the traditionalists making most of the adjustments. In Brunswick, Georgia, for example, Temple Beth Tefilloh seems to have enticed the Orthodox Agudath Israel into a merger in 1927. Initially the Reformers conceded that any rabbi hired for the High Holidays would be "suitable to both congregations," but it is clear which group had the upper hand from the fact that only the name Beth Tefilloh was retained. The history prepared by the Brunswick temple on the occasion of its seventy-fifth anniversary proclaims that such a negotiated merger of Reform and Orthodox groups was "unprecedented in American Jewish life," but in fact this process was replicated in many other small communities during the interwar period.[27]

In Marion, Indiana, where Orthodox leaders had walked out of a merger meeting in 1924 rather than agree to be part of a Reform congregation, the complete independence of the more religiously observant group lasted only about a decade. When the Reform Sinai Temple erected a synagogue in 1936, the Orthodox group finally agreed to move its services into that building. Although this still did not constitute a formal consolidation of the two groups, it was nonetheless, as the son of one of the Orthodox leaders described it, "a hell of a concession." In the same vein, in 1939 the Orthodox Tree of Life Congregation in Clarksburg, West Virginia, entered into an uneasy merger with the town's Reform congregation, Temple Emanuel. Tree of Life had been established around 1917 by Russian immigrants to Clarksburg, but now, even though they avoided adopting Reform practice wholesale, they were conceding that the days of Orthodox worship in their town were over.[28]

Reinforcing the tendency of traditionalist Jews to accept the demise of Orthodoxy in small-town America was the Reform movement's active involvement in outreach to immigrants and their children, as it sought to promote its liberal interpretation of Jewish beliefs and practices. Not only were local Reform congregations involved in this work, but also traveling Reform rabbis who visited small communities, both those with temples and those without, seeking to win over more and more small-town Jews. In Michigan, for example, in the very early years of the twentieth century, Rabbi Leo Franklin of Detroit, Rabbi Moses Bergman of Grand Rapids, and Rabbi George Zepin of Kalamazoo each traveled to towns such as Battle Creek, Lansing, Bay City, and Saginaw in an effort to plant and reinforce Reform congregations in those places.[29] Indeed, throughout the early decades of the twentieth century, the Reform movement was the only one that actively labored to recruit adherents in small communities. As early as 1894 the movement's central agency, the Union of American Hebrew Congregations, had already established a Committee on Circuit Preaching with the aim of providing smaller Jewish settlements with educational and rabbinic support. In 1903 this body was transformed into the Department of Synagogue Extension, and in 1905, taking on some additional educational functions, it became known as the Department of Synagogue and School Extension. Among other activities, this agency published sermons to be used in congregations that were without rabbis, provided Sunday school materials, continued to oversee the activities of visiting rabbis, and eventually supervised the work of regional rabbis and the placement of student rabbis in small communities.[30]

Throughout most of the first half of the twentieth century, the work of the UAHC's Department of Synagogue and School Extension was under the direction of George Zepin, who in 1903 had left the Kalamazoo temple to which he had gone after his ordination in order to take up his administrative duties at the Reform movement's headquarters in Cincinnati. Zepin has been called "the real builder" of the UAHC, "attempting to encompass in its reach almost every phase of American Jewish life and activity," and he was resolutely devoted to the concept of outreach.[31] As early as 1904, following a tour of

*Rabbi George Zepin, head of the Department of Synagogue and School Extension of the*
*Union of American Hebrew Congregations. Zepin was especially eager to promote Reform*
*Judaism among Jews in small towns. Courtesy of the Jacob Rader Marcus Center of the*
*American Jewish Archives.*

forty-five cities in the states of Ohio, Indiana, Mississippi, and Louisiana, Zepin expressed the opinion that what he called the "Country Jews" of small-town America already had "a dim consciousness that the only form of religion compatible with their changed conditions is Reform Judaism," and he made it clear that he felt Jews in small communities were a natural constituency for the UAHC to cultivate. In later years, too, the activities of the Department of Synagogue and School Extension were directed toward spreading the influence of Reform primarily through direct contact. One account of the work of the South East District of the UAHC reported, for example, that between 1929 and 1935 the extension's regional rabbi and various resident rabbis in the area had visited ninety-six towns, sometimes making an effort to encourage the establishment of a local congregation and sometimes (where the number of Jews was very small) simply attempting to "stimulate" the local Jews "to maintain their Jewish interests."[32]

Rabbis affiliated with Judaism's nascent Conservative movement in the early decades of the century recognized the zeal of Reform in its efforts to win over Jews in small communities, and some lamented the success Reform was achieving. These traditionalists, usually graduates of the Jewish Theological Seminary of America in New York (JTS), had no objection to the Americanization of Judaism, but they believed that this could be accomplished without abandoning traditional Jewish ritual and law. In 1910, when JTS graduate Samuel Rosinger arrived in Beaumont, Texas, a town with a Jewish population of about 400 at the time, he discovered that the influence of the Reform movement's seminary in Cincinnati, Hebrew Union College, had entrenched Reform practice quite firmly there. "The *goyim* [gentiles] of the H.U.C. wrought untold harm in this community," he anguished, dismissing the legitimacy of the type of Judaism preached by Reform rabbis. The following year Rabbi Moses Abels, also ordained at JTS, allowed that he had had "ample occasion to observe conditions in the smaller communities" and that he was "more than ever convinced that had it not been for the radical Rabbis the Jewish congregations [in those places] would never have drifted to radical reform."[33]

The Reform movement's philosophy of outreach to East Europeans in small communities was articulated most frankly, perhaps, in a World War II–era pamphlet prepared by Jacob Weinstein when he was working with the UAHC's Department of Synagogue and School Extension. Weinstein argued that in order to function in small communities, where the majority of Jews were by then of East European background, the Reform movement had to gain "the confidence of men who think they have extremely different theological notions" and work to maintain rabbinic leadership in these communities that was "modern in every way" but still possessed of "a sympathetic understanding of all of orthodox life and customs." He marveled at "how far the recently orthodox [individual] will travel on the road to religious liberalism, provided he is certain that his guide is not temperamentally a stranger." Cynically, Weinstein asserted that even observant Orthodox Jews "will listen respectfully to the most heretical opinions" as long as those views were "expressed in Yiddish."[34]

Throughout the years before midcentury, then, traditionalist Jews in small towns were increasingly coming to accept the notion that they could not sustain Orthodox congregations. In any given town, the number of those truly devoted to Orthodox practice was almost bound to be very limited, and in any case the small-town environment was hardly conducive to the maintenance of any kind of exotic lifestyle with a strict discipline. So successful was Reform Judaism in appealing to Jews in small communities that at least a few small-town congregations founded around the turn of the twentieth century adopted Reform practice from the outset, even if most of their founders were men of East European background. This was the case in Muncie, Indiana, for example, where Beth El was organized as a Reform temple in 1897. It is true that some Jews in Muncie rejected Reform and affiliated with Orthodox congregations in Indianapolis and that one family even attempted to influence Beth El to move toward traditionalism in the late 1920s, but the congregation remained firmly within the Reform camp nonetheless.[35]

To be sure, not all the small-town congregations founded by East Europeans as Orthodox shuls were forced to disband over the years, or to merge with Reform temples. However, those initially Orthodox congregations that did survive well into the twentieth century seldom retained their original outlook and standards of practice. Even without pressure from competing liberal congregations or from the outreach programs of the Reform movement, over the decades traditionalist synagogues altered their characters substantially. Certain congregations established under an Orthodox banner came to adopt a Reform identity with remarkable speed. In Hancock, Michigan, for example, the Congregation of Israel constructed its synagogue along Orthodox lines in 1912, but already by the mid-1920s it had embraced Reform practice.[36] More commonly, however, small-town traditionalist congregations moved away from Orthodoxy more gradually. Some analysts of Jewish life in the hinterland have even suggested that liberalization and Americanization came more slowly to East European congregations in smaller cities than it did to those in big ones.[37] Moreover, where they were the only congregations in their towns (and this was very common), Orthodox assemblies frequently attempted to maintain communal unity by accommodating a wide variety of religious practices, at least for a time, even as their journey away from Orthodox modes proceeded apace.

The history of philosophical and liturgical transformation in Clarksdale, Mississippi, provides a case in point. There the Beth Israel congregation was established by Lithuanian immigrants in the mid-1890s, and it remained the dominant local Jewish institution throughout the twentieth century. When Beth Israel erected its first synagogue in 1910, the services conducted in the building were Orthodox, and those few people in the community who wanted an alternative met elsewhere. When Beth Israel constructed a new synagogue in 1929, however, it became home to a wide range of religious services, and by 1940, Reform, Conservative, and Orthodox prayer meetings were all being held in the building. As one observer reported at the time, "all three denominations of the Jewish faith . . . find free expression under one roof." After World War II, Beth Israel's character continued to evolve. "As younger people moved up to high office," the synagogue's rabbi recalled in the 1960s, "Reform became dominant, an organ was installed . . . and the congregation joined . . . the Union of American Hebrew Congregations." In 1963 separate Orthodox services were abolished completely at Beth Israel, and a new "universally satisfying" liturgy was adopted, one that was "Reform with a Conservative tinge."[38]

Similar stories of transformation are recorded in the annals of many other small communities. In Muskegon, Michigan, where B'nai Israel was established with a clear Orthodox identity even while accommodating local German-Jewish reformers, it did not take long before the status quo began to face challenges. Even the official history of the congregation admits that in its early years "there were some disagreements," almost certainly centering on questions of liberalization, "and occasional bitter squabbles, a few of which continued for many years." Ultimately, by the 1930s, "as the leadership of the congregation was transferred to a younger generation and new families moved to the area," again to quote from its official history, "Congregation B'nai Israel increasingly reflected the views and practices of Reform." In 1945 the congregation hired a Reform rabbi for the first time and joined the UAHC.[39]

Another example of transformation comes from Topeka, Kansas, which saw the creation of two congregations early in the twentieth century, both Orthodox. B'nai Israel was founded in 1905, apparently by traditionalists of Central European background, and B'nai Abraham was founded in 1915 by East European immigrants. These two congregations agreed to merge in 1919 (the new body was initially called B'nai Israel and Abraham), and they soon acquired a synagogue building and hired a rabbi. By the 1920s, however, the commitment of the Topeka congregation to Orthodoxy was waning. Its leaders had come to believe that in order to survive, the congregation had to attract the membership and the financial support of more religiously liberal Jews in the city. Thus in 1928 they reinvented their congregation as Temple Beth Sholom and adopted Reform practice, agreeing, however, that during their lifetimes the original Orthodox members of the congregation would be allowed to conduct their own services in a room set aside for that purpose.[40]

A history prepared in honor of the hundredth anniversary of Congregation B'nai Abraham in Hagerstown, Maryland, tells yet one more tale of the gradual renunciation of Orthodoxy in favor of Reform. Speaking of religious practice in the congregation, the history relates that in the period between the two world wars, "the old ways began to die out, and demand for the new ways grew continually." Already during the 1920s a member with Reform sympathies was elected president, "giving evidence of the impending liberalization of the congregation," and by 1940 B'nai Abraham considered itself unequivocally Reform. The congregation joined the UAHC in 1947, although there was enough of a residual traditionalism among its members that as late as 1952 there was a flare-up over the installation of an organ.[41]

As the comments of several observers of congregational change suggest, the adoption of Reform in small-town America often came when the immigrant generation began to lose its influence and younger leadership emerged. To American-born Jews who had never known life in an intensively Jewish milieu, the appeal of the Reform style was very powerful. Even where many immigrants remained ambivalent about the shift away from Orthodoxy, they were willing to accept it as a way of giving their children a viable connection to the Jewish faith. As Samuel M. Silver, a student rabbi in Logan, West Virginia, in the 1930s reported, most of the older people in his congregation "miss the warmth of old-fashioned services," but he concluded that "on reflection" most of them were willing to accept Reform because they realized that the influence of Hebrew Union College and its liberal philosophy would "keep religion in their children." Years later an older East European Jew in Williamson, West Virginia, echoed these sentiments: "What turned me toward Reform," he acknowledged, "was that my son liked Reform so much."[42]

Certainly not every small-town Orthodox congregation that underwent change, nor even the majority, made the journey all the way to Reform Judaism by the middle of the twentieth century. Rather, a large number tried to maintain something of a traditionalist flavor even as they followed a trajectory away from Orthodox liturgies and practices. Thus, by midcentury many Orthodox shuls in small towns had become not Reform temples, but rather Conservative synagogues. In Petersburg, Virginia, for instance, Brith Achim began moving from Orthodoxy toward Conservative practice as early as 1927 in order to prevent members (as their minutes said) "from drifting away altogether to competitive synagogues and temples." Most likely Brith Achim was concerned especially about the attraction of Petersburg's Reform congregation, Rodef Sholom. In Benton Harbor, Michigan, what the Children of Israel's fiftieth anniversary history called "the difficult transmutation from strict orthodox to conservative services and rituals" was begun under Rabbi Moses Schwab, who arrived in 1937. Rabbi Schwab referred to his approach variously as "conservative," "semi-orthodox," and "modern orthodox," but it was clear that under his guidance the gravitation toward liberalization had begun. Change was in the air at Benton Harbor's Ohava Shalom congregation as well. Sometime before World War II, this synagogue adopted mixed seating, perhaps in an attempt to forestall defections to Temple Beth-El, the Reform congregation that had been established in Benton Harbor in 1934.[43]

In Pittston, Pennsylvania, Agudath Achim signaled its changing character when it hired Rabbi Harry Katchen, a graduate of the Conservative movement's Jewish Theological Seminary, in 1930. In Iron Mountain, Michigan, Anshe Knesseth Israel adopted mixed seating in 1938, even though some in town still considered it an Orthodox institution. In North Carolina, Durham's Beth El hired a Conservative rabbi in place of an Orthodox leader for the first time in 1948, and in Georgia, Macon's Sherah Israel made the move from Orthodoxy to Conservatism at about the same time, adopting a new prayerbook and affiliating with the Conservative movement's umbrella organization, the United Synagogue of America. In Iowa City the community's nominally Orthodox Agudas Achim dedicated a new building in 1950, but at the time even the wife of the congregation's rabbi admitted that "the shul has [only] one Orthodox member, old Mr. Worton."[44]

Clearly, then, by the time the generation of East European immigrants who had settled in small communities began to die out, the extinction of Orthodox Judaism in small towns was well advanced. Certainly by 1960, if not earlier, it became very difficult to find a congregation that still identified itself as Orthodox in any of the towns that had been home to a triple-digit Jewish community in the late 1920s. In the first place, to judge by the most complete compilation of contemporary information available, 122 of the 490 triple-digit communities of 1927 (25 percent) had no functioning congregations at all in 1960. More to the point, of those communities in our sample that still had synagogues, only sixty-two (13 percent) were home to congregations that still called themselves Orthodox in 1960, and at least nineteen of these sixty-two communities had Jewish populations that had climbed beyond the 1,000 mark by then.[45] Furthermore, many of the congregations still designated as Orthodox at midcentury were, in reality, hardly adhering to Orthodox standards. Ahavas Achim in Newburyport was still calling itself Orthodox, for example, even though it had long before adopted policies such as mixed seating that had, in effect, moved the congregation into the Conservative camp. Similarly, the Moses Montefiore Synagogue of Appleton, Wisconsin, was still listed as an Orthodox congregation in 1960, even though it, too, was permitting men and women to sit together and allowing bat mitzvah ceremonies for girls, a very modern innovation.[46]

Altogether, of the 490 towns that make up the sample for this study, 349 still had Jewish populations under 1,000 and functioning congregations in the year 1960. Of these 349 towns, eighty-four (24 percent) were home to nothing but a single Reform temple as the twentieth century entered its seventh decade, and 124 (36 percent) were home to only a single Conservative synagogue. Another twenty-seven towns (8 percent) supported a lone congregation with more than one denominational affiliation or with no designated affiliation in 1960, suggesting that it was attempting to accommodate a wide variety of religious philosophies. In addition, seventy-four of the 349 towns in question (21 percent) supported two or more congregations, but in fully sixty-five of these places (88 percent of the seventy-four towns) all the congregations were either Reform, Conservative, or unaffiliated.

In a great many ways, the history of small-town congregations mirrored that of their counterparts in larger communities. Congregations both in small-town environments and in larger cities were organized for fundamentally the same purposes, and they shared some basic assumptions about the role of the synagogue in Jewish life. They even followed similar trends in the design of their buildings. But the small-town setting did nonetheless make a substantial difference. The limited population base in small communities meant that acquiring and maintaining synagogue buildings there could be a more challenging task than it was in larger Jewish centers, and it also meant that small-town synagogues were more likely to be the only physical structures associated with local Jewish life. Independent Jewish schools, YM/YWHA buildings, and Jewish lodge halls were not completely unknown in smaller Jewish settlements, but they were few and far between. Thus, almost invariably, synagogues in small towns served as the hubs of Jewish life in a much more intensive way than they did in the more fragmented communities of larger cities. In towns with only a single congregation, this reality was only intensified.

Perhaps most significantly, however, it was the nearly complete disappearance of Orthodox congregations from small communities by the middle of the twentieth century that distinguished those settlements from larger Jewish centers, where at least something of an Orthodox presence survived. Large and even midsize cities were far more likely than small towns to sustain separate Orthodox subcommunities, with their own social and religious networks. Moreover, Orthodox refugees from Europe arriving just before World War II and Orthodox survivors of the Shoah reinforced the religiously observant populations of at least some large and midsize cities, but they did not settle in small towns. Thus, like other aspects of Jewish life in small communities, the patterns of their synagogue history can be fully understood only in light of the fact that limited size and the small-town setting were powerful environmental factors.

# 9 Patterns of Religious Leadership

In much the same way that small Jewish communities strove to construct synagogue buildings to house their communal activities, they also aspired to find rabbis who would guide their congregations. Despite the crucial role played by prominent lay leaders in small towns, and despite the fact that Jewish religious law does not require the participation of rabbis in worship services, small-town Jews tended to consider their communal infrastructure to be truly complete only when they had a spiritual leader in their midst. Nonetheless, smaller communities were not always able to find ordained clergymen to fill the pulpits of their temples and synagogues, nor did they necessarily retain the rabbis they did attract. Thus, small communities often had to address the need for religious leadership in the absence of fully trained rabbis, and this they did with a number of creative strategies.

The emphasis that Reform congregations placed on decorum in their temples, and on the sermon, helps explain why they considered rabbis to be almost essential as officiants at prayer services and life cycle events such as weddings and funerals. Moreover, Reform congregations believed that rabbis could best represent the Jewish community to the larger society, since their prestige was seen to be on a par with that of local ministers. These congregations took great pride in the visibility and the accomplishments of their spiritual leaders, and they expected them to be ambassadors to the gentile community, engaged in a variety of efforts that would demonstrate the integration of Jews into local town life.

Not surprisingly, just about every account of the achievements of late nineteenth- and early twentieth-century Reform rabbis serving in small towns alludes to their participation in local civic affairs. So, for example, Solomon L. Kory, the long-serving spiritual leader of Vicksburg's congregation Anshe Chesed, was said to be deeply involved in relief efforts during World War I and an active Democrat who took a strong interest in political developments. As one contemporary biographical sketch observed, "his voice and his pen hav[e] on numerous occasions rendered effective service in behalf of good local government." Characteristically, Kory held membership not only in B'nai B'rith but also in the Vicksburg Masonic lodge, the Knights of Pythias, and the Elks. Similarly, Edmund Landau, the son of a rabbi from Bay City, Michigan, and the spiritual leader of congregation B'nai Israel in Albany, Georgia, for almost half a century beginning in 1898, served as a Boy Scout leader and as president of the local Kiwanis Club. Rabbi Samuel Rabinowitz, who occupied a pulpit in Greenville, Mississippi, from the early 1920s until after World War II, worked hard to improve local relations between African Americans and whites, and he was remembered as "one who bound the races closer, and brought the tensioned groups to mutual respect."[1]

Small-town Jews concerned with their public image hoped and expected that their rabbis would garner praise in the local press. The Reform Jews of Congregation Albert in Albuquerque, New Mexico, for example, must have been pleased when a local newspaper described a sermon delivered in 1898 by William Greenburg, their first rabbi, as a "rare treat for those fortunate to hear him." "His ideas are bright and original," the paper remarked; "his language is beautiful, and his view of life extremely optimistic." Likewise, the Reform Jews of Lafayette, Indiana, must have been proud of the way a local paper showered praise on their rabbi, Nathan Krass, when it was announced in 1908 that he was leaving to take a pulpit in Rochester, New York. The paper noted that Rabbi Krass "has taken an interest in charitable work and has been an active and valuable member of the community," and it asserted that he "has made a lasting impression by his intellectuality, eloquence and personal qualities."[2]

Small-town Reform congregations also considered it important for their rabbis to cultivate amicable ties with clergymen of other faiths. Congregants anticipated that they would hear from their spiritual leaders the kinds of sentiments that Irving Levey expressed about his experience in Topeka, Kansas. Levey, who was later rabbi at Temple Israel in Boston and director of the library at Hebrew Union College in Cincinnati, recalled that when he was the rabbi of Topeka's Temple Beth Sholom around 1930 his synagogue "enjoyed excellent relations with all the other churches, even as I did with all the members of the ministerial association." Rabbis who actually headed interdenominational associations of clergymen, as Fred Rypins did in Greensboro, North Carolina, in the early 1930s, were viewed as having achieved a major success. So, too, were rabbis who could air regular programs on local radio stations, as Alexander Kline of Beth Ha-'Tephillah in Asheville, North Carolina, did in the mid-1930s.[3]

For small-town Orthodox congregations in the immigrant era, having rabbis who could represent Jews as acculturated citizens of their towns was far less of a concern, although this became an issue for them, too, as midcentury approached and their constituents became increasingly Americanized. Nonetheless, even at the turn of the century, small-town Orthodox congregations also strove to hire rabbis for their shuls, for there were a great many functions for these rabbis to perform. They were expected not only to act as the local authorities on *halachah* (Jewish law), but often to serve as cantors, Torah readers, and teachers as well. Frequently they were also expected to perform *shechitah* (ritual slaughtering of animals) and *milah* (ritual circumcision).

Occasionally a small-town congregation attempting to attract a trained rabbi to its pulpit met with notable success. Especially in the annals of well-established Reform congregations, there are examples of extremely capable clergymen who settled down in small towns and became beloved and highly visible leaders in their communities. Solomon Kory of Vicksburg and Edmund Landau of Albany, Georgia, are two examples. Another is the European-educated Leopold Freudenthal, who arrived in Trinidad, Colorado, in 1889 as the second rabbi to serve in that city, and remained for twenty-seven years until his death in 1916. One source suggests that Freudenthal was such a popular figure in Trinidad, and so much in demand, that his congregation eventually had to bar him from officiating at the life cycle events of individuals who were not Jewish. Yet another example of a Reform rabbi with a long and successful career in a small community is Isaac E. Marcuson, who became rabbi of Temple Beth Israel in Macon, Georgia, in 1894, soon after he was ordained at HUC, and served until his death in 1952, with only one short interruption. As was expected in such situations, while Marcuson served as the spiritual leader of his congregation, he was also heavily engaged with the larger community. He was a chaplain to the wounded during the Spanish-American War and a frequent visitor to the local state hospital, for example, and he was also a leader of the Macon library board, the Boy Scouts, and the Red Cross.[4]

Like Reform assemblies, traditionalist congregations also now and then found rabbis who served long tenures and rose to prominence in their small communities. In Oshkosh, Wisconsin, for instance, the Lithuanian-born Louis Edelson served from 1901 until his death in 1934, overseeing a slow liberalization of Orthodox practice at Congregation B'Nai Israel. So devoted to him were his congregants that at one point, when Edelson was seriously considering moving to El Paso, Texas, they mobilized not only to raise his salary substantially, but also to convince his wife that El Paso was a place to avoid because of its unhealthy environment and its dangerous "mixed ethnic population." Similarly, Nahum Kreuger, born in Philadelphia and ordained at the Conservative movement's Jewish Theological Seminary in 1918, arrived at Congregation Beth Abraham in the southern New Jersey town of Bridgeton around 1930 and

*Solomon L. Kory, rabbi of Congregation Anshe Chesed, Vicksburg, Mississippi, from 1903 to 1936. Some rabbis, like Kory, remained in their small-town pulpits for long periods, but a frequent turnover of spiritual leaders was more common. Courtesy of the Jacob Rader Marcus Center of the American Jewish Archives.*

remained there until his death some two decades later. Like many of his Reform counterparts in their small towns, he was said to be "always regarded by the residents of Bridgeton as a leader of civic affairs and a spokesman for the entire community" who was "loved and revered" by Christians as well as Jews. In Manchester, New Hampshire, Rabbi Abraham Hefterman served from about 1926 until his retirement around the end of World War II. A native of Bessarabia, Hefterman routinely fulfilled the variety of tasks often assigned to an Orthodox rabbi in a small community and stayed long enough to become the subject of dissent within his congregation, as younger members began to voice their desire for a rabbi whose native tongue was English and who would be more open to liberal practices.[5]

Despite these examples of long-serving religious leaders, it was quite unusual for congregations in triple-digit communities to identify rabbis who were well suited to their needs and to create conditions that would induce them to take up small-town posts. Men who had chosen the rabbinate, perhaps more than individuals in other fields, were reluctant to settle in places where they would be without a rich Jewish cultural environment and the opportunity to interact with colleagues. Moreover, the most accomplished rabbis looking for positions were sometimes wary of settings in which they would be required to fulfill a wide range of functions, rather than ones for which they felt they were especially well equipped. All these factors made the search for a rabbi a very difficult task.[6]

In a sense, a congregation's recruitment of a suitable spiritual leader was a venture akin to the pairing of potential mates, and just as there were intricate networks that reached into Jewish communities both large and small to facilitate matrimonial matchmaking, there were informal networks that connected Jewish functionaries looking for employment with congregations that had vacant positions. So, for example, Bernhard Henry Gotthelf, who had served as only the second Jewish chaplain of the United States during the Civil War, found his rabbinic post in Vicksburg, Mississippi, shortly after the war because some members of the Vicksburg congregation had family ties to Louisville, where Gotthelf was employed before moving south. So, too, in the 1890s the Talmud student Jacob Goldfarb found his small-town rabbinic posts through personal connections. Having left his native Lithuania, Goldfarb came first to New York and then to Pittsburgh. There the leading Orthodox rabbi in the city, Moshe Sivitz, took Goldfarb under his wing and sent him out to appropriate rabbinic positions in the region, first in the Pennsylvania town of Connellsville, and then in Washington, Pennsylvania.[7]

The career of Ferdinand Hirsch provides yet another illustration of the way in which personal contacts helped communities find rabbis and rabbis find positions. Hirsch relocated several times in the course of his rabbinic career, and each time personal connections with key individuals played a role. In 1908 Hirsch's relocation from a pulpit in Bessemer, Alabama, to one in Athens, Georgia, was facilitated by the fact that a leading member of the Athens congregation was married to a woman from Bessemer. In 1919 Hirsch's move from Athens to Sumter, South Carolina, was based largely upon a recommendation from the highly respected Rabbi David Marx of Atlanta. In 1928 Hirsch's final move, this time to Monroe, Louisiana, was made possible by a friend in Monroe who intervened on Hirsch's behalf.[8] Word-of-mouth connections and contacts based on kin and professional ties remained important elements in the recruitment of small-town rabbis throughout the classic era of small-town Jewish life.

Aside from informal channels of communication, however, there were more systematic methods of finding rabbis for vacant small-town pulpits. Sometimes small communities advertised open positions in the national Jewish press, and by the beginning of the twentieth century they were also turning increasingly to America's various rabbinic seminaries for assistance. Chief among these institutions were Hebrew Union College in Cincinnati, which began training Reform rabbis in 1875; the Jewish Theological Seminary in New York, founded in 1887 and revitalized in 1902 as the rabbinic training program of the emerging Conservative movement; and the Rabbi Isaac Elchanan Theological Seminary (RIETS), also in New York, founded in 1897 and soon the nucleus around which Yeshiva University was created.

Often the small-town congregations that turned to these rabbinical schools were quite explicit about their requirements, perhaps assuming that there was no shortage of qualified candidates. In April 1924, for instance, the newly organized Temple Sinai in Michigan City, Indiana, wrote to HUC indicating that the congregation "would like to secure a Rabbi from your next graduating class" and stipulating, among other things, that "this Rabbi is to put his full time in Michigan City." Later the same year the Bnai Israel Congregation in Wilmington, North Carolina, wrote to RIETS to say that it had "at present an opening for a modern Orthodox rabbi," and requested that the yeshiva send someone who was "a first class Hebrew teacher, translating the Hebrew to the children in a good grammatical english." Reflecting the fact that small-town rabbis were routinely asked to undertake multiple tasks, the letter advised that the person they were seeking "must also be a Shochet, Chazon [cantor], Mohel and inspiring english lecturer" and that "he should be married, and of respectfull appearance in dress and manners." Lastly, the letter concluded, he should be "a GENTLEMAN of amicable disposition and a good social mixture [mixer?]."[9]

In reality, however, there was far more demand for rabbis than there were rabbinical students to fill vacant positions, and even though faculty members and placement officers at America's rabbinical seminaries had a great deal of influence over the destinations of their graduates, seeking help from these schools was no guarantee of success in finding a rabbi. Hebrew Union College in Cincinnati was the seminary most responsive to appeals from small communities, for it considered Reform to be the ideal variety of Judaism for small-town settings and saw the spread of Reform as part of its mission. For this reason, small-town congregations that identified with Reform could always harbor some hope that rabbis at the beginning of their careers would be directed to their pulpits. Still, neither HUC nor the Central Conference of American Rabbis (CCAR), the umbrella organization of Reform clergy, could cater to the needs of every small-town congregation looking for a spiritual leader. In 1927, for example, Reform rabbis who were members of the CCAR were serving in only 42 of America's 490 triple-digit Jewish communities.[10] Clearly, many a Reform temple hoping to hire an ordained rabbi was disappointed.

Small-town traditionalist congregations looking for rabbis were even less likely than Reform congregations to find help in the country's premier rabbinical schools or in the main organizations of Orthodox rabbis in America. Neither JTS nor RIETS was especially anxious to dispatch its recent graduates to small congregations in the hinterland, both because newly minted Orthodox and Conservative rabbis were in great demand in larger communities and because these young men were even more reluctant than their Reform counterparts to settle in places that lacked an extensive Jewish infrastructure. In the early decades of the century, JTS graduates complained even about assignments in cities such as Minneapolis, Toledo, and Washington, D.C., places where the Jewish population at the time ran into the thousands.[11] No wonder they shunned pulpits in truly small communities.

Of the ninety-two rabbis who were members of the JTS Alumni Association in 1914, for example, only eight were serving congregations in cities that had Jewish populations under 1,000 at the time, and four of these places had growing communities that would number over 1,000 individuals by the 1920s. Of the 203 living graduates of JTS in 1929, it appears that no more than nine were serving congregations in communities of less than 1,000 Jews, while six or seven others were living in smaller communities without having pulpits. These six or seven included Rabbi Jacob Mendelsohn, who was teaching at the Hebrew Institute in Greenwich, Connecticut; and Rabbi Isidor Hoffman, who was directing the Hillel student organization at Cornell University in Ithaca, New York; while the others were probably in retirement or between rabbinic posts. To be sure, some Conservative rabbis who found themselves in small towns were content to stay there (the JTS-trained Rabbi William Ackerman remained for many years at the Reform congregation Beth Israel in Meridian, Mississippi, for example), but most would have far preferred to be someplace else.[12] The data on rabbis trained at RIETS tell a similar story, even in the period after Bernard Revel introduced a modernized curriculum there and began to attract more Americanized students to the yeshiva. Of the thirty-three rabbis who graduated under the newly revised curriculum between 1919 and 1923, for instance, only one was serving in a small community in the mid-1920s, that of Ellenville, New York.[13]

Not surprisingly, accomplished European-trained Orthodox rabbis serving in America also tended to avoid very small communities. One indicator here is the scarcity of members of major Orthodox rabbinical organizations among the leaders of small-town congregations. Of the 377 members listed in the 1934 directory of the Union of Orthodox Rabbis of the United States and Canada (the Agudat Harabanim), most were serving in New York City or in other leading Jewish centers such as Baltimore, Pittsburgh, Cleveland, Detroit, and St. Louis. There were also a few dozen rabbis from this organization in less prominent midsize communities. However, only two of the organization's members were in towns identified as having a triple-digit Jewish community in the late 1920s: Burlington, Vermont, and Roselle, New Jersey. Members of the country's other major Orthodox group, the Rabbinical Council of America (the Histadrut Harabanim), were also extremely underrepresented in small communities. Of the 125 members of the organization in 1941, only seventeen were in towns that had reported Jewish populations in triple digits in the 1920s, and five of these seventeen towns were quite near New York City.[14]

Given the reluctance of thoroughly trained rabbis to locate in small communities, small-town temples and synagogues counted themselves fortunate even if they could attract competent spiritual leaders without formal ordination. As one immigrant to a small town on the Minnesota Iron Range put it, "We weren't fussy. We needed a rabbi, we took anybody we could get."[15] Of course, some communities found rabbi-surrogates, often given the honorific title "Reverend," with a fair amount of learning and ability. Such, it seems, were Henry Loewenthal, who served the Bickur Cholim congregation of San Jose, California, as an unordained minister, *shochet,* and teacher from 1881 until 1893; and Joseph Bleeden, who arrived to join his Lithuanian *landsleit* in Muscatine, Iowa, around 1892 and served as the spiritual leader there until his death in 1916. On the other hand, many small communities had to settle for freelance rabbi-surrogates who were less accomplished or less personable. One example here is the curmudgeonly and abusive Fishel Shilsky, the supposed Orthodox rabbi who figures prominently in the African-American writer James McBride's memoir, *The Color of Water.* As was typical of many self-styled rabbis in the prewar era, Shilsky had a series of brief contracts in places such as Port Jervis and Glens Falls, New York; Belleville, New Jersey; and Suffolk, Virginia.[16]

At least some Jewish leaders saw the proliferation of freelancers who usurped the title "Rabbi" as a serious problem. They protested that these ersatz clergymen not only compromised the standards that were supposed to be maintained in the rabbinate, but also encroached unfairly upon the territory of properly ordained rabbis, often providing a wide range of services at reduced salaries, especially in small towns. Twice before conventions of the Conservative movement's Rabbinical Assembly during the 1930s, for example, Rabbi Jacob Freedman railed against freelancers, calling them "noxious growths in the Vineyard of Israel."[17] Nonetheless, for small-town Jews in need of religious leaders, engaging a rabbi-surrogate was often the most reasonable option.

Reliable numerical data about rabbinic leadership in small communities are difficult to uncover, but to judge from information available from the year 1919 concerning the 490 triple-digit Jewish communities that constitute our sample, it appears that the chances were only about one in five that a typical small-town community would have the benefit of a resident rabbi as the period of mass migration to America was coming to an end. A total of ninety-five of our 490 communities reported the presence of one rabbi in 1919, and a mere sixteen communities reported the presence of two.[18] Of course, the information available from 1919 does not make a clear distinction between ordained rabbis and those who claimed the title for themselves, and it reveals the situation at only one point in time. It is certainly possible that some communities in our sample were able to attract rabbis either before or after 1919, and it is also possible that some communities with resident rabbis simply failed to report their presence. Still, it is quite certain that only a minority of small-town Jews could count on having properly ordained yeshiva- or seminary-trained clergymen in their midst.

If most small-town congregations found it difficult to attract rabbis to their pulpits in the first place, they had at least as much trouble retaining those who did come. Whether they were formally ordained or not, most individuals hired as the spiritual leaders of synagogues and temples in small communities did not stay in one place for very long. This pattern was set already in the middle decades of the nineteenth century, as is suggested by the story of rabbinic leadership at congregation B'er Chayim in Cumberland, Maryland. There, the history of the congregation explains, Rabbi Juda Wechsler was hired in 1853 and "remained in charge one year." He was followed by Rabbi Hermann, who led the congregation for two years; then by Rabbi Strauss, who stayed for one year; then by Rabbi Freundlich for also remained only a year; and then by Rabbi Laser, who officiated for two years and left in 1860.[19] From one small town after another come similar sagas of rapid turnover throughout the late nineteenth and into the twentieth centuries, and of frequent periods without rabbinic leadership at all.

The history of the Bickur Cholim congregation in San Jose (later Temple Emanu-El) reflects the checkered pattern of rabbinic leadership that was common during the classic era of America's small communities. Bickur Cholim hired its first ordained rabbi, Myer Sol Levy of London, in 1873, and he stayed until 1881. The congregation then came under the leadership of Reverend Henry Loewenthal, who has already been mentioned. During the 1890s two rabbis whose tenures were quite short served Bikur Cholim, and from 1900 to 1902 the congregation was left with no rabbi at all. Then, however, Rabbi Julius Nathanson arrived and served for fourteen years until his death. For five years afterward, Bickur Cholim was again without a rabbi, and then

Harvey Franklin came for about a decade. During the Great Depression, lay leadership held sway, with a local judge, Joseph Karesh, often leading services. Only in 1939 was the congregation able to hire a rabbi once again.[20]

At San Bernardino's Congregation Emanu El the situation was similar. The first resident rabbi there was Samuel Margolis, who arrived in 1923. Margolis died the following year, however, and three other rabbis followed him in quick succession between 1925 and 1929. When the Depression began, the San Bernardino congregation had to forgo rabbinic leadership for a while, and even when it was able to hire Rabbi Jacob Alkow under precarious circumstances in 1931 (the rabbi sold insurance on the side to make ends meet), he stayed only until 1937. Rabbi Norman Feldheym was hired shortly after Rabbi Alkow's departure, but from 1942 to 1945 he was absent from his congregation while serving in the military.[21]

Back east, the story was much the same. A roster of those who served as the spiritual leaders of congregation Beth Israel in Plattsburg, New York, between 1862 and 1923 lists fifteen men with the title "Reverend," followed by two ordained rabbis. A list of the rabbis who served B'nai Abraham in Hagerstown, Maryland, between 1891 and 1947 runs to sixteen names. In Annapolis, Maryland, Kneseth Israel had twelve different spiritual leaders between 1909 and 1945, half of them ordained clergymen and the other half not. In Alexandria, Louisiana, eight men with the title "Reverend" served Congregation Gemiluth Chassodim between 1873 and 1901, with several gaps, and they were followed by ten ordained rabbis between 1901 and 1951, only two of whom stayed more than four years. In the twenty-five years before 1949, nine different rabbis served Congregation Agudas Achim in Leominster, Massachusetts; on average, each stayed less than three years. Paul Kronick, who grew up in North Adams, Massachusetts, in the period before World War II, recalled that the Orthodox synagogue there was served by rabbis who were "hired on two-year contracts, never renewed more than once," and, although he surely exaggerated, a St. Louis rabbi visiting Lexington, Kentucky, once referred to that city's Ohavay Zion as a congregation "where they get a [new] rabbi every six months."[22]

Given the transience of so many small-town rabbis, it is not surprising that many of those whose names appear in census documents were recorded as boarders living in the homes of others, rather than as occupants of their own homes. In 1880 the Hebrew "minister" Samuel Egen was listed as living in the home of Samuel Levy in Jackson, Michigan, for example, while in 1920 Rabbi Pinchus Magidson was registered as living with Jacob Kloin in Fitchburg, Massachusetts, and Rabbi Solomon Radinovsky was recorded as living with Joseph Katcher in Modesto, California. When David Greenberg arrived in Fresno, California, to assume his rabbinic duties there in 1931, he was advised to rent an apartment instead of buying a house. Although he remained in Fresno for sixty years, initially his congregants simply assumed he would not be around for long.[23]

There were a great many reasons why congregations in small communities had trouble holding on to their rabbis. Some of these reasons were not peculiar to small towns, but others certainly were. For one thing, small-town congregations, with their limited membership rosters, often found themselves hard pressed to pay rabbinic salaries. Thus, for example, when he first came to serve as the rabbi of the Beth Israel synagogue in Washington, Pennsylvania, Jacob Goldfarb was forced to help support himself by charging ten cents a head for the kosher slaughtering of chickens (he killed about 150 each week) and by holding a second job as an insurance agent. Although Goldfarb stayed on in Washington for over fifty years, dying there in 1941, other rabbis were not as willing to put up with low salaries. Rabbi Edward Chapman left Congregation Albert in Albuquerque, New Mexico, in 1910, for instance, because he deemed his salary there too low. Despite the fact that some of his congregants agreed, saying that the pay offered Chapman was "too measly for a man of the rabbi's ability and learning," no additional funds could be found. Similarly, Rabbi Allan Summers left Congregation Beth Shalom in Santa Ana, California, because that congregation, which had been struggling to maintain a rabbi beginning in the era of World War I, could not meet his salary demands in 1944.[24]

Funding a rabbinic position in a small community was especially problematic during the Great Depression, when even big-city congregations with huge constituencies found themselves in financial straits. The Reform congregation in Decatur, Illinois, for example, was forced to dismiss its rabbi, Efraim Rosenzweig, a 1928 graduate of HUC, when it found that it could no longer pay his salary in the early 1930s. At the time, Decatur had a Jewish population of about eighty-five people. In 1933 Rosenzweig went to Topeka, Kansas, and found that the congregation there was in financial trouble as well. Often when it came time to pay the rabbi's salary, funds were so scarce that the president of the synagogue had to "run around collecting the unpaid dues from the members."[25]

Another reason some rabbis left small towns was that they became involved in disputes with the lay leaders of their congregations. Although rabbis were the titular heads of their communities, the lay leaders of small-town synagogues were powerful individuals in their own right and often wielded much more authority than the clergymen they hired. In some cases, control over the rabbi was even written into congregational constitutions. The rules drafted in 1890 for the Reform Congregation Rodef Sholem in Wabash, Indiana, for example, stipulated the duties of the rabbi in great detail: he was to "attend all divine services in the Temple promptly," to be at every funeral conducted by the congregation, and to "deliver a sermon every Friday evening and Saturday morning and on all Holidays." The rabbi was not permitted to allow anyone to officiate in his stead "without special permission of the President"; he could not officiate at any rites of nonmembers "without the consent of the congregation"; and he had to perform any services "consistent with his station, whenever requested to do so by the President." At about the same time the constitution of the Tree of Life Congregation in Columbia, South Carolina, stipulated that the assembly's rabbi was not allowed to leave town without the permission of the synagogue's president. Sometimes congregations even attempted to control the most intimate affairs of their rabbis' lives. When the twenty-three-year-old Reuben Grafman was hired as the spiritual leader of the Orthodox synagogue in Bradford, Pennsylvania, in 1897, for instance, the congregation insisted that he get married before assuming his duties on the High Holidays. The elders of the community even had a bride in mind for Grafman, a local young woman by the name of Amelia Lipnotsky. Sure enough, after only a brief courtship, the couple wed in August 1897, and Grafman assumed his post.[26]

Among the religious leaders of small-town congregations, there were certainly some who were willing to abide by the conditions imposed upon them without question. Reverend Isaac Fall, who served as spiritual leader of B'nai Israel in Davenport, Iowa, during the latter years of the nineteenth century, was described by Simon Glazer, an early twentieth-century observer of Iowa Jewry, as "ever ready to yield to the demands of his flock." Even though he himself was "most Orthodox," according to Glazer, he "never raised a voice of protest against any radical measure ventured by his constituents and was ever ready to follow every sort of naïve customs [sic] promulgated by them."[27] It is unlikely, however, that most rabbinic leaders were as pliant as the Reverend Fall, and those who wanted to exert their own influence were particularly vulnerable whenever congregational controversies arose. Especially in small towns where a single congregation was expected to fulfill the needs of a broad membership, rabbis who attempted to follow their own instincts had trouble surviving. As early as 1902 one observer of small-town Jewish life lamented that every time a congregation in a place with a single synagogue found a rabbi who, "wonder of wonders," appeared able to deal with a diverse constituency ("He is liberal enough to please the radical, and quotes Hebrew glibly enough to please the conservative"), it turned out that he was too controversial. His situation became "very unpleasant," and before long he would decide to seek "greener fields and pastures new."[28]

As if to illustrate this perceptive early twentieth-century analysis, the nephew of Rabbi Julius Nathanson, who served in pre–World War I San Jose, recalled that his uncle "was trying to please the Orthodox and . . . the Reform and he was getting squeezed in the middle." In a similar vein, the untenable position of many small-town rabbis was reflected in the fact that when Congregation Beth Shalom in Frederick, Maryland, dismissed Rabbi Meyer Goldman in 1936 in the midst of a debate over whether the congregation would continue with an Orthodox or Reform identity, it charged him with the "repudiation of the established principles of Judaism and the flagrant violation of the conditions of his contract." The published history of the House of Israel in Sharon, Pennsylvania, recognized quite specifically the difficulties faced by assertive rabbis trying to balance the various demands of a diverse congregation, observing that in Sharon "the Rabbi was never really given a free hand to lead the Congregation and thus it was that no Rabbi ever stayed very long."[29]

It was not only problems arising within a congregation that could lead to a rabbi's departure, but also involvements outside the synagogue. Though Reform temples were especially eager to have their spiritual leaders active in civic affairs and social action, even they were uncomfortable if their rabbis became too visible in support of controversial causes. Since most small-town Jews were businesspeople who depended for their livelihood on the goodwill of their fellow citizens, they did not want their rabbis involved in the more sensitive social issues of the day. Foreshadowing the kinds of problems that would arise for the rabbis of some southern congregations in the civil rights era, in 1907 Rabbi J. H. Kaplan resigned rather abruptly from the pulpit of Congregation Albert in Albuquerque in part because his passionate objection to lynching had become controversial. Similarly, Rabbi A. L. Krohn was forced out of the same pulpit in 1938 because many in the congregation objected to his strong support for local farmers suffering during the Depression.[30]

Of course, it did not always take disputes to motivate small-town rabbis to leave their posts. Some, it seems, simply tired of the rabbinate. In 1920 Rabbi David Fishmon left his congregation in Lake Charles, Louisiana, to begin work with a charitable society in New Orleans, for instance; and in 1933 Rabbi Lawrence Broh Kahn abandoned Congregation Adath Israel in Lexington, Kentucky, for a career as a lawyer. Earlier, in 1891, Rabbi Samuel Freuder had resigned from his pulpit in Davenport, Iowa. An 1886 graduate of HUC, he had lost interest not only in the rabbinate, but in Judaism itself. Following his resignation, Freuder converted to Christianity.[31]

Certainly the most compelling reason that rabbis vacated their small-town pulpits, however, was that they had their sights set on moving up to more prestigious positions in larger communities. Even though there were some rabbis who spent their entire careers in a single small community, or in a succession of such communities—Joseph Utschen, for example, served as rabbi in Athens, Georgia; Petersburg, Virginia; Topeka, Kansas; Gastonia, North Carolina; and Gadsden, Alabama, between 1926 and 1963—most aspired to serve in larger Jewish centers. Indeed, most notably in the Reform movement, there seems to have been a sort of hierarchy of pulpits. Rabbis were more or less expected to start their careers in smaller communities but to use their initial positions as stepping stones to appointments at more substantial congregations in large or at least midsize cities. So, for example, Rabbi Edward Calisch, who served as president of the CCAR from 1921 to 1923, held a pulpit in Peoria, Illinois, for four years after his ordination at HUC in 1887 and then moved on to Beth Ahabah in Richmond, Virginia, where he remained for over fifty years. Rabbi Jacob Raisin, who came to the United States from Poland in 1892 and graduated from HUC in 1900, occupied pulpits in Port Gibson, Mississippi; Butte, Montana; Las Vegas, New Mexico; and Troy, New York, before assuming a position at Beth Elohim in Charleston, South Carolina, the cradle of Reform Judaism in America, and serving there from 1915 until 1944. Similarly, the Brooklyn-born Rabbi Samuel J. Levinson occupied pulpits in Greenwood, Mississippi; Lincoln, Illinois; and Muncie, Indiana, before returning to his birthplace in 1911 to serve for thirty-six years as spiritual leader of Temple Beth Emeth in Flatbush.[32]

When Rabbi Nathan Krass died in 1949, his colleague Max Raisin observed that Krass's life story read "like a fairy-tale" because of "the way he rose from comparative obscurity in the rabbinate to what is regarded as the top-most rabbinical position in the land." Graduating from HUC in 1903, Krass had occupied pulpits in several small communities, including those of Owensboro, Kentucky, and Lafayette, Indiana, before being called to more visible posts, initially in Rochester, then in Brooklyn, and finally in Manhattan, where he served first New York's Central Synagogue and then Temple Emanu-El, perhaps the most prestigious pulpit in American Reform. So common was the practice of starting in a small-town pulpit and then advancing to a big-city congregation that one observer of the Reform rabbinate has reported that over the decades "rabbis questioned the success of their colleagues who had chosen to serve a small city congregation," noting that it was not uncommon to hear talk about this or that rabbi who was " 'stuck' in a small city because he [was] not suited for anything better."[33]

Among Orthodox and Conservative rabbis who found themselves in small communities, escape seemed to be the usual goal as well. The most accomplished traditionalists were always on the lookout for opportunities to relocate to larger communities with a greater number of observant Jews and more resources. So, for instance, in 1904 the Hungarian rabbi Henry Einhorn was attracted away from Beth Abraham in Zanesville, Ohio, to Tifereth Israel in Columbus. Similarly, in 1911 the Polish-born Israel Rosenberg, who had been educated at the famous yeshiva of Slobodka and had come to America in 1909, left Burlington, Vermont, for New York City, where he eventually became head of the Union of Orthodox Rabbis of the United States and Canada. Of the nine JTS-trained rabbis who held pulpits in triple-digit Jewish communities in 1929, four had left by 1931. Rabbi Jacob Cohen, for example, departed Agudath B'nai Israel in Lorain, Ohio, for Temple Emanuel in Lawrence, Mas-

sachusetts, a community of some 4,000 Jews at the time, while Rabbi Nathan
Lublin left Adath Yeshurun in Manchester, New Hampshire, for Beth Elohim
in the Bronx. The first ordained rabbi hired by the Orthodox Kneseth Israel
congregation in Annapolis, Maryland, was Morris E. Gordon, who arrived in
1935. He was an energetic leader who organized youth activities, inaugurated
a Friday-evening lecture series, brought his sisters to town to teach in the
congregation's Hebrew school, and helped found the local B'nai B'rith lodge.
Nonetheless, offered a position in New York City, he was gone by 1937.[34]

Local observers of the situation understood very well how common it was
for small towns to lose their best rabbis to more substantial congregations in
larger Jewish centers. Murry Milkman, who lived in Pittston, Pennsylvania,
from 1929 until 1947, has explained, for instance, that his town "was a 'starting' place" that had "a steady succession of 'starter' rabbis," including a
brother of the entertainer Jackie Mason, whom Milkman remembered as "a
pretty funny guy." Similarly, in 1955 Rabbi Julius Kerman explained the fact
that since 1913 eleven rabbis had preceded him in Natchez, Mississippi, by
simply pointing out that "larger cities with wider fields lured rabbis away from
here." The Jews of Topeka, Kansas, too, understood the nature of rabbinic
careers. The published history of their community remarks that many of the
problems associated with finding rabbinic leadership "stemmed from the fact
that Topeka was considered a beginner's pulpit. Often a rabbi would expect to
move on to a larger, more prestigious, and better funded congregation," the
history concludes, "and usually the congregation expected it too."[35]

Despite their reluctance to remain in small towns, many of the rabbis
who assumed leadership positions in small communities enjoyed their early
tenures and recognized the value of their experience there. So, for example,
Efraim Rosenzweig, who had served in Topeka during the Depression and
then moved on to Scranton, Pennsylvania, and Hillel work in North Carolina,
later thanked Topeka's Temple Beth Sholom for "helping me, a young rabbi,
deepen my understanding of what being a rabbi was all about." Similarly,
Rabbi Albert M. Lewis, who was ordained at HUC in 1939 and served Adath
Israel in Lexington, Kentucky, in the era of World War II, acknowledged that
both his understanding of how a congregation functions and his commitments
to social justice and to Zionism were shaped by his early experiences in Kentucky. Many rabbis who began their careers in small towns would have identified with Rabbi Max Raisin's comments when he noted in his memorial for
Rabbi Nathan Krass that each of the early ministries Krass had served in a
small community had functioned as "a stage in the process which made him
the distinguished man of his later years."[36]

The fondness that many rabbis had for their early small-town posts was
only reinforced if they forged some sort of personal connection to the places
where they had started out. It was not uncommon, for instance, for small-

town rabbis to meet their future wives in the local community. After all, many rabbis arrived to serve small-town synagogues or temples at just the time that they were ready to get married. Thus, Rabbi Ferdinand Hirsch married Nellie Levinson in 1909 soon after serving in her home town of Bessemer, Alabama, and Rabbi Max Handman married Della Doppelmayer, daughter of a Marshall, Texas, pioneer, while he was serving that community in 1910. Similarly, "the handsome young Rabbi Lowenstein" married Leonora Berger, daughter of one of La Crosse's wealthiest nineteenth-century Jews, after he met her when he came from Cincinnati to Wisconsin to conduct High Holiday services.[37]

Although congregations that experienced a rapid turnover of clergy would certainly have preferred greater stability, the fact that they were more or less prepared for the early departure of their best rabbis can only have smoothed the experience of the men they attracted by forestalling the development of unrealistic expectations. Some congregations actually expressed satisfaction that they had benefited, if only briefly, from the presence of able young rabbis early in their careers. When Rabbi G. George Fox died in 1960, a colleague observed that long after he had left his first pulpit in Bloomington, Illinois, where he had gone immediately after his ordination in 1908, the congregation there "retained fond memories of his ministry and frequently availed itself of his services." A member of the Temple Israel congregation in Lafayette, Indiana, writing at the midpoint of the twentieth century, expressed happiness that "through a great good fortune" his synagogue "was served by a number of gifted Rabbis in the early days of their ministry. Many of these men later came to occupy pre-eminent posts in American Jewish religious life," he wrote, and in this, his little congregation "rejoiced with almost paternal pride."[38]

Given the paucity of rabbis serving long tenures in small-town congregations, many small communities found themselves developing ways to function without resident rabbis for at least some periods. Some places came to rely on itinerant functionaries who were engaged to lead services only on special occasions, most notably the High Holidays. In more traditional congregations, visiting prayer leaders were engaged mainly for their cantorial skills. In liberal congregations, the premium was on sermonizing. Although the visiting clergymen hired had at least some talents that were lacking among local Jewish residents, the abilities and qualifications of these individuals were not always beyond question. The distiller and philanthropist Isaac Bernheim, who spent the first part of his career in Paducah, Kentucky, has left a very colorful description of the "traveling reader" who would find employment in one small town or another around the turn of the twentieth century. Such a person "almost always styled himself a Rabbi," Bernheim related, although in reality he was likely to be either "an unsuccessful German teacher" or "an individual who claimed to have attended some Yeshiba in

Poland." He might even be "a foreign clerk, without a job, who had a smatter-
ing of Hebrew knowledge." During the High Holiday season "the woods were
full of them," Bernheim asserted, and these traveling prayer leaders were, in
general, "a peculiar and none too conscientious lot." Still, it is likely that few of
the itinerant rabbis who showed up in small towns were as bad as the Reverend Moses Cohen, who is reported to have raised a hundred dollars during his
Yom Kippur appeal in Davenport, Iowa, in 1867 and then to have absconded
with the money.[39]

Other communities that had to rely on outsiders for religious leadership
depended on rabbinical students who would visit periodically. The most consistent supplier of seminarians was Hebrew Union College, which had a well-
established system for dispatching student rabbis to serve isolated Jewish
settlements. HUC sent students not only to places in which Reform Judaism
was already firmly rooted, but also to those in which there was only a potential
for formal affiliation with the Reform movement. The idea was that students
from the college would gain valuable on-the-job training while also spreading
the gospel of Reform.

In some small communities, senior HUC students would visit as often as
once or twice a month. In 1922–23, for example, fifteen students were serving
midwestern congregations on a biweekly basis. In Ohio these students were
going to Hamilton, Lima, Portsmouth, Springfield, Steubenville, and Zanesville. In Kentucky they were going to Lexington, Owensboro, and Ashland.
Sheldon Blank, later a professor of Bible at HUC, was traveling to Jackson,
Tennessee; and Nelson Glueck, a future president of HUC, was going to Saginaw, Michigan. During the High Holiday season, HUC students served an
even greater number of hinterland communities. In 1928, for instance, sixty-
one seminarians were dispatched to small towns all over the country. They
went to places such as Jackson, Michigan, and Jackson, Mississippi; Springfield, Ohio, and Springfield, Missouri; Danville, Illinois, and Danville, Pennsylvania. A list of the rabbinical students who served the Reform congregation
Beth El in Danville, Illinois, between 1919 and the mid-1960s runs to thirty-
four names.[40]

HUC was not alone in providing visiting rabbinical students to small-town
congregations, however. Certainly by the 1920s, if not earlier, JTS and RIETS
were dispatching their students to assist with High Holiday services as well,
both as a way of building connections with more isolated congregations and in
order to give their students some practice in preaching. Indeed, small communities composed of traditionalist Jews were actively encouraged to invite
student rabbis to officiate on Rosh Hashanah and Yom Kippur. Samuel L. Sar,
who was in charge of placements for RIETS, wrote in 1924 to one congregation
in Haverstraw, New York, that "the Yeshiva will be more than delighted to
send you for the high holidays a man who will deliver sermons in both English

and Yiddish." To North Adams, Massachusetts, Sar wrote that he was prepared to send a young man who would "deliver sermons that will be both instructive and entertaining." One list of rabbinical students dispatched from RIETS to High Holiday pulpits in 1927 indicates that the seminary accommodated the needs of Orthodox congregations in small towns such as Fitchburg in Massachusetts, Bristol on the Virginia-Tennessee border, and Mount Carmel, Oil City, and Norristown in Pennsylvania.[41]

Yet another approach adopted in many small communities that found themselves without resident rabbis was to establish some sort of ongoing relationship with a rabbi or a congregation in a larger city in the region. Thus, Edward Calisch of Beth Ahabah in Richmond made trips on many occasions to Charlottesville and to Staunton, Virginia. Similarly, for a time after World War I, Charles A. Rubenstein, the retired rabbi of the Har Sinai Temple in Baltimore, commuted to Cumberland, Maryland, on a biweekly basis. Beginning in 1926 and for the next twenty years, Rabbi Arthur Bonnheim commuted from Chicago to serve as the spiritual leader of the Sinai Congregation in Michigan City, Indiana; and for several years beginning in 1927, Rabbi Morris Goldblatt commuted from JTS in New York to conduct services on a part-time basis at congregation Shomrei Emunah in Montclair, New Jersey.[42] Sometimes small-town congregations even altered the schedule of their weekly worship services in order to accommodate visiting rabbis. In the 1920s the main religious service in Williamson, West Virginia, was held on Sunday evenings, when Rabbi Abraham Feinstein was able to come from Huntington; and in the late 1930s Rabbi Jerome Mark of Knoxville commuted to Bristol, Virginia, where he conducted Sunday afternoon "spiritual meetings" once a month. In Danville, Illinois, even the essentially traditionalist congregation had Sabbath services on Thursday evenings for a time so that they could be led by a commuting rabbi, probably from Chicago.[43]

Of course, any system of clerical leadership that depended on intermittent visitors left a lot to be desired, and in the end most small-town congregations without resident rabbis looked for ways to sustain their religious activities on a more regular basis. In order to do this, they often came to rely upon knowledgeable laypeople from within their own ranks to conduct services and to perform other rabbinic functions. In congregations established by German Jews in the nineteenth century, this was possible because each community was likely to have at least a few residents who brought the necessary linguistic and liturgical skills with them from Europe. In early Petersburg, Virginia, for example, the local congregation was at times led by A. S. Naustedler, who had come to America from Augsburg in Germany. One member of the local community in 1877 remembered Naustedler as a man "profoundly versed in the Talmud and in the traditions," whose "mind was stored with rabbinical lore and who was generally called 'Rabbi' by his friends and acquaintances." In Albany, Georgia, the local Jewish community chose the merchant and later journalist Charles Wessolowsky as their religious leader. He remained in that role for twenty-three years, until the Albany community was able to hire its first ordained rabbi in 1889. As his biographer has noted, Wessolowsky's "extensive biblical and talmudic training, his fluency in Hebrew, his knowledge of ritual and ceremony and his oratorical ability were credentials [the local community] could not ignore."[44]

Even as the number of immigrants in America's German-Jewish settlements diminished, a reliance on lay leadership remained an option because virtually all of the country's German-Jewish congregations adopted Reform. As a result English became the main language of prayer, rituals were simplified, and considerations of *halachah* became more or less irrelevant. Despite the fact that Reform Jews were more likely than traditionalists to see rabbis as essential for the conduct of a proper prayer service—when the Reform Jews of Rockford, Illinois, were unable to secure the services of a student rabbi for Passover in 1923, they canceled their arrangements for a communal seder—they generally preferred a lay-led service to none at all. A story about the newly established Reform congregation in Boise, Idaho, that appeared in the Jewish press in 1899 is instructive. It explained that although the congregation understood that their temple "was not complete without a rabbi," its members were nonetheless conducting services themselves and even delivering sermons "that would do credit to regularly ordained ministers."[45]

Examples abound of Reform temples that functioned for long periods without resident rabbinic figures of any sort. In Charlottesville, Virginia, a rabbi was hired by the Beth Israel congregation soon after it built its first synagogue in 1882, but a few years after that lay leaders took over, and Charlottesville was not served by a full-time rabbi again until 1939, when one was hired jointly by the congregation and the Jewish student union at the University of Virginia (soon to be one of the country's early Hillel chapters). For many decades in Springfield, Missouri, the president of Temple Israel generally "read the service," for only on the High Holidays was the congregation able to bring a student from HUC, and only in 1940 was it able to hire its first rabbi, Karl Richter, a refugee from Nazi Germany who had previously led a large congregation in Mannheim. In Trinidad, Colorado, Leopold Freudenthal, whose tenure came to an end in 1916, was the last full-time rabbi at the town's Temple Aaron, and after he died members of the local Sanders family took charge of conducting services: Leopold Sanders until his death in 1935 and then his brother Gilbert until his death in 1952. Gilbert's widow, Beatrice, took over after that and kept the congregation going into the 1980s.[46]

In congregations established by East European Jews around the turn of the twentieth century, lay leadership was less of a conceptual problem than it was in Reform temples, and perhaps less of a practical problem as well, since a fair number of East European immigrants brought with them some training in Jewish texts and liturgy. The claim by the historian of the La Crosse Jewish community that the East European Jews who arrived there "were nearly all learned in Judaic law and many came from distinguished rabbinic backgrounds" is probably an exaggeration,[47] but there is no doubt that in La Crosse and similar small towns there were enough East Europeans educated in traditional practice to provide most of the skills needed in an Orthodox community. The lay leaders who conducted services in small-town shuls were likely to be individuals who were already serving the Jewish community in some other capacity. They may have come to town first as kosher butchers, for instance, or as *melamdim*, old-fashioned Hebrew teachers. Indeed, they were probably prized at least as much for their role in providing kosher meat and for their willingness to try to educate the children as they were for their more specifically "clerical" abilities. Clearly reflecting the sense that every Orthodox community needed someone to act as ritual slaughterer and teacher even if it had no rabbi is a 1908 letter from the Cohn Brothers, scrap dealers in Waterloo, Iowa, to the Industrial Removal Office in New York. The communication informed the IRO that one Jacob Bobrov would soon be applying for assistance in reaching Waterloo. "We beg of you to help him out and to send him to our city," the Cohn Brothers pleaded, "as we need him for a schochet and a melomed."[48]

The laymen who assumed rabbinic duties in small-town Orthodox communities were perhaps provided some additional remuneration for their efforts, and, like many of the full-time functionaries who served American congregations without benefit of ordination, they were often accorded the title "Reverend." Examples of small communities in which teachers, kosher butchers, and grocers became the key figures in Orthodox congregations are numerous. In Englewood, New Jersey, the *shochet* Benjamin Sher helped organize congregation Ahavath Torah in 1895 and then served as its spiritual leader for several decades. In the early days of the Orthodox community of Ann Arbor, Michigan, services were held in the home of the *shochet* Pincus Gropstein, who not only led prayers but also taught children at his house during the week. Gropstein left in 1921 and was replaced in 1924 by Jacob Kamenetzky, who performed the same functions as his predecessor.[49]

Aaron Zussman, a native of Minsk, arrived in Appleton, Wisconsin, in 1910 and from 1912 until 1919 served as "cantor, teacher, 'shochet,' and spiritual leader" of the Moses Montefiore congregation. In later years he continued to assist the rabbis hired by the congregation while also running a grocery. In Kankakee, Illinois, the *shochet* Joseph Mirovetz was also "rabbi" when Congregation B'nai Israel built its first synagogue in 1922, and he continued in both his roles until his death in 1940. In Lexington, Kentucky, it was "Reverend" Harry Goller, owner of a kosher food store, who oversaw activities at the Orthodox Ohavay Zion synagogue whenever that congregation was without a rabbi. A list of early twentieth-century leaders of Congregation Beth Jacob in Plymouth, Massachusetts, includes not only the names of several rabbis, but also "old 'Melamed' Nathanson" and " 'Sheched' [i.e., *shochet*] Steinberg."[50]

The same survey in which about a quarter of the 490 triple-digit Jewish communities in our sample reported having a resident rabbi in 1919 also indicates that congregations in at least forty-six of these communities reported that they were led by religious functionaries with other titles. These individuals were identified variously as "reader," "cantor," "acting rabbi," "rabbi-cantor," and, in Lima, Ohio, even "shohet and reader."[51] Small communities were so accustomed to dealing with having no permanent rabbinic leadership that some responded with near amazement when they did secure a rabbi. In 1939, when the Jews of Rome, Georgia, were able to recruit a rabbi for the first time, they enthused that "he was not a student rabbi, not a shochet, not even a visitor from Atlanta—but a rabbi who had come from New York City expressly to care for the spiritual needs of Rome Jewry."[52]

Clearly, religious leadership meant something very different in small towns than it did in larger Jewish centers. For one thing, those rabbis who were most successful as the leaders of small-town congregations, including those who chose to stay in small communities throughout their careers, were often quite different in their attitudes and expectations from rabbis serving in larger communities. They were likely to be content living in places without other Jewish professionals with whom they could interact and likely to be very comfortable fulfilling a multiplicity of roles. So, too, they were likely to be willing to forgo large salaries, and sometimes even to work at more than one job in order to make ends meet. Perhaps most of all, successful small-town rabbis were ones who were able to accommodate the needs of Jews with a variety of religious inclinations in places where their congregants usually did not have the option of moving to other temples or synagogues.

Furthermore, religious leadership in small communities was different because only in small communities did congregations so frequently have to develop strategies for keeping Jewish life alive without the benefit of ordained rabbis. Only in small towns were visiting rabbis and rabbinical students so critical to the continuity of local religious activity, and only in smaller Jewish settlements were Hebrew teachers, kosher butchers, and others with a grounding in religious texts so frequently thrust into positions as the primary religious authorities for their communities. Thus, the story of religious leadership in the classic era of America's smaller Jewish centers serves as yet another powerful reminder of just how distinctive Jewish life was in small-town America.

# 10   Patterns of Culture: The German Jews

Among the primary goals of the families that founded those small Jewish communities whose history stretched back into the middle decades of the nineteenth century were rapid acculturation and swift entry into the ranks of the comfortable middle class. The occupational choices made by the heads of these pioneer families tended to facilitate their economic success, and to the extent that their businesses prospered, these individuals became widely recognized and centrally involved in the day-to-day life of their towns. To their gentile fellow citizens, these small-town Jewish storekeepers, livestock dealers, skilled artisans, and professionals, almost invariably of Central European background, constituted an important element of the population that provided valuable links to the larger world. And the German Jews of small-town America forged ties with their gentile neighbors in other ways as well. They often became involved in the civic and political affairs of their towns, for instance, and their organizations took their place as integral elements of the local institutional infrastructure.

Still, the German Jews of America's small communities were not totally absorbed into the social fabric of their towns. Not only did their religion set them apart, but, because of the fundamental character of their communities and because of a lingering anti-Jewish prejudice, both the men and the women of America's small-town German-Jewish communities sought to maintain at least something of a distinctive social and cultural life, one often centered on membership organizations such as B'nai B'rith and the National Council of Jewish Women. As we shall discover, even in the relatively comfortable atmosphere of small-town America, German Jews always felt a certain tension between their identity as citizens well known to their neighbors and their identity as Jews operating within their own cultural milieu.

One indication that the early Jewish families of small-town America were strongly linked to the general culture of their surroundings is that German-

*Photo opposite page: The Beth Israel synagogue in Macon, Georgia, constructed in 1902. The architectural style of this temple erected by the German-Jewish families of Macon reflects their status as citizens well integrated into their local environment. Photo by the author.*

Jewish men often became members, and frequently officers, of local fraternal lodges. So, too, they commonly participated in efforts to establish hospitals, libraries, and even communal organizations with Christian identities, such as YMCAs. In late nineteenth-century Phoenix, Jews were even members of the earliest volunteer fire companies, which not only provided a valuable public service but also functioned as prestigious social organizations.[1] The integration of early Jewish settlers into the society of their small towns was facilitated by their frequent identification with Germanic culture generally and their consequent association with gentiles of German background. In Wilmington, North Carolina, for instance, it was Rabbi Samuel Mendelssohn who led a memorial service marking the death of Kaiser Wilhelm in 1888, and German Jews there were leading members of organizations such as the German-American Alliance and the Wilmington German Club into the early decades of the twentieth century.[2] In the racially bifurcated society of the South, moreover, the acceptance of Jews as part of the white population further reinforced their participation in the social mainstream.

In one small town after another during the late nineteenth and early twentieth centuries, it was common to encounter men of German-Jewish stock who had emerged as prominent citizens deeply engaged in local affairs. Some such individuals have already been mentioned in our consideration of immigrants who became firmly rooted in various secondary urban centers, and there is no shortage of additional examples. In Williamsport, Pennsylvania, for instance, there was the storeowner and real estate investor Abraham Hart, who was not only a president of Temple Beth Ha-Shalom but also "an active and liberal supporter of the . . . Chamber of Commerce industrial fund" and "a member of several Masonic bodies, taking a keen interest in the rites of the lodge." In Anniston, Alabama, there was the clothier Joseph Saks, a fifty-year resident once described as a "Mason, a Shriner, a member of the Knights of Pythias, an Elk, and a charter member of the local Red Cross, the Rotary Club, and the Anniston Country Club." Saks also funded a school on the outskirts of Anniston that became the core of the hamlet of Saks, Alabama. In Davenport, Iowa, there was Emanuel Adler, who arrived to manage the local newspaper in 1899 and eventually served as president of the Greater Davenport Committee, a trustee of the Davenport Museum, a director of the Mississippi Valley Fair and of the YMCA, chairman of the local Red Cross, and a founder of the Davenport Industrial Commission. It is little wonder that congregations dominated by Jewish men such as these expected their rabbis to be joiners as well.[3]

Perhaps the ultimate manifestation of the involvement of German Jews in the prevailing culture of their towns was their willingness, even eagerness, to enter local politics. Just about every small Jewish community of the late nineteenth century could claim at least a few Jews who, while making contributions to civic affairs in other ways as well, became aldermen, postmasters, mayors, state assemblymen, and the like. In Albany, Georgia, during the 1870s, for instance, the merchant and community leader Charles Wessolowsky served as alderman, clerk of the county superior court, state representative, and state senator. For fifty-five years after Wessolowsky prepared the way, there was always a member of the Jewish community on the Albany city council. In Rome, Georgia, Max Meyerhardt, an officer of the local Masonic lodge for thirty-nine years, was elected city court judge in 1887. It is said that in deference to his religious background, he would not hold court on Saturdays, and so after four years in office he stepped down rather than continue to impose the schedule dictated by his religious sensibilities on his fellow townspeople. In Charlottesville, Virginia, Moses Leterman, who helped create the local chamber of commerce in 1888, and who raised funds for restoration work at the University of Virginia after a fire there in 1896, also served as president of the city council. Leterman's father, Simon, had served on the town council even before Charlottesville was incorporated as a city, and his mother Hannah had been one of the founders of the local temperance league.[4]

In Cumberland, Maryland, Isaac Hirsch was president of the city council in 1895. He also played a key role in establishing the municipal lighting plant in 1898 and helped create a new city waterworks in 1908. In Bradford, Pennsylvania, Joseph Greenewald was elected to the city council in 1881 and, as an advocate of municipal ownership of essential services such as the water company, went on to serve as president of the council and later as mayor of Bradford. In Muscatine, Iowa, Morris Neidig served as an alderman from 1876 to 1878 and was followed in that position by his brother Benjamin in the 1880s and by David Rothschild Jr., another member of the local Jewish community. In Trinidad, Colorado, Sam Jaffa was elected chairman of the town council when Trinidad was incorporated in 1876, and two other Jews were elected to the city's board of trustees. In Albuquerque, New Mexico, Henry Jaffa, a relative of Trinidad's Sam, was elected mayor in 1885, and in 1890 another Jew, Mike Mandell, succeeded him. In Phoenix, Arizona, Emil Ganz held the office of mayor twice toward the end of the nineteenth century.[5]

The pattern of political service established by Central European Jews in the 1800s continued well into the twentieth century. In Danville, Illinois, for instance, Louis Platt became mayor in the first decade of the century, and his son Casper became a federal judge. In Boise, Idaho, Moses Alexander was elected mayor in 1897, and from 1915 to 1919 he served two terms as governor of his state, the first Jew in America to hold such a post. In Natchez, Mississippi, Saul Laub, whose family had got its start in the city with a modest drygoods store soon after the Civil War, served as mayor from 1929 to 1936. In Greensboro, North Carolina, where the textile manufacturing Cone family was a major presence in the community (Laura Cone was the first women to

*Moses Alexander, mayor of Boise and governor of Idaho from 1915 to 1919. German Jews were well represented among political officeholders in small-town America. Courtesy of the Jacob Rader Marcus Center of the American Jewish Archives.*

serve as president of the Greensboro Community Chest, for example, and the family created the Moses H. Cone Memorial Hospital), Benjamin Cone served as mayor from 1949 to 1951.[6]

Of course, accounts of the history of America's various small Jewish communities are far more likely to record examples of civic virtue than examples of dissolute behavior. Nonetheless, some of the documentary evidence available suggests that in their zeal to acculturate, the Jewish citizens of small-town America adopted many of the corruptions of the majority culture, just as they took upon themselves many of its more attractive attributes. A case in point is the involvement of middle-class Jewish men in the small towns of the South in illicit interracial sexual relationships. Census records from 1880 Alexandria, Louisiana, for instance, reveal a number of cases of mulatto children living with their black or biracial mothers but bearing the surnames of local Jewish families. For example, the mulatto James Heyman, an eight-year-old living with his black mother, Ann, then twenty-four years old, and his stepfather, Adolph Anderson, was almost certainly fathered by a Jewish Alexandrian, as was the biracial Mary Heyman, a nine-year-old living with both her widowed mother, a forty-four-year-old woman of mixed race herself, and her eighty-five-year-old grandmother. Similarly revealing is the composition of the household of Morris Weil, a forty-five-year-old Jewish peddler who had never been married. Living with Weil were an unmarried twenty-year-old mulatto cook named Martha Hayes and Martha's five-year-old daughter, tellingly named Julia Weil. The fact that in all these cases the biracial children who were born out of wedlock carried Jewish surnames suggests that their Jewish fathers at least acknowledged their offspring and thus probably provided them some support.[7]

In the same way that the behavior of individuals reflected the high degree to which German Jews were integrated into the culture of their small towns, so, too, did many of the activities of their communal institutions. For all their eagerness to found congregations and to establish their own charitable societies, these Jews always envisioned such institutions as elements within the larger constellation of local civic society. Nothing better reveals the extent to which the German Jews of small-town America saw their religious activities as bound up with public life than the way in which they included their Christian fellow citizens in the dedication ceremonies of their synagogues. In one town after another, whenever a German-Jewish congregation laid the cornerstone for a temple or consecrated a new house of worship, the festivities surrounding the event became occasions to involve many segments of their small-town society. The procession that marched to the cornerstone laying of the new B'Nai Sholom temple in Quincy, Illinois, in 1869, for example, included, among others, the mayor of Quincy and members of the city council, judges of the local courts, clergymen of several faiths, members of the Masonic order, and reporters from the press. When Rodeph Shalom of Petersburg, Virginia, laid the cornerstone for its first temple in 1876, the procession to the site of the new building came down the town's main street led by a brass band, and all the Masonic lodges in Petersburg, as well as the mayor, participated in the ceremonies. The cornerstone laying for Temple Israel in Paducah, Kentucky, in 1893 was described as "a joyous meeting of Jew and Gentile"; and when Beth Israel's new temple was dedicated in Boise, Idaho, in 1896, the large audience present consisted principally of Christians "who were interested in God, worshipped from a Jewish standpoint on this occasion."[8]

The ease with which Jewish and Christian congregations made use of each other's buildings also reveals the extent to which small-town Jews were able to create parallels between their religious activities and those of their Christian neighbors. In Bloomington, Illinois, for instance, the earliest Jewish services were held in the Boston Shoe Store owned by a Jewish merchant, but they were later moved to the basement of the town's Free Congressional Church. In 1901 and 1902 Beth Israel in Macon, Georgia, used the First Baptist Church for its functions while its second synagogue building was under construction (the first building had been abandoned because the neighborhood in which it stood had become a noisy market area—at one point the congregation had petitioned the city council to prohibit the eating of watermelon on its steps). When the B'nai Israel temple in Natchez, Mississippi, burned down in 1903, the congregation received offers from the Methodist, Baptist, and Episcopal churches in the neighborhood to hold services in their buildings. By the same token, the Baptist congregation in Macon that later lent its building to Beth Israel had itself used the temple's facilities when its church had burned in 1883. Toward the end of the nineteenth century, both the English Lutheran Church and the Methodist Church of Cumberland, Maryland, made use of the synagogue of Congregation B'er Chayim when their buildings were under construction or being repaired. Apparently the rabbi of B'er Chayim even preached to the Lutherans. In Albuquerque the First Methodist Episcopal Church was invited to use Temple Albert for its services in 1904 while its own building was being completed, and when a Methodist church in Vicksburg, Mississippi, burned down in 1929, Anshe Chesed offered its facilities for use by that church's congregation.[9]

That Christians frequently contributed funds for the construction of synagogue buildings can also be seen as evidence of how successful Jewish congregations were in fostering good relations with the Christian majority in their small towns and forging links between their sectarian activities and their identities as part of the larger society. When a new temple was dedicated in Columbia, South Carolina, in 1905, the local newspaper made specific reference to the good feelings between Christians and Jews in that town. Noting that both Jews and gentiles had contributed money to erect the structure and had attended its dedication, the paper editorialized that although "evidence of breadth and the utmost religious tolerance in this community is nothing new . . . it is well that it be emphasized." In an apparent reference to the pogroms in Russia in 1905, the paper added that it was especially important to highlight cooperation between Christians and Jews when "in some of the countries of Europe bigotry is carried to the extremes of barbarity—in the name of Christianity."[10] Given the atmosphere of interfaith cooperation that prevailed in Columbia, it is not surprising that in the early decades of the twentieth century the local Hebrew Benevolent Society, dominated by well-established men connected with the local Reform congregation, made its two largest contributions to civic causes rather than to exclusively Jewish concerns. The group gave one large donation to the county antituberculosis association and another to the victims of a storm that had killed fifteen children when a local schoolhouse collapsed.[11] In their attempts to connect their religious activities with the larger civic culture of their surroundings, the German Jews of Columbia were far from unusual.

Part of what facilitated the gentile acceptance of small-town German Jews on such equal terms was the adoption by their congregations of a Reform ideology that deemphasized Jewish particularism, stressed decorum in the conduct of worship services, and mimicked many mainstream Protestant practices. Indeed, one reason that Reform congregations so welcomed gentile interest in their activities and press scrutiny of their affairs was that openness to the public enabled Jews to reassure their Christian neighbors that they were very much like their fellow citizens. Even though members of the public were often drawn to synagogues in the hope of observing strange and unfamiliar customs, the Reform congregations themselves wanted non-Jews to understand that Jewish rites were not all that exotic. As one small-town Jew told a Reform rabbi at the turn of the twentieth century, it was important to open synagogue services to public view in order "to show the gentiles that we don't lead out a White Elephant at our services."[12]

Also facilitating the integration of German Jews in small communities was their general lack of distinctive religious behavior as individuals. Because the religious culture of Reform Judaism increasingly focused on synagogue life at the expense of domestic observances, small-town German Jews rapidly abandoned the more particularistic elements of traditional Jewish practice in their personal lives. Those immigrants from Central Europe who resisted this trend were few in number, and their determination was often short-lived. In their desire to conform to the culture of the majority, even those who maintained their identity as part of a religious community quickly gave up the observance of the Jewish dietary laws, for example. While the abandonment of *kashrut* was a general trend among Reform Jews, it may have proceeded even more rapidly in smaller Jewish settlements, given the greater difficulty of obtaining kosher foods in those places. Not only did small-town Jews commonly violate the restriction on serving dairy and meat products at the same meal, but they even began eating pork products and shellfish, foods whose prohibition most symbolized the Jewish dietary tradition. Illustrative is the Friday-night practice of one German-Jewish family in Anniston, Alabama, around 1900, as reported by the author Eli Evans. Although the mother in this family blessed the Sabbath candles before dinner, the meal itself often in-cluded traditionally forbidden foods such as oyster stew and ham.[13]

Even at events most closely associated with Jewish life, German Jews flagrantly disregarded traditional foodways. At the wedding celebration of Moses Goldsmith and Fannie Speyer in Lexington, Kentucky, in 1884, for instance, the meal served may have been a "feast fit for the gods," but it began with oyster soup and included both beef tenderloin *aux champignons* and vanilla ice cream. Similarly, the meal marking the wedding of Sam Adler and Anna York in Alexandria, Louisiana, started with "lobster *à la* York" and in-cluded both squab and ice cream. At the banquet accompanying the dedica-tion of the Moses Montefiore temple in Bloomington, Illinois, in 1889, again, according to the local paper, "a feast fit for the Gods," the menu included not only meat and milk products at the same meal (chicken, tongue, veal, and ice cream) but also shrimp.[14]

For the most part, small-town German Jews also cast aside prohibitions against work on the Sabbath and on holidays. They did so both because main-taining the usual workweek was another way of adapting to their environ-ment and because keeping businesses open on Saturday brought with it de-cided economic advantages. Some would say it was an economic necessity in small-town America, where Saturday was the traditional market day, bringing many shoppers in from the rural surroundings that most small towns served. In any case, the last thing small-town Jews wanted was to call undue attention to their distinctive practices. So neglected was the Sabbath in Vicksburg, Mis-sissippi, in the 1870s that Rabbi Bernhard Gotthelf of the town's Anshe Chesed synagogue was moved to deliver a powerful sermon in 1874 decrying the absence of his congregants from temple on what should have been a day of rest and prayer. "Whilst we remain behind our counters, or seated around the tables for a social game," he preached, "whilst we are deaf and blind against every attempt at spiritual elevation; whilst our whole time is money, and money only; and whilst we, by our own bad examples of stubbornly and totally neglecting the Sabbath and worship, also keep aloof our rising genera-tion from the house of God . . . Judaism will perish!!!"[15]

Of course the most extreme indication of a retreat from Jewish particular-ism was a willingness to subscribe to the beliefs and to follow the practices of another faith. Examples of Jewish men who allowed their children to be raised with the religious beliefs of their Christian mothers are not difficult to uncover, and there are even instances in which small-town Jews adopted Christianity themselves. In the decades after the Civil War in Durham, North Carolina, for instance, the German-born Jewish tailor Isaac Wissburg became "identified with the Episcopal Church," while the wife of one of the Baptist ministers in town was apparently of Jewish background.[16] There are also plenty of examples of Jews who never abandoned their Jewish identity but nonetheless lived a very Christian lifestyle. Only in an extremely assimilated household could Clara Lowenburg, growing up in Natchez, Mississippi, in the 1870s, report that she "received Christmas presents from Santa Claus and often ate boiled river shrimp during the summer." Only in an environment of little Jewish consciousness could Birdie Feld and her sister Anne, who lived in Vicksburg in the 1920s, serve as Christian Science practitioners, even though Birdie was a charter member of the Anshe Chesed sisterhood.[17]

All in all, the goals of economic success and cultural integration that most Central European Jews set for themselves when they migrated to small towns were largely achieved. Especially in places where they were among the founders of their cities, German Jews were deeply involved in civic, cultural, and political affairs and were at times made welcome even in the most exclusive social circles and prestigious local organizations.[18] Generally speaking, anti-Jewish sentiment was relatively muted in small-town settings, in part because anti-immigrant and antisemitic biases were more likely to be focused on the masses of foreigners congregated in large cities. Moreover, even the most prejudiced individuals found it harder to maintain negative attitudes toward men and women with whom they had frequent personal contact. Here again, the small-town environment conditioned the Jewish experience.

All this is not to say that Jews in small communities were unequivocally within the mainstream of society. There is no question that certain stereotypes about Jews persisted in small-town America, some positive but most negative, and that Jews continued to be seen as at least slightly out of place in an overwhelmingly Christian milieu.[19] For all their acceptance as fellow citizens, and for all the recognition that they received for playing a disproportionate role in the commercial and civic affairs of their towns, there was still a sense that Jews were a separate element within society and a people apart. Even the widespread favorable notice given Jews in the small-town press had a certain edge. In 1867, for example, the La Crosse Daily Democrat observed that "the Jews of this city are among our very best citizens . . . they always mind their own business and never get into trouble." The paper pointed out as well that the local Jews "give to all charitable objects with great liberality and are always willing to help others." Similarly, in 1912 Albert Perry, a local historian in Illinois, observed that "the Jewish people, who have resided in Galesburg during the past sixty years . . . are public spirited, patriotic and law-abiding." Further, he commented, "they always favor public improvements, are liberal contributors to public enterprise, never turn down a worthy charity, and never refuse to help the deserving poor." While observations such as these are essentially positive, they nonetheless reflect a sense that Jews were a separate category of citizens, and they might even be taken to imply that the laudable behavior of Jews was counterintuitive.[20]

The perception that nineteenth- and early twentieth-century German

Jews constituted a distinct, cohesive, and even clannish element within small-town society was only reinforced by the fact that nearly all small-town Jews were associated with middle-class or even more highly prosperous entrepreneurial households. Moreover, many small-town German-Jewish families were interrelated, and most lived in comfortable residential settings close to one another and not far from their downtown places of business. The situation in Trinidad, Colorado, around the turn of the twentieth century was representative, with most of the Jews living "within a few blocks of the court house well within the original town site."[21]

So common was the assumption among the gentile inhabitants of small-town America that Jewish people were somehow different and perhaps suspect in their moral and ethical behavior that when individual Jews in their midst were singled out for acclaim, they were often characterized as "Christian." Noting that the Jewish entrepreneur Hardy Solomon had made many contributions to the community in the latter years of the nineteenth century, for example, the editor of the *Wichita Eagle* referred to him as "a Christian in his impulse and judgments." In much the same way, when Rabbi Wolff Willner died in Frederick, Maryland, in 1932, the local newspaper eulogized him in a manner that was almost apologetic about his Jewish identity. "Although a leader of a Synagogue, and a gifted exponent of the Jewish Faith," the paper said, "he could and did stand reverently within the sacred precincts of any Church and feel the presence of a Universal [God]." A similar sentiment was expressed a short time later by William Foster Hayes, a local notable in Owensboro, Kentucky, when he wrote about Clemmie Wolf, the selfless daughter of a prominent Jewish merchant, who had died in Owensboro while working as a volunteer nurse during the influenza epidemic of 1918. Hayes was moved to write that although "Clemmie Wolf was doubtless a faithful adherent to the religion of her fathers," she was imbued with "the spirit of Jesus, the spirit of self-sacrificing love," and that she was therefore "an unconscious but shining exemplar of Christianity . . . a practical example of the highest Christian character."[22]

And so, even while Jews found broad acceptance in small towns, a certain element of prejudice lurked in the shadows. Thus, in a well-publicized murder trial that took place in Fresno, California, in 1893, one of the defense attorneys tried to impugn the credibility of a witness by pointing to his Jewish identity; and even in the highly tolerant environment of Columbia, South Carolina, in 1904, the Jewish city councilman Aaron David lost in his bid to become mayor in a race "tainted with references to his religion." The daughter of one prominent German-Jewish merchant in nineteenth-century Santa Ana, California, was certainly echoing a common perception among small-town Jews when she recalled that "although her father and uncles were very respected in Santa Ana, they were always conscious of an underlying anti-

Semitism there." Likewise, the historian of the Jewish community of Wichita could have been speaking about a great many other small communities, as well, when he wrote that "tolerance existed, but it could be uneasy." Clearly, even towns on the American frontier were not completely free of anti-Jewish prejudice, although it might have been expected that Old World attitudes would dissipate more quickly there than they did in the more conservative cities of the East.[23]

Occasionally the antisemitism that festered under the surface in small towns burst out into the open. Indeed, several of the most notorious anti-Jewish incidents of nineteenth-century America were played out in small-town settings. In 1862, during the Civil War, the citizens of Thomasville in Confederate Georgia voted to expel all Jews from their city and to prohibit future Jewish settlement there. In the same year General Ulysses S. Grant issued his infamous "General Orders Number 11," which banished Jews "as a class" from the district under his command and led to the disruption of Jewish life in several small cities, most notably Paducah, Kentucky. The decision taken in Thomasville was never implemented, it seems, and Grant's order was rescinded once protests over the measure reached Washington; but the way in which some residents of small towns turned against their Jewish neighbors, or at least failed to support them in their hour of distress, was not easily forgotten. Nor could manifestations of antisemitism in small-town America be explained by the stresses of domestic upheaval alone. Perhaps the best-known antisemitic incident of the late nineteenth century transpired in a small-town locale in a period of general domestic calm. This was the 1877 case in which the New York banker Joseph Seligman was turned away from a fashionable hotel in Saratoga Springs, New York, simply because of his faith. At the time this incident took place, Saratoga Springs itself had about three dozen Jewish residents.[24]

The Jews of America's small communities were well aware that they were frequently judged as a group and viewed with at least some suspicion. As Leo Weinberg of Frederick, Maryland, reminded the members of his small community in 1917, "we are treated as a unit in our relations and transactions with the world," with "all being blamed for the wrongs of one." Indeed, the main reason that well-established German Jews in smaller cities were so apprehensive about cooperating with the Industrial Removal Office in bringing unemployed East European immigrants to their towns was their fear that if the newcomers behaved improperly, these greenhorns might reflect badly on them. The historian Jack Glazier has written perceptively that "American Jews found their reputations particularly vulnerable in small towns" because in those places "missteps among Jews and unwanted public attention were especially liable to the scrutiny of non-Jewish opinion and judgment."[25]

Under the circumstances, it is not surprising that Jews sometimes adopted a defensive posture as they asserted their right to be considered integral members of their small-town societies. Leo Weinberg argued in 1917, for example, that the Jew was often seen "as the innovating crusader, the unwelcome visitor" in what he called "rural communities" such as that of Frederick, and that Jews had to convince their fellow citizens that they had come "not to tear down but to build up, not to hinder but to help." Similarly, in the fiftieth year of the Anshe Emeth congregation in Pine Bluff, Arkansas, also in 1917, one of its members, Raphael Goldenstein, observed that celebrating the congregation's anniversary would allow the community to "emphasize the fact that the Jewish people of the city are no interlopers on the scene, but old settlers who have labored for decades to build up the life of the city with their energy, their means, and their enthusiasm." Goldenstein anticipated that "among their fellow Christian citizens," a realization of the place of the Jews in Pine Bluff's early development "is bound to evoke a large measure of appreciation."[26]

Because feelings of group solidarity lingered even among the most acculturated German Jews, and because these Jews remained aware of the persistent if subtle currents of anti-Jewish sentiment in small towns, the Jewish pioneers of America's small communities always maintained not just a distinctive religious identity, but some sort of separate cultural identity as well. Even as they became highly integrated into their local environments, they also engaged in behaviors that perpetuated their Jewish sense of self and their cohesiveness. Just as their counterparts did in larger Jewish centers, Jews in small communities had an inclination to remain within their own social circles, which often overlapped with family circles, and, despite their frequent participation in mainstream fraternal organizations, they routinely established their own fellowships as well. Part of the attraction of these fraternal groups was the mutual benefit programs they offered, but the opportunity they afforded for Jewish camaraderie in nonreligious settings was also a factor in their appeal. In some small towns, lodges of the fraternal order B'nai B'rith were the first Jewish institutions to be organized. In Bloomington, Illinois, for instance, a B'nai B'rith chapter was established in 1872, ten years before Bloomington Jews founded a congregation. In Albuquerque, New Mexico, as well, the first Jewish institution was a lodge of B'nai B'rith, organized in 1883, and it was this body that established the town's Jewish Cemetery Association in 1892.[27]

By 1900 there were B'nai B'rith chapters not only in a great many of America's primary Jewish communities and in cities that were on their way to becoming urban places with substantial Jewish populations, but also in sixty-five towns that would still have only triple-digit Jewish communities in the 1920s. There were also chapters in some places that would have Jewish populations well under 100 in the 1920s. These included Meadville, Pennsylvania; Ligonier, Indiana; Ottawa, Illinois; Keokuk, Iowa; Eufaula, Alabama; Bastrop,

Louisiana; and Helena, Montana. In 1907, one of the few years for which comprehensive records exist, the number of B'nai B'rith chapters in towns that would have triple-digit Jewish populations in the 1920s stood at eighty-three. Moreover, other small-town chapters of B'nai B'rith continued to appear throughout the early decades of the twentieth century as additional small communities were in formation. In Phoenix, for instance, a chapter of thirty members was organized in 1916, just three years after the first Phoenix congregation had been founded.[28]

Nor was B'nai B'rith the only Jewish fraternal organization with mutual benefit programs and social activities that functioned in small towns where German Jews had settled. The Free Sons of Israel had been founded in 1849 with the original purpose of securing a burial place for Jews in New York City. By 1907, however, this organization had chapters widely scattered throughout the United States, including seven in communities that would have only triple-digit Jewish populations in the 1920s. These cities were Newport, Rhode Island; Amsterdam, New York; Williamsport, Pennsylvania; Leavenworth, Kansas; and Greenville, Meridian, and Vicksburg, Mississippi. Most likely, the appearance of chapters of the Free Sons of Israel in these places can be explained by the migration of individuals who had first affiliated with the group during a sojourn in New York or in some other primary urban center.[29]

Two other fraternal orders represented in small towns were Brith Abraham, which had been founded by Hungarian and German Jews as a self-help organization in 1859, and the dissident Independent Order of Brith Abraham, which had broken away from its parent organization in 1887 amid allegations of mismanagement and which would become the single largest Jewish fraternal organization in the land in the decades before World War II. In 1907 Brith Abraham had chapters in nine of the small Jewish communities that constitute the sample for our study, while the Independent Order also had a chapter in one of these nine communities (that of Manchester, New Hampshire) and in eight other small communities. Several other Jewish fraternal groups also were represented by scattered chapters in small-town America. In 1907 there were lodges of the Sons of Benjamin in Ithaca, New York; Bradford, Pennsylvania; and Zanesville, Ohio, for instance, and affiliates of the Chicago-based Independent Western Star Order in Benton Harbor, Michigan; Oshkosh, Wisconsin; and Chicago Heights, Illinois. In the same year there were "circles" of the Jewish Chautauqua Society, an organization that disseminated information about Judaism and sponsored annual vacation-time popular assemblies, in twenty of our sample communities.[30]

In some small towns, in addition to chapters of national or regional Jewish organizations, German Jews established local social clubs as institutions that would bring them together in an exclusively Jewish milieu. In Kalamazoo, Michigan, for instance, there was the New Allemania Club, created in

1859 and boasting forty-three members as of 1907. In Fort Smith, Arkansas, there was the Progress Club, founded in 1892 for "social activities, culture, good fellowship, and [the] mental development of [its] members." In a few small towns Jewish social clubs even had their own facilities, thus compromising the monopoly that synagogue buildings usually had in smaller communities as the only definitively Jewish spaces in the environment. In Fort Smith, for instance, the Progress Club erected a three-story building in 1910, and in Wilmington, North Carolina, the Harmony Club was housed above a downtown store in quarters that were "comfortable, but not elegant." Its facilities consisted of a lounge, a large ballroom, and a kitchen, and the club was the scene of a weekly poker game, as well as occasional weddings and holiday celebrations.[31]

In Vicksburg, Mississippi, the local social club was originally known as the Young Men's Hebrew Benevolent Association, but it later changed its name for tax purposes to the B'nai B'rith Literary Stock Company, and it bought its first building in 1889. In 1892 this building was replaced with a much more elaborate downtown facility, to which an indoor swimming pool was added in 1904. One description of the Vicksburg club from 1895 reports that it was known throughout the region "as the centre of the most lavish, yet refined, hospitality, while its cuisine under the direction of its accomplished caterers, past and present, is no less celebrated."[32]

Throughout the second half of the nineteenth century and into the early twentieth, the concept of separate spheres that held sway in bourgeois society helped to shape the social and cultural life of small-town German Jews, just as it helped to shape their family life. Because men were expected to operate primarily in the "public" arena of business, politics, and civic affairs, while women were expected to fulfill "private" nurturing roles such as those of homemaker, mother, and perhaps nurse or teacher, the social lives of the two sexes were organized quite apart from each other. Even when couples participated in family or communal activities, it was generally clear whether they were taking place within a predominantly masculine or feminine domain.

Congregations, the fundamental Jewish organizations of small communities, were clearly dominated by men, at least officially. Although entire families were expected to attend services, synagogues were essentially "public" institutions and thus a preserve of male authority. It was men who created congregations, drew up constitutions and by-laws, and served as officers. A few Reform congregations in small-town America did count women as full members from rather early in their history. Congregation Albert in Albuquerque voted to give women equal voting privileges on all matters as early as 1898, and B'er Chayim in Cumberland, Maryland, altered its constitution to give women full membership rights in 1924.[33] But such examples are quite rare. In general, pre–World War II congregations counted men alone as members, routinely making exceptions only for independent adult single women or for widows. Congregational meetings, often mandated in constitutions, meant gatherings of men. Burial societies, social clubs, and most of the other organizations that gave structure to small-town Jewish life were male dominated as well. Of course, fraternal lodges were by definition exclusively male preserves.

Nonetheless, women in small communities felt the need to develop social networks as much as men did, and to be involved in communal life on their own terms. Thus, the German-Jewish women of America's small-town communities created their own institutions, some of which predated the establishment of local congregations, but most of which were tied in one way or another to the local religious infrastructure. Sometimes these women's groups were know as Ladies' Aid Societies or as Ladies' Benevolent Societies. Because the congregations with which the families of these women were affiliated were almost invariably Reform, it was also common for women's sodalities to take on the guise of temple sisterhood organizations and eventually to affiliate with the Reform movement's National Federation of Temple Sisterhoods, which was organized in 1913.[34]

Another common pattern in places where Reform continued to shape local congregational life was for female temple members to constitute a chapter of the Council of Jewish Women, known later as the National Council of Jewish Women (NCJW), founded in 1893 as an association to aid Jewish families and individuals in distress. Although the council was not intended to be a synagogue-affiliated organization, it was dominated by middle-class women of Central European background and was thus closely associated with the Reform movement. Given its concern with aid to the Jewish underclasses, the NCJW functioned primarily in large and midsize Jewish communities, but as early as 1900 it already had chapters, or "sections," in a few smaller Jewish settlements as well. These included the communities of Oil City, Pennsylvania; Petoskey, Michigan; Quincy, Illinois; Natchez, Mississippi; Mobile, Alabama; Alexandria, Louisiana; and Tyler, Texas. Moreover, some Jewish leaders hoped to see the council increase its efforts to recruit members in small communities precisely because they saw the organization as a vehicle not only for providing welfare services, but also for maintaining Jewish identity. As one Mrs. Pappe, a leader of the Council of Jewish Women from Sioux City, Iowa, argued in 1902, because it was ideally suited to fostering Jewish involvement among those living in relatively isolated locales, "the Council is needed much more in small towns than in large cities."[35]

Rabbi George Zepin, the Reform activist and astute observer of small-town Jewish life, was also eager to see the expansion of the Council of Jewish

Women into a greater number of small communities. He recognized that the council could be a vehicle for maintaining Jewish life in isolated environments, and he believed that, as a women's organization, it could serve to promote Reform Judaism specifically. Writing in 1904, he argued that women were both more cultured and more adaptable to new conditions than were men, that in this respect "womankind forms the superior sex," and he anticipated that females would welcome the "emancipation of woman" offered by Reform Judaism. He contrasted his own movement's liberal approach to that of Orthodoxy, which, "with its legacy of orientalism, clung to the view that deprecated woman." With his attitude firmly grounded both in the doctrine of separate spheres that informed gender roles in America, and in the negative attitude toward Orthodoxy common in Reform circles, Zepin put great faith in the ability of women to influence the religious sentiments of their communities in general. "More keenly sensitive [than men] to the ideals of our day, they will be first to appreciate the electric thrill of the coming change, their brows will catch the first rays of the rising sun," Zepin wrote. "In the women of Israel lies our hope."[36]

By the time the NCJW held its tenth triennial convention in 1923, it was evident that the organization had indeed gained a foothold among small-town Jewish women. By then there were sections in at least sixty of the small towns that were home to triple-digit Jewish communities during the late 1920s. Still, the survival of sections of the council, like the continued existence of chapters of other Jewish organizations, was always more precarious in small towns than it was in larger cities. In 1923, for example, sections in places such as Lewiston and Rockland, Maine; Coatesville and Du Bois, Pennsylvania; Lorain and Lima, Ohio; and Albuquerque, New Mexico, had all recently been forced to disband. In Lynchburg, Virginia; Joliet, Illinois; and Bellingham, Washington, sections organized as recently as 1920 had not survived to 1923.[37]

Because few German-Jewish communities or subcommunities in small towns could support more than one female sodality, the women's groups that were oriented toward Reform Judaism in these places tended to perform multiple functions. In many communities it was essentially impossible to distinguish between nominally independent women's societies, congregational ladies' auxiliaries, and chapters of the National Council of Jewish Women. Indeed, without altering their basic character or membership base, small-town women's organizations sometimes simply changed their names as their identities evolved. In Macon, Georgia, for instance, the women of the Reform community were organized at various times as the Ladies Aid, the Temple Guild, and the Sisterhood. In Greensboro, North Carolina, the local Ladies Aid Society was transformed into a chapter of the NCJW in 1919, and in the late 1930s it joined with the Temple Emanuel sisterhood to create a body that called itself the Council-Sisterhood. In Topeka, Kansas, the local section of the National Council simply metamorphosed into a chapter of the National Federation of Temple Sisterhoods in 1943, since it had been functioning as the sisterhood organization of Temple Beth Sholom for over a decade.[38]

Whatever the organizations that German-Jewish women established in small communities were called, the various activities in which they were engaged were quite similar. It was common for them to serve in part as literary societies, and, especially in the period before World War I, many also had formal mutual-aid arrangements for dispensing funds and providing comfort to the sick and bereaved. Some women's groups even acted as burial societies. Sodalities that were euphemistically known as "sewing circles" probably took this name because originally they performed the task of preparing shrouds in which the dead could be interred.[39]

One of the most important activities in which women's organizations engaged was fundraising. Because involving themselves in charitable endeavors was viewed by middle-class society as a natural extension of women's nurturing roles, their participation in such activity was expected, and especially in small towns that had limited Jewish manpower, the involvement of women in fundraising was almost essential. Frequently women's groups would raise money by assessing their own members various dues and fees, and also fines. The members of the Hebrew Ladies Aid Society of Trinidad, Colorado, organized in 1889, could, for example, be assessed for failing to fulfill assignments and even for talking during the business portion of the group's meetings.

At least as vital for their fundraising efforts, however, was the work of women's organizations in sponsoring a variety of social events, including teas, parties, and bazaars, which often featured the sale of items such as baked goods and needlework that the women themselves had prepared. Although German-Jewish women commonly planned fundraising balls around the Jewish holiday of Purim, a traditional occasion for merrymaking, most of the events they sponsored were connected more to the culture of the larger society around them than to Judaism itself. Again the example of Trinidad is illustrative; there the affairs organized by the Hebrew Ladies Aid Society included Halloween balls and strawberry festivals open to the public, as well as regular whist evenings for members and their husbands. Indeed, even the idea of invoking the tradition of masquerading at Purim had its counterpart in Christian culture, for costume balls were in vogue as entertainments among all classes of society in nineteenth- and early twentieth-century Europe and America. Thus, Purim balls provided opportunities for Jews not only to mark an occasion on their own religious calendar, but also to demonstrate their absorption of the larger popular culture. At the Purim ball held at the Masonic

Hall in Lexington, Kentucky, in 1886, for example, two women came dressed as the Gilbert and Sullivan character Yum-Yum, two men came dressed as the controversial writer Oscar Wilde, and one young lady came dressed as a nun.[40]

Some of the money that was raised by Jewish women's organizations went to support their own mutual benefit activities, of course, but most was contributed to a variety of other causes deemed worthy by their members. Given the social service concerns of many of these groups, especially if they were affiliated with the NCJW, some chose to support the work of national institutions such as the Jewish Orphan Asylum established by B'nai B'rith in Cleveland in 1868 and the National Jewish Hospital for Consumptives in Denver. Small-town women's societies also contributed to causes that were not specifically Jewish. After all, like their male counterparts, the German-Jewish women of small-town America saw themselves not only as Jews, but also as engaged members of the larger civic community. Thus, for instance, the Ladies Benevolent Society of La Crosse, founded in 1873, "aided not only needy Jews, but any family that needed help, whether Jew or Gentile." Similarly, the Ladies Hebrew Benevolent Society of Anniston, Alabama, made donations not only to Jewish philanthropies, but also to a local free kindergarten for disadvantaged children. Among the contributions of the Ladies' Aid Society of the Reform congregation in Lafayette, Indiana, were donations to the local Flower Mission, which presumably sent flowers to anyone who was ill.[41]

Above all else, however, the money raised by German-Jewish women was used to support their local Reform congregations. Women's groups often helped to fund synagogue construction, for example, and they routinely provided money for maintenance and for beautification. As the historian Karla Goldman has demonstrated, German-Jewish women in America transformed the synagogue into an institution as important for their own expression of Jewishness as it was for men's. In this sense, German-Jewish women were unlike their counterparts in Europe, for whom the home remained the main locus of Jewish identity even in a period of modernization. Although women's involvement in synagogue life was in some ways a novel intrusion into the realm of the "public," it was at the same time a natural extension of their roles as moral and spiritual guides. In a sense, in small towns as in big cities, the close involvement of women with the "home" of the congregation was seen as an extension of their accepted role as homemakers for their own families.[42] Thus, in Boise, Idaho, the Judith Montefiore Association, formed at the same time Congregation Beth Israel came into existence, completely furnished the temple built by the community in 1896. In the same year a congregational women's organization was established in Bellaire, Ohio, and one of its first accomplishments, too, was to help furnish the local synagogue. In Macon, Georgia, the sisterhood of Temple Beth Israel purchased "everything from tables and chairs to modern electrical equipment, carpeting, and an organ," and it was this organization, together with the local chapter of the NCJW, that "kept the Temple solvent during the depression years." In Michigan City, Indiana, also, the Sisterhood carried the burden of the local Reform congregation's mortgage on the church building it had renovated in 1930, finally paying it off in 1937.[43]

In addition to providing money for the maintenance of temple facilities and for the conduct of services, another major responsibility women took upon themselves in Reform congregations was providing religious instruction for the children. Again, all concerned seemed to view the involvement of women in Jewish education as a natural outgrowth of their obligations as nurturing caregivers and moral guides. As in Williamsport, Pennsylvania, temple Sunday schools frequently were said to be under the "full jurisdiction" of the sisterhood.[44] What this meant in practice, in Williamsport and elsewhere, was that women took charge of organizing classes and that they constituted most or all of the teaching staff, designing and imparting a rudimentary curriculum, usually in consultation with a rabbi, whether he served the congregation full-time or came to town only occasionally.

The variety of activities in which temple sisterhoods and similar organizations were engaged in support of congregational life is reflected in the committee structure established by the Ladies Auxiliary Society that was created in 1904 at Congregation Anshe Chesed in Vicksburg. First there was the Building and Furnishings Committee, which dealt with maintenance of the temple. Then there were the Publication Committee and the Religious School Committee, which concerned themselves with education. There was also a Worship Committee, which was probably in charge of the temple choir and other matters related to religious services; and, finally, there was the Finance and Entertainment Committee, which was in charge of fundraising, much of which was tied to congregational and communal social events.[45]

So deeply involved were women's organizations in synagogue affairs that in some small towns they became the primary force behind communal initiatives. In Anniston, Alabama, in the early 1890s, it was the Ladies Hebrew Benevolent Society that took the lead in seeing that a synagogue was erected in town. This group planned the temple, raised all the money for its construction, and even appointed and instructed a building committee, although, in keeping with the gender conventions of the time, the committee itself was composed of the members' husbands and other men. Similarly, in turn-of-the-century Jackson, Michigan, at a time when the local congregation had suspended its operation, it was the Jewish women in town who took charge of the community's cemetery, arranged social events, and provided a modicum of Jewish education for the children. In 1903 Rabbi Leo Franklin, visiting from Detroit, wrote that in Jackson "the saving element—we confess it—are the young women." Soon after Franklin's visit, Jackson's Jewish women formed a Temple Aid Society and played a large part in acquiring a downtown Lutheran church and remodeling it as a synagogue.[46]

While women's groups in small communities were significant for the material and practical support they provided, both for their own members and for others, these societies were also very important for the less tangible benefits they provided their participants. Through their various projects, these groups afforded women an opportunity to experiment with American-style organizational politics, for instance, and they allowed them to develop their leadership skills. This was especially significant in light of the fact that women were almost never allowed to assume formal leadership positions in congregational or communal life more generally. In fact it was considered quite a victory for gender equality even when a sisterhood representative was finally allowed on a synagogue board, as happened in Sharon, Pennsylvania, in 1943.[47]

Perhaps most important in terms of intangibles, however, small-town women's organizations served as the main elements in their members' social lives. Indeed, Jewish women's groups in small communities were probably more focused on social interaction than were their counterparts in larger communities, both because in the small-town setting it was likely that all the women from German-Jewish families already knew one another, and because there was less practical social service work for these women to do. Beyond raising funds, running a Sunday school for the temple, or helping a member of the community or a transient through some hard times, there were few projects to which small-town Jewish women could turn their attention. Unlike their counterparts in larger communities, these women did not have occasion to throw themselves into the work of establishing settlement houses or providing visiting services for the kinds of destitute families that crowded the Jewish neighborhoods of big cities. In small towns, it simply did not make sense for chapters of the NCJW, for example, to establish schools for slum children, provide vocational classes and employment bureaus, manage model tenements, and offer free baths, as some chapters of the organization did in larger cities.

So fundamental was the social role of German-Jewish women's organizations in small towns that at some times and in some places these groups contented themselves with fulfilling that role exclusively. Even the official history of the B'er Chayim sisterhood in Cumberland, Maryland, for instance, admits that when the group was first organized in 1876, its meetings were "little more than 'koffee klatches'" to which members brought their knitting and sewing. The group did collect dues of twenty-five cents at each meeting and used the money for charity or for repair projects at its temple, but its overriding purpose was to provide a venue for pleasant conversation. The women of the Cumberland sisterhood were apparently so unconcerned with the actual business of their group, and perhaps so accustomed to leadership by males, that they elected a man as their first secretary![48]

In Lexington, Kentucky, too, the ladies of the city's German-Jewish families created a club notable for its lack of any purpose beyond socializing. They called their circle the As You Like It Club, and at its very first meeting in 1900, they turned down a specific suggestion that the group raise money to help start a congregation in Lexington, which had none at the time. They also rejected the notion that the club should function as a benevolent society. Instead, they endorsed the idea "that the soul [sic] object [of the club] be a social one." Over the next two years, the women of the As You Like It Club reaffirmed their limited agenda on several occasions. They pointedly ignored a suggestion that they offer aid to a poor family in "destitute circumstances," they turned down a proposal that they "form a branch of the Jewish Chautauqua," and they rejected the idea of devoting one day a week to sewing for a local hospital. In December 1902 the club finally did take a step in the direction of charitable work when it voted to contribute two dollars to each of two needy families that had been identified by members of the group; but the very next week the club members rescinded their decision, citing their initial agreement "that the funds collected weekly from the members, in the form of dues, were to be set apart [exclusively] for the purpose of entertaining." Indeed, the issue of greatest concern for the As You Like It Club seems to have been what food to serve at its regular Wednesday meetings. It took a protracted debate before agreement was reached that only two items were to be put out as refreshments at each gathering, and that if a hostess wanted to prepare more food, she could do so only "by paying the penalty of twenty five cents." Whether a beverage counted as one of the two items allowed was yet another matter of contention.[49]

Picking up on the matter of women's socializing, Rabbi Max Raisin of Meridian, Mississippi, was so concerned about the obsession with cards that the women in his community seem to have developed that he raised the issue in his annual address to his congregation in 1913. He agonized about "the gambling mania which has seized upon many a Jewish man, and, what is infinitely worse, upon many a Jewish woman, making of card-playing a fetich [sic] before which all things else, however sacred and ennobling, are relegated to the limbo of disuse and neglect." Rabbi George Zepin suggested early in the twentieth century that women's groups in the South were more likely than those in the North to be solely concerned with socializing, but we have no evidence to confirm his impression. As in so many other matters of small-town Jewish history, it is unlikely that region was a decisive factor. Examples of small-town women's clubs with an interest in little more than socializing and amusement come from all sections of the country. The women of Wichita, Kansas, for instance, met in the 1870s and 1880s as the Entre Nous Club, its very name suggesting the group's lack of concern with specifically Jewish affairs or with others outside their own circle. In Galesburg, Illinois, the Jewish Ladies Aid organized in 1904 by the women of the Reform families in town quickly evolved into little more than an exclusive bridge club from which newly arrived East European Jewish women were routinely excluded.[50]

In many ways, then, German-Jewish men's fraternal organizations and women's sodalities played similar roles in America's small Jewish communities. Both served certain practical purposes such as providing mutual aid benefits and raising money for charitable causes, and both functioned as focal points for social networks that provided camaraderie in times of joy and comfort in times of trouble, illness, and death. Moreover, both men's and women's organizations served as vehicles to help their members navigate the cultural terrain of small-town society. On the one hand, they provided additional opportunities for Jews to mimic the ways of their middle-class Christian neighbors, with whom they had a great deal in common. On the other hand, these organizations also allowed Jews to separate themselves from their gentile fellow citizens, among whom they were never totally accepted, and to create their own social space. So, too, in places where a subcommunity of Central Europeans survived well into the twentieth century, clubs and societies dominated by German Jews served to create a certain distance between their members and the East Europeans who were migrating to small towns in increasing numbers by the turn of the twentieth century, bringing with them a whole new set of cultural norms.

Although the German-Jewish organizations of small towns were in many ways similar to those in larger communities, there were some significant differences based on environmental factors. Because they served such a limited populace, small-town societies were usually very few in number, and they generally brought together all or nearly all the members of the German-Jewish settlements they served. Moreover, Jewish men and women living as a tiny minority in the sometimes intrusive atmosphere of small-town America were likely to be even more eager than their big-city counterparts to maintain at least a bit of exclusive social and cultural space into which they could retreat. As we shall see, for the East Europeans arriving in the country's smaller cities and towns, the creation of a separate and distinctive cultural space was even more crucial.

# 11 Patterns of Culture: The East Europeans

In considering matters of culture, as in considering just about any other aspect of small-town Jewish life in the United States, we must keep in mind that most of the small Jewish communities that dotted the American landscape in the early decades of the twentieth century did not get their start as German-Jewish settlements in the middle decades of the nineteenth. Rather, the vast majority of the small communities of the interwar period came into being only with the arrival of East Europeans. Consequently, in most small-town Jewish centers, Jewish cultural norms in the decades just before World War II were those of East European Jewish immigrants. Moreover, even in small communities where a German-Jewish population had fashioned its own way of life during the nineteenth century, East Europeans tended to create their own separate subculture. Although in some ways the culture of East Europeans in small-town America was similar to that created by their German-Jewish predecessors, it was in many ways quite different. As we shall see, the culture of small-town East European Jews was characterized by a deep-seated and enduring sense of ethnic solidarity, closely associated with traditional Jewish practice, an attachment to Zionism, and a strong bond to the Yiddish language and the outlook on life that it represented.

Of course, to say that East Europeans were the first to create a Jewish culture in most of America's classic small-town Jewish settlements does not mean that German Jews were completely absent from these environments even in places where they never established true German-Jewish communities. In fact a few isolated Central European Jews had appeared in some of the towns that became fully developed Jewish centers only in the era of mass migration. Very commonly, however, these individuals did not become firmly established in their small towns, and their sojourns in those places were merely stopovers on the way to larger cities.[1] Moreover, those isolated

---

*Photo previous page: A meeting of the Anshe Knesses Israel Sisterhood, Danville, Illinois, ca. 1926. East European women, as well as men, created their own social and organizational networks in America's small towns. Courtesy of the Anshe Knesses Israel Sisterhood, Danville, Illinois.*

German Jews who might still have been present in this or that town as East Europeans began to arrive proved to be more or less invisible to the newcomers. The pioneer Central Europeans in places without true communities were likely to have become highly integrated into the civic and social affairs of their cities and to have abandoned virtually all their Jewish attachments. One example here is the dry-goods merchant Samson Levy, who settled in Newburyport, Massachusetts, married a local gentile woman, and served as an alderman around 1872, when he was likely to have been the only Jew in town. Another example is the clothier Moses Bloom, reported to have been the first Jewish settler in Iowa City, Iowa. He became a Mason, a member of the Odd Fellows, and a director of two local banks, and he was elected mayor of Iowa City in the 1870s, when the town probably had fewer than a dozen Jewish residents.

Yet another example of an early settler cut off from Jewish contacts is Solomon Elias, who came from San Francisco in 1879, together with his father, uncle, and grandfather, to open the first men's clothing store in Modesto, California. Elias eventually became a prominent businessman in his own right and a widely read local historian. A member of the Stanford University Alumni Association, the bar association, the Masons, the Elks, and the Native Sons of the Golden West, he served as mayor of Modesto from 1922 until 1931, just as a Jewish community was developing there. Even then, however, Elias did not become involved in the city's Jewish life.[2] In those small towns where the East Europeans arriving during the era of mass migration had been preceded only by individual Jewish settlers such as Levy in Newburyport, Bloom in Iowa City, and Elias in Modesto, the new immigrants had to create both a religious infrastructure and a local Jewish cultural milieu from scratch, just as they had to do in towns where there had been no previous Jewish presence whatsoever.

Indeed, even in places where East European immigrants did encounter a full-fledged community planted earlier by German Jews, the newcomers found that they had to give local Jewish life an entirely new form. The historian Hal Rothman, writing about the Wichita Jewish community at the turn of the twentieth century, claims that the Jews of Central European background in the city greeted newly arrived East Europeans enthusiastically, seeing them "as an entrepreneurial class like they themselves had been twenty years earlier." "There were so few Jews," Rothman asserts, "that the established families welcomed the newcomers, feeling both that they restored a kind of Jewishness absent in Wichita and increased the pool of potential spouses for children." However, if this attitude was prevalent in Wichita, the situation in that town was an exception. Generally, small-town German Jews were quite wary of newly arrived East Europeans and anxious to incorporate them into their communities only on condition that they conform to the Jewish cultural standards to which the Germans themselves were adhering. Even Rothman allows that as the number of East Europeans in Wichita increased, a desire grew for their "rapid assimilation" and their transformation into American-ized Kansans.[3]

For their part, the East Europeans who migrated to small towns had little inclination to adopt the model of cultural adaptation that had been pioneered by their German-Jewish predecessors. Even though they often came to small communities by way of larger American cities, these East Europeans were products of an environment in which Orthodoxy was the standard for reli-gious practice, whatever the degree to which it was observed, and in which a strong Jewish ethnic identity was still the norm. In the same way that East Europeans were frequently uncomfortable with the Reform rituals and ideology that were nearly universal in congregations dominated by German Jews, they rejected the assimilationist bent of the German's general approach to small-town life. As a result, in those towns where German Jews had devel-oped a communal life before East Europeans arrived, the two groups came to constitute distinct subcommunities, each with its own character. Much as in larger Jewish centers, a sort of unease, even antagonism, characterized the relationship between the two groups.

From one town after another come personal reflections that testify to the division that existed between German Jews and East Europeans even in the smallest communities. Edna Ferber, for example, remembered that when she arrived in Appleton, Wisconsin, as a girl in 1897, some thirty of the forty Jewish families in town were of German background and that "the German-born Jew practiced the most absurd snobbery toward the Russian or the Polish Jew." "To the average Gentile a Jew is a Jew," she observed, but "in the mind of the Jew himself there exist gradations based on ridiculous standards." Similarly, the novelist Fannie Hurst reported that her mother, a product of German-Jewish society in Hamilton, Ohio, objected to one of her early boyfriends, an East European Jew, because he was a "kike," and thus even less desirable than a gentile. Along the same lines, the future rabbi Ferdinand Hirsch, a Jew of German background who grew up in Hamilton and Marion, Ohio, and in Bloomington, Illinois, reported that until the beginning of the twentieth cen-tury, all the marriages that took place within his family were with other German Jews and that "the first marriage to an Eastern European was looked upon with disfavor."[4]

Among contemporaries who had occasion to notice the Jewish cultural divide within small communities were agents of the Industrial Removal Of-fice. The IRO field worker who attempted to organize the group's efforts in Steubenville, Ohio, in 1908, for instance, found that he had to set up two separate local committees, one composed of German Jews and one of East

Europeans. "I found conditions from a Jewish standpoint (communally speaking) very bad," he wrote. "Petty jealousies exist which make concerted action almost impossible." Another agent, writing about the German and East European Jews in Marion, Indiana, also in 1908, reported that he found "a woeful lack of entente cordiale between the two factions."[5]

Like contemporary observers, more recent historians also have called attention to the division that existed within small Jewish communities. Writing about the La Crosse community, for example, Myer Katz reports that by 1900 the local Reform Jews of German background "were for all practical purposes completely Americanized and a few had already intermarried with non-Jews." In contrast to the East Europeans in town, he notes, these German Jews "moved only in the self-styled elite strata of local society." Similarly, Carolyn Gray LeMaster writes that new immigrants arriving in early twentieth-century Fort Smith, Arkansas, "were struck deeply by the class contempt shown them and other East European Jews by the well-established German-Jewish community."[6]

Clearly, then, the lack of harmony between Reform and Orthodox congregations that we have already noted in many small communities reflected a more general cultural subdivision. The friction that kept Reformers and traditionalists from uniting, even when doing so might have made practical sense, was based as much on cultural differences between Germans and East Europeans as it was on strictly religious considerations. In Galesburg, Illinois, for example, even though throughout the early decades of the twentieth century neither the German Jews nor the East Europeans met for religious services more than a few times a year (essentially on the High Holidays), they insisted on maintaining the trappings of two separate congregations, the Reform Sons of Judah and the Orthodox Ohav Zedek. More to the point, even as late as 1939, when the national office of B'nai B'rith organized a chapter of the fraternal organization in Galesburg, some of the older leaders of the Sons of Judah still objected to bringing together individuals from the two local subcommunities in what was essentially a secular joint venture. By the same token, in 1945 it took an outsider to unite the women of the two groups in the effort to create a community Sunday school. The key person behind this project was a newcomer to Galesburg who had "the education, charm, 'know-how,' and economic advantage" to be accepted by the Reform faction, even though she was a traditionalist who kept "a strictly Orthodox home."[7]

In other small communities, too, the persistence of distinctive Central European and East European identities was remarkable. One commentator on the Jewish history of Muscatine, Iowa, observed that as late as the 1950s the main body of the city's Jewry, composed of those with an East European background, did not even know of the existence of a German-Jewish

cemetery in their town. In Wilmington, North Carolina, as well, Jews inter-
viewed in the 1970s still focused upon how little contact there had been between the town's German Jews and its East Europeans earlier in the century.[8]

Whether they were establishing a local Jewish community for the first
time or creating a subcommunity parallel to an existing one of German Jews,
the East Europeans who settled in smaller urban centers generally erected
rather broad, if small-scale, institutional frameworks. In some respects, the
East Europeans copied the ways of their Americanized German-Jewish predecessors. Both German Jews and East Europeans placed synagogues at the
center of their communal lives, for example, and both established separate
organizational networks for men and for women. These similarities were
largely structural and superficial, however. Beneath them lay some fundamental differences of approach and attitude. In the case of East European
Jews, synagogue activities tended to complement rather than replace domestic observances such as adherence to traditional dietary laws, at least at some
level. So, too, the creation of separate women's organizations among East
Europeans was less the result of their exposure to the American middle-class
doctrine of "separate spheres" than a consequence of their origins in a traditionalist society where men and women were assigned very distinct roles. In
the end, despite the influence of German-Jewish models on East European
immigrants, and despite the persistence of a distinctive German-Jewish sub-
group in some of America's classic small communities, by the second quarter
of the twentieth century, if not earlier, it was predominantly East Europeans
who set the tone for local Jewish culture in just about every one of America's
smaller Jewish centers.

The creation of new Orthodox congregations in so many places was the
clearest sign that East Europeans were putting their own stamp on small-town
Jewish life. The establishment of these shuls proclaimed that the East Europeans rejected the religious norms of the German Jews they encountered in
older communities and that they were intent on maintaining at least some of
the practices and values of their Old World society. But the infrastructure of
Jewish life that immigrants from places such as Russia and Poland created in
small towns consisted of much more than just synagogues. Among the most
conspicuous indicators of the intention of East Europeans to perpetuate their
own cultural modes was their creation of their own burial societies and cemeteries. These institutions were generally established either shortly before or
shortly after local Orthodox congregations came into being, and in this sense
East Europeans replicated a pattern observable in many mid-nineteenth-
century German-Jewish communities. In Manchester, New Hampshire, for
example, Adath Yeshurun began meeting for services about 1889 and acquired
land for a cemetery around 1896, although the congregation was not char-

tered formally until 1900, following the passage of a state law requiring the incorporation of all religious organizations.[9]

Given the attitudes of East European immigrants and their desire to safeguard at least some aspects of traditional religious practice, it is not surprising that in towns that already had Jewish burial grounds under Reform auspices, the newcomers commonly established their own separate cemeteries. In Macon, Georgia, for instance, the local German Jews had acquired a burial ground within the city's Rose Hill Cemetery as early as 1845, and the Reform Temple Beth Israel had expanded that burial ground in 1879. At the beginning of the twentieth century, however, Macon's Orthodox congregation, Sherah Israel, established its own separate section within Rose Hill. In Davenport, Iowa, the Orthodox B'nai Emes Congregation, organized in 1888, declined to bury its deceased members in the cemetery owned by the Reform Temple Emanuel; instead it purchased its own burial ground around 1901. In Alexandria, Louisiana, the original Jewish cemetery was laid out across the Red River in Pineville in 1861, but the city's Orthodox Jews refused to make use of it and secured their own burial place on the eastern outskirts of Pineville in 1914.[10]

The main reason that East Europeans so frequently established burial grounds separate from those controlled by Reform temples was that Reform congregations were usually quite lax in their rules governing who could be interred in their cemeteries. Despite their reluctance to condone intermarriage, Reform temples often allowed the non-Jewish spouses of their members to be buried in their cemeteries, for example, while small-town Orthodox congregations would not countenance the burial of gentiles together with Jews. To have done so would have offended both their religious standards and their cultural sensibilities. The rules of the Orthodox cemetery in Lafayette, Indiana, to take but one example, provided that no uncircumcised Jewish male could be buried on its grounds, nor anyone who had been cremated, in violation of Jewish practice. Moreover, the rules mandated that "if a [Jewish] male or female marries a non-Jew, it is strictly forbidden for either of the parties to be buried on our cemetery." These provisions were not to be waived "regardless of any compensation offered."[11]

Just as small-town East Europeans sought to establish burial grounds that would meet the needs of religious traditionalists, they also tried to find ways to provide for many of the other requirements of an observant Jewish lifestyle. For instance, throughout the early decades of the twentieth century, small communities of East Europeans usually made some provision for a supply of kosher meat to be available. At times these communities provided enough of a clientele that butchers trained in ritual slaughtering, *shechitah*, could operate full-scale markets. In Lexington, Kentucky, Samuel Krasne served as the first resident *shochet,* succeeded by Harry Goller around 1915. In Topeka, Kansas, in the very early 1900s, a grocer by the name of Katz kept live chickens at this store, slaughtering them according to the laws of *kashrut* for his Jewish customers, and once a week he slaughtered a cow as well. Even in small communities fairly close to large cities, kosher meat markets were often a part of the local Jewish scene, thus sparing the residents of these communities trips into the city and reinforcing the character of small-town Jewish centers as self-contained settlements. In Rockville Centre, on New York's Long Island, for instance, Ruben Fleischer would stock his kosher market by arising every weekday at 4 A.M. to travel to Manhattan to buy meat or to go farther east on Long Island to buy live poultry. The actual slaughtering of the chickens would be done in his shop by the rabbi of the local congregation, at least in the late 1920s, allowing those who wanted kosher poultry to abandon their former practice of placing live chickens in a sack and bringing them to be killed by the rabbi.[12]

Of course, even in small towns with a large percentage of religiously observant Jews, the demand for kosher food was limited, and this fact helps explain why so many of those able to practice *shechitah* were inclined to serve their communities in other capacities as well: as synagogue cantors, teachers, and ritual circumcisers, for example. The limited client base for kosher meat also meant that in some small communities kosher butchers sold not only food that conformed to Jewish dietary laws, but nonkosher products as well, mainly to a gentile clientele. There were even some cases in which the purveyor of kosher meat in a small town was a gentile butcher who had made some sort of special arrangement to supply the Jewish community. In turn-of-the-century Sharon, Pennsylvania, for instance, a local butcher agreed to purchase a separate chopping block for kosher meats and to allow the local *shochet* to come to his store two mornings a week to serve his Jewish clients, although once a full-scale kosher meat market opened in Sharon, sometime around 1909, this arrangement was no longer necessary.[13]

The situation in Kalamazoo, Michigan, illustrates how supplying kosher meat for a small community often depended on a variety of unconventional arrangements. There, early in the twentieth century, a Mr. Finkelstein acted as cantor in the synagogue and as teacher for the Jewish children while also providing the service of ritual slaughtering, although it is said that he would refuse the five-cent fee due him for killing poultry, urging his customers to donate the money to charity instead. Later, a gentile butcher by the name of Maxam provided kosher meat, despite the fact that this scheme was far from ideal from the point of view of Jewish observance. One longtime resident of Kalamazoo, remembering that Maxam's efforts to stock kosher food resulted in "some years of comedy," explained that "half his shop had Kosher meat with a moo, and on the other side was trafeh [nonkosher] meat with a grunt."

Still later, around the 1930s, kosher meat in Kalamazoo was made available in a shop that Rabbi Herman Price operated with his wife, Ida, so that they could supplement their income.[14]

In communities of East Europeans that were unable to support a resident kosher butcher or *shochet* themselves, or at times when the services of such a specially trained individual were unavailable, there were nonetheless always some mechanisms in place to provide for the needs of those who observed *kashrut*. In some places a circuit-riding *shochet* would make the rounds of small communities, often going door to door to slaughter home-raised poultry. This was the case for some time in the upper peninsula of Michigan, for instance, and in Durham, North Carolina, during the 1920s. In other places without a local kosher butcher, the common practice was to obtain meat from another community in the region. Some of the more observant families in early twentieth-century Charlottesville, Virginia, had kosher food shipped in by bus from Lynchburg, for example; and in Topeka, after the grocer Katz left town and before a new grocery with kosher meat opened around 1918, those who observed the dietary laws either awaited an itinerant *shochet* or had their meat shipped in from Kansas City. Rather than arranging for delivery, some residents of small communities traveled to get kosher meat themselves. Belle Stock's mother would made a weekly trip from Ambridge, Pennsylvania, to Pittsburgh to buy kosher products, for instance, and Morris Nasatir would make a similar weekly trip from Santa Ana, California, to Los Angeles, although eventually Nasatir learned to do *shechitah* himself so that he could raise and slaughter his own chickens. In Bessemer, Alabama, Charles Weinstein sometimes killed chickens according to the laws of *kashrut* for the local Jews, but more commonly the Weinstein family and others who kept kosher homes would drive to Birmingham to buy provisions.[15]

Another concern for East Europeans in small communities was providing a ritual bath, a *mikvah*, for the convenience of those women who continued to obey the Jewish "family purity" laws that required ritual immersion, most notably before resuming intercourse after each menstrual period. This was seen as such a high priority that even when small-town Orthodox congregations had only temporary quarters, they often installed a *mikvah* in those buildings. This was the case in Sharon, Pennsylvania; La Crosse, Wisconsin; Nashua, New Hampshire; and Newburyport, Massachusetts, among many other places.[16] Naturally, when small-town Orthodox congregations built more permanent houses of worship, it was usual for them to include ritual baths among the basic facilities of those buildings. In Hagerstown, Maryland, for example, the B'nai Abraham congregation bought a city lot in 1892 and moved the house that stood there to the back of the property for use as a school building. At the front of the lot the congregation erected a synagogue that included a *mikvah* in a small room at the rear of the structure. In the same

year the Jews of North Adams, Massachusetts, put up a two-story frame building that included a worship hall, school facilities, a residence for the *shammas*
(the sexton), and a ritual bath. In Plymouth, Massachusetts, the synagogue
erected in 1912 was said to be superlatively equipped, having "seats, three
rooms, a Mikvah, and steam heat." The Children of Israel synagogue built in
Benton Harbor, Michigan, in 1925 had a place for ritual immersion in the
basement, as did the Sons of Abraham synagogue in Lafayette, Indiana, during the interwar period.[17]

In those small communities where the synagogue did not provide a *mikvah*, there was likely to be one in a private home. This was the case in Muscatine, Iowa, where the residence of Charles Fryer housed a ritual bath and
seems to have served as the center of Jewish life in the late nineteenth century. In Aberdeen, South Dakota, in the early part of the twentieth century,
the *mikvah* available to the community was in the home of Gussie Amdur, and
in Lexington, Kentucky, it was in the home of the Lithuanian-born merchant
Joe Rosenberg and his wife. The Rosenbergs were the parents of four daughters, as well as six sons, and so even within their own family there were
several women for whom a *mikvah* was considered essential.[18]

Beyond establishing elements of an infrastructure that would serve their
specifically defined religious needs, the East European Jews who established
communities in small towns also created institutions that had no particular tie
to ritual observance per se. Even more than the German Jews who preceded
them in some places, the East Europeans, with their strong ethnic consciousness, saw a need for secular organizations that would address some of their
practical needs, on the one hand, and provide opportunities for social interaction, on the other. In some towns, it is true, existing institutions, such as B'nai
B'rith lodges that had been founded by German Jews, did welcome East European newcomers, but just as often the two subgroups simply moved in different circles and developed parallel sets of organizations. Not only were the
German Jews who dominated existing communal institutions inclined to be
uncomfortable with the immigrants, but the immigrants themselves were
likely to find it difficult to identify with individuals who rejected the traditionalist mentality and the sense of ethnic distinctiveness that infused the
self-image of most small-town East Europeans. As a result of this situation, in
some communities, once-vibrant chapters of B'nai B'rith and similar societies
identified with the German-Jewish establishment languished in the era of
East European settlement. The B'nai B'rith chapter in La Crosse, Wisconsin,
established in 1881, returned its charter to the parent body and was revived
only as the children of East European immigrants, not the immigrants themselves, took an interest in the organization. By the same token, in many of the
towns populated almost exclusively by East Europeans, B'nai B'rith chapters
were not founded until well into the twentieth century. The B'nai B'rith lodge

serving Fitchburg and Leominster, Massachusetts, for example, was not created until 1936. In Durham, North Carolina, an attempt had been made to organize a B'nai B'rith chapter in 1910, but its founders were forced to return their charter in 1912, and the group was not reconstituted until 1937.[19]

Typical of the self-help organizations that cropped up among East European Jews in small communities were free loan societies. Much as they did in larger cities, these organizations adapted the traditional Jewish practice of lending funds to indigent members of the community at no interest to situations in which new immigrants might need money for basic necessities or to get started in business. In Muscatine, Iowa, for instance, a free loan society functioned from 1896 until about 1920, and in Lafayette, Indiana, an Orthodox Hebrew Free Loan Association was established in 1907 with twenty-four members and an initial capital of $28.60. The lending capital of the Lafayette society had grown to over $400 by 1910 and to over $2,250 by 1928, a year in which the organization made fifty-four small loans to help individuals in one way or another. In Manchester, New Hampshire, the local free loan society was called the Chase Memorial Free Loan Association in honor of E. M. Chase, who made the largest single contribution to its initial capitalization and who remained one of its foremost champions. In Fitchburg, Massachusetts, the loan society was the Jewish Fitchburg Credit Union, which held monthly meetings at the town's synagogue and could provide up to $300 to any member of the local congregation. As the scheduling of regular meetings in Fitchburg suggests, gatherings of free loan society and credit union members served as opportunities not only to transact business but to socialize as well.[20]

In general, small Jewish communities dominated by East Europeans, like all American Jewish communities, prided themselves on looking after their own needy, a task made easier in small towns by the fact that the number of Jewish poor there was usually quite small. A self-congratulatory reporter writing about the Jewish community of Fargo, North Dakota, in 1913 declared triumphantly that he could "state without fear of contradiction that there is not a Jew in the city of Fargo that is in any way dependent upon [public] charity." Similarly, the author of the history of the La Crosse Jewish community observed in the middle of the twentieth century that "never has a La Crosse Jew been on the city or county welfare rolls or even applied for such assistance. . . . When special needs arose, their fellow Jews took from their own meager means and came to the rescue."[21]

Yet another indication that East European Jews with a strong ethnic identity created their own cultural framework in small towns was the appearance there of Zionist societies. In the decades before World War II, America's acculturated German-Jewish families were unlikely to support the concept of Jewish nationalism; thus Zionist activity at the local level served as a clear marker for the development of an East European subculture. As early as 1907 the

*American Jewish Year Book* recorded the existence of Zionist groups not only in many large and midsize Jewish communities, but also in small towns such as Lewiston, Maine; Pawtucket, Rhode Island; Hagerstown, Maryland; Beaver Falls, Pennsylvania; Bellaire, Ohio; and Tyler, Texas. As the twentieth century progressed, new Zionist circles continued to appear in other small communities. In Texarkana, straddling the Texas-Arkansas border, Zionists formed an association in 1917, for example, and by 1919 individuals from Petersburg, Virginia, were traveling to Zionist conventions, although they did not formally establish a local Zionist organization until fifteen years later. In 1920 about half of the Jewish population of Eveleth, Minnesota, belonged to the local Zionist society, and there were Zionist groups in nearby Chisholm and Hibbing as well.[22]

Even Zionist youth groups appeared in a surprising number of small towns. By the mid-1930s there were chapters of Young Judaea in at least twenty-six of the triple-digit communities of the late 1920s, including places such as Burlington, Vermont; Framingham, Massachusetts; Massena, New York; Palisades Park, New Jersey; Butler, Pennsylvania; Newport, Kentucky; Hattiesburg, Mississippi; St. Augustine, Florida; Iron Mountain, Michigan; Racine, Wisconsin; Cedar Rapids, Iowa; Minot, North Dakota; Aberdeen, South Dakota; and Cheyenne, Wyoming.[23] In some small communities, East European Jews were so immersed in Zionist activity that they supported chapters of factional Zionist groups. By 1918 there was a chapter of the Labor Zionist Poalei Zion in Iowa City, for instance, and by the early 1940s there was a chapter of the religious Zionist organization Mizrachi in Steubenville, Ohio. The East European Jews of Durham, North Carolina, supported a chapter of Mizrachi by the early 1940s, as well as a chapter of the Labor Zionist youth movement Habonim.[24]

The appearance of affiliates of national Zionist societies and of chapters of other Jewish organizations in small communities reflects the importance of long-distance ties in helping the residents of small towns sustain their Jewish identities so fervently. The survival of Jewish life in small communities had always been predicated to some extent on maintaining connections with larger Jewish centers, and, despite the essential self-sufficiency of smaller Jewish settlements, the significance of their contact with the larger Jewish world should not be overlooked. Already during the second half of the nineteenth century, Isaac Mayer Wise, the most influential figure in American Reform Judaism, had been among those who realized how important ties between communities were, and that is why he put so much effort into maintaining a national Jewish press and why he spent so much time crisscrossing the country staying in touch with various Jewish settlements. Indeed, Wise saw a union of Hebrew congregations that would link America's various Jewish centers as being especially important for small communities, and he frequently traveled to small towns to bring his message in person. So, for example, Wise was in Davenport, Iowa, in 1855; in Lafayette, Indiana, in 1860; and in Cumberland, Maryland, in 1867, although he inadvertently arrived there a week late for the dedication of the town's synagogue. He was in Quincy, Illinois, in 1870 and in San Jose, California, in 1874. According to James Heller, one of Wise's biographers, "between 1855 and 1873 he had visited almost every Jewish community, large and small, from Missouri to the Atlantic, and from New Orleans to New York." In the course of his travels "he had lectured to large and attentive audiences, he laid the cornerstones of numerous synagogues, and then usually dedicated them after their completion." Eventually, Heller reports, Wise's name became "a household word in American Israel." Nor was Wise the only prominent Jewish figure whose travels helped maintain contacts between various Jewish communities during the nineteenth century. Charles Wessolowsky, for instance, as lecturer and subscription agent for the Atlanta-based periodical the *Jewish South*, visited some sixty cities, towns, and villages in seven states in the years 1878 and 1879 alone.[25]

Like Wise and Wessolowsky, the founders of the Jewish Publication Society of America (JPS) were committed to making contacts in small towns, and their efforts, too, contributed to the maintenance of a national Jewish network that incorporated small communities. Founded in Philadelphia in 1888 to promote the publication of books of Jewish content in English, the JPS sought the financial support and subscriptions of "members" not only in America's major Jewish centers, but also in smaller Jewish settlements all over the country. As early as 1900, when the JPS had only a single agent traveling around the United States to solicit subscribers and when many of America's classic small Jewish communities were still in their formative stage, the society nonetheless had at least one member in 156 of the 490 towns that would have triple-digit communities by the late 1920s. The society also had members in a fair number of small towns that would be home to even fewer than 100 Jews in the 1920s. The JPS had thirty-two subscribers in Mobile, Alabama, in 1900, for example; nineteen in Macon, Georgia; eighteen in Wilmington, North Carolina; fourteen in Appleton, Wisconsin; thirteen in Corsicana, Texas; nine in Hamilton, Ohio; eight in Kalamazoo, Michigan; and five in Plattsburgh, New York. Places with a single subscriber in 1900 included Fitchburg, Massachusetts; Somerville, New Jersey; Punxsutawney, Pennsylvania; Martinsburg, West Virginia; Fayetteville, North Carolina; Bessemer, Alabama; Aurora, Illinois; Muscatine, Iowa; and Tucson, Arizona.[26]

The intensity of contact between national Jewish institutions and small Jewish communities only increased during the early decades of the twentieth century, as East Europeans with a strong ethnic identity came to dominate small-town Jewish life. The leaders of America's major Jewish organizations recognized that even in the most remote small communities, Jews stayed abreast of developments in the larger Jewish world and would welcome such contact. Furthermore, these leaders understood that small-town Jews represented a source of financial and moral support that should not remain untapped. By 1927 the Jewish Publication Society, for example, had at least one member in 254 of the 490 triple-digit Jewish communities identifiable in that year. In Pennsylvania, for instance, Pottstown was home to twelve JPS members, while Bradford and York each had eight members. Coatesville, Greensburg, and Oil City each had six JPS subscribers, while Butler, Donora, New Castle, and Wilkensburg each had five. Beaver Falls, Pittston, and Shenandoah had four members each, and in addition there were four towns with triple-digit communities that had three members in each, twelve towns with two members in each, and twenty-one towns with one member in each.

In North Carolina, to take another example, Goldsboro was home to eight members of the JPS in 1927, while Asheville was home to seven. Charlotte and Wilmington each had four members, and there were also eight towns with triple-digit communities that had either one or two members in each. In Illinois, Rockford had eight JPS members; Springfield, six; Aurora and Champaign, four each. In addition, there were eight triple-digit communities in Illinois with one to three JPS members in each. Obviously, the number of JPS subscribers in triple-digit communities and in even smaller Jewish settlements paled in comparison to the membership in places such as Baltimore (287 members in 1927), Detroit (179 members), Minneapolis (72 members), and Los Angeles (121 members), to say nothing of Philadelphia and New York City. Nonetheless, the fact that there were JPS subscribers in so many secondary cities and towns helps confirm the significance of these places as components of America's Jewish communal cosmos.[27]

Like the Jewish Publication Society of America, a wide range of Jewish charitable organizations maintained contact with small communities, their efforts in these places perhaps even more important in providing for the expression of Jewish loyalty than they were for fundraising. Small-town Jews of both German and East European background not only supported institutions such as the orphan homes that served American Jewry and the Jewish tuberculosis hospital in Denver, but they also responded to appeals to assist victims of the pogroms that wracked the Russian Empire at the beginning of the century and contributed to various fundraising drives to help those suffering from the disruptions caused by World War I in Eastern Europe and in Palestine. As one author described the reaction to appeals in Newburyport, Massachusetts, during World War I, "nearly every Jewish resident . . . pledged himself to contribute weekly, according to his means, for the needs of his suffering race."[28]

By the second decade of the twentieth century, those institutions whose constituents were to be found primarily among Jewish immigrant families became increasingly active in seeking out contacts with smaller communities. An account of the fundraising efforts of the Central Relief Committee that was organized during World War I by the New York–based Union of Orthodox Congregations to aid Jews in distress in Europe and in the Middle East provides a useful illustration. The Central Relief Committee, which, through the Joint Distribution Committee, coordinated its efforts with other agencies such as the American Jewish Relief Committee and the socialist People's Relief Committee, engaged in a wide range of fundraising activities, including the sale of war relief stamps and certificates, the promotion of a Jewish Relief Day, and the sponsorship of cross-country fundraising tours.

Although the Central Relief Committee focused its activities mainly on Jews in large and midsize cities, its attempts to enlist support in smaller communities were substantial. The statements reporting all donations of over $100 that the committee issued periodically during World War I convey some idea of its outreach efforts. One typical statement from 1917 or 1918, which reports total contributions of $59,493.40, shows twenty-six donations of $100 or more coming from various synagogues and organizations around New York City; twenty-five donations from relief committees and other groups in midsize cities such as Newark, Cleveland, St. Louis, and Jacksonville; and another eighteen contributions coming from smaller cities and towns that had Jewish populations of well under 1,000. The statement reveals, for example, that Congregation Beth Jacob of Tupper Lake, New York, had donated $460; that the Ladies Aid Society of Westfield, Massachusetts, had provided $150; that a collection in Carnegie, Pennsylvania, had yielded $367; and that fundraising in Green Bay, Wisconsin, had netted $851.90. From several small towns, donations came in from local committees that had been set up specifically to raise funds for relief: $140 from Attleboro, Massachusetts; $400 from Marietta, Ohio; $1,000 from Eveleth, Minnesota.

Another typical statement issued by the Central Relief Committee shows a huge contribution of $100,000 from the committee's affiliate in Chicago, but smaller contributions from about thirty other cities, both large and small. The Relief Committee of Chicopee, Massachusetts, sent in $109, and the Committee of Newport, Rhode Island, sent $228.35. The Ladies Aid Society in Freehold, New Jersey, contributed $100; the Sons of Abraham Congregation of Lafayette, Indiana, donated $105; the Hebrew Congregation of Fargo, North Dakota, sent $179.50; and a collection in Columbus, Georgia, raised $100. Yet another periodic statement shows contributions from places such as Oswego, New York; Hagerstown, Maryland; Ambridge, Pennsylvania; Middletown and Barberton, Ohio; Jackson, Michigan; Winston Salem, North Carolina; Clarksdale, Mississippi; Mobile, Alabama; Waterloo, Iowa; and Aberdeen, South Dakota.[29]

Another example of a New York–based organization that reached out to small towns was the Jewish Labor Committee, founded in 1934 to provide a voice for Jewish labor interests both within the American trade union movement and within mainstream American Jewish organizations. Drawing its support from groups such as the International Ladies' Garment Workers Union, the socialist-oriented Workmen's Circle, and the readers of the Yiddish-language daily, *The Forward*, the Jewish Labor Committee was active before World War II in promoting a boycott of goods produced in Nazi Germany and supporting other antifascist activities. During World War II the committee built links to underground resistance movements in Europe, supported émigrés in America, and mobilized union locals to assist refugees and continue antifascist activities. Its work on behalf of refugees continued after the war as well.

Even though Jewish industrial workers were few and far between in smaller communities, the Jewish Labor Committee saw a benefit in turning to small-town Jews for support. Like so many of the country's more visible Jewish organizations, the Labor Committee recognized that a broad appeal to American Jewry had to include interaction with small communities as well as large. It reasoned that at least some of those who had made their way to smaller Jewish settlements would be sympathetic to its agenda and its progressive credentials, even if they themselves had no connection with union activism. Thus, in the years from 1934 to 1947 the organization had correspondence with individuals in scores of smaller cities and towns. In Michigan, for example, the committee had contacts in Ann Arbor, Battle Creek, Bay City, Benton Harbor, Lansing, Mount Clemens, Muskegon, Pontiac, and Saginaw, all of which had triple-digit Jewish populations at the time. In Wisconsin, the committee had contacts in Beloit, Fond du Lac, Green Bay, Manitowoc, Oshkosh, and Racine.[30]

Another organization that maintained communication with East European Jews in small towns was Yeshiva University (YU). Even though, as we have seen, rabbis trained at YU's Rabbi Isaac Elchanan Theological Seminary seldom ended up serving congregations in smaller communities, Yeshiva's leaders expected that the East European Jews in those places still identified with the culture of Orthodoxy and that it was worthwhile approaching them for support and financial assistance. The records of YU indicate that during the first half of the twentieth century, the school solicited funds to sustain its programs not only in dozens of large and midsize Jewish communities, as might have been expected, but in scores of small towns as well. Indeed, it was perhaps because YU was attempting to Americanize the Orthodoxy of the old country that its leaders thought small-town Jews might be especially inclined to aid its efforts.

From 1917 to 1950, fundraisers for YU had correspondence with groups or individuals in at least 142 of the 490 triple-digit Jewish communities of the

1920s, and in some parts of the country the institution's search for support in small towns was remarkably intense. In New Jersey, for example, YU was in touch with people in Bergenfield, Bound Brook, Caldwell, Carteret, Clifton, Dover, Englewood, Freehold, Garfield, Guttenberg, Hackensack, Kearny, Keyport, Millville, Montclair, Morristown, Palisades Park, Pleasantville, Princeton, Rahway, Red Bank, Roselle, South River, Summit, Vineland, Westfield, and Wildwood. In New Hampshire, Yeshiva University made contacts in Berlin, Claremont, Concord, Manchester, Nashua, and Portsmouth. In Maryland, financial support was sought in Annapolis, Cumberland, Frederick, and Hagerstown. Even in Alabama, seldom perceived as a bastion of Orthodoxy, funds were solicited in Anniston, Bessemer, Gadston, Mobile, Selma, and Tuscaloosa.[31]

While East European men in small towns managed the congregations, cemetery associations, free loan societies, and other such institutions that were considered to be in their domain, East European women found ways to involve themselves in the institutional frameworks of their communities as well. As was the case with their husbands, these women were sometimes welcomed into groups that had been established by their German-Jewish predecessors. The Ladies' Benevolent Society organized by Central European Jewish women in Topeka, Kansas, in 1885 did not hesitate to offer membership to East Europeans when they arrived in town, for example. In most small-town settings, however, women of East European background had to establish service organizations and other female sodalities of their own. In some cases, they did so because existing women's organizations snubbed the newcomers. In Galesburg, Illinois, when East European women found that they were excluded from the primarily social and occasionally philanthropic activities of the Jewish Ladies Aid, they established their own Judean Club as a sewing circle and institutional base. In other cases, however, the creation of new women's groups was simply the result of there having been no local Jewish infrastructure in place before the arrival of East Europeans.[32]

In many ways, echoing the way their husbands' institutions often copied older models, the societies organized by East European women followed the patterns established by earlier German-Jewish female sodalities. These groups sometimes took on mutual aid functions, for example, and they often served as the equivalent of congregational sisterhood organizations. Furthermore, like older German-Jewish organizations, it was not unusual for the newer groups to change their names over time, and occasionally it was difficult to distinguish between groups that were affiliated with synagogues and those that were nominally independent of congregations. In Manchester, New Hampshire, for instance, what began as a Ladies' Aid and Benevolent Association in 1910 eventually became known as the Sisterhood of Congregation Adath Yeshurun.[33] Especially as the twentieth century progressed and women who were born or at least raised in America began to play a larger role in small-town Jewish life, the women's organizations there took on a familiar look.

A fundamental way in which the groups established by East European women resembled earlier societies is that they frequently engaged in important fundraising tasks. They collected money for their own activities, for various charitable causes, and for the synagogues with which they were associated. Of course, in the case of East European women, these synagogues were primarily Orthodox or, later, Conservative, rather than Reform. In La Crosse, Wisconsin, the Orthodox women's Hebrew Ladies Aid Society, which functioned from 1903 until around 1930, collected dues of twenty-five cents a month from each member and made a contribution to one worthy cause or another each time it had accumulated ten dollars. The Orthodox Ladies' Aid Society of Lafayette, Indiana, is known to have raised some $450 in early 1917 for the relief of war sufferers in Europe. In Plymouth, Massachusetts, the Ladies Aid Society not only purchased the first Torah mantles for the Beth Jacob synagogue and later provided silver Torah crowns and breastplates which they "polished . . . constantly with their loving hands," but also helped pay off the Beth Jacob mortgage. One list of fundraising activities undertaken by the Ladies Aid Society of the Orthodox Cnesses Israel congregation in Green Bay, Wisconsin, though it is purported to be "far from complete," includes several kinds of events whose exact nature can only be imagined: "rummage sales, card parties, trolley parties, theatre parties, keno parties, bridge luncheons, dances, musicales, tooth-brush sales, marathon bridge tourneys, cake sales, thimble parties, raffles (of almost anything), food sales, [and] hard-times parties."[34]

The full range of activities that could be undertaken by even a single organization of East European Jewish women in small-town America is illustrated by the workings of the Ladies Aid Society of Muskegon, Michigan, organized in 1902. This sodality, affiliated with the B'nai Israel synagogue, provided relief, sent flowers, and paid visits to women in the congregation who were sick or had fallen on hard times. By the 1920s the society was also making contributions to a local school milk fund and to several out-of-town organizations: a social service agency in Chicago, the Jewish tuberculosis sanatorium in Denver, a relief organization helping Jews in Eastern Europe, various institutions in Palestine, and a group providing aid to Ethiopian Jews. Furthermore, the Ladies Aid was also serving as a major resource for B'nai Israel itself. Among other things, it covered the cost of visiting rabbis when the congregation was without its own spiritual leader.[35]

So important was the work of East European women's organizations in fundraising that soon after the House of Israel Congregation was founded in Sharon, Pennsylvania, the men who served as its leaders entreated the women of the synagogue to form a ladies' auxiliary in anticipation of the financial help the group could provide. Among the things funded by the Sharon sisterhood in ensuing years were a stove and various utensils for the synagogue kitchen and "a long line of paint jobs." In Hagerstown, Maryland, the Hebrew Ladies Auxiliary, organized in 1915, was able to erect an entire school building adjacent to the B'nai Abraham synagogue. Dedicated in 1921, it was complete with a kitchen and space for meetings and social events. In Auburn, Maine, the sisterhood of the Orthodox congregation Beth Abraham helped with the reconstruction of the music hall the community had purchased for use as a synagogue when the newly acquired and uninsured building burned in a huge fire that left only the outer walls standing. As a newspaper story later recalled, "the men of the parish still wonder how they ever could have paid off the mortgage if it had not been for the Beth Abraham Sisterhood."[36]

Although the women of smaller Jewish settlements were generally not in a position to support a profusion of female associations, sometimes the congregational divisions that emerged even within East European communities were reflected also in the multiplication of women's societies. In Torrington, Connecticut, for example, where internal dissension had resulted in the creation of two separate Orthodox synagogues, each had its own sisterhood. The group affiliated with the Sons of Jacob had started out as the Torrington Hebrew Ladies Aid Society even before the town's first congregation was chartered, while the sisterhood connected with Beth El got its start around 1929. Moreover, Torrington's community also supported a chapter of the National Federation of Temple Sisterhoods, even though there was no Reform congregation in the city with which it could affiliate. It seems that this group, probably composed of American-educated women, eventually played a key role in moving Torrington's Jews away from their adherence to Orthodoxy.[37]

One thing that clearly distinguished the early twentieth-century cultural life of East European women from that of their German-Jewish predecessors in small communities was the prominent role played by Zionism in the organizational activities of the more recently arrived. Jewish women of East European background, like their husbands, were possessed of an ethnic consciousness that was mostly absent among their German-Jewish counterparts, and so, for these women, as for East European men, Jewish nationalism was an attractive ideology. Certainly the most visible of all women's Zionist societies in America during the interwar period was Hadassah, founded by Henrietta Szold in 1912 to raise funds for health care and other projects in Palestine and to promote Jewish education in the United States. Thus, in the years before midcentury, the presence of a Hadassah chapter in a community was a good indicator that there were women there who were devoted to Zionist ideals. It is significant, therefore, that in the period before World War II, Hadassah chapters sprang up not only in all of America's principal cities but also in many of the small towns in which East European immigrants had settled. In

1937, for instance, Hadassah had chapters in ninety-four of our sample triple-digit communities, and in some places that had even fewer than 100 Jewish residents in the 1920s. Moreover, although Hadassah seems to have ceased publishing comprehensive lists of its local groups after 1937, other sources suggest that the number of its chapters in small towns continued to grow considerably in subsequent years. In 1939, for example, brand-new Hadassah chapters were organized in three small cities in Mississippi: Clarksdale, Hattiesburg, and Jackson. So, too, while Fargo was the only North Dakota town with a Hadassah chapter in 1937, by 1942 there were chapters in Grand Forks and Minot as well.[38]

For all the work that East European women's societies accomplished in fundraising, in support of congregational functions, and in Zionist activism, these organizations, like earlier groups established by German-Jewish women, also fulfilled a very important social role. Meetings of these organizations were opportunities for camaraderie and conversation as much as they were occasions for conducting business, and they seldom took place without food and drink being served. In La Crosse, for instance, when the Orthodox women of the community got together, "refreshments invariably consisted of hot tea served in glasses and sweetened with raspberry or strawberry preserves . . . and each lady vied with the others to see who could bake the tallest [sponge] cake." What is more, as the younger generation of East European women Americanized, some of their gatherings took on a character that was overwhelmingly social, much as some of the gatherings of German-Jewish ladies had in the late nineteenth century. Indeed, in Newburyport, Massachusetts, some older immigrant women were quite dismayed at the Americanized ways that the younger members of the community were adopting by the 1930s. One older woman, asked about the bridge parties of young wives in the community, echoed what Rabbi Max Raisin had said two decades earlier in Meridian, Mississippi, when she opined that bridge games represented "a regular epidemic and a sickness." Some of the women who spent so much time at cards, she fumed, "should be taken out and shot." "They don't take care of their own children," she groused, and "their husbands come home and find no supper."[39]

Besides the existence of religious institutions guided by Orthodox practice and an infrastructure of men's and women's organizations that gave immigrant Jewish life its contours, there were also other, less tangible, factors that promoted a sense of cultural cohesion among small-town East European Jews. For one thing, to an even greater extent than the Central European Jews who had preceded them, the East Europeans tended to live near one another, creating neighborhoods that were closely associated with the local Jewish experience. Thus, even small towns with Jewish populations of no more than a few hundred could claim some miniature version of the quasi-mythical

"Lower East Side" of New York City.[40] Of course, these small-town Jewish precincts were in no sense completely Jewish in character, nor were they home to all the local Jewish families. Nonetheless, they served as emotionally compelling focal points for local Jewish life.

David Rome, who was born in Fitchburg, Massachusetts, in 1914, reported that as early as 1900 Boutelle Street could be identified as "the principal Jewish street of the city," with his own family, owners of a downtown clothing store, living at number 6. Rome also had memories of the synagogue, just two doors from his home; of Krevoruck's Kosher Butcher Shop, just beyond the synagogue; and of a grocery store at the corner of Boutelle and Lunenburg Streets, run by Joseph Miller, a stalwart of the Fitchburg congregation, and his wife. Census reports confirm Rome's impressions, revealing that anyone walking past the double-digit even-numbered houses of Boutelle Street in 1920 would have encountered the homes of seven families headed by some-one born in New England, three families headed by French-Canadians, one family headed by a Swede, but sixteen Jewish families.[41]

Though memory can exaggerate and even distort historical reality, the way so many individuals remember their experiences leaves little doubt that in the early decades of the twentieth century those who grew up in small towns perceived the districts inhabited by East European immigrants and their families as vibrant Jewish enclaves. One man who spent his youth in Portsmouth, New Hampshire, reported that the Jews there tended to settle near the synagogue that was established in 1912, and that the area around the shul, recently restored as the Strawbery Banke district, was home to "two kosher butcher stores, a Jewish bakery, and three Jewish grocery stores." A local history of the Beth Israel Congregation in Latrobe, Pennsylvania, written in the mid-1950s, reports that the majority of the East European Jewish fam-ilies in the city lived in the First Ward, and that "in time this section became known as 'Jew Town.'" A woman who grew up in Warren, Ohio, reported that the first Jews who settled there "brought the mores of their community with them, forming a ghetto of their own." Using the same imagery, a resident of Kalamazoo observed that "the South St. area near the old Schul, was what could be called a Little Ghetto."[42] In Charlottesville, Virginia, the Russian Jews in town were so concentrated in one neighborhood that they became known as the Ridge Street community; and a recent interviewer who spoke with several individuals who grew up in Bessemer, Alabama, in the 1920s and 1930s concluded that Jews there settled mainly on Clarendon Avenue, Berk-ley Avenue, and Sixth Avenue, near the temple, reflecting an "old-country shtetl desire" to live near one another. In Modesto, California, too, most of the Jewish families lived within easy walking distance of the synagogue that was constructed in 1922 at the corner of Fourteenth and F Streets.[43]

The most detailed study of pre–World War II Jewish residence patterns in a small city, conducted in Newburyport in the 1930s, also points to the propensity of Jews to gravitate toward one another in small towns, just as they did in larger urban centers. The sociologists who investigated the situation in Newburyport found that, although Jews there were beginning to lose their "residential coherence" as they became more entrenched in the local society, they were still heavily settled in only two of the twelve geographic segments into which the researchers had divided the city. These sociologists also found that other groups in Newburyport made at least some attempts to contain the spread of Jews beyond their core residential areas. In 1933, when Newburyport's Jewish congregation purchased a former church building in a relatively upscale neighborhood to use as a synagogue, several families living in the area circulated a petition addressed to the mayor asking him to keep the Jews out. This episode suggests that the creation of Jewish neighborhoods in towns such as Newburyport was the result of both the instinctive desire of Jews to locate near one another and a certain amount of anti-Jewish prejudice.[44]

East European Jewish families of the immigrant generation not only lived near one another, but worked near one another as well. One woman who arrived in Augusta, Georgia, in 1921 remembered that "the localism for the Jewish neighborhood was Kugel Avenue, which in reality was Ellis Street," and that "all the Jewish merchants in Augusta were on one block of Broad Street." The historian Louis Schmier has observed that in Valdosta, Georgia, where the Jewish population seems to have hovered just below 100 in the interwar period, the geographic location of homes and businesses not only reflected a cohesiveness among the East European Jews there, but also reinforced a certain estrangement that many of them felt from the dominant gentile society. "Hill Avenue was the only really acceptable street on which to live," Schmier reports, but Troup Street, which the locals often called "Jew Street," was "at the lower end of the scale." Similarly, "Patterson Street was the only 'proper' commercial street . . . [while] Ashley Street, where the Jews located their stores, was degradingly known as 'Nigger Street' because on it were located the saloons and stores where blacks traded."[45]

Accounts of Jewish life in other small towns reflect the geographic concentration of Jewish businesses as well, and serve as further reminders that some people had the impression that Jews actually dominated small-town trade. One man who grew up in Arkansas before World War II recalled that his father was generally able to gather the quorum required for daily prayers by "sending him down Pine Bluff's Main Street to notify various Jewish businessmen that a minyan . . . was needed." In Topeka, stores owned by Jews were found on nearly every block of the Kansas Avenue shopping district, and, according to the published history of the community, the thoroughfare "would have seemed deserted without them." When Rabbi Norman Feldheym arrived in San Bernardino, California, in 1937, he found that the majority of the members of his congregation "either owned or were associated with small businesses, most of which were at or near Third and E Streets." Later he recalled that when he needed to attend to congregational affairs, he "used to gravitate between Mr. Greenhood's print shop, the Harris Company and the pawn shop," all within close proximity downtown.[46]

Notwithstanding the fact that synagogues were the prime centers of Jewish life in just about every small community, often there were specific places of business in small towns where Jews routinely encountered one another and which thus became Jewish spaces, to some extent, in their own right. Often these were grocery stores carrying kosher meat and delicatessen products. In Topeka, in the period after World War I, Ben and Anna Kross's Kansas Avenue grocery served as "an important hub of the Jewish community." In Fitchburg, Massachusetts, at about the same time, it was the Krevoruck Butcher Shop that David Rome remembered; and in Lexington, Kentucky, it was the grocery store owned by Harry Goller, described by one resident as "the most colorful character in this town." In Muskegon, Michigan, especially during the Depression, Rosenbaum's grocery store functioned as "a local gathering place for those with time on their hands" and as a place of diversion for "youngsters who dipped spoonsful out of the sauerkraut barrel and begged pieces of penny candy out of the jars on the counter."[47]

Along the same lines, a map showing "locations of Jewish Interest" in Manchester, New Hampshire, highlights the pre–World War II grocery store of Abraham Savan, who was "affectionately remembered for the barrel of pickles and the hefty corned beef sandwiches on bulkie rolls that he dispensed" and the Hideaway Restaurant run by a Mrs. Silverman between 1938 and 1956, which was a "popular Jewish eating- and meeting-place." In Newburyport in the early decades of the twentieth century, while the older men tended to congregate at the synagogue, the younger men came together at a Jewish-owned grocery store on the main downtown square. One member of the community described this establishment as "the clubhouse" and recalled that "on a hot summer night there may have been as many as twenty-five or thirty men sitting around on boxes reading papers and discussing."[48]

Probably the most powerful factor that gave East European immigrants in small towns an identity separate from both the German Jews who may have preceded them and from the larger society around them was their pervasive use of Yiddish as the language of everyday life. Unfortunately, the enumerators employed by the U.S. Census Bureau in the early twentieth century were not always careful about how they ascertained and recorded the native languages of the individuals they listed, so even though information on mother tongue is provided in some census documents, it is difficult to discover exactly how many small-town Jews in America considered Yiddish their vernacular. Many of those recorded as having Russian or Polish or some other language as their mother tongue were likely to have spoken Yiddish on a daily basis, and those whose native language was registered as Hebrew were even more likely to have been, in fact, Yiddish speakers, since the use of Hebrew for mundane conversation was quite rare in the early decades of the twentieth century, both in Europe and in America. Because of all this, the number of native Yiddish speakers in small-town census documents is certainly underreported. Still, it is striking how often Yiddish does appear in census records as the native tongue of Jews in small communities. In Nashua, New Hampshire, in 1920, for instance, thirty-five heads of household are listed as having Yiddish or "Jewish" as their native language, and twenty-six more are listed as native Hebrew speakers. In Hamilton, Ohio, in the same year, twenty-three heads of household are listed as being native Yiddish speakers, and twelve more are listed as native speakers of Hebrew. In Lexington, Kentucky, twenty-nine heads of household are listed as having Yiddish or "Jewish" as their mother tongue, and twenty-three more are listed as having Hebrew.[49]

Furthermore, a wealth of anecdotal evidence attests to the persistence of Yiddish among Jewish immigrants in small-town America. In Wakefield, Massachusetts, for example, the first "Hebrew School," organized in 1910 with twelve students in the home of Morris Slotnick, had a curriculum consisting of the translation of biblical texts from Hebrew to Yiddish, and practice in Yiddish orthography as well. The Hebrew School of Plymouth, Massachusetts, also taught Yiddish reading and writing, along with the Hebrew language, "and also music." The storyteller Shlomo Noble reported that when he arrived in Beaver Falls, Pennsylvania, in 1920, "Everybody—even the American born —spoke Yiddish" and that those in the immigrant generation "knew very little English." Even in the early twentieth-century West, still something of a frontier, Yiddish survived as a common medium of discourse. Fannie Wisman recalled that as a young child growing up in Topeka, she heard only Yiddish at home and that she had a very hard time when she started school because her English was so poor. Only after her father took a night-school course so he could converse with her in English did she begin to "love school, and achieve high marks." So, too, Rabbi Irving Levey recalled "vividly" that at the reception held in his honor when he arrived in Topeka in 1929, "the congregants kept talking in Yiddish about us—especially about my wife Sarah." Yiddish was also frequently heard in the Jewish community of Wichita, although the situation in Topeka renders inaccurate historian Hal Rothman's assertion that in the World War I era, the neighborhood in which most of Wichita's East European Jews lived was "most certainly the only place in early twentieth-century Kansas where Yiddish was commonly spoken."[50]

Although the small Jewish communities of the South have never been perceived as vital repositories of East European Jewish culture, the Yiddish language remained alive there, as well. From turn-of-the-century Durham,

North Carolina, for example, comes the story of two East European immigrants who went before a local judge in a dispute involving contested ownership, business rivalry, and intimations of sexual improprieties, arguing out the entire case in Yiddish, with the court supplying a translator. And from Lexington, Kentucky, comes the tale of the highly regarded Yiddish poet I. J. Schwartz, who lived and wrote in the heart of the Bluegrass region for over a decade just after World War I, producing, among other things, the epic poem cycle he called "Kentucky." Schwartz found in Lexington an entire Yiddish-speaking microcosm. Myer Godhelff, who grew up there in the 1920s and 1930s, reported that the people with whom his parents associated "all spoke Yiddish in person and on the telephone." Although they knew Russian, Godhelff's parents seldom used that language, and they were reticent about conversing in English as well. "Only at home in our circle of Jewish friends and at the synagogue did they speak all out," he recalled, "and it was always Yiddish."[51]

Although the story of I. J. Schwartz in Lexington is perhaps the best illustration of the way a Yiddish cultural identity could thrive in small-town America, it is by no means the only such illustration. Other stories point to the perpetuation of highly sophisticated Jewish learning in small communities throughout the early decades of the twentieth century, not only in Yiddish but also in Hebrew. In Kearny, New Jersey, for instance, lived the Latvian-born Ephraim Deinard, an active bibliographer and polemicist who wrote over fifty Hebrew books and pamphlets attacking Hasidism, Reform Judaism, and Christianity. His extensive private holdings eventually helped build the Judaica collections of both the Library of Congress and Harvard University. In Greensburg, Pennsylvania, lived Isaac Kahanowitz, who in the early twentieth century amassed the greatest private collection of Yiddish and Hebrew books and periodicals in western Pennsylvania, meaning that his library surpassed anything that could be found even in Pittsburgh, with a Jewish population of over 50,000 in the 1920s.[52]

Steubenville, Ohio, was the home of Rebecca Altman, born in Lithuania in 1880 and recognized as early as 1904 as a translator of Yiddish, Hebrew, and German works and as the author of "essays, poems [and] sketches" in Hebrew and in English for the American Jewish press. Colorado Springs, Colorado, was the home of Bernard Lewis, who died there at age forty-five in 1925 and whose tombstone, which identifies him as a "Yiddish and Hebrew poet," bears the entire nineteen-line text of one of his Yiddish compositions. Indeed, small-town Jewish cemeteries all over the United States yield examples of eloquent tombstone inscriptions, some of them involving inventive acrostics using the names of the deceased, testifying to an impressive linguistic ability on the part of at least a few residents of small communities.[53]

So omnipresent was Yiddish as the language of daily life among small-town Jews that there were a few cases of immigrants who survived in smaller Jewish settlements without learning English at all, at least for a time. The 1920 census of Lexington, Kentucky, lists the fifty-year-old Esther Levy and the seventy-five-year-old Lena Levesky as individuals who did not speak English. Levy had come to America only in 1919, but Levesky had been in the country for seven years. In Newburyport, Massachusetts, the fifty-eight-year-old Hannah Wagman could not speak English, even though she had come to America in 1906, nor could the seventy-five-year-old Hyman Walter, a widower living with his daughter and son-in-law. As late as the 1930s, a few older Jewish women in Newburyport still had trouble carrying on even simple conversations in English. Likewise, the grandmother of Faye Moskowitz continued to conduct her life entirely in Yiddish, even while she was living with Faye's parents in Jackson, Michigan, during the Great Depression. Paul Kronick's grandfather, who ran a grocery business with his three sons in pre–World War II North Adams, Massachusetts, never learned to speak English either.[54]

Occasionally, it seems, East European immigrants in small towns attempted to use Yiddish even when communicating with their gentile neighbors. The historian of the Jewish community of Racine, Wisconsin, reports that one Mrs. Gordon was renowned for her amiability and thoughtfulness and that she had many friends beyond the Jewish community. "She would talk to them in Yiddish and they to her in Danish," he writes, "and both of them thought they were speaking English." Similarly, Mollie Scrinopskie recalled that her mother, an immigrant in Topeka, "was never proficient in English and always spoke Yiddish" but that since she had such an outgoing personality, before long "she had all her neighbors learning Yiddish."[55]

That Yiddish newspapers commonly circulated among East European Jews in small towns is yet another manifestation of the centrality of the language in the lives of these people. From all over America, recollections of small-town Jewish life are likely to include memories of Yiddish papers in the home. The Grossmans, one of the most prominent Jewish families in turn-of-the-century Corpus Christi, Texas, subscribed to the Yiddish-language *Tageblatt* in the years before World War I, and Julia Rome was subscribing to the same paper in Fitchburg, Massachusetts, in the era of World War II. In Jackson, Mississippi, early in the twentieth century, the local butcher, a Mr. Harris, regularly received issues of the country's leading Yiddish daily, *The Forward*, from New York; and a little later in Modesto, California, the Arnopole and Zeff families both subscribed as well. In Benton Harbor, Michigan, in the period between the wars, Fannie Marcus used to read human-interest stories to her children from *The Forward* on Saturday afternoons, and Faye Moskowitz writes that her family in Depression-era Jackson "didn't own any books, but the *Jewish Daily Forward* came in the mail each morning." Rabbi Abraham Hefterman of Manchester, New Hampshire, wrote a regular column for *The Forward*, often relating thinly disguised tales about his own community.[56]

Further evidence of the pervasiveness and persistence of Yiddish in small-town settings comes from the fact that many of the institutions established by East Europeans in these places conducted their business in the old-country vernacular. The first prayer group in Plymouth, Massachusetts, penciled its minutes in Yiddish in a large ledger book, for example; and both the Orthodox Hebrew Free Loan Association and the Sons of Abraham synagogue in Lafayette, Indiana, kept their minutes in Yiddish as late as 1939. The Ladies' Auxiliary of the Kneseth Israel congregation in Annapolis, Maryland, conducted its meetings and kept its records in Yiddish until the late 1930s as well, introducing English and parliamentary procedure only when the group elected its first American-born president, Lena Eisenstein. Congregation Brith Achim in Petersburg, Virginia, where the rabbi preached in Yiddish during the interwar years, kept its records in Yiddish at least until the 1920s, and the Orthodox *chevrah kadishah*, the burial society in town, used Yiddish until 1946.[57]

So, too, there were Yiddish-speaking chapters of the socialist-oriented Workmen's Circle organization (the Arbeiter Ring) in Butler, Pennsylvania, and in Macon, Georgia, early in the twentieth century, while in Burlington, Vermont, a local Yiddisher Kultur Verein was organized in 1922. By the 1930s there was even a Workmen's Circle "Labor Lyceum" building in Ellenville, New York. Furthermore, a number of small-town congregations advertised that they conducted worship services using a Yiddish vernacular in addition to the usual Hebrew. In 1919 these could be found in places such as Wallingford, Connecticut; Clearfield, Pennsylvania; Wheeling, West Virginia; and Bellingham, Washington. In pre–World War II Donora, Pennsylvania, even some American-born boys still delivered their bar mitzvah speeches in Yiddish.[58]

Clearly, the East European immigrants who created the vast majority of America's small-town Jewish communities and who revitalized others in the era of mass migration brought with them a strong sense of their cultural identity, and at least for a time they were able to perpetuate a way of life based on their distinctive background, including their powerful ties to the Yiddish language. That they could do so despite their small local numbers is a story that has long been overlooked. Of course, the immigrant culture of small-town Jews was by no means monolithic, nor did it replicate the Yiddish culture that developed in the leading Jewish communities of the United States, let alone the Yiddish culture of the Old World. Nonetheless, the ability of East European immigrants to maintain so much of their traditional lifestyle in the less than ideal environment of small-town America is testimony to the positive feelings that these settlers had toward their cultural roots. Whether East European Jewish immigrants would have been allowed full integration into the life of their small towns had they sought it remains an open question, however, as does the question of what these immigrants might have done differently to ensure the perpetuation of their culture into future generations.

# 12 Patterns of Prejudice and of Transformation

"YOUR UNCLE," LEOPOLD DRYFUS.

With a purpose that's been steadfast "Uncle" has made his way;
With a motto that is classic he's made his business pay.
Black face lambs and little hams have been his stock in trade—
Hams and lambs as sweet as honey have Uncle's fortune made—
'Cause "Uncle needs the money."

A firm grounding in traditional Jewish practice, the creation of a multi-faceted religious and organizational infrastructure, the persistence of certain residential and occupational patterns, and an abiding attachment to Yiddish culture were the main factors that helped create cohesive and distinctive East European Jewish communities or subcommunities in the small towns where immigrants settled during the era of mass migration. However, there is no doubt that the persistence of anti-Jewish sentiments also played a part in defining the East European Jews of small-town America as a group cut off from the social and cultural mainstream. Of course, by the early decades of the twentieth century, Jews of Central European background were highly integrated into the gentile society of the towns in which they lived. Most were native-born and highly acculturated, and some had even intermarried. Indeed, in small towns where German-Jewish families had settled during pioneer days, their presence is likely to have smoothed the way for new arrivals by conveying a sense that Jews had always been a part of the local social fabric.[1]

Nonetheless, anti-Jewish feelings, or at least a lack of concern with Jewish sensibilities, had hardly disappeared from small-town America. Even well-integrated Jews of Central European background felt the sting of antisemitism intermittently, and prejudice against Jews was only intensified as it came to be directed against East Europeans who still retained much of their immigrant culture. In all sections of the country, small-town Jews encountered lingering anti-Jewish stereotypes, a resentment of them as middlemen in business, and a perception that they were somehow different, whether they were one of several foreign-born population groups in their towns or the only one. Even as their gentile neighbors continued to marginalize the Jews, however, the Americanization of their small communities continued. Throughout the early

---

*Photo previous page: A caricature of the meat-packing magnate Leopold Dryfus of Lafayette, Indiana, 1910. Although some Jewish citizens of small towns were counted as local notables, Jews were seldom completely accepted in elite society. From* Lafayette Men of Affairs as Seen by Those Who Know Them *(Lafayette, Ind., 1910).*

decades of the twentieth century, East European immigrants diluted their own adherence to Orthodox religious norms and encountered numerous obstacles in their efforts to pass their cultural outlook on to their children.

To be sure, as in the period when most Jews in America were of Central European origin, antisemitism in the early decades of the twentieth century was less openly pronounced in small towns than it was in metropolitan centers. The most flagrant manifestations of prejudice were still more likely to target large masses of Jews in big cities, rather than the enclaves present in small towns. Moreover, East European Jews in small communities, like their German-Jewish predecessors, were known to the public as individuals, and this fact, too, made it less likely that they would be subjected to the most vicious demonstrations of antisemitism. Jews in small towns seldom felt immediately threatened, even by the most openly anti-Jewish groups. One man who grew up in Haverstraw, New York, in the years just before World War II, for example, had a sense that while there was probably "latent anti-Semitism within the community, it did not relate itself to the local Jewish population." He recalled that even when members of the pro-Nazi German-American Bund held rallies in the 1930s, "not once did they come into the village."[2]

Similarly, student rabbis in small towns in the 1930s reported little antisemitism in the local environment, except perhaps in periods when the Ku Klux Klan was especially active. Even the Klan, however, tended to direct its venom at blacks and at Catholics more often than at Jews. Joseph Klein, the student rabbi in Muskogee, Oklahoma, in 1935, echoed the perception of others when he declared that the Klan's attacks against Jews in his town "have been in the main comparatively light." While small-town Jews were certainly alert to Klan activities, they were seldom alarmed.[3] No wonder an apocryphal story has often surfaced about a small-town Jewish merchant who watched a parade of hooded Klansmen with a mixture of apprehension and bemusement, naming the supposedly anonymous racists individually as they went by, identifying each by the shoes he had bought at the merchant's store.[4]

Harry Golden, the best-known commentator on southern Jewish life in the middle of the twentieth century, has gone so far as to suggest that in the small communities of the South "segregation of Jew and Gentile disappears entirely" and that small-town Jews, far from being singled out for contempt or hatred, were actually protected "with a zeal and devotion otherwise bestowed only on the Confederate monument in the square." Golden's views reflect his regional loyalties and are certainly too enthusiastic, but there can be no doubt that Jews in the South continued to benefit from the perception that they were important to the economic viability of their small towns and that they were certainly much more integral to the local citizenry than their black fellow townspeople. It also did not hurt that many small-town southerners viewed Jews as the People of the Bible incarnate.[5]

All this about relatively mild manifestations of antisemitism having been said, however, it remains true that East European Jews in small communities were often perceived through the lens of conventional anti-Jewish canards. In the popular imagination, they were apt to be viewed as avaricious, domineering, untrustworthy, and clannish. In Fitchburg, Massachusetts, in 1913, for example, a character dressed as a stereotypical Jew marched in a Fourth of July parade carrying a dollar bill as his flag, an incident to which, on the other hand, 150 citizens responded by signing a petition of protest. So, too, the first Jewish child born in Williamson, West Virginia, later reported that when he arrived, "people came from all over to see the 'Jew-baby'—expecting horns." East European Jews also suffered ridicule because of their unfamiliar names and distinctive patterns of speech. As the historian of La Crosse Jewry has observed caustically about the East Europeans there, "these Jews, most of whom were well educated in Europe in their own Jewish academies and who were multi-lingual, were often laughed at locally because of their accented English, generally by persons who spoke only one language—poor English."[6]

Because so many small-town Jews were main-street merchants dealing directly with the public, they also were easily subject to the very old and persistent prejudices against shopkeepers and businessmen in general. Negative feelings about Jewish entrepreneurs were only reinforced in places where Jewish storeowners and tradesmen replicated the relationships Jews had had with neighboring ethnic groups in the old country, relationships that were always fraught with a certain degree of tension. This was the case in the coal towns of western Pennsylvania and of southern West Virginia, for example, where Jewish shopkeepers frequently found themselves selling dry goods, clothing, and hardware to Polish, Slovak, Hungarian, and Ukrainian laborers, much as Jews had sold similar goods to peasants from these same ethnic groups in Eastern Europe.[7]

In other parts of the country as well, it was not uncommon for a variety of European immigrant groups to be found in towns where triple-digit Jewish communities developed, thus providing fertile ground for latent antisemitism based on centuries-old attitudes to come to the surface. In Newburyport, Massachusetts, for instance, the 300 or 400 resident Jews of the 1930s were living in a city that also included about 700 Polish immigrants, perhaps 150 Russians, and about 6,000 other ethnics whose background was rural and agricultural. Other towns that were home to both a triple-digit Jewish community and a population of at least 5,000 non-Jewish immigrants during the interwar period included Cranston, Rhode Island; Bristol, Connecticut; Montclair, New Jersey; Lorain, Ohio; Saginaw, Michigan; and Kenosha, Wisconsin.[8]

Some Jews who grew up in ethnically diverse small towns in the Northeast and Midwest came to feel that they and their coreligionists were a well-accepted part of the local ethnic and cultural mix. In many instances, Jews have reported that they got along very well with neighbors of Polish or Italian or Irish background. Typical is the recollection of Fay Taylor Holtzman of Englewood, New Jersey, about her close childhood relationships with her non-Jewish neighbors. "I used to know a lot of the catechism," she reported, "because I used to listen to little Irish Mary . . . and I'd have to hold the book while she repeated the catechism and everything else!" Deborah Weiner, who has studied the Jews of the West Virginia coalfields, has even argued that ethnic diversity in a town was likely to facilitate Jewish acceptance and integration, especially where Jews were present along with other ethnic groups from the outset. Nonetheless, under the social and economic conditions that held sway in ethnically diverse towns, it is not surprising that some of the mutual suspicions and antagonisms that had existed between Jews and other groups in Europe would crop up in America as well.[9]

Nor were Jewish businesspeople spared the affects of bigotry in places where the local population was largely native-born, as it was especially in the small towns of the South. There, just as in more ethnically diverse places, Jews were invariably the only non-Christians in sight and thus the subject of some suspicion. Furthermore, in cities where the white population was relatively homogeneous, it is likely that many or even most of the foreigners that the rest of the townspeople encountered were Jews, thus making the "otherness" of the Jews even more glaring and rendering them the most convenient targets for nativist prejudice. In Lexington, Kentucky, in 1920, for example, 42 percent of all the Jews in town had been born outside the United States, and even though these Jews represented less than one half of 1 percent of Lexington's total population, they accounted for over 20 percent of all the nonnative Americans in the city. The 160 natives of Ireland in town constituted the only group of foreign-born residents in Lexington that even came close to having the visibility that Jews did.[10]

The demographic profiles of other small towns in the South suggest that in certain places Jews were likely to have constituted an even larger percentage of the foreign-born population than they did in Lexington, even a majority. Around 1930, when about half of all the Jews in the United States were foreign-born, the 420 or so Jews of Fort Smith, Arkansas, were living in a town with only about 600 immigrants in all. In Monroe, Louisiana, and in Wichita Falls, Texas, each of which was home to about 500 Jews, the total number of foreign-born residents was also about 500; and in Hagerstown, Maryland, with some 650 Jewish residents, the total number of immigrants was only about half that number. In Columbus, Georgia, where there were about 700 Jews, the total number of foreign-born residents was a mere 260, a figure suggesting the possibility that nearly all the nonnatives in town were members of the local Jewish community.[11]

Although most of the manifestations of antisemitism that small-town

Jews encountered were rather subtle, they surfaced in a variety of circumstances. In the public schools, for instance, children commonly faced situations in which they were made to feel uncomfortable because of their Jewish identity. In Wichita early in the twentieth century, young Mel Witrogen was told by a teacher that he could not be both a Jew and an American, and in Dover, New Jersey, Vivian Barnert was assigned to a teacher who had her students "read from the New Testament in the morning" and was "noted for her outspoken hatred of Jews." In 1918 the Jewish community of Alexandria, Louisiana, waged an unsuccessful campaign against a proposal to hold public school classes on Saturday in order to make up days missed as a result of that year's flu epidemic. When Janyce Pearlstein reported for school in Warren, Ohio, in 1940, her preregistration card recorded her "nationality" as "Jewish," while all the other students in her room were classified as "American." At about the same time in Bessemer, Alabama, Betty Beck was a member of her high school Honor Society and Thespian Club, as well as being on the staffs of the newspaper and yearbook, but because she was Jewish she was not allowed to join the Cotillion Club that sponsored the Debutante Ball. Small-town Jews, certainly more than those in large communities, had to deal with the common assumption that everyone celebrated Christmas. As Faye Moskowitz wrote about her experience, "somehow the concept of separation of church and state hadn't trickled down yet to Jackson, Michigan, when I was raised there in the late thirties and early forties."[12]

Memories of good intergroup relations in small towns notwithstanding, there were lots of cases in which non-Jewish young people singled out Jews to be the victims of their antisocial behavior. In Iowa City in the 1920s, for example, Ansel Chapman was so harassed by local Irish Catholic children on his way home from Hebrew school that he stopped going in order to avoid further abuse. In Fitchburg, Massachusetts, as well, young Max Sarkin was frequently attacked by the Irish Catholic boys in his neighborhood and often had to be rescued by the local priest. One native of Ellwood City, Pennsylvania, reported that although "there was little anti-Semitism" in his ethnically mixed town, "occasionally there were 'kid gangs' from other sections that would harass us or settle around the synagogue and throw stones or shoot BB guns at the windows."[13]

In the world of adults, too, there were constant reminders that Jews were not quite equal as participants in small-town life. In Donora, Pennsylvania; in Danville, Illinois; in Hibbing, Minnesota; in Fort Smith, Arkansas; in Wilmington, North Carolina, and in scores of other small cities all over the country, Jews were routinely excluded from membership in the most prestigious country clubs or limited to no more than a handful of token members, almost always individuals from long-established families of Central European background. In times of increased xenophobia, Jews were banished from some clubs into which they had previously been accepted. In Michigan, for example, the Muskegon Country Club attempted to expel the prominent merchant Leo Rosen, who won his case against the club in court before resigning in protest.[14]

A certain degree of discrimination in housing was common in small towns as well, just as it was in larger cities. Again, the exclusionary attitudes and practices of gentiles reinforced the inclination of Jews to live in proximity to one another. Jews who moved to Montclair, New Jersey, for instance, "tended to see it as a beautiful place to live in but not especially friendly to Jews." One woman who came to Montclair in 1939 reported that when she was refused a house there, the potential seller explained that she did not mind selling to Jews, but that "her neighbors would not like it." Janyce Pearlstein, who had experienced marginalization as a Jewish child in public school, also remembered that in Warren, Ohio, even after World War II, "there remained areas where Jews were unwelcome to live" and that "no one forced this issue because civil rights were yet unknown." In Muncie, Indiana, a story circulated that when the subdivision of Westwood was plotted, the idea of keeping Jews out was actually suggested by a Jewish confidant of the developer, who wanted to be sure his friend's venture would succeed.[15]

Amid all the manifestations of "social" antisemitism in small towns, there were also occasional expressions of more flagrant and unmitigated anti-Jewish attitudes, especially in times of social or economic crisis. At the dedication of a synagogue in Attleboro, Massachusetts, in 1968, for instance, one speaker asserted that in the early part of the century the Jewish community there "met secretly in secluded places to pray to the Almighty because of the 'intolerance and bigotry' that surrounded them." Even though this claim is unsubstantiated, its persistence suggests that the memory of anti-Jewish feelings in Attleboro had left a powerful legacy. Better documented is the fact that during a particularly bitter shoeworkers' strike in Newburyport in 1933, much of the laborers' anger was directed against Jews, both those who were the absentee owners of some of the local factories and those who were shoe distributors and had a great deal of influence on the industry. Some of the anger unleashed may have been justified, but it was articulated in the most vitriolic and racist terms. "Jews always ruin everything they get into—once a Kike gets into anything, decent people have to get out," proclaimed one disgruntled Newburyport worker. And when a certain Jewish manufacturer tried to convince striking employees that he had their interests at heart, their reaction was only anger: "picture that goddamned New York Kike . . . trying to get away with that kind of stuff. Why those bastards wouldn't give you the sweat off their balls!"[16]

So, too, small-town Jews were likely to be touched by eruptions of a more general xenophobia. During World War I the Jews of Iowa City were directly affected by the governor's proclamation forbidding the use of any language other than English in schools, public places, on the telephone, and even in religious services outside the home. This made the Talmud Torah school that functioned in Iowa City technically illegal between 1918 and 1923, when the U.S. Supreme Court finally overturned the governor's ruling. His proclamation may also have delayed the acquisition of a synagogue building by Iowa City's Agudas Achim congregation, which had been founded in 1916.[17]

Ultimately, even though antisemitism never dominated Jewish life in small-town America, and even though many of the Jews who lived there recalled with fondness some of their interactions with their gentile neighbors, few members of small Jewish communities felt completely comfortable. Every interaction between Jews and non-Jews had a certain edge. Again an example from the much-scrutinized community of Newburyport in the mid-1930s is illustrative. When the town was preparing to observe the tercentenary of its founding, the organizing committee for the celebration decided that various groups should be asked to take part in a parade featuring major characters and events from the history of Newburyport and the country in general. Thus, the local Knights of Columbus would represent the voyages of Christopher Columbus, and the local Harvard Club would represent the first graduates of Harvard. Initially the Jewish community was assigned the role of representing Benedict Arnold, who had massed troops in Newburyport during the American Revolution in preparation for an attack on Quebec. It seems that the organizers of the Newburyport celebration simply overlooked the fact that Arnold later became one of the great villains of American history, associated foremost with betrayal and treason. This association might well have remained obscure had it not been for the fact that the representation of Arnold was now linked with Newburyport's Jews. Both the notables in charge of the tercentenary celebration and the leaders of the local Jewish community realized the unfortunate situation that had been created and within a day professed that a mistake had been made when the pairing was announced. As the team of sociologists who studied Newburyport concluded, "when the Jewish connection [with Arnold] was made, the ambiguous history of the relationship between Jewish and Christian groups" and the "separation from full integration into the larger community [of Newburyport's Jews] were brought into focus. All the deep anxieties and concerns of both groups were mobilized."[18]

In a similar vein, the sociologist Benjamin Kaplan, an astute observer of southern Jewish life, writing in 1951, summed up the situation in small towns throughout the country. Jews in small communities, he observed, "live out their lives, on the surface at least, as other people do, but [they] are never quite at ease, never completely secure, and seldom imbued with the sense of worthwhileness that members of other religious groups are. Outwardly they may be calm," he concluded, "but inwardly they are worried." A longtime resident of Williamson, West Virginia, put this same sentiment even more succinctly. "In a small town, being Jewish one has to be careful what one does and says," he explained; "I can't be myself except when I'm with fellow Jews."[19]

It was, then, a variety of religious, social, and cultural forces promoting Jewish identity and the reluctance of gentile society to fully accept the Jewish minority within it, that combined to foster a clearly distinguishable Jewish subculture in the hundreds of smaller Jewish settlements that were scattered across the United States in the early decades of the twentieth century. Although their separation from the mainstream was brought about in part by negative forces, it was to a large extent self-imposed, and it carried with it a welcome sense of cohesiveness and solidarity, which many small-town Jews remember as a feeling that they belonged to one large family. This feeling was buttressed by the fact that many of those who settled in small towns had true kin connections within their communities, and by the fact that many were conditioned by the way East European *landsleit* related to each other. The sense of kinship felt by Jewish immigrants in small communities tended to carry over to their children, and even to small-town Jews who were less attached to traditionalist culture. Lynne Applebaum Waggoner, daughter of a shoe store owner in Bessemer, Alabama, recalled that she "really felt a sense of belonging" within the town's lone congregation "because I knew everyone"; and Murray Milkman, who was born in Pittston, Pennsylvania, in 1929, observed that in many respects a Jewish community in a small town "acts as an extended family." A similar sentiment was expressed in an anniversary history of the Adath Yeshurun congregation of Manchester, New Hampshire, when its author recalled that bar mitzvah celebrations there in the pre–World War II era "had about them a home-made, family feeling."[20]

The concern members of small communities had for each other's welfare is a common theme in the recollections of Jews who lived in small towns in the early decades of the twentieth century. It was said, for example, that David Sax, a kosher butcher in Benton Harbor, Michigan, "knew exactly how many mouths each family had to feed and which one needed more than the 25-cents worth of 'flanken' it could afford." Likewise, Frieda Perry remembered that if she and her shopkeeper husband were absent from their synagogue in Cumberland, Maryland, on a Friday evening, "invariably the next day someone from the congregation . . . would drop by the store and say, 'We didn't see you at services last night. Were you sick?'" One woman from Englewood, New Jersey, summed up the feeling in the Jewish community there by observing that "everything was like a family. Your problem was my problem—my problem was your problem. If there were any affairs or a funeral we were all there." In a sense, the Jews of America's smaller communities had developed a sort of New World *landsmanschaft* mentality in the interwar decades. As their ties to their places of origin in the old country faded, they began to think of the other Jews in their small-town communities as *landsleit*.[21]

For all the positive feelings that East European immigrants in small towns had about traditional Judaism and about the Yiddish culture that sustained their sense of connectedness, these people did not necessarily maintain traditional Jewish practices in a strict sense, nor did they find it easy to pass on their religious and cultural attachments to their children. This was evident from the fact that so many small-town Orthodox shuls had become Conservative or even Reform synagogues by the middle of the twentieth century. Indeed, even though the ideals of Sabbath observance, conformity to *kashrut,* and adherence to the so-called family purity laws continued to resonate in the minds of East European immigrants, often they began to stray from Orthodox practice in their personal behavior well before their congregations began their drift away from Orthodox ritual and identity.

A few East European immigrants made a decision very early to try to blend as fully as possible into the larger gentile environment of their small towns, mimicking what most nineteenth-century German-Jewish settlers had done. In Wichita, Kansas, for example, Henry Yabrof decided to join the Reform Holy Emanu-El congregation rather than the Orthodox Ahavat Achim when he came to town, and he named a son Henry Jr., adopting a gentile naming custom that was quite foreign to traditional East European Jews. East European immigrants who quickly immersed themselves in the Americanization process were quite exceptional, however. It certainly goes much too far to say, as Robert Davis has done on the basis of his study of small-town Jews in Texas, that "the bond of Orthodoxy was largely sentimental and easily broken" and that "its influence on small-town life was practically irrelevant."[22]

Still, it was common for East European traditionalists to make compromises in their lifestyles without going to extremes. Even those who truly wanted to maintain as much Jewish practice as possible found very quickly that they would have to alter their patterns of personal observance in their new surroundings. For example, even though most small-town Jewish merchants closed their stores for the High Holidays each fall, they kept their businesses open on the Sabbath, and some did so even on major religious festivals such as Passover. It was not unusual to find notices in the press such as the seemingly paradoxical item that appeared in the *Benton Harbor News-Palladium* in 1919 announcing that with the arrival of Rosh Hashanah, "local Jewish stores which annually celebrate the event will be closed Thursday and Friday, but open on Saturday." Although religious leaders occasionally made efforts to promote stricter Sabbath observance in small communities, their attempts proved to be futile. When Rabbi Morris Gordon arrived in Annapolis, Maryland, in 1935 and found that Jewish shopkeepers there invariably kept their stores open on Saturday, for instance, he set out to combat what he considered the "sorrowful plight and state of utter neglect of Judaism" in the city. In the end, however, he met with much resistance and only limited success. At about the same time an Orthodox rabbi in Englewood, New Jersey, made a pledge that he would not stay in his position if he could not convince his congregants to close their stores on the Sabbath. Eventually he had to resign.[23]

The motivation for keeping stores open on Saturday was, of course, primarily economic. After all, Saturday remained the major shopping day in small towns all across America. As one member of the Jewish community of Newburyport noted in the 1930s, "the men here would like to observe the Sabbath, but competition forces them to keep their places open." Robert Davis, in arguing for the irrelevance of Orthodoxy in the small towns of Texas, has suggested that although "not keeping a store closed on Rosh HaShanah or Yom Kippur showed a lack of self-respect," not keeping a store open on Saturday "was in most cases a form of economic suicide." Apart from a purely economic motivation for keeping businesses open on Saturdays, there was also perhaps a desire on the part of small-town Jews to minimize perceptions of Jewish "otherness." Even immigrant East European businessmen who were very comfortable with their distinctive religious and ethnic identity realized that it was in their interest to avoid having their customers feel that they were dealing with strangers. Conducting business on Saturday was a way to avoid what the historian Hal Rothman has called "the mortifying experience" of having to explain the Jewish calendar to non-Jews.[24]

In the same way that nominally Orthodox Jews in small communities quickly gave up many elements of Sabbath observance, few participated in the daily prayer services that are, in theory, the obligation of every adult Jewish male. In small communities it was at times difficult to find the required *minyan* even for Saturday morning services, and it would have been unrealistic to expect many individuals to commit themselves to participation in daily prayers. In responding to the survey that informed the directory of local Jewish institutions published in the *American Jewish Year Book* in 1919, for example, 143 congregations located in towns that had triple-digit Jewish communities in the 1920s supplied information on their schedule of services. Of these congregations, only nine (6 percent) reported that they sponsored daily prayer services. By contrast, for the country as a whole, 504 congregations outside New York City supplied information about their schedules, and of these, 154 (31 percent) reported having a daily *minyan*. In New York, naturally, daily services were a matter of course throughout the city. Given the situation in small communities, it is no wonder that when Lewis Rome died in Fitchburg, Massachusetts, in 1930, it was difficult to find even ten men who would attend daily morning services in the year following his passing so that the *kaddish* could be recited in his memory; this, even though Rome had been a leader of the Jewish community in Fitchburg and had two sons living in town.[25]

Observance of the laws of *kashrut* was another element of Orthodox practice that tended to give way in the face of practical considerations. Despite the fact that most small communities did try to make some arrangement for a supply of kosher meat to be available, keeping kosher was never as easy in the hinterland as it was in larger urban centers. Moreover, as the immigrant generation began to die out and a more Americanized second generation came to dominate small-town Jewish life, all domestic observances began to taper off. Bernice Hyman kept kosher in Modesto, California, for about nine years after she was married in 1921, for example, but then she stopped because of the difficulty of storing kosher meat in the days before reliable refrigeration. A student rabbi visiting Beckley, West Virginia, in 1935 noted that none of the East European Jews in that town used kosher food because "conditions don't allow it"; and another student rabbi visiting New Bern, North Carolina, in the same year observed that "none [of the local Jewish families] seem to keep strictly kosher, though some few observe certain dietary rules." Years later a resident of Williamson, West Virginia, recalled that "my grandfather kept kosher, but [discovered] it's too hard to keep kosher in a small town"; and another reported that "when we moved to Williamson [in the interwar period] . . . mother realized she couldn't keep a kosher home [but] she still would not mix milk and meat."[26]

As midcentury approached, small-town kosher grocers and butchers found it increasingly difficult to stay in business, as fewer and fewer residents of small communities maintained the dietary laws. Even in towns where there had been a strong commitment to *kashrut* in the early decades of the century, demand was greatly diminished. By the 1940s the last kosher butcher shop had closed in Sharon, Pennsylvania, for example, where the Orthodox presence had once been vital; and in Lafayette, Indiana, there were so few households keeping kosher that the local purveyor of kosher meat found it no longer worthwhile to continue serving the community. As early as January 1940 the local butcher, a Mr. Friedman, declared that he "wished to discontinue the kosher meat business as quickly as possible," and the leaders of the community had to appoint a two-man "Meat committee" to make alternative arrangements. By 1945 only very careful monitoring made it possible to maintain a supply of kosher meat. In August of that year, for example, the secretary of the Sons of Abraham synagogue was instructed to write letters to two persons who were "taking kosher chickens," presumably from the shop where they were sold, without being members of the organization charged with providing kosher food for Lafayette. These two people were told that " if they want to continue getting kosher killed chickens they'll have to become members with a minimum pay of $1.00 monthly dues."[27]

The use of ritual baths in small communities also declined as the twentieth century advanced. Reflecting similar developments elsewhere, at mid-century the *mikvah* was eliminated from the Beth Abraham synagogue in Zanesville, Ohio, in order to facilitate an "improvement of the kitchen." In Michigan there were no ritual baths remaining at all by 1960 outside Detroit, even though at that time the state had at least a dozen triple-digit Jewish communities, as well as three communities of between 1,000 and 3,000 Jews.[28]

In terms of perpetuating their distinctive small-town subculture, the greatest challenge that East European immigrants faced was passing on their outlook and their practices to a second generation. One serious problem was that small communities could seldom provide the extensive educational opportunities available (if not always utilized) in larger cities. The recorded histories of America's smaller Jewish centers almost always mention the importance those communities attached to educating their children. Speaking of the Jewish pilgrims who settled in early twentieth-century Plymouth, Massachusetts, for example, the history of the community asserts that educating their children Jewishly "was foremost in the minds of these staunch men and women."[29] Providing a coherent and comprehensive Jewish education in a small town was, however, always an uphill battle.

As early as 1904, George Zepin, the Reform rabbi so involved in outreach to Jews in small communities, noticed the dismal state of Jewish education there. He recognized that the East European immigrants just then arriving in small towns brought with them a certain degree of Jewish knowledge, but he noted that the first generation of German Jews in small communities was quickly dying out, and he lamented that members of the second generation "have for the most part grown up in woeful ignorance of what Judaism means." Indeed, it seems that by the turn of the twentieth century many German-Jewish congregations were already without any members who could lead even a simplified Reform temple service. So lacking was lay leadership among the 250 or so Jews of Paducah, Kentucky, for example, that in 1898 the town's Temple Israel took the step of reducing payments to its organist until such time as the congregation could "succeed of getting a Minister" so that it could resume "regular meetings." Meanwhile Temple Israel sent out appeals to religious functionaries in Cincinnati and in Mount Vernon, Indiana, asking if they could travel to Paducah from time to time to lead services.[30]

A rare systematic appraisal of the generally weak state of small-town Jewish education is made possible by the survey of American Jewish communities that was used to create the directory of local institutions published in the 1919 *American Jewish Year Book*, the same survey that revealed the paucity of daily *minyanim* in small towns. For 323 of the 490 small communities in our sample, no information on schooling is provided in the *Year Book* directory, and it seems reasonable to assume that in most of these places, if not all, little or no organized Jewish education was being provided. Furthermore, in the 167 towns where some formal Jewish schooling was reported to be available, that schooling was far from intensive. Only a handful of the communities in our sample had institutions concerned exclusively with education in 1919. There was an independent supplementary Talmud Torah school in Pawtucket, Rhode Island, and also one in Butte, Montana. In Burlington, Vermont, there were both a Talmud Torah and a Hebrew Educational Society. Elsewhere, however, Jewish education was left completely in the hands of temples and synagogues, and it often consisted of Sunday school and nothing more. If the goal was to have children learn the Hebrew language and to become conversant with the basic texts of the Jewish faith, as it was in most traditionalist homes, this could hardly even be attempted on such a limited schedule. It appears that in the period just after World War I, formal Jewish education was provided four days a week or more in only about 85 of the 490 triple-digit Jewish communities of the 1920s (17 percent).[31]

Of course, the data on Jewish education published in 1919 are not totally reliable, and some Jewish educational opportunities were provided in small communities on a more informal basis, often by private tutors, especially for boys who were preparing for a bar mitzvah ceremony. Moreover, in some places the circumstances might have improved after 1919. In Lafayette, Indiana, where the Orthodox Sons of Abraham congregation reported no educational program at all in 1919 and where the Reform congregation Temple Israel reported only a Sunday school, the situation had changed dramatically by 1939. In that year the children of the Orthodox congregation, at least, were offered Hebrew school classes on Tuesday, Wednesday, and Thursday of each week from 4:00 to 6:00 P.M., on Friday afternoons from 3:45 to 5:30, and on Saturday at 10:00 A.M., presumably in conjunction with Sabbath morning services. In addition, in 1939 there were special sessions for two advanced students on Saturday and Sunday mornings and a regular Sunday school that met from 10:00 until noon.[32]

Overall, however, the picture of Jewish education in America's small towns throughout the late nineteenth and early twentieth centuries was rather bleak. Not infrequently, an organized system of Jewish education was absent altogether, and parents had to search elsewhere if they wanted any religious schooling for their children. Some families in towns without programs of Jewish education went so far as to send their children to church-run Sunday schools rather then deprive them of religious instruction completely, although this practice was bound to come in for criticism from Jewish leaders. George Zepin, for one, argued that Judaism had a very distinctive "conception of life" and that "it is most emphatically true that our children cannot learn morality in Christian Sunday Schools."[33]

Other small-town families hoping to educate their youngsters sent them to school in larger Jewish communities that were not too far away. Early in the twentieth century a few children from South River, New Jersey, attended Hebrew school in New Brunswick, for example. But having children travel even to nearby cities on a regular basis was problematic, and in the pre–World War II era, psychological distances between small towns and adjacent cities were as significant as the actual mileage involved. Albert Danoff of Nanticoke in the Wyoming River Valley of Pennsylvania recalled, for instance, that at one point during the 1930s his parents decided to send him to Hebrew school at the Anshe Emes synagogue in the larger Jewish community of Wilkes-Barre. Although Nanticoke and Wilkes-Barre are only about eight miles apart, Danoff remembered the journey to class as an arduous trek involving two streetcar rides and a long uphill climb on foot to reach his destination.[34]

Even where small-town Jewish communities did sponsor their own classes, moreover, these were not necessarily of high quality. Occasionally small-town Jews remembered their prewar Jewish education in very positive terms. Seymour Horowitz recalled his time in the *cheyder* of Englewood, New Jersey, as "good days," and he remembered that "kids learned a lot." Much more often, however, the opposite was true. Pearl Feldman, also of Englewood, remembered that the Hebrew school there "never had the same principal for more than a couple of months" and that her parents sent her brother all the way to New York City for lessons, an arrangement facilitated by the fact that her father was part owner of a bus line and that all the drivers knew her brother and watched out for him. "He used to teach them the Alef-Bais [the Hebrew alphabet]," she recalled. Other small-town Jews had even more negative things to say about their school experiences and about how little opportunity they had to acquire an understanding of Jewish beliefs and practices. Julian Feibelman, who later became a Reform rabbi, remembered that his religious school in Jackson, Mississippi, around 1910 was "at best a makeshift that left no permanent recollection or impression." "I can't recall we learned anything about religion," he observed, thinking back to preparation for his confirmation; "we were constantly rehearsing our parts for the ceremony." Similarly, a man who grew up in Williamson, West Virginia, before World War II reported that "our religious school was a farce—I learned nothing"; and another man recalled that his bar mitzvah ceremony "was a sham . . . . We were growing up in a Christian world," he reflected, and "we ourselves knew so little about Judaism." Writing about Jewish "education" in Dover, New Jersey, at midcentury, the local commentator Arthur Spear explained that he placed "education" in quotation marks "because the education standard in the Hebrew School is very low."[35]

One factor that hindered the delivery of high-quality Jewish education was that small-town school facilities were often woefully inadequate. Classes were commonly held in the synagogue sanctuary, vestry room, or basement, hardly ideal settings for classroom management. One account of the synagogue in Cumberland, Maryland, in the World War I era, before the building was renovated, describes how "a pot-bellied heating stove graced the center of the vestry rooms, and around its doubtful warmth the young ones used to gather for their religious instruction." Perry Peskin recalled that even later, when he went to school in Cumberland in the period just before World War II, classes were still held "in small, somewhat dismal rooms in our ancient temple." In South River, New Jersey, where some elements of formal Jewish education were introduced after the local community built a synagogue in 1920, instruction took place in a small room that doubled as a social hall behind the synagogue sanctuary and also, for a time, in the basement of a factory owned by the congregant who oversaw the school program. The chronicler of the Jewish history of Muscatine, Iowa, has described the *cheyder* there in the early twentieth century as being conducted in a "small, damp and dingy room" in the basement of the community's synagogue, where children were taught in such a way that later they had "no leader, no service and no school."[36]

Even more detrimental to proper Jewish schooling was the perennial problem of finding qualified teachers, whether for Sunday school lessons in Reform temples or for the afternoon classes of traditional synagogues. Unlikely to have trained educators already in town, and too strapped financially to import them, small communities usually had to make do with local volunteer instructors. Often congregational rabbis were asked to add teaching children to the many other tasks they were expected to perform, and occasionally an East European community would recruit an old-fashioned *melamed* from out of town, but having the services of even one professionally trained and highly qualified educator was generally out of the question for a small community. Already at the turn of the twentieth century, George Zepin noticed that while many small-town congregations were making an attempt to introduce a Sabbath school, even more in the South than in the North, "the inability to find able teachers hampers its realization." Another rabbi who recognized how difficult it was to find adequate teachers for small-town schools was Joseph Raffaeli. When he arrived at Brith Achim in Petersburg, Virginia, in 1929, he rendered a scathing critique of the education being provided at the congregation's religious school and suggested that its poor state was probably "due to the influence of changing teachers or of lengthy interruption." The Brith Achim school had thirty students, and almost all of them "read a Hebrew that was ungrammatical," he observed. Furthermore, "they could not write anywhere near fair. They could not translate at all. Knew nothing of Jewish holidays. Had no conception of the Jewish calendar. No appreciation of Jewish customs and ceremonials."[37]

Many other accounts of Jewish education during the classic era of small-town Jewish life also highlight the absence of well-prepared teachers. Early twentieth-century reports from Santa Ana, California, indicate that although the Jews there sought to organize a congregation and a religious school so that their children "might enjoy the privileges of a Jewish education and a Jewish religious atmosphere," in 1921 the town had "a Hebrew school consisting of eighteen students, but no teacher." At about the same time Jewish education in Topeka, Kansas, was apparently in the hands of one Ike Gilberg, described variously as "untaught scholastically, but . . . highly intelligent"; "a little strange"; and "a spiritualist [who] claimed he could cure anything." "Since there was no rabbi, he taught all ages for no compensation," one member of the Topeka community remembered; "there were very few books available." "I was not particularly qualified as a teacher," admitted a woman who served as a Sunday school instructor in San Bernardino, California, in the interwar period. "In fact," she confessed, "I'd never been to Sunday School [myself]."[38]

The situation was no better in the East. One man who was born in Ellwood City, Pennsylvania, in 1909 recalled that the Jewish education available at his Orthodox synagogue was only intermittent. "No teacher, or melamed, remained long," he remarked, "and each succeeding instructor would always start from the beginning." David Rome, who grew up in Fitchburg, Massachusetts, in the 1920s, remembered Hebrew school as being one of the "burdens" endured by Jewish children there. He described going to *cheyder* from the age of six to bar mitzvah at age thirteen four afternoons a week (this was besides Sunday school) and being taught by the rabbi of the local congregation, a man who was "ill prepared to handle the young American boys whose interest was far from learning." The rabbis who served congregations like his and were asked to fulfill a multiplicity of roles may have been learned themselves, Rome concluded, but they were not effective educators. "The rod was the only tool they knew and they did not spare it," he recalled, observing that the "frustrations" of the teachers were met with the "resentments" of the students. Ben Deutschman, who grew up in Shamokin, Pennsylvania, concluded that the instructional methods used in small-town Hebrew schools "would give our progressive education fanatics a traumatic experience that would take years of psychiatry to overcome."[39]

Even accounts of synagogue history prepared by small-town congregations, accounts that might be expected to gloss over the less successful aspects of synagogue life, often lament the inadequacies of the Jewish education available to local children. The fiftieth-anniversary history of Temple Israel in Springfield, Missouri, for example, reported that religious instruction for its children was organized soon after the congregation was founded in 1893, but that "only occasionally a professional teacher could be engaged." A chronicle prepared by Temple Beth Israel reported that in Sharon, Pennsylvania, *melamdim* from out of town were hired to help the community's one full-time teacher in the early decades of the twentieth century but that, even though "these men had a knowledge of Hebrew," they had no pedagogical skills. In their classes "there was a general confusion, as rough discipline supplanted understanding as a tool of teaching." Similarly, the centenary history of Adath Yeshurun in Manchester, New Hampshire, reported that in 1938 that congregation and the other Orthodox shul in town agreed that "neither was having much success in teaching the younger generation," and together they embarked on a project to centralize Jewish education at the city's Young Men's and Young Women's Hebrew Association, newly transformed into the Jewish Community Center. That effort yielded an improved situation, but only "for a few years."[40]

The serious shortcomings of Jewish educational efforts in small towns, coupled with declining levels of religious observance and the great difficulty parents of the immigrant generation had in passing on their attitudes to their offspring, helps account for the fact that children of East European settlers in small-town America came to adopt a lifestyle that was far less intensively Jewish than that of their mothers and fathers. Almost inevitably, young people who were born in America, or who had come at a very early age, rejected domestic practices such as observing *kashrut* and strayed from anything near regular synagogue attendance. "I go to shul on New Year's but that's all," admitted an eighteen-year-old in Newburyport around 1932; "I don't know what it's all about."[41]

Even when the Americanized children of immigrants were familiar with traditional observances and customs, they found little meaning in them. It did not help that particularistic Jewish practices were even more likely to mark their followers as alien in small towns than in larger urban settings. Speaking of the time when the children of Durham's Orthodox families first began to depart from the ways of their parents, the local historian Leonard Rogoff observes that "the young girls giggled when they passed the mikvah, and boys more interested in baseball and football had no interest in [the Yom Kippur folk practice of] swinging chickens around their head to expiate sin." The author Eli Evans describes the younger members of Durham's Beth El synagogue as men less concerned with maintaining Orthodox tradition than with "attracting new membership, building a new building, driving to services in a new car, and streamlining the service." He speaks of the founding members of the congregation who were still present in the era of World War II as attempting "to talk across the chasm to another generation already lost to Orthodoxy." Similarly, Joe Marcus, who grew up on a farm on the outskirts of Benton Harbor, Michigan, in the interwar period, suggested that the reason a Reform congregation was established in his town in 1934 was that the children of East European immigrants in Benton Harbor wanted a place where lack of Jewish education would not be as keenly felt as it was in traditionalist shuls. "If you

*A bar mitzvah at Congregation B'nai Abraham, Hagerstown, Maryland. The education of children in small towns was approached in a variety of ways, but not always effectively. Courtesy of The Jewish Museum of Maryland, 1988.150.1.*

didn't have a Jewish education and walked into the synagogue they'd frown upon you," he explained, "so here's a temple where you could be Jewish and you weren't embarrassed because you had no Jewish education."[42]

The third generation of small-town Jews was even less likely than the second to be steeped in the traditions of the immigrants who first came to America. Yetta Brandt, whose parents spent their early years in Augusta, Georgia, and Durham, North Carolina, explained it this way: "My parents did not really know a lot about the Jewish religion themselves. They could not possibly pass on to us what they did not know . . . I guess their parents, my grandparents, never taught them to be Jewish the way that they had learned in Europe."[43]

Those few families that might have tried to provide an intensive Jewish education for their children and to rear them in a highly traditional lifestyle found themselves struggling to do so in nearly total isolation. The daughter of the most observant family in Newburyport reported, for example, that in the early 1930s hers was the only Jewish home in town that did not allow the playing of the radio on the Sabbath. This made the day "awfully quiet and boring," she complained, and she and her siblings fought their father fiercely over this matter, though to no avail. The children of small-town Orthodox rabbis were always in a precarious position. The daughter of Rabbi Barnet

Kramer, who spent the years from 1918 to 1923 in Muskegon, Michigan, remembered with some bitterness not only that her father had been mistreated by his congregation but that, as a teenager, she had been nicknamed "The Genius" and ostracized at school. Her difficult experience spilled forth in the novel *Hour upon the Stage*, which she published under the pen name Anne Pinchot in 1929. This thinly veiled account of life in Muskegon pillories several Jewish families in the community and occupies a place in the genre of works that purport to depict the provincialism and pettiness of small-town life in the 1920s. In much the same vein, the author Melissa Fay Greene has described the early years of Rachel Shilsky, a rabbi's daughter who endured both a dysfunctional family life and an Orthodox upbringing in pre–World War II Suffolk, Virginia, as an "ugly duckling childhood" because Rachel, "raised so far from the swans of Jewish New York . . . scarcely [knew] that the possibility existed for undespised Jewish life."[44]

Just as a familiarity and engagement with traditional religious observance invariably diminished from one generation to another, so, too, did involvement with other aspects of East European culture, including the use of Yiddish. As Myer Godhelff, the Lexington resident who reported on his parents' circle of Yiddish-speaking friends, recalled, "I understood Yiddish very well but hardly spoke it, as I now was learning English and being educated through the Lex[ington] school system and later at U. K. [the University of Kentucky]." Indeed, some in the younger generation were quite adamant about abandoning Yiddish. One boy in Newburyport allowed as how "it gets me mad when I hear some of the Jewish women speaking Jewish out loud on the street. This is America!" Similarly, a woman who spent her childhood in Kingston, Pennsylvania, in the 1930s recalled: "I hated it when I was in a public situation (like the movies) with my mother and grandmother, and they would speak Yiddish to each other."[45]

East Europeans of the immigrant generation seem to have had mixed feelings about the way their children and grandchildren were drifting away from traditional culture. On the one hand, many idealized the lifestyle of the old country, where it was possible for Jews to be insulated from the surrounding religious and cultural environment, and they mourned the disappearance of some elements of the way of life an isolated existence had allowed. In Russia, one observant Jewish immigrant living in Newburyport reminisced, the Sabbath was beautiful. "When the family sat down to the table on Friday night, even the poorest became rich," he recalled. "Everybody was excited; it was a real holiday." But in America, he lamented, "Shabas is lifeless."[46] On the other hand, even the most nostalgic immigrants realized that a certain price had to be paid for reaping the benefits of an open society that promised such material advantages. These immigrants would not have remained in a small city if they had not accepted the trade-off. In the same way that so many of those with an Orthodox outlook were willing to countenance the transformation of their Orthodox shuls into Conservative or even Reform synagogues, they were willing to see their children abandon traditional observances in order to fit into the milieu of small-town America.

Still, some observers of small-town Jewry believed that the immigrant generation was by no means as open to change as it should have been. The UAHC's Jacob Weinstein, who had urged his Reform colleagues to promote liberal Judaism aggressively among small-town East Europeans, was exasperated that immigrant parents were not more accepting of the worldview he championed. He groused that "these dyed-in-the-wool orthodox are not worried about their children" and considered them blind to the potential of Reform to address the problem of raising Jewishly conscious youngsters even in small communities. Weinstein contended that the second generation's "ignorance of Jewish life and the indifference and apostasy [that comes] in the wake of such ignorance only confirms the elders in their own stiff-necked righteousness."[47]

While the erosion of traditional Jewish practices and the weakness of Jewish education were increasingly wearing away at the distinctive East European Jewish subculture of small-town America, other factors were at work as well to expand the contact that East Europeans had with mainstream society. As the small communities established around the turn of the twentieth century began to mature, more and more elements of a lifestyle once associated only with assimilationist German Jews began to pervade small communities dominated by East Europeans. To a greater extent than in larger Jewish communities, the East Europeans of smaller Jewish settlements found that they both wanted and needed to associate with their non-Jewish neighbors, especially those who shared their middle-class status. Their communities were simply too limited in size to support a completely self-contained existence, and their success in business depended on building connections with the larger society. Thus, while the most intimate social interactions of small-town East Europeans continued to be primarily with other Jews, these immigrants, and especially their children, became increasingly involved with civic and political activities in their towns. Over time, they began to join service organizations and social clubs and to seek public office.

Thus, Max Rogalsky was on the city council of Hibbing, Minnesota, as early as the first decade of the twentieth century, and the Russian-born Abe Gellman, who owned first a pawn shop and later a jewelry business in Petersburg, Virginia, supported the organization of a municipal golf course and was a charter member of the local Kiwanis Club. In Rome, Georgia, the Riga-born community stalwart Pressley Esserman not only became a member of the Masons, the Kiwanis Club, and the Knights of Pythias, but also joined the men's club of the local Presbyterian church, "as a goodwill gesture to correctly interpret and represent Judaism," he asserted, "rather than as a convert." To be sure, social antisemitism kept East European Jews out of some organizations with which they might have affiliated, and it slowed their entry into politics to a greater extent than it had that of their German-Jewish predecessors, but the groundwork was being laid for even fuller Jewish integration in the latter decades of the twentieth century.[48]

Furthermore, while East European Jews did not seek out gentile involvement in the internal affairs of their communities to the extent their German-Jewish forerunners had, for these traditionalists, too, activities such as synagogue dedications and interfaith programs provided opportunities for interaction with the larger society. When the Jews of Virginia, Minnesota, dedicated their Orthodox synagogue in 1910, for example, one of the speakers was the minister of the local Presbyterian church; and when the Jews of Manchester, New Hampshire, held an open house at their new synagogue in 1912, several local businesses advertised in the program booklet published for the occasion, and a number of local dignitaries offered remarks. When the Orthodox congregation Agudas Achim in Leominster, Massachusetts, dedicated its building in 1924, those present included the mayor, the city council, clergy from Leominster and several surrounding communities, and perhaps as many as 1,500 members of the general public. Another sign of barriers coming down was that during the interwar period traditionalist rabbis began to participate in interfaith services and to join ministerial associations, just as their Reform counterparts had been doing for a long time. During the 1930s the rabbi of the Orthodox Beth Jacob synagogue in Plymouth, Massachusetts, became a member of the Plymouth Council of Churches, for example, and the rabbi of Beth El in Durham, North Carolina, joined the local ministerial association. The first interfaith Thanksgiving service involving congregation B'nai Abraham in Hagerstown, Maryland, took place in 1939.[49]

That organizations created by East European Jews began to sponsor such all-American institutions as sports teams and scout troops was yet another sign that Jewish leaders understood the need for acculturation and that the public-school-educated children and grandchildren of the immigrant generation were entering the American mainstream. The YMHA in Benton Harbor had a baseball team as early as 1913, for example; and in Red Bank, New Jersey, when Boy Scout Troop 60 was organized at the B'nai Israel synagogue in 1923, the congregation's rabbi became its scoutmaster. Also during the 1920s, Annapolis had a "Jewish Mohawks" basketball team, and the YMHA basketball team of North Adams, Massachusetts, won a state championship. In pre–World War II Bradford, Pennsylvania, the local youth baseball scene was dominated for a time by a Jewish team called the Maccabees, known locally also as the "Yiddish Yankees" and the "Kosher Kids." Of course, the fact that certain sports teams and scout troops were identified with the Jewish minority, even in small-town America, is a reminder that gentile society still had a certain hesitancy about the full social integration of Jews and that Jewish youngsters themselves maintained a certain pride in their distinctive identity.[50]

In small towns where East European and German-Jewish subcommunities had coexisted in the era of mass migration, yet another factor that mitigated the isolation and distinctiveness of the East Europeans was their growing cooperation with German Jews as midcentury approached. Just as there were forces that drove small-town Reform and Orthodox congregations to cooperate, and in some cases even to merge, and just as some German-Jewish clubs and organizations recognized that they needed to welcome East European newcomers in order to survive, environmental pressures also compelled a more general consolidation of the various factions within small-town Jewish communities. The Jews in such communities increasingly realized that they did not have the resources to maintain a wide range of institutions, and at the same time the rationale for communal subdivisions became less compelling. A few small-town institutions had made it their goal to bridge the gap between subcommunities already in the era of mass migration. In Columbia, South Carolina, for example, very soon after the establishment of a liberal congregation in 1896 and an Orthodox assembly in 1906, the local Benevolent Society, which maintained the town's Jewish cemetery, adopted an amendment to its constitution that stipulated that it would "never be combined with any other Society, religious or otherwise." The intention here was clearly to maintain support for the Benevolent Society from all the elements of Columbia's Jewish population.[51] Such efforts in the direction of communal consolidation increased markedly in the period just before World War II.

The most important manifestation of this consolidation was the creation of centralized charity agencies whose purpose was not only to avoid duplication of efforts and competition among various local philanthropies, but also to insulate the collection of funds for worthy causes from internal communal divisions, congregational or otherwise. By 1939 there were federations of Jewish charities in at least eighty-four of the triple-digit settlements in our sample. These included Jewish communities as seemingly unlikely to need centralized agencies as those of Butler, Pennsylvania; Lima, Ohio; Anderson, Indiana; Joliet, Illinois; Manitowoc, Wisconsin; Virginia, Minnesota; Dubuque, Iowa; Joplin, Missouri; Gadsden, Alabama; Port Arthur, Texas; Reno, Nevada; and Bakersfield, California. During World War II centralized agencies appeared in other small towns as well. The United Jewish Charities was created in Muskegon, Michigan, in 1941, for instance, and over the next five years it distributed over $100,000 to groups ranging from local health care institutions to international Zionist groups, and from the Jewish Theological Seminary in New York to various European relief organizations. Moreover, some small towns that did not have their own centralized welfare agencies were specifically included in the territory covered by the welfare federations of nearby cities, as the very beginnings of highly integrated regional Jewish networks appeared. Thus, for example, Bellingham and Everett in Washington State fell under the purview of the Federated Jewish Fund of Seattle, organized in 1936, while Derby and Wallingford, Connecticut, were under the umbrella of the Jewish Community Council of New Haven, organized in 1938.[52]

Among its other effects, the transformation of Jewish life that was taking place in small communities was making it increasingly difficult to distinguish between the Americanized culture of small-town Jews whose heritage was East European and those whose background was Central European. On the eve of World War II, it was clear that the days were numbered for the distinctive subculture that East European immigrants had constructed in small towns all over the country, flavored by Orthodoxy and inflected with Yiddish. Of course, a decline in Orthodox religious observance and the abandonment of Yiddish culture among the children of East European immigrants was by no means unique to small-town Jewry. These changes were under way all over the United States. But what is most significant here is that the transformation of East European communities was much more complete in America's smaller Jewish settlements than it was in the country's larger cities. In more substantial Jewish communities, even those of midsize cities, the population was sufficiently large and diverse to allow for the survival of at least some religiously observant or intensively ethnic Jewish elements. In small communities, on the other hand, after a very few decades no critical mass remained to allow for such survival. In the words of one resident of Newburyport in the 1930s, "in the cities Jews live compactly. They influence each other and keep each other Jews," but "here in the small town we have the Gentile influence very strong and we live loosely and are assimilating."[53] Once again, as in so many other connections, community size and the small-town setting were decisive factors. "Place" really mattered.

# Epilogue: Patterns of Endurance and Decline

In the years immediately following World War II, there was a palpable sense of optimism in America's small-town Jewish communities. By the middle of the twentieth century, these communities had achieved a character all their own, and, as a class, they appeared to have a permanent place in the American Jewish landscape. Those families that constituted America's smaller Jewish settlements had a sense that although the nature of their communities had evolved since the early 1900s, the equilibrium they had achieved would remain largely unaltered into the future. Developments during the latter part of the twentieth century would prove, however, that this expectation was unfounded. As we shall see, by the turn of the twenty-first century, some of America's classic small-town Jewish centers would grow considerably, while many others would be transformed into little more than appendages of larger communities or would actually disappear. Moreover, even those small-town communities that survived would be very different in character from those that flourished during the classic age of small-town Jewish life. New Jewish demographic patterns, urban sprawl, and changes in the technology of transportation and communication would all have an impact on the small-town Jewish experience and bring its classic era to an end.

One factor that may have provided small-town Jews with a sense of assured continuity in the period just after World War II was that the majority of the smaller Jewish centers that had existed in the 1920s had neither grown nor shrunk dramatically by the middle of the twentieth century. Although population information is not available for all the towns in our sample, the data that are at hand reveal that at the midpoint of the century no fewer than 295 of the triple-digit communities of 1927 (60 percent) were still home to at least 100 but fewer than 1,000 Jews, with another 19 of our sample communities (4 percent) having Jewish populations of between 1,000 and 1,500. So, too, although the war years themselves had been difficult ones, a conviction that small communities had before them a period of tranquility and economic prosperity energized their residents.

In the aftermath of World War II, many of the Jewish families of small-town America could take satisfaction in the fact that their businesses had weathered the Depression, and all could take pride in the way their communities had responded to the war itself. Not only had small communities sent their children off to fight, but they had participated in the war effort in many other ways as well. In one small town after another, rabbis had been given leave to serve as military chaplains, congregational vestry rooms and social halls had been made available for Red Cross work, visits had been arranged to patients in local military hospitals, and synagogues and homes had been opened to Jewish servicemen stationed at nearby bases. The Jews of Hagerstown, Maryland, had made soldiers at nearby Fort Ritchie feel welcome in the community, for example, while the Jews of Michigan City, Indiana, had embraced sailors training at the naval armory in town. Temple Beth Sholom in Topeka had provided programs for men and women at nearby Forbes Air Base and Winter General Army Hospital, and in Greensboro, North Carolina, a lounge for servicemen had been set up at Temple Emanuel.[1] In addition, small-town Jews were influenced by many of the same monumental developments that affected all of American Jewry. The involvement of Jews in the war had given them a new sense of security as part of American society, while the horror of the Shoah had reinforced their identification with the fate of the Jewish people everywhere. At the same time, the creation of the State of Israel in 1948 gave them a new sense of pride in their Jewishness.

Furthermore, a majority of small-town Jews were quite content with their individual lives. When B'nai B'rith conducted a survey among its members in 168 American towns with Jewish populations of 1,000 or fewer in the early 1950s, it discovered that about 40 percent of them felt that in their communities both the quality of Jewish education and opportunities for Jews to marry within the faith were "poor," but that nonetheless, given the choice, more than half would remain where they were. Of all respondents to the survey, 62 percent said their chances of feeling comfortable as Jews in their towns were good, and a majority believed that Jews in their communities could have a satisfactory social life, obtain positions of prestige, and achieve their economic aspirations. Only 14 percent of respondents expressed the opinion that their chances of leading a satisfactory social life in a small community were poor, and only 4 percent said their chances of feeling comfortable there as Jews were meager.[2]

Nothing better symbolized the optimism and the apparent vigor of small-town Jewish communities in the ten or twenty years after World War II than the synagogue building boom that took place there. This upsurge in construction, which shared many characteristics with the rush to build new synagogues in larger Jewish centers, was sparked by the aging of early twentieth-century structures and by a new sense of communal purpose. Small-town Jews who had endured the Depression and the war years now wanted to settle into a more comfortable lifestyle, and, from the point of view of their communal priorities, this desire often involved modernizing their synagogue facilities. Building also meant a certain psychological triumph for the generation of men and women who had led most of America's small Jewish communities through their formative period and through the difficult 1930s and early 1940s. That young men returning from military service were eager to settle down and begin raising families only reinforced the desire of their elders to bolster local Jewish life. Moreover, as the younger cohort assumed the leadership of small communities to an ever-greater extent, its members were much concerned with providing proper facilities for the children who constituted the postwar baby boom.

Several practical developments also facilitated the postwar wave of synagogue construction in America's small towns. For one thing, despite all its negative consequences, the coming of World War II had meant a definitive end to the Great Depression and expanded employment opportunities for all Americans. These developments brought a revival of business activity and even some accumulation of savings. Building campaigns that had been contemplated in the early 1940s generally had been deferred during the war, both because the attention of Jewish communities was focused elsewhere, and because rationing and the emphasis on war production would have made embarking on construction difficult. With the war over, however, new construction projects became feasible.

All over the country, old buildings were renovated and new ones went up. In Muskegon, Michigan, for example, the Jewish community erected a new temple in 1948, replacing an old frame house, by then totally inadequate, that had been in use since 1918. In Greensboro, North Carolina, where plans for enlarging the Temple Emanuel building had been put on hold during the war, the congregation completed a renovation of its synagogue and the construction of a new religious school wing by December 1949. Moreover, a second synagogue was dedicated in Greensboro during that year as well, this one commissioned by a group of people who had left Temple Emanuel to form a Conservative congregation that eventually took the name Beth David. In Sharon, Pennsylvania, the House of Israel, now called Temple Beth Israel, dedicated a new synagogue in 1950, complete with classrooms and a state-of-the-art social hall that boasted a stage with concealed lighting and facilities for motion picture projection.[3]

Throughout the 1950s and into the early 1960s, small-town synagogue construction projects continued to proliferate. Examples abound. In Michigan

City, Indiana, the Sinai Temple had taken over the community's cemetery association and had eclipsed the local Orthodox shul by 1952, and in that year it built a modern multipurpose synagogue away from the downtown area. At about the same time the Jews of Warren, Ohio, sold both their synagogue building and the house they had been using for Sunday school classes and erected the Beth Israel Temple Center to take their place. The year 1953 saw the erection of a new synagogue to replace an old one in San Bernardino, California, and in 1955 the Jews of Danbury, Connecticut, left the converted private home they had been using since the 1920s and relocated to a new synagogue building. In Middletown, Connecticut, Adath Israel more than doubled the size of its 1929 synagogue with the addition of classrooms and a social hall. In 1958 Temple Israel of Columbus, Georgia, dedicated a new building, as did Congregation B'nai Israel of Kankakee, Illinois, vacating the synagogue it had erected in 1922. In recording this event, the historian of the Kankakee congregation gushed with pride. "Not only people passing through and not only our Christian friends and neighbors are caught in rapt awe and admiration of our glorious House of God," the chronicler wrote, "but we ourselves often wonder at how beautifully did so few build the house of our people's history, learning and spirit."[4]

In Hagerstown, Maryland, a building program completed in 1959 saw the enlargement and remodeling of Congregation B'nai Abraham's Talmud Torah building, the renovation of its synagogue sanctuary, including the installation of stained-glass windows, and the addition of a social hall. In Annapolis, Kneseth Israel bought land for a new synagogue complex in the mid-1950s and constructed its new facilities there in the early 1960s. B'nai Israel in Jackson, Tennessee, which had accomplished the rare feat of dedicating a new synagogue in the early 1940s, added a school wing to the building in 1962. In Jackson, Michigan, where Temple Beth Israel had completed a new building in 1949, the structure's school facilities were expanded in 1966.[5] As some of these examples suggest, in many small towns, new construction meant a migration away from the downtown neighborhoods where most nineteenth- and early twentieth-century synagogues had stood. This relocation reflected Jewish population shifts that were taking place in small towns and replicated in miniature the suburbanization of Jews in America's larger cities.

Despite the self-confidence of the period immediately after World War II, by the mid-1960s it was becoming apparent that few of America's classic small Jewish communities would retain their prewar character. For one thing, American Jewish migration patterns in the latter decades of the twentieth century meant that at least some small communities were beginning to grow into much more substantial Jewish centers, with expanded Jewish populations and a greater variety of communal agencies and services. Of the 490 triple-digit Jewish settlements of the late 1920s, about 10 percent had been transformed into more significant communities by the early 1980s, with populations above 1,000 and expanded Jewish infrastructures.

Small communities that were on the periphery of major urban centers and that attracted Jews moving out of older areas of settlement were among those that were apt to experience substantial growth. Greenwich, Connecticut, for example, was home to only 250 Jews on the eve of World War II and still had only 850 Jewish residents as late as 1960. Situated on Long Island Sound within a reasonable commuting distance of New York City, however, Greenwich saw its Jewish population grow to nearly 4,000 by the 1990s. Similarly, the community of Englewood, New Jersey, just across the Hudson River from the Bronx, still had only a triple-digit Jewish population and a single synagogue on the eve of World War II. By 1950, however, Englewood had a Jewish population of 2,500, and by 1960 there were three congregations in the town: the original Orthodox Ahavath Torah, the Conservative Temple Emanu-El, and the Reform Temple Sinai. By the early 1980s the Jewish population of Englewood was close to 10,000.[6]

In Massachusetts, the town of Framingham had a reported Jewish population of 360 in 1927, 450 in 1937, and 600 in 1950, but the city was so situated that it drew migrants moving outward from Boston; it was home to over 4,000 Jews by 1960 and to about 10,000 by the mid-1980s. One of the most spectacular examples of the growth of a small community near a major city is that of Newton, Massachusetts, also adjacent to Boston, but even closer to the metropolis than Framingham. The Jewish population of Newton was reported to be only 850 in 1937, and in the early 1940s it still supported only two synagogues, one Reform and one Conservative. By the beginning of the 1990s, however, there were some 34,000 Jews living in Newton and at least nine congregations functioning there.[7]

Also likely to grow in size during the final decades of the twentieth century were small communities in the Sunbelt South, Southwest, and West, as Jews, along with other Americans, were attracted increasingly to these regions. In California, for instance, the Jewish population of Santa Monica grew from 700 in 1927 to 8,000 by the early 1990s, and that of Santa Barbara expanded from 150 to about 5,000 in the same period. In Albuquerque, New Mexico, there were some signs of communal expansion even before World War II, as a new Conservative congregation called B'nai Israel was created there around 1940. After the war, however, the city became home to a considerable number of new Jewish residents who had encountered New Mexico as airman during their military service, and Albuquerque continued to lure more Jewish settlers as it grew and prospered (Albuquerque's total population was just under 10,000 in 1950 but close to 400,000 by 1990). The city had a

Jewish population of only about 450 in the late 1930s, but that population had grown to about 2,000 by 1960 and perhaps 4,000 by 1990.[8]

Without a doubt, the most spectacular examples of the growth of small Jewish communities in the Sunbelt involve the triple-digit Jewish settlements of Tucson and Phoenix in Arizona. Each of these towns had Jewish populations of about 400 in the late 1920s, and each supported only one or two congregations in that period. In the years just after World War II, however, both communities grew to around 4,000, and by the early 1990s the Jewish population of Tucson had reached about 20,000, while that of Phoenix stood at about 50,000. Toward the end of the twentieth century, the Jews of Tucson supported at least six congregations and a Jewish day school, while those of Phoenix supported at least seven congregations in the city proper, nine more in surrounding suburban towns, and two day schools.[9]

At the same time that about one in ten of America's classic small-town Jewish settlements was losing its original character as the result of substantial growth, other small communities were losing their identities by becoming completely integrated into huge metropolitan collectivities with major cities as their hubs. As a result of advances in transportation and communication, along with urban sprawl, many smaller Jewish centers, like the towns in which they were located, lost the sense of geographic integrity and distinctiveness that they had preserved in the nineteenth and early twentieth centuries. Instead they now became elements within a vast urban conglomeration. Indeed, even some of the small communities on the periphery of large cities that grew into major points of Jewish settlement themselves (communities such as those of Englewood, New Jersey, or Newton, Massachusetts) could not escape being folded into the greater metropolitan Jewish communities of their nearby central cities. This was part of the price paid, often willingly, for the convenience of ubiquitous automobiles and superhighways, and for the economic prosperity represented by suburbanization.

Reflecting the frequent amalgamation of once individual communities is the fact that in many places Jewish institutions, and especially welfare federations, came to think of themselves as serving extended metropolitan areas, rather than the specific cities in which they were based. Also indicative of this transformation is the fact that, as we noted earlier, various Jewish agencies began to aggregate population data for entire regions. Thus, for example, toward the end of the twentieth century, the once-distinct Jewish communities of towns such as Haverstraw, Nyack, Spring Valley, and Suffern, New York, became elements of a more amorphous "Rockland County" region in the orbit of New York City, with a Jewish population in 1984 rounded to 25,000. Similarly, the Jewish communities of towns such as Highland Park, Maywood, and Chicago Heights, previously identified as distinct entities, became only components of the Jewish community of the Chicago Metropolitan Area. In California, communities such as those of Alhambra and Glendale became simply elements in the Jewish community of Greater Los Angeles.[10]

Yet another development that altered the geography of American Jewish life during the final decades of the twentieth century and helped bring the classic era of small-town Jewry to an end was the unmistakable deterioration of many small communities. Notwithstanding the renewal that numerous smaller settlements experienced immediately after World War II, the general tendency of young people who grew up in these places was to move away as they matured. Although it was certainly not unheard of for children to take over the small-town businesses that their parents or grandparents had established, after midcentury many more of these young people went off to college or to the big city and did not return. Indeed, already in the early 1960s, only 40 percent of all Americans born in rural settings still lived in such places,[11] and Jews were especially prone to migrate to major metropolitan centers. The historian of the Jewish community of La Crosse, Wisconsin, could have been speaking about a great many other small communities as well when he observed that while many East European immigrants in his town made their living in lowly pursuits such as junk or fruit peddling, their children sought out opportunities in higher education and made their way in a wider universe. Thus, among the children of La Crosse's Jewish immigrants were "many school teachers, several physicians, attorneys, accountants, a concert pianist, a radio and television writer, [and] a famous football star." These were individuals who were likely to find a small city such as La Crosse just too confining.[12]

To be sure, as we have seen, the tendency of young people to leave their small towns was already evident to a certain extent even before midcentury. The sociologists who studied Newburyport, Massachusetts, in the 1930s noticed the departure of some second-generation Jews and suggested that they were simply following the example of their elders. As the researchers put it, "in a manner analogous to that of their immigrant parents, they [began] to seek 'new worlds.' "[13] Nonetheless, the outward migration of Jews who grew up in small towns accelerated greatly in the latter decades of the twentieth century, and in most cases it was not counterbalanced by the arrival of new settlers. One important factor that prompted Jews to abandon so many of America's classic small communities was a changing business environment that was inauspicious for mercantile establishments that were still in the hands of Jewish families. In an age when consumers came to value retail outlets offering discount prices, a wide range of goods, and uniformity of facilities more highly than they valued locally owned stores whose main attractions were personalized service and a long-established presence, the kinds of businesses that were owned by small-town Jews were bound to founder. In other words, in smaller cities and towns all over the country, Jewish shops on

Main Street were losing out to immense chain stores built on the outskirts of town. As the historian of the Jewish community of Danville, Illinois, has written mournfully, "when the downtown was alive and well, there were many Jewish merchants with fine stores." More recently, however, "the children of most of the large families have been educated as professionals and left Danville."[14]

Where the local economy took a sharp downward turn and where a town's population actually diminished in the second half of the twentieth century, the situation for Jewish merchants was even worse than it was in the face of simple competition from retail chains. As the early twentieth-century demise of communities in places such as Keokuk, Iowa; Madison, Indiana; and Port Gibson, Mississippi, had already demonstrated, a Jewish settlement based on mercantile activity could do little to survive when confronted with urban stagnation and a declining customer base. In the once-thriving steel center of Farrell, Pennsylvania, to take but one example, the total population declined from 13,644 in 1950 to only 6,841 by 1990, and much of the city came to look like a bombed-out war zone.[15] By 1980 the Jewish population of Farrell was down to 150 from a prewar peak of nearly 700, and by the 1990s no Jewish presence remained in the town at all.

As the end of the twentieth century approached, there were many small towns in which only a handful of individuals remained as reminders that these places once had been home to vibrant Jewish communities. Thus, for example, when Louis Kariel's son graduated from high school in Marshall, Texas, in the mid-1970s, he left not a single Jewish child anywhere in the town's school system, and he found himself in a Jewish community that revolved around no more than six aging adults; this in a town that had had a Jewish population of over 100 as early as the 1870s and a Jewish community of 170 individuals in the 1920s. Similarly, an account of Jewish life in Marion, Indiana, in the mid-1970s reported that of the more than thirty young Jews who had grown up in the town and then gone off to college elsewhere, only three had returned to Marion to live. Moreover, two of these three were married to non-Jews, an indication that they were unlikely to be contributing to the continuity of local Jewish life.[16]

Not far away, in Wabash, Indiana, where the Jewish population had remained well above 100 continuously from at least the 1870s until the 1920s, no more than four Jewish families were still represented in town by the 1970s. Sam Sposeep, whose father, Abe, had arrived in Wabash in 1913, was still around, running the family scrap yard, and so was Sam's son Michael, serving as city judge. Also still in Wabash was Harold Wolf, co-owner of the Beitman and Wolf dry goods store that had been founded in 1846. Individuals such as these, however, could do nothing to forestall the demise of Wabash Jewry as the community around them disappeared. In Williamson, West Virginia, which may have had a Jewish community of as many as seventy families at its peak, only eight families remained by the early 1990s, trying to maintain some semblance of communal life. The only youngsters in the community in 1994 were the three grandchildren of Bill and Betty Rosen, recently retired proprietors of the Cinderella Boot Shop.[17]

Even for small-town communities that did not face complete extinction, the general trajectory in the final decades of the twentieth century was very often one of decline. Of the 183 triple-digit Jewish communities of 1927 that were still identifiable as communities of at least 100 but fewer than 1,000 Jews in 1983, some 108 (59 percent) had lost population since their heyday in the period before World War II. In many cases the decline was dramatic. In Pennsylvania, for instance, the reported Jewish population of Williamsport dropped from 825 to 415 between 1937 and 1983, and that of Donora dropped from 400 to 100. The reported Jewish population of New Castle, Pennsylvania, stood at 850 in 1937, but at only 400 in 1983 and 200 by 1991. In Wisconsin, the Jewish population of Racine went from 850 to 405 between 1937 and 1983, and that of Kenosha fell from 950 to 250. In the same period the reported Jewish population of Cumberland, Maryland, diminished from 820 to 265, and that of Greenwood, Mississippi, went from 300 to 100. In Pine Bluff, Arkansas, the Jewish population dropped from 375 to 175 between the late 1930s and the early 1980s, while in Sioux Falls, South Dakota, it fell from 425 to 125. In Watertown in upstate New York the number of Jews declined from 460 to 250 between 1937 and 1983, and the number was down to 120 by 1991. Steubenville, Ohio, which had a reported Jewish population of close to 1,000 from the late 1920s until 1960, counted only 220 Jews among its residents in 1983 and only 175 by 1991.

The sagas of specific local Jewish families can provide arresting evidence of the deterioration of small-town communities, even those that still endured. Two examples from Benton Harbor, Michigan, are instructive. The first involves the descendants of the junk dealer Joseph Sandler and his wife, Jennie, who had moved to Benton Harbor in 1888 and had witnessed the birth of fifteen children, eleven of whom had survived to adulthood. By 1995 these eleven offspring had produced twenty grandchildren, forty-one great-grandchildren, fifty-one great-great-grandchildren, and five great-great-great-grandchildren. Of all these Sandler progeny, however, only one great-granddaughter and her two children were still living in Benton Harbor in the last decade of the twentieth century. The second example involves the family of the horse trader Joseph Litowich and his wife, Sarah, who had arrived in Benton Harbor around 1907 and had raised two daughters and five sons there. The two Litowich daughters moved to Chicago after they married, but the sons all stayed in their hometown. Nonetheless, of the third generation of the Litowich family, not a single member remained in Benton Harbor.[18]

With declining populations and dimming prospects for future growth in so many of America's small Jewish communities, the merger of congregations there, a trend already apparent in the years before World War II, continued apace. In more and more small towns that had once maintained two congregations, consolidation was the order of the day. Sometimes the merger of previously distinct congregations was seen as the only way to facilitate the construction of badly needed new facilities, but often it was a matter of sheer survival. Trying to put the best face on the reality of an increasingly less variegated Jewish community, the historian of La Crosse Jewry, for example, observed that the two main Jewish factions in his town once had "maintained a separate social culture and even independent synagogues" but that toward the end of the twentieth century all the Jews of La Crosse had come to "cooperate beautifully as a single Jewish unit—socially, culturally, and even religiously—with no friction."[19]

In a few cases, retrenchment in a small community was achieved through the merger of rival congregations that had similar theological perspectives. Thus, the two traditionalist congregations that had coexisted for several decades in different neighborhoods of North Adams, Massachusetts, joined in 1958 and dedicated a new building in 1962. In other cases, consolidation meant that a Reform congregation closed its doors, leaving only a nominally Conservative or so-called Traditional synagogue to try to meet the needs of an entire community. This is what happened in Danville, Illinois, for example, where the Reform Temple Beth El disbanded around 1960 after over half a century of operation, leaving the Conservative Congregation Israel (originally Anshe Knesses Israel) as the only synagogue in town.[20]

Not surprisingly, there were also a great many instances in which the consolidation of religious life in a small town meant the ascendancy of Reform. Thus, in 1958, in the long-divided community of Galesburg, Illinois, the merger of the town's original liberal congregation, Sons of Judah, and the Orthodox congregation Ohav Zedek resulted in the creation of a new Reform assembly with the name Temple Sholom and a new building. At about the same time the Reform Beth Zion and the Orthodox Beth Israel finally joined together in Bradford, Pennsylvania, and there, too, the resulting assembly took a new name, Temple Beth El. Like Temple Shalom in Galesburg, Beth El became affiliated with the Reform movement and commissioned a new building, completed in 1961. Yet another example of the ascendancy of Reform Judaism comes from East Liverpool, Ohio, where the community's two congregations consolidated in 1963 and moved into the local Reform temple.[21]

To judge from information available about the 136 triple-digit Jewish communities of 1927 that could still be identified as independent triple-digit communities in the early 1990s, the consolidation of congregational activity was quite sweeping in those classic small-town Jewish centers that survived throughout the twentieth century. In 1991 there were two congregations still in operation in only 12 of the 136 communities identified, while there were no congregations at all in 20 of these communities. The 104 remaining small-town Jewish centers each had only one surviving congregation in 1991, and of these, 45 were affiliated with the Reform movement, 45 were affiliated with Conservatism, and 4 were identified as "Traditional." In nine other towns, the lone congregation was not affiliated with any specific branch of Judaism.[22]

Despite the presence of synagogues that identified with Conservative or even Traditional practice in numerous places, the ongoing transformation of congregational life in small towns invariably involved a continuation of the long-term trend away from the Orthodox orientation of those who established most of America's smaller Jewish settlements. Traditionalists in late-1940s Muskegon, where a new synagogue building had just been erected, perceived what was happening there as "a stampede toward Reform."[23] Indeed, even where the only congregation in town was a Conservative synagogue, its tendency was often to stray from Conservative principles in order to accommodate those in the community with more liberal religious perspectives. Again, developments in Benton Harbor provide a case in point. There the two traditionalist congregations that had coexisted for half a century, the Children of Israel and Ohava Sholom, merged in 1959, taking on a Conservative identity and the name B'nai Sholom. In 1968, however, the Reform Temple Beth-El combined with the recently created B'nai Sholom, and even though the resulting assembly maintained its official affiliation with the Conservative movement, it made a number of changes to accommodate its newest members. It altered its name to Temple B'nai Shalom, for example, and it introduced organ music at Friday evening services.[24] Also reflecting the triumph of liberal Judaism in small-town America is the fact that of all the triple-digit Jewish communities of 1927 that could still be seen as independent small communities in the early 1990s, only two had congregations that identified with Orthodoxy. One of these was the congregation of the historic Touro Synagogue in Newport, Rhode Island; the other was a barely functioning congregation in Fargo, North Dakota, a town that was also home to a Reform temple.[25]

With the absorption of some small-town Jewish centers into larger metropolitan conglomerates and with the decline or even demise of others, it was increasingly difficult by the end of the twentieth century to find small communities that functioned much as they had in the classic era of small-town Jewry. Altogether, by 1983, 253 of the 490 triple-digit communities in our core sample, or 52 percent, had disappeared from the Jewish population listings published periodically in the *American Jewish Year Book*. Either they no longer had an identity independent of other Jewish centers or their populations had dropped below 100 and they had ceased to be viable Jewish settlements for all intents and purposes. By 1991, 304 of our 490 sample communities, or 62 percent, had dropped from sight in *Year Book* listings.

Like *Year Book* population statistics, data on small-town congregations also point to the collapse of a great many of the smaller Jewish centers that had flourished in the early decades of the twentieth century. As of 1991, some 195 of the 490 triple-digit communities of 1927 (40 percent) were without even a single congregation surviving, and 252 of these prewar communities (over 50 percent) were without a rabbi to serve them. Moreover, some of the small-town congregations that still existed in the final decade of the twentieth century were only limping along. The Reform temple in Martinsburg, West Virginia, was holding services only once a month, for example, as was the unaffiliated synagogue in Bennington, Vermont. The congregations in Montpelier, Vermont, and in Paducah, Kentucky, convened only twice a month. The synagogue in Petoskey, Michigan, was opened only in the summer, and that in Catskill, New York, only in the winter. The congregations in Bath, Maine; Bristol, Rhode Island; and Bismarck, North Dakota, held services only on the High Holidays. If the fifty or so triple-digit communities of 1927 that became larger Jewish centers were excluded from our tally, and if those communities that had become, in effect, elements of big-city networks were left out, the decline of small-town Jewish life would be even more apparent. As a brochure distributed by the Museum of the Southern Jewish Experience observed in the early 1990s, "in many small towns, the story of [the] Jewish experience survives only as a cherished memory." A few years earlier the sociologist Eugen Schoenfeld had put the same sentiment more starkly. The once-thriving Jewish communities of small towns, he asserted, "have become merely the skeletal remnants of their former selves."[26]

By the turn of the twenty-first century, in small towns all across America, only cemeteries with few if any fresh graves, visited on occasion by the big-city children or grandchildren of those buried there, provided evidence of once-thriving Jewish communities.[27] In other places there were also synagogue buildings empty of Jews that served as poignant reminders of communities that had faded away. In Ashland, Kentucky, virtually devoid of Jewish residents, two synagogue buildings still stand, one transformed into a church and the other into an insurance office. In Ligonier, Indiana, and in Stevens Point, Wisconsin, the synagogues have become municipal museums. In Virginia, Minnesota, the last of the town's Jewish residents worked to have the local shul protected by landmark status in the hope that it would be "saved forever"; and in Natchez, Mississippi, the Museum of the Southern Jewish Experience has concluded a preservation agreement to maintain the magnificent B'nai Israel temple in a town with only about twenty-five Jewish residents.[28] Many small-town burial grounds and synagogues, no longer serving

*Monument in the Jewish cemetery of Vicksburg, Mississippi. In many small towns, seldom-visited burial grounds have become reminders of once thriving Jewish communities. Photo by the author.*

their original purposes, have become powerful "places of memory." They are not only sites where actual events transpired, but also places that have been suffused with a larger meaning because they have come to be reminders of an entire historical experience that has reached its end.[29]

All this is not to say, of course, that small communities are on the verge of disappearing completely as elements in the geography of American Jewish life. A few long-standing communities have survived in a familiar enough form so that in places such as Pottstown, Pennsylvania; Saginaw, Michigan; Appleton, Wisconsin; and Tyler, Texas, one can still get some sense of what Jewish life was like in the classic era of small-town Jewry. Moreover, new communities have continued to spring up in smaller cities and towns since World War II. Many of these are in expanding industrial centers. A case in point is the community of Dalton, Georgia. Just before World War II, Dalton had a reported Jewish population of only forty individuals, and there was no organized Jewish life in the town. In the years after 1940, however, Dalton began developing into one of the world's foremost carpet manufacturing centers, and the Jewish population increased rapidly. In 1983 Dalton's Jewish population was reported to be 235, and its synagogue had just concluded its fourth decade of operation. Similarly, in Spartanburg, South Carolina, the Jewish population never surpassed 100 in the pre–World War II era, but in the decades after the war Spartanburg blossomed as one of the South's major textile centers, and by the early 1980s its Jewish population approached 300.[30]

The growth of educational institutions in some of America's smaller cities also has stimulated the development of new Jewish communities with populations in the triple-digit range. Chapel Hill, for example, a town dominated by the University of North Carolina, was reported to have only thirty-two Jewish residents in 1937 but 230 by 1968. Fayetteville, home of the University of Arkansas, had no reported Jewish inhabitants at all before the middle of the twentieth century, but by 1983 it was home to 120 Jews. Bloomington, Indiana, where Indiana University is located, had only eighteen Jewish residents in 1927 but some 300 in 1983 and as many as 1,000 by the 1990s. Indeed, some of the small communities of the early 1900s that retained their viability in the latter decades of the twentieth century did so precisely because they were in college towns. In Charlottesville, Virginia, for instance, the Jewish community was clearly on the wane at midcentury, and in the 1940s the local Jews even turned their cemetery over to the city in an effort to ensure that it would be maintained when all of them were gone. In the 1960s, however, the University of Virginia, which had been "virtually closed to Jewish faculty throughout much of its history," began to hire Jewish professors, and their arrival helped spark a revitalization of Charlottesville Jewish life. In the 1980s the local temple reclaimed its cemetery from the municipality. Similarly, towns such as Ithaca, New York; Champaign, Illinois; and Iowa City, Iowa, all home to major universities, saw their Jewish populations rise dramatically in the decades after World War II.[31]

In recreation and retirement meccas such as Myrtle Beach, South Carolina; Vero Beach, Florida; and Aspen, Colorado, as well, new triple-digit Jewish communities developed in the second half of the twentieth century. These towns drew both Jews of the leisure class who could afford to take up residence in idyllic settings and Jewish businesspeople who catered to the growing populations of these places. In short, there was a certain parallel between the kinds of small towns that were prospering in the latter decades of the twentieth century and the kinds of places in which small Jewish communities either survived or developed anew. In an age of increased mobility and rampant acculturation, it is not surprising that a certain number of Jews were among the Americans who were taking up residence in semirural bedroom communities, in new industrial centers, in college towns, in Sunbelt retirement villages, and in resort locations. Just as in the late 1800s and the early 1900s, again in the late twentieth century the economic health of a small town and its attractiveness to migrants were good predictors of the development of a Jewish settlement there.[32]

Still, the triple-digit Jewish communities that appeared in the latter decades of the twentieth century bore little resemblance to the small-town Jewish settlements that had proliferated across the country in the decades before World War II. Whereas the typical communities of earlier times had been established by enterprising immigrant families whose personal identities often became closely linked to the towns in which they settled, the new small-town communities of the late twentieth century depended heavily on the arrival of transplanted professionals and business executives, cosmopolitan scholars and teachers, retirees from big cities, and recreation enthusiasts, many of them transient. Even in small communities with a longer history, a great deal had changed. The complete disappearance of the immigrant generation, the professionalization of small-town Jews, the continuing difficulty of providing a solid Jewish education in the absence of a critical mass of people, and a rising incidence of intermarriage all left their mark. Both the intensity and the distinctiveness that once characterized Jewish life in small communities became greatly diluted.

What the local historian Dennis Devlin has written about Muskegon, Michigan, is emblematic. He has noted that the people who came to dominate Jewish life there after midcentury were no longer inclined to bond together as part of a well-defined religious and ethnic minority. They had "become 'Americans' and either left Muskegon or moved out into the broader community," Devlin writes; "the Jewish community ceased to be the focus of their lives." By the early 1980s the youth group of Muskegon's congregation B'nai Israel had disbanded, the town's B'nai B'rith chapter had become moribund, and the two women's organizations in the community, the temple sisterhood and Hadassah, had merged.[33] In general, Jewish families rooted in a small-town way of life had almost completely disappeared from America's smaller Jewish communities by the end of the twentieth century, just as that way of life itself had largely dissipated, a victim of the technological and sociological changes that were linking together cities and towns throughout the country, homogenizing many of their features, and facilitating the fragmentation of American culture by providing individuals with greater independence and choice. Like other Americans, small-town Jews scaled back their sense of collective identity and weakened the connections they made between place and self.[34]

Toward the end of the twentieth century, with the classic era of small-town Jewry a thing of the past, Jewish life in the self-contained small communities that had been so numerous before World War II, or an idealized version of that life, became the stuff of nostalgia, no less than the small-town main-street culture that so many Americans craved to recover.[35] Jews whose origins were in small towns but who had left for greener pastures frequently remembered their early years with great warmth. Mike Maidenberg, who had left Marion, Indiana, to go to school at the University of Michigan and Columbia, recalled in 1977 that he and others of his generation had been "directed by our parents to look at a wider horizon" and that he had simply got into a line of work that was "really beyond Marion." Nonetheless, he said, "I've always regretted that I had to leave. I've always had fond feelings for Marion." Similarly, the chroniclers of the Jewish history of Charlottesville, Virginia, have observed that "few of the first immigrant families to settle in Charlottesville remained for more than two or three generations" but that "their scattered descendents remain proud and close to the city their grandparents and parents helped build."[36] So intense have been the feelings of affection expressed by many small-town Jews for their places of origin that events organized to bring them back for visits have drawn hundreds, as one such program did in Natchez, Mississippi, in 1994, and another did in Selma, Alabama, in 1997.[37] Also reflecting sorrow over the loss of small communities are the newspaper accounts that began to appear with some regularity toward the end of the twentieth century, reporting on dead or dying Jewish enclaves and conveying a sense of the lost world of small-town Jewry.[38] Still, very few of those who had left small communities gave any indication that they would consider returning.

To a certain degree, the fate of America's smaller Jewish communities has mirrored the fate of small-town America. During the late nineteenth and the early twentieth centuries, every small city, even if it was not very far from a major urban center, functioned as a sort of microcosm. The same can be said of small Jewish communities during their classic era. After the middle of the twentieth century, however, both small towns and their Jewish settlements shed much of their intimacy and autonomy to became elements of huge regional or national networks inexorably bound together by gigantic business systems, multilane expressways, and instantaneous electronic communication. Thus, just as observers concerned about the deterioration of a distinctive small-town culture have said that "the viability of a small town's Main Street gives a good indication of the overall health of a community," it might also be said that the vigor of a small town's Jewish community has been able to give a good indication of the viability of its Main Street.[39] In any event, an understanding of small-town Jewry provides a useful window on the history of small-town America in general, even as it underscores the role that Jews played in the economic and civic culture of smaller urban centers and highlights the often-ignored diversity of small-town society in times past.

More to the point, discovering the history of America's smaller Jewish communities provides a new perspective on the way geography has helped to condition the Jewish experience in the United States. Our study of the classic era of small-town Jewish life has demonstrated unequivocally that the limited size of small-town Jewish settlements and their location within America's less prominent urban places had a decided influence on the very nature of those Jewish enclaves. The relative isolation of the individuals and families who lived in these Jewish centers and their encounters with small-town society were crucial factors conditioning both their everyday existence, at home, at work, and in the civic arena, and the character of their religious and cultural experience as Jews. To be sure, the story of small communities was in some ways similar to that of larger ones. In communities both small and large, migration was the key to growth and development, subcommunities sometimes arose (most often along the fault line between German Jews and East Europeans), and both traditional religious practice and Yiddish cultural identity tended to decline over time. But the classic small-town Jewish settlements of the pre–World War II era were very much unlike large and midsize communities in some fundamental ways as well. As we have seen, smaller Jewish communities were essentially settlements of entrepreneurs in an age when America's more visible Jewish centers invariably included a significant working-class element. Furthermore, for all their internal tensions, small communities often witnessed a kind of cooperation across liturgical and social lines that was mostly absent in larger Jewish centers. So, too, small communities were ones in which, for better or for worse, it was extremely difficult to develop an idiosyncratic Jewish identity or to be anonymous.

For tens of thousands of American Jews in the late nineteenth and early twentieth centuries, the very fact of living in a smaller Jewish community in a small town surpassed other cultural and environmental factors, including regional location, as an influence on the contours of their lives. In this sense, the end of the classic era of small-town Jewish life meant the disappearance of a singular aspect of the Jewish encounter with America. Ultimately, understanding the ways in which small-town Jewish life sometimes resembled the Jewish experience in major communities and sometimes diverged from that experience can help us appreciate both the complex character of American Jewry and the tremendously powerful role of place in shaping the patterns of American Jewish history.

# Reading the Manuscript Census

At several points in this study of smaller Jewish communities, I report on certain aspects of small-town Jewish life on the basis of information gleaned from the manuscript records of the U.S. Census. In the course of my research, I attempted, in essence, to reconstruct the entire Jewish population of several triple-digit Jewish communities. Using original census registers that are available on microfilm from the Census Bureau, I sought to identify all the Jews living in the year 1880 in Bradford, Pennsylvania; Appleton, Wisconsin; Jackson, Michigan; Lafayette, Indiana; Hamilton, Ohio; Lexington, Kentucky; Vicksburg, Mississippi; and Alexandria, Louisiana. I also sought to reconstruct the Jewish communities of these eight towns as they were constituted in 1920 using census data gathered in that year. In addition, I attempted to develop a picture of the Jewish communities of 1920 in four towns in which Jewish communal life had not yet emerged as of 1880: Nashua, New Hampshire; Newburyport and Fitchburg, Massachusetts; and Modesto, California. Trying to identify all the Jewish inhabitants of a town using the hundreds of handwritten register sheets completed by census takers many decades ago was tedious work. Nonetheless, it allowed me to become familiar with several classic small-town Jewish communities not only on the basis of institutional records and anecdotal information about individual families, but also on the basis of composite profiles of those communities at one or two specific points in time.

The twelve towns I selected for close examination were chosen because they represented a variety of regions around the United States and because they did not seem to be anomalous in a way that would prevent their Jewish communities from reflecting the usual situation in triple-digit Jewish settlements. Another factor that influenced the selection of these towns was that for each I was able to discover records such as synagogue rosters and cemetery listings that could help me identify Jewish individuals and households as I systematically examined census records. In the case of Vicksburg, Mississippi, for example, I had access both to a list of burials in the local Jewish cemetery and to a 1904 list of the eighty-one founding members of Congregation Anshe Chesed's ladies' auxiliary. For Jackson, Michigan, I was able to consult the cashbook of the local B'nai B'rith lodge for the period 1919–1924 and the burial list for Jackson's Temple Beth Israel Cemetery.[1] The availability of at least some records providing the names of local Jewish residents is crucial for the reconstruction of Jewish communities using census documents because the U.S. Census Bureau itself never asked Americans about their religious affiliation. As a result, much of the work of reconstruction depends upon matching census information with that in other sources.

This essay describes in some detail how I went about using manuscript census rolls to identify the Jewish inhabitants of the twelve towns on which I focused, and it is intended, in part, to demonstrate the possibility of using census materials to determine the composition of any small Jewish community in given years with a certain degree of precision and confidence. On the other hand, however, it is also intended to alert readers to the many pitfalls encountered in using census data to identify Jewish individuals and households and to make it clear that there is no way to guarantee complete accuracy in this endeavor. While there is good reason to believe that my work with census materials yielded a rather precise portrait of the small Jewish communities I studied, it is impossible to be certain that I was able to produce an absolutely perfect picture of the make-up of those communities. Ultimately, my hope is that this description of how I pursued my analysis of manuscript census documents will prove valuable to future researchers who may wish to use census materials for their own work in local Jewish history.

In order to identify the Jews listed in the 1880 and 1920 manuscript census records I reviewed, I began by scanning the many ledger pages of each local enumeration, concentrating initially on the columns indicating the places of birth of the parents of each individual listed. I was looking for individuals with at least one parent born in Europe, or perhaps in the Middle East. This was a productive way to begin because in 1880 there were few adult Jews in America who did not have at least one parent born in Central Europe, and even in 1920 there were still many American-born Jews of Central European background who had mothers or fathers who had been born in Germany or in a neighboring region such as Alsace in France. Similarly, nearly all adults of East European background in the United States in 1920 were either immigrants themselves or the children of immigrants. The 1920 census records not only the place of birth of those listed and of their parents, but also the native language of each of these people, and this makes the identification of individuals with foreign-born parents even easier.

Whenever I located a person with one or both parents born in Central Europe, Eastern Europe, England or the Middle East, I examined the entire census entry for that person's household to determine if any or all of the people in it were Jewish. Obviously, if I found a person whose own native tongue was listed as Yiddish, or "Jewish," or Hebrew, or if I came across someone whose parents spoke one of these languages, I knew that I had come upon a Jewish individual. Also, if the name of the individual in question or of someone else in his or her family appeared on one of the lists of known Jews that I had available, I was able to confirm a Jewish identity. Once I identified a specific individual in a household as Jewish, it was generally easy to determine who else in the household was Jewish, especially if the individual initially identified was the head of a family. There were some cases, however, in which the Jews I encountered were not living in households headed by Jews. They might have been lodgers in the homes of non-Jewish families, for example, or tenants in a boarding house.

On a computerized spreadsheet, I recorded all of the Jewish households and individuals I discovered by focusing on parents' origin and native language, and then I went through the entire census manuscript for each of the towns I had selected yet again, this time scanning the documents for individual names. I looked for surnames very commonly used by Jews (sometimes referred to by researchers as Distinctive Jewish Names, or DJNs) and for names of local Jewish families known from other sources.[2] Whenever I encountered a relevant surname, I made a judgment about the Jewish identity of the individual who bore that name. In this way I was able to uncover some Jewish individuals and households that I had missed in my first review and to increase my chances of finding all the Jews listed in the census of each of the towns I was studying. In other words, my second review was not only a way to crosscheck the first review, but also a way to identify the grandchildren and great-grandchildren of Jewish immigrants. If such individuals were the heads of their own households or boarding with others, they would certainly have been missed had I focused only on people with foreign-born parents. Without the second review I conducted of each manuscript census roll, I would never have spotted Bessie Cohen in 1880 Lexington, for example. In a town renowned for its girls' boarding schools, she was a pupil in the academy of W. S. Ryland. Although her name indicates that she was almost certainly Jewish, neither she nor her parents had been born abroad. The second reading of each manuscript census also provided a way to spot individuals whose census entries were flawed in one way or another. I discovered Jesse Cohen only in my second review of the 1920 census of Modesto, California, for instance, because the column listing the native tongue of his father had been left blank inadvertently, and this omission caused me to miss the fact that his father had been born in Russia.

Although my second review of census documents did reveal some Jewish residents previously overlooked, it tended to confirm that my first scrutiny had located nearly all the Jewish inhabitants that could be identified in each of the towns I studied. In the case of 1880 Vicksburg, for example, my second reading yielded only one household that I had missed in the first round, that of the fifty-two-year-old grocer Solomon Rothschild. In the case of Lafayette, Indiana, in 1920, my second review yielded no more than eight new households, out of a total of nearly 100. In the case of Nashua, New Hampshire, in 1920, my second round of review uncovered only two additional households.

In both rounds of manuscript review there were, of course, many cases in which the Jewish identity of some individual or household was not easy to determine. Where the native tongue listed for a person's parents was German, French, Russian, Polish, or some other language of a region from which Jews migrated to the United States (or where the place of birth involved was England) and where there was no definitive collateral evidence from the lists available for cross-matching, other indicators had to be considered in order to make a determination about Jewish identity. For example, if a person's full name did not appear on a local list of synagogue members or the like, the presence of his or her surname was at least an indication that the family in question was probably represented in the local Jewish community and thus a clue suggesting the Jewish identity of the individual I was considering. Sometimes the name of a relative in the household provided the circumstantial evidence on which a determination of Jewish identity was based. Unfortunately, the lists of names I had available for cross-referencing did not always overlap with the census years 1880 and 1920, and this fact made the task of record matching somewhat more complicated.

In cases in which only a Jewish-sounding name suggested that a person might be counted in the local Jewish population, that name itself was sufficient evidence of a Jewish identity if the name was unmistakable. I included Mendel Hymowitz in my inventory of Jewish householders in Newburyport without hesitation, for example, even though his native language was recorded in the manuscript census as Russian and he did not appear on any of the lists I had available for cross-referencing. In general, however, great caution had to be exercised when it came to a reliance on names alone, since many surnames that can be indicators of Jewish ethnicity are nonetheless ambiguous. In Hamilton, Ohio, for example, many gentile families of German background had surnames often borne by Jews as well. These names include Goodman, Hoffman, Mayer, and Miller. The task of identifying Jewish households in Hamilton was further complicated by the fact that the town was home to both Jewish and non-Jewish families with the names Sauer, Smith, and Wolf. Similarly, in Vicksburg in the 1920s there were black families named Brown and Jacobs and Winston, a white gentile family named Nelson, an Arab family named Abraham, and Jewish families with the very same surnames.

Even family names such as Cohen, Levy, and their variants could be misleading. For example, I concluded that the widow Catherine Kohen of Appleton, Wisconsin, was probably not Jewish. My determination was based not only on her characteristically Christian first name and on the fact that I had no evidence of Appleton Jews with the name Kohen from other sources, but also on the fact that Catherine was the sister of a man named Frank Mader. Of course it is possible that Kohen's deceased husband had been Jewish, but even so, there is no evidence that she identified with Judaism in any way.

Obviously, each determination about the religious and ethnic identity of a person with a possibly Jewish surname had to be made on a case-by-case basis. As in the example of Catherine Kohen, sometimes first names provided a clue. If I had no additional information to go on, I was more likely to conclude that an Abraham and Sarah with an ambiguous surname were Jewish than I was to accept as Jewish a Christopher and Maria with the same surname. More commonly, however, a combination of hints led me to a conclusion about a person's identity. I decided that Daniel Steinberg of Appleton, whose father was born in Prussia, was probably not Jewish, for example, because Steinberg's son was given the same name as his father, a practice rare among Jews, because Steinberg's daughter was named Mary, and because his mother-in-law had been born in Kentucky. Of course, it is possible that Steinberg himself was Jewish but that his wife was not, or even that the entire family was Jewish, but in general my inclination was to err on the side of caution. In my attempts to reconstruct local Jewish communities as accurately as possible, I was somewhat less concerned about excluding a few Jewish individuals or households than I was about including too many people who were not in fact Jewish.

Along these same lines, I excluded from my inventories of Jewish residents those descendents of Jewish settlers who were known to have disassociated themselves from their Jewish past. Thus, I excluded Howard Gratz from the inventory of Lexington Jewry in 1880. Although he was the son of Benjamin Gratz and thus descended from a famous Jewish merchant family of eighteenth-century Philadelphia, his mother was not Jewish, and he seems to have maintained no contact with Lexington's Jewish community. Similarly, I excluded Julius Levy from my inventory of Jews in Newburyport in 1920. Although his father was a German Jew, neither his mother nor his wife was Jewish, and he did not participate in local Jewish affairs.

Ultimately, in deciding about a person's Jewish identity, it was often necessary to combine the diverse clues available with sheer intuition. A few further examples drawn from the way I dealt with the manuscript census data for Newburyport in 1920 will illustrate the kinds of judgments that I had to make. In reconstructing the Jewish community of that Massachusetts town, I concluded, for example, that one A. Krakovsky was almost certainly Jewish, even though his native tongue was recorded as Russian and I had no other record of this individual. I made this assessment because Krakovsky's wife and children had first names frequently used by Jews, because his household was adjacent to that of a man who was known to be an East European Jew, and because I knew of another man named Krakovsky elsewhere in Newburyport who was definitely Jewish. Moreover, Russian, rather than Yiddish, was listed as the native tongue of Krakovsky's Jewish neighbor as well as of Krakovsky himself, an indication that the census taker in their section of Newburyport simply listed Russian as the native language of all those born in Russia without asking further questions.

On the other hand, I excluded Charles Barth from my inventory of Jewish householders in Newburyport even though there were other Barths in town who were known to be Jewish. I made this decision because the other Barths were all born in Russia and spoke Yiddish as their mother tongue, while Charles was born in Germany and spoke German as his native language. Moreover, Charles was married to a woman born in Scotland whose native tongue was Scottish. Somewhat more reluctantly, I excluded from my inventory of Newburyport Jewish residents one Charles Fellman, even though there were three Fellman households in the city that were known to be Jewish. Charles was rejected because, unlike the other Fellmans, his wife was born in Massachusetts rather than in Russia and he had an obviously non-Jewish boarder in his home. The decision to exclude Charles Fellman from my inventory of Jewish households was strengthened by the fact that, as a house carpenter, he practiced a trade not typically associated with Jewish occupational patterns in smaller cities and towns.

While I am confident that I was able to identify nearly all the Jews who were listed in the census rosters for the towns I studied, I suspect that I did overlook a few and that the methodology I employed probably led me to miss Jews in some categories more frequently than those in others. For example, transient Jews with ambiguous surnames were more likely to have been excluded from my inventories than Jews with ambiguous surnames who remained in their towns for a long time, because the latter were far more likely than the former to show up in the local Jewish organizational directories or cemetery lists that I had available. So, too, Jews living in households headed by gentiles were liable to be excluded from my inventories when household composition was the only criterion available for determining Jewish identity. Finally, Jews of German background had a somewhat greater chance of being overlooked than Jews of East European background because the native tongue recorded for Central European Jews was invariably the same as that recorded for their gentile fellow immigrants, and their surnames were more frequently indistinguishable from those of their gentile neighbors.

Although most of the difficulties I confronted in reconstituting Jewish communities were associated with determining the Jewish identity of the individuals listed in census registers, some of the problems I encountered were inherent in the way the registers themselves were produced. For one thing, both in 1880 and in 1920 the U.S. Census was conducted by individual enumerators sent door to door to record information about all the members of every household they visited, and in many instances the census takers simply made mistakes. In Bradford, Pennsylvania, for example, at least one of the census agents employed in 1880 routinely left blank the column listing the relationships of the people in a household to one another, making it difficult at times to identify boarders, servants, and various family members whose surnames differed from that of the household head. So, too, the manuscript registers for Lafayette, Indiana, contain several cases in which English is recorded as the native language of an individual born in Germany, and this seems another indication of errors on the part of enumerators.

The appearance of individuals in more than one place on the census rolls complicated the job of reconstructing Jewish communities as well. In 1880 Bradford, the entire family of Coppell Rothstein was recorded as living in two places at once. Rothstein, his wife, Amelia, his children, Benjamin and Esther, and his brothers Myer and Abram appear once as residents of Congress Street and again as residents of Boylston Street, perhaps because they moved during the period the census was being conducted. The fact that Rothstein is listed as a twenty-seven-year-old saloonkeeper at one address and as a twenty-five-year-old restaurateur at the other only reinforces the impression that census takers were not always as careful as they should have been in verifying and recording information.

The double entry for the Rothstein family is far from being the only indication of problems with the way census takers did their canvassing. A further example is the fact that the census registers for 1920 Vicksburg report the twenty-five-year-old Charles Feith as a member of two different households. Charles's father-in-law, Newman Loewenberg, reported Charles, his wife, and their daughter as living in the Loewenberg home, while Charles's mother, Ida, reported Charles as a married son living in her home without his family. Similarly, the household of Heyman and Sophie Bohrer is recorded twice in the 1920 census records for Alexandria, Louisiana. The Bohrer household appears once on Holly Street and once on Monroe Street. On Holly Street, Heyman is a German-speaking native of Austria, while on Monroe he speaks "Jewish" and hails from Germany. Again a lack of consistency concerning biographical information raises doubts about the care taken by census enumerators in general. Indeed, it appears that in some cases census takers did not even ask householders for complete information, but instead used their own discretion in completing census registers. As we have seen, some enumerators simply assumed that the mother tongue of anyone born in Russia was Russian and thus failed to recognize many native speakers of Yiddish.

Mundane but often frustrating problems associated with spelling and orthography also complicated the work of identifying Jewish residents and reconstructing Jewish communities. Some enumerators had better handwriting than others, and some were more careful than others with the spelling of the names of those they encountered. In the case of Alexandria, Louisiana, where the handwriting of at least one census taker working in the part of town where many Jews lived was a tiny scrawl, the problem of legibility was compounded by the fact that the available microfilm of the 1920 census manuscript was somewhat out of focus.

Finally, the fact that canvassers employed by the Census Bureau almost certainly failed to encounter some of the Jewish residents of the districts to which they were assigned also makes it impossible to be certain that I was reconstructing Jewish communities in their entirety. For example, the 1921 city directory for Appleton, Wisconsin, lists a Jewish resident of the city named Oscar Friedman, and it is likely that he was living in Appleton the previous year as well. However, Friedman does not figure in my inventory of Appleton Jewish residents in 1920 because the manuscript census from that year yielded a record neither of Friedman nor of a visit to the address at which Friedman was living in 1921. Similarly, spot-checking in Vicksburg, Mississippi, led me to identify fifteen Jewish heads of household (seven men and eight women) whose names appeared in the local city directories of 1918 and 1921, but whose names I was unable to find in the 1920 manuscript census (a 1920 city directory for Vicksburg was unavailable).

Given the multiple problems inherent in the source materials available, and given my generally conservative approach in determining Jewish identity in the census records, it is likely that in reconstructing the twelve communities upon which I focused, I undercounted the number of individuals and households that constituted those Jewish settlements. Indeed, in a few cases the number of Jewish residents I discovered was considerably lower than the number reported in contemporary surveys conducted by Jewish agencies, although, as I have demonstrated in chapter 1 of this volume, the figures provided by those agencies are far from being completely reliable. I identified only 106 Jewish inhabitants of Appleton, Wisconsin, in 1880, for example, while the Union of American Hebrew Congregations' *Statistics of the Jews*, published in that same year, reported 143; and I found only 174 Jews in Lafayette, Indiana, in 1880, while *Statistics of the Jews* reported 225. In Fitchburg, Massachusetts, I discovered 372 Jews in 1920, while the *American Jewish Year Book* reported 528 Jews two years earlier. In 1920 Jackson, Michigan, I found 109 Jews, while the *Jewish Year Book* reported 300, although in this case I am especially suspicious of the accuracy of the *Year Book* estimate.

On the other hand, in many more cases, the number of individuals represented in the population inventories I developed and the number reported in contemporary sources are remarkably similar. I counted 96 Jews in Hamilton, Ohio, in 1880, for example, and *Statistics of the Jews* reported 110. I found 191 Jews in Alexandria, Louisiana, in 1880, and *Statistics of the Jews* reported 206.

For 1920 I counted 393 Jews in Lexington, Kentucky, while the *American Jewish Year Book* reported 385 in 1918. In Nashua, New Hampshire, I counted 325 Jewish inhabitants in 1920, and the *Year Book* reported 350 two years earlier. For 1920 Vicksburg, my count was 471 Jews, whereas the *Year Book* estimated the number at 532. In the end, however, even where my population figures diverged from those published in contemporary sources, the number of individuals and households included in each of my communal inventories was large enough to give me confidence that the problems I encountered in the course of creating those inventories were not great enough to distort my analysis of local Jewish life.

# Bibliographic Essay

I present here an extended bibliographic essay concerning the sources I consulted in preparing this study of America's small-town Jewish communities because such an essay should be of much greater value to the readers of this volume than a standard inventory of works cited. Those who may wish to pursue further information about the many individual communities discussed in this book or about the various topics upon which it touches can fruitfully turn to the endnotes to the text in their search for relevant references. On the other hand, those who wish to get a sense of the nature of the sources upon which I relied will learn much more from this discussion than from a mere cataloguing of books, articles, and the like. In essence, the purpose of this essay is to alert readers to the vast array of resources that are available to supply information about the history of America's smaller Jewish communities and to provide some guidance for other researchers who may want to pursue their own studies in local Jewish history.

All the general population figures cited in this study come from standard reference volumes issued by the U.S. Bureau of the Census. Basic data about the number of inhabitants in America's various cities and towns and about their fundamental demographic characteristics can be found in the reports customarily issued after each decennial census, publications such as *Fourteenth Census of the United States Taken in the Year 1920, Volume I, Population 1920: Number and Distribution of Inhabitants* (Washington, D.C., 1921) and *Sixteenth Census of the United States: 1940, Population, Volume I: Number of Inhabitants* (Washington, D.C., 1942). Much basic information can also be found in the very useful summaries published by the Census Bureau, volumes such as *Compendium of the Tenth Census (June 1, 1880)* (1883; reprint, New York, 1976) and *Abstract of the Fourteenth Census of the United States* (1923; reprint, New York, 1976). Of course, the published volumes produced by the Census Bureau provide only aggregate statistics based on the household-by-household enumeration undertaken by census agents every ten years. For a dozen towns that figure prominently in this study, I mined the actual census registers that were completed by those agents to discover a tremendous amount of information relevant to small-town Jewish life. How I did so is the topic of a separate essay in this volume, "Reading the Manuscript Census."

This book's chapter titled "Patterns of Evidence" presents a full discussion of the Jewish population statistics available for the United States, but it seems worthwhile to cite the most important sources of Jewish population data covering the classic era of small-town Jewish life again here. For the period around 1830, when there were only about 4,000 Jews in the entire United States, one may consult Ira Rosenwaike's *On the Edge of Greatness: A Portrait of American Jewry in the Early National Period* (Cincinnati, 1985). For the time around 1878, there is *Statistics of the Jews of the United States,* published by the Union of American Hebrew Congregations (Philadelphia, 1880). Although *The Jewish Encyclopedia* published some Jewish population statistics for 1905 in its entry "United States," the prime source of published Jewish population data throughout the rest of the century is the *American Jewish Year Book*. Population listings for 1907 appear in volume 9 of the *Year Book* (1907–08), and population information for 1918 appears in both volume 20 (1918–19) and volume 21 (1919–20). The data for 1927 appear most conveniently in volume 30 (1928–29), and those for 1937 appear in volume 42 (1940–41). The most extensive compilation of American Jewish population statistics currently available in one place is Jacob Rader Marcus's *To Count a People: American Jewish Population Data, 1585–1984* (Lanham, Md., 1990). Although this reference volume brings together information from many population surveys and supplements that information with figures from numerous local histories, it can not be relied upon exclusively, because it has some serious shortcomings. For example, it is missing some of the figures available in the 1880 *Statistics of the Jews,* and it completely ignores the population data available in the 1907 *American Jewish Year Book*.

Along with various census reports, city directories constituted an essential resource for my study of small Jewish communities. These directories were the standard reference books providing information about local residents and businesses in cities and towns all across the United States from the early nineteenth century until at least the middle of the twentieth. Typically, these volumes were issued annually and contained alphabetical listings of individuals, commercial enterprises, and local institutions. The standard directory entry for an individual male head of household generally included both his name and that of his wife, their residential address, and information about his occupation or place of business. In some cases, additional items of information such as a telephone number and, in the case of widows, the name of a deceased husband were included as well. City directories also commonly featured classified sections that provided information about goods and services locally available, civic sections that dealt with local government and community life, and advertising sections that helped to defray the cost of publication. Not uncommonly, directories also provided street guides that indicated the occupants of every structure in a city, building by building. Maps, brief local histories, and postal information might appear in directories as well.

Late nineteenth- and early twentieth-century city directories were printed by a variety of publishing houses. In the early 1920s, for instance, there were over three dozen members of the Association of North American Directory Publishers, including such firms as the Sampson and Murdock Company in Boston, the Caron Directory Company in Louisville, the Cleveland Directory Company, the Chicago Directory Company, the Minneapolis Directory Company, and the Los Angeles Directory Company. Certainly the most prominent name in directory publishing was Ralph Lane Polk, who began producing city guides in Indianapolis in 1869. By the time its founder died in 1923, Polk and Company was the largest publisher of city directories in the world. By then the firm had its home offices in Detroit and New York, and it had also spun off the Polk-Gould Directory Company, based in St. Louis; the Polk-Husted Directory Company, based in Oakland, California; and Polk's Southern Directory Company, based in Little Rock, Arkansas.[1]

Almost invariably, only one publishing house issued a city directory for any given town in any given year, and so the only pieces of information needed to locate a specific directory are the name of the city and the year of the volume. Unfortunately, searches for directories for specific cities in specific years are not always successful. In some cases, a directory for a given year was simply not published; in other cases, all copies of a volume that appeared in a certain year have disappeared. By their very nature these books quickly became obsolete and were routinely discarded. Full series of past city directories are quite rare, with the most complete sets generally preserved in the collections of local libraries and historical societies and at the Library of Congress. I was able to consult city directories for many of the small towns whose Jewish communities I studied during visits to those towns. I also took advantage of some of the directories made available in the microform series *City Directories of the United States*, published during the 1990s by Research Publications International of Woodbridge, Connecticut, although most of the directories reproduced in this collection are for larger cities.

Given the nature of this book, my research relied heavily on work done previously by scores of writers who have chronicled the histories of individual small-town Jewish communities. Their works fall into several categories. Some of the writings I consulted are full-length monographs covering the history of small communities or, occasionally, the history of small-town congregations. Although the content and organization of many of these books betray the amateur status of their writers, a few of them, such as Belinda and Richard Gergel's *In Pursuit of the Tree of Life: A History of the Early Jews of*

*Columbia, South Carolina, and the Tree of Life Congregation* (Columbia, S.C., 1996) and Leonard Rogoff's *Homelands: Southern Jewish Identity in Durham and Chapel Hill, North Carolina* (Tuscaloosa, Ala., 2001), reflect thorough research and are very well written. I also had access to a few exhibition catalogues that help to tell the story of Jewish life in specific towns. Examples include *The Jewish Community of Newburyport: A Photographic Exhibit* (Newburyport, Mass., 1986) and *To Seek the Peace of the City: Jewish Life in Charlottesville,* prepared by Carol Ely, Jeffrey Hantman, and Phyllis Leffler (Charlottesville, Va., 1994).

Another category of works that were very helpful in the preparation of this book consists of journal articles dealing with the history of individual Jewish communities. Again, the quality of publications in this category varies widely, but the best are carefully researched and nicely crafted, whether they are authored by trained historians or by others, whether they are published in journals of specifically Jewish interest or journals with a more general readership. Representative of the best articles are William Toll's "The Domestic Basis of Community: Trinidad, Colorado's Jewish Women, 1889–1910," *Rocky Mountain Jewish Historical Notes* 8 and 9 (summer and fall 1987); Hal Rothman's "'Same Horse, New Wagon': Tradition and Assimilation among the Jews of Wichita, 1865–1930," *Great Plains Quarterly* 15 (spring 1995); and Sherry Blanton's "Lives of Quiet Affirmation: The Jewish Women of Early Anniston, Alabama," *Southern Jewish History* 2 (1999). Similar to journal articles are pamphlets such as Todd Endelman's *A Short History of the Jews of the Ann Arbor Area* (Ann Arbor, Mich., 1997).

The largest category of local history narratives on which I relied comprises individual synagogue histories produced by congregations, usually on the occasion of an anniversary or at the time of a building dedication, and published in booklets or program brochures with titles such as *Seventy-Fifth Anniversary of Beth Israel Congregation* (Plattsburg, N.Y., 1936); *Dedication Journal: Temple Beth Abraham* (Nashua, N.H., 1960); *Moses Montefiore Temple: A Time to Remember* (Bloomington, Ill., 1982); *A Century of Jewish Commitment, 1887–1987: Congregation Kneses Tifereth Israel* (Port Chester, N.Y., 1987); and *Congregation Kneseth Israel: Looking Back, Moving Forward* (Annapolis, 1996). Although some of these histories are extensive and detailed accounts penned by identified authors, most are cursory narratives by anonymous writers. Nonetheless, all these congregational profiles provide just the kind of specific information that is essential to building a global understanding of small-town Jewish life.

In addition to published accounts of the history of various small-town Jewish communities, I made use of several unpublished works. Some of these writings, such as Harry Tecler's "A History of the Jewish Community of Auburn, N.Y.," composed in 1947 and preserved at the American Jewish Archives in Cincinnati, and Arnold Hirsch's "Remembering Donora's Jewish Community," written about 1995 and preserved in the Historical Society of Western Pennsylvania Archives in Pittsburgh, were prepared simply to create a record of the history of a specific small community. Other unpublished essays were composed as undergraduate research papers at colleges or universities. Examples here include David J. Goldberg's "In Dixie Land, I Take my Stand: A Study of Small-city Jewry in Five Southeastern States," written at Columbia College in 1974; Patricia L. Dean's "The Jewish Community of Helena, Montana: 1866–1900," written as an undergraduate honors thesis at Carroll College in 1977; Jennifer Kraft's "Children of Israel Synagogue and the Jewish Community of Benton Harbor, Michigan: A History," written at the Jewish Theological Seminary of America in 1992; and Aaron Kohen's "Five Small Jewish Communities in Illinois: Place and Time in Ottawa, Spring Valley, LaSalle, Joliet and Aurora," presented as an undergraduate thesis at the University of Chicago in 1995.

Other unpublished works I consulted were the result of research by graduate students, works such as Jerome Paul David's "Jewish Consciousness in the Small Town," a rabbinic thesis submitted at Hebrew Union College in 1974; and Karen R. Goody's "The Greensboro Jewish Community: Keeping the Memories under Glass," a master's thesis completed at Wake Forest University in 1984. A few truly excellent doctoral dissertations deal either in whole or in part with small Jewish communities. Among the most important of these are Rochelle Berger Elstein's "Synagogue Architecture in Michigan and the Midwest: Material Culture and the Dynamics of Jewish Accommodation, 1865–1945" (Michigan State University, 1986); Chester Jay Proshan's "Eastern European Jewish Immigrants and Their Children on the Minnesota Iron Range, 1890s–1980s" (University of Minnesota, 1998); and Deborah R. Weiner's "A History of Jewish Life in the Central Appalachian Coalfields, 1870s to 1970s" (West Virginia University, 2002).

Newspaper and magazine stories constitute yet another class of documents very important for the study of small-town Jewish history. Although it was beyond the scope of my research to systematically examine entire runs of local newspapers, I was able to conduct a few random searches of local papers and to examine clippings preserved in the files of various libraries and archives. Everything in local newspapers from advertisements for businesses owned by Jews to obituaries for members of the Jewish community helped to flesh out the picture of local Jewish life. Occasionally I also came across extensive accounts of developments in a local Jewish community. Some of these stories, with titles such as "Jewish Citizens Play Prominent Part in All Affairs of City," in the *Lexington Herald* of April 15, 1917, and "New Synagogue of Congregation Ahavas Achim Dedicated," in the *Newburyport News* of September 11, 1933, came directly out of the classic era of small-town Jewish life. Other such comprehensive stories, such as Walt Williams' "City's Jewish Heritage: Sol Elias to Mark Spitz," in the *Modesto Bee* of March 3, 1974, and Patty Hiemstra's "Kalamazoo Lured Jewish Pioneers," in the *Kalamazoo Gazette* of April 8, 1984, were produced in more recent decades. A significant subcategory among newspaper stories includes those fairly recent articles that document the decline of Jewish life in once-vital Jewish centers all across America. Examples include Tim Klass's "Jewish Communities Vanishing from Small Towns," in the *Detroit News* of July 31, 1994, and Sue Anne Pressley's "Southern Jews Close Up Shop," in the *Washington Post* of May 23, 1999.

Although most of the works I consulted took only single Jewish centers as their subjects, occasionally I was able to glean information about triple-digit Jewish settlements from books or collections of essays dealing with entire states or even entire regions. For small communities in the Northeast and in the Middle Atlantic states, I benefited from books such as *Jews in Berkshire Country*, written by Pink Horwitt and Bertha Skole and dealing with western Massachusetts (Williamstown, Mass., 1972); *Peddler to Suburbanite: The History of the Jews of Monmouth County, New Jersey*, by Alan S. Pine, Jean C. Hershenov, and Aaron H. Lefkowitz (Deal Park, N.J., 1981); and *The Jewish Experience in Western Pennsylvania: A History, 1755–1945*, by Jacob S. Feldman (Pittsburgh, 1986). For small communities in the South, I drew upon works such as *Jewish Roots in the Carolinas: A Pattern of American Philo-Semitism*, by Harry Golden (Charlotte, N.C., 1955); *Jews in Early Mississippi*, by Leo and Evelyn Turitz (Jackson, Miss., 1983); *A Corner of the Tapestry: A History of the Jewish Experience in Arkansas, 1820s–1990s*, by Carolyn Gray LeMaster (Fayetteville, Ark., 1994); and *Turn to the South: Essays on Southern Jewry*, edited by Nathan M. Kaganoff and Melvin I. Urofsky (Charlottesville, Va., 1979). In seeking information on small-town Jewry in the Southwest and the West, I profited from books such as *Deep in the Heart: The Lives and Legends of Texas Jews*, by Ruthe Winegarten and Cathy Schechter (Austin, 1990); *History of the Jews in Utah and Idaho*, by Juanita Brooks (Salt Lake City, 1973); and *Exploring Jewish Colorado*, by Phil Goodstein (Denver, 1992).

At times I also found information on small-town Jewish centers in works concerned with local history in general. Perhaps the most interesting such sources are the richly detailed and often enchantingly illustrated city and county histories produced by the dozens in the last few decades of the nineteenth century and the first few of the twentieth, works such as J. F. Everhart's *History of Muskingum County, Ohio, with Illustrations and Biographical Sketches* (1882; reprint, Evansville, Ind., 1974); H. P. Chapman and J. F. Battaile's *Picturesque Vicksburg* (Vicksburg, Miss., 1895); R. P. DeHart's *Past and Present of Tippecanoe County, Indiana* (Indianapolis, 1909); and George H. Tinkham's *History of Stanislaus County, California* (Los Angeles, 1921). In their sections on religious life, such works often provide insight into the origins of the local

Jewish community, and they sometimes offer biographical information on prominent Jewish residents as well. More recent local histories, many of them again illustrated, were also a source of information. Examples include volumes such as *A Guide to Macon's Architecture and Historical Heritage*, edited by John J. McKay (Macon, Ga., 1972); *Around the World in Fitchburg*, written by Doris Kirkpatrick for the Fitchburg Historical Society (Fitchburg, Mass., 1975); and *Jackson: An Illustrated History*, authored by Brian Deming and dealing with Jackson, Michigan (Woodland Hills, Calif., 1984).

Several documentary films have been produced touching on Jewish life in the American hinterland. Although I seldom relied on these productions as significant sources of new information, I often found them interesting and useful for the visual dimension they add to the historical record. Among the documentary films and videos that I came across in the course of preparing this volume are *The Fitchburg Mosaic: the Jewish Experience*, produced by the Fitchburg Public Library, Fitchburg State College, and the Fitchburg Historical Society (ca. 1980); *Tales from Raisin-Land: A Conversation with Rabbi David Greenberg*, produced by Gregg Rossen (ca. 1991); *The Righteous Remnant: Jewish Survival in Appalachia*, produced by Maryanne Reed (1997); *Delta Jews: A Film about Jews in the "Land of the Blues,"* produced by Mike DeWitt (1998); and *Pushcarts and Plantations: Jewish Life in Louisiana*, produced by Brian Cohen (1998).

Depending on what aspect of a community's experience I was considering, texts such as local histories, synagogue chronicles, and newspaper accounts could serve as either primary sources or secondary sources of information. More clearly falling into the category of primary documents, however, are the institutional records of individual congregations and other local Jewish organizations. Documents such as congregational minute books from Danville, Pennsylvania; B'nai B'rith application and initiation certificates from Lafayette, Indiana; and rabbi's reports from Hamilton, Ohio, all of which I consulted at the American Jewish Archives, proved extremely helpful. Also among the holdings of the American Jewish Archives and invaluable for this study is a set of questionnaires completed by rabbinical students in 1935 concerning the small-town pulpits that they served as part of their training.

Falling into the category of primary sources, as well, are reports and pamphlets issued under the auspices of various institutions during the early decades of the twentieth century. These include texts such as one Mrs. Pappe's "The Small Towns and the Scattered Groups," published in the *Proceedings of the Council of Jewish Women* after that organization's annual meeting in 1902; Rabbi George Zepin's "Jewish Religious Conditions in Scattered Communities," published in the *Year Book of the Central Conference of American Rabbis* in 1904; Jacob J. Weinstein's *The Religious Situation among Small Town Jewries*, a pamphlet issued by the Union of American Hebrew Congregations around the time of World War II; and Robert Shosteck's *Small-Town Jewry Tell their Story*, published by B'nai B'rith (Washington, D.C.,1953).

Letters and other correspondence that I came upon in various archives and libraries, or sometimes in the back rooms of small-town synagogues, also helped shed light on the story of America's smaller Jewish communities. Among the most valuable collections of correspondence that I consulted are that relating to the work of the Industrial Removal Office, preserved by the American Jewish Historical Society in New York; that dealing with the placement of Reform rabbis trained at Hebrew Union College, held at the American Jewish Archives; and that concerning the placement of Orthodox rabbis ordained by the Rabbi Isaac Elchanan Theological Seminary, preserved in the Yeshiva University Archives.

Another rich source of information for this study was the body of memoir literature created by individuals whose origins were in small towns or whose families lived in small towns at one time or another. Examples include Edna Ferber's *A Peculiar Treasure* (New York, 1939); Ben Deutschman's *In a Small Town a Kid Went to Shul* (Nashville, 1971); Julian Feibelman's *The Making of a Rabbi* (New York, 1980); Faye Moskowitz's *A Leak in the Heart: Tales from a Woman's Life* (Boston, 1985); David Rome's *Ancestors, Descendants, and Me* (Beverly Hills, 1986); and Edward Cohen's *The Peddler's Grandson: Growing Up Jewish in Mississippi* (Jackson, Miss., 1999). Also in the category of relevant memoirs are Eli N. Evans' widely read *The Provincials: A Personal History of the Jews in the South*, rev. ed. (New York, 1997); and a number of unpublished writings such as Abraham Isaacson's manuscript "Leaps and Bounds: From the Russian Ghetto to the Mississippi Delta," preserved on microfilm at the American Jewish Archives.

Deserving of special mention in the context of memoir literature is the volume *Jews in Small Towns: Legends and Legacies* (Santa Rosa, Calif., 1997), a collection of 140 autobiographical sketches assembled by Howard Epstein, a retired professor of social work with a small-town background himself. Epstein solicited the essays he gathered by placing notices in various Jewish periodicals during the 1990s. In publishing what he calls a record of "the thoughts and emotions of Jews who have had the experience of living in small towns," he fulfilled a "lifelong goal."[2] Although many of the autobiographical essays in Epstein's collection were prepared by people who grew up in small communities only in the latter decades of the twentieth century and many others reflect the experiences of individuals from towns in which there was no organized Jewish life at all, some did provide information about one or another of the small-town communities that are the focus of this study.

Similar to Epstein's volume are several other collections of transcribed oral histories relating to small-town Jewish communities. These include *Middletown Jews: The Tenuous Survival of an American Jewish Community*, edited by Dan Rottenberg (Bloomington, Ind., 1997), which preserves the recollections of Jewish residents of Muncie, Indiana; and *Listen to our Words: Oral Histories of the Jewish Community of Westmoreland County, Pennsylvania*, edited by Richard David Wissolik, Jennifer Campion, and Barbara Wissolik (Latrobe, Pa., 1997). Also to be mentioned in this connection is *A Storyteller's Worlds: The Education of Shlomo Noble in Europe and America* (New York, 1994), a volume based on author Jonathan Boyarin's conversations with Noble and including a fascinating chapter on Noble's experience in Beaver Falls, Pennsylvania. Related to published oral histories are those preserved in electronic media. Examples here include a set of audio tapes archived at Temple Adath Israel in Lexington, Kentucky; and a video project undertaken in 1984 by the United Synagogue Youth chapter of Congregation Beth Shalom in Modesto, California. Despite certain reservations I have about helping to create the evidence upon which I rely, I also conducted a limited number of oral history interviews of my own and asked several individuals to complete a questionnaire that I designed.

Essays in the two major English-language Jewish encyclopedias published during the first half of the twentieth century, especially those entries covering individual states, constitute yet another source from which I was able to glean information about small-town communities. These reference works are *The Jewish Encyclopedia,* published in New York between 1901 and 1916, and *The Universal Jewish Encyclopedia*, published in the same city in 1939–1943. As for many other topics in Jewish studies, the more recent *Encyclopaedia Judaica,* CD-ROM ed. (Jerusalem, 1997), was a helpful reference tool as well.

Various guidebooks published for Jewish travelers also proved to be important resources. These guidebooks provide the only available comprehensive listings of small-town congregations and other Jewish organizations at various points in time after 1919, when the *American Jewish Year Book* published its last all-inclusive directory of local Jewish institutions. Jewish guidebooks from the middle and late twentieth century include *A Jewish Tourist's Guide to the U.S.* (Philadelphia, 1954) and *Jewish Landmarks of New York* (New York, 1978), both authored by Bernard Postal and Lionel Koppman; *The Standard American-Jewish Directory, 1960* (n.p., 1960), published by Meyer Barkai; and *Traveling Jewish in America*, 3d ed. (Lodi, N.J., 1991), edited by Ellen Chernofsky.

Because my approach to research on small-town Jewry was so eclectic, many of the sources from which I gathered information defy easy classification. It is not easy to fit into standard categories items such as the *Membership List of the Union of Orthodox Rabbis of the United States and Canada,* published in New York in 1934; or the "Book of Remembrance," a manuscript volume prepared around 1960 and kept in the lobby of the B'nai Israel synagogue in

Kankakee, Illinois; or the forms completed in 1992 in order to list the Temple of Israel synagogue in Amsterdam, New York, on the National Register of Historic Places. Nonetheless, my use of these kinds of sources certainly deserves mention.

The study of any aspect of America's Jewish history must rely not only on sources of information related to that specific topic, but also on the treasure trove of secondary works that approach both American and Jewish history from other perspectives. Thus, I was able to learn a lot about small-town Jewish life from the works of various scholars in Jewish history who did not have an interest in smaller communities per se, but whose works illuminate some larger themes that have important implications for small-town Jewry. Examples include Andrew R. Heinze's *Adapting to Abundance: Jewish Immigrants, Mass Consumption, and the Search for American Identity* (New York, 1990); Shelly Tenenbaum's *A Credit to Their Community: Jewish Loan Societies in the United States, 1880–1945* (Detroit, 1993); Leonard Dinnerstein's *Antisemitism in America* (New York, 1994); Jack Glazier's *Dispersing the Ghetto: The Relocation of Jewish Immigrants across America* (Ithaca, N.Y., 1998); David Kaufman's *Shul with a Pool: The "Synagogue-Center" in American Jewish History* (Hanover, N.H., 1999); and Karla Goldman's *Beyond the Synagogue Gallery: Finding a Place for Women in American Judaism* (Cambridge, Mass., 2000).

Here should also be mentioned individual articles that helped put the small-town Jewish experience in context—contributions such as Jonathan D. Sarna's essays "The 'Mythical Jew' and the 'Jew Next Door' in Nineteenth-Century America" in *Anti-Semitism in American History,* edited by David A. Gerber (Urbana, Ill., 1986); and "The Debate over Mixed Seating in the American Synagogue," in *The American Synagogue: A Sanctuary Transformed,* edited by Jack Wertheimer (Cambridge, 1987); Jack Wertheimer's own "Pioneers of the Conservative Rabbinate: Reports from the Field by Graduates of 'Schechter's Seminary,'" *Conservative Judaism* 47 (spring 1995); and Clive Webb's "Jewish Merchants and Black Customers in the Age of Jim Crow," *Southern Jewish History* 2 (1999). Of the various surveys of American Jewish history that I consulted at one point or another, the most useful were Hasia R. Diner's *A Time for Gathering: The Second Migration, 1820–1880*; and Gerald Sorin's *A Time for Building: The Third Migration, 1880–1920,* two volumes in the series The Jewish People in America, edited by Henry L. Feingold (Baltimore, 1992).

The concerns of this study intersect in many places with subjects that are far from being of exclusively Jewish interest, and whenever I turned my attention to one such subject or another, I took advantage of the writings of many experts whose fundamental areas of scholarship are far from my own. In exploring the general character of small-town America, for example, I consulted analyses such as Park Dixon Goist's *From Main Street to State Street: Town, City, and Community in America* (Port Washington, N.Y., 1977); Richard

Lingeman's "The Small Town in America: The Recent Past, the Near Future," in *Change and Tradition in the American Small Town,* edited by Robert Craycroft and Michael Fazio (Jackson, Miss., 1983); and Richard Francaviglia's *Main Street Revisited: Time, Space, and Image Building in Small-Town America* (Iowa City, 1996). Similarly, in considering issues of xenophobia, I read works such as John Higham's *Strangers in the Land: Patterns of American Nativism, 1860–1925,* 2d ed. (New Brunswick, N.J., 1988); and Walter P. Zenner's *Minorities in the Middle: A Cross-Cultural Analysis* (Albany, N.Y., 1991). In order to understand the role of servants in American society, I consulted Daniel E. Sutherland's *Americans and their Servants: Domestic Service in the United States from 1800 to 1920* (Baton Rouge, La., 1981); and Phyllis Palmer's *Domesticity and Dirt: Housewives and Domestic Servants in the United States, 1920–1945* (Philadelphia, 1989).

Clearly, in considering the history of America's smaller Jewish settlements, there is much to be learned by comparing them with the country's large and midsize Jewish communities. Thus, I profited immensely from reading in the vast literature of local Jewish history covering more substantial Jewish centers. This literature includes some studies that deal with Jewish settlements only slightly larger than those treated in this volume, works such as Ewa Morawska's superlative book about Johnstown, Pennsylvania, *Insecure Prosperity: Small-Town Jews in Industrial America, 1890–1940* (Princeton, 1996); and Wendy Lowe Besmann's recent *A Separate Circle: Jewish Life in Knoxville, Tennessee* (Knoxville, 2001).[3] The literature of local Jewish history also includes studies that deal with more prominent midsize communities, volumes such as Louis J. Swichkow and Lloyd P. Gartner's *The History of the Jews of Milwaukee* (Philadelphia, 1963); Steven Hertzberg's *Strangers within the Gate City: The Jews of Atlanta, 1845–1915* (Philadelphia, 1978); Marc Lee Raphael's *Jews and Judaism in a Midwestern Community: Columbus, Ohio, 1840–1975* (Columbus, 1979); and Judith E. Endelman's *The Jewish Community of Indianapolis, 1849 to the Present* (Bloomington, Ind., 1984). The literature of local Jewish history also includes studies that focus on Jewish life in one or another of America's premier Jewish centers, books such as *The Making of an American Jewish Community: The History of Baltimore Jewry from 1773 to 1920,* by Isaac M. Fein (Philadelphia, 1971); and *The Jews of Boston: Essays on the Occasion of the Centenary (1895–1995) of the Combined Jewish Philanthropies of Greater Boston,* edited by Jonathan D. Sarna and Ellen Smith (Boston, 1995). Academic studies exploring the history of New York City's unique Jewish community constitute a separate category in its own right and range from pioneering publications such as Moses Rischin's *The Promised City: New York's Jews, 1870–1914* (Boston, 1962) to much newer offerings such as *Remembering the Lower East Side: American Jewish Reflections,* edited by Hasia Diner, Jeffrey Shandler, and Beth Wenger (Bloomington, Ind., 2000).

Finally, as a study produced at the turn of the twenty-first century, my project frequently took advantage of the resources available on the Internet. Many surviving small-town congregations have posted accounts of their own origins on their web sites, for example, and the annals of many smaller cities and towns are also on line. Those wishing to get a small taste of the vast amount of material available on the web to aid in the exploration of small-town Jewish history might visit a site such as "Virtual Restoration of Small-town Synagogues," http://geocities.com/txsynvr/txsyn.html; or individual web pages such as "My Grandfather's Butcher Shop," http://www.lihistory.com/specfam/fambreit.htm; or "Shapiro House," http://www.strawbery banke.org/museum/shapiro/shapiro.html.

# Appendix of Tables

### Table 1: The Triple-Digit Jewish Communities of the United States in 1927, with Reported Jewish Populations in Selected Years

| Town | State | Total Pop. 1920 | Reported Jewish Population | | | | | |
|---|---|---|---|---|---|---|---|---|
| | | | ca. 1878 | ca. 1907 | 1918 | 1927 | 1937 | ca. 1950 |
| Anniston | Ala. | 17,734 | | 250 | 220 | 125 | 90 | |
| Bessemer | Ala. | 18,674 | | 100 | 110 | 111 | 105 | 100 |
| Demopolis | Ala. | 2,779 | | 124 | 107 | 150 | 90 | |
| Gadsden | Ala. | 14,737 | | | 107 | 116 | 100 | |
| Mobile | Ala. | 60,777 | 566 | 1,000 | 2,200 | 950 | 1,050 | 850 |
| Selma | Ala. | 15,589 | 200 | 315 | 340 | 281 | 325 | 210 |
| Tuscaloosa | Ala. | 11,996 | 22 | 106 | 55 | 208 | 300 | 187 |
| Douglas | Ariz. | 9,916 | | 90 | 100 | 108 | 16 | |
| Phoenix | Ariz. | 29,053 | 6 | 75 | 150 | 425 | 1,000 | 4,300 |
| Tucson | Ariz. | 20,292 | | | 40 | 400 | 480 | 4,000 |
| El Dorado | Ark. | 3,887 | | | | 124 | 65 | |
| Fort Smith | Ark. | 28,870 | 66 | 200 | 300 | 420 | 350 | 370 |
| Helena | Ark. | 9,112 | 180 | 160 | 250 | 400 | 220 | 177 |
| Hot Springs | Ark. | 11,695 | | 225 | 309 | 250 | 325 | 300 |
| North Little Rock | Ark. | 14,048 | | | | 500 | 65 | |
| Pine Bluff | Ark. | 19,280 | 250 | 463 | 400 | 400 | 375 | 275 |
| Texarkana | Ark./Tex. | 19,737 | 44 | 150 | 350 | 375 | 160 | |
| Alameda | Calif. | 28,806 | | | 200 | 400 | 445 | 350 |
| Alhambra | Calif. | 9,096 | | | | 240 | 310 | 660 |
| Bakersfield | Calif. | 18,638 | 18 | | 125 | 240 | 425 | 600 |
| Berkeley | Calif. | 56,036 | | | 300 | 300 | 460 | 1,800 |
| Fresno | Calif. | 45,086 | | | 400 | 700 | 935 | 1,200 |
| Glendale | Calif. | 13,536 | | | | 200 | 930 | |
| Modesto | Calif. | 9,241 | 34 | | | 350 | 360 | 267 |
| Petaluma | Calif. | 6,226 | 86 | | | 500 | 340 | 600 |
| Piedmont | Calif. | 4,282 | | | | 150 | 100 | |
| Pomona | Calif. | 13,505 | | | | 125 | 130 | |
| San Bernardino | Calif. | 18,721 | 133 | 100 | 250 | 250 | 560 | 750 |
| San Jose | Calif. | 39,642 | 265 | 225 | 200 | 375 | 580 | 1,300 |
| San Mateo | Calif. | 5,979 | | | | 450 | 265 | |
| San Rafael | Calif. | 5,512 | 26 | | | 200 | 150 | |
| Santa Ana | Calif. | 15,485 | 12 | | 87 | 300 | 315 | 693 |
| Santa Barbara | Calif. | 19,441 | 20 | | | 150 | 275 | 400 |
| Santa Monica | Calif. | 15,252 | | | | 700 | 1,335 | 5,000 |
| Taft | Calif. | 3,317 | | | | 104 | 22 | |
| Colorado Springs | Colo. | 30,105 | | 188 | 660 | 500 | 550 | 400 |
| Greeley | Colo. | 10,958 | 3 | | | 100 | 96 | |
| Trinidad | Colo. | 10,906 | | 138 | 250 | 110 | 70 | |
| Bristol | Conn. | 20,620 | | | | 250 | 240 | 250 |
| Danbury | Conn. | 18,943 | 43 | 500 | 300 | 400 | 525 | 1,000 |
| Derby | Conn. | 11,238 | | | 250 | 150 | 200 | |
| Greenwich | Conn. | 5,939 | | | | 160 | 250 | 350 |
| Middletown | Conn. | 13,638 | 55 | | 128 | 565 | 510 | 1,000 |
| Putnam | Conn. | 7,711 | | | | 100 | 95 | 120 |

**Table 1:** *continued*

| Town | State | Total Pop. | Reported Jewish Population | | | | | |
|------|-------|-----------|----------|----------|------|------|------|---------|
| | | 1920 | ca. 1878 | ca. 1907 | 1918 | 1927 | 1937 | ca. 1950 |
| Torrington | Conn. | 20,623 | | | | 168 | 250 | 310 | |
| Wallingford | Conn. | 9,648 | | | | 200 | 120 | 280 | |
| Willimantic | Conn. | 12,330 | | | | 250 | 340 | 400 | 425 |
| Daytona Beach | Fla. | 6,841 | | | | | 250 | 390 | 800 |
| Orlando | Fla. | 9,282 | | | | | 290 | 550 | 1,000 |
| St. Augustine | Fla. | 6,192 | | | | 54 | 300 | 225 | 180 |
| St. Petersburg | Fla. | 14,237 | | | | | 100 | 510 | 1,800 |
| West Palm Beach | Fla. | 8,659 | | | | | 600 | 500 | 2,000 |
| Albany | Ga. | 11,555 | 100 | 238 | 265 | 275 | 290 | 350 |
| Athens | Ga. | 16,748 | 110 | 139 | 340 | 185 | 90 | |
| Augusta | Ga. | 52,548 | 240 | 313 | 2,500 | 970 | 950 | 600 |
| Bainbridge | Ga. | 4,792 | 53 | | 103 | 220 | 42 | |
| Brunswick | Ga. | 14,413 | | 200 | 138 | 120 | 84 | 108 |
| Columbus | Ga. | 31,125 | 275 | 543 | 300 | 700 | 735 | 550 |
| Macon | Ga. | 52,995 | 350 | 550 | 550 | 650 | 850 | 676 |
| Rome | Ga. | 13,252 | 46 | 102 | 250 | 225 | 200 | |
| Boise | Idaho | 21,393 | 34 | 51 | 200 | 316 | 300 | 170 |
| Pocatello | Idaho | 15,001 | | | | 120 | 50 | 114 |
| Alton | Ill. | 24,682 | | | 90 | 160 | 190 | 148 |
| Aurora | Ill. | 36,397 | | | 300 | 480 | 540 | 432 |
| Belleville | Ill. | 24,823 | 69 | | 150 | 206 | 250 | 165 |
| Bloomington | Ill. | 28,725 | 115 | 146 | 275 | 350 | 215 | 160 |
| Cairo | Ill. | 15,203 | 57 | 150 | 375 | 75 | 60 | |
| Champaign | Ill. | 15,873 | 83 | | 150 | 300 | 380 | 404 |
| Chicago Heights | Ill. | 19,653 | | 200 | | 325 | 320 | 400 |
| Cicero | Ill. | 44,995 | | | | 250 | 545 | |
| Danville | Ill. | 33,776 | | 175 | 625 | 335 | 380 | 250 |
| Elgin | Ill. | 27,454 | | | 500 | 300 | 565 | 480 |
| Evanston | Ill. | 37,234 | | | 250 | 315 | 460 | |
| Forest Park | Ill. | 10,768 | | | | 100 | 100 | |
| Galesburg | Ill. | 23,834 | 51 | 120 | 220 | 150 | 120 | 144 |
| Glencoe | Ill. | 3,381 | | | | 100 | 548 | |
| Granite City | Ill. | 14,757 | | | | 275 | 190 | |
| Highland Park | Ill. | 6,167 | | | | 125 | 956 | |
| Joliet | Ill. | 38,442 | 25 | 100 | 1,100 | 630 | 590 | 555 |
| Kankakee | Ill. | 16,026 | | | 260 | 120 | 215 | 272 |
| Maywood | Ill. | 12,072 | | | 700 | 400 | 1,040 | |
| North Chicago | Ill. | 5,839 | | | | 100 | 45 | |
| Quincy | Ill. | 35,978 | 500 | 126 | 400 | 350 | 235 | 152 |
| Rockford | Ill. | 65,651 | 28 | | 900 | 500 | 720 | 715 |
| Springfield | Ill. | 59,183 | 150 | 425 | 700 | 600 | 1,120 | 1,250 |
| Anderson | Ind. | 29,767 | 30 | | 150 | 150 | 100 | 100 |
| East Chicago | Ind. | 35,967 | | | | 220 | 780 | 1,000 |
| Elkhart | Ind. | 24,277 | 45 | | | 102 | 122 | 140 |
| Kokomo | Ind. | 30,067 | 20 | 75 | 130 | 100 | 90 | 181 |

**Table 1:** *continued*

| Town | State | Total Pop. 1920 | ca. 1878 | ca. 1907 | 1918 | 1927 | 1937 | ca. 1950 |
|------|-------|-----------------|----------|----------|------|------|------|----------|
| | | | Reported Jewish Population | | | | | |
| Lafayette | Ind. | 22,486 | 225 | 220 | 300 | 350 | 300 | 416 |
| Marion | Ind. | 23,747 | | 100 | 400 | 500 | 380 | 165 |
| Michigan City | Ind. | 19,457 | | 275 | 450 | 300 | 235 | 320 |
| Mishawaka | Ind. | 15,195 | | | | 159 | 155 | |
| Mount Vernon | Ind. | 5,284 | 86 | 114 | 85 | 120 | 23 | |
| Muncie | Ind. | 36,524 | | 96 | 200 | 131 | 135 | 340 |
| Valparaiso | Ind. | 6,518 | | | | 100 | 25 | |
| Wabash | Ind. | 9,872 | 100 | 174 | 150 | 150 | 53 | |
| Burlington | Iowa | 24,057 | 121 | 100 | 225 | 107 | 115 | |
| Cedar Rapids | Iowa | 45,566 | 6 | | 700 | 697 | 735 | 450 |
| Council Bluffs | Iowa | 36,162 | | | 1,000 | 600 | 535 | 450 |
| Davenport | Iowa | 56,727 | 204 | 227 | 600 | 690 | 710 | 850 |
| Dubuque | Iowa | 39,141 | 55 | 325 | 450 | 420 | 275 | 208 |
| Fort Dodge | Iowa | 19,347 | | | 155 | 140 | 110 | 116 |
| Iowa City | Iowa | 11,267 | 9 | | | 151 | 130 | 150 |
| Marshalltown | Iowa | 15,731 | 26 | | | 139 | 175 | 222 |
| Muscatine | Iowa | 16,068 | | | 429 | 300 | 215 | 120 |
| Waterloo | Iowa | 36,230 | 28 | | 325 | 385 | 420 | 556 |
| Leavenworth | Kans. | 16,912 | 455 | 350 | 600 | 800 | 420 | 160 |
| Topeka | Kans. | 50,022 | | 139 | 1,000 | 900 | 675 | 147 |
| Wichita | Kans. | 72,217 | 32 | 150 | 300 | 700 | 1,315 | 1,000 |
| Ashland | Ky. | 14,729 | | | 86 | 170 | 150 | 200 |
| Covington | Ky. | 57,121 | | | 350 | 500 | 350 | |
| Lexington | Ky. | 41,534 | 140 | 238 | 385 | 750 | 660 | 550 |
| Newport | Ky. | 29,317 | | | 300 | 600 | 475 | |
| Paducah | Ky. | 24,735 | 203 | 247 | 250 | 800 | 600 | 150 |
| Alexandria | La. | 17,510 | 206 | 600 | 450 | 560 | 585 | 660 |
| Baton Rouge | La. | 21,782 | 94 | 50 | 165 | 750 | 590 | 750 |
| Bogalusa | La. | 8,245 | | | 65 | 100 | 80 | |
| Lafayette | La. | 7,855 | | 57 | 63 | 100 | 110 | 194 |
| Lake Charles | La. | 13,088 | | 125 | 286 | 320 | 295 | 100 |
| Monroe | La. | 12,675 | 128 | 200 | 350 | 500 | 520 | 900 |
| Plaquemine | La. | 4,632 | 61 | 125 | 55 | 132 | 55 | |
| Auburn | Maine | 16,985 | | 175 | 300 | 480 | 825 | |
| Bath | Maine | 14,731 | | | 93 | 300 | 180 | 150 |
| Biddeford | Maine | 18,008 | | | | 325 | 250 | |
| Gardiner | Maine | 5,475 | | | 70 | 120 | 87 | |
| Hallowell | Maine | 2,764 | | | | 147 | | |
| Lewiston | Maine | 31,791 | 65 | 100 | 275 | 650 | 1,100 | 1,400 |
| Rockland | Maine | 8,109 | | | 150 | 100 | 90 | 130 |
| Rumford Falls | Maine | 7,016 | | | | 231 | 176 | |
| Waterville | Maine | 13,351 | 43 | | | 150 | 215 | 120 |
| Annapolis | Md. | 11,214 | | 150 | 240 | 300 | 570 | 1,000 |
| Cumberland | Md. | 29,837 | 140 | 183 | 600 | 720 | 820 | 510 |
| Frederick | Md. | 11,066 | 75 | | 144 | 102 | 125 | 150 |

**Table 1:** *continued*

| Town | State | Total Pop. 1920 | Reported Jewish Population | | | | | |
|------|-------|------|----------|----------|------|------|------|----------|
| | | | ca. 1878 | ca. 1907 | 1918 | 1927 | 1937 | ca. 1950 |
| Hagerstown | Md. | 28,064 | 42 | 231 | 250 | 650 | 445 | 306 |
| Athol | Mass. | 9,792 | | | 85 | 180 | 185 | 240 |
| Attleboro | Mass. | 19,731 | | | 530 | 200 | 130 | 180 |
| Chicopee | Mass. | 36,214 | | | 250 | 430 | 320 | |
| Clinton | Mass. | 12,979 | | | 185 | 105 | 100 | 120 |
| Everett | Mass. | 40,120 | | | 500 | 200 | 1,920 | |
| Fitchburg | Mass. | 41,029 | | 300 | 528 | 580 | 610 | |
| Framingham | Mass. | 17,033 | | | | 360 | 450 | 600 |
| Gardner | Mass. | 16,971 | | | 146 | 150 | 250 | 130 |
| Gloucester | Mass. | 22,947 | | | 243 | 260 | 200 | 280 |
| Greenfield | Mass. | 15,462 | | | | 185 | 250 | 250 |
| Hudson | Mass. | 7,607 | | | | 100 | 28 | |
| Leominster | Mass. | 19,744 | | | 210 | 120 | 185 | |
| Lexington | Mass. | 6,350 | | | 540 | 163 | 155 | |
| Longmeadow | Mass. | 2,618 | | | | 100 | 150 | |
| Maynard | Mass. | 7,086 | | | | 135 | 100 | |
| Medford | Mass. | 39,038 | | | 250 | 680 | 630 | |
| Medway | Mass. | 2,956 | | | 250 | 265 | 182 | 150 |
| Milford | Mass. | 13,471 | | | 130 | 220 | 300 | 450 |
| Newburyport | Mass. | 15,618 | | 150 | 149 | 300 | 290 | 320 |
| Newton | Mass. | 46,054 | | | 400 | 520 | 850 | |
| North Adams | Mass. | 22,282 | | 400 | 500 | 800 | 725 | 560 |
| Northampton | Mass. | 21,951 | | 150 | 400 | 500 | 560 | 300 |
| Norwood | Mass. | 12,627 | | | 80 | 140 | 125 | |
| Plymouth | Mass. | 13,045 | | | 510 | 132 | 231 | 220 |
| Saugus | Mass. | 10,874 | | | | 150 | 150 | |
| Stoughton | Mass. | 6,865 | | | 63 | 250 | 180 | |
| Swampscott | Mass. | 8,101 | | | | 150 | 150 | |
| Taunton | Mass. | 37,137 | | | 750 | 785 | 760 | 600 |
| Wakefield | Mass. | 13,025 | | | 114 | 105 | 100 | |
| Waltham | Mass. | 30,915 | | | 300 | 725 | 760 | |
| Watertown | Mass. | 21,457 | | | 60 | 102 | 190 | |
| Westfield | Mass. | 18,604 | | | 160 | 110 | 102 | |
| Woburn | Mass. | 16,574 | | | 153 | 100 | 75 | |
| Ann Arbor | Mich. | 19,516 | | | 300 | 150 | 200 | 240 |
| Bay City | Mich. | 47,554 | 153 | 900 | 1,000 | 695 | 770 | 736 |
| Benton Harbor | Mich. | 12,233 | | 432 | 580 | 800 | 870 | 830 |
| Escanaba | Mich. | 13,103 | 25 | | 83 | 115 | 95 | |
| Hamtramck | Mich. | 48,615 | | | | 575 | 640 | |
| Hancock | Mich. | 7,527 | 36 | 90 | 83 | 140 | 40 | |
| Iron Mountain | Mich. | 8,251 | | | | 130 | 90 | 104 |
| Ironwood | Mich. | 15,739 | | | | 228 | 200 | |
| Jackson | Mich. | 48,374 | 141 | | 300 | 250 | 200 | 200 |
| Kalamazoo | Mich. | 48,487 | 217 | 288 | 900 | 345 | 400 | 640 |
| Lansing | Mich. | 57,327 | | 32 | 450 | 200 | 500 | 550 |

**Table 1:** *continued*

| Town | State | Total Pop. 1920 | ca. 1878 | ca. 1907 | 1918 | 1927 | 1937 | ca. 1950 |
|---|---|---|---|---|---|---|---|---|
| Monroe | Mich. | 11,573 | | | 30 | 140 | 140 | |
| Mount Clemens | Mich. | 9,488 | 2 | | | 500 | 305 | 300 |
| Muskegon | Mich. | 36,570 | | 60 | 300 | 275 | 300 | 400 |
| Petoskey | Mich. | 5,064 | | 75 | 89 | 120 | 75 | |
| Pontiac | Mich. | 34,273 | | | | 375 | 550 | 700 |
| Port Huron | Mich. | 25,944 | | 60 | 500 | 180 | 220 | 130 |
| Saginaw | Mich. | 61,903 | 52 | 100 | 1,000 | 410 | 475 | 600 |
| South Haven | Mich. | 3,829 | | | | 250 | 300 | 450 |
| Chisolm | Minn. | 9,039 | | 85 | 83 | 134 | 125 | |
| Eveleth | Minn. | 7,205 | | | 110 | 200 | 125 | |
| Hibbing | Minn. | 15,089 | | 162 | 165 | 275 | 285 | 280 |
| Virginia | Minn. | 14,022 | | | 250 | 160 | 135 | 180 |
| Canton | Miss. | 3,252 | 150 | 100 | 75 | 108 | 85 | |
| Clarksdale | Miss. | 7,552 | | | 220 | 200 | 412 | 380 |
| Greenville | Miss. | 11,560 | 320 | 500 | 350 | 375 | 450 | 283 |
| Greenwood | Miss. | 7,793 | | 125 | 58 | 250 | 300 | 160 |
| Hattiesburg | Miss. | 13,270 | | | 125 | 148 | 215 | 184 |
| Jackson | Miss. | 22,817 | 88 | 108 | 126 | 169 | 235 | 300 |
| Meridian | Miss. | 23,399 | 160 | 394 | 400 | 575 | 350 | 250 |
| Natchez | Miss. | 12,608 | 220 | 513 | 261 | 151 | 125 | 153 |
| Vicksburg | Miss. | 18,072 | 520 | 688 | 532 | 467 | 378 | 280 |
| Columbia | Mo. | 10,392 | 25 | 36 | 175 | 115 | 115 | |
| Joplin | Mo. | 29,902 | 63 | 175 | 250 | 350 | 275 | 350 |
| Springfield | Mo. | 39,613 | | | 165 | 360 | 285 | 200 |
| Butte | Mont. | 41,611 | | 275 | 1,000 | 540 | 570 | 206 |
| Great Falls | Mont. | 24,121 | | | | 125 | 96 | |
| Fremont | Nebr. | 9,592 | 30 | | 100 | 130 | 110 | |
| Reno | Nev. | 12,016 | 89 | | | 164 | 245 | 350 |
| Berlin | N.H. | 16,104 | | | 117 | 250 | 275 | |
| Claremont | N.H. | 9,524 | | | | 100 | 177 | 200 |
| Concord | N.H. | 22,167 | 2 | | 158 | 120 | 75 | 160 |
| Laconia | N.H. | 10,897 | | | | 117 | 150 | 120 |
| Manchester | N.H. | 78,384 | | 650 | 600 | 935 | 1,150 | 1,485 |
| Nashua | N.H. | 28,379 | | 160 | 350 | 435 | 500 | 360 |
| Portsmouth | N.H. | 13,569 | 29 | 400 | 550 | 225 | 350 | 480 |
| Bergenfield | N.J. | 3,667 | | | | 150 | 110 | 260 |
| Boonton | N.J. | 5,372 | | | 50 | 128 | 212 | 195 |
| Bound Brook | N.J. | 5,906 | | | | 130 | 200 | 350 |
| Bridgeton | N.J. | 14,323 | 33 | | | 300 | 500 | 600 |
| Burlington | N.J. | 9,049 | | | 83 | 650 | 500 | 250 |
| Caldwell | N.J. | 3,776 | | | | 300 | 470 | 730 |
| Carteret | N.J. | 11,047 | | | 150 | 500 | 550 | 600 |
| Clifton | N.J. | 26,470 | | | | 625 | 900 | |
| Dover | N.J. | 9,803 | 35 | 125 | 300 | 800 | 580 | 700 |
| Edgewater | N.J. | 3,530 | | | | 120 | 120 | |

**Table 1:** *continued*

| Town | State | Total Pop. 1920 | Reported Jewish Population | | | | | |
|------|-------|----------------|---------------------------|--|--|--|--|--|
| | | | ca. 1878 | ca. 1907 | 1918 | 1927 | 1937 | ca. 1950 |
| Englewood | N.J. | 11,627 | 6 | | 99 | 750 | 650 | 2,500 |
| Freehold | N.J. | 4,768 | | | 36 | 400 | 600 | 500 |
| Garfield | N.J. | 19,381 | | | | 600 | 650 | |
| Glen Ridge | N.J. | 4,620 | | | 41 | 450 | 580 | |
| Guttenberg | N.J. | 6,726 | | | | 150 | 150 | |
| Hackensack | N.J. | 17,667 | | | 200 | 500 | 930 | 1,200 |
| Kearny | N.J. | 26,724 | | | | 750 | 1,200 | 302 |
| Keyport | N.J. | 4,415 | | 30 | 166 | 175 | 125 | 327 |
| Metuchen | N.J. | 3,334 | | | | 105 | 200 | 250 |
| Millville | N.J. | 14,691 | 9 | | 170 | 560 | 310 | 260 |
| Montclair | N.J. | 28,810 | | | 75 | 450 | 750 | 890 |
| Morristown | N.J. | 12,548 | | | 40 | 850 | 930 | 1,000 |
| Newton | N.J. | 4,125 | | | 44 | 100 | 75 | 232 |
| Palisades Park | N.J. | 2,633 | | | | 400 | 250 | 400 |
| Pennsgrove | N.J. | 6,060 | | | | 103 | 70 | |
| Pleasantville | N.J. | 5,887 | | | | 150 | 200 | |
| Princeton | N.J. | 5,917 | | | | 100 | 160 | 300 |
| Rahway | N.J. | 11,042 | | | 93 | 500 | 375 | 800 |
| Red Bank | N.J. | 9,251 | | | 500 | 520 | 850 | 1,200 |
| Ridgefield Park | N.J. | 8,575 | | | 30 | 220 | 200 | 410 |
| Roselle | N.J. | 5,737 | | | | 150 | 900 | |
| Salem | N.J. | 7,435 | 2 | | | 168 | 220 | 235 |
| Somerville | N.J. | 6,718 | | 120 | 250 | 600 | 500 | 634 |
| South Amboy | N.J. | 7,897 | | | 74 | 115 | 125 | 145 |
| South River | N.J. | 6,596 | | | | 375 | 400 | 400 |
| Summit | N.J. | 10,174 | | | | 115 | 200 | 400 |
| Vineland | N.J. | 6,432 | | 225 | | 700 | 950 | 2,000 |
| Westfield | N.J. | 9,063 | | | 80 | 140 | 150 | |
| West Orange | N.J. | 15,573 | | | | 560 | 540 | |
| Wildwood | N.J. | 2,790 | | | | 400 | 425 | 360 |
| Albuquerque | N.Mex. | 15,157 | | 165 | 220 | 240 | 450 | 850 |
| Amsterdam | N.Y. | 33,524 | | 250 | 300 | 720 | 655 | 500 |
| Auburn | N.Y. | 36,192 | | 80 | 250 | 480 | 340 | 275 |
| Babylon | N.Y. | 2,523 | | | | 200 | 135 | |
| Baldwinsville | N.Y. | 3,685 | | | | 260 | | |
| Batavia | N.Y. | 13,541 | | | 141 | 126 | 160 | 300 |
| Beacon | N.Y. | 10,996 | | | | 200 | 335 | 525 |
| Catskill | N.Y. | 4,728 | 16 | | | 200 | 240 | 240 |
| Cedarhurst | N.Y. | 2,838 | | | | 900 | 1,350 | |
| Cohoes | N.Y. | 22,987 | 27 | | 200 | 142 | 110 | 100 |
| Dunkirk | N.Y. | 19,336 | 25 | | 164 | 112 | 75 | 168 |
| Ellenville | N.Y. | 3,116 | | | 330 | 425 | 540 | 800 |
| Endicott | N.Y. | 12,803 | | | | 120 | 220 | |
| Freeport | N.Y. | 8,599 | | | 300 | 950 | 1,440 | |
| Glen Cove | N.Y. | 8,664 | | | 281 | 350 | 280 | |

**Table 1:** *continued*

| Town | State | Total Pop. 1920 | Reported Jewish Population | | | | | |
|---|---|---|---|---|---|---|---|---|
| | | | ca. 1878 | ca. 1907 | 1918 | 1927 | 1937 | ca. 1950 |
| Glens Falls | N.Y. | 16,638 | 27 | 100 | 500 | 560 | 630 | 962 |
| Hastings-on-Hudson | N.Y. | 5,526 | | | | 130 | 110 | |
| Haverstraw | N.Y. | 5,226 | | 232 | 220 | 450 | 360 | 420 |
| Hempstead | N.Y. | 6,382 | | | 88 | 250 | 1,185 | |
| Hoosick Falls | N.Y. | 4,896 | | | 87 | 100 | 55 | |
| Hudson | N.Y. | 11,745 | 105 | | 450 | 680 | 700 | 700 |
| Ithaca | N.Y. | 17,004 | 55 | 110 | 221 | 200 | 424 | 400 |
| Jamestown | N.Y. | 38,917 | 8 | | 125 | 150 | 170 | 260 |
| Lawrence | N.Y. | 2,861 | | | | 200 | 1,100 | |
| Little Falls | N.Y. | 13,029 | 49 | | 150 | 112 | 90 | 212 |
| Mamaroneck | N.Y. | 6,571 | | | 72 | 350 | 750 | |
| Massena | N.Y. | 5,993 | | | | 102 | 150 | 108 |
| Middletown | N.Y. | 18,420 | | | 153 | 520 | 950 | 1,100 |
| Mount Kisco | N.Y. | 3,944 | | | 29 | 225 | 350 | |
| Nyack | N.Y. | 4,444 | 28 | | | 250 | 275 | 276 |
| Ogdensburg | N.Y. | 14,609 | 100 | 75 | 55 | 150 | 140 | 180 |
| Olean | N.Y. | 20,506 | | 109 | 150 | 175 | 250 | 330 |
| Ossining | N.Y. | 10,739 | | 120 | 114 | 300 | 655 | |
| Oswego | N.Y. | 23,626 | 45 | | 31 | 125 | 120 | 108 |
| Patchogue | N.Y. | 4,031 | | 150 | 500 | 625 | 685 | |
| Plattsburgh | N.Y. | 10,909 | 125 | 125 | 205 | 416 | 240 | 370 |
| Port Chester | N.Y. | 16,573 | | 300 | 1,000 | 850 | 2,200 | 2,700 |
| Port Jervis | N.Y. | 10,171 | | | 150 | 260 | 200 | 400 |
| Rockville Center | N.Y. | 6,262 | | | | 505 | 1,600 | 5,176 |
| Rome | N.Y. | 26,341 | 20 | | 250 | 257 | 165 | 240 |
| Saranac Lake | N.Y. | 5,174 | | | | 300 | 335 | 100 |
| Saratoga Springs | N.Y. | 13,181 | 35 | 40 | 126 | 250 | 450 | 500 |
| Spring Valley | N.Y. | 3,818 | | | 28 | 900 | 1,335 | 2,100 |
| Suffern | N.Y. | 3,154 | | | | 250 | 325 | 544 |
| Tarrytown | N.Y. | 5,807 | 38 | | 400 | 500 | 625 | |
| Watertown | N.Y. | 31,285 | 9 | 160 | 230 | 450 | 460 | 460 |
| Asheville | N.C. | 28,504 | | 100 | 250 | 700 | 950 | 600 |
| Charlotte | N.C. | 46,338 | 104 | | 350 | 400 | 720 | 770 |
| Durham | N.C. | 21,719 | | 200 | 500 | 375 | 360 | 360 |
| Fayetteville | N.C. | 8,877 | 52 | | | 116 | 148 | 228 |
| Goldsboro | N.C. | 11,296 | 147 | 188 | 165 | 120 | 143 | 135 |
| Greensboro | N.C. | 19,861 | | 150 | 187 | 400 | 535 | 525 |
| Henderson | N.C. | 5,222 . | | | | 190 | 35 | |
| Hendersonville | N.C. | 3,720 | | | | 115 | 103 | |
| High Point | N.C. | 14,302 | | | | 101 | 210 | 215 |
| Raleigh | N.C. | 24,418 | 78 | 39 | 120 | 150 | 334 | 350 |
| Wilmington | N.C. | 33,372 | 200 | 850 | 400 | 390 | 330 | 303 |
| Wilson | N.C. | 10,612 | 16 | | | 140 | 70 | |
| Winston-Salem | N.C. | 48,395 | | | 116 | 325 | 315 | 340 |
| Bismarck | N.Dak. | 7,122 | | | 22 | 400 | 300 | 114 |

**Table 1:** *continued*

| Town | State | Total Pop. 1920 | Reported Jewish Population | | | | | |
|------|-------|------|------|------|------|------|------|------|
| | | | ca. 1878 | ca. 1907 | 1918 | 1927 | 1937 | ca. 1950 |
| Devils Lake | N.Dak. | 5,004 | | | | 180 | 51 | |
| Fargo | N.Dak. | 21,961 | | 250 | 600 | 500 | 473 | 442 |
| Grand Forks | N.Dak. | 14,010 | | 250 | 124 | 350 | 485 | 240 |
| Minot | N.Dak. | 10,476 | | | 61 | 130 | 128 | 110 |
| Alliance | Ohio | 21,603 | 50 | | 100 | 208 | 175 | |
| Barberton | Ohio | 18,811 | | | | 220 | 190 | |
| Bellaire | Ohio | 15,061 | 64 | 220 | 440 | 300 | 275 | 260 |
| East Cleveland | Ohio | 27,292 | | | | 850 | 1,160 | |
| East Liverpool | Ohio | 21,411 | | | 300 | 500 | 535 | 365 |
| Elyria | Ohio | 20,474 | | | 148 | 310 | 475 | 360 |
| Geneva | Ohio | 3,081 | | | | 152 | 100 | |
| Hamilton | Ohio | 39,675 | 110 | 150 | 260 | 450 | 410 | 418 |
| Lakewood | Ohio | 41,732 | | | | 555 | 555 | |
| Lima | Ohio | 41,326 | 47 | 147 | 300 | 400 | 420 | 418 |
| Lorain | Ohio | 37,295 | | 150 | 300 | 975 | 935 | 715 |
| Mansfield | Ohio | 27,824 | 28 | 50 | 50 | 160 | 270 | 308 |
| Marietta | Ohio | 15,140 | | | 80 | 100 | 80 | |
| Massillon | Ohio | 17,428 | | | 138 | 128 | 130 | 130 |
| Middletown | Ohio | 23,594 | | 52 | 225 | 215 | 310 | 310 |
| Norwood | Ohio | 24,966 | | | | 200 | 215 | |
| Portsmouth | Ohio | 33,011 | 84 | 105 | 128 | 200 | 175 | 196 |
| Springfield | Ohio | 60,840 | 148 | 250 | 400 | 580 | 475 | 550 |
| Steubenville | Ohio | 28,508 | 37 | 200 | 400 | 920 | 1,000 | 780 |
| Warren | Ohio | 27,050 | | | | 710 | 635 | 800 |
| Wooster | Ohio | 8,204 | | | | 101 | 150 | 135 |
| Zanesville | Ohio | 29,569 | 100 | 150 | 250 | 260 | 370 | 300 |
| Muskogee | Okla. | 30,277 | | | 225 | 200 | 155 | 150 |
| Okmulgee | Okla. | 17,430 | | | | 125 | 100 | |
| Aliquippa | Pa. | 2,931 | | | 300 | 115 | 410 | 400 |
| Ambridge | Pa. | 12,730 | | | | 200 | 290 | 300 |
| Beaver Falls | Pa. | 12,802 | | | 121 | 300 | 415 | |
| Berwick | Pa. | 12,181 | | | 157 | 100 | 90 | |
| Bradford | Pa. | 15,525 | | 400 | 560 | 400 | 250 | 416 |
| Bristol | Pa. | 10,273 | | | 92 | 120 | 125 | 161 |
| Brownsville | Pa. | 2,502 | | | | 400 | 450 | 250 |
| Butler | Pa. | 23,778 | | 150 | 150 | 300 | 325 | 500 |
| Canonsburg | Pa. | 10,632 | | | | 240 | 330 | 240 |
| Carbondale | Pa. | 18,640 | 26 | | 1,000 | 600 | 750 | 320 |
| Carnegie | Pa. | 11,516 | | | 320 | 422 | 335 | 268 |
| Chambersburg | Pa. | 13,171 | 19 | | 90 | 100 | 70 | 205 |
| Charleroi | Pa. | 11,516 | | | 75 | 300 | 225 | 144 |
| Clearfield | Pa. | 8,529 | | | 68 | 180 | 50 | |
| Coatesville | Pa. | 14,515 | | | 300 | 675 | 630 | 400 |
| Collingdale | Pa. | 3,834 | | | | 110 | 110 | |
| Connellsville | Pa. | 13,804 | | | 383 | 100 | 150 | 160 |

**Table 1:** *continued*

| Town | State | Total Pop. 1920 | Reported Jewish Population | | | | | |
|------|-------|-----------------|----------|----------|------|------|------|---------|
| | | | ca. 1878 | ca. 1907 | 1918 | 1927 | 1937 | ca. 1950 |
| Coraopolis | Pa. | 6,162 | | | | 200 | 180 | 152 |
| Danville | Pa. | 6,952 | 132 | 150 | 104 | 140 | 55 | |
| Darby | Pa. | 7,922 | | | | 190 | 355 | |
| Dickson City | Pa. | 11,049 | | | 174 | 150 | 175 | |
| Donora | Pa. | 14,131 | | 164 | 81 | 800 | 400 | 160 |
| Dubois | Pa. | 13,681 | | | 186 | 240 | 200 | 240 |
| Dunmore | Pa. | 20,250 | | | 109 | 218 | 165 | |
| Duquesne | Pa. | 19,011 | | | 350 | 920 | 750 | 230 |
| East Pittsburgh | Pa. | 6,527 | | | | 500 | 640 | 660 |
| East Stroudsburg | Pa. | 4,855 | | | | 180 | 240 | |
| Ellwood City | Pa. | 8,958 | | | 39 | 150 | 120 | 147 |
| Exeter | Pa. | 4,176 | | | 198 | 150 | 180 | |
| Farrell | Pa. | 15,586 | | 275 | 550 | 500 | 690 | |
| Glassport | Pa. | 6,959 | | | 120 | 140 | 210 | 120 |
| Greensburg | Pa. | 15,033 | | 250 | 130 | 450 | 480 | 440 |
| Greenville | Pa. | 8,101 | 18 | | | 391 | 35 | |
| Grove City | Pa. | 4,944 | | | | 121 | 20 | |
| Indiana | Pa. | 7,043 | 3 | | | 106 | 165 | 130 |
| Jeannette | Pa. | 10,627 | | | 80 | 200 | 360 | 200 |
| Jenkintown | Pa. | 3,366 | | | | 250 | 250 | |
| Kingston | Pa. | 15,286 | | | | 400 | 550 | |
| Kittanning | Pa. | 7,153 | | | 145 | 109 | 167 | |
| Lansdowne | Pa. | 4,797 | | | | 200 | 200 | |
| Latrobe | Pa. | 9,484 | | | 87 | 100 | 100 | 130 |
| Lebanon | Pa. | 24,643 | 37 | | 100 | 135 | 570 | 582 |
| Lehighton | Pa. | 6,102 | | | 53 | 325 | 85 | |
| Lewistown | Pa. | 9,849 | 29 | | 81 | 150 | 235 | 250 |
| Lock Haven | Pa. | 8,557 | | | 200 | 125 | 360 | 350 |
| Luzerne | Pa. | 5,998 | | | 131 | 140 | | |
| Mahanoy City | Pa. | 15,599 | 18 | | 244 | 200 | 175 | 100 |
| McKees Rocks | Pa. | 16,713 | | | 220 | 240 | 330 | 260 |
| Media | Pa. | 4,109 | | | 157 | 110 | | |
| Middletown | Pa. | 5,920 | | 75 | 85 | 100 | 55 | |
| Minersville | Pa. | 7,845 | 19 | | | 140 | 75 | |
| Monessen | Pa. | 18,179 | | | 265 | 280 | 250 | |
| Monongahela City | Pa. | 8,688 | | | 142 | 65 | | |
| Mount Carmel | Pa. | 17,469 | | | 550 | 325 | 210 | 272 |
| Mount Pleasant | Pa. | 5,862 | | | 197 | 175 | | |
| Nanticoke | Pa. | 22,614 | | | 150 | 200 | 220 | |
| New Castle | Pa. | 44,938 | 50 | 110 | 610 | 750 | 850 | 800 |
| New Kensington | Pa. | 11,987 | | | 375 | 640 | 735 | 640 |
| Norristown | Pa. | 32,319 | | | 220 | 750 | 675 | 560 |
| Oil City | Pa. | 21,274 | 58 | 320 | 380 | 500 | 375 | 360 |
| Olyphant | Pa. | 10,236 | | | 280 | 600 | 525 | |
| Philipsburg | Pa. | 3,900 | | | 35 | 140 | 135 | 136 |

**Table 1:** *continued*

| Town | State | Total Pop. | Reported Jewish Population | | | | | |
|------|-------|-----------|------|------|------|------|------|------|
| | | 1920 | ca. 1878 | ca. 1907 | 1918 | 1927 | 1937 | ca. 1950 |
| Phoenixville | Pa. | 10,484 | 9 | | 220 | 128 | 100 | 202 |
| Pittston | Pa. | 18,497 | | 150 | 320 | 160 | 425 | |
| Plymouth | Pa. | 16,500 | 40 | 90 | | 165 | 275 | |
| Pottstown | Pa. | 17,431 | 26 | | 328 | 700 | 635 | 450 |
| Punxsutawney | Pa. | 10,311 | | 200 | 275 | 125 | 90 | |
| Shamokin | Pa. | 21,204 | 43 | | 235 | 450 | 235 | 250 |
| Sharon | Pa. | 21,747 | 89 | 50 | 500 | 700 | 585 | |
| Shenandoah | Pa. | 24,726 | | | 550 | 600 | 563 | 444 |
| South Brownsville | Pa. | 4,675 | | | | 500 | 275 | |
| Steelton | Pa. | 13,428 | | | 250 | 200 | 95 | |
| Stroudsburg | Pa. | 5,278 | 5 | | | 100 | 115 | 226 |
| Sunbury | Pa. | 15,721 | 30 | | 150 | 300 | 230 | 160 |
| Swissvale | Pa. | 10,908 | | | 375 | 150 | 200 | |
| Swoyersville | Pa. | 6,876 | | | | 125 | 110 | |
| Tamaqua | Pa. | 12,363 | | | | 125 | 100 | |
| Tarentum | Pa. | 8,925 | | | | 300 | 180 | 160 |
| Titusville | Pa. | 8,432 | 500 | | 205 | 400 | 175 | 120 |
| Washington | Pa. | 21,480 | | 200 | 400 | 575 | 450 | 500 |
| West Chester | Pa. | 11,717 | | | 117 | 350 | 450 | 360 |
| Wilkensburg | Pa. | 24,403 | | | 125 | 200 | 300 | |
| Williamsport | Pa. | 36,198 | 158 | 215 | 350 | 500 | 825 | 800 |
| York | Pa. | 47,512 | 101 | 300 | 700 | 750 | 935 | 1,000 |
| Bristol | R.I. | 11,375 | | | 300 | 200 | 60 | |
| Cranston | R.I. | 29,407 | | | 400 | 400 | 220 | |
| Newport | R.I. | 30,255 | | 163 | 500 | 750 | 950 | 750 |
| Pawtucket | R.I. | 64,248 | | 200 | 500 | 570 | 1,100 | 1,300 |
| Camden | S.C. | 3,930 | 80 | | 75 | 108 | 67 | |
| Columbia | S.C. | 37,524 | 100 | 150 | 281 | 590 | 680 | 500 |
| Georgetown | S.C. | 4,579 | 54 | 65 | 60 | 135 | 100 | |
| Greenville | S.C. | 23,127 | 35 | | | 195 | 183 | 260 |
| Sumter | S.C. | 9,508 | 89 | 158 | 300 | 200 | 235 | 250 |
| Aberdeen | S.Dak. | 14,537 | | | 150 | 130 | 180 | 107 |
| Sioux Falls | S.Dak. | 25,202 | | | 200 | 210 | 425 | 350 |
| Bristol | Tenn./Va. | 14,776 | | 110 | 125 | 203 | 107 | |
| Brownsville | Tenn. | 3,062 | 92 | 74 | 28 | 100 | 60 | |
| Jackson | Tenn. | 18,860 | 46 | | 160 | 188 | 110 | 155 |
| Austin | Tex. | 34,876 | 100 | 213 | 300 | 490 | 575 | 750 |
| Corpus Christi | Tex. | 10,522 | | 60 | 110 | 200 | 645 | 1,100 |
| Corsicana | Tex. | 11,356 | 90 | 380 | 200 | 330 | 360 | 188 |
| Laredo | Tex. | 22,710 | | | 93 | 128 | 175 | 184 |
| Marshall | Tex. | 14,271 | 113 | 200 | 135 | 170 | 130 | |
| Mercedes | Tex. | 3,414 | | | | 250 | 315 | |
| Palestine | Tex. | 11,039 | 58 | | 95 | 120 | 56 | |
| Port Arthur | Tex. | 22,251 | | | 110 | 173 | 250 | 248 |
| Tyler | Tex. | 12,085 | | 257 | 350 | 500 | 650 | 450 |

**Table 1:** *continued*

| Town | State | Total Pop. 1920 | Reported Jewish Population | | | | | |
|------|-------|------|------|------|------|------|------|------|
| | | | ca. 1878 | ca. 1907 | 1918 | 1927 | 1937 | ca. 1950 |
| Wichita Falls | Tex. | 40,079 | | | | 505 | 385 | 276 |
| Ogden | Utah | 32,804 | | 75 | 125 | 290 | 175 | |
| Bennington | Vt. | 7,230 | | | 103 | 175 | 102 | 120 |
| Burlington | Vt. | 22,779 | | 575 | 850 | 900 | 1,000 | 1,000 |
| Montpelier | Vt. | 7,125 | 2 | | 100 | 100 | 75 | |
| Rutland | Vt. | 14,954 | 24 | | 134 | 160 | 250 | 280 |
| Alexandria | Va. | 18,060 | | 116 | 72 | 140 | 700 | 650 |
| Charlottesville | Va. | 10,688 | 100 | 91 | 50 | 112 | 85 | 120 |
| Danville | Va. | 21,539 | 68 | 114 | 150 | 180 | 290 | 200 |
| Hampton | Va. | 6,138 | | 110 | 80 | 144 | 145 | 175 |
| Harrisonburg | Va. | 5,875 | 67 | 116 | 102 | 105 | 104 | 112 |
| Lynchburg | Va. | 30,070 | 100 | 195 | 300 | 425 | 520 | 204 |
| Petersburg | Va. | 31,012 | 163 | 61 | 400 | 705 | 393 | 500 |
| Roanoke | Va. | 50,842 | | 175 | 300 | 455 | 470 | 650 |
| Staunton | Va. | 10,623 | | 43 | 85 | 108 | 70 | |
| Suffolk | Va. | 9,123 | | | | 114 | 135 | 180 |
| Bellingham | Wash. | 25,585 | | | 250 | 200 | 154 | 148 |
| Everett | Wash. | 27,644 | | | 150 | 500 | 135 | 125 |
| Bluefield | W.Va. | 15,282 | | | 152 | 220 | 210 | 300 |
| Clarksburg | W.Va. | 27,869 | | | 245 | 235 | 300 | 270 |
| Fairmont | W.Va. | 17,851 | 3 | | 95 | 140 | 235 | 160 |
| Logan | W.Va. | 2,998 | | | | 116 | 83 | |
| Martinsburg | W.Va. | 12,515 | 8 | | | 304 | 120 | |
| Morgantown | W.Va. | 12,127 | | | 120 | 250 | 132 | 211 |
| Parkersburg | W.Va. | 20,050 | 77 | 100 | 440 | 392 | 125 | 100 |
| Wheeling | W.Va. | 56,208 | 300 | 475 | 1,000 | 750 | 1,150 | 800 |
| Williamson | W.Va. | 6,819 | | | | 128 | 135 | 173 |
| Appleton | Wis. | 19,561 | 143 | 194 | 140 | 215 | 510 | 573 |
| Beloit | Wis. | 21,284 | | | 167 | 125 | 150 | 160 |
| Eau Clair | Wis. | 20,906 | 19 | | 183 | 280 | 55 | 158 |
| Fond du Lac | Wis. | 23,427 | | | 5 | 142 | 175 | 160 |
| Green Bay | Wis. | 31,017 | | 200 | 300 | 350 | 440 | 448 |
| Kenosha | Wis. | 40,472 | | | 200 | 900 | 950 | 600 |
| La Crosse | Wis. | 30,421 | 106 | 150 | 235 | 190 | 200 | 166 |
| Manitowoc | Wis. | 17,563 | | | 130 | 160 | 167 | 184 |
| Marinette | Wis. | 13,610 | | | 275 | 220 | 180 | 158 |
| Oshkosh | Wis. | 33,162 | | 100 | 100 | 135 | 195 | 160 |
| Racine | Wis. | 58,593 | | 300 | 400 | 735 | 850 | 850 |
| Wausau | Wis. | 18,951 | | 90 | 225 | 200 | 250 | 151 |
| West Allis | Wis. | 13,745 | | | | 100 | 125 | |
| Cheyenne | Wyo. | 13,829 | 40 | 300 | 113 | 800 | 650 | |

*Total population figures for 1920 are from U.S. Bureau of the Census,* Abstract of the Fourteenth
Census of the United States *(1923; reprint, New York, 1976), supplemented by idem,* Abstract of the
Fifteenth Census of the United States *(1933; reprint, New York, 1976). All towns listed are urban places as*

*defined in the U.S. Census of 1920. The names of the towns given, their boundaries, and their populations are as they were in 1927. A blank space indicates that population information for the town in question is unavailable.*

*Jewish population figures for ca. 1878 are from Union of American Hebrew Congregations, Statistics of the Jews of the United States (Philadelphia, 1880). An 1878 Jewish population of 100 has been estimated for Wabash, Ind.; Ogdensburg, N.Y.; Zanesville, Ohio; Columbia, S.C.; and Austin, Texas, simply because each of these towns is listed in Statistics of the Jews even though no population data are provided and because each was home to a Jewish congregation. The population figure given for Mobile, Ala., is based on ambiguous data in the Statistics.*

*Jewish population figures for ca. 1907 are from The Jewish Encyclopedia, s.v. "United States," 371–74; and American Jewish Year Book (AJYB) 9 (1907–08): 123–430. In cases in which divergent population figures are reported in these two sources, the figures provided have been averaged. Jewish population figures for 1918 are from AJYB 20 (1918–19): 52–65; and AJYB 21 (1919–20): 337–583. Jewish population figures for 1927 are from AJYB 30 (1928–29): 180–96; and AJYB 31 (1929–30): 223–31. When the population figures in these two sources do not agree, the figure published in 1928 is provided. Jewish population figures for 1937 are from AJYB 42 (1940–41): 239–65 and figures for ca. 1950 are from AJYB 52 (1951): 17–21.*

**Table 2: Number of Triple-Digit and Larger Jewish Communities in the United States, 1927, by Region and State**

| Region | State | Triple-Digit Communities | % of Total | Larger Communities | % of Total | Jewish population | % of Total |
|---|---|---|---|---|---|---|---|
| New England | Connecticut | 9 | | 11 | | 91,538 | |
| | Maine | 9 | | 2 | | 8,480 | |
| | Massachusetts | 33 | | 23 | | 225,634 | |
| | New Hampshire | 7 | | 0 | | 2,779 | |
| | Rhode Island | 4 | | 2 | | 25,003 | |
| | Vermont | 4 | | 0 | | 2,036 | |
| Regional Totals | | 66 | 13 | 38 | 19 | 355,470 | 8 |
| Middle Atlantic | New Jersey | 40 | | 24 | | 225,306 | |
| | New York | 45 | | 22 | | 1,903,890 | |
| | Pennsylvania | 84 | | 20 | | 404,979 | |
| Regional Totals | | 169 | 34 | 66 | 34 | 2,534,175 | 60 |
| South Atlantic | Delaware | 0 | | 1 | | 5,310 | |
| | Dist. of Columbia | 0 | | 1 | | 16,000 | |
| | Florida | 5 | | 4 | | 13,402 | |
| | Georgia | 8 | | 2 | | 23,179 | |
| | Maryland | 4 | | 1 | | 70,871 | |
| | North Carolina | 13 | | 0 | | 8,252 | |
| | South Carolina | 5 | | 1 | | 6,851 | |
| | Virginia | 10 | | 4 | | 25,656 | |
| | West Virginia | 9 | | 2 | | 7,471 | |
| Regional Totals | | 54 | 11 | 16 | 8 | 176,992 | 4 |
| East North Central | Illinois | 23 | | 6 | | 345,980 | |
| | Indiana | 12 | | 7 | | 27,244 | |
| | Michigan | 19 | | 4 | | 89,462 | |
| | Ohio | 22 | | 9 | | 173,976 | |
| | Wisconsin | 13 | | 4 | | 35,935 | |
| Regional Totals | | 89 | 18 | 30 | 15 | 672,597 | 16 |
| East South Central | Alabama | 7 | | 2 | | 12,891 | |
| | Kentucky | 5 | | 1 | | 19,533 | |
| | Mississippi | 9 | | 0 | | 6,420 | |
| | Tennessee | 3 | | 4 | | 22,532 | |
| Regional Totals | | 24 | 5 | 7 | 4 | 61,376 | 1 |
| W. North Central | Iowa | 10 | | 3 | | 16,404 | |
| | Kansas | 3 | | 1 | | 7,792 | |
| | Minnesota | 4 | | 3 | | 43,197 | |
| | Missouri | 3 | | 3 | | 80,687 | |
| | Nebraska | 1 | | 2 | | 14,209 | |
| | North Dakota | 5 | | 0 | | 2,749 | |
| | South Dakota | 2 | | 0 | | 1,584 | |
| Regional Totals | | 28 | 6 | 12 | 6 | 166,622 | 4 |

**Table 2:** *continued*

| Region | State | Triple-Digit Communities | % of Total | Larger Communities | % of Total | Jewish population | % of Total |
|---|---|---|---|---|---|---|---|
| West South Central | Arkansas | 7 | | 1 | | 8,850 | |
| | Louisiana | 7 | | 2 | | 16,432 | |
| | Oklahoma | 2 | | 2 | | 7,823 | |
| | Texas | 10 | | 8 | | 46,648 | |
| Regional Totals | | 26 | 5 | 13 | 7 | 79,753 | 2 |
| Mountain | Arizona | 3 | | 0 | | 1,455 | |
| | Colorado | 3 | | 2 | | 20,321 | |
| | Idaho | 2 | | 0 | | 1,141 | |
| | Montana | 2 | | 0 | | 1,578 | |
| | Nevada | 1 | | 0 | | 264 | |
| | New Mexico | 1 | | 0 | | 1,052 | |
| | Utah | 1 | | 1 | | 2,854 | |
| | Wyoming | 1 | | 0 | | 1,319 | |
| Regional Totals | | 14 | 3 | 3 | 2 | 29,984 | 1 |
| Pacific | California | 18 | | 8 | | 123,284 | |
| | Oregon | 0 | | 1 | | 13,075 | |
| | Washington | 2 | | 3 | | 14,698 | |
| Regional Totals | | 20 | 4 | 12 | 6 | 151,057 | 4 |
| Grand Totals | | 490 | 99 | 197 | 101 | 4,228,026 | 100 |

The number of triple-digit Jewish communities in the United States and the number of communities of 1,000 or more is calculated from information in AJYB 30 (1928–29): 180–96; and AJYB 31 (1929–30): 223–31. When the population figures in these two sources do not agree, the figure published in 1928 has been used. The regions indicated are those designated by the U.S. Bureau of the Census for 1920. State-by-state Jewish population figures for 1927 are from AJYB 42 (1940–41): 227–28. Grand totals of percentages may not equal 100 because of rounding.

**Table 3: The Triple-Digit Jewish Communities of the United States, ca. 1878, with Reported Jewish Populations in Selected Years**

| Town | State | Total Pop. 1880 | Reported Jewish Population ca. 1878 | ca. 1907 | 1927 |
|------|-------|-----------------|-------------------------------------|----------|------|
| Eufaula | Ala. | 3,836 | 105 | 128 | 29 |
| Mobile | Ala. | 29,132 | 566 | 1,000 | 950 |
| Montgomery | Ala. | 16,713 | 600 | 1,250 | 3,000 |
| Selma | Ala. | 7,529 | 200 | 315 | 281 |
| Helena | Ark. | 3,652 | 180 | 160 | 400 |
| Little Rock | Ark. | 13,138 | 655 | 1,150 | 3,000 |
| Pine Bluff | Ark. | 3,203 | 250 | 463 | 400 |
| Los Angeles | Calif. | 11,183 | 330 | 4,500 | 65,000 |
| Oakland | Calif. | 34,555 | 227 | 2,000 | 6,000 |
| San Bernardino | Calif. | 1,673 | 133 | 100 | 250 |
| San Jose | Calif. | 12,567 | 265 | 225 | 375 |
| Santa Cruz | Calif. | 3,898 | 100 | | 90 |
| Stockton | Calif. | 10,282 | 200 | 443 | 1,150 |
| Woodland | Calif. | | 110 | | |
| Denver | Colo. | 35,629 | 260 | 4,500 | 17,000 |
| Georgetown | D.C. | 12,578 | 133 | | |
| Jacksonville | Fla. | 7,650 | 130 | 656 | 4,000 |
| Albany | Ga. | 3,216 | 100 | 238 | 275 |
| Athens | Ga. | 6,099 | 110 | 139 | 185 |
| Atlanta | Ga. | 37,409 | 525 | 2,750 | 11,000 |
| Augusta | Ga. | 21,891 | 240 | 313 | 970 |
| Columbus | Ga. | 10,123 | 275 | 543 | 700 |
| Macon | Ga. | 12,749 | 350 | 550 | 650 |
| Savannah | Ga. | 30,709 | 603 | 2,500 | 3,800 |
| Bloomington | Ill. | 17,180 | 115 | 146 | 350 |
| Ottawa | Ill. | 7,834 | 130 | | 59 |
| Peoria | Ill. | 29,259 | 400 | 1,500 | 1,500 |
| Quincy | Ill. | 27,268 | 500 | 126 | 350 |
| Rock Island | Ill. | 11,659 | 153 | 200 | 1,675 |
| Springfield | Ill. | 19,743 | 150 | 425 | 600 |
| Attica | Ind. | 2,150 | 138 | 32 | 51 |
| Evansville | Ind. | 29,280 | 375 | 775 | 1,800 |
| Fort Wayne | Ind. | 26,880 | 275 | 464 | 1,800 |
| Goshen | Ind. | 4,123 | 125 | 139 | 51 |
| Indianapolis | Ind. | 75,056 | 400 | 3,900 | 10,000 |
| Lafayette | Ind. | 14,860 | 225 | 220 | 350 |
| Laporte | Ind. | 6,195 | 142 | | 50 |
| Madison | Ind. | 8,945 | 253 | 50 | 24 |
| Terre Haute | Ind. | 26,042 | 100 | 400 | 1,000 |
| Wabash | Ind. | 3,800 | 100 | 174 | 150 |
| Burlington | Iowa | 19,450 | 121 | 100 | 107 |
| Davenport | Iowa | 21,831 | 204 | 227 | 690 |
| Des Moines | Iowa | 22,408 | 260 | 1,750 | 4,200 |
| Keokuk | Iowa | 12,117 | 152 | 68 | 27 |

**Table 3:** *continued*

| Town | State | Total Pop. 1880 | Reported Jewish Population ca. 1878 | ca. 1907 | 1927 |
|---|---|---|---|---|---|
| Leavenworth | Kans. | 16,546 | 455 | 350 | 800 |
| Lexington | Ky. | 16,656 | 140 | 238 | 750 |
| Owensboro | Ky. | 6,231 | 213 | 153 | 49 |
| Paducah | Ky. | 8,036 | 203 | 247 | 800 |
| Alexandria | La. | 1,800 | 206 | 600 | 560 |
| Bayou Sara | La. | 710 | 133 | | |
| Donaldsonville | La. | 3,600 | 179 | 85 | 80 |
| Monroe | La. | 2,070 | 128 | 200 | 500 |
| Shreveport | La. | 8,009 | 900 | 975 | 2,000 |
| Portland | Maine | 33,810 | 185 | 1,600 | 3,500 |
| Cumberland | Md. | 10,693 | 140 | 183 | 720 |
| Bay City | Mich. | 20,693 | 153 | 900 | 695 |
| Grand Rapids | Mich. | 32,016 | 201 | 450 | 1,780 |
| Jackson | Mich. | 16,105 | 141 | | 250 |
| Kalamazoo | Mich. | 11,937 | 217 | 288 | 345 |
| Minneapolis | Minn. | 46,887 | 172 | 5,500 | 22,000 |
| St. Paul | Minn. | 41,473 | 225 | 3,500 | 13,500 |
| Canton | Miss. | 2,083 | 150 | 100 | 108 |
| Columbus | Miss. | 3,955 | 100 | 69 | 80 |
| Greenville | Miss. | 2,191 | 320 | 500 | 375 |
| Meridian | Miss. | 4,008 | 160 | 394 | 575 |
| Natchez | Miss. | 7,058 | 220 | 513 | 151 |
| Port Gibson | Miss. | | 109 | 151 | 48 |
| Vicksburg | Miss. | 11,814 | 520 | 688 | 467 |
| Kansas City | Mo. | 55,785 | 240 | 6,750 | 22,000 |
| St. Joseph | Mo. | 32,431 | 325 | 1,600 | 3,500 |
| Helena | Mont. | 3,624 | 112 | 300 | 79 |
| Eureka | Nev. | 4,207 | 172 | | |
| Virginia Cty | Nev. | 10,917 | 305 | | |
| Hoboken | N.J. | 30,999 | 600 | 1,500 | 2,760 |
| Jersey City | N.J. | 120,722 | 450 | 8,000 | 18,000 |
| New Brunswick | N.J. | 17,166 | 173 | 400 | 5,000 |
| Paterson | N.J. | 51,031 | 427 | 5,500 | 22,300 |
| Santa Fe | N.Mex. | 6,635 | 108 | 25 | 40 |
| Buffalo | N.Y. | 155,134 | 775 | 8,500 | 20,000 |
| Elmira | N.Y. | 20,541 | 300 | 1,650 | 1,500 |
| Gloversville | N.Y. | 7,133 | 103 | 800 | 1,500 |
| Hudson | N.Y. | 8,670 | 105 | | 680 |
| Kingston (incl. Rondout) | N.Y. | 18,344 | 818 | 690 | 1,750 |
| Newburgh | N.Y. | 18,049 | 158 | 500 | 1,735 |
| Ogdensburg | N.Y. | 10,341 | 100 | 75 | 127 |
| Plattsburgh | N.Y. | 5,245 | 125 | 125 | 416 |
| Poughkeepsie | N.Y. | 20,207 | 262 | 138 | 1,850 |
| Schenectady | N.Y. | 13,655 | 100 | 775 | 3,500 |
| Troy | N.Y. | 56,747 | 500 | 2,400 | 2,500 |

**Table 3:** *continued*

| Town | State | Total Pop. 1880 | Reported Jewish Population ca. 1878 | Reported Jewish Population ca. 1907 | Reported Jewish Population 1927 |
|------|-------|-----------------|-------------------------------------|-------------------------------------|---------------------------------|
| Utica | N.Y. | 33,914 | 900 | 2,000 | 5,000 |
| Charlotte | N.C. | 7,094 | 104 | | 400 |
| Goldsboro | N.C. | 3,286 | 147 | 188 | 120 |
| Wilmington | N.C. | 17,350 | 200 | 850 | 390 |
| Akron | Ohio | 16,512 | 165 | 1,250 | 7,500 |
| Columbus | Ohio | 51,647 | 420 | 2,750 | 8,500 |
| Dayton | Ohio | 38,678 | 500 | 1,850 | 4,900 |
| Hamilton | Ohio | 12,122 | 110 | 150 | 450 |
| Springfield | Ohio | 20,730 | 148 | 250 | 580 |
| Toledo | Ohio | 50,137 | 350 | 3,000 | 10,000 |
| Youngstown | Ohio | 15,435 | 140 | 2,000 | 8,000 |
| Zanesville | Ohio | 18,113 | 100 | 150 | 260 |
| Portland | Oreg. | 17,577 | 625 | 4,500 | 12,000 |
| Allegheny | Pa. | 78,682 | 100 | | |
| Danville | Pa. | 8,346 | 132 | 150 | 140 |
| Easton | Pa. | 11,924 | 255 | 200 | 1,500 |
| Erie | Pa. | 27,737 | 165 | 600 | 1,575 |
| Franklin | Pa. | 5,010 | 131 | | 34 |
| Harrisburg | Pa. | 30,762 | 100 | 900 | 5,000 |
| Lancaster | Pa. | 25,769 | 115 | 1,000 | 1,500 |
| Meadville | Pa. | 8,860 | 120 | 28 | 80 |
| Pottsville | Pa. | 13,252 | 283 | 400 | 1,000 |
| Reading | Pa. | 43,278 | 142 | 800 | 2,500 |
| Scranton | Pa. | 45,850 | 245 | 5,500 | 9,000 |
| Titusville | Pa. | 9,046 | 500 | | 400 |
| Wilkes-Barre | Pa. | 23,339 | 500 | 1,900 | 5,500 |
| Williamsport | Pa. | 18,934 | 158 | 215 | 500 |
| York | Pa. | 13,940 | 101 | 300 | 750 |
| Providence | R.I. | 104,857 | 375 | 10,000 | 21,000 |
| Charleston | S.C. | 49,984 | 700 | 1,150 | 2,100 |
| Columbia | S.C. | 10,036 | 100 | 150 | 590 |
| Chattanooga | Tenn. | 12,892 | 178 | 450 | 3,385 |
| Austin | Tex. | 11,013 | 100 | 213 | 490 |
| Dallas | Tex. | 10,358 | 260 | 2,600 | 7,500 |
| Fort Worth | Tex. | 6,663 | 116 | 900 | 2,100 |
| Houston | Tex. | 16,413 | 461 | 2,500 | 11,000 |
| Marshall | Tex. | 5,624 | 113 | 200 | 170 |
| San Antonio | Tex. | 20,550 | 302 | 1,300 | 8,000 |
| Waco | Tex. | 7,295 | 158 | 600 | 1,500 |
| Salt Lake City | Utah | 20,768 | 180 | 750 | 2,000 |
| Charlottesville | Va. | 2,676 | 100 | 91 | 112 |
| Lynchburg | Va. | 15,959 | 100 | 195 | 425 |
| Norfolk | Va. | 21,966 | 500 | 1,600 | 7,800 |
| Petersburg | Va. | 21,656 | 163 | 61 | 705 |
| Wheeling | W. Va. | 30,737 | 300 | 475 | 750 |

**Table 3:** *continued*

| Town | State | Total Pop. 1880 | Reported Jewish Population | | |
|------|-------|-----------------|---------------------------|---|---|
| | | | ca. 1878 | ca. 1907 | 1927 |
| Appleton | Wis. | 8,005 | 143 | 194 | 215 |
| La Crosse | Wis. | 14,505 | 106 | 150 | 190 |

Total population figures for 1880 are from U.S. Department of the Interior, Census Office, Compendium of the Tenth Census (June 1, 1880) (Washington, D.C., 1883), 452–63, supplemented by, for the smallest towns in this study, idem, Compendium of the Eleventh Census: 1890, Part I—Population (Washington, D.C., 1892), 442–67.

Jewish population figures for ca. 1878 are from Union of American Hebrew Congregations, Statistics of the Jews of the United States (Philadelphia, 1880), except that the Los Angeles figure is for 1870, from Norton B. Stern, ed., The Jews of Los Angeles (Los Angeles, 1981); and the Utica figure is based on 225 heads of families in 1871, from EJ, s.v. "Utica." Also, a Jewish population of 100 has been estimated for Wabash, Ind.; Ogdensburg, N.Y.; Schenectady, N.Y.; Zanesville, Ohio; Allegheny, Pa.; Columbia, S.C.; and Austin, Texas, simply because each of these towns is listed in Statistics of the Jews even though no population data are provided and because each was home to a Jewish congregation. The population figures for Mobile, Ala., and for Wilkes-Barre, Pa., are based on ambiguous data in the Statistics.

Jewish population figures for ca. 1907 are from The Jewish Encyclopedia, s.v. "United States," 371–74; and AJYB 9 (1907–08): 123–430. In cases in which divergent population figures are reported in these two sources, the figures provided have been averaged. Jewish population figures for 1927 are from AJYB 30 (1928–29): 180–96; and AJYB 31 (1929–30): 223–31. When the population figures in these two sources do not agree, the figure published in 1928 is provided.

**Table 4: Composition of Selected Small-Town Jewish Communities, 1880**

| Community | Total Number of Jews Identified | Number of Jewish Boarders Identified | Number of Jewish Households Identified | Male without Family | Female without Family | Couple without Family | Parent(s) and Children Only | Extended Families (e.g., brothers, grand-children present) | Of Households Evaluated, Number with Boarders | Of Households Evaluated, Number with Servants |
|---|---|---|---|---|---|---|---|---|---|---|
| | | | | | | | | | **Composition of Jewish Households** | |
| Alexandria, La. | 191 | 4 | 41 | 3 | 1 | 2 | 28 | 7 | 2 | 8 |
| Appleton, Wis. | 106 | 3 | 16 | 0 | 0 | 0 | 13 | 3 | 1 | 13 |
| Bradford, Pa. | 318 | 21 | 40 | 5 | 0 | 1 | 26 | 8 | 11 | 14 |
| Hamilton, Ohio | 96 | 0 | 16 | 0 | 0 | 2 | 12 | 2 | 0 | 4 |
| Jackson, Mich. | 121 | 2 | 22 | 0 | 0 | 1 | 18 | 3 | 3 | 10 |
| Lafayette, Ind. | 174 | 2 | 36 | 2 | 0 | 3 | 18 | 13 | 1 | 16 |
| Lexington, Ky. | 98 | 8 | 20 | 2 | 0 | 2 | 11 | 5 | 6 | 7 |
| Vicksburg, Miss. | 454 | 41 | 60 | 0 | 0 | 4 | 30 | 26 | 10 | 26 |

*Data derived from the manuscript rosters of the U.S. Census for 1880, available from the Census Bureau on microfilm (publication T-9).*

**Table 5: Composition of Selected Small-Town Jewish Communities, 1920**

| Community | Total Number of Jews Identified | Number of Jewish Boarders Identified | Number of Jewish Households Identified | Composition of Jewish Households | | | | | | |
|---|---|---|---|---|---|---|---|---|---|---|
| | | | | Male without Family | Female without Family | Couple without Family | Parent(s) and Children Only | Extended Families (e.g., brothers, grand-children present) | Of Households Evaluated, Number with Boarders | Of Households Evaluated, Number with Servants |
| Alexandria, La. | 467 | 24 | 96 | 3 | 0 | 10 | 52 | 31 | 9 | 7 |
| Appleton, Wis. | 214 | 4 | 45 | 1 | 0 | 4 | 37 | 3 | 3 | 8 |
| Bradford, Pa. | 566 | 9 | 130 | 2 | 1 | 18 | 81 | 28 | 5 | 8 |
| Fitchburg, Mass. | 372 | 10 | 64 | 0 | 0 | 2 | 49 | 13 | 5 | 0 |
| Hamilton, Ohio | 327 | 11 | 67 | 0 | 0 | 8 | 47 | 12 | 4 | 4 |
| Jackson, Mich. | 109 | 5 | 28 | 0 | 1 | 3 | 21 | 3 | 2 | 2 |
| Lafayette, Ind. | 380 | 8 | 88 | 2 | 1 | 12 | 64 | 9 | 5 | 15 |
| Lexington, Ky. | 393 | 15 | 88 | 4 | 1 | 7 | 63 | 13 | 5 | 4 |
| Modesto, Calif. | 151 | 13 | 35 | 1 | 0 | 4 | 27 | 3 | 7 | 3 |
| Nashua, N.H. | 325 | 3 | 70 | 2 | 1 | 11 | 50 | 6 | 4 | 1 |
| Newburyport, Mass. | 360 | 18 | 72 | 0 | 0 | 6 | 59 | 7 | 17 | 1 |
| Vicksburg, Miss. | 471 | 29 | 107 | 1 | 1 | 8 | 51 | 46 | 8 | 6 |

*Data derived from the manuscript rosters of the U.S. Census for 1920, available from the Census Bureau on microfilm (publication T-625). In Jackson, Mich., in addition to the 109 Jewish residents identified, 21 identifiable Jewish inmates of Jackson State Prison appear on census rosters.*

# Notes

*Abbreviations*

AJA:  American Jewish Archives, Cincinnati

*AJYB: American Jewish Year Book*

*EJ: Encyclopaedia Judaica,* DC-ROM edition, Jerusalem, 1997

IRO Coll.:  Industrial Removal Office Collection (code *I-91), American Jewish Historical Society, New York

Ms. Census:  Manuscript census of the United States on microfilm (publication T-9 for 1880; publication T-625 for 1920, National Archives and Records Aministration, Washington, D.C.)

*UJE: Universal Jewish Encyclopedia* (New York, 1939–43)

*Introduction. Searching for Patterns*

1. On immigration restrictions, see, for example, John Higham, *Strangers in the Land: Patterns of American Nativism, 1860–1925,* 2d ed. (New Brunswick, N.J., 1988), esp. chap. 11; and Jack Glazier, *Dispersing the Ghetto: The Relocation of Jewish Immigrants across America* (Ithaca, N.Y., 1998), chap. 2.

2. For the sources of the population data employed throughout this study, see chapter 1 and the Bibliographic Essay.

3. See, for example, Moses Rischin, *The Promised City: New York's Jews, 1870–1914* (Boston, 1962); Arthur A. Goren, *New York Jews and the Quest for Community: The Kehillah Experiment, 1908 1922* (New York, 1970); Jeffrey S. Gurock, *When Harlem was Jewish, 1870–1930* (New York, 1979); Deborah Dash Moore, *At Home in America: Second Generation New York Jews* (New York, 1981); Beth S. Wenger, *New York Jews and the Great Depression: Uncertain Promise* (New Haven, 1996); and Hasia R. Diner, *Lower East Side Memories: A Jewish Place in America* (Princeton, 2000).

4. See, for example, Louis J. Swichkow and Lloyd P. Gartner, *The History of the Jews of Milwaukee* (Philadelphia, 1963); Isaac M. Fein, *The Making of an American Jewish Community: The History of Baltimore Jewry from 1773 to 1920* (Philadelphia, 1971); Steven Hertzberg, *Strangers within the Gate City: The Jews of Atlanta, 1845–1915* (Philadelphia, 1978); Marc Lee Raphael, *Jews and Judaism in a Midwestern Community: Columbus, Ohio, 1840–1975* (Columbus, 1979); Judith E. Endelman, *The Jewish Community of Indianapolis, 1849 to the*

*Present* (Bloomington, Ind., 1984); Jonathan D. Sarna and Ellen Smith, eds., *The Jews of Boston: Essays on the Occasion of the Centenary (1895–1995) of the Combined Jewish Philanthropies of Greater Boston* (Boston, 1995); and Walter Ehrlich, *Zion in the Valley: The Jewish Community of St. Louis,* vol. 1: *1807–1907* (Columbia, Mo., 1997).

5. Lance J. Sussman, *Beyond the Catskills: Jewish Life in Binghamton, New York, 1850–1975* (Binghamton, N.Y., 1989); Ewa Morawska, *Insecure Prosperity: Small-Town Jews in Industrial America, 1890–1940* (Princeton, 1996).

6. Swichkow's statement appears in his review of Frank J. Adler, *Roots in a Moving Stream: The Centennial History of Congregation B'nai Jehudah of Kansas City, 1870–1970, American Jewish Historical Quarterly* 63 (March 1974): 292. Swichkow evaluates Adler's book favorably, in contrast to other congregational histories. See also Jeffrey Gurock, *American Jewish History: A Bibliographical Guide* (New York, 1983), 11–13; and Jonathan D. Sarna, "Jewish Community Histories: Recent Non-Academic Contributions," *Journal of American Ethnic History* 6 (fall 1986): 62–70.

7. Helene Gerard, "Yankees in Yarmulkes: Small-Town Jewish Life in Eastern Long Island," *American Jewish Archives* 38 (April 1986): 25; Dennis S. Devlin, *Muskegon's Jewish Community: A Centennial History, 1888–1988* (Muskegon, Mich., 1988), 9; Carol Ely, Jeffrey Hantman, and Phyllis Leffler, *To Seek the Peace of the City: Jewish Life in Charlottesville,* exhibition catalogue (Charlottesville, Va., 1994), preface; Louis Ginsberg, *History of the Jews of Petersburg, 1789–1950* (Petersburg, Va., 1954), 1.

8. Gerald Sorin, *A Time for Building: The Third Migration, 1880–1920,* vol. 3 of Henry L. Feingold, series ed., The Jewish People in America (Baltimore, 1992), chap. 5, quotation from 161. For an earlier example of the misleading use of the term "smaller cities," see Jacob Lestschinsky, "Economic and Social Development of American Jewry," in *The Jewish People, Past and Present,* vol. 4 (New York, 1955), 89–90. Lestschinsky reports on Jewish employment patterns during the 1930s in what he calls "47 smaller cities," even though these include places such as Atlanta, Columbus, Dallas, Denver, Memphis, Minneapolis, and Patterson, New Jersey, all major cities with Jewish populations of at least 10,000 at the time. Compare Nathan Goldberg, "Occupational Patterns of American Jews, II," *Jewish Review* 3 (October–December 1945).

9. See, for example, Richard Lingeman, "The Small Town in America: The Recent Past, the Near Future," in Robert Craycroft and Michael Fazio, eds., *Change and Tradition in the American Small Town* (Jackson, Miss., 1983); Anselm L. Strauss, "Some Varieties of American Urban Symbolism," in Alexander B. Callow, Jr., ed., *American Urban History: An Interpretive Reader with Commentaries,* 3d ed. (New York, 1982); and Park Dixon Goist, *From Main Street to State Street: Town, City, and Community in America* (Port Washington, N.Y., 1977).

10. See, for example, Ima Honaker Herron, *The Small Town in American Literature* (Durham, N.C., 1939); and Anthony Channell Hilfer, *The Revolt from the Village, 1915–1930* (Chapel Hill, N.C., 1969).

11. Shelby M. Harrison, *Social Conditions in an American City: A Summary of the Findings of the Springfield Survey* (New York, 1920), 20. See also Jean M. Converse, *Survey Research in the United States: Roots and Emergence, 1890–1960* (Berkeley, 1987), 35.

12. See esp. Robert S. Lynd and Helen Merrell Lynd, *Middletown: A Study in American Culture* (New York, 1929); Robert S. Lynd and Helen Merrell Lynd, *Middletown in Transition: A Study in Cultural Conflicts* (New York, 1937); and W. Lloyd Warner and Paul S. Lunt, *The Social Life of a Modern Community,* Yankee City Series, vol. 1 (New Haven, 1941).

13. Lingeman, "The Small Town in America," 6; and Maurice R. Stein, *The Eclipse of Community: An Interpretation of American Studies* (Princeton, 1960), 48. See also Don Martindale and R. Galen Hanson, *Small Town and the Nation: The Conflict of Local and Translocal Forces* (Westport, Conn., 1969), 10.

14. Literary Digest, *Zanesville and 36 Other American Communities: A Study of Markets and of the Telephone as a Market Index* (New York, 1927), 14; Norris F. Schneider, *Y Bridge City: The Story of Zanesville and Muskingum County, Ohio* ([1950]; reprint, Evansville, Ind., 1977), 327.

15. Harrison, *Social Conditions in an American City,* 21; Lynd and Lynd, *Middletown,* 8; Warner and Lunt, *Social Life,* 38. Volume 3 of the Yankee City Series is W. Lloyd Warner and Leo Srole, *The Social Systems of American Ethnic Groups* (New Haven, 1945). For an interesting discussion of some of the problems with the Newburyport study, see Stephan Thernstrom, " 'Yankee City' Revisited: The Perils of Historical Naïveté," in Michael Aiken and Paul E. Mott, eds., *The Structure of Community Power* (New York, 1970).

16. See Melvin I. Urofsky, "Preface: The Tip of the Iceberg," in Nathan M. Kaganoff and Melvin I. Urofsky, eds., *Turn to the South: Essays on Southern Jewry* (Charlottesville, Va., 1979), xii; Hal Rothman, " 'Same Horse, New Wagon:' Tradition and Assimilation among the Jews of Wichita, 1865–1930," *Great Plains Quarterly* 15 (spring 1995): 84; and Mark K. Bauman, *The Southerner as American: Jewish Style* (Cincinnati, 1996), esp. 29–30.

17. See Devlin, *Muskegon's Jewish Community*; Myer Katz, "The Jews of La Crosse Past and Present," *Encounters,* ca. June 1973; Joy Cumonow and Fred N. Reiner, *The Spirit Unconsumed: A History of the Topeka Jewish Community* (Topeka, 1979); and Leonard Rogoff, *Homelands: Southern Jewish Identity in Durham and Chapel Hill, North Carolina* (Tuscaloosa, Ala., 2001).

## Chapter 1. Patterns of Evidence: Identifying Small Communities

1. Ira Rosenwaike, *On the Edge of Greatness: A Portrait of American Jewry in the Early National Period* (Cincinnati, 1985), esp. table on 31.

2. See Uriah Zvi Engelman, "Jewish Statistics in the U.S. Census of Religious Bodies (1850–1936)," *Jewish Social Studies* 9 (April 1947): 127–74.

3. See, for example, Joseph Jacobs, "Jewish population of the United States," *AJYB* 16 (1914–15): 339.

4. Jacques J. Lyons and Abraham de Sola, *Jewish Calendar for Fifty Years* (Montreal, 1854), 148–73.

5. See Allan Tarshish, "The Board of Delegates of American Israelites (1859–1878)," in Abraham Karp, ed., *The Jewish Experience in America,* 5 vols. (Waltham, Mass., 1969), 3: 132.

6. Union of American Hebrew Congregations, *Statistics of the Jews of the United States* (Philadelphia, 1880).

7. The manuscript ledger book from which *Statistics of the Jews* was complied is preserved in Ms. Coll. 10, 66/2, AJA.

8. Judith E. Endelman, *The Jewish Community of Indianapolis, 1849 to the Present* (Bloomington, Ind., 1984), 30; Benjamin Band, *Portland Jewry: Its Growth and Development* (Portland, Maine, 1955), 20.

9. *The Jewish Encyclopedia,* s.v. "United States," 371–74; "Directory of Jewish Local Organizations in the United States," *AJYB* 9 (1907–08): 123–430.

10. "Directory of Local Organizations," *AJYB* 2 (1900–01): 185–490.

11. *The Jewish Encyclopedia,* s.v. "United States," 371; "Directory," *AJYB* 9 (1907–08), 21, 24.

12. See Harry S. Linfield, "Jewish Population in the United States, 1927," *AJYB* 30 (1928–29): 104.

13. For Jewish immigration data, see Paul Mendes-Flohr and Jehuda Reinharz, *The Jew in the Modern World,* 2d ed. (New York, 1995), 706, table IV. For purposes of analysis in this study, in cases in which divergent population figures are reported in *The Jewish Encyclopedia* and the 1907 *Year Book,* the figures are averaged.

14. *UJE,* s.v. "American Jewish Committee" and "Synagogue Council of America."

15. See Joseph Jacobs, "Jewish Population of the United States," *AJYB* 16 (1914–15): 339–78. The actual population figures appear in the appendix on 359–78.

16. See Samson D. Oppenheim, "The Jewish Population of the United States," *AJYB* 20 (1918–19): 31–74; quotation from introduction to this *AJYB* volume, V.

17. Ibid., 48.

18. See Oppenheim, "Jewish Population," AJYB 20 (1918–19): 49–74; and "Directory of Jewish Local Organizations in the United States," *AJYB* 21 (1919–20): 337–583.

19. "Directory," *AJYB* 21 (1919–20): 330.

20. On Keokuk, see "Directory," *AJYB* 21 (1919–20): 374; Union of American Hebrew Congregations, *Statistics of the Jews,* 42; "Directory," *AJYB* 2 (1900–01): 254; and "Directory," *AJYB* 9 (1907–08): 180. On Brunswick, see "Directory," *AJYB* 21 (1919–20): 357; *UJE,* s.v. "Georgia"; and *Seventy-fifth Anniversary: Temple Beth Tefilloh* (Brunswick, Ga., 1961). On Keyport, see "Directory," *AJYB* 21 (1919–20): 422; and Alan S. Pine, Jean C. Hershenov, and Aaron H. Lefkowitz, *Peddler to Suburbanite: The History of the Jews of Monmouth County, New Jersey* (Deal Park, N.J., 1981), 50.

21. See, for example, "Jewish Local Organizations in the United States (Supplementary Directory)," *AJYB* 22 (1920–21): 322–39; *AJYB* 24 (1922–23): 264–85; *AJYB* 26 (1924–25): 522–45; and *AJYB* 29 (1927–28): 191–214.

22. See Linfield, "Jewish Population . . . 1927," 180–96 (general table F); Harry S. Linfield, "The Communal Organization of the Jews in the United States, 1927," *AJYB* 31 (1929–30): 223–31 (general tables A and B); and idem, "Jewish Communities of the United States," *AJYB* 42 (1940–41): 239–65 (table F).

23. On San Mateo, see city directory for San Mateo, California, 1930; Joan C. Abrams, *Peninsula Temple Beth El, San Mateo, California: A Congregational History* (San Mateo, Calif., 1985); and Mitchell P. Postel, *The History of the Peninsula Golf and Country Club* (San Mateo, Calif., 1993), 7–19. On Paducah, see 1927 Temple Israel membership list (copy in author's possession); and "Directory of Jewish Federations and Welfare Funds, 1937," *AJYB* 39 (1937–38): 706.

24. In this study, when 1927 population figures published in the *American Jewish Year Book* in 1928 and 1929 do not agree, the figures provided in 1928 are used.

25. Linfield, "Jewish Communities," *AJYB* 42 (1940–41): 215; Ben B. Seligman, "Changes in Jewish Population in the United States, 1949–50," *AJYB* 52 (1951): 4.

26. See Alvin Chenkin, "Jewish Population in the United States, 1983," *AJYB* 84 (1984): 167–74 (table 3).

27. Alvin Chenkin, "Jewish Population in the United States, 1961," *AJYB* 63 (1962): 139.

28. For an insightful contemporary critique of the population data available before World War II, see Uriah Zevi Engelman, *The Jewish Community in Figures: Guess-Work and Speculation That Pass for Statistics* (New York, 1937).

29. See, for example, Park Dixon Goist, *From Main Street to State Street: Town, City, and Community in America* (Port Washington, N.Y., 1977), 3–9; Roland L. Warren, *The Community in America*, 3d ed. (Chicago, 1978), esp. chap. 2.

30. See Rose O'Brien, "Beth Abraham's Congregation Observes 50th Anniversary," *Lewiston Journal Magazine Section*, December 6, 1952; and Meyer Barkai, publisher, *The Standard American-Jewish Directory, 1960* (n.p., 1960), 74.

31. See U.S. Bureau of the Census, *Thirteenth Census of the United States Taken in the Year 1910—Volume 1: Population* (Washington, D.C., 1913), 73–77 (quotation from 73); and idem, *Abstract of the Fifteenth Census of the United States* (1933; reprint, New York, 1976), 77–79. On the history of Metropolitan Districts, see idem, *Geographic Areas Reference Manual* (Washington, D.C., 1994), 13–3; and Charles N. Glaab and A. Theodore Brown, *A History of Urban America*, 2d ed. (New York, 1976), 245–48.

32. See Michael H. Ebner, *Creating Chicago's North Shore: A Suburban History* (Chicago, 1988); James Borchert, "Residential City Suburbs: The Emergence of a New Suburban Type, 1880–1930," *Journal of Urban History* 22 (March 1996): 283–307; idem, "Cities in the Suburbs: Heterogeneous Communities on the U.S. Urban Fringe, 1920–1960," *Urban History* 23 (August 1996): 211–27; and Daniel J. Elazar, *Building Cities in America: Urbanization and Suburbanization in a Frontier Society* (Lanham, Md., 1987), 4.

33. See, for example, "A 20th Century Diaspora," clipping from the *Pittsburgh Post*

*Gazette,* "Donora, Pennsylvania" Nearprint file, AJA; William M. Katz, "Reminiscences of the Jewish Community of Canonsburg," document prepared for the *Jefferson College Times,* ca. 1990, Historical Society of Western Pennsylvania Archives, Pittsburgh; Arnold W. Hirsch, "Remembering Donora's Jewish Community," document MFF #2044, ca. 1995, ibid.; *Celebration of the Century: Northern Kentucky Jewish Families,* program booklet (Cincinnati, 1994).

34. Bernard Postal and Lionel Koppman, *Jewish Landmarks of New York* (New York, 1978), 261; *Congregation Ahavath Torah: An Oral History,* centennial booklet (Englewood, N.J., 1995), 15; William B. Helmreich, *The Enduring Community: The Jews of Newark and Metrowest* (New Brunswick, N.J., 1999), 58, 62–63 (quotation).

35. Lloyd P. Gartner, *History of the Jews of Cleveland* (Cleveland, 1978), 269–71.

36. See Jonathan D. Sarna and Nancy H. Klein, *The Jews of Cincinnati* (Cincinnati, 1989); Louis Swichkow and Lloyd P. Gartner, *The History of the Jews of Milwaukee* (Philadelphia, 1963), esp. 327; Max Vorspan and Lloyd P. Gartner, *History of the Jews of Los Angeles* (San Marino, Calif., 1970), esp. 276–77.

37. See Sidney Bolkosky, *Harmony and Dissonance: Voices of Jewish Identity in Detroit, 1914–1967* (Detroit, 1991), 99; Walter Ehrlich, *Zion in the Valley: The Jewish Community of St. Louis,* vol. 1: *1807–1907* (Columbia, Mo., 1997), xi.

38. Oppenheim, "Jewish Population," *AJYB* 20 (1918–19): 49–73.

39. See Linfield, "Jewish Population . . . 1927," 101–98.

40. See Linfield, "Communal Organization . . . 1927," 99–100, 223–31. Linfield employed the same concept of "principal" and "subordinate" communities in his 1937 study; see Linfield, "Jewish Communities," *AJYB* 42 (1940–41): 216–17.

41. Rudolph Glanz, "The Spread of Jewish Communities through America before the Civil War," *YIVO Annual of Jewish Social Science* 15 (1974): 7–45.

42. See, for example, Joseph Brandes with Martin Douglas, *Immigrants to Freedom: Jewish Communities in Rural New Jersey since 1882* (Philadelphia, 1971); Uri D. Herscher, *Jewish Agricultural Utopias in America, 1880–1910* (Detroit, 1981); Gertrude Wishnick Dubrovsky, *The Land Was Theirs: Jewish Farmers in the Garden State* (Tuscaloosa, Ala., 1992); Ellen Eisenberg, *Jewish Agricultural Colonies in New Jersey, 1882–1920* (Syracuse, 1995); and Abraham D. Lavender and Clarence B. Steinberg, *Jewish Farmers of the Catskills: A Century of Survival* (Gainesville, Fla., 1995). For purposes of analysis in this study, "urban places" are those defined as such by the 1920 U.S. Census.

43. On New Bern, see "Directory," *AJYB* 21 (1919–20): 523; and *UJE,* s.v. "North Carolina." On Helena, see Patricia L. Dean, "The Jewish Community of Helena, Montana: 1866–1900" (undergraduate honors thesis, Carroll College, 1977; copy in file SC-4871, AJA), 53, 66–67. On La Porte, see Nettie K. Stern and Edith J. Backus, "History of B'ne Zion Jewish Congregation" in H. H. Martin, comp., "Laporte, Indiana: History of First Hundred Years," 5–6, typescript, 1932, Public Library of Michigan City, Ind.

44. See "Statistics of Jews," *AJYB* 21 (1919–20): 608–09 (table X).

45. Lee J. Levinger, "The Disappearing Small-Town Jew," *Commentary* 14 (Au-

gust 1952): 157–63 (quotation from 157); Erich Rosenthal, "Studies of Jewish Intermarriage in the United States," *AJYB* 64 (1963): 11.

46. These towns were Arlington, Belmont, Canton, Franklin, Great Barrington, Marlborough, Montague, Ware, and Webster.

## Chapter 2. Patterns of Settlement: The Early Years

1. The discussion in this paragraph and the next is based on total population information from 1930.

2. Patty C. Hiemstra, "Kalamazoo Lured Jewish Pioneers," *Kalamazoo Gazette*, April 8, 1984; Joseph Levine, "Jewish Community Small," in Linda Robertson, ed., *Wabash County History: Bicentennial Edition, 1976* (Marceline, Mo., 1976), 167; Isaac W. Bernheim, *History of the Settlement of Jews in Paducah and the Lower Ohio Valley* (Paducah, Ky., 1912), 22–23; Carolyn Gray LeMaster, *A Corner of the Tapestry: A History of the Jewish Experience in Arkansas, 1820s–1990s* (Fayetteville, Ark., 1994), 27; Leo E. Turitz and Evelyn Turitz, *Jews in Early Mississippi* (Jackson, Miss., 1983), 116–17.

3. See, for example, Rudolf Glanz, "Notes on Early Jewish Peddling in America," *Jewish Social Studies* 7 (1945): 119–36; and Elliott Ashkenazi, *The Business of Jews in Louisiana, 1840–1875* (Tuscaloosa, Ala., 1988), 132–35.

4. Benjamin Hirsh, "Ninety-five Years of Beth Ha-Sholom," *Journal of the Lycoming County Historical Society* 12, no. 1 (1976): 6–7.

5. Ashkenazi, *The Business of Jews*, 134; Jacob S. Feldman, *The Jewish Experience in Western Pennsylvania: A History, 1755–1945* (Pittsburgh, 1986), 59.

6. Newton J. Friedman, "A History of Temple Beth Israel of Macon, Georgia" (D.Th. diss., Burton Seminary of Colorado, 1955), 7; Oscar Fleishaker, *The Illinois-Iowa Jewish Community on the Banks of the Mississippi River* (n.p., 1971), 83; Sybil Stern Mervis, "History of the Jewish Community of Danville," in *Congregation Israel Synagogue, 1916–1991*, 75th anniversary booklet (Danville, Ill., 1991), 17.

7. Compare the title of Leonard Winograd, *The Horse Died at Windber: A History of Johnstown's Jews of Pennsylvania* (Bristol, Ind., 1988). Windber, a town not far from Johnstown, is not included in this study because its reported Jewish population in 1927 was only seventy.

8. Louis Ginsberg, *History of the Jews of Petersburg, 1789–1950* (Petersburg, Va., 1954), 7; Carol Ely, Jeffrey Hantman, and Phyllis Leffler, *To Seek the Peace of the City: Jewish Life in Charlottesville*, exhibition catalogue (Charlottesville, Va., 1994), 3, 2; Julius Kerman, "Story of Temple B'nai Israel, Natchez, Mississippi" (mimeographed document, 1955; copy at Hebrew Union College Library, Cincinnati), 1; Turitz and Turitz, *Jews in Early Mississippi*, 11.

9. *The Kentucky Encyclopedia* (Lexington, Ky., 1992), s.v. "Gratz, Benjamin"; Myer Katz, "The Jews of La Crosse Past and Present," *Encounters*, ca. June 1973, 40–43.

10. Ginsberg, *Jews of Petersburg*, 13–15; Bertrand E. Pollans and Ben Hirsh, eds., "Eighty Years of Temple Beth Ha-Sholom in Williamsport," in *80th*

*Anniversary Celebration, 1866–1946* (Williamsport, Pa., 1946), 5; Feldman, *Jewish Experience in Western Pennsylvania*, 58.

11. On Lafayette specifically, see Robert M. Taylor Jr. et al., *Indiana: A New Historical Guide* (Indianapolis, 1989), 485. On San Bernardino, see Sunny Rabenstock, "Emanu El—God Is with Us: A History of Congregation Emanu El, San Bernardino, California," in *100th Anniversary, Congregation Emanu El* (San Bernardino, Calif., 1991), 1–3. For an interesting perspective on the role of secondary river towns in nineteenth-century regional economic networks, see Timothy R. Mahoney, "Urban History in a Regional Context: River Towns of the Upper Mississippi, 1840–1860," *Journal of American History* 72 (September 1985): 318–39.

12. On Cumberland, see Writers Program of the Work Projects Administration, *Maryland: A Guide to the Old Line State* (New York, 1940), 265–66. On Meridian, see Turitz and Turitz, *Jews in Early Mississippi*, 89. For rail connections in 1868, see *Travelers' Official Railway Guide for the United States and Canada* (1868; reprint, New York, 1968), index.

13. Ely, Hantman, and Leffler, *To Seek the Peace of the City*, 3, 5; Paul P. Gordon and Rita S. Gordon, *The Jews beneath the Clustered Spires* (Hagerstown, Md., 1971), 107; *The Kentucky Encyclopedia*, s.v. "Gratz, Benjamin"; Martin I. Hinchin, *Fourscore and Eleven: A History of the Jews of Rapides Parish, 1828–1919* (Alexandria, La.[?], 1984), 1–3.

14. See, for example, Hasia R. Diner, *A Time for Gathering: The Second Migration, 1820–1880*, vol. 2 of Henry L. Feingold, series ed., The Jewish People in America (Baltimore, 1992), 94; Jacob Rader Marcus, *United States Jewry, 1776–1985*, 4 vols. (Detroit, 1989–1992), 2: 197.

15. Irving I. Katz, "History of Temple Beth Israel, Jackson, Michigan," 1–4, typescript, 1952, Histories file, AJA, including quotation from *The Israelite*, November 12, 1858.

16. On Macon, see John J. McKay, ed., *A Guide to Macon's Architecture and Historical Heritage* (Macon, Ga., 1972), 10–14; Friedman, "History of Temple Beth Israel of Macon," 7 ff.; "The Way It Was: Macon's Temple Beth Israel Celebrates 125th," *Southern Israelite*, May 4, 1984, 7. On Paducah, see Bernheim, *History of the Settlement of Jews in Paducah*, 29, 56–62.

17. Gertrude Philippsborn, *The History of the Jewish Community of Vicksburg (from 1820 to 1968)* (Vicksburg, Miss., 1969), 10–13; On Lafayette, see "The First Century of Temple Israel," in *Temple Israel, Lafayette, Indiana: One Hundred Years, 1849–1949* (Lafayette, Ind., 1949; copy in "Lafayette—Temple Israel" Nearprint file, AJA), 20–21.

18. *Temple Emanu-El of San José*, 125th anniversary booklet (San Jose, Calif., 1987), unpaginated; Spinoza Society Minute Book, entry of October 28, 1877, AJA.

19. On Wheeling, see *Temple Shalom: Congregation L'Shem Shomayim, 1849–1989*, 140th anniversary booklet (Wheeling, W.Va., 1989), 6. On La Crosse, see Gordon H. Feinberg, "History of La Crosse Jewish Community to 1948," in *Dedication: Congregation Sons of Abraham Synagogue* (La Crosse, Wis., 1948), 31;

Katz, "Jews of La Crosse," 59–60; and "Directory of Jewish Local Organizations in the United States," *AJYB* 9 (1907–08): 426. On Kalamazoo, see *History of Kalamazoo County, Michigan* (Philadelphia, 1880), 247. On Charlottesville, see Ely, Hantman, and Leffler, *To Seek the Peace of the City*, 12–13.

20. See Pollans and Hirsh, "Eighty Years of Temple Beth Ha-Sholom," 5–6; Hirsh, "Ninety-five Years of Beth Ha-Sholom," 7–8; and *L'dor va-dor: Ohev Sholom 75th Anniversary* (Williamsport, Pa., 1982), 31.

21. *Seventy-fifth Anniversary of Beth Israel Congregation* (Plattsburg, N.Y., 1936), 5–7; Kerman, "Story of Temple B'nai Israel," 1.

22. *The Anniversary Story of Congregation B'er Chayim,* centennial booklet (Cumberland, Md., 1953), chap. 2; Ginsberg, *Jews of Petersburg*, 27–28; Herman Eliot Snyder, "A Brief History of the Jews in Springfield, Illinois, and of Temple Brith Sholom," in *History of Temple Brith Sholom Compiled in Commemoration of the Seventieth Anniversary* (Springfield, Ill., 1935); *Congregation Temple Israel: A Commemorative History* (Springfield, Ill., 1958); *History of Temple B'rith Sholom Compiled in Commemoration of Its 125th Anniversary* (Springfield, Ill., 1983).

23. On the places of origin of America's mid-nineteenth-century Jews, see esp. Diner, *Time for Gathering*, chap. 1.

24. Ms. Census, Alexandria, Rapides Parish, Louisiana, 1880.

25. Ms. Census, Hamilton, Butler County, Ohio, 1880; Ms. Census, Appleton, Outagamie County, Wisconsin, 1880.

26. Ms. Census, Bradford, McKean County, Pennsylvania, 1880.

27. See William Henry Perrin, ed., *History of Fayette County, Kentucky* (Chicago, 1882), 644–45; "A Prominent Citizen: Short Sketch of the Life of Mr. S. Siesel," *A Picture of Macon, Georgia: Macon Evening News Industrial Issue*, 1889.

28. Ms. Census, Appleton, 1880; Ms. Census, Jackson, Jackson County, Michigan, 1880.

29. Katz, "Jews of La Crosse," 38.

30. On the Reinachs, see Louis Ginsberg, *Chapters on the Jews of Virginia, 1658–1900* (Petersburg, Va., 1969), 18–19. On the Sterns, see idem, *Jews of Petersburg,* 39–40.

31. On the Sonneborns, see *Anniversary Story of Congregation B'er Chayim*, chap. 1. On the Dreyfuses, see R. P. DeHart, *Past and Present of Tippecanoe County, Indiana*, vol. 2 (Indianapolis, 1909), 889.

32. On the Livingstons, see *Moses Montefiore Temple: A Time to Remember*, centennial booklet (Bloomington, Ill., 1982), unpaginated. On the Meises, see Mervis, "History of the Jewish Community of Danville," 17.

33. Ruthe Winegarten and Cathy Schechter, *Deep in the Heart: The Lives and Legends of Texas Jews* (Austin, 1990), 44–45; William Toll, "The Domestic Basis of Community: Trinidad, Colorado's Jewish Women, 1889–1910," *Rocky Mountain Jewish Historical Notes* 8 and 9 (summer and fall 1987): 4; Norton B. Stern, "Santa Ana, California: Its First Jews and Jewish Congregations," *Western States Jewish Historical Quarterly* 14, no. 3 (April 1982): 249–51.

34. Hirsh, "Ninety-five Years of Beth Ha-Sholom," 7; Edna Ferber, *A Peculiar*

*Treasure* (New York, 1939), 59; Stephen Udelsohn, "Jewish Community and Cemetery Study of Brownsville," research paper, 1975, file SC-1453, AJA; Martin Zwelling, "A Brief History of the Jews of Zanesville" (typescript, n.d.; copy in the author's possession); Marcus, *United States Jewry*, 2: 190.

35. See Union of American Hebrew Congregations, *Statistics of the Jews of the United States* (Philadelphia, 1880). In seven cases in which this volume lists a town but provides no Jewish population figure, an estimate of 100 individuals has been assumed on the basis of the presence of a congregation. The towns are Allegheny, Pennsylvania; Austin, Texas; Columbia, South Carolina; Ogdensburg, New York; Schenectady, New York; Wabash, Indiana; and Zanesville, Ohio. Also, because *Statistics of the Jews* provides no population figure for Hartford, Connecticut, the figure for that city is taken from Morris Silverman, *Hartford Jews, 1659–1970* (Hartford, 1970), 31. The population figure used for Los Angeles, California, is for 1870, from Norton B. Stern, ed., *The Jews of Los Angeles* (Los Angeles, 1981); and the figure used for Utica, New York, is based on 225 heads of families in 1871, from *EJ*, s.v. "Utica."

36. Diner, *Time for Gathering*, 58–59.

37. This figure is based on the 134 cases for which total population data for 1880 are available.

38. Two of the 136 triple-digit communities identifiable in 1878 disappeared from the records by the 1920s because they were absorbed into the communities of adjacent cities. The community of Allegheny became part of the Pittsburgh community when these two cities merged, and the community of Georgetown became part of the community of Washington, D.C.

39. On Keokuk, see Bernard Postal and Lionel Koppman, *A Jewish Tourist's Guide to the U.S.* (Philadelphia, 1954), 173. On Madison, see Elizabeth Weinberg, "And Then There Was Only One" (unpublished paper, ca. 1990; copy in the author's possession), 1.

40. See Feldman, *Jewish Experience in Western Pennsylvania*, 65.

41. See, for example, Rudolf Glanz, *The Jews of California from the Discovery of Gold until 1880* (New York, 1960); Robert E. Levinson, *The Jews in the California Gold Rush* (New York, 1978); and Susan Morris, *A Traveler's Guide to Pioneer Jewish Cemeteries of the California Gold Rush* (Berkeley, 1996).

42. Eureka had a total population of 4,207 in 1880, but by 1900 it no longer existed as a separate corporate entity, and the entire precinct of which the town had once been a part was home to only 877 people. Virginia City's population plunged from 10,917 in 1880 to only 2,695 in 1900.

## Chapter 3. Patterns of Settlement: The Era of Mass Migration

1. See Union of American Hebrew Congregations, *Statistics of the Jews of the United States* (Philadelphia, 1880).

2. Jerry Miller, "Marion's Chosen Few," *Marion Chronicle-Tribune Magazine*, July 17, 1977, 4; Dan Rottenberg, ed., *Middletown Jews: The Tenuous Survival of an American Jewish Community* (Bloomington, Ind., 1997), xvii–xviii; I. A. Cas-

per, *A Short History of the Jews of Middletown* (Middletown, Ohio[?], 1956), unpaginated; Gunther Rothenberg, *Congregation Albert, 1897–1972* (Albuquerque, 1972), 9.

3. "An Historic Outline of Manchester Jews," in *Silver Anniversary, 1912–1937: Adath Yeshurun Synagogue*, 25th anniversary booklet (Manchester, N.H., 1937), 23, with reference to *The Israelite*, October 17, 1862; Joy Cumonow and Fred N. Reiner, *The Spirit Unconsumed: A History of the Topeka Jewish Community* (Topeka, 1979), 1.

4. Todd M. Endelman, *A Short History of the Jews of the Ann Arbor Area* (Ann Arbor, 1997), 2; Paul P. Gordon and Rita S. Gordon, *The Jews beneath the Clustered Spires* (Hagerstown, Md., 1971), 110; Douglas W. Jones, "Jewish Life at Iowa" (typescript, 1997; copy in the author's possession), 4. Valdosta, Georgia, which had just under 100 Jews in 1927, provides another example of a town that was abandoned by its early German Jews; see Louis Schmier, "Jews and Gentiles in a South Georgia Town," in *Jews of the South: Selected Essays from the Southern Jewish Historical Society*, ed. Samuel Proctor and Louis Schmier with Malcolm Stern (Macon, Ga., 1984).

5. See, for example, Steven Hertzberg, *Strangers within the Gate City: The Jews of Atlanta, 1845–1915* (Philadelphia, 1978); Charles Reznikoff and Uriah Z. Engelman, *The Jews of Charleston: A History of an American Jewish Community* (Philadelphia, 1950); Elaine H. Maas, *The Jews of Houston: An Ethnographic Study* (New York, 1989); Isaac M. Fein, *The Making of an American Jewish Community: The History of Baltimore Jewry from 1773 to 1920* (Philadelphia, 1971); Myron Berman, *Richmond's Jewry, 1769–1976: Shabbat in Shockoe* (Charlottesville, Va., 1979); and Carol Ely, *Jewish Louisville: Portrait of a Community* (Louisville, 2003).

6. This observation about the first decade of the twentieth century is based on the absence of certain towns from both of the main listings of communities in that period. See *The Jewish Encyclopedia,* s.v. "United States"; and "Directory of Jewish Local Organizations in the United States," *AJYB* 9 (1907–08): 123–430.

7. George J. Fogelson, "Rudolph Anker. San Bernardino Pioneer," *Western States Jewish History* 17 (January 1985): 129–30; Dennis S. Devlin, *Muskegon's Jewish Community: A Centennial History, 1888–1988* (Muskegon, Mich., 1988), 3–4.

8. Sherry Blanton, "Lives of Quiet Affirmation: The Jewish Women of Early Anniston, Alabama," *Southern Jewish History* 2 (1999): 26; Rothenberg, *Congregation Albert*, 9–13, 23; William Toll, "The Domestic Basis of Community: Trinidad, Colorado's Jewish Women, 1889–1910," *Rocky Mountain Jewish Historical Notes* 8 and 9 (summer and fall 1987): 2.

9. Ms. Census, Newburyport, Essex County, Massachusetts, 1920; Ms. Census, Fitchburg, Worcester County, Massachusetts, 1920.

10. Ms. Census, Modesto, Stanislas County, California, 1920.

11. Ms. Census, Hamilton, Butler County, Ohio, 1920.

12. Ms. Census, Lexington, Fayette County, Kentucky, 1920.

13. Ms. Census, Alexandria, Rapides Parish, Louisiana, 1920.

14. Ms. Census, Vicksburg, Warren Country, Mississippi, 1920; Ms. Census, Appleton, Outagamie County, Wisconsin, 1920.

15. Abraham P. Nasatir, "The Nasatir Family in Santa Ana, California, 1898 to 1915," *Western States Jewish Historical Quarterly* 15 (April 1983): 254-55; Cumonow and Reiner, *Spirit Unconsumed*, 3.

16. Chester Jay Proshan, "Eastern European Jewish Immigrants and Their Children on the Minnesota Iron Range, 1890s-1980s" (Ph.D. diss., University of Minnesota, 1998), 89, 102; Alan S. Pine, Jean C. Hershenov, and Aaron H. Lefkowitz, *Peddler to Suburbanite: The History of the Jews of Monmouth County, New Jersey* (Deal Park, N.J., 1981), 87; Louis Ginsberg, *History of the Jews of Petersburg, 1789-1950* (Petersburg, Va., 1954), 62-64; *Temple B'nai Shalom, Benton Harbor, Mich., 1895-1995*, centennial booklet (Benton Harbor, Mich., 1995), unpaginated.

17. Helene Gerard, "Yankees in Yarmulkes: Small-Town Jewish Life in Eastern Long Island," *American Jewish Archives* 38 (April 1986): 28; Rochelle Berger Elstein, "The Jews of Houghton-Hancock and Their Synagogue," *Michigan Jewish History* 38 (November 1998): 2-3; Cumonow and Reiner, *Spirit Unconsumed*, 7.

18. Karen R. Goody, "The Greensboro Jewish Community: Keeping the Memories under Glass" (master's thesis, Wake Forest University, 1984), 17; letter from Isaac Kuhn to David Bressler, February 7, 1911, quoted in Robert A. Rockaway, *Words of the Uprooted: Jewish Immigrants in Early Twentieth-Century America* (Ithaca, N.Y., 1998), 97-98; Miller, "Marion's Chosen Few," 11.

19. *Temple Shaare Tefilah: Bar Mitzvah*, 83d anniversary booklet (Norwood, Mass., 1991), unpaginated; autobiographical essay by Vivian Barnert in Howard V. Epstein, ed., *Jews in Small Towns: Legends and Legacies* (Santa Rosa, Calif., 1997), 284; William B. Helmreich, *The Enduring Community: The Jews of Newark and Metrowest* (New Brunswick, N.J., 1999), 63; autobiographical essay by Howard Brody in Epstein, *Jews in Small Towns*, 471.

20. Interviews of Rebecca Zeff and Harriet Eisberg Kirschen by the author, Modesto, California, October 26, 1999; Phil Goodstein, *Exploring Jewish Colorado* (Denver, 1992), 99-100.

21. See David J. Goldberg, "In Dixie Land, I Take my Stand: A Study of Small-City Jewry in Five Southeastern States" (undergraduate thesis, Columbia College, 1974), 11.

22. Jacob S. Feldman, *The Jewish Experience in Western Pennsylvania: A History, 1755-1945* (Pittsburgh, 1986), 105, 207, 204-5; Proshan, "Eastern European Jewish Immigrants," 105; Robert P. Davis, "Port Arthur, Rodef Shalom," on the Internet site "Virtual Restoration of Small-Town Synagogues" at http://geo cities.com/txsynvr/txsyn.html (accessed March 26, 2000).

23. Pine, Hershenov and Lefkowitz, *Peddler to Suburbanite*, 51; Deborah R. Weiner, "Middlemen of the Coal Fields: The Role of Jews in the Economy of Southern West Virginia Coal Towns, 1890-1950," *Journal of Appalachian Studies* 4 (spring 1998): 33-34; Toll, "Domestic Basis of Community," 2; Juanita Brooks, *History of the Jews in Utah and Idaho* (Salt Lake City, 1973), 145;

Charles N. Glaab and A. Theodore Brown, *A History of Urban America*, 2d ed. (New York, 1976), 115, 103. For a good general discussion of the role of railroads in urban development around the turn of the twentieth century, see ibid., 103–10.

24. Robert P. Davis, "Settlement," on the Internet site "Virtual Restoration of Small-Town Synagogues."

25. Hal Rothman, "'Same Horse, New Wagon': Tradition and Assimilation among the Jews of Wichita, 1865–1930," *Great Plains Quarterly* 15 (spring 1995): 86; Glaab and Brown, *History of Urban America*, 115–16; Carolyn Gray LeMaster, *A Corner of the Tapestry: A History of the Jewish Experience in Arkansas, 1820s–1990s* (Fayetteville, Ark., 1994), 141; Norton B. Stern, "Santa Ana, California: Its First Jews and Jewish Congregations," *Western States Jewish Historical Quarterly* 14 (April 1982): 249; *Facsimile of the June 1893 Travelers' Official Railway Guide* (New York, 1972), 793–884 (index); *The Official Guide of the Railways and Steam Navigation Lines of the United States . . .* (New York, October 1910), 1223–1439 (index).

26. Rothenberg, *Congregation Albert*, 9. See also Abraham I. Shinedling with Milton Taichert, "The Las Vegas, New Mexico, Congregation (the Montefiore Congregation) and the Jewish Community of Las Vegas, N. Mex.," typescript, 1964, Histories file, AJA.

27. "For Historic Adirondack Shul, a New Beginning," clipping from *Jewish Advocate,* December 14, 1984, "Tupper Lake" Nearprint file, AJA; Weiner, "Middlemen of the Coal Fields," 34; Deborah R. Weiner, "A History of Jewish Life in the Central Appalachian Coalfields, 1870s to 1970s" (Ph.D. diss., West Virginia University, 2002), 95–101.

28. Helmreich, *Enduring Community*, 58; Ginsberg, *History of the Jews of Petersburg,* 69; Logan Esarey, *History of Indiana from Its Exploration to 1922,* (Dayton, 1923–28), 3:153.

29. See Michael S. Arnold, "Fading Tradition: Bogalusa Losing Jewish Presence," *New Orleans Times Picayune,* November 24, 1995; Rothman, "'Same Horse, New Wagon,'" 95; Proshan, "Eastern European Jewish Immigrants," 87; "Beth Israel's 75th Year to Be Celebrated," *Clarksdale* (Mississippi) *Press Register,* October 10, 1969.

30. Elstein, "The Jews of Houghton-Hancock," 8; [Marjorie Abrams and Meyer M. Cohen], *Dedication: Congregation Cnesses Israel* (Green Bay, Wis., 1951), 27; Cumonow and Reiner, *Spirit Unconsumed,* 11.

31. Debra [Deborah] Weiner, "The Jews of Clarksburg: Community Adaptation and Survival, 1900–1960," *Southern Jewish Historical Society Newsletter,* March 1995, 4–5; "Mayer Brauser Marking 60th Anniversary in City," *Bradford Era,* May 2, 1978; LeMaster, *Corner of the Tapestry,* 283.

32. Oscar Fleishaker, *The Illinois-Iowa Jewish Community on the Banks of the Mississippi River* (n.p., 1971), 149; *Sisterhood of Ohavay Zion Congregation*, 45th anniversary booklet (Lexington, Ky., 1959), unpaginated; Ms. Census, Newburyport, 1920; Pink Horwitt and Bertha Skole, *Jews in Berkshire Country* (Williamstown, Mass., 1972), 50.

33. Sybil Stern Mervis, "History of the Jewish Community of Danville," in *Congregation Israel Synagogue, 1916–1991*, 75th anniversary booklet (Danville, Ill., 1991), 13–14, 18.

34. The best single study of the IRO is Jack Glazier, *Dispersing the Ghetto: The Relocation of Jewish Immigrants across America* (Ithaca, N.Y., 1998). On the Galveston Movement, see ibid., 59–61; Rockaway, *Words of the Uprooted*, 27–29; and Gary Dean Best, "Jacob H. Schiff's Galveston Movement: An Experiment in Immigrant Deflection, 1907–1914," *American Jewish Archives* 30 (April 1978): 43–79.

35. Cumonow and Reiner, *Spirit Unconsumed*, 41.

36. Letters from Stanley Bero to David Bressler, November 19, 1907, and January 27, 1910, box 18, IRO Coll.

37. Letter from Stanley Bero to David Bressler, November 20, 1907, box 18, IRO Coll.; Elias Margolis to Bressler, June 25, 1908, quoted in Rockaway, *Words of the Uprooted*, 53; Abraham Solomon to David Bressler, October 14, 1912, quoted in ibid., 63.

38. Form completed by A. Braverman, December 20, 1904, Box 15, IRO Coll.; letter from Julian Morganstern to David Bressler, January 23, 1905, box 28, IRO Coll.; Bressler to Lewis Mayer, June 5, 1906, ibid.

39. See *Tenth Annual Report of the Industrial Removal Office for the Year Nineteen Hundred and Ten* (New York, 1911), table 1. Rockaway, *Words of the Uprooted*, reproduces many letters concerning IRO placements in cities both large and small.

## Chapter 4. Patterns of Stability and Mobility

1. Benjamin Hirsh, "Ninety-five Years of Beth Ha-Sholom," *Journal of the Lycoming County Historical Society* 12, no. 1 (1976): 9–10.

2. Myer Katz, "The Jews of La Crosse Past and Present," *Encounters*, ca. June 1973, 52–56.

3. Alan S. Pine, Jean C. Hershenov, and Aaron H. Lefkowitz, *Peddler to Suburbanite: The History of the Jews of Monmouth County, New Jersey* (Deal Park, N.J., 1981), 51–53.

4. See "Lazard Kahn, Manufacturer, Outstanding Man, Dies," *Hamilton Evening Journal*, March 8, 1928.

5. [Marjorie Abrams and Meyer M. Cohen], *Dedication: Congregation Cnesses Israel* (Green Bay, Wis., 1951), 31.

6. On Levinsohn, see *Congregation Ahavath Torah: An Oral History*, centennial booklet (Englewood, N.J., 1995), 9, 15. Information on Stein is from "History" on the Internet site "Stein Mart" at http://www.steinmart.com (accessed April 3, 2000).

7. Form completed by Prof. A. Gideon of Greeley, Colorado, September 27, 1904; form completed by Rabbi David Liknaitz of Leavenworth, Kansas, January 24, 1905; form completed by Charles Bernstein of Marshalltown, Iowa, October 26, 1904; all box 15, IRO Coll.

8. Letter from Stanley Bero to David Bressler, February 10, 1910, box 18, IRO Coll. Reports from Beloit, Wisconsin, August 9 and November 4, 1912; report from Alex Kahn of Bay City, Michigan, November 6, 1912; all box 17, ibid. Report from Rabbi Sol Kory of Vicksburg, Mississippi, June 30, 1904, box 15, ibid.

9. Letter from Rabbi E. Frisch of Pine Bluff, Arkansas, October 31, 1905, box 15, IRO Coll.

10. Form completed by A. Braverman of Cedar Rapids, Iowa, October 26, 1904, box 15, IRO Coll.; report from Macon, Georgia, November 4, 1912, box 17, ibid.; report from I. Warsaw of Lake Charles, Louisiana, November 30, 1905, box 15, ibid.; letter from Sam Rostoff of Lafayette, Indiana, March 18, 1907, quoted in Robert A. Rockaway, *Words of the Uprooted: Jewish Immigrants in Early Twentieth-Century America* (Ithaca, N.Y., 1998), 18.

11. Letter from Rabbi Emanuel Kahn of Joplin, Missouri, January 24, 1905; form completed by S.[?] Z. Levy of Paducah, Kentucky, June 14, 1905; both box 15, IRO Coll. Amy Hill Shevitz, "The Industrial Removal Office and the Vagaries of Americanization: Case Studies from the Ohio River Valley," 7–8, paper presented at the annual meeting of the Association for Jewish Studies, Boston, December 1997.

12. Letter from J. Sachs of Dubuque, Iowa, to David Bressler, June 7, 1907, box 98, IRO Coll., reproduced in Rockaway, *Words of the Uprooted,* 202.

13. Letter from Leo Stamm of Meridian, Mississippi, to the IRO, undated, quoted in Jack Glazier, *Dispersing the Ghetto: The Relocation of Jewish Immigrants across America* (Ithaca, N.Y., 1998), 120–21.

14. (Industrial Removal Office) *Monthly Bulletin,* August 1914, 3, quoted in David J. Goldberg, "In Dixie Land, I Take my Stand: A Study of Small-City Jewry in Five Southeastern States" (undergraduate thesis, Columbia College, 1974), 8.

15. Martin I. Hinchin, *Fourscore and Eleven: A History of the Jews of Rapides Parish, 1828–1919* (Alexandria, La.[?], 1984), A-167; *Congregation Kneseth Israel: Looking Back, Moving Forward,* 90th anniversary booklet (Annapolis, 1996), unpaginated.

16. See, for just three examples, Albert W. Levin, "The History of the Jewish Community of Racine, Wisconsin" (mimeographed document, 1942; copy in the author's possession), 1–6; Marilyn A. Posner, *The House of Israel—A Home in Washington: 100 Years of Beth Israel Congregation* (Washington, Pa., 1991), 5–17; Carol Ely, Jeffrey Hantman, and Phyllis Leffler, *To Seek the Peace of the City: Jewish Life in Charlottesville,* exhibition catalogue (Charlottesville, Va., 1994), 8–19.

17. On Paducah, see Congregation Temple Israel Minute Book for 1880–1893, 109; and Congregation Temple Israel Minute Book for 1893–1910, 2; both box 679, AJA. On Danville, see Congregation B'nai Zion Minute Book for 1890–1946, Ms. Coll. 476, AJA.

18. See Stephen Udelsohn, "Jewish Community and Cemetery Study of Brownsville," research paper, 1975, file SC-1453, AJA.

19. On Hammerslough, see Herman Eliot Snyder, "A Brief History of the Jews in

Springfield, Illinois, and of Temple Brith Sholom," in *History of Temple Brith Sholom Compiled in Commemoration of the Seventieth Anniversary* (Springfield, Ill., 1935), unpaginated; and *History of Temple B'rith Sholom Compiled in Commemoration of Its 125th Anniversary* (Springfield, Ill., 1983), unpaginated. On Bernheim, see Isaac W. Bernheim, *The Story of the Bernheim Family* (Louisville, 1910).

20. On Cohen, see Dan Rottenberg, ed., *Middletown Jews: The Tenuous Survival of an American Jewish Community* (Bloomington, Ind., 1997), xix. On the Kerns, see obituary of Heine Kern, newspaper clipping in Minute Book of Temple Israel, Lafayette, Indiana, for 1923–1941, box X-356, AJA. On Heymann, see city directories for Oshkosh, Wisconsin, 1903–04, 1910, 1919, and 1930.

21. *EJ*, s.v. "Rosenwald, U.S. family." See also *Seventy-fifth Anniversary of Beth Israel Congregation, 1861–1936* (Plattsburgh, N.Y., 1936), 29–33.

22. On the Gimbels, see *EJ*, s.v. "Gimbel, U.S. merchant family"; Sybil Stern Mervis, "History of the Jewish Community of Danville," in *Congregation Israel Synagogue, 1916–1991,* 75th anniversary booklet (Danville, Ill., 1991), 12. Information on May is from "Corporate History" on the Internet site "The May Company Department Stores" at http://www.mayco.com/may/about/history.html (accessed April 3, 2000). For the Mostov quotation, see Stephen G. Mostov, "Dun and Bradstreet Reports as a Source of Jewish Economic History," *American Jewish History* 72 (March 1983): 342.

23. On Kuhn, see Carol Bloom, comp., "The 150-Year History of the Temple Israel Congregation," in *Ahavath Achim, 1849–1999,* 150th anniversary booklet (West Lafayette, Ind., 1999), 13; and "The First Century of Temple Israel," in *Temple Israel, Lafayette, Indiana: One Hundred Years, 1849–1949* (Lafayette, Ind., 1949), 20. On Ferber, see *EJ*, s.v. "Ferber, Edna"; and Paula E. Hyman and Deborah Dash Moore, eds., *Jewish Women in America* (New York, 1997), s.v. "Ferber, Edna." See also Edna Ferber's autobiography, *A Peculiar Treasure* (New York, 1939). On Weisz, see *EJ*, s.v. "Houdini, Harry"; and Ruth Brandon, *The Life and Many Deaths of Harry Houdini* (New York, 1993), esp. 10–13. On the Warners, see *EJ*, s.v. "Warner, family of pioneers of the motion picture industry"; and Jacob S. Feldman, *The Jewish Experience in Western Pennsylvania: A History, 1755–1945* (Pittsburgh, 1986), 171.

24. See *EJ*, s.v. "Adler, Max"; "Baruch, prominent U.S. family"; "Lasky, Jesse L."; "Hurst, Fannie"; "Wiener, Norbert"; "Friedman, Milton"; and "James, Harry." On Hurst, see also Hyman and Moore, *Jewish Women in America*, s.v. "Hurst, Fannie."

25. See *EJ*, s.v. "Philipson, David"; "Goldstein, Sidney Emanuel"; "Feibelman, Julian Beck"; "Feinberg, Abraham L."; and "Liebman, Joshua Loth." See also Julian Feibelman's autobiography, *The Making of a Rabbi* (New York, 1980).

26. On Schilkerat, see Ms. Census, Appleton, Outagamie County, Wisconsin, 1920; and city directory for Appleton, 1940. On Krasnowitz, see memorial by Max Raisin in *Year Book of the Central Conference of American Rabbis* 60 (1950): 272–75; and city directories for Owensboro, Kentucky, 1903–1907. On Krakofsky, see Ms. Census, Newburyport, Essex County, Massachusetts,

1920; and city directory for Newburyport, 1925. On Shubovitz, see David Rome, *Ancestors, Descendants, and Me* (Beverly Hills, 1986), 47.

27. William Toll, "The Domestic Basis of Community: Trinidad, Colorado's Jewish Women, 1889–1910," *Rocky Mountain Jewish Historical Notes* 8 and 9 (summer and fall 1987): 5.

28. For Jackson, membership in 1863 is from Irving I. Katz, "History of Temple Beth Israel, Jackson, Michigan," 4, typescript, 1952, Histories file, AJA. For Paducah, membership in 1880 is from Congregation Temple Israel Minute Book for 1880–1893, 19; and membership in 1893 is from Congregation Temple Israel Minute Book for 1893–1910, 2.

29. See Ms. Census, Lafayette, Tippecanoe County, Indiana, 1880; city directory for Lafayette, 1889; Ms. Census, Appleton, 1880; city directory for Appleton, 1891.

30. See Ms. Census, Lexington, Fayette County, Kentucky, 1880; city directory for Lexington, 1902.

31. See Adath Israel Minute Book, 1903–1909, pp. 94–97, box 673, AJA; city directories for Lexington, Kentucky, 1908, 1919, and 1927.

32. See Congregation B'nai Zion Minute Book, 1890–1946.

33. See Ms. Census, Newburyport, 1920; city directories for Newburyport, 1925–26 and 1931–32; Ms. Census, Bradford, McKean County, Pennsylvania, 1920; city directories for Bradford, 1925 and 1929; Ms. Census, Jackson, Jackson County, Michigan, 1920; and city directory for Jackson, 1925.

34. See Ms. Census, Lafayette, 1880; city directories for Lafayette, 1889 and 1899; Ms. Census, Appleton, 1880; city directory for Appleton, 1901; Ms. Census, Hamilton, Butler County, Ohio, 1880; city directory for Hamilton, 1902.

35. See Ms. Census, Appleton, 1920; city directories for Appleton, 1940 and 1950; Ms. Census, Bradford, 1920; city directory for Bradford, 1940.

36. See Hinchin, *Fourscore and Eleven*, 162; obituary of Lena Allen, *Bradford Era*, March 16, 1921; obituary of Bettie Netter Benjamin, clipping in "Kleisdorff family" file, Small Collections, AJA.

37. See Minute Book of Temple Israel, Lafayette, for 1923–1941. On Bernard Sobel, see *EJ*, s.v. "Sobel, Bernard."

38. The obituaries studied appeared in the *Lexington Herald*, the *Lexington Leader*, and the *Lexington Sunday Herald-Leader* between 1915 and 1978.

39. Dennis S. Devlin, *Muskegon's Jewish Community: A Centennial History, 1888–1988* (Muskegon, Mich., 1988), 6, 11; Works Progress Administration for Mississippi, *Source Material for Mississippi History*, vol. 44 (Jackson, Miss.[?], 1938), 523.

40. See Ms. Census, Lexington, 1880; city directory for Lexington, 1902; Ms. Census, Appleton, 1880; city directories for Appleton, 1891 and 1901. On David Hammel, see also Ferber, *Peculiar Treasure*, 58.

41. This analysis is based on membership lists in Congregation B'nai Zion Minute Book, 1890–1946.

42. The Lafayette analysis (involving thirty-four homeowners and forty-eight renters) is based on information in Ms. Census, Lafayette, 1920; and city

directory for Lafayette, 1929. The Newburyport analysis (forty-seven home-owners and twenty-five renters) is based on information in Ms. Census, Newburyport, 1920; and city directory for Newburyport, 1931. The Vicksburg analysis (fifty-six homeowners and forty-eight renters) is based on information in Ms. Census, Vicksburg, Warren County, Mississippi, 1920; and city directory for Vicksburg, 1929.

43. The Jackson analysis is based on information in Ms. Census, Jackson, 1920; and city directory for Jackson, 1925. The Alexandria analysis (involving fifty-five homeowners and thirty-seven renters) is based on information in Ms. Census, Alexandria, Rapides Parish, Louisiana, 1920; and city directory for Alexandria, 1931. The Bradford analysis (105 cases) is based on information in Ms. Census, Bradford, 1920; and city directories for Bradford, 1929 and 1940.

44. See Ms. Census, Appleton, 1880; city directory for Appleton, 1891; Ms. Census, Lafayette, 1920; city directory for Lafayette, 1924; Ms. Census, Jackson, 1920; and city directory for Jackson, 1925.

45. See Ms. Census, Bradford, 1920; city directories for Bradford, 1925, 1929, and 1940; Ms. Census, Newburyport, 1920; and city directories for Newburyport, 1925–26 and 1931–32.

46. See city directories for Newburyport, 1919–20, 1922–23, 1925–26, and 1931–32.

47. See obituary of L. M. Krienson, *Bradford Era,* January 3, 1921; and Dunbar Rowland, *History of Mississippi, Heart of the South,* vol. 4 (1925; reprint, Spartanburg, S.C., 1978), 320–21.

48. Paul P. Gordon and Rita S. Gordon, *The Jews beneath the Clustered Spires* (Hagerstown, Md., 1971), 104–05.

49. Carolyn Gray LeMaster, *A Corner of the Tapestry: A History of the Jewish Experience in Arkansas, 1820s–1990s* (Fayetteville, Ark., 1994), 80–81; Ruthe Winegarten and Cathy Schechter, *Deep in the Heart: The Lives and Legends of Texas Jews* (Austin, 1990), 89; Abraham P. Nasatir, "The Nasatir Family in Santa Ana, California, 1898 to 1915," *Western States Jewish Historical Quarterly* 15 (April 1983): 257.

50. On Gloversville, see Herbert M. Engel, *Shtetl in the Adirondacks: The Story of Gloversville and Its Jews* (Fleischmanns, N.Y., 1991), 36. Various *AJYB* listings report Gloversville's Jewish population as 650 in 1918, 1,500 in 1927, and 1,375 in 1937. On the Iron Range, see Chester Jay Proshan, "Eastern European Jewish Immigrants and Their Children on the Minnesota Iron Range, 1890s–1980s" (Ph.D. diss., University of Minnesota, 1998), 153–54. On Petaluma, see Kenneth L. Kann, *Comrades and Chicken Ranchers: The Story of a California Jewish Community* (Ithaca, N.Y., 1993); and Bonnie Burt and Judy Montell, directors, *A Home on the Range* (video, 2002).

51. See Dean R. Esslinger, *Immigrants and the City: Ethnicity and Mobility in a Nineteenth-Century Midwestern Community* (Port Washington, N.Y., 1975), 43; Gordon W. Kirk, *The Promise of American Life: Social Mobility in a Nineteenth-Century Immigrant Community: Holland, Michigan, 1847–1894* (Philadelphia,

1978), 51; and John Bodnar, *Immigration and Industrialization: Ethnicity in an American Mill Town, 1870–1940* (Pittsburgh, 1977), 69.

## Chapter 5. Patterns of Livelihood and Class

1. See, for example, Nathan Goldberg, "Occupational Patterns of American Jews, II," *Jewish Review* 3 (1945): 173; Ida Cohen Selavan, "Jewish Wage Earners in Pittsburgh, 1890–1930," *American Jewish Historical Quarterly* 65 (March 1976): 272–85; and Judith E. Endelman, *The Jewish Community of Indianapolis, 1849 to the Present* (Bloomington, Ind., 1984), 84–85.
2. See Nathan Goldberg, "Occupational Patterns of American Jews," *Jewish Review* 3 (1945): 11–12; Joel Perlmann, "Beyond New York: The Occupations of Russian Jewish Immigrants in Providence, R.I., and in Other Small Jewish Communities, 1900–1915," *American Jewish History* 72 (March 1983), esp. 374 (table 2).
3. On peddling see, for example, Hasia R. Diner, *A Time for Gathering: The Second Migration, 1820–1880,* vol. 2 of Henry L. Feingold, series ed., The Jewish People in America (Baltimore, 1992), 66–73; on entrepreneurship, see ibid., 76–81.
4. Rudolf Glanz, "Notes on Early Jewish Peddling in America," *Jewish Social Studies* 7 (1945): 135–36.
5. See Doris Kirkpatrick, *Around the World in Fitchburg* (Fitchburg, Mass., 1975), 143–44; David Rome, *Ancestors, Descendants, and Me* (Beverly Hills, 1986), 6, 32, 145–48; Ms. Census, Fitchburg, Worcester County, Massachusetts, 1920.
6. See Harry L. Golden, *Jewish Roots in the Carolinas: A Pattern of American Philo-Semitism* (Charlotte, N.C., 1955), 38; Hal Rothman, " 'Same Horse, New Wagon': Tradition and Assimilation among the Jews of Wichita, 1865–1930," *Great Plains Quarterly* 15 (spring 1995): 94.
7. See *Congregation Ahavath Torah: An Oral History,* centennial booklet (Englewood, N.J., 1995), 9; Ms. Census, Lexington, Fayette County, Kentucky, 1920; Ms. Census, Nashua, Hillsborough County, New Hampshire, 1920.
8. See Daniel Soyer, "Class Conscious Workers and Immigrant Entrepreneurs: The Ambiguity of Class among Eastern European Jewish Immigrants to the United States at the Turn of the Century," *Labor History* 42 (February 2001): 45–59. See also Edward Shapiro, "American Jews and the Business Mentality," *Judaism* 27 (spring 1978): 214–21.
9. Paul P. Gordon and Rita S. Gordon, *The Jews beneath the Clustered Spires* (Hagerstown, Md., 1971), 116.
10. For an interesting discussion of both cultural and structural factors in the development of American Jewish entrepreneurship, see Shelly Tenenbaum, *A Credit to Their Community: Jewish Loan Societies in the United States, 1880–1945* (Detroit, 1993), chaps. 1–2. See also Moses Kligsberg, "Jewish Immigrants in Business: A Sociological Study," *American Jewish Historical Quarterly* 56 (March 1967): 283–318. On ethnic solidarity among Jews and other "mid-

dleman minorities," see Walter P. Zenner, *Minorities in the Middle: A Cross-Cultural Analysis* (Albany, N.Y., 1991), esp. 19–21 and chap. 4. On these themes, see also Chester Jay Proshan, "Eastern European Jewish Immigrants and Their Children on the Minnesota Iron Range, 1890s–1980s" (Ph.D. diss., University of Minnesota, 1998), 99–111; Deborah R. Weiner, "A History of Jewish Life in the Central Appalachian Coalfields, 1870s to 1970s" (Ph.D. diss., West Virginia University, 2002), esp. 202; and Robert P. Davis, "Business" on the Internet site "Virtual Restoration of Small-town Synagogues" at http://geocities.com/txsynvr/txsyn.html (accessed March 26, 2000).

11. Douglas W. Jones, "A Brief History of Congregation Agudas Achim of Iowa City," 2, lecture delivered at the congregation, September 19, 1997; copy in the author's possession.

12. Robert Shosteck, *Small-Town Jewry Tell Their Story* (Washington, D.C., 1953), 11–16. See also Jacob Lestschinsky, "Economic and Social Development of American Jewry," in *The Jewish People, Past and Present,* vol. 4 (New York, 1955), 90.

13. See, for example, Proshan, "Eastern European Jewish Immigrants," 200.

14. City directory for Middletown, New York, 1905, 69; Joy Cumonow and Fred N. Reiner, *The Spirit Unconsumed: A History of the Topeka Jewish Community* (Topeka, 1979), 74; Gordon and Gordon, *Jews beneath the Clustered Spires,* 146; Blaine P. Lamb, "Frontiersmen in Broadcloth: Jews in Early Phoenix, 1870–1920," *Western States Jewish History* 25 (October 1992): 9; city directory for Vicksburg, Mississippi, 1929, 127.

15. See, for example, Golden, *Jewish Roots in the Carolinas,* 38; and Stella Suberman, *The Jew Store* (Chapel Hill, N.C., 1998), although the latter tells the story only of a lone Jewish family in a pseudonymous small town in Tennessee.

16. Abraham Isaacson, "Leaps and Bounds: From the Russian Ghetto to the Mississippi Delta," part 2, p. 75, typescript, n.d., Microfilm 1975, AJA.

17. On Jewish storekeepers and their black clientele, see Clive Webb, "Jewish Merchants and Black Customers in the Age of Jim Crow," *Southern Jewish History* 2 (1999): 55–80; and Golden, *Jewish Roots in the Carolinas,* 47.

18. Carol Ely, Jeffrey Hantman, and Phyllis Leffler, *To Seek the Peace of the City: Jewish Life in Charlottesville,* exhibition catalogue (Charlottesville, Va., 1994), 9, 15.

19. John Barnhart and Donald Carmony, *Indiana: From Frontier to Industrial Commonwealth,* vol. 3 (New York, 1954), 206.

20. See city directory for Danbury, Connecticut, 1924; "$300,000 in Dry Goods: S. Waxelbaum & Son," in *A Picture of Macon, Georgia: Macon Evening News, Industrial Issue,* 1889; Melanie Torbett, "Building a Downtown," *CENLA: The Magazine of Central Louisiana,* May/June 1993, 10; Leo E. Turitz and Evelyn Turitz, *Jews in Early Mississippi* (Jackson, Miss., 1983), 103; Jerry Miller, "Marion's Chosen Few," *Marion Chronicle-Tribune Magazine,* July 17, 1977, 4; Carolyn Gray LeMaster, *A Corner of the Tapestry: A History of the Jewish Experience in Arkansas, 1820s–1990s* (Fayetteville, Ark., 1994), 153; Ruthe Winegarten and Cathy Schechter, *Deep in the Heart: The Lives and Legends of Texas*

*Jews* (Austin, 1990), 44; Proshan, "Eastern European Jewish Immigrants," 180; city directories for Leavenworth, Kansas, 1898–99, 1900–01, 1909, 1913–14, and 1917–18.

21. Myer Katz, "The Jews of La Crosse Past and Present," *Encounters,* ca. June 1973, 52; Fern Honeywell Martin and Paula Alexander Woods, *Greater Lafayette: A Pictorial History* (St. Louis, 1989), 106; Rothman, " 'Same Horse, New Wagon,' " 86, 90; Lamb, "Frontiersmen in Broadcloth," 7.

22. Autobiographical essay by Sanford Glickson in Howard V. Epstein, ed., *Jews in Small Towns: Legends and Legacies* (Santa Rosa, Calif., 1997), 458; city directory for Mobile, Alabama, 1900; Norton B. Stern, "Santa Ana, California: Its First Jews and Jewish Congregations," *Western States Jewish Historical Quarterly* 14 (April 1982): 252; Miller, "Marion's Chosen Few," 5.

23. Gordon and Gordon, *Jews beneath the Clustered Spires,* 146; city directory for Oshkosh, Wisconsin, 1908; city directory for Oswego, New York, 1931–32; city directory for Bristol, Connecticut, 1929; Oscar Fleishaker, *The Illinois-Iowa Jewish Community on the Banks of the Mississippi River* (n.p., 1971), 84.

24. Ms. Census, Lafayette, Tippecanoe County, Indiana, 1880; Ms. Census, Newburyport, Essex County, Massachusetts, 1920; Ms. Census, Modesto, Stanislas County, California, 1920.

25. Ms. Census, Jackson, Jackson County, Michigan, 1880; Ms. Census, Lexington, 1880; Ms. Census, Vicksburg, Warren County, Mississippi, 1880; Ms. Census, Fitchburg, 1920; Ms. Census, Bradford, McKean County, Pennsylvania, 1920; Ms. Census, Alexandria, Rapides Parish, Louisiana, 1920; Deborah R. Weiner, "The Jews of Keystone: Life in a Multicultural Boomtown," *Southern Jewish History* 2 (1999): 4, 6; Ms. Census, Hamilton, Butler County, Ohio, 1920; Marilyn A. Posner, *The House of Israel—A Home in Washington: 100 Years of Beth Israel Congregation* (Washington, Pa., 1991), 26.

26. Dunbar Rowland, *History of Mississippi, Heart of the South,* vol. 4 (1925; reprint, Spartanburg, S.C., 1978), 128–31.

27. Phil Goodstein, *Exploring Jewish Colorado* (Denver, 1992), 88; Walt Williams, "City's Jewish Heritage: Sol Elias to Mark Spitz," *Modesto Bee,* March 3, 1974. On the Plato family, see also George H. Tinkham, *History of Stanislaus County, California* (Los Angeles, 1921), 340.

28. Ely, Hantman, and Leffler, *To Seek the Peace of the City,* 17–19; Cumonow and Reiner, *Spirit Unconsumed,* 9, 74; Proshan, "Eastern European Jewish Immigrants," 280–81; Anita Shafer Goodstein, "History of the Jews of Ithaca" (mimeographed report, 1955; copy in the author's possession), 5; "Keiler Family," Biographies file, AJA.

29. Edna Ferber, *A Peculiar Treasure* (New York, 1939), 93; Lippman quotation in Proshan, "Eastern European Jewish Immigrants," 199. For a good discussion of the role of Jews in the spread of consumer culture to small-town America, see Weiner, "History of Jewish Life in the Central Appalachian Coalfields," 220–35.

30. Ely, Hantman, and Leffler, *To Seek the Peace of the City,* 15; Arnold W. Hirsch, "Remembering Donora's Jewish Community," 5, document MFF 044, ca.

1995, Historical Society of Western Pennsylvania Archives, Pittsburgh; *Congregation Ahavath Torah: An Oral History,* centennial booklet (Englewood, N.J., 1995), 2.

31.  Goodstein, *Exploring Jewish Colorado,* 86; city directory for Paducah, Kentucky, 1881–82; city directories for Leavenworth, Kansas, 1898–99 and 1909; city directory for Mobile, Alabama, 1900; city directory for Alexandria, Louisiana, 1931.

32.  City directory for Vicksburg, Mississippi, 1929, street listings.

33.  Miller, "Marion's Chosen Few," 5; Tony Fargo, "Whither Ashland's Jewish Community?" *Ashland Daily Independent,* December 6, 1994 (special issue on "Religion").

34.  "A Few San Bernardino Businessmen in 1892," *Western States Jewish Historical Quarterly* 15 (January 1983): 171; Gordon and Gordon, *Jews beneath the Clustered Spires,* 141; David J. Goldberg, "In Dixie Land, I Take my Stand: A Study of Small-City Jewry in Five Southeastern States" (undergraduate thesis, Columbia College, 1974), 29; Segal advertisement in city directory for Oshkosh, Wisconsin, 1919.

35.  Ms. Census, Appleton, Outagamie County, Wisconsin, 1880; Ferber, *Peculiar Treasure,* 59; "Jewish Citizens Play Prominent Part in All Affairs of City," *Lexington Herald,* April 15, 1917; Kirkpatrick, *Around the World in Fitchburg,* 149–50; Ms. Census, Modesto, 1920.

36.  See Glanz, "Notes on Early Jewish Peddling," 124–25. On Deutsch, see Fleishaker, *Illinois-Iowa Jewish Community,* 84. On Levy and Isaac, see Ms. Census, Lafayette, 1920; and obituary of Maurice Levy, newspaper clipping in Minute Book of Temple Israel, Lafayette, Indiana, for 1923–1941, box X-356, AJA. On Meyer, see *Biographical Memoirs of Wabash County, Indiana* (Chicago, 1901), 450–52. On the Rissman brothers and Friedman, see Sybil Stern Mervis, "History of the Jewish Community of Danville," in *Congregation Israel Synagogue, 1916–1991,* 75th anniversary booklet (Danville, Ill., 1991), 14, 18.

37.  Golden, *Jewish Roots in the Carolinas,* 40; Richard L. Zweigenhaft, "Two Cities in North Carolina: A Comparative Study of Jews in the Upper Class," *Jewish Social Studies* 41 (1979): 297.

38.  See quotation from Habacht in Ruth Marcus Patt, *The Jewish Scene in New Jersey's Raritan Valley, 1698–1948* (New Brunswick, N.J., 1978), 26; David G. Stahl, "Our History," in *Temple Adath Yeshurun Centennial, 1891–1991* (Manchester, N.H., 1991), 28–29.

39.  City directory for Mobile, Alabama, 1906; Proshan, "Eastern European Jewish Immigrants," 97; Kirkpatrick, *Around the World in Fitchburg,* 153–54; Dennis S. Devlin, *Muskegon's Jewish Community: A Centennial History, 1888–1988* (Muskegon, Mich., 1988), 25, 33.

40.  See, for example, W. Lloyd Warner and Leo Srole, *The Social Systems of American Ethnic Groups,* Yankee City Series, vol. 3 (New Haven, 1945), 200–203; and S. Joseph Fauman, "The Jews in the Waste Industry in Detroit," *Jewish Social Studies* 3 (January 1941): 41–56.

41. City directory for Leavenworth, Kansas, 1909; city directory for Colorado Springs, Colorado, 1926; city directory for Oswego, New York, 1931–32; city directory for Oshkosh, Wisconsin, 1930; Ms. Census, Appleton, 1920.

42. City directory for Modesto, California, 1935, 195; advertisements in *Lafayette Morning Journal,* April 18, 1906, and in *Lafayette Journal,* July 6, 1914. On the situation in Michigan in the decades before World War II, where Jews were said to "control" the scrap business in towns such as Ann Arbor, Lansing, and Port Huron, see Rochelle Berger Elstein, "Synagogue Architecture in Michigan and the Midwest: Material Culture and the Dynamics of Jewish Accommodation, 1865–1945" (Ph.D. diss., Michigan State University, 1986), 304.

43. Letter from Adolph Traub of Jackson, Michigan, to IRO, n.d., in reply to letter of August 30, 1913, box 48, IRO Coll.

44. Katz, "Jews of La Crosse," 61; Brian Deming, *Jackson: An Illustrated History* (Woodland Hills, Calif., 1984), 124; Max Friedman, "Kalamazoo Jewish Family History," typescript, ca. 1983, vertical file "Jews," Kalamazoo Public Library, Kalamazoo, Mich.; Mervis, "History of the Jewish Community of Danville," 18.

45. City directory for Mobile, Alabama, 1900. See also Elliott Ashkenazi, *The Business of Jews in Louisiana, 1840–1875* (Tuscaloosa, Ala., 1988); and "A Brief History of the Montgomery and Selma Jewish Communities," *Circa* (Museum of the Southern Jewish Experience) 5 (spring 1995), unpaginated.

46. Rothman, " 'Same Horse, New Wagon,' " 85–86; Lamb, "Frontiersmen in Broadcloth," 5, 8.

47. See city directory for Paducah, Kentucky, 1881–82; *A Newspaper Reference Work: Men of Affairs of Paducah and Western Kentucky* (Paducah, Ky., 1912), s.v. "Joseph L. Friedman" and "John William Keiler"; "Bernheim Brothers," *Paducah Sun-Democrat,* March 28, 1968; letter from Sol Dreyfus to Temple Israel of Paducah, Kentucky, February 21, 1910 (copy in the author's possession).

48. Amy Hill Shevitz, "The Industrial Removal Office and the Vagaries of Americanization: Case Studies from the Ohio River Valley," 10, paper presented at the annual meeting of the Association for Jewish Studies, Boston, December 1997; Ms. Census, Bradford, 1920; Rochelle Berger Elstein, "The Jews of Houghton-Hancock and Their Synagogue," *Michigan Jewish History* 38 (November 1998): 4.

49. On Belmer, see Alan S. Pine, Jean C. Hershenov, and Aaron H. Lefkowitz, *Peddler to Suburbanite: The History of the Jews of Monmouth County, New Jersey* (Deal Park, N.J., 1981), 75–76. On Benton Harbor, see Jennifer R. Kraft, "Children of Israel Synagogue and the Jewish Community of Benton Harbor, Michigan: A History" (term paper, Jewish Theological Seminary of America, 1992), 6. On Mount Clemens, see Dorothy M. Magee, ed., *Centennial History of Mount Clemens, Michigan, 1879–1979* (Mount Clemens, Mich., 1980), esp. 118–20, available on the Internet site "Mount Clemens Local History" at http://www.macomb.lib.mi.us/mountclemens/local.htm (accessed September 13, 2002). On the approach of American Jews to vacationing, see

Andrew R. Heinze, *Adapting to Abundance: Jewish Immigrants, Mass Consumption, and the Search for American Identity* (New York, 1990), 124–30.

50. Proshan, "Eastern European Jewish Immigrants," 97.

51. See Katz, "Jews of La Crosse," 41, 48.

52. See *Biographical Memoirs of Wabash County,* 507–09; Miller, "Marion's Chosen Few," 4.

53. On Katz, see Sunny Rabenstock, "Emanu El—God Is with Us: A History of Congregation Emanu El, San Bernardino, California," in *100th Anniversary, Congregation Emanu El* (San Bernardino, Calif., 1991), 6–7; and Norton B. Stern, "Introduction" to Marcus Katz, "The Jewish New Year 5650 in San Bernardino," *Western States Jewish History* 26 (January 1994): 113–15. On Ganz, see Lamb, "Frontiersmen in Broadcloth," 8. On Slater, see Norton B. Stern, "Log of California Jewish History Trip," file SC-1547, AJA.

54. On Kaufman, see Ely, Hantman, and Leffler, *To Seek the Peace of the City,* 11. On Lowenstein, see Gordon and Gordon, *Jews beneath the Clustered Spires,* 141, 142. On Kramer, see autobiographical essay by Anne G. Kramer in Epstein, *Jews in Small Towns,* 382.

55. See Winegarten and Schechter, *Deep in the Heart,* 70; Devlin, *Muskegon's Jewish Community,* 25.

56. Fleishaker, *Illinois-Iowa Jewish Community,* 84; Aaron Kohen, "Five Small Jewish Communities in Illinois: Place and Time in Ottawa, Spring Valley, LaSalle, Joliet and Aurora" (undergraduate thesis, University of Chicago, 1995), 59; Belinda Gergel and Richard Gergel, *In Pursuit of the Tree of Life: A History of the Early Jews of Columbia, South Carolina, and the Tree of Life Congregation* (Columbia, S.C., 1996), 61; *Biographical Memoirs of Wabash County,* 560; Ms. Census, Lafayette, 1920; Ms. Census, Vicksburg, 1920.

57. James C. Cobb, ed., *The Mississippi Delta and the World: The Memoirs of David L. Cohn* (Baton Rouge, 1995), preface; Kirkpatrick, *Around the World in Fitchburg,* 156–57; Rothman, "'Same Horse, New Wagon,'" 98.

58. See Simon Litman, *Looking Back: An Autobiographical Sketch* (n.p., ca. 1960).

59. Ely, Hantman, and Leffler, *To Seek the Peace of the City,* 23; Jules Janick, "A Jewish History of Purdue, 1920–1940," *Purdue University Jewish Studies Program Newsletter* 46 (January–February 1991): 1–7; Douglas W. Jones, "Jewish Life at Iowa" (typescript., 1997; copy in the author's possession), 18–23.

60. Shosteck, *Small-Town Jewry Tell Their Story,* 13–14.

61. Rothman, "'Same Horse, New Wagon,'" 95.

62. Helene Gerard, "Yankees in Yarmulkes: Small-Town Jewish Life in Eastern Long Island," *American Jewish Archives* 38 (April 1986): 29–30; Pine, Hershenov, and Lefkowitz, *Peddler to Suburbanite,* 86; *Temple Shaare Tefilah: Bar Mitzvah,* 83d anniversary booklet (Norwood, Mass., 1991), unpaginated; city directory for Newburyport, Massachusetts, 1922–23; Ms. Census, Newburyport, 1920; Ms. Census, Lafayette, 1920; autobiographical essay by Evelyn Rose Benson in Epstcin, *Jews in Small Towns,* 564.

63. On Durham, see Leonard Rogoff, *Homelands: Southern Jewish Identity in Dur-*

*ham and Chapel Hill, North Carolina* (Tuscaloosa, Ala., 2001), chap. 4; Leonard Rogoff, "Jewish Proletarians in the New South: The Durham Cigarette Rollers," *American Jewish History* 82 (1994–95): 141–57; and Eli N. Evans, *The Provincials: A Personal History of the Jews in the South,* rev. ed. (New York, 1997), 14–17. On Setauket, for which Jewish population figures are unavailable, see Gerard, "Yankees in Yarmulkes," 32–33. On Middletown, see "One Hundred Years of Jewish Congregations in Connecticut: An Architectural Survey," *Connecticut Jewish History* 2 (fall 1991): 97. On Wabash, see Joseph Levine, "Jewish Community Small," in Linda Robertson, ed., *Wabash County History: Bicentennial Edition, 1976* (Marceline, Mo., 1976), 164; and *Biographical Memoirs of Wabash County,* 450–53. On Northumberland, see "Jewish Cemetery" (reference citation from Local History Room, Priestley-Forsyth Memorial Library, Northumberland, Pennsylvania; copy in the author's possession).

64. Ferber, *Peculiar Treasure,* 63; Katz, "Jews of La Crosse," 62.

65. On domestic service in the late nineteenth and early twentieth centuries, see, for example, Daniel E. Sutherland, *Americans and Their Servants: Domestic Service in the United States from 1800 to 1920* (Baton Rouge, 1981), esp. 34 and chap. 10; and Phyllis Palmer, *Domesticity and Dirt: Housewives and Domestic Servants in the United States, 1920–1945* (Philadelphia, 1989), esp. 69–71. On domestic servants on the Iron Range, see Proshan, "Eastern European Jewish Immigrants," 115.

66. W. Lloyd Warner and Paul S. Lunt, *The Social Life of a Modern Community,* Yankee City Series, vol. 1 (New Haven, 1941), 224–25.

67. Ernest I. Jacob, "Fifty Years of Jewish Life in Springfield, Mo.," in *Fifty Years— Temple Israel, Springfield, Missouri: Invitation to the Anniversary Celebration* (Springfield, Mo., 1943), unpaginated; autobiographical essay by Herschel Rubin in Epstein, *Jews in Small Towns,* 537; Goodstein, "History of the Jews of Ithaca," 4.

68. Newton J. Friedman, "A History of Temple Beth Israel of Macon, Georgia" (D.Th. diss., Burton Seminary of Colorado, 1955), 18.

69. On the founding of Adath Israel, see the following two sources, which do not agree in all respects. Adath Israel Minute Book, 1903–1909, box 673, AJA; and *Temple Adath Israel, Lexington, Kentucky, Seventy Fifth Anniversary* (Lexington, Ky., 1979), 5–7. Biographical information about the first seatholders at Adath Israel was gleaned from several sources, chief among them the *Microcode Index to the 1910 Federal Population Census for Kentucky* (Washington, D.C., ca. 1982) and the city directory for Lexington, Kentucky, 1908.

70. Letter from Abraham Solomon to David Bressler, October 14, 1912, quoted in Robert A. Rockaway, *Words of the Uprooted: Jewish Immigrants in Early Twentieth-Century America* (Ithaca, N.Y., 1998), 63–64.

71. See "Lafayette, Indiana—B'nai B'rith Barzillai Lodge No. 111, Application and initiation certificates 1868–1946," Microfilm 2515, AJA.

72. William Toll, "The Domestic Basis of Community: Trinidad, Colorado's Jewish Women, 1889–1910, *Rocky Mountain Jewish Historical Notes* 8 and 9

(summer and fall 1987): 4–5; Jane Manaster, "Synagogue Architecture of Corsicana, Texas, and Gabin, Poland: Copy or Coincidence," 23, typescript, ca. 1984; copy in file SC-7691, AJA.

73. Ms. Census, Alexandria, 1880; Ms. Census, Hamilton, 1880; Ms. Census, Bradford, 1880; Ms. Census, Jackson, 1880.
74. Ms. Census, Alexandria, 1920; Ms. Census, Hamilton, 1920.
75. Ms. Census, Bradford, 1920.
76. Ms. Census, Alexandria, 1920; Ms. Census, Lexington, 1920.
77. Ms. Census, Fitchburg, 1920; Ms. Census, Nashua, 1920.

## Chapter 6. Patterns of Family Life

1. Hal Rothman, " 'Same Horse, New Wagon': Tradition and Assimilation among the Jews of Wichita, 1865–1930," *Great Plains Quarterly* 15 (spring 1995): 96.
2. *A Century of Living Judaism,* Temple Sholom centennial booklet (Galesburg, Ill., 1967), unpaginated; Myer Katz, "The Jews of La Crosse Past and Present," *Encounters,* ca. June 1973, 51; J. F. Everhart, *History of Muskingum County, Ohio, with Illustrations and Biographical Sketches* (1882; reprint, Evansville, Ind., 1974), 202–03.
3. Ms. Census, Alexandria, Rapides Parish, Louisiana, 1880; Ms. Census, Jackson, Jackson County, Michigan, 1880; Ms. Census, Appleton, Outagamie County, Wisconsin, 1880; Edna Ferber, *A Peculiar Treasure* (New York, 1939), 59; Juanita Brooks, *History of the Jews in Utah and Idaho* (Salt Lake City, 1973), 134.
4. Louis Ginsberg, *History of the Jews of Petersburg, 1789–1950* (Petersburg, Va., 1954), 67–68; Ms. Census, Alexandria, 1920; Ms. Census, Lexington, Fayette County, Kentucky, 1920; Ms. Census, Newburyport, Essex County, Massachusetts, 1920; autobiographical essay by Paul Kronick in Howard V. Epstein, ed., *Jews in Small Towns: Legends and Legacies* (Santa Rosa, Calif., 1997), 168.
5. Paul P. Gordon and Rita S. Gordon, *The Jews beneath the Clustered Spires* (Hagerstown, Md., 1971), 102.
6. *Dedication: Temple Beth Israel* (Sharon, Pa., 1950), 7; Wendy Machlovitz, *Clara Lowenburg Moses: Memoir of a Southern Jewish Woman* (Jackson, Miss., 2000), 3–4; Gunther Rothenberg, *Congregation Albert, 1897–1972* (Albuquerque, 1972); questionnaire completed by Bernard Wolf Barron of Lexington, Kentucky, 1993, in the author's possession; *Temple B'nai Shalom, Benton Harbor, Mich., 1895–1995,* centennial booklet (Benton Harbor, Mich., 1995), unpaginated.
7. Samuel W. Durant, *History of Kalamazoo County, Michigan* (Philadelphia, 1880), 247; William Toll, "The Domestic Basis of Community: Trinidad, Colorado's Jewish Women, 1889–1910," *Rocky Mountain Jewish Historical Notes* 8 and 9 (summer and fall 1987): 5; Katz, "Jews of La Crosse," 59; *The Anniversary Story of Congregation B'er Chayim,* centennial booklet (Cumberland, Md., 1953), chap. 4.
8. For the specific examples given, see Ms. Census, Vicksburg, Warren County,

Mississippi, 1880; and Ms. Census, Bradford, McKean County, Pennsylvania, 1920.

9. See Ms. Census, Appleton, 1880; Ms. Census, Lafayette, Tippecanoe County, Indiana, 1880; and Ms. Census, Bradford, 1880.

10. See Ms. Census, Hamilton, Butler County, Ohio, 1920; Ms. Census, Fitchburg, Worcester County, Massachusetts, 1920; Ms. Census, Nashua, Hillsborough County, New Hampshire, 1920.

11. See Ms. Census, Alexandria, 1920; and Martin I. Hinchin, *Fourscore and Eleven: A History of the Jews of Rapides Parish, 1828–1919* (Alexandria, La.[?], 1984), passim.

12. Ms. Census, Vicksburg, 1920; Ms. Census, Appleton, 1920.

13. Ms. Census, Jackson, 1880; Ms. Census, Vicksburg, 1880; Ms. Census, Alexandria, 1920; Ms. Census, Fitchburg, 1920; Ms. Census, Vicksburg, 1920.

14. W. Lloyd Warner and Leo Srole, *The Social Systems of American Ethnic Groups,* Yankee City Series, vol. 3 (New Haven, 1945), 80–81; Ms. Census, Newburyport, 1920; Toll, "Domestic Basis of Community," 5.

15. See, for example, Karla Goldman, *Beyond the Synagogue Gallery: Finding a Place for Women in American Judaism* (Cambridge, Mass., 2000), 9–11; Jenna Weissman Joselit, "The Special Sphere of the Middle-Class American Jewish Woman: The Synagogue Sisterhood, 1890–1940," in Jack Wertheimer, ed., *The American Synagogue: A Sanctuary Transformed* (Cambridge, 1987), 206–10. On nineteenth- and early twentieth-century concepts of proper middle-class womanhood in general, see Barbara Welter, "The Cult of True Womanhood, 1820–1860," *American Quarterly* 18 (summer 1966); and Karen Blair, *The Clubwoman as Feminist: True Womanhood Redefined, 1868–1914* (New York, 1980).

16. Warner and Srole, *Social Systems,* 113–14.

17. Katz, "Jews of La Crosse," 43–44; Rothman, "'Same Horse, New Wagon,'" 96.

18. Joy Cumonow and Fred N. Reiner, *The Spirit Unconsumed: A History of the Topeka Jewish Community* (Topeka, 1979), 43; Chester Jay Proshan, "Eastern European Jewish Immigrants and Their Children on the Minnesota Iron Range, 1890s–1980s" (Ph.D. diss., University of Minnesota, 1998), 109; city directory for Alexandria, Louisiana, 1931; Susan Fleischer Breitburg, "My Grandfather's Butcher Shop," on the Internet site "Long Island: Our Story" at http://www.lihistory.com/specfam/fambreit.htm (accessed October 8, 1999).

19. Ms. Censuses, Alexandria, 1880, 1920; Ms. Census, Appleton, 1920; Ms. Census, Fitchburg, 1920; autobiographical essay by Evelyn Rose Benson in Epstein, *Jews in Small Towns,* 564. On Malachowsky, see also Hinchin, *Fourscore and Eleven,* 74.

20. David J. Goldberg, "An Historical Community Study of Wilmington Jewry, 1738–1925" (seminar paper, school unknown, 1976; available at Hebrew Union College Library, Cincinnati), 36–37.

21. City directory for Lafayette, Indiana, 1924; city directory for Bradford, Pennsylvania, 1925; David Rome, *Ancestors, Descendants, and Me* (Beverly Hills, 1986), 32.

22. See Mary Beth Norton et al., *A People and a Nation: A History of the United States,* vol. 2 (Boston, 1982), 584.

23. Katz, "Jews of La Crosse," 59, 37; Warner and Srole, *Social Systems,* 150; notice regarding Rosen in *American Jewish Times,* May 1936, 15. On the development of high school education in the late nineteenth and early twentieth centuries, see Joel Spring, *The American School, 1642–1985* (New York, 1986), 149–81, 193–207. The World War I era attendance figures are from 194.

24. Questionnaires completed by Joseph Klein, Edward Ellenbogen, Meyer H. Marx, and Leonard Mervis, 1935, in "Student Survey, 1935–1936," Ms. Coll. 5, AJA.

25. Paula E. Hyman and Deborah Dash Moore, eds., *Jewish Women in America* (New York, 1997), s.v. "Landau, Sara"; Ms. Census, Fitchburg, 1920; Leonard Rogoff, *Homelands: Southern Jewish Identity in Durham and Chapel Hill, North Carolina* (Tuscaloosa, Ala., 2001), 82.

26. "Gertrude Weil" exhibit in "Women of Valor," on the Internet site "Jewish Women's Archive" at http://www.jwa.org/exhibits/weil/ (accessed December 1, 2002); David G. Stahl, "Our History," in *Temple Adath Yeshurun Centennial, 1891–1991* (Manchester, N.H., 1991), 21; Goldberg, "Historical Community Study of Wilmington Jewry," 32.

27. Ms. Census, Appleton, 1920; Ms. Census, Hamilton, 1920; Deborah R. Weiner "A History of Jewish Life in the Central Appalachian Coalfields, 1870s to 1970s" (Ph.D. diss., West Virginia University, 2002), 203; James McBride, *The Color of Water: A Black Man's Tribute to His White Mother* (New York, 1996), 47, 83.

28. Ms. Census, Hamilton, 1880; Ms. Census, Lafayette, 1880; Ms. Census, Vicksburg, 1880.

29. Interview of Sid Weiner of Newburyport, Massachusetts, by Caitlin Sklarz and Bertha Woodman, February 14, 1996 (transcript in the author's possession); Ms. Census, Nashua, 1920; Ms. Census, Vicksburg, 1920.

30. Ms. Census, Lafayette, 1880; Ms. Census, Lexington, 1920.

31. Toll, "Domestic Basis of Community," 5.

32. Ms. Census, Alexandria, 1920; Ms. Census, Hamilton, 1920.

33. Dennis S. Devlin, *Muskegon's Jewish Community: A Centennial History, 1888–1988* (Muskegon, Mich., 1988), 24–25, 63.

34. Devlin, *Muskegon's Jewish Community,* 4; Rome, *Ancestors, Descendants, and Me,* 83.

35. On the Wabash example, see *Biographical Memoirs of Wabash County, Indiana* (Chicago, 1901), 509; and Joseph Levine, "Jewish Community Small," in Linda Robertson, ed., *Wabash County History: Bicentennial Edition, 1976* (Marceline, Mo., 1976), 167.

36. On the La Crosse examples, see Katz, "Jews of La Crosse," 57. On the Charlottesville example, see Carol Ely, Jeffrey Hantman, and Phyllis Leffler, *To Seek the Peace of the City: Jewish Life in Charlottesville,* exhibition catalogue (Charlottesville, Va., 1994), 11. On the Jackson example, see Dunbar Rowland, *History of Mississippi, Heart of the South,* 4 vols. (1925; reprint, Spartan-

burg, S.C., 1978), 4: 128. On the Muskegon example, see Devlin, *Muskegon's Jewish Community,* 5, 14. On the Danbury example, see Eric Roman, "The Jews of Danbury: A History," 38, typescript, ca. 1976, file SC-2616, AJA.

37. Robert Shosteck, *Small-Town Jewry Tell Their Story* (Washington, D.C., 1953), 46. See also Erich Rosenthal, "Studies of Jewish Intermarriage in the United States," *AJYB* 64 (1963): 12–14.

38. Calculated from data in Ms. Censuses for Hamilton, 1880, 1920; Bradford, 1880, 1920; Vicksburg, 1880, 1920; Nashua, 1920; and Modesto, 1920.

39. Ms. Census, Alexandria, 1920; Ms. Census, Bradford, 1920; Ms. Census, Hamilton, 1920.

40. See Harry L. Golden, *Jewish Roots in the Carolinas: A Pattern of American Philo-Semitism* (Charlotte, N.C., 1955), 28.

41. Questionnaire completed by Roland Gittlesohn, 1935, in "Student Survey 1935–1936"; Max Raisin, *Rabbi's Message: Address Delivered at the Annual Meeting of Congregation Beth Israel* (Meridian, Miss., 1913), 7.

42. Questionnaires completed by S. Glasner and by Joseph Klein, in "Student Survey, 1935–1936." For a commentary on this phenomenon in the South, see Golden, *Jewish Roots in the Carolinas,* 25–26.

43. See "Jewish Synagogue," *Donaldsonville Chief Sesquicentennial Edition,* August 17, 1972; Judith Saul Stix, "The Jewish Demography of Ligonier, Indiana, 1860–1910," typescript, ca. 1990, file SC-13625, AJA; Elizabeth Weinberg, "Families and Personalities [of Madison]" (unpublished paper, ca. 1990), 8.

44. George Zepin, "Jewish Religious Conditions in Scattered Communities," *Year Book of the Central Conference of American Rabbis* 14 (1904): 218.

45. On rates of intermarriage before the mid-twentieth century, see Egon Mayer and Carl Sheingold, *Intermarriage and the Jewish Future* (New York, 1979), 1–2; and Egon Mayer, *Love and Tradition: Marriage between Jews and Christians* (New York, 1985), 7.

46. Gertrude Philippsborn, *The History of the Jewish Community of Vicksburg (from 1820 to 1968)* (Vicksburg, Miss., 1969), 65–66; *Temple Emanu-El of San José,* 125th anniversary booklet (San Jose, Calif., 1987), unpaginated; Norton B. Stern, "Introduction" to Marcus Katz, "The Jewish New Year 5650 in San Bernardino," *Western States Jewish History* 26 (January 1994): 118; Carol Bloom, comp., "The 150-Year History of the Temple Israel Congregation," in *Ahavath Achim, 1849–1999,* 150th anniversary book (West Lafayette, Ind., 1999), 49.

47. Alan S. Pine, Jean C. Hershenov, and Aaron H. Lefkowitz, *Peddler to Suburbanite: The History of the Jews of Monmouth County, New Jersey* (Deal Park, N.J., 1981), 86; "An Historic Outline of Manchester Jews," in *Silver Anniversary, 1912–1937: Adath Yeshurun Synagogue,* 25th anniversary booklet (Manchester, N.H., 1937), 29; Ms. Census, Fitchburg, 1920; interviews of Rebecca Carlin Zeff and Sarah Arnopole by the author, Modesto, Calif., October 26, 1999.

48. "Constitution of the Hebrew Congregation of Galesburg," quoted in Barbara Atwood, "A Study of Social Class in the Jewish Ethnic Group in Galesburg" (sociology essay, college unknown, 1947; copy in Miscellaneous file, AJA), 4;

"Constitution and By-Laws of Congregation Rodef Sholem" (1890), in Ronald L. Woodward, comp., "Records Relating to the Rodef Sholem Cemetery, Wabash, Indiana," typescript, 1977, Wabash Carnegie Public Library, Wabash, Ind.; Brith Achim constitution quoted in Ginsberg, *History of the Jews of Petersburg,* 66; Albert W. Levin, "The History of the Jewish Community of Racine, Wisconsin" (mimeographed document, 1942; copy in the author's possession), 7; Melvin S. Harris, *The Columbia Hebrew Benevolent Society: One Hundred and Twenty-Five Years of Benevolence* (Columbia, S.C., 1947), 36, 39.

49. See Goldberg, "Historical Community Study of Wilmington Jewry," 3; autobiographical essay by Sanford Glickson in Epstein, *Jews in Small Towns,* 458.

50. See Proshan, "Eastern European Jewish Immigrants," 155; (Lafayette, Ind.) *Jewish Community Journal* 1 (December 1, 1916).

51. *American Jewish Times,* April 1936, 19.

52. Ely, Hantman, and Leffler, *To Seek the Peace of the City,* 26; Rome, *Ancestors, Descendants, and Me,* 48; autobiographical essay by Anne G. Kramer in Epstein, *Jews in Small Towns,* 383–84.

53. Autobiographical essay by Anita Behn in Epstein, *Jews in Small Towns,* 358; Cumonow and Reiner, *Spirit Unconsumed,* 15; interview of Zeff; Golden, *Jewish Roots in the Carolinas,* 27–28.

54. Edward Cohen, *The Peddler's Grandson: Growing Up Jewish in Mississippi* (Jackson, Miss., 1999), 11–12. See also Rowland, *History of Mississippi,* 3: 611.

55. Rosa K. Drackman, "From New York to Tucson in 1868," *Western States Jewish History* 22 (October 1989): 18–21; autobiographical essay by Rose B. Orenstein in Epstein, *Jews in Small Towns,* 597–98; Rothman, " 'Same Horse, New Wagon,' " 89; Abraham P. Nasatir, "The Nasatir Family in Santa Ana, California, 1898 to 1915," *Western States Jewish Historical Quarterly* 15 (April 1983): 255; *Temple B'nai Shalom, Benton Harbor.*

56. Gordon and Gordon, *Jews beneath the Clustered Spires,* 99; Rowland, *History of Mississippi,* 4: 662–65; Rome, *Ancestors, Descendants, and Me,* 59; Goldberg, "Historical Community Study of Wilmington Jewry," 31.

57. The marriage announcements studied appeared in the *Lafayette Journal and Courier* between 1905 and 1925.

58. See Raisin, *Rabbi's Message,* 16–17.

59. *Temple Adath Yeshurun Centennial,* 23; Cumonow and Reiner, *Spirit Unconsumed,* 55; interview of Arnopole.

60. [Audrey Gorwitz, ed.], *Fox Valley Jewish Centennial* (Oshkosh, Wis., 1991), unpaginated; *The Jewish Community of Newburyport: A Photographic Exhibit,* exhibit catalogue (Newburyport, Mass., 1986), 9.

61. Devlin, *Muskegon's Jewish Community,* 14–15; autobiographical essay by Herschel Rubin in Epstein, *Jews in Small Towns,* 537; *Temple B'nai Shalom, Benton Harbor;* Karen R. Goody, "The Greensboro Jewish Community: Keeping the Memories under Glass" (master's thesis, Wake Forest University, 1984), 46. See also Rogoff, *Homelands,* 178.

62. Levine, "Jewish Community Small," 157; Goldberg, "Historical Community

Study of Wilmington Jewry," 25–26; Adolph Rosenberg, "Between Rome's Rivers," *Southern Israelite,* October 29, 1948, 15.

63. Philippsborn, *History of the Jewish Community of Vicksburg,* 36–37; Julian B. Feibelman, *The Making of a Rabbi* (New York, 1980), 38; William Foster Hayes, *Sixty Years of Owensboro, 1883–1943* (Owensboro, Ky., 1943), 32–33. For more on Gotthelf, see John E. Kleber, ed., *The Encyclopedia of Louisville* (Lexington, Ky., 2001), s.v. "Gotthelf, Bernhard Henry." On the epidemic of 1878 itself, see Khaled J. Bloom, *The Mississippi Valley's Great Yellow Fever Epidemic of 1878* (Baton Rouge, 1993).

64. Devlin, *Muskegon's Jewish Community,* 18; Proshan, "Eastern European Jewish Immigrants," 223; "Struck Down . . . Heroes Return," *Bradford Era,* June 10, 1921; Myron Samuelson, *The Story of the Jewish Community of Burlington, Vermont* (Burlington, Vt., 1976), 167–68; *A Century of Jewish Commitment, 1887–1987: Congregation Kneses Tifereth Israel,* centennial booklet (Port Chester, N.Y., 1987), 11.

65. Questionnaire completed by S. Glasner, in "Student Survey 1935–1936"; Jerome Folkman, "Autobiography [written in 1947]," typescript, 1969, file SC-3502, AJA; autobiographical essay by Vivian Barnert in Epstein, *Jews in Small Towns,* 286; Goody, "Greensboro Jewish Community," 36–37.

66. Rome, *Ancestors, Descendants, and Me,* 55, 71–72; Devlin, *Muskegon's Jewish Community,* 29; Rogoff, *Homelands,* 150; Judith E. Endelman, *The Jewish Community of Indianapolis, 1849 to the Present* (Bloomington, Ind., 1984), 161.

67. Compare Nathan Goldberg, "Occupational Patterns of American Jews, II," *Jewish Review* 3 (1945): 170–71.

68. Questionnaires completed by Meyer H. Marx and Roland Gittlesohn, in "Student Survey 1935–1936"; autobiographical essay by Perry Peskin in Epstein, *Jews in Small Towns,* 156.

69. Autobiographical essays by Janyce B. Pearlstein and Howard Fink in Epstein, *Jews in Small Towns,* 531, 106; Devlin, *Muskegon's Jewish Community,* 34; Faye Moskowitz, *A Leak in the Heart: Tales from a Woman's Life* (Boston, 1985), 116.

70. Rose Sherman Geller, "History of Congregation Beth Jacob," booklet essay, 1988, vertical file "Churches," Plymouth Public Library, Plymouth, Mass.; Doris Kirkpatrick, *Around the World in Fitchburg* (Fitchburg, Mass., 1975), 159; *Congregation B'nai Abraham: Celebrating 100 Years* (Hagerstown, Md., 1992), 15; *Congregation Ahavath Torah: An Oral History,* centennial booklet (Englewood, N.J., 1995), 18; Karl Richter, "The History of Sinai Temple," in *Sinai Temple, Michigan City, Indiana,* dedication booklet (Michigan City, Ind., 1953), 12; Levin, "History of the Jewish Community of Racine," 19–23.

*Chapter 7. Patterns of Congregational Organization*

1. Quoted in Stephen J. Whitfield, *In Search of American Jewish Culture* (Hanover, N.H., 1999), 13.

2. On Danville, see Congregation B'nai Zion Minute Book. 1890–1946, Ms. Coll.

476, AJA. On Columbus, see *Temple B'nai Israel 100th Anniversary Service* (Columbus, Miss., 1979), unpaginated; and James W. Parker et al., comps., *Friendship Cemetery, Columbus, Mississippi: Tombstone Inscriptions and Burial Records* (Columbus, Miss., 1979), 336–41.

3. The main sources on which this observation is based are Union of American Hebrew Congregations, *Statistics of the Jews of the United States* (Philadelphia, 1880); "Directory of Local Organizations," *AJYB* 2 (1900–01): 185–490; and "Directory of Jewish Local Organizations in the United States," *AJYB* 9 (1907–08): 123–430.

4. See "Lakewood Jewish Mothers to Organize Sunday School," *Lakewood Press,* May 2, 1918, 1. See also "Jewish Sabbath School for Lakewood," (Cleveland) *Jewish Review and Observer,* August 2, 1918, 1.

5. Isaac W. Bernheim, *History of the Settlement of Jews in Paducah and the Lower Ohio Valley* (Paducah, Ky., 1912), 67–68; Louis Ginsberg, *History of the Jews of Petersburg, 1789–1950* (Petersburg, Va., 1954), 51; "The Way It Was: Macon's Temple Beth Israel Celebrates 125th," *Southern Israelite,* May 4, 1984, 7.

6. *History of Temple B'rith Sholom Compiled in Commemoration of Its 125th Anniversary* (Springfield, Ill., 1983), unpaginated. On the transition to reform in general, see, for example, Jonathan D. Sarna, "The Debate over Mixed Seating in the American Synagogue," in Jack Wertheimer, ed., *The American Synagogue: A Sanctuary Transformed* (Cambridge, 1987), 363–94; and Karla Goldman, *Beyond the Synagogue Gallery: Finding a Place for Women in American Judaism* (Cambridge, Mass., 2000), esp. chaps. 3–5.

7. On Zanesville, see Martin Zwelling, "A Brief History of the Jews of Zanesville" (typescript, n.d.; copy in the author's possession); and J. F. Everhart, *History of Muskingum County, Ohio, with Illustrations and Biographical Sketches* (1882; reprint, Evansville, Ind., 1974), 185. On Quincy, see *Centennial Anniversary: B'Nai Sholom Temple* (Quincy, Ill., 1970), 1–2; and David Frolick, "The Children of Abraham in Quincy, Illinois" (manuscript, ca. 2000; copy in the author's possession).

8. The number of triple-digit Jewish communities in the United States in the early twentieth century was determined on the basis of data in *The Jewish Encyclopedia,* s.v. "United States," 371–74; and "Directory," *AJYB* 9 (1907–08): 123–430. Congregational affiliation was determined on the basis of information in both the latter source and "Directory of Jewish Organizations in the United States," ibid.,115–18 (list of member congregations of the UAHC).

9. *The Anniversary Story of Congregation B'er Chayim,* centennial booklet (Cumberland, Md., 1953), chap. 3; Amy Hill Shevitz, "The Industrial Removal Office and the Vagaries of Americanization: Case Studies from the Ohio River Valley" 6, paper presented at the annual meeting of the Association for Jewish Studies, Boston, December 1997.

10. *Anniversary Story of Congregation B'er Chayim,* chap. 3. See also Earl Pruce, *Synagogues, Temples, and Congregations of Maryland, 1830–1990* (Baltimore, 1993), 1–2. As a result of the situation at B'er Chayim, Cumberland's was one of the very few triple-digit Jewish communities in the United States to be

listed as supporting three separate congregations in Harry S. Linfield, "The Communal Organization of the Jews in the United States, 1927," *AJYB* 31 (1929–30): 223–30 (general table A).

11. Carol Ely, Jeffrey Hantman, and Phyllis Leffler, *To Seek the Peace of the City: Jewish Life in Charlottesville,* exhibition catalogue (Charlottesville, Va., 1994), preface, 14, 25.

12. Gertrude Philippsborn, *The History of the Jewish Community of Vicksburg (from 1820 to 1968)* (Vicksburg, Miss., 1969), 43–44.

13. Harvey B. Franklin, "Memories of a California Rabbi: Stockton, San Jose and Long Beach," *Western States Jewish Historical Quarterly* 9 (January 1977): 124; and [Harvey B. Franklin], *The San Jose Experiment* (San Jose, Calif., 1928). See also *Temple Emanu-El of San José,* 125th anniversary booklet (San Jose, Calif., 1987), unpaginated.

14. Carolyn Gray LeMaster, *A Corner of the Tapestry: A History of the Jewish Experience in Arkansas, 1820s–1990s* (Fayetteville, Ark., 1994), 89–90; Robert P. Davis, "Temple Bnai Israel, Laredo, Texas" and "Identity," on the Internet site "Virtual Restoration of Small-Town Synagogues" at http://geocities.com/txsynvr/txsyn.html (accessed March 26, 2000).

15. Mississippi Historical Records Survey Project, *Inventory of the Church and Synagogue Archives of Mississippi: Jewish Congregations and Organizations* (Jackson, Miss., 1940), 23–24; interview of Herbert Heuman of Jackson, Michigan, by the author, January 24, 1996.

16. These dates were gleaned from the following sources: "Directory," *AJYB* 9 (1907–08): 192, 396, 418; "Directory of Jewish Local Organizations in the United States," *AJYB* 21 (1919–20): 350, 359, 400, 417; and Alan S. Pine, Jean C. Hershenov, and Aaron H. Lefkowitz, *Peddler to Suburbanite: The History of the Jews of Monmouth County, New Jersey* (Deal Park, N.J., 1981), 75.

17. See Walter I. Deacon Jr., "List History of Agudas Achim Congregation as Observance Date Nears," *Leominster Daily Enterprise,* August 27, 1949; and Ruth Marcus Patt, *The Jewish Scene in New Jersey's Raritan Valley, 1698–1948* (New Brunswick, N.J., 1978), 46.

18. Dennis S. Devlin, *Muskegon's Jewish Community: A Centennial History, 1888–1988* (Muskegon, Mich., 1988), 12–13.

19. See Linfield, "Communal Organization," but the composite tables presented there contain some errors. In Danville, Illinois, only one congregation is reported in 1927, for example, even though there were two congregations functioning there at the time; see Sybil Stern Mervis, "History of the Jewish Community of Danville," in *Congregation Israel Synagogue, 1916–1991,* 75th anniversary booklet (Danville, Ill., 1991); and "History of Temple Beth El [Danville, Ill.]," typescript, ca. 1964, file SC-2627, AJA.

20. Herman Eliot Snyder, "A Brief History of the Jews of Springfield, Illinois, and of Temple Brith Sholom," in *History of Temple Brith Sholom compiled in Commemoration of the Seventieth Anniversary* (Springfield, Ill., 1935), unpaginated; *History of Temple B'rith Sholom . . . 125th Anniversary;* "Directory," *AJYB* 21 (1919–20): 368.

21. On Petersburg, see Ginsberg, *History of the Jews of Petersburg,* 65–66; and "Directory," *AJYB* 9 (1907–08): 420. On Wilmington, see *UJE,* s.v. "North Carolina." On Macon, see *History of Our Congregation,* leaflet (Macon, Ga., 1987[?]), 1; and "The Way It Was," 7. On Pine Bluff, see LeMaster, *Corner of the Tapestry,* 84.

22. On Hamilton, see "Our History," on the Internet site "Beth Israel Synagogue, Hamilton, Ohio" at http://www.uscj.org/glr/hamilton (accessed September 13, 2002); and *1866–1941: Congregation Bene Israel, Hamilton, Ohio,* 75th anniversary booklet (Hamilton, Ohio, 1941). On Danville, see Mervis, "History of the Jewish Community of Danville," 12–13. On Plattsburg, see Henry K. Freedman, *The Jewish Congregations of Plattsburgh, N.Y.* (Plattsburgh, N.Y., 1975), 5, 21. On Wichita, see Hal Rothman, " 'Same Horse, New Wagon': Tradition and Assimilation among the Jews of Wichita, 1865–1930," *Great Plains Quarterly* 15 (spring 1995): 90, 94. On Boise, see *UJE,* s.v. "Idaho"; and "Congregation Beth Israel, Boise, Idaho in 1899," *Western States Jewish History* 22 (July 1990): 334–35.

23. On Bradford, see *Temple Beth El, Bradford, Pennsylvania,* building dedication booklet (Bradford, Pa., 1961). Beth Israel was also known as the First Hebrew Orthodox Congregation. On Michigan City, see Karl Richter, "The History of Sinai Temple," in *Sinai Temple, Michigan City, Indiana,* dedication booklet (Michigan City, Ind., 1953), 10.

24. *Twenty-fifth Anniversary: Temple Israel, New Castle, Pennsylvania, 1926–1951,* 25th anniversary booklet (New Castle, Pa., 1951), unpaginated; *UJE,* s.v. "Steubenville."

25. Belinda Gergel and Richard Gergel, *In Pursuit of the Tree of Life: A History of the Early Jews of Columbia, South Carolina, and the Tree of Life Congregation* (Columbia, S.C., 1996), 63, 69–72; *UJE,* s.v. "South Carolina."

26. Phil Goodstein, *Exploring Jewish Colorado* (Denver, 1992), 102; Ruthe Winegarten and Cathy Schechter, *Deep in the Heart: The Lives and Legends of Texas Jews* (Austin, 1990), 129; Meyer Barkai, publisher, *The Standard American-Jewish Directory, 1960* (n.p., 1960), 236.

27. On Marion, see Jerry Miller, "Marion's Chosen Few," *Marion Chronicle-Tribune Magazine,* July 17, 1977, 8. On Bradford, see "Proposal for Merger of Orthodox and Reform Congregations in Bradford, Pennsylvania, 1923," Miscellaneous files, AJA; *Temple Beth El, Bradford, Pennsylvania;* and John H. Spitzer, "A History of the First Bradford Hebrew Orthodox Congregation from 1940–1948 as Seen in the Minutes of the Congregation" (research paper, Hebrew Union College, 1971; copy in box 539, AJA).

28. See "Directory," *AJYB* 21 (1919–20): 359, 371, 568; and Linfield, "Communal Organization," 223, 224, 227.

29. On Zanesville, see "Directory," *AJYB* 9 (1907–08): 366; and "Directory," *AJYB* 21 (1919–20): 535. On Appleton, see Viola Hellermann, "Appleton, Worship Center for Jews in Area, Has Orthodox, Conservative, Reformed Congregations," *Appleton Post-Crescent,* July 23, 1938; and Gordon Bubolz, ed., *Land of the Fox: Saga of Outagamie County* (Appleton, Wis., 1949), 184.

30. On Petersburg, see Ginsberg, *History of the Jews of Petersburg,* 72. On Benton Harbor, see Jennifer R. Kraft, "Children of Israel Synagogue and the Jewish Community of Benton Harbor, Michigan: A History" (term paper, Jewish Theological Seminary of America, 1992), 16; and *Temple Beth-El, Benton Harbor, Michigan, Dedication Program* (Benton Harbor, Mich., 1949). On Fresno, see David L. Greenberg, "Notes on the Early History of the Fresno Area Jewish Community," typescript, June 5, 1979, file SC-3724, AJA.

31. On Bloomington, see *Moses Montefiore Temple: A Time to Remember,* centennial booklet (Bloomington, Ill., 1982), unpaginated. On Springfield, see questionnaire completed by Sidney Ballon in "Student Survey, 1935–1936," Ms. Coll. 5, AJA. On Williamsport, see Bertrand E. Pollans and Ben Hirsh, eds., "Eighty Years of Temple Beth Ha-Sholom in Williamsport," in *80th Anniversary Celebration, 1866–1946* (Williamsport, Pa., 1946), 8; and presentation by Carol Mantinband Ginsburg at the annual meeting of the Southern Jewish Historical Society, Cincinnati, November 4, 2000. On Columbia, see Gergel and Gergel, *In Pursuit of the Tree of Life,* 73.

32. On Hamilton, see Arthur J. Lelyveld, "Report of the Rabbi," typescript, May 1940, in "Hamilton, Ohio—Temple Bene Israel," Nearprint file, AJA. On Springfield, see *History of Temple B'rith Sholom . . . 125th Anniversary.*

33. On Zanesville, see J. Hope Sutor, *Past and Present of the City of Zanesville and Muskingum Country, Ohio* (Chicago, 1905), s.v. "Hebrew Congregations"; Zwelling, "A Brief History"; and "Directory," *AJYB* 21 (1919–20): 535. On Farrell, see Jacob S. Feldman, *The Jewish Experience in Western Pennsylvania: A History, 1755–1945* (Pittsburgh, 1986), 208–09. On Manchester, see David G. Stahl, "Our History," in *Temple Adath Yeshurun Centennial, 1891–1991* (Manchester, N.H., 1991), 21, 24–25; and "An Historic Outline of Manchester Jews," in *Silver Anniversary, 1912–1937: Adath Yeshurun Synagogue* (Manchester, N.H., 1937), esp. 27, 29.

34. On North Adams, see Pink Horwitt and Bertha Skole, *Jews in Berkshire Country* (Williamstown, Mass., 1972), 50; "Directory," *AJYB* 9 (1907–08): 213; and "Directory," *AJYB* 21 (1919–20): 399. On Aliquippa, see Feldman, *Jewish Experience in Western Pennsylvania,* 205. On Newport, see letter from Morris Weintraub, former president of the United Hebrew Congregation, to the author, August 28, 1990; and Lee Shai Weissbach, *The Synagogues of Kentucky: Architecture and History* (Lexington, Ky., 1995), 139–40, 151. On Benton Harbor, see Kraft, "Children of Israel Synagogue," 7, 10, 13; and Michael Eliasohn, "The First 100 Years," in *Temple B'nai Shalom, Benton Harbor, Mich., 1895–1995,* centennial booklet (Benton Harbor, Mich., 1995), unpaginated.

35. On North Adams, see autobiographical essay by Paul Kronick in Howard V. Epstein, ed., *Jews in Small Towns: Legends and Legacies* (Santa Rosa, Calif., 1997), 171. On Benton Harbor, see Kraft, "Children of Israel Synagogue," 15.

36. On Port Huron, see Rochelle Berger Elstein, "Synagogue Architecture in Michigan and the Midwest: Material Culture and the Dynamics of Jewish Accommodation, 1865–1945" (Ph.D. diss., Michigan State University, 1986), 364. On Newburyport, see W. Lloyd Warner and Leo Srole, *The Social Systems*

*of American Ethnic Groups,* Yankee City Series, vol. 3 (New Haven, 1945), 116–17, 205–17. A solution to the problem of seating similar to that adopted in Newburyport was adopted also at the Temple of Abraham synagogue in Bay City, Michigan, in 1934; see Elstein, "Synagogue Architecture in Michigan," 365.

37. See *Dedication: Temple Beth Israel* (Sharon, Pa., 1950), 15, 25.

38. On Appleton, see Hellermann, "Appleton, Worship Center for Jews." On Iron Mountain, see Elstein, "Synagogue Architecture in Michigan," 376, n. 52. On Ashland, see letter from Harold Freedman of Ashland, Kentucky, to the author, June 13, 1990.

39. On Davenport, see Oscar Fleishaker, *The Illinois-Iowa Jewish Community on the Banks of the Mississippi River* (n.p., 1971), 119. On Torrington, see *Dedication Journal . . . of the New Building of the Beth El Synagogue, Torrington, Connecticut* (Torrington, Conn., 1951), unpaginated.

40. Information on Bradford is based on interview of Lester Brauser of Bradford, Pennsylvania, by the author, June 4, 1996. On Sheboygan, see Andrew Muchin, "Down, but not Out," *Jewish Heartland,* October–November 1999, 23.

41. Rose Sherman Geller, "History of Congregation Beth Jacob," booklet essay, 1988, vertical file "Churches," Plymouth Public Library, Plymouth, Mass.; Pine, Hershenov and Lefkowitz, *Peddler to Suburbanite,* 87.

42. On Vineland, see "Directory," *AJYB* 9 (1907–08): 256–57. On Grand Forks, see ibid., 349; and "Directory," *AJYB* 21 (1919–20): 525. On Auburn, see "Directory," *AJYB* 21 (1919–20): 381; Rose O'Brien, "Beth Abraham's Congregation Observes 50th Anniversary," *Lewiston Journal Magazine Section,* December 6, 1952; and *Beth Abraham Synagogue Golden Jubilee,* 50th anniversary booklet (Auburn, Maine, 1952).

*Chapter 8. Patterns of Synagogue History*

1. On Kalamazoo, see Samuel W. Durant, *History of Kalamazoo County, Michigan* (Philadelphia, 1880), 247. On Nashua, see "A History of the Nashua Jewish Community," in *Dedication Journal: Temple Beth Abraham* (Nashua, N.H., 1960), unpaginated. On Amsterdam, see National Register of Historic Places Registration Form for Temple of Israel, Amsterdam, New York (1992; copy in Geography Nearprint file, AJA). On Bloomington, see *Moses Montefiore Temple: A Time to Remember,* centennial booklet (Bloomington, Ill., 1982), unpaginated. On Wichita, see Hal Rothman, " 'Same Horse, New Wagon': Tradition and Assimilation among the Jews of Wichita, 1865–1930," *Great Plains Quarterly* 15 (spring 1995): 93. On Engelwood, see *Congregation Ahavath Torah: An Oral History,* centennial booklet (Englewood, N.J., 1995), introduction.

2. Louis Ginsberg, *History of the Jews of Petersburg, 1789–1950* (Petersburg, Va., 1954), 49; "The Way It Was: Macon's Temple Beth Israel Celebrates 125th," *Southern Israelite,* May 4, 1984, 7; *The Jewish Community of Newburyport: A Photographic Exhibit,* exhibit catalogue (Newburyport, Mass., 1986), 6.

3. On Manchester, see David G. Stahl, "Our History," in *Temple Adath Yeshurun Centennial, 1891–1991* (Manchester, N.H., 1991), 22; and *Silver Anniversary, 1912–1937: Adath Yeshurun Synagogue,* 25th anniversary booklet (Manchester, N.H., 1937), 29–31. On Lexington, see Lee Shai Weissbach, *The Synagogues of Kentucky: Architecture and History* (Lexington, Ky., 1995), 26–28. On Auburn, see Harry Tecler, "A History of the Jewish Community of Auburn, N.Y.," 5–6, manuscript, 1947, file SC-578, AJA.

4. [Marjorie Abrams and Meyer M. Cohen], *Dedication: Congregation Cnesses Israel* (Green Bay, Wis., 1951), 7.

5. Rochelle Berger Elstein, "The Jews of Houghton-Hancock and Their Synagogue," *Michigan Jewish History* 38 (November 1998): 6; Ginsberg, *History of the Jews of Petersburg,* 52; Patricia L. Dean, "The Jewish Community of Helena, Montana: 1866–1900" (undergraduate honors thesis, Carroll College, 1977; copy in file SC-4871, AJA), 52.

6. On Quincy, see *Centennial Anniversary, B'Nai Sholom Temple* (Quincy, Ill., 1970), 2. On Bloomington, see *Moses Montefiore Temple,* unpaginated. On Paducah, see Weissbach, *Synagogues of Kentucky,* 68–70. On Corsicana, see Jane Manaster, "Synagogue Architecture of Corsicana, Texas and Gabin, Poland: Copy or Coincidence," typescript, ca. 1984; copy in file SC-7691, AJA. On late nineteenth- and early twentieth-century American synagogue architecture in general, see Rachel Wischnitzer, *Synagogue Architecture in the United States: History and Interpretations* (Philadelphia, 1955); and *Two Hundred Years of American Synagogue Architecture,* exhibit catalogue (Waltham, Mass., 1976). On the naming of American Jewish institutions in honor of Montefiore, see Moshe Davis, *Sir Moses Montefiore: American Jewry's Ideal* (Jerusalem, 1985).

7. On Lafayette, see, for example, Carol Bloom, comp., "The 150-Year History of the Temple Israel Congregation," in *Ahavath Achim, 1849–1999,* 150th anniversary booklet (West Lafayette, Ind., 1999), 12, 19. On Warren, see *Beth Israel Temple Center,* 80th anniversary booklet (Warren, Ohio, 1998), unpaginated. On Plymouth, see Marjorie Levin, ed., *The Jews of Wilkes-Barre: 150 Years (1845–1995) in the Wyoming Valley of Pennsylvania* (Wilkes-Barre, Pa., 1999), 81. On Benton Harbor, see Michael Eliasohn, "The First 100 Years," in *Temple B'nai Shalom, Benton Harbor, Mich., 1895–1995,* centennial booklet (Benton Harbor, Mich., 1995), unpaginated. On Middletown, see "One Hundred Years of Jewish Congregations in Connecticut: An Architectural Survey," *Connecticut Jewish History* 2 (fall 1991): 97–99. On Lansing, see Rochelle Berger Elstein, "Synagogue Architecture in Michigan and the Midwest: Material Culture and the Dynamics of Jewish Accommodation, 1865–1945" (Ph.D. diss., Michigan State University, 1986), 428–29, 503.

8. Gertrude Philippsborn, *The History of the Jewish Community of Vicksburg (from 1820 to 1968)* (Vicksburg, Miss., 1969), 25; Carol Ely, Jeffrey Hantman, and Phyllis Leffler, *To Seek the Peace of the City: Jewish Life in Charlottesville,* exhibition catalogue (Charlottesville, Va., 1994), 13; "Congregation Beth Israel Formed in 1904," *Stevens Point Daily Journal,* June 28, 1958.

9. On Macon, see "The Way It Was," 7. On Greenville, see Leo E. Turitz and Evelyn Turitz, *Jews in Early Mississippi* (Jackson, Miss., 1983), 66. On Monroe, see *Congregation B'nai Israel, Monroe, Louisiana, 85th Anniversary* (Monroe, La., 1953), unpaginated. On Springfield, see *History of Temple B'rith Sholom Compiled in Commemoration of Its 125th Anniversary* (Springfield, Ill., 1983), unpaginated.

10. Edna Ferber, *A Peculiar Treasure* (New York, 1939), 72.

11. Stahl, "Our History," 22.

12. On Springfield, see Ernest I. Jacob, "Fifty Years of Jewish Life in Springfield, Mo." in *Fifty Years—Temple Israel, Springfield, Missouri: Invitation to the Anniversary Celebration* (Springfield, Mo., 1943), unpaginated. On Wabash, see Joseph Levine, "Jewish Community Small," in Linda Robertson, ed., *Wabash County History: Bicentennial Edition, 1976* (Marceline, Mo., 1976), 167. On Oshkosh, see [Audrey Gorwitz, ed.], *Fox Valley Jewish Centennial* (Oshkosh, Wis., 1991), unpaginated. On Colorado Springs, see Phil Goodstein, *Exploring Jewish Colorado* (Denver, 1992), 100. Information on Portsmouth is from "Shapiro House," on the Internet site "Strawbery Banke" at http://www.strawberybanke.org/museum/shapiro/shapiro.html (accessed July 23, 2002). On Lexington, see Weissbach, *Synagogues of Kentucky,* 27–28. On Newburyport, see *Congregation Ahavas Achim: Fiftieth Anniversary of the Dedication of Our House of Worship* (Newburyport, Mass., 1983), unpaginated; and "New Synagogue of Congregation Ahavas Achim Dedicated," *Newburyport News,* September 11, 1933.

13. *Congregation B'nai Jacob (First Hebrew Congregation of Kern County): 50 Years* (Bakersfield, Calif., 1965), unpaginated; Helen Motto[?], "Hear Ye! Hear Ye! O Israel of Santa Barbara!" in *Congregation B'nai B'rith,* congregational brochure (Santa Barbara, Calif., 1962), 4; Paul P. Gordon and Rita S. Gordon, *The Jews beneath the Clustered Spires* (Hagerstown, Md., 1971), 123–27; autobiographical essay by Paul Kronick in Howard V. Epstein, ed., *Jews in Small Towns: Legends and Legacies* (Santa Rosa, Calif., 1997), 171.

14. On Lexington, see Weissbach, *Synagogues of Kentucky,* 26, 77–79. On Auburn, see Rose O'Brien, "Beth Abraham's Congregation Observes 50th Anniversary," *Lewiston Journal Magazine Section,* December 6, 1952; and *Beth Abraham Synagogue Golden Jubilee,* 50th anniversary booklet (Auburn, Maine, 1952), unpaginated.

15. Gordon and Gordon, *Jews beneath the Clustered Spires,* 123; *Beth Israel Temple Center*; Weissbach, *Synagogues of Kentucky,* 25; Adolph Rosenberg, "Between Rome's Rivers," *Southern Israelite,* October 29, 1948, 19.

16. Elstein, "Synagogue Architecture in Michigan," 232; Leonard Rogoff, "Synagogue and Jewish Church: A Congregational History of North Carolina," *Southern Jewish History* 1 (1998): 49–50; Levin, *The Jews of Wilkes-Barre,* 80.

17. *Moses Montefiore Temple*; Sherry Blanton, "Lives of Quiet Affirmation: The Jewish Women of Early Anniston, Alabama," *Southern Jewish History* 2 (1999): 37; Belinda Gergel and Richard Gergel, *In Pursuit of the Tree of Life: A History*

*of the Early Jews of Columbia, South Carolina, and the Tree of Life Congregation* (Columbia, S.C., 1996), 64; Chester Jay Proshan, "Eastern European Jewish Immigrants and Their Children on the Minnesota Iron Range, 1890s–1980s" (Ph.D. diss., University of Minnesota, 1998), 149–50.

18. Published discussions of synagogue board meetings based on their minutes are abundant. See, as examples, *Dedication: Temple Beth Israel* (Sharon, Pa., 1950); Gunther Rothenberg, *Congregation Albert, 1897–1972* (Albuquerque, 1972), 20–21, 24, 30–31; and Gorwitz, *Fox Valley Jewish Centennial.*

19. *The Anniversary Story of Congregation B'er Chayim,* centennial booklet (Cumberland, Md., 1953), chap. 2.

20. W. Lloyd Warner and Leo Srole, *The Social Systems of American Ethnic Groups,* Yankee City Series, vol. 3 (New Haven, 1945), 258–59; Robert P. Davis, "Settlement," on the Internet site "Virtual Restoration of Small-Town Synagogues" at http://geocities.com/txsynvr/txsyn.html (accessed March 26, 2000).

21. Sunny Rabenstock, "Emanu El—God Is with Us: A History of Congregation Emanu El, San Bernardino, California," in *100th Anniversary, Congregation Emanu El* (San Bernardino, Calif., 1991), 10–11; "History of our Synagogue" (document from Newburyport, Mass., 1949; copy in the author's possession).

22. On Dover, see "The Dover Jewish Center: How We Grew" (document from Dover, N.J., ca. 1981; copy in the author's possession). On Freehold, see *Freehold Jewish Center,* congregational directory (Freehold, N.J., 1999), unpaginated. On San Jose, see *Temple Emanu-El of San José,* 125th anniversary booklet (San Jose, Calif., 1987), unpaginated; and [Harvey B. Franklin], *The San Jose Experiment* (San Jose, Calif., 1928).

23. On Belmar, see Alan S. Pine, Jean C. Hershenov, and Aaron H. Lefkowitz, *Peddler to Suburbanite: The History of the Jews of Monmouth County, New Jersey* (Deal Park, N.J., 1981), 77. On South River, see Ruth Marcus Patt, *The Jewish Scene in New Jersey's Raritan Valley, 1698–1948* (New Brunswick, N.J., 1978), 46. On Annapolis, see Eric L. Goldstein, "Our History," in *Congregation Kneseth Israel: Looking Back, Moving Forward,* 90th anniversary booklet (Annapolis, 1996), unpaginated. On Sharon, see *Dedication: Temple Beth Israel,* 17, 35.

24. Ginsberg, *History of the Jews of Petersburg,* 76; autobiographical essay by Evelyn Rose Benson in Epstein, *Jews in Small Towns,* 563; *Congregation Ahavath Torah,* 18. On the concept of the "synagogue center," see David Kaufman, *Shul with a Pool: The "Synagogue-Center" in American Jewish History* (Hanover, N.H., 1999).

25. Carolyn Gray LeMaster, *A Corner of the Tapestry: A History of the Jewish Experience in Arkansas, 1820s–1990s* (Fayetteville, Ark., 1994), 80–81, 84, 87.

26. Rothenberg, *Congregation Albert,* 31; *Centennial Anniversary B'Nai Sholom,* 4.

27. The situation in Brunswick was reconstructed from two partially contradictory sources: *Seventy-fifth Anniversary: Temple Beth Tefilloh* (Brunswick, Ga., 1961), unpaginated; and *UJE,* s.v. "Georgia."

28. Jerry Miller, "Marion's Chosen Few," *Marion Chronicle-Tribune Magazine,* July

17, 1977, 8; Debra [Deborah] Weiner, "The Jews of Clarksburg: Community Adaptation and Survival, 1900–1960," *Southern Jewish Historical Society Newsletter,* March 1995, 4–5.

29. Elstein, "Synagogue Architecture in Michigan," 199–200.

30. See "A Brief Biography of the Union," in *An Intimate Portrait of the Union of American Hebrew Congregations: A Centennial Documentary* (Cincinnati, 1973), 7–8; "An Inventory to the Union of American Hebrew Congregation Records (1873–1985)" (locating aid, ca. 1985, AJA), 4.

31. "A Brief Biography of the Union," 8. See also Jacob S. Schwarz, "Rabbi George Zepin," typescript biography, 1936, file 1/1, Ms. Coll. 50 (George Zepin papers), AJA.

32. For Zepin's comment, see George Zepin, "Jewish Religious Conditions in Scattered Communities," *Year Book of the Central Conference of American Rabbis* 14 (1904): 208. On visits of rabbis in the South East District, see *Sixty-second Annual Report of the Union of American Hebrew Congregations,* June 1936, 94–95.

33. See Jack Wertheimer, "Pioneers of the Conservative Rabbinate: Reports from the Field by Graduates of 'Schechter's Seminary,'" *Conservative Judaism* 47 (spring 1995): 55, 61.

34. Jacob J. Weinstein, *The Religious Situation among Small Town Jewries* (n.p., n.d.), 11.

35. See Dan Rottenberg, ed., *Middletown Jews: The Tenuous Survival of an American Jewish Community* (Bloomington, Ind., 1997), xxiv–xxv, 81. The founding date of Beth El is from "Directory of Jewish Local Organizations in the United States," *AJYB* 21 (1919–20): 372.

36. Elstein, "The Jews of Houghton-Hancock," 7–8.

37. See, for example, Ewa Morawska, *Insecure Prosperity: Small-Town Jews in Industrial America, 1890–1940* (Princeton, 1996), chap. 4; and Eric L. Goldstein, "Beyond Lombard Street: Jewish Life in Maryland's Small Towns," in Karen Falk and Avi Y. Dechter, eds., *We Call This Place Home: Jewish Life in Maryland's Small Towns,* exhibit catalogue (Baltimore, 2002), 59–62.

38. See "Beth Israel's 75th Year to Be Celebrated," *Clarksdale Press Register,* October 10, 1969; and Mississippi Historical Records Survey Project, *Inventory of the Church and Synagogue Archives of Mississippi: Jewish Congregations and Organizations* (Jackson, Miss., 1940), 21–22, 24.

39. Dennis S. Devlin, *Muskegon's Jewish Community: A Centennial History, 1888–1988* (Muskegon, Mich., 1988), 12–13, 38, 41.

40. Joy Cumonow and Fred N. Reiner, *The Spirit Unconsumed: A History of the Topeka Jewish Community* (Topeka, 1979), 4–6.

41. *Congregation B'nai Abraham: Celebrating 100 Years* (Hagerstown, Md., 1992), 15–16.

42. See questionnaire completed by Samuel Silver in "Student Survey, 1935–1936," Ms. Coll. 5, AJA; and Jerome Paul David, "Jewish Consciousness in the Small Town" (rabbinic thesis, Hebrew Union College, 1974), 15.

43. See Ginsberg, *History of the Jews of Petersburg,* 81; Jennifer R. Kraft, "Chil-

dren of Israel Synagogue and the Jewish Community of Benton Harbor, Michigan: A History" (term paper, Jewish Theological Seminary of America, 1992), 11, 14.

44. On Pittston, see Levin, *The Jews of Wilkes-Barre,* 83. On Iron Mountain, see Elstein, "Synagogue Architecture in Michigan," 364; and *UJE,* s.v. "Michigan." On Durham, see Leonard Rogoff, *Homelands: Southern Jewish Identity in Durham and Chapel Hill, North Carolina* (Tuscaloosa, Ala., 2001), 203–04. On Macon, see *History of Our Congregation,* leaflet (Macon, Ga., 1987[?]), 1–2. On Iowa City, see Douglas W. Jones, "A Brief History of Congregation Agudas Achim of Iowa City," 5, lecture delivered at the congregation, September 19, 1997.

45. For synagogues in the United States in 1960, see Meyer Barkai, publisher, *The Standard American-Jewish Directory, 1960* (n.p., 1960).

46. On Newburyport, see the discussion of the controversy over seating at Ahavas Achim in chapter 7. On Appleton, see *Moses Montefiore Synagogue Dedication* (Appleton, Wis., 1970), 15.

## Chapter 9. Patterns of Religious Leadership

1. On Kory, see Dunbar Rowland, *History of Mississippi, Heart of the South,* vol. 3 (1925; reprint, Spartanburg, S.C., 1978), 161–62; and Gertrude Philippsborn, *The History of the Jewish Community of Vicksburg (from 1820 to 1968)* (Vicksburg, Miss., 1969), 45–46. On Landau, see the memorial by Louis Wolsey in *Year Book of the Central Conference of American Rabbis* 55 (1945): 208–09. On Rabinowitz, see the memorial by Julian Feibelman in ibid., 59 (1949): 252–53.

2. Gunther Rothenberg, *Congregation Albert, 1897–1972* (Albuquerque, 1972), 15; "Dr. Krass Resigns," *Lafayette Morning Journal,* September 10, 1908.

3. Joy Cumonow and Fred N. Reiner, *The Spirit Unconsumed: A History of the Topeka Jewish Community* (Topeka, 1979), 33–34; Karen R. Goody, "The Greensboro Jewish Community: Keeping the Memories under Glass" (master's thesis, Wake Forest University, 1984), 39; *American Jewish Times,* May 1936, 15.

4. Phil Goodstein, *Exploring Jewish Colorado* (Denver, 1992), 88–89; "The Way It Was: Macon's Temple Beth Israel Celebrates 125th," *Southern Israelite,* May 4, 1984, 7.

5. On Edelson, see [Audrey Gorwitz, ed.], *Fox Valley Jewish Centennial* (Oshkosh, Wis., 1991), unpaginated. On Kreuger, see eulogy by Martin Berkowitz, *Proceedings of the Rabbinical Assembly of America* 14 (1950): 323–24. On Hefterman, see David G. Stahl, "Our History," in *Temple Adath Yeshurun Centennial, 1891–1991* (Manchester, N.H., 1991), 25–28.

6. Robert Orkand, "The Rabbi in the Small City," *Journal of Reform Judaism* 28 (winter 1981): 66–75, based on a survey of fifty Reform rabbis serving in small towns in the 1970s, discusses many issues that would have been of concern to small-town rabbis earlier in the century as well. See also the chapter "Small-Town Rabbi," in Murray Polner, *Rabbi: The American Experience* (New York, 1977), 171–99.

7. On Gotthelf, see Philippsborn, *History of the Jewish Community of Vicksburg*, 15. On Goldfarb, see Marilyn A. Posner, *The House of Israel—A Home in Washington: 100 Years of Beth Israel Congregation* (Washington, Pa., 1991), 1.

8. Questionnaire completed by Ferdinand Kilsheimer Hirsch, 1955, file 1/10, Ms. Coll. 264, AJA.

9. Letter from A. K. Hoodwin, Michigan City, Indiana, to Julian Morgenstern, president of HUC, April 30, 1924, file B-13/6, Ms. Coll. 5 , AJA; and letter from I. Shain, Wilmington, North Carolina, to RIETS, November 26, 1924, file 9-3-8, Sar Collection, Yeshiva University Archives, New York.

10. See *Central Conference of American Rabbis Yearbook* 37 (1927): 465–75.

11. See Jack Wertheimer, "Pioneers of the Conservative Rabbinate: Reports from the Field by Graduates of 'Schechter's Seminary,'" *Conservative Judaism* 47 (spring 1995): 55, 56–57, 68–69.

12. *Jewish Theological Seminary of America Register, 1914–15,* 29–31; *Jewish Theological Seminary of America Register, 1929–30,* 38–49. On Ackerman, see *UJE*, s.v. "Mississippi."

13. On the reforms at RIETS under Revel, see Jeffrey S. Gurock, *The Men and Women of Yeshiva: Higher Education, Orthodoxy, and American Judaism* (New York, 1988), chap. 4. For the location of graduates in the mid-1920s, see *The Rabbi Isaac Elchanan Theological Seminary Register* (1924–25).

14. See *Membership List of the Union of Orthodox Rabbis of the United States and Canada* (New York, 1934); *Rabbinic Registry, 1941: Rabbinical Council of America* (New York, 1941).

15. Quoted in Chester Jay Proshan, "Eastern European Jewish Immigrants and Their Children on the Minnesota Iron Range, 1890s–1980s" (Ph.D. diss., University of Minnesota, 1998), 132.

16. On Loewenthal, see *Temple Emanu-El of San José,* 125th anniversary booklet (San Jose, Calif., 1987), unpaginated. On Bleeden, see Oscar Fleishaker, *The Illinois-Iowa Jewish Community on the Banks of the Mississippi River* (n.p., 1971), 141–52. On Shilsky, see James McBride, *The Color of Water: A Black Man's Tribute to His White Mother* (New York, 1996), esp. 29–31.

17. See Jacob Freedman, "The Problem of the 'Free Lance' Rabbis in America," *Rabbinical Assembly of America: Proceedings, 1933–38* (1939): 487–90. Appended to this article are a call from the Philadelphia Board of Jewish Ministers to eliminate "unauthorized rabbis" and a supportive editorial from the *Jewish Exponent.*

18. Information on rabbis is based on data in "Directory of Jewish Local Organizations in the United States," *AJYB* 21 (1919–20): 330–583.

19. *The Anniversary Story of Congregation B'er Chayim,* centennial booklet (Cumberland, Md., 1953), chap. 2.

20. *Temple Emanu-El of San José.*

21. Sunny Rabenstock, "Emanu El—God Is with Us: A History of Congregation Emanu El, San Bernardino, California," in *100th Anniversary, Congregation Emanu El* (San Bernardino, Calif., 1991), 27–31.

22. *Seventy-fifth Anniversary of Beth Israel Congregation, 1861–1936* (Plattsburgh,

N.Y., 1936), 19; *Congregation B'nai Abraham: Celebrating 100 Years* (Hagerstown, Md., 1992), 27; Eric L. Goldstein, "Our History," in *Congregation Kneseth Israel: Looking Back, Moving Forward,* 90th anniversary booklet (Annapolis, 1996), unpaginated; Martin I. Hinchin, *Fourscore and Eleven: A History of the Jews of Rapides Parish, 1828–1919* (Alexandria, La.[?], 1984), A-167; Walter I. Deacon Jr., "List History of Agudas Achim Congregation as Observance Date Nears," *Leominster Daily Enterprise,* August 27, 1949. For Paul Kronick's memories, see his autobiographical essay in Howard V. Epstein, ed., *Jews in Small Towns: Legends and Legacies* (Santa Rosa, Calif., 1997), 177. On Lexington, see *Sisterhood of Ohavay Zion Congregation,* 45th anniversary booklet (Lexington, Ky., 1959), unpaginated.

23. Ms. Census, Jackson, Jackson County, Michigan, 1880; Ms. Census, Fitchburg, Worcester County, Massachusetts, 1920; Ms. Census, Modesto, Stanislas County, California, 1920; Gregg Rossen, producer and director, *Tales from Raisin-Land: A Conversation with Rabbi David Greenberg* (video, ca. 1991).

24. On Goldfarb, scc Posner, *The House of Israel,* 18–19, 27, 32; and Jacob S. Feldman, *The Jewish Experience in Western Pennsylvania: A History, 1755–1945* (Pittsburgh, 1986), 199. On Chapman, see Rothenberg, *Congregation Albert,* 21. On Summers, see Norton B. Stern, "Santa Ana, California: Its First Jews and Jewish Congregations," *Western States Jewish Historical Quarterly* 14 (April 1982): 255.

25. Cumonow and Reiner, *The Spirit Unconsumed,* 33–34.

26. On Wabash, see "Constitution and By-Laws of Congregation Rodef Sholem [1890]," in Ronald L. Woodward, comp., "Records Relating to the Rodef Sholem Cemetery, Wabash, Indiana," typescript, 1977, Wabash Carnegie Public Library, Wabash, Ind. On Columbia, see Belinda Gergel and Richard Gergel, *In Pursuit of the Tree of Life: A History of the Early Jews of Columbia, South Carolina, and the Tree of Life Congregation* (Columbia, S.C., 1996), 63. On Bradford, see Stephen W. Grafman, "Out of the Pale, A Grafman Family History" (typescript, ca. 1990; selections in the author's possession), 130–31, 192–93.

27. Simon Glazer, *The Jews of Iowa* (Des Moines, 1904), quoted in Fleishaker, *Illinois-Iowa Jewish Community,* 111.

28. Mrs. Pappe, "The Small Towns and the Scattered Groups," *Proceedings of the Council of Jewish Women,* 1902, 79.

29. On Nathanson, see *Temple Emanu-El of San José.* On Goldman, see Paul P. Gordon and Rita S. Gordon, *The Jews beneath the Clustered Spires* (Hagerstown, Md., 1971), 136–37. On Sharon, see *Dedication: Temple Beth Israel* (Sharon, Pa., 1950), 29.

30. See Rothenberg, *Congregation Albert,* 21–22, 33–34. On the problems faced by southern rabbis involved in the civil rights movement, see Mark K. Bauman and Berkley Kalin, eds., *The Quiet Voices: Southern Rabbis and Black Civil Rights, 1880s to 1990s* (Tuscaloosa, Ala., 1997).

31. On Fishmon, see letter from Barney J. Sugar of Lake Charles, Louisiana, to Kaufman Kohler, president of HUC, March 30, 1920, file B-13/1, Ms. Coll. 5,

AJA. On Kahn, see "Biographies of the Graduates of the Hebrew Union College: Living Alumni," typescript, 2 vols., 1946, AJA, s.v. "Kahn, Lawrence Earl Broh." On Freuder, see Fleishaker, *Illinois-Iowa Jewish Community,* 112–13.

32. On Utschen, see the memorial by William F. Rosenblum, *Central Conference of American Rabbis Yearbook* 73 (1963): 139; and Cumonow and Reiner, *The Spirit Unconsumed,* 36. On Calisch, see the memorial by Aliel Goldburg, *Central Conference of American Rabbis Yearbook* 56 (1946): 259–61. On Raisin, see the memorial by David Lefkowitz, ibid., 267–68. On Levinson, see the memorial by Sidney Tedesche, ibid., 58 (1948): 226–27.

33. On Krass, see the memorial by Max Raisin, *Central Conference of American Rabbis Yearbook* 60 (1950): 272–75. For comments on the rabbinate, see Orkand, "Rabbi in the Small City," 70.

34. On Einhorn, see Marc Lee Raphael, *Jews and Judaism in a Midwestern Community: Columbus, Ohio, 1840–1975* (Columbus, 1979), 184. On Rosenberg, see Myron Samuelson, *The Story of the Jewish Community of Burlington, Vermont* (Burlington, Vt., 1976), 154–55. On the JTS rabbis, see *Jewish Theological Seminary of America Register, 1929–30,* 38–49; and *Jewish Theological Seminary of America Register, 1931–1933,* 42–56. On Gordon, see Goldstein, "Our History."

35. For Milkman's memories, see his autobiographical essay in Epstein, *Jews in Small Towns,* 591. For Kerman's comments, see Julius Kerman, *Story of Temple B'nai Israel, Natchez, Mississippi* (mimeographed document, 1955; copy at Hebrew Union College Library, Cincinnati), 7. On Topeka, see Cumonow and Reiner, *The Spirit Unconsumed,* 33.

36. Cumonow and Reiner, *The Spirit Unconsumed,* 34; Lee Shai Weissbach, "Lexington, Kentucky's Jewish History: Why It Matters," *Proceedings of the Eleventh World Congress of Jewish Studies* (Jerusalem,1994), 127; memorial by Max Raisin, 272–73.

37. See questionnaire completed by Ferdinand Kilsheimer Hirsch; Ruthe Winegarten and Cathy Schechter, *Deep in the Heart: The Lives and Legends of Texas Jews* (Austin, 1990), 45, 72, 151; Myer Katz, "The Jews of La Crosse Past and Present," *Encounters,* ca. June 1973, 52.

38. Memorial for G. George Fox by Samuel Schwartz, *Year Book of the Central Conference of American Rabbis* 71 (1961): 201; "The First Century of Temple Israel" in *Temple Israel, Lafayette, Indiana: One Hundred Years, 1849–1949* (Lafayette, Ind., 1949), 23.

39. Isaac W. Bernheim, *History of the Settlement of Jews in Paducah and the Lower Ohio Valley* (Paducah, Ky., 1912), 57; Fleishaker, *Illinois-Iowa Jewish Community,* 90, 98.

40. Letter from Dora Aaronson of HUC to Louis Egelson of the Department of Synagog and School Extension, February 6, 1923, file B-9/6; and document concerning 1928 placements, file B-9/1; both Ms. Coll. 5, AJA. On Danville, see "History of Temple Beth El [Danville, Ill.]," 2, typescript, ca. 1964, file SC-2627, AJA.

41. Letter from Samuel Sar to K. Ebb of Haverstraw, New York, September 4, 1924, file 9-3-7; letter from Samuel Sar to L. Spitzer of North Adams, Mas-

sachusetts, September 22, 1924, file 9–3–7; and documents regarding placement, file 9–3-11; all Sar Collection, Yeshiva University Archives.

42. Louis Ginsberg, *Chapters on the Jews of Virginia* (Petersburg, Va., 1969) 35; *Anniversary Story of Congregation B'er Chayim,* chap. 3; Karl Richter, "The History of Sinai Temple," in *Sinai Temple, Michigan City, Indiana,* dedication booklet (Michigan City, Ind., 1953), 10; "Congregation Shomrei Emunah," on the Internet site "The Joseph and Miriam Ratner Center for the Study of Conservative Judaism" at http://www.jtsa.edu/research/ratner/archives/conrec/inst_shomreiemunah.shtml (accessed June 29, 2001).

43. Jerome Paul David, "Jewish Consciousness in the Small Town" (rabbinic thesis, Hebrew Union College, 1974), 4; "Bristol, Va.-Tenn.: History of Congregation B'nai Sholom," file SC-1384, AJA; Sybil Stern Mervis, "History of the Jewish Community of Danville," in *Congregation Israel Synagogue, 1916–1991,* 75th anniversary booklet (Danville, Ill., 1991), 14.

44. Louis Ginsberg, *History of the Jews of Petersburg, 1789-1950* (Petersburg, Va., 1954), 17; Louis Schmier, ed., *Reflections on Southern Jewry: The Letters of Charles Wessolowsky, 1878-1879* (Macon, Ga., 1982), 13–14.

45. See letter from W. Shanhouse Sons of Rockford, Illinois, to Julian Morgenstern, president of HUC, April 3, 1923, file B-9/6, Ms. Coll. 5, AJA; and "Congregation Beth Israel, Boise, Idaho in 1899," *Western States Jewish History* 22 (July 1990): 336.

46. Carol Ely, Jeffrey Hantman, and Phyllis Leffler, *To Seek the Peace of the City: Jewish Life in Charlottesville,* exhibition catalogue (Charlottesville, Va., 1994), 13, 21; Ernest I. Jacob, "Fifty Years of Jewish Life in Springfield, Mo.," in *Fifty Years—Temple Israel, Springfield, Missouri: Invitation to the Anniversary Celebration* (Springfield, Mo., 1943), unpaginated; Goodstein, *Jewish Colorado,* 90–91.

47. Katz, "The Jews of La Crosse," 58–59.

48. Letter from the Cohn Brothers of Waterloo, Iowa, to the IRO, June 2, 1908, box 98, IRO Coll.

49. On Sher, see *Congregation Ahavath Torah: An Oral History,* centennial booklet (Englewood, N.J., 1995), 3. On Gropstein and Kamenetzky, see Todd M. Endelman, *A Short History of the Jews of the Ann Arbor Area* (Ann Arbor, Mich., 1997), 4; and Rochelle Berger Elstein, "Synagogue Architecture in Michigan and the Midwest: Material Culture and the Dynamics of Jewish Accommodation, 1865–1945" (Ph.D. diss., Michigan State University, 1986), 283, n. 134.

50. On Zussman, see *Moses Montefiore Synagogue Dedication* (Appleton, Wis., 1970), 8–9; and "Rev. Zussman Is Dead at 75," *Appleton Post-Crescent,* January 21, 1952. On Mirovetz, see "Book of Remembrance" (manuscript volume, ca. 1960, in lobby of B'nai Israel synagogue, Kankakee, Ill.), unpaginated. On Goller, see *Sisterhood of Ohavay Zion Congregation*; Goller was the grandfather of the author's wife. On Nathanson and Steinberg, see Rose Sherman Geller, "History of Congregation Beth Jacob," booklet essay, 1988, vertical file "Churches," Plymouth Public Library, Plymouth, Mass.

51. "Directory," *AJYB* 21 (1919–20): 330–583.

52. Sol H. Marshall, "New Spiritual Values for Rome," *Southern Israelite,* November 24, 1939, 5.

*Chapter 10. Patterns of Culture: The German Jews*

1. See Blaine P. Lamb, "Frontiersmen in Broadcloth: Jews in Early Phoenix, 1870–1920," *Western States Jewish History* 25 (October 1992): 10.
2. David J. Goldberg, "An Historical Community Study of Wilmington Jewry, 1738–1925" (seminar paper, school unknown, 1976; available at Hebrew Union College Library, Cincinnati), 30.
3. On Hart, see Benjamin Hirsh, "Ninety-five Years of Beth Ha-Sholom," *Journal of the Lycoming County Historical Society* 12 (fall 1976): 21. On Saks, see Sherry Blanton, "Lives of Quiet Affirmation: The Jewish Women of Early Anniston, Alabama," *Southern Jewish History* 2 (1999): 27–28. On Adler, see Oscar Fleishaker, *The Illinois-Iowa Jewish Community on the Banks of the Mississippi River* (n.p., 1971), 87.
4. On Wessolowsky, see Louis Schmier, ed., *Reflections on Southern Jewry: The Letters of Charles Wessolowsky, 1878–1879* (Macon, Ga., 1982), 17. On Meyerhardt, see Adolph Rosenberg, "Between Rome's Rivers," *Southern Israelite,* October 29, 1948. On Leterman, see Carol Ely, Jeffrey Hantman, and Phyllis Leffler, *To Seek the Peace of the City: Jewish Life in Charlottesville,* exhibition catalogue (Charlottesville, Va., 1994), 15.
5. On Hirsch, see *UJE,* s.v. "Maryland." On Greenewald, see Vernelle A. Hatch, ed., *Illustrated History of Bradford, McKean County, Pa.* (Bradford, Pa., 1901), 43–45. On Neidig and Rothschild, see Fleishaker, *Illinois-Iowa Jewish Community,* 144. On Sam Jaffa and his colleagues, see Phil Goodstein, *Exploring Jewish Colorado* (Denver, 1992), 87. On Henry Jaffa and Mike Mandell, see Gunther Rothenberg, *Congregation Albert, 1897–1972* (Albuquerque, 1972), 11; and *UJE,* s.v. "New Mexico." On Ganz, see Lamb, "Frontiersmen in Broadcloth," 10.
6. On the Platts, see Sybil Stern Mervis, "History of the Jewish Community of Danville" in *Congregation Israel Synagogue, 1916–1991,* 75th anniversary booklet (Danville, Ill., 1991), 14. On Alexander, see Alan Minskoff, *Keeping the Faith: A Centennial Celebration of Organized Jewish Life in Boise, Idaho* (Boise, Idaho, 1997), 14–17; and Juanita Brooks, *History of the Jews in Utah and Idaho* (Salt Lake City, 1973), 134. On Laub, see Wendy Machlovitz, *Clara Lowenburg Moses: Memoir of a Southern Jewish Woman* (Jackson, Miss., 2000), 7. On the Cones, see Harry L. Golden, *Jewish Roots in the Carolinas: A Pattern of American Philo-Semitism* (Charlotte, N.C., 1955), 40–41; Karen R. Goody, "The Greensboro Jewish Community: Keeping the Memories under Glass" (master's thesis, Wake Forest University, 1984), 49–50; and Richard L. Zweigenhaft, "Two Cities in North Carolina: A Comparative Study of Jews in the Upper Class," *Jewish Social Studies* 41 (1979): 297.
7. See Ms. Census, Alexandria, Rapides Parish, Louisiana, 1880.
8. On Quincy, see *Centennial Anniversary B'Nai Sholom Temple* (Quincy, Ill.,

1970), 6. On Petersburg, see Louis Ginsberg, *History of the Jews of Petersburg, 1789–1950* (Petersburg, Va., 1954), 52. On Paducah, see "Paducah, Ky.: Cong. Temple Israel Minute Book for 1893–1910," 8, box 679, AJA. On Boise, see (Portland, Ore.) *American Hebrew News,* September 22, 1899, quoted in "Congregation Beth Israel, Boise, Idaho in 1899," *Western States Jewish History* 22 (July 1990): 336. For yet other examples of similar dedication ceremonies, see Belinda Gergel and Richard Gergel, *In Pursuit of the Tree of Life: A History of the Early Jews of Columbia, South Carolina, and the Tree of Life Congregation* (Columbia, S.C., 1996), 64; Ely, Hantman, and Leffler, *To Seek the Peace of the City,* 13; and Rothenberg, *Congregation Albert,* 16–17.

9. On Bloomington, see *Moses Montefiore Temple: A Time to Remember,* centennial booklet (Bloomington, Ill., 1982), unpaginated. On Macon, see "The Way It Was: Macon's Temple Beth Israel Celebrates 125th," *Southern Israelite,* May 4, 1984, 7. On Natchez, see Machlovitz, *Clara Lowenburg Moses,* 13. On Cumberland, see *The Anniversary Story of Congregation B'er Chayim,* centennial booklet (Cumberland, Md., 1953), chap. 2. On Albuquerque, see Rothenberg, *Congregation Albert,* 22. On Vicksburg, see Gertrude Philippsborn, *The History of the Jewish Community of Vicksburg (from 1820 to 1968)* (Vicksburg, Miss., 1969), 45.

10. Quoted in Gergel and Gergel, *In Pursuit of the Tree of Life,* 68.

11. See Melvin S. Harris, *The Columbia Hebrew Benevolent Society: One Hundred and Twenty-five Years of Benevolence* (Columbia, S.C., 1947), 37.

12. See George Zepin, "Jewish Religious Conditions in Scattered Communities," *Year Book of the Central Conference of American Rabbis* 14 (1904): 223.

13. See Eli N. Evans, *The Provincials: A Personal History of the Jews in the South,* rev. ed. (New York, 1997), 90.

14. See *Lexington Daily Press,* October 9, 1884; *Alexandria Daily Town Talk,* February 17, 1916, reprinted in Martin I. Hinchin, *Fourscore and Eleven: A History of the Jews of Rapides Parish, 1828–1919* (Alexandria, La.[?], 1984), A-142; and *Moses Montefiore Temple.*

15. "Lecture of Rabbi Gotthelf of Vicksburg delivered in 1874," typescript, Bernhard Gotthelf Collection, AJA.

16. Leonard Rogoff, *Homelands: Southern Jewish Identity in Durham and Chapel Hill, North Carolina* (Tuscaloosa, Ala., 2001), 34.

17. Machlovitz, *Clara Lowenburg Moses,* 11; Ms. Census, Vicksburg, Warren County, Mississippi, 1920.

18. See, for example, Zweigenhaft, "Two Cities in North Carolina." Compare also John Higham, "Social Discrimination against Jews in America, 1830–1930," *Publications of the American Jewish Historical Society* 47 (September 1957): 23–27.

19. On American attitudes toward Jews during the nineteenth century in general, see Jonathan D. Sarna, "The 'Mythical Jew' and the 'Jew Next Door' in Nineteenth-Century America," in David A. Gerber, ed., *Anti-Semitism in American History* (Urbana, Ill., 1986); Leonard Dinnerstein, *Antisemitism in America* (New York, 1994), chaps. 2–3; and Hasia R. Diner, *A Time for Gathering:*

*The Second Migration, 1820–1880,* vol. 2 of Henry L. Feingold, series ed., The Jewish People in America (Baltimore, 1992), 169–200.

20. *La Crosse Daily Democrat,* November 12, 1867, quoted in Myer Katz, "The Jews of La Crosse Past and Present," *Encounters,* ca. June 1973, 65; Albert Perry is quoted in Allen I. Freebling, "The Galesburg Jewish Community— One Hundred Years in Review," in *A Century of Living Judaism,* centennial booklet (Galesburg, Ill., 1967), unpaginated.

21. William Toll, "The Domestic Basis of Community: Trinidad, Colorado's Jewish Women, 1889–1910," *Rocky Mountain Jewish Historical Notes* 8 and 9 (summer and fall 1987): 3.

22. See Hal Rothman, "'Same Horse, New Wagon': Tradition and Assimilation among the Jews of Wichita, 1865–1930," *Great Plains Quarterly* 15 (spring 1995): 92; Paul P. Gordon and Rita S. Gordon, *The Jews beneath the Clustered Spires* (Hagerstown, Md., 1971), 131; and William Foster Hayes, *Sixty Years of Owensboro, 1883–1943* (Owensboro, Ky., 1943), 32–33.

23. See "A Gentile Reproves an Anti-Semite: Fresno—1893," *Western States Jewish Historical Quarterly* 9 (July 1977): 299–300; Gergel and Gergel, *In Pursuit of the Tree of Life,* 58–59, 70–71; Norton B. Stern, "Santa Ana, California: Its First Jews and Jewish Congregations," *Western States Jewish Historical Quarterly* 14 (April 1982): 251; Rothman, "'Same Horse, New Wagon,'" 90.

24. On the incidents cited, see, for example, Dinnerstein, *Antisemitism in America,* 32–33, 39. On Grant's orders, see also "Jewish Victims of 'General Orders No. 11,'" on the Internet site "Jewish American History on the Web" at http://theoccident.com/go11.htm (accessed September 17, 2002).

25. See Leo Weinberg, "Jews in Rural Communities," *Baltimore Jewish Comment,* December 7, 1917, 250; Jack Glazier, *Dispersing the Ghetto: The Relocation of Jewish Immigrants across America* (Ithaca, N.Y., 1998), 171.

26. Weinberg, "Jews in Rural Communities," 249; Ralph Goldenstein, ed., *History and Activities of Congregation Anshe-Emeth, Pine Bluff, Arkansas, 1867–1917* (Pine Bluff, Ark.[?], 1917), 18–19.

27. See *Moses Montefiore Temple*; Rothenberg, *Congregation Albert,* 10, 12.

28. See "Directory of National Organizations," *AJYB* 2 (1900–01): 92–112; "Directory of Jewish Organizations in the United States," *AJYB* 9 (1907–08): 69–81; Lamb, "Frontiersmen in Broadcloth," 14.

29. See "Directory of Jewish Organizations," AJYB 9 (1907–08): 62–65. On Jewish fraternal organizations in general, see *UJE,* s.v. "Fraternal Orders."

30. See "Directory of Jewish Organizations," AJYB 9 (1907–08): 50–60, 82–85, 87–89, 90–94, 101–9. See also *UJE,* s.v. "Brith Abraham, Independent Order," and "Jewish Chautauqua Society."

31. See "Directory of Jewish Local Organizations in the United States," *AJYB* 9 (1907–08): 221; Carolyn Gray LeMaster, *A Corner of the Tapestry: A History of the Jewish Experience in Arkansas, 1820s–1990s* (Fayetteville, Ark., 1994), 74; and Goldberg, "Historical Community Study of Wilmington Jewry," 31.

32. See Philippsborn, *History of the Jewish Community of Vicksburg,* 62–64; and

H. P. Chapman and J. F. Battaile, *Picturesque Vicksburg* (Vicksburg, Miss., 1895), 105–07 (quotation from 107).

33. Rothenberg, *Congregation Albert*, 16; *Anniversary Story of Congregation B'er Chayim*, chap. 3.

34. See *UJE*, s.v. "National Federation of Temple Sisterhoods."

35. See *Proceedings of the Council of Jewish Women* (Baltimore, 1902), i–iii (list of "sections"), 82 (quotation from Mrs. Pappe).

36. See Zepin, "Jewish Religious Conditions," 212–13.

37. Compare *Proceedings of the Council of Jewish Women: Second Triennial Convention* (Chicago, 1900), i; and *National Council of Jewish Women: Official Report of the Tenth Triennial Convention* (St. Louis, 1923), 104–06.

38. "The Way It Was," 7; Goody, "The Greensboro Jewish Community," 43; Joy Cumonow and Fred N. Reiner, *The Spirit Unconsumed: A History of the Topeka Jewish Community* (Topeka, 1979), 42–44.

39. See, for example, Blanton, "Lives of Quiet Affirmation," 28; and Cumonow and Reiner, *Spirit Unconsumed*, 41.

40. On Trinidad, see Toll, "Domestic Basis of Community," 7–8. On Lexington, see *Lexington Morning Transcript*, March 23, 1886. For a description of the Purim ball in Alexandria, Louisiana, in 1887, similar to that held in Lexington the previous year, see *Louisiana Democrat*, March 16, 1887, reprinted in Hinchin, *Fourscore and Eleven*, A-65–67. On costume balls in Europe see, for example, Frederic Morton, *A Nervous Splendor: Vienna, 1888/89* (New York, 1979), 191–95.

41. See Katz, "Jews of La Crosse," 61; Blanton, "Lives of Quiet Affirmation," 43; and (Lafayette, Ind.) *Jewish Community Journal*, December 1, 1916, 7.

42. See Karla Goldman, *Beyond the Synagogue Gallery: Finding a Place for Women in American Judaism* (Cambridge, Mass., 2000), esp. chap. 1. See also Jenna Weissman Joselit, "The Special Sphere of the Middle-Class American Jewish Woman: The Synagogue Sisterhood," in Jack Wertheimer, ed., *The American Synagogue: A Sanctuary Transformed* (Cambridge, 1987), 206–30.

43. "Congregation Beth Israel, Boise," 335; Goldman, *Beyond the Synagogue Gallery*, 190; "The Way it Was," 7; Karl Richter, "The History of Sinai Temple," in *Sinai Temple, Michigan City, Indiana*, dedication booklet (Michigan City, Ind., 1953), 12.

44. Bertrand E. Pollans and Ben Hirsh, eds., "Eighty Years of Temple Beth Ha-Sholom in Williamsport," in *80th Anniversary Celebration, 1866–1946* (Williamsport, Pa., 1946), 20.

45. Minute Book of the Ladies Auxiliary Society, 1904–1917, 4–6, "Vicksburg, Mississippi—Congregation Anshe Chesed" file, Small Collections, AJA.

46. See Blanton, "Lives of Quiet Affirmation," 25–53; and Rochelle Berger Elstcin, "Synagogue Architecture in Michigan and the Midwest: Material Culture and the Dynamics of Jewish Accommodation, 1865–1945" (Ph.D. diss., Michigan State University, 1986), 237. Women's groups also played key roles in organizing synagogue construction in Natchez, Mississippi, and Baton Rouge, Louisiana; see Goldman, *Beyond the Synagogue Gallery*, 144–46.

47. *Dedication: Temple Beth Israel* (Sharon, Pa., 1950), 35.

48. "Our Sisterhood," in *Anniversary Story of Congregation B'er Chayim.*

49. Minute Book of the As You Like It Club for 1900–03, Histories file, AJA.

50. Zepin, "Jewish Religious Conditions," 217; Max Raisin, *Rabbi's Message: Address Delivered at the Annual Meeting of Congregation Beth Israel* (Meridian, Miss., 1913), 6; Rothman, " 'Same Horse, New Wagon,' " 90; Barbara Atwood, "A Study of Social Class in the Jewish Ethnic Group in Galesburg" (sociology essay, college unknown, 1947; copy in Miscellaneous file, AJA), 8.

## *Chapter 11. Patterns of Culture: The East Europeans*

1. See Stephen G. Mostov, "Dun and Bradstreet Reports as a Source of Jewish Economic History: Cincinnati, 1840–1875," *American Jewish History* 72 (March 1983): 343.

2. On Levy, see *The Jewish Community of Newburyport: A Photographic Exhibit,* exhibit catalogue (Newburyport, Mass., 1986), 5; and city directory for Newburyport, Massachusetts, 1886–87. On Bloom, see Douglas W. Jones, "Jewish Life at Iowa" (manuscript, 1997; copy in the author's possession), 2; Union of American Hebrew Congregations, *Statistics of the Jews of the United States* (Philadelphia, 1880), 42; and Michael J. Bell, " 'True Israelites of America': The Story of the Jews of Iowa," *Annals of Iowa* 53 (spring 1994): 89–90. On Elias, see Walt Williams, "City's Jewish Heritage: Sol Elias to Mark Spitz," *Modesto Bee,* March 3, 1974; and George H. Tinkham, *History of Stanislaus County, California* (Los Angeles, 1921), 340–43.

3. Hal Rothman, " 'Same Horse, New Wagon': Tradition and Assimilation among the Jews of Wichita, 1865–1930," *Great Plains Quarterly* 15 (spring 1995): 95.

4. See Edna Ferber, *A Peculiar Treasure* (New York, 1939), 59; Brooke Kroeger, *Fannie: The Talent for Success of Writer Fannie Hurst* (New York, 1999), 7, 33, 274; and questionnaire completed by Ferdinand Kilsheimer Hirsch, 1955, file 1/10, Ms. Coll. 264, AJA.

5. Letter from Henry Goldstein to David Bressler, June 3, 1908, quoted in Amy Hill Shevitz, "The Industrial Removal Office and the Vagaries of Americanization: Case Studies from the Ohio River Valley," 5, paper presented at the annual meeting of the Association for Jewish Studies, Boston, December 1997; and letter from Elias Margolis to David Bressler, May 8, 1908, quoted in Jack Glazier, *Dispersing the Ghetto: The Relocation of Jewish Immigrants across America* (Ithaca, N.Y., 1998), 156.

6. Myer Katz, "The Jews of La Crosse Past and Present," *Encounters,* ca. June 1973, 58; Carolyn Gray LeMaster, *A Corner of the Tapestry: A History of the Jewish Experience in Arkansas, 1820s–1990s* (Fayetteville, Ark., 1994), 300.

7. Barbara Atwood, "A Study of Social Class in the Jewish Ethnic Group in Galesburg" (sociology essay, college unknown, 1947; copy in Miscellaneous file, AJA), 5–7. See also Allen I. Frecbling, "The Galesburg Jewish Community—One Hundred Years in Review," in *A Century of Living Judaism,* centennial booklet (Galesburg, Ill., 1967), unpaginated.

8. Oscar Fleishaker, *The Illinois-Iowa Jewish Community on the Banks of the Mississippi River* (n.p., 1971), 143; David J. Goldberg, "An Historical Community Study of Wilmington Jewry, 1738–1925" (seminar paper, school unknown, 1976; available at Hebrew Union College Library, Cincinnati), 39.

9. David G. Stahl, "Our History," in *Temple Adath Yeshurun Centennial, 1891–1991* (Manchester, N.H., 1991), 22.

10. On Macon, see *History of our Congregation,* leaflet (Macon, Ga., 1987[?]), 1; "The Way It Was: Macon's Temple Beth Israel Celebrates 125th," *Southern Israelite,* May 4, 1984, 7; and John C. Butler, *Historical Record of Macon and Central Georgia* (1879; reprint, Macon, Ga., 1958), 325. On Davenport, see Fleishaker, *The Illinois-Iowa Jewish Community,* 119. On Alexandria, see "Jewish Cemetery" and "B'nai Israel Jewish Cemetery," in Mary Parker Partain, *Gone but Not Forgotten: Cemetery Inscriptions of Rapides Parish* (Pineville, La., 1992[?]).

11. See "Sons of Abraham Congregation, Lafayette, Ind., Minutes 1943–60," Microfilm 2632, AJA.

12. *Sisterhood of Ohavay Zion Congregation,* 45th anniversary booklet (Lexington, Ky., 1959), unpaginated; Joy Cumonow and Fred N. Reiner, *The Spirit Unconsumed: A History of the Topeka Jewish Community* (Topeka, 1979), 4; Susan Fleischer Breitburg, "My Grandfather's Butcher Shop," on the Internet site "Long Island: Our Story" at http://www.lihistory.com/specfam/fambreit.htm (accessed October 8, 1999).

13. *Dedication: Temple Beth Israel* (Sharon, Pa., 1950), 11.

14. Max Friedman, "Kalamazoo Jewish Family History," typescript, ca. 1983, vertical file "Jews," Kalamazoo Public Library, Mich.

15. Rochelle Berger Elstein, "Synagogue Architecture in Michigan and the Midwest: Material Culture and the Dynamics of Jewish Accommodation, 1865–1945" (Ph.D. diss., Michigan State University, 1986), 320; Leonard Rogoff, *Homelands: Southern Jewish Identity in Durham and Chapel Hill, North Carolina* (Tuscaloosa, Ala., 2001), 144; Carol Ely, Jeffrey Hantman, and Phyllis Leffler, *To Seek the Peace of the City: Jewish Life in Charlottesville,* exhibition catalogue (Charlottesville, Va., 1994), 26; Cumonow and Reiner, *Spirit Unconsumed,* 4, 8; "A 20th Century Diaspora," clipping from the *Pittsburgh Post Gazette,* "Donora, Pennsylvania" Nearprint file, AJA; Abraham P. Nasatir, "The Nasatir Family in Santa Ana, California, 1898 to 1915," *Western States Jewish Historical Quarterly* 15 (April 1983): 255–56; Terry Barr, "A Shtetl Grew in Bessemer: Temple Beth-El and Jewish Life in Small-Town Alabama," *Southern Jewish History* 3 (2000): 13.

16. *Dedication: Temple Beth Israel,* 9; Katz, "Jews of La Crosse," 62; "A History of the Nashua Jewish Community," in *Dedication Journal: Temple Beth Abraham* (Nashua, N.H., 1960), unpaginated; W. Lloyd Warner and Leo Srole, *The Social Systems of American Ethnic Groups,* Yankee City Series, vol. 3 (New Haven, 1945), 195.

17. *Congregation B'nai Abraham: Celebrating 100 Years* (Hagerstown, Md., 1992), 13–14; Pink Horwitt and Bertha Skole, *Jews in Berkshire Country* (Williamstown,

Mass., 1972), 50; Rose Sherman Geller, "History of Congregation Beth Jacob," booklet essay, 1988, vertical file "Churches," Plymouth Public Library, Plymouth, Mass.; Jennifer R. Kraft, "Children of Israel Synagogue and the Jewish Community of Benton Harbor, Michigan: A History" (term paper, Jewish Theological Seminary of America, 1992), 10; Minutes of December 7, 1939, in "Minutes of Orthodox Hebrew Free Loan Association, Lafayette Ind., 1923–77," Microfilm 2632, AJA.

18. See Fleishaker, *The Illinois-Iowa Jewish Community,* 145; Bernice Premack, "A History of the Jewish Community of Aberdeen, South Dakota, 1887–1964" (typescript, ca. 1998; copy in the author's possession), 7; and "Mr. and Mrs. Rosenberg to Celebrate Anniversary," *Lexington Press Herald,* April 30, 1944.

19. Katz, "Jews of La Crosse," 61; Doris Kirkpatrick, *Around the World in Fitchburg* (Fitchburg, Mass., 1975), 161; Rogoff, *Homelands,* 117, 184. On B'nai B'rith in the late nineteenth and early twentieth centuries in general, see Deborah Dash Moore, *B'nai B'rith and the Challenge of Ethnic Leadership* (Albany, N.Y., 1981), chaps. 2–5.

20. On Muscatine, see Fleishaker, *The Illinois-Iowa Jewish Community,* 149. On Lafayette, see "Minutes of Orthodox Hebrew Free Loan Association, Lafayette"; and Chester F. Elsinger, "A Brief History of the Lafayette Orthodox Hebrew Free Loan Association, 1907–1960," *Indiana Jewish Historical Society Publication* 9 (July 1977). On Manchester, see "An Historic Outline of Manchester Jews," in *Silver Anniversary, 1912–1937: Adath Yeshurun Synagogue,* 25th anniversary booklet (Manchester, N.H., 1937), 33–35. On Fitchburg, see Kirkpatrick, *Around the World in Fitchburg,* 160. On Jewish free loan societies in general, see Shelly Tenenbaum, *A Credit to Their Community: Jewish Loan Societies in the United States, 1880–1945* (Detroit, 1993).

21. Special issue on "The Jews of Fargo," *Reform Advocate,* December 13, 1913, 6; Katz, "Jews of La Crosse," 37.

22. See "Directory of Jewish Organizations in the United States," *AJYB* 9 (1907–08): 37–44; LeMaster, *Corner of the Tapestry,* 72; Louis Ginsberg, *History of the Jews of Petersburg, 1789–1950* (Petersburg, Va., 1954), 79–80; Chester Jay Proshan, "Eastern European Jewish Immigrants and Their Children on the Minnesota Iron Range, 1890s-1980s" (Ph.D. diss., University of Minnesota, 1998), 151. For an interesting discussion of the hostility of Reform Jews to Zionism in many of the small communities of the South as late as the 1940s, see Eli N. Evans, *The Provincials: A Personal History of the Jews in the South,* rev. ed. (New York, 1997), chap. 8.

23. See *Young Judaea Yearbook: 1935–1936* (New York, 1936), 33–41a. For indications of Young Judaea chapters in the North Carolina towns of Asheville, Charlotte, and Kinston (which had a Jewish population of about seventy-five in 1927), see *American Jewish Times,* May 1936, 15.

24. See Jones, "Jewish Life at Iowa," 11; *UJE,* s.v. "Steubenville" and "North Carolina."

25. On Wise's travels, see James G. Heller, *Isaac M. Wise: His Life, Work and*

*Thought* (New York, 1965), esp. 405 (quoted), 662. On Wise in Cumberland, see *The Anniversary Story of Congregation B'er Chayim,* centennial booklet (Cumberland, Md., 1953), chap. 2. Wise's travels are also documented in the pages of his newspaper, *The Israelite;* see, for example, the issues of February 12, 1864 (visit to Jackson, Mich.); August 13, 1869 (visit to Quincy, Ill.); July 12, 1872 (visit to Titusville, Pa.); September 20, 1872 (visit to Hudson, N.Y.); and September 12, 1889 (visit to Ligonier, Ind.). On Wessolowsky, see Louis Schmier, ed., *Reflections on Southern Jewry: The Letters of Charles Wessolowsky, 1878-1879* (Macon, Ga., 1982), esp. 23.

26. For membership in 1900, see "Members," *AJYB* 2 (1900): 669–731.

27. For membership in 1927, see "Members," *AJYB* 29 (1927): 291–371.

28. See, for example, (Lafayette, Ind.) *Jewish Community Journal,* May 30, 1917, 8; Proshan, "Eastern European Jewish Immigrants and Their Children," 143–45; Melvin S. Harris, *The Columbia Hebrew Benevolent Society: One Hundred and Twenty-five Years of Benevolence* (Columbia, S.C., 1947), 31, 34, 36; Gunther Rothenberg, *Congregation Albert, 1897-1972* (Albuquerque, 1972), 20, 25, 29; and Blaine P. Lamb, "Frontiersmen in Broadcloth: Jews in Early Phoenix, 1870–1920," *Western States Jewish History* 25 (October 1992): 13. The quotation is from Minnie Atkinson, *Newburyport in the World War* (Newburyport, Mass., 1938), 171.

29. See Roger S. Kohn, Alizah Zinberg, and Barbara Martin, "An Inventory to the Records of the Central Relief Committee, 1914–1918," locating aid, 1986, Yeshiva University Archives, New York. Unfortunately, the wartime statements prepared by the Central Relief Committee are undated, and it is not clear at what intervals they were produced; the examples cited here are all from box 3, folder 3, Records of the Central Relief Committee, 1914–1918, Yeshiva University Archives.

30. See "Holocaust-Era Records of the Jewish Labor Committee, Part I: 1934–1947," locating aid, 1997, Robert F. Wagner Labor Archives, New York University. See also the Internet site produced to accompany the Wagner Archives Jewish Labor Committee holdings at http://www.nyu.edu/library/bobst/collections/exhibits/tam/JLC/opener/html (accessed July 6, 1999).

31. See "Yeshiva University Fundraising Collection (1917–1953)," locating aid, n.d., Yeshiva University Archives.

32. On Topeka, see Cumonow and Reiner, *Spirit Unconsumed,* 41. On Galesburg, see Atwood, "A Study of Social Class," 8.

33. Stahl, "Our History," 23.

34. Katz, "Jews of La Crosse," 63; (Lafayette, Ind.) *Jewish Community Journal,* March 1, 1917, 9; Geller, "History of Congregation Beth Jacob"; [Marjorie Abrams and Meyer M. Cohen], *Dedication: Congregation Cnesses Israel* (Green Bay, Wis., 1951), 10.

35. Dennis S. Devlin, *Muskegon's Jewish Community: A Centennial History, 1888-1988* (Muskegon, Mich., 1988), 13, 21–22.

36. On Sharon, see *Dedication: Temple Beth Israel,* 17, 26–27. On Hagerstown, see

*Congregation B'nai Abraham,* 14. On Auburn, see Rose O'Brien, "Beth Abraham's Congregation Observes 50th Anniversary," *Lewiston Journal Magazine Section,* December 6, 1952.

37. See *Dedication Journal . . . of the New Building of the Beth El Synagogue, Torrington, Connecticut* (Torrington, Conn., 1951), unpaginated.

38. See *Hadassah Year Book,* 1937, 106–14; Mississippi Historical Records Survey Project, *Inventory of the Church and Synagogue Archives of Mississippi: Jewish Congregations and Organizations* (Jackson, Miss., 1940), 13; and *UJE,* s.v. "North Dakota."

39. See Katz, "Jews of La Crosse," 63; and Warner and Srole, *Social Systems,* 115.

40. On the "Lower East Side" in American Jewish culture, see Hasia R. Diner, *Lower East Side Memories: A Jewish Place in America* (Princeton, 2000).

41. David Rome, *Ancestors, Descendants, and Me* (Beverly Hills, 1986), 32–33; Ms. Census, Fitchburg, Worcester County, Massachusetts, 1920.

42. On Portsmouth, see autobiographical essay by George Sherman in Howard V. Epstein, ed., *Jews in Small Towns: Legends and Legacies* (Santa Rosa, Calif., 1997), 279; and "Shapiro House," on the Internet site "Strawbery Banke" at http://www.strawberybanke.org/museum/shapiro/shapiro.html (accessed July 23, 2002). On Latrobe, see Louis Goldman, "Beth Israel Congregation, Latrobe, Pennsylvania," in Richard David Wissolik, Jennifer Campion, and Barbara Wissolik, eds., *Listen to Our Words: Oral Histories of the Jewish Community of Westmoreland County, Pennsylvania* (Latrobe, Pa., 1997), 207. On Warren, see autobiographical essay by Janyce B. Pearlstein in Epstein, *Jews in Small Towns,* 531. On Kalamazoo, see Friedman, "Kalamazoo Jewish Family History."

43. On Charlottesville, see Ely, Hantman and Leffler, *To Seek the Peace of the City,* 24; On Bessemer, see Barr, "Shtetl Grew in Bessemer," 14; On Modesto, see Sarah Arnopole and Martha Loeffler, "Pathways to Today," in *Congregation Beth Shalom, 1988/5749,* 70th anniversary booklet (Modesto, Calif., 1988), unpaginated.

44. See W. Lloyd Warner and Paul S. Lunt, *The Social Life of a Modern Community,* Yankee City Series, vol. 1 (New Haven, 1941), 232–33; and Warner and Srole, *Social Systems,* 45, 51.

45. On Augusta, see Myrna Katz Frommer and Harvey Frommer, *Growing up Jewish in America: An Oral History* (New York, 1995), 44–45. On Valdosta, see Louis Schmier, "Jews and Gentiles in a South Georgia Town," in *Jews of the South: Selected Essays from the Southern Jewish Historical Society,* ed. Samuel Proctor and Louis Schmier with Malcolm Stern (Macon, Ga., 1984), 12.

46. LeMaster, *Corner of the Tapestry,* 84; Cumonow and Reiner, *Spirit Unconsumed,* 73; Sunny Rabenstock, "Emanu El—God Is with Us: A History of Congregation Emanu El, San Bernardino, California," in *100th Anniversary, Congregation Emanu El* (San Bernardino, Calif., 1991), 30.

47. Cumonow and Reiner, *Spirit Unconsumed,* 8, 74; Rome, *Ancestors,* 32; audiotape interview of Jane Scherago, ca. 1980, archives of Temple Adath Israel, Lexington, Kentucky; Devlin, *Muskegon's Jewish Community,* 31–32.

48. On Manchester, see Stahl, "Our History," 26 (map), 29. On Newburyport, see Warner and Srole, *Social Systems,* 257–58.

49. Ms. Census, Nashua, Hillsborough County, New Hampshire, 1920; Ms. Census, Hamilton, Butler County, Ohio, 1920; Ms. Census, Lexington, Fayette County, Kentucky, 1920.

50. On Wakefield, see *Temple Emmanuel, Wakefield, Massachusetts,* 50th anniversary booklet (Wakefield, Mass., 1997), unpaginated. On Plymouth, see survey form of the Works Progress Administration, "Survey of State and Local Historical Records: 1936" (copy on Microfilm 3088, AJA). On Beaver Falls, see Jonathan Boyarin, *A Storyteller's Worlds: The Education of Shlomo Noble in Europe and America* (New York, 1994), 113. On Topeka, see Cumonow and Reiner, *Spirit Unconsumed,* 33, 44. On Wichita, see Rothman, " 'Same Horse, New Wagon,' " 96.

51. On Durham, see Rogoff, *Homelands,* 104–05. On Lexington, see Gertrude W. Dubrovsky, introduction to I. J. Schwartz, *Kentucky,* trans. Gertrude W. Dubrovsky (Tuscaloosa, Ala., 1990); and questionnaire completed by Myer B. Godhelff, 1996, in the author's possession.

52. On Deinard, see William B. Helmreich, *The Enduring Community: The Jews of Newark and Metrowest* (New Brunswick, N.J., 1999), 58. On Kahanowitz, see Ida Jean Selavan, "Ike Kahanowitz of Greensburg: Jewish Bibliophile of the Boondocks," in Wissolik, Campion and Wissolik, *Listen to Our Words,* 199–203.

53. On Altman, see "Biographical Sketches of Jews Prominent in the Professions, etc., in the United States," *AJYB* 6 (1904–05): 56. Information on Lewis is from his tombstone in the Sons of Israel Cemetery, Colorado Springs, Colorado.

54. Ms. Census, Lexington, 1920; Ms. Census, Newburyport, 1920; Warner and Srole, *Social Systems,* 230; Faye Moskowitz, *A Leak in the Heart: Tales from a Woman's Life* (Boston, 1985), 4–5; autobiographical essay by Paul Kronick in Epstein, *Jews in Small Towns,* 168.

55. Albert W. Levin, "The History of the Jewish Community of Racine, Wisconsin" (mimeographed document, 1942; copy in the author's possession), 3; Cumonow and Reiner, *Spirit Unconsumed,* 3.

56. Ruthe Winegarten and Cathy Schechter, *Deep in the Heart: The Lives and Legends of Texas Jews* (Austin, 1990), 129; Rome, *Ancestors,* 30; Julian B. Feibelman, *The Making of a Rabbi* (New York, 1980), 57; interviews of Rebecca Carlin Zeff and Sarah Arnopole by the author, Modesto, California, October 26, 1999; Joseph Marcus, "The Way Things Used to Be," in *Temple B'nai Shalom, Benton Harbor, Mich., 1895–1995,* centennial booklet (Benton Harbor, Mich., 1995), unpaginated; Moskowitz, *Leak in the Heart,* 72; Stahl, "Our History," 25.

57. On Plymouth, see Geller, "History of Congregation Beth Jacob." On Lafayette, see "Minutes of Orthodox Hebrew Free Loan Association, Lafayette"; and "Sons of Abraham Congregation, Lafayette, Ind., Minutes." On Annapolis, see Eric L. Goldstein, "Our History," in *Congregation Kneseth Israel: Looking Back, Moving Forward,* 90th anniversary booklet (Annapolis, 1996), unpaginated. On Petersburg, see Ginsberg, *History of the Jews of Petersburg,* 80–83.

58. On Butler, see "Directory of Jewish Organizations," *AJYB* 9 (1907–08): 28. On

Macon, see Newton J. Friedman, "A History of Temple Beth Israel of Macon, Georgia" (D.Th. diss., Burton Seminary of Colorado, 1955), 69. On Burlington, see Myron Samuelson, *The Story of the Jewish Community of Burlington, Vermont* (Burlington, Vt., 1976), 169. On Ellenville, see Y. Kaminsky, comp., *Forty Years—Workmen's Circle: A History in Pictures* (New York, 1940), 40. On services in Yiddish, see "Directory of Jewish Local Organizations in the United States," *AJYB* 21 (1919–20). On Donora, see Arnold W. Hirsch, "Remembering Donora's Jewish Community," 7, document MFF 2044, ca. 1995, Historical Society of Western Pennsylvania Archives, Pittsburgh).

## Chapter 12. Patterns of Prejudice and of Transformation

1. See, for example, Richard L. Zweigenhaft, "Two Cities in North Carolina: A Comparative Study of Jews in the Upper Class," *Jewish Social Studies* 41 (1979): 297–98; and Deborah R. Weiner, "A History of Jewish Life in the Central Appalachian Coalfields, 1870s to 1970s" (Ph.D. diss., West Virginia University, 2002), 321–23. On the view that local Jews were not seen as outsiders even by fervent Populists and Klansmen in small towns, see John Higham, "Social Discrimination against Jews in America, 1830–1930," *Publications of the American Jewish Historical Society* 47 (1957): 32.

2. See autobiographical essay by Melvin H. Klingher in Howard V. Epstein, ed., *Jews in Small Towns: Legends and Legacies* (Santa Rosa, Calif., 1997), 378–79.

3. See questionnaires completed by Joseph Klein, Leonard Mervis, and Roland Gittelsohn in "Student Survey, 1935–1936," Ms. Coll. 5, AJA. On the Klan in Muncie, Indiana, see Dan Rottenberg, ed., *Middletown Jews: The Tenuous Survival of an American Jewish Community* (Bloomington, Ind., 1997), 50–51. On the Klan in Iowa City, Iowa, see Douglas W. Jones, "Jewish Life at Iowa" (manuscript, 1997; copy in the author's possession), 24. On the Klan in Modesto, California, see interview of Bernice Hyman in Beth Shalom chapter of United Synagogue Youth, producer, *History of the Jewish Community of Modesto* (video, Modesto, Calif., 1984). On the Klan in Durham, North Carolina, see Leonard Rogoff, *Homelands: Southern Jewish Identity in Durham and Chapel Hill, North Carolina* (Tuscaloosa, Ala., 2001), 132–33. On the Klan in Williamson and other towns of southern West Virginia, see Weiner, "History of Jewish Life in the Central Appalachian Coalfields," 479–80.

4. Edward Cohen, for example, tells this story about his own grandfather in Jackson, Mississippi; see Edward Cohen, *The Peddler's Grandson: Growing Up Jewish in Mississippi* (Jackson, Miss., 1999), 9–10.

5. Harry L. Golden, *Jewish Roots in the Carolinas: A Pattern of American Philo-Semitism* (Charlotte, N.C., 1955), 55–56.

6. See Doris Kirkpatrick, *Around the World in Fitchburg* (Fitchburg, Mass., 1975), 164–65; Jerome Paul David, "Jewish Consciousness in the Small Town" (rabbinic thesis, Hebrew Union College, 1974), 3; and Myer Katz, "The Jews of La Crosse Past and Present," *Encounters*, ca. June 1973, 59.

7. See Ewa Morawska, "A Replica of the 'Old Country' Relationship in the Ethnic

Niche: East European Jews and Gentiles in Small-town Western Pennsylvania, 1880s–1930s," *American Jewish History* 77 (September 1987): 27–86; and Weiner "History of Jewish Life in the Central Appalachian Coalfields." On the prejudice against merchants in general, see Walter P. Zenner, *Minorities in the Middle: A Cross-Cultural Analysis* (Albany, N.Y., 1991), esp. chap. 3 and 140–42.

8. On Newburyport, see W. Lloyd Warner and Leo Srole, *The Social Systems of American Ethnic Groups,* Yankee City Series, vol. 3 (New Haven, 1945), 28. Data on immigrants within the population are from U.S. Census Bureau, *Abstract of the Fifteenth Census of the United States* (1933; reprint, New York, 1976), 170–72.

9. See *Congregation Ahavath Torah: An Oral History,* centennial booklet (Englewood, N.J., 1995), 2; and Weiner, "History of Jewish Life in the Central Appalachian Coalfields," esp. chap. 6. On tensions between Jews and other ethnics in the small towns of Minnesota, see Chester Jay Proshan, "Eastern European Jewish Immigrants and Their Children on the Minnesota Iron Range, 1890s–1980s" (Ph.D. diss., University of Minnesota, 1998), 212–13.

10. Data on the number of foreign-born Jews in Lexington are from Ms. Census, Lexington, Fayette County, Kentucky, 1920. Data on other components of the foreign-born population in Lexington are from U.S. Bureau of the Census, *Fourteenth Census of the United States Taken in the Year 1920, Volume II: Population, 1920* (Washington, D.C., 1922), 762–63.

11. Data on the number of foreign-born residents in the cities cited are from U.S. Census Bureau, *Abstract of the Fifteenth Census,* 170–72. The conclusion that about half the Jews in the United States around 1930 were foreign-born is based on the estimate that about 66 percent of American Jews were foreign-born in 1920 and that about 39 percent of American Jews were foreign-born in ten midsize U.S. cities "studied before World War II." The percentage of foreign-born Jews in 1920 was calculated from information in Harry S. Linfield, "The Jewish Population of the United States, 1927," *AJYB* 30 (1928–29): 167–68 (note D). The percentage of foreign-born Jews in ten cities before World War II is from C. Bezalel Sherman, *The Jew within American Society* (Detroit, 1961), 91.

12. On Wichita, see Hal Rothman, " 'Same Horse, New Wagon': Tradition and Assimilation among the Jews of Wichita, 1865–1930," *Great Plains Quarterly* 15 (spring 1995): 98. On Dover, see autobiographical essay by Vivian Barnert in Epstein, *Jews in Small Towns,* 289. On Alexandria, see Martin I. Hinchin, *Fourscore and Eleven: A History of the Jews of Rapides Parish, 1828–1919* (Alexandria, La.[?], 1984), 186. On Warren, see autobiographical essay by Janyce B. Pearlstein in Epstein, *Jews in Small Towns,* 532. On Bessemer, see Terry Barr, "A Shtetl Grew in Bessemer: Temple Beth-El and Jewish Life in Small-Town Alabama," *Southern Jewish History* 3 (2000): 32. For the quotation from Moskowitz, see Faye Moskowitz, *A Leak in the Heart: Tales from a Woman's Life* (Boston, 1985), 58. For examples of students facing Christmas at school, see also autobiographical essays by Howard Fink (Marion, Ind.), Tevis M.

Goldhaft (Vineland, N.J.), and Roxsene Plafker (Dubois, Pa.) in Epstein, *Jews in Small Towns,* 106, 304, 600–601.

13. On Iowa City, see Jones, "Jewish Life at Iowa," 24. On Fitchburg, see Kirkpatrick, *Around the World in Fitchburg,* 164. On Ellwood City, see autobiographical essay by Aaron Caplan in Epstein, *Jews in Small Towns,* 567. For other examples of Jews being taunted by non-Jewish youngsters, see also the autobiographical essays by Leo Lappin (Norwood, Mass.) and Vivian Barnert (Dover, N.J.) in Epstein, *Jews in Small Towns,* 180, 285.

14. On Donora, see "A 20th Century Diaspora," clipping from the *Pittsburgh Post Gazette,* "Donora, Pennsylvania" Nearprint file, AJA. On Danville, see Sybil Stern Mervis, "History of the Jewish Community of Danville," in *Congregation Israel Synagogue, 1916–1991,* 75th anniversary booklet (Danville, Ill., 1991), 15. On Hibbing, see Proshan, "Eastern European Jewish Immigrants and Their Children," 244. On Fort Smith, see Carolyn Gray LeMaster, *A Corner of the Tapestry: A History of the Jewish Experience in Arkansas, 1820s–1990s* (Fayetteville, Ark., 1994), 298. On Wilmington, see David J. Goldberg, "An Historical Community Study of Wilmington Jewry, 1738–1925" (seminar paper, school unknown, 1976; available at Hebrew Union College Library, Cincinnati), 39. On Muskegon, see Dennis S. Devlin, *Muskegon's Jewish Community: A Centennial History, 1888–1988* (Muskegon, Mich., 1988), 37.

15. See William B. Helmreich, *The Enduring Community: The Jews of Newark and Metrowest* (New Brunswick, N.J., 1999), 61; autobiographical essay by Janyce B. Pearlstein in Epstein, *Jews in Small Towns,* 531; and Eugene J. Lipman and Albert Vorspan, eds., *A Tale of Ten Cities: The Triple Ghetto in American Religious Life* (New York, 1962), 117.

16. See *Congregation Agudas Achim Building Rededication* (Attleboro, Mass., 1998), unpaginated; and W. Lloyd Warner and J. O. Low, *The Social System of the Modern Factory,* Yankee City Series, vol. 4 (New Haven, 1947), 5, 141.

17. Jones, "Jewish Life at Iowa," 10, 15–16.

18. W. Lloyd Warner, *The Living and the Dead: A Study of the Symbolic Life of Americans,* Yankee City Series, vol. 5 (New Haven, 1959), 197–203.

19. See Benjamin Kaplan, *The Eternal Stranger: A Study of Jewish Life in the Small Community* (New York, 1957), 158; David, "Jewish Consciousness," 52.

20. Barr, "Shtetl Grew in Bessemer," 17; autobiographical essay by Murray Milkman in Epstein, *Jews in Small Towns,* 592; David G. Stahl, "Our History," in *Temple Adath Yeshurun Centennial, 1891–1991* (Manchester, N.H., 1991), 23.

21. Michael Eliasohn, "The First 100 Years," in *Temple B'nai Shalom, Benton Harbor, Mich., 1895–1995,* centennial booklet (Benton Harbor, Mich., 1995), unpaginated; autobiographical essay by Perry Peskin in Epstein, *Jews in Small Towns,* 159; *Congregation Ahavath Torah,* 3.

22. Rothman, " 'Same Horse, New Wagon,' " 98; Robert P. Davis, "Identity," on the Internet site "Virtual Restoration of Small-Town Synagogues" at http://geocities.com/txsynvr/txsyn.html (accessed March 26, 2000).

23. See Jennifer R. Kraft, "Children of Israel Synagogue and the Jewish Commu-

nity of Benton Harbor, Michigan: A History" (term paper, Jewish Theological Seminary of America, 1992), 8; Eric L. Goldstein, "Our History," in *Congregation Kneseth Israel: Looking Back, Moving Forward,* 90th anniversary booklet (Annapolis, 1996), unpaginated; and *Congregation Ahavath Torah,* 2.

24. See Warner and Srole, *Social Systems,* 201; Davis, "Identity"; Rothman, "'Same Horse, New Wagon,'" 98. Compare also David J. Goldberg, "In Dixie Land, I Take My Stand: A Study of Small-City Jewry in Five Southeastern States" (undergraduate thesis, Columbia College, 1974), 13.

25. See "Directory of Jewish Local Organizations in the United States," *AJYB* 21 (1919–20): 332, 337–583; David Rome, *Ancestors, Descendants, and Me* (Beverly Hills, 1986), 41.

26. See interview of Bernice Hyman in "History of the Jewish Community of Modesto"; questionnaires completed by Morton Applebaum and Louis Josephson in "Student Survey, 1935–1936"; David, "Jewish Consciousness," 34.

27. On Sharon, see *Dedication: Temple Beth Israel* (Sharon, Pa., 1950), 11. On Lafayette, see minutes of January 3, 1940, in Minutes of Orthodox Hebrew Free Loan Association, Lafayette Ind., 1923–77; and minutes of August 27, 1945, in Sons of Abraham Congregation, Lafayette, Ind., Minutes 1943–60, both on Microfilm 2632, AJA.

28. *Dedication: Congregation Beth Abraham* (Zanesville, Ohio, 1959), unpaginated; Rochelle Berger Elstein, "Synagogue Architecture in Michigan and the Midwest: Material Culture and the Dynamics of Jewish Accommodation, 1865–1945" (Ph.D. diss., Michigan State University, 1986), 321.

29. Rose Sherman Geller, "History of Congregation Beth Jacob," booklet essay, 1988, vertical file "Churches," Plymouth Public Library, Plymouth, Mass.

30. George Zepin, "Jewish Religious Conditions in Scattered Communities," *Year Book of the Central Conference of American Rabbis* 14 (1904): 215; "Paducah, Ky., Cong. Temple Israel Minute Book for 1893–1910," 111, box 679, AJA.

31. See "Directory," *AJYB* 21 (1919–20): 330–583.

32. See minutes of November 1, 1939, in Minutes of Orthodox Hebrew Free Loan Association, Lafayette Ind., 1923–77.

33. Zepin, "Jewish Religious Conditions," 222.

34. Ruth Marcus Patt, *The Jewish Scene in New Jersey's Raritan Valley, 1698–1948* (New Brunswick, N.J., 1978), 59; Marjorie Levin, ed., *The Jews of Wilkes-Barre: 150 Years (1845–1995) in the Wyoming Valley of Pennsylvania* (Wilkes-Barre, Pa., 1999), 98.

35. See *Congregation Ahavath Torah,* 18, 20; Julian B. Feibelman, *The Making of a Rabbi* (New York, 1980), 54–55; David, "Jewish Consciousness," 16–17; Arthur Spear, "The Jewish Community of Dover New Jersey (a Short History)," 15, typescript, 1951, file SC-2943, AJA.

36. *The Anniversary Story of Congregation B'er Chayim,* centennial booklet (Cumberland, Md., 1953), chap. 3; Peskin in Epstein, *Jews in Small Towns,* 160; Patt, *Jewish Scene,* 59; Oscar Fleishaker, *The Illinois-Iowa Jewish Community on the Banks of the Mississippi River* (n.p., 1971), 152.

37. Zepin, "Jewish Religious Conditions," 212; Louis Ginsberg, *History of the Jews of Petersburg, 1789–1950* (Petersburg, Va., 1954), 82.

38. Norton B. Stern, "Santa Ana, California: Its First Jews and Jewish Congregations," *Western States Jewish Historical Quarterly* 14 (April 1982): 253–54; Joy Cumonow and Fred N. Reiner, *The Spirit Unconsumed: A History of the Topeka Jewish Community* (Topeka, 1979), 4; Sunny Rabenstock, "Emanu El—God Is with Us: A History of Congregation Emanu El, San Bernardino, California" in *100th Anniversary, Congregation Emanu El* (San Bernardino, Calif., 1991), 21.

39. Caplan in Epstein, *Jews in Small Towns,* 566–67; Rome, *Ancestors, Descendants, and Me,* 33–34; Ben Deutschman, *In a Small Town a Kid Went to Shul* (Nashville, 1971), 32.

40. Ernest I. Jacob, "Fifty Years of Jewish Life in Springfield, Mo.," in *Fifty Years— Temple Israel, Springfield, Missouri: Invitation to the Anniversary Celebration* (Springfield, Mo., 1943), unpaginated; *Dedication: Temple Beth Israel,* 19; Stahl, "Our History," 27.

41. Warner and Srole, *Social Systems,* 198.

42. See Leonard Rogoff, "Small-Town Orthodoxy, Southern Style," 9–10, paper presented at the annual meeting of the Southern Jewish Historical Society, New Orleans, 1995; Eli N. Evans, *The Provincials: A Personal History of the Jews in the South,* rev. ed. (New York, 1997), 115–16; Kraft, "Children of Israel Synagogue," 14.

43. See Rogoff, *Homelands,* 143.

44. See Warner and Srole, *Social Systems,* 196; Devlin, *Muskegon's Jewish Community,* 25–27; Melissa Fay Greene, "In Search of a New Vocabulary," *CommonQuest,* fall 1996, 58. Greene's essay is a review of James McBride, *The Color of Water* (New York, 1996), of which Rachel Shilsky is the subject.

45. Questionnaire completed by Myer B. Godhelff, 1996, in the author's possession; Warner and Srole, *Social Systems,* 138; autobiographical essay by Judith Falk in Epstein, *Jews in Small Towns,* 578.

46. Warner and Srole, *Social Systems,* 201.

47. Jacob J. Weinstein, *The Religious Situation among Small Town Jewries* (n.p., n.d.), 8.

48. Proshan, "Eastern European Jewish Immigrants and Their Children," 166; Ginsberg, *History of the Jews of Petersburg,* 62–65; Adolph Rosenberg, "Between Rome's Rivers," *Southern Israelite,* October 29, 1948, 17; and Sol H. Marshall, "New Spiritual Values for Rome," *Southern Israelite,* November 24, 1939, 17. For the example of the entry of East European Jews into politics in Durham, North Carolina, see Rogoff, *Homelands,* 172–73.

49. On Virginia, see Proshan, "Eastern European Jewish Immigrants and Their Children," 228. On Manchester, see Stahl, "Our History," 22–23. On Leominster, see "Impressive Ceremonies Mark Dedication of New Synagogue," *Worcester Telegram,* September 15, 1924; and Walter I. Deacon Jr., "List History of Agudas Achim Congregation as Observance Date Nears," *Leominster Daily Enterprise,* August 27, 1949. On Plymouth, see Geller, "History of Congregation Beth Jacob." On Durham, see Rogoff, *Homelands,* 170. On Hagers-

town, see *Congregation B'nai Abraham: Celebrating 100 Years* (Hagerstown, Md., 1992), 16.

50. On Benton Harbor, see Kraft, "Children of Israel Synagogue," 9. On Red Bank, see Alan S. Pine, Jean C. Hershenov, and Aaron H. Lefkowitz, *Peddler to Suburbanite: The History of the Jews of Monmouth County, New Jersey* (Deal Park, N.J., 1981), 89. On Annapolis, see Goldstein, "Our History." On North Adams, see Pink Horwitt and Bertha Skole, *Jews in Berkshire Country* (Williamstown, Mass., 1972), 50. On Bradford, see Francis X. Sculley, "Maccabees Ruled Ball Diamonds in Bradford," *Bradford Era,* September 11, 1975, 16.

51. Melvin S. Harris, *The Columbia Hebrew Benevolent Society: One Hundred and Twenty-five Years of Benevolence* (Columbia, S.C., 1947), 28.

52. For the situation in 1939, see "1939 Directory of Jewish Federations, Welfare Funds, Community Councils and Their Local Affiliated Agencies," *AJYB* 41 (1939–40): 517–558. On Muskegon, see Devlin, *Muskegon's Jewish Community,* 41.

53. Warner and Srole, *Social Systems,* 203.

## Epilogue. Patterns of Endurance and Decline

1. On Hagerstown, see *Congregation B'nai Abraham: Celebrating 100 Years* (Hagerstown, Md., 1992), 16. On Michigan City, see Karl Richter, "The History of Sinai Temple," in *Sinai Temple, Michigan City, Indiana,* dedication booklet (Michigan City, Ind., 1953), 12. On Topeka, see Joy Cumonow and Fred N. Reiner, *The Spirit Unconsumed: A History of the Topeka Jewish Community* (Topeka, 1979), 12–13. On Greensboro, see Karen R. Goody, "The Greensboro Jewish Community: Keeping the Memories under Glass" (master's thesis, Wake Forest University, 1984), 45–46.

2. Robert Shosteck, *Small-Town Jewry Tell Their Story* (Washington, D.C., 1953), 36–48.

3. Dennis S. Devlin, *Muskegon's Jewish Community: A Centennial History, 1888–1988* (Muskegon, Mich., 1988), 40; Goody, "Greensboro Jewish Community," 38, 42; *Dedication: Temple Beth Israel* (Sharon, Pa., 1950), 41–43.

4. Richter, "History of Sinai Temple," 10, 15; autobiographical essay by Janyce B. Pearlstein in Howard V. Epstein, ed., *Jews in Small Towns: Legends and Legacies* (Santa Rosa, Calif., 1997), 532; Sunny Rabenstock, "Emanu El—God Is with Us: A History of Congregation Emanu El, San Bernardino, California," in *100th Anniversary, Congregation Emanu El* (San Bernardino, Calif., 1991), 12–13; "One Hundred Years of Jewish Congregations in Connecticut: An Architectural Survey," *Connecticut Jewish History* 2 (fall 1991): 58, 98; Jean Kiralfy Kent, *Temple Israel of Columbus, Georgia, 1854–2000* (Columbus, Ga., 2000), 49; "Book of Remembrance" (manuscript volume, ca. 1960, in lobby of B'nai Israel synagogue, Kankakee, Ill.), unpaginated.

5. Earl Pruce, *Synagogues, Temples, and Congregations of Maryland, 1830–1990* (Baltimore, 1993), 4, 166; site visit by the author, Jackson, Tennessee, 1995; site visit by the author, Jackson, Michigan, 1996.

6. On congregations in Englewood, see *UJE*, s.v. "New Jersey"; and Meyer Barkai, publisher, *The Standard American-Jewish Directory, 1960* (n.p., 1960), 110.

7. On congregations in Newton, see *UJE*, s.v. "Massachusetts"; and Ellen Chernofsky, ed., *Traveling Jewish in America*, 3d ed. (Lodi, N.J., 1991), 180–81. On the development of Newton, see also Gerald H. Gamm, "In Search of Suburbs, Boston's Jewish Districts, 1843–1994," in Jonathan D. Sarna and Ellen Smith, eds., *The Jews of Boston: Essays on the Occasion of the Centenary (1895–1995) of the Combined Jewish Philanthropies of Greater Boston* (Boston, 1995), 150–54.

8. On Albuquerque, see Gunther Rothenberg, *Congregation Albert, 1897–1972* (Albuquerque, 1972), 35, 40–54.

9. On congregations in Tucson and Phoenix, see Chernofsky, *Traveling Jewish*, 5–8.

10. Alvin Chenkin, "Jewish Population in the United States, 1983," *AJYB* 84 (1984): 167–74 (table 3).

11. Robert E. Tournier, "Small Towns at the Crossroads: Outcome Scenarios in Non-Metropolitan Change," in Robert Craycroft and Michael Fazio, eds., *Change and Tradition in the American Small Town* (Jackson, Miss., 1983), 32.

12. See Myer Katz, "The Jews of La Crosse Past and Present," *Encounters,* ca. June 1973, 59.

13. W. Lloyd Warner, *The Living and the Dead: A Study of the Symbolic Life of Americans,* Yankee City Series, vol. 5 (New Haven, 1959), 66.

14. Sybil Stern Mervis, "History of the Jewish Community of Danville," in *Congregation Israel Synagogue, 1916–1991,* 75th anniversary booklet (Danville, Ill., 1991), 14.

15. Site visit by the author, Farrell, Pennsylvania, 1997.

16. On Marshall, see Murray Polner, *Rabbi: The American Experience* (New York, 1977), 172. See also Robert P. Davis, "Marshall, Moses Montefiore," on the Internet site "Virtual Restoration of Small-Town Synagogues" at http://geocities.com/txsynvr/txsyn.html (accessed March 26, 2000). On Marion, see Jerry Miller, "Exodus—Marion style," *Marion Chronicle-Tribune Magazine,* July 17, 1977, 9–10.

17. On Wabash, see Joseph Levine, "Jewish Community Small," in Linda Robertson, ed., *Wabash County History: Bicentennial Edition, 1976* (Marceline, Mo., 1976), 168. On Williamson, see Gustav Niebuhr, "Dwindling Synagogue Holds On, and Worries," *New York Times,* September 15, 1994.

18. See *Temple B'nai Shalom, Benton Harbor, Mich., 1895–1995,* centennial booklet (Benton Harbor, Mich., 1995), unpaginated.

19. Katz, "Jews of La Crosse," 40.

20. On North Adams, see Pink Horwitt and Bertha Skole, *Jews in Berkshire Country* (Williamstown, Mass., 1972), 51. On Danville, see Mervis, "History of the Jewish Community of Danville," 12–13.

21. On Galesburg, see Allen I. Freebling, "The Galesburg Jewish Community—One Hundred Years in Review," in *A Century of Living Judaism,* centennial booklet (Galesburg, Ill., 1967), unpaginated; and Barkai, *Standard American-*

*Jewish Directory*, 62. On Bradford, see *Temple Beth El, Bradford, Pennsylvania,* building dedication booklet (Bradford, Pa., 1961), 4. On East Liverpool, see autobiographical essay by Herschel Rubin in Epstein, *Jews in Small Towns,* 539.

22. See Chernofsky, *Traveling Jewish.*

23. Devlin, *Muskegon's Jewish Community,* 51.

24. See Jennifer R. Kraft, "Children of Israel Synagogue and the Jewish Community of Benton Harbor, Michigan: A History" (term paper, Jewish Theological Seminary of America, 1992), 15–16, 18; and Michael Eliasohn, "The First 100 Years," in *Temple B'nai Shalom, Benton Harbor, Mich., 1895–1995.*

25. See Chernofsky, *Traveling Jewish.* On the relationship between the two congregations in Fargo, see Robert J. Lazar, "From Ethnic Minority to Socio-Economic Elite: A Study of the Jewish Community of Fargo, North Dakota" (Ph.D. diss., University of Minnesota, 1968), chap. 3.

26. On congregations around 1991, see Chernofsky, *Traveling Jewish.* The quotations are from *Welcome to the Museum of the Southern Jewish Experience,* brochure (Jackson, Miss.[?], 1993[?]); and Thomas Goldwasser, "Jews in Small Towns," *Baltimore Sun,* March 23, 1983.

27. See, for example, autobiographical essays by Geraldine Stregevsky and by Murray Milkman in Epstein, *Jews in Small Towns,* 543, 593.

28. Lee Shai Weissbach, *The Synagogues of Kentucky: Architecture and History* (Lexington, Ky., 1995), 80, 98; site visits by the author, Ligonier, Indiana, 1992, and Stevens Point, Wisconsin, 1996; autobiographical essay by Sandra Kaufman Harris in Epstein, *Jews in Small Towns,* 224; and "Natchez site" on the Internet site "Museum of the Southern Jewish Experience" at http://www.msje.org/museum_natchez.html (accessed September 5, 2002).

29. On the concept of "places of memory" in the context of the Shoah, see, for example, James E. Young, *The Texture of Memory: Holocaust Memorials and Meaning* (New Haven, 1993), chaps. 2 and 5. See also James E. Young, "The Art of Memory: Holocaust Memorials in History," esp. 23–24; and Jack Kugelmass, "Why We Go to Poland: Holocaust Tourism as Secular Ritual," esp. 180–81, both in James E. Young, ed., *The Art of Memory: Holocaust Memorials in History* (New York, 1994).

30. On Dalton, see *Temple Beth El, Dalton, Georgia, 1940–1980,* 40th anniversary booklet (Dalton, Ga., 1980).

31. On Charlottesville, see Carol Ely, Jeffrey Hantman, and Phyllis Leffler, *To Seek the Peace of the City: Jewish Life in Charlottesville,* exhibition catalogue (Charlottesville, Va., 1994), 1–2, 12. The reported Jewish population of Ithaca was 424 in 1937 and 1,000 in 1984; that of Champaign, together with Urbana, was 404 in 1937 and 2,000 in 1984; and that of Iowa City was 130 in 1937 and 750 in 1984.

32. On the fate of small towns in America in the 1970s and 1980s, see, for example, Tournier, "Small Towns at the Crossroads," 31–47. On the search of late twentieth-century Americans for places to live where they could escape the drawbacks of big cities, see, among others, Terry Pindell, *A Good Place to Live:*

*America's Last Migration* (New York, 1995). For a discussion of the disappearance of some small Jewish communities and the creation of others in the South during the final decades of the twentieth century, see Ira M. Sheskin, "The Dixie Diaspora: The 'Loss' of the Small Southern Jewish Community," *Southeastern Geographer* 40 (May 2000): 52–74.

33. See Devlin, *Muskegon's Jewish Community,* 66, 73.

34. The erosion of place as a marker of community is one of the main themes in David Jacobson, *Place and Belonging in America* (Baltimore, 2002).

35. See, for example, Roland L. Warren, *The Community in America,* 3d ed. (Chicago, 1978), esp. chap. 3; and Craig Wilson, "Vanishing America: 'Good Simplicity' Falls by the Wayside," *USA Today,* July 2, 1999.

36. See Miller, "Exodus—Marion style," 9; and Ely, Hantman and Leffler, *To Seek the Peace of the City,* preface.

37. On Natchez, see *Natchez Jewish Homecoming!,* brochure (Jackson, Miss.[?], 1994). On Selma, see E. Thomas Wood, "Jews Return to Selma, Underscoring Exodus," *New York Times,* October 6, 1997.

38. See, for example, Mary T. Schmich, "Jews Are Consigned to History in South: Proud Heritage Dies in Small Towns," *Chicago Tribune,* November 1, 1987; Peter Applebome, "Small-Town South Clings to Jewish History," *New York Times,* September 29, 1991; Tim Klass, "Jewish Communities Vanishing from Small Towns," *Detroit News,* July 31, 1994; Fred Mogul, "A Light Still Burning," *Omaha World Herald,* December 7, 1996; Gayle White, "In Small Towns, a Cloudy Outlook," *Atlanta Journal / Atlanta Constitution,* September 27, 1997; and Sue Anne Pressley, "Southern Jews Close Up Shop," *Washington Post,* May 23, 1999.

39. Manon Pavy and Fritz Wagner, "Focusing the Old Downtown on Specialty Retail for Economic Survivals: The Transition of Ponchatoula, Louisiana," *Small Town* 24 (November–December 1993): 18, quoted in Richard V. Francaviglia, *Main Street Revisited: Time, Space, and Image Building in Small-Town America* (Iowa City, 1996), xviii.

*Reading the Manuscript Census*

1. Walter and Annie S. Salassi, comps., "Anshe Chesed Cemetery, Vicksburg, Mississippi," typescript, 1986, file SC-12594, AJA; Congregation Anshe Chesed: Minute Book of the Ladies Auxiliary Society, 1904–1917, "Vicksburg, Mississippi" file, Small Collections, AJA; Cashbook of the B'nai B'rith David Heuman Lodge No. 807, Jackson, Michigan, 1919–1924, microfilm 2115, AJA; computerized burial listing provided to the author by Victor Burstein, chairman, Temple Beth Israel Cemetery, Jackson, Michigan, January 1996.

2. On the use of DJNs in contemporary social scientific research, see, for example, Harold S. Himmelfarb, R. Michael Loar, and Susan H. Mott, "Sampling by Ethnic Surnames: The Case of American Jews," *Public Opinion Quarterly* 47 (summer 1983): 247–60. Several lists of DJNs in America have been compiled; see, for example, Steven M. Cohen, *A Case Study of an Abbreviated*

*Demographic Survey: The New Haven Jewish Population "Mini-Study" of 1987* (New York, 1988), 16.

*Bibliographic Essay*

1. See *Who Was Who in America,* vol. 1 (Chicago, 1897), s.v. "Polk, Ralph Lane"; and Dorothea N. Spear, *Bibliography of American Directories through 1860* (Worcester, Mass., 1961), 5–10.
2. Howard V. Epstein, ed., *Jews in Small Towns: Legends and Legacies* (Santa Rosa, Calif., 1997), xvi–xviii.
3. For the author's review of *Insecure Prosperity,* see *American Jewish History* 84 (September 1996): 274–76. For the author's review of *A Separate Circle,* see *Journal of Southern History* 69 (February 2003): 172–73.

# Index

*Note: Only the names of individuals likely to have been widely known beyond their own communities have been indexed. Names of businesses, congregations, and other local institutions have not been indexed. However, information about many individuals and institutions can be located by referring to the entries for their towns. The names of cities with larger Jewish communities have not been indexed, but see the entry "Larger Jewish communities."*